TITLE
E.S.E.A.

St. Mary High School Library

St. Mary's H. S. Library
South Amboy, N. J.

L.C. 12/82

EUROPE
**The World
of the Middle Ages**

EUROPE
The World of the Middle Ages

EDWARD PETERS
University of Pennsylvania

PRENTICE-HALL, INC., ENGLEWOOD CLIFFS, NEW JERSEY 07632

Library of Congress Cataloging in Publication Data
PETERS, EDWARD (date)
  Europe, the world of the Middle Ages.

  Bibliography: p. 586
  Includes index.
  1. Middle Ages—History. 2. Civilization,
Medieval. I. Title.
D118.P45   940.1   76-20673
ISBN 0-13-291898-6

© 1977 by Prentice-Hall, Inc., Englewood Cliffs, New Jersey 07632

All rights reserved. No part of this book may be reproduced, in any form or by any means, without permission in writing from the publisher.

PRINTED IN THE UNITED STATES OF AMERICA

10 9 8 7 6 5 4 3 2 1

PRENTICE-HALL INTERNATIONAL, INC., *London*
PRENTICE-HALL OF AUSTRALIA PTY. LIMITED, *Sydney*
PRENTICE-HALL OF CANADA LTD., *Toronto*
PRENTICE-HALL OF INDIA PRIVATE LIMITED, *New Delhi*
PRENTICE-HALL OF JAPAN, INC., *Tokyo*
PRENTICE-HALL OF SOUTHEAST ASIA PTE. LTD., *Singapore*

TO MY CHILDREN
Nicole Marie Peters
Moira Anne Peters
Edward Murray Peters III

CONTENTS

Preface xiii

Introduction:
The Discovery and Invention of the Middle Ages 1

PART ONE: EUROPE AND THE ANCIENT WORLD 9

1 A Map of the Medieval Environment: The Geography and Climate of Mediterranean and North Temperate Europe 11
Physical Europe: Lands and Waters 11
The Climate of North Temperate and Mediterranean Europe, 500 B.C.–1850 A.D. 16
Society and Environment in Early Europe 18

2 The First Europeans 23
The Celtic World 23
Mediterranean Societies to the Second Century A.D. 27
The Early Germans 31

3 The Transformation of the Eurasian World, 200–400 A.D. 34
The Imperial Crisis of the Third Century 34
The World beyond the Empire, 150–375 A.D. 42
The Intellectual and Spiritual Worlds of Late Antiquity 47

4 The Fourth Century 56
The Empire and the Triumph of Christianity 56
The Structure of the Church in the Fourth Century 59
Paganism and Christianity in the Fourth Century:
 Learned and Popular Culture 65
The Second Rome and the Old Empire, 330–395 74

PART TWO: THE LEGACY OF MEDITERRANEAN ANTIQUITY 77

5 East and West Rome and the Invasions, 395–530 79
Emperors and Churchmen 79
The World of Galla Placidia:
 Visigoths and Romans in the West 86
The Breaching of the Rhine Frontier:
 Vandals, Burgundians, and Huns 89
Romania: The Impact of the Invasions
 on East and West Rome 81

6 The Barbarian West 96
The Tragedy of the "Good" Barbarians: Ostrogothic Italy 96
The Franks in Gaul 102
From Frontier Provinces to Barbarian Kingdoms:
 Britain, Spain, and Africa, 450–550 106
Monasticism and Culture in the Barbarian West 110

7 The Making of Byzantium 117
The Emperor Who Never Sleeps 117
Constantinople: The Eye of the World 125
After Justinian:
 Avars, Slavs, and the Flowering of Sasanid Persia 129
Heraclius and the Defense of the Empire 132

8 Germanic Kingdoms and the Church in the West, 565–700 135
Lombard Italy and the First Rome 135
God's Consul 139
Roman and Celtic Christianity in Anglo-Saxon England 145
Visigothic Spain 148
Frankish Gaul under the Successors of Clovis, 511–683 151

9 The New Mediterranean World: The Rise of Islam 158
The Imperial African Provinces 158
The Arab World and the Revelations of Mohammed 160
Mohammed's Successors and the Spread of Islam to 750 163
The Abbasid Dynasty
 and the Divisions of the Islamic World 165

CONTENTS ix

PART THREE: THE BOOK AND THE SWORD, 650–950 **169**

10 The World of Bede and Boniface, 650–750 **171**
Bede: "The Light Within the Church" **171**
The English Continental Mission and Saint Boniface,
  Exul Germanicus **176**
Ecclesiastical Reform and the New Rulers of the Franks **177**

11 From Frankish Kingdom to Christian Empire **182**
Frankish Kingship, the Church, and the Institutions of Royal
  Governance under Pepin and Charlemagne, 751–800 **182**
The Expansion of Frankish Power in the
  Eighth and Ninth Centuries **195**
Byzantium, Lombard Italy, and the Papacy **199**
The Carolingian Renaissance **204**
Frankish King and *Imperator Romanorum* **210**

12 Politics, Society, and Economy in Ninth-Century Europe **220**
From *Respublica Christiana* to Separate Kingdoms,
  814–888 **220**
Population and Forms of Settlement **226**
The Distribution of Wealth and Power **230**
Trade and Communication **231**

13 Byzantium and the Crisis of the West, 802–950 **235**
Central and Eastern Europe to 900 **235**
Crisis and Recovery in Byzantium, 802–904 **238**
The New Invasions of Europe:
  Arabs, Magyars, and Vikings **241**
The Macedonian Dynasty
  and the Flowering of Byzantine Civilization **247**
Rome, the Papacy,
  and the Fragments of the Carolingian Ideal **249**

PART FOUR: CHRISTENDOM: MATERIAL CIVILIZATION AND CULTURE, 950–1150 **255**

14 The Social and Economic Transformation of the Eleventh and Twelfth Centuries **257**
Population Growth and New Patterns of Settlement **257**
Sustenance and Surplus: European Agriculture **262**
Market, Town, and City in an Agricultural World **268**
Communication and Trade, Technology and Industry **276**

15
Power and Society 282
Lordship and Political Communities 282
The New German Monarchy and the Imperial Revival 287
Christendom and the East:
   The Byzantine Sphere and Kievan Russia 292
Royal Lordship in the Eleventh Century 297

16
Spiritual Reform and the Concept of Christendom 306
Lordship: Power and Culture in the Eleventh Century 306
Imperial Reform and the Eleventh-Century Papacy 315
The Pontificate of Gregory VII and the Imperial Conflict 322
Christianitas: The Consequences of Reform and Conflict 327

17
Christendom East and West, 1025–1150 330
Christianitas: The Acculturation of an Idea 330
The Crisis of the Byzantine Empire
   in the Eleventh Century 335
Holy War and Sinful Society:
   Pope Urban II and the "Pilgrimage" to Jerusalem 339
Byzantium, Islam, and the Latin Kingdom of Jerusalem,
   1099–1144 345

PART FIVE: CHRISTENDOM: AUTHORITY AND ENTERPRISE, 1150–1300 351

18
The Materials of a New Learning 353
Schools, Curricula, and Objects of Study 353
Readers, Books, and Libraries: The Materials of Literacy 358
Language and Culture 362
The Market for Learning and Letters:
   Education and Careers in the Twelfth Century 369

19
The Content of the New Learning 374
Anselm and Abelard: From Dialectic to Philosophy 374
The Invention of Theology 379
The Professions: Law 383
The Medieval University 388

20
The Church and the World, 1098–1250 392
Monasticism and Civilization 392
New Forms of Devotion, Order, and Dissent 397
The New Pastoralism, Heretics, and Jews 410
Christendom as Polity: Papacy and Empire, 1123–1250 418

21
The Road to the World 431
Courtly Society and Secularization 431
The Flowering of Vernacular Literature 434
Arsitotle, Aquinas, and the Place of Nature 439
Secularization of the Active Life 442

22
Temporal Authority: From Territorial Principality to Territorial Monarchy 448
The King and the Kingdom 448
Traditional Status in a Changing Political World 463
The Conflict between Spiritual and Temporal Authority 466

23
Latin Christendom and Beyond 475
Byzantium, Outremer, and the Latin West, 1144–1261 475
Kingdom and Community in Central and Eastern Europe 480
The Mongol Empire, 1227–1350 487
Geography, Travel, and Commerce:
  The Opening of China and the Atlantic 491

PART SIX: THE HUMAN CONDITION 495

24
The Individual and Society in the Thirteenth Century 497
Birth and Death, Diet, Sickness and Health 497
Marrying and Giving in Marriage, Friendship,
  Love, and Hate, 501
Ceremony and Festival: The Human Year 506

25
The World of Dante 512
Italy and the Italian City-Republics 512
Civic Culture 516
Exul Immeritus 520

26
Material Civilization in Crisis: The Fourteenth Century 523
Famine, Plague, and Warfare 523
The Financial Crisis 530
The Problems of the Social Order 541

27
The Roots of Traditional Europe 546
Spirituality and Secularism 546
Power and Order 558
The Shape of Europe and the New World 574
The Frames of Time: Visions of a New Past and Present 582

Bibliography I General Bibliographies 587
  II Selective Bibliography 601

Index 617

PREFACE

The subject of this book is the settlement of Europe by its historical populations and the formation of a distinctively European material and spiritual culture that lasted, in some respects at least, until the Industrial Revolution and the political upheavals of the nineteenth and early twentieth centuries. The title of the last chapter, "The Roots of Traditional Europe," suggests one way of summing up this subject.

The emergence of a distinctively European civilization out of the worlds of Mediterranean antiquity and western and central Eurasia, and the forms of early culture, technology, and communication it assumed requires that such a study concern itself, even if in a highly selective way, with a slightly wider and more diverse map than that which describes Europe alone. For our purposes, the world of the Middle Ages is bounded by Greenland and the Urals, Norway and the northern Sahara, the valleys of the Shannon and the Euphrates. Its largest time-frames are those of the palaeoclimatologist and the demographer, although its practical limits may be conveniently considered as falling between the establishment of Roman colonies in southern Gaul and Spain in the late second century B.C. and a series of dates in the late fourteenth and fifteenth centuries A.D. Between these two periods, the Middle Ages can be, and has been more precisely defined, but, as the Introduction suggests, one of the most interesting chapters in European intellectual history lies in the shifting meanings of the term "Middle Ages" as it applies to the early settlement and culture of Europe.

I have chosen some conspicuously wide frames of inquiry for this book. The geographical and climatic sections with which it begins cover very long periods of time and large areas of space. The remainder of Part One treats both the general character of Mediterranean expansion and the encounter of Greeks and Romans with Celtic and Germanic peoples throughout the history of the Roman Empire and the transformation of the internal character of the Roman Empire itself. Part Two, dealing approximately with the period 395 to 650, traces the further divisions of the Mediterranean ecumenical world of Hellenism and Rome and the particular forms that the survivals of earlier tradition took in the face of new peoples settling in the areas of North Africa, the Near East, and Europe. Part Three, 650 to 950, characterizes the shaping of the first distinctive European culture since that of the Iron Age Celts and Rome, the culture supported and spread by the peoples ruled by Charlemagne and characterized by the book—the Bible—and the sword—the power of military force in the expansion of Frankish power. By 950 the problems of migration and settlement, cultural change and adaptation, and the similarities and differences among the worlds of the Frankish West, Byzantium, and Islam had produced open, vulnerable societies, of which only Byzantium, the surviving Eastern Roman Empire with its capital at Constantinople, may be said to have had deep roots both in the ancient Roman past and in its own internal structure. Both Islam and the Latin West were subjected to yet further change in the centuries that followed.

Part Four, 950 to 1150, studies the basis of the new material civilization and culture of the Latin West and the growing use of the concept of Christendom to designate it on a territorial and cultural basis. Part Five, 1150 to 1300, focuses in considerable detail upon the articulation of the material and cultural world of Christendom, and Part Six, "The Human Condition," considers, not the "end" of the Middle Ages, but the transformation of material life and the roots of traditional Europe.

The history of a civilization, or of any part of one, is a vast, intricate, and frequently opaque subject, one that requires if not expertise in, then at least awareness of the potential contributions of many disciplines. Only a few of these chapters are conventionally narrative, and most are highly selective. To have treated each of a wide variety of subjects as if they were relentlessly homogeneous would be to oversimplify the character of historical knowledge—and vastly to overestimate my own, as well as to lengthen this book beyond measure. One advantage of the final arrangement should be to inspire reflection upon the character of historical knowledge itself and to ask the question, "How do we know and what do we know that permits us to think about the life of the inhabitants of large areas through long periods of time and to make intelligible statements about them?" The bibliographies, both general and serial, suggest crucial further reading and are designed to give quick access to important areas of modern scholarship. If the term *humanities* retains its original meaning, the citation of major works in languages other than English is justified.

This book grew out of the needs of a teacher and his students, and it is addressed primarily to teachers and students of all ages, sexes, shapes, colors, sizes, and levels. To the students, day and evening, who have studied medieval history with me under a number of different catalogue designations at several universities, I am particularly grateful, partly for having shown me the particular shape of a pedagogical problem, and partly for having helped me, for a time, at least, to solve it. To my colleagues, particularly those in and out of the Department of History at the University of Pennsylvania, I am also grateful, because they let me badger them with problems that it would not have been fair to inflict upon students.

I am most grateful, however, to my own family, who alone know the amount of time—their time—that went into this project and made my life considerably easier, as they always do, while I finished it. To offer my children this book in dedication is only a clumsy sign of affection, certainly not a hint of even partial repayment.

EDWARD PETERS

EUROPE
**The World
of the Middle Ages**

INTRODUCTION:
The Discovery and Invention of the Middle Ages

"As we walked over the walls of the shattered city [of Rome], or sat there, the fragments of the ruins were under our very eyes. Our conversation turned toward history, which we appear to have divided up between us in such a fashion that in modern history you, in ancient history I, seemed the more expert; and ancient were called those events which took place before the name of Christ was celebrated in Rome, and adored by the Roman emperors, modern, however, the events from that time to the present." In these words written to his friend Giovanni Colonna in 1343, the Italian scholar, poet, man of letters, and sometime historian Francesco Petrarca introduced one of the fundamental distinctions of modern historical thought: that between the world of Mediterranean antiquity and the European world that followed it. The act of dividing the past into distinctive and intelligible periods did not,

2 Introduction

however, originate with Petrarca. Both Greek and Roman historical thought had concerned themselves with successive ages, cycles, and distinctive periods, as had, in a very different way, the historical literature of the Old Testament. From the fourth to the fourteenth centuries a series of combinations of Old Testament and classical ideas made a number of recognized divisions of past time the common property of many European thinkers. Some of these appear to resemble more recent divisions, whereas others seem to derive from myth, legend, prophecy, and literary exegesis. Both kinds, however, derived equally from a religious cosmology, and both reflected sets of criteria that were fundamentally religious in character. From Petrarca on, the religious ground of historical thought was not, to be sure, lost, but other grounds and sets of criteria were added to it, creating a number of different kinds of historical views that flourished between Petrarca's time and the nineteenth century. Among those new historical views there occurred the discovery and invention of the Middle Ages.

Petrarca's interests, which centered primarily in the character of the Latin language and the relation between moral philosophy and civil life, certainly colored his view that a distinctive period in history ended during the fourth century A.D. Others who later took up his distinction had other interests, equally limited and equally passionate. It is the limited character of many of these interests and the limited resources of historical investigation on the part of those who held them that produced the wide variety of definitions of the period after the fourteenth century that prompt me to suggest that a combination of these interests and limited resources led first to an "invention" of the Middle Ages— or, rather, many inventions, which suited the purposes of those who concocted them. Invoking theories of history to illustrate or justify confessional or ideological views is a technique that was not limited to the period between Petrarca and the nineteenth century, of course, but the effects of such invocation were much greater before the advent of critical methods for the study of history. For in a number of different areas, usually unknown or indifferent to each other, thinkers between the fifteenth and the nineteenth centuries did in fact discover critical means of investigating the past and broadened their ideas of historical periodization. This second thread, manifesting itself in the expansion and broadening of historical inquiry, the insistence upon critical methodologies, and the influence, to be sure, of changing cultural values in the eighteenth and nineteenth centuries, led to what may be called the "discovery" of the Middle Ages. As a result of the process leading to the discovery and invention of the Middle Ages, then, it is possible to study both the early history of Europe and the history of various ideas concerning the early history of Europe. An awareness of both the results of historical method and the history of historical thought is necessary to the student of history, for history is not an absolute or infinite art, and an awareness of what one historian has called "the disguises of history" aids us in reflecting critically upon our own historical knowledge.

Petrarca, of course, had not set out to revolutionize historical thought when he wrote to Colonna in 1343, nor did his criteria for historical periodization extend far beyond linguistic and civil interests, although he strongly urged the Holy Roman Emperor of his own day, Charles IV, to reassert imperial authority in Italy, and in doing so revealed a distinctly characteristic prophetic strain. There is no question either, of Petrarca or any of his successors being "pagan revivalists." Petrarca's significance in the train of historical thought in which we are considering him lay precisely in his Christian beliefs and in his use of what may conveniently be called secular criteria to add another dimension to the idea of history. For Petrarca's secularism was in one respect, at least, highly original. He knew about ancient Rome and the life and language that had once thrived there better than anyone before him; he had spent a lifetime studying these subjects, and although his dividing line between ancient and modern history falls in the period of the Christianization of the Roman Empire, he drew no explicitly causal connections between the acceptance of Christianity by the emperors and the "decline" of Rome. Later thinkers, however, did.

In the century and a half following Petrarca's casual distinction between "ancient" and "modern" history—and it should be noted that Petrarca did not especially admire what he termed "modern" history—historians and chroniclers adapted that distinction and focused on interests different from his. By the fifteenth century some writers had cast off Petrarca's pessimism about "modern" history and begun to talk of their own times as recapturing some of the glories of ancient life and thought. The terms of their inquiry broadened to include not only letters, language, and civil life, but the arts, architecture, religion, and, somewhat improbably, even medicine, science, magic, and technology as contributing to a revival, a "rebirth," of classical values. By the end of the fifteenth century some writers had divided Petrarca's "modern" period into two periods: a long, nameless, undistinguished period lasting from the fourth to the fourteenth centuries, and a new "modern" period, from Petrarca's lifetime onward, characterized by the rescue of classical values from a thousand years of neglect.

Some of these writers even coined the modern terms for the division. By the fifteenth century the term *antiquitas* (antiquity) designated the Roman world, and the term *modernitas* (modernity) came more frequently to designate, not Petrarca's "from the time [when] the name of Christ was celebrated in Rome, and adored by the Roman emperors . . . to the present," but from Petrarca's own lifetime (1306-1372) onward. What modernity represented to the first people who used the term was a "rebirth," a "revival" (in later French, *renaissance*) of Roman classical culture. Classical antiquity, revived, reborn, brought from darkness into light, became a widely admired ideal, and in comparison the nameless period between what fifteenth-century metaphorical thought called *ab inclinatione imperii* ("from the decline of the Empire") and the period of rebirth appeared grimmer and grimmer. The cultural and political splendors of ancient Rome had "fallen," "declined," and "died." Thinkers of the fifteenth and sixteenth centuries had "revived" them, "reawakened," "resurrected," and "restored" them from the "darkness," "shadows," "murk," "gloom," and "ignorance" into which they had tumbled so long ago.

The metaphorical language of such historical periodization as this illuminates the minds of those who used it. In it, empires "decline and fall," cultures pass from "light" into "darkness" and back again, and the life of the ancient past is "reborn." The first of these images is from the realm of architecture and the rest are from that of theology. As Theodor Mommsen once pointed out, the terms darkness and light, death and rebirth in these writings were borrowed from the vocabulary of theology, particularly from the language of baptism and spiritual reform and renewal. This linguistic evidence is but one example of the secularizing of religious motifs that governed much of the historical thought of early modern Europe.

In the sixteenth and seventeenth centuries, a religious revolution contributed a further dimension to the divisions of history. Theologians of the Reformation, from Luther to Calvin and beyond, not only attacked the Christian Church of their own time but quickly proposed a view of history, particularly ecclesiastical history, that regarded the Christianization of the Roman Empire and the subsequent history of the Western Latin Church as a spectacular betrayal of the principles of early Christianity. The formation of a number of regional and national churches after the Reformation further generated local interest in local history, in establishing the antiquity and independence from Rome of regional churches, and in combing through historical documents that they collected painstakingly for evidence against Rome. These historical controversies and collections of documents became one of the most important seedbeds of later historical methodology. In 1604 the German legal historian Melchior Goldast coined one more of a variety of labels that have been applied to the period between *antiquitas* and *modernitas*. He called the period a *medium aevum,* a "middle age," and in 1675 a hack writer of history books, Christopher Kellarius, wrote a popular history called *The Nucleus of Middle History between Ancient and Modern*. After Kellarius, the label stuck. The Middle Ages had been invented.

Not all interest in the Middle Ages, however, was generated by cultural and confessional styles. Some areas of interest did not permit the period to be treated with quite the kind of scorn that we have seen developing above. The pride of rulers and subjects in the history of their own kingdoms and churches, the legal problems of the continuity of families, property titles, and governmental institutions, aristocratic interest in family history—in short, all of the complex and widely dispersed roots in the past that sixteenth- and seventeenth-century societies necessarily possesed generated subtle tenions between hostility and appreciation, indifference and interest. And in the arenas of law, scholarship, and constitutional crises, questions of the authenticity of laws, rights, and documents and of the accuracy of information about the past generated new critical methods as well as means for their dissemination. The debate as to whether the rights of Englishmen descended from an "Ancient Constitution" or were created and defined by the conquest of William of Normandy in 1066 troubled the constitutional upheavals of seventeenth-century England. At the same time, the decision of a group of Jesuit scholars in the Netherlands to publish an authentic calendar of the saints along with critical editions of saints' lives led to the inauguration of the longest ongoing collaborative research project in Western history, the *Acta Sanctorum* of the Bollandists, and generated disputes among religious sectors about scholarly accuracy and partisanship. The Benedictine monks of St. Maur and their greatest representative, Jean Mabillon, the father of modern paleography, were yet another group. Isolated antiquarians, legal researchers, enthusiastic local amateurs, and court historians all drew upon this loose and unorganized body of technique and knowledge throughout the seventeenth and eighteenth centuries. At the same time, popular interest in stories of chivalry and romantic adventure remained at a high level, barely scratched by the scathing satire of Cervantes's *Don Quixote*.

The philosophical historians of the eighteenth century launched an even more furious attack on the Middle Ages. Imbued with the notion that there was an absolute standard according to which all periods of history and societies could be judged—and that this standard consisted largely of how closely their values resembled those of the philosophical historians who were doing the judging—such writers as Hume and Voltaire heaped eloquent scorn upon what they considered the servility, superstition, ignorance, and barbarity of early European society. Their critical, rational, anticlerical, and antifabulist temper led them to criticize not only the past itself, but also the dusty and pedantic antiquarians and uncouth ecclesiastics who continued to interest themselves seriously in that past. In 1776, however, there appeared the first volume of Edward Gibbon's *Decline and Fall of the Roman Empire*, a work that incorporated many of the values of the critics of the Middle Ages, but also, and for the first time, much of the technique worked out by scholars, antiquarians, and local amateurs. Gibbon's scorn for what he contemptuously called "The Triumph of Barbarism and Religion" was not unlike that of Hume and Voltaire, but Gibbon's massive erudition, his obvious mastery of antiquarian and scholarly detail, and his insistence upon a critical use of these scholarly techniques translated the debate over the Middle Ages to a different technical level. The discovery of the Middle Ages began in freeing historical thought and literature from ideology, confession, and taste and subjecting its formation to a critical and tested scholarly methodology.

Within Gibbon's lifetime (1737–1794) not only did the basis of historical periodization change, but so did the cultural sensibility of Europe. By the end of the eighteenth century, a new and sometimes grotesque taste for the Middle Ages had emerged from the welter of shifting attitudes and interests of many Europeans. In the stirrings of a new kind of interest in the regional and national past that began to consider language, folklore, and tradition as well as political and legal history, and in the philosophical approaches of thinkers such as Hegel and the aesthetic sensibility of the Romanticists in literature and art, the spectrum of historical inquiry widened once more. At its most awful, the Romantic taste for the Middle Ages was no less bizarre and hallucinatory than the hostility of eighteenth-century philosophers. At its most effective, however, the Romantic interest supported and made respectable the techniques of scholarly research that Gibbon had first begun to pull together. From the early nineteenth century date a number of important collective publishing enterprises that began for the first time on a large scale to make available in print many of the most important documentary sources of medieval history. In 1826, under the able and dedicated direction of the Prussian statesman Baron Karl von Stein, a group of able scholars published the first volume of the *Monumenta Germaniae Historica,* a vast undertaking to print well-edited versions of all the sources of German history from the end of the Roman Empire in the West to the age of print. The *MGH,* as it is popularly known, is still in operation, now in Munich, and with the *Acta Sanctorum* of the Bollandists and the *Histoire Littéraire de la France* of the Maurists represents the cultural impact of nineteenth-century editing technique and public support of historical research at its best. Private and state-supported research and publication facilities were joined later in the century by the increasing work of scholars at universities, particularly that of Leopold von Ranke, who brought his researches in archives and libraries into the classroom and laid the foundations for extremely influential historical seminars at Göttingen and Berlin. By the end of the nineteenth century, Romantic interest, private and public patronage, and the increasing professionalization of historical research and teaching in the universities of Germany, then of France and England, had substantially transformed both historical thought and critical method and had brought the Middle Ages into the arena where Europe for the first time discovered Europe.

The increasing practice of professionalizing the study of history in universities and the spreading influence of German scholarly techniques links the world of Stein and Ranke to that of the United States at the end of the nineteenth and the beginning of the twentieth century. Presidents Andrew Dickson White of Cornell, Daniel C. Gilman of Johns Hopkins, and Charles W. Eliot of Harvard assembled new faculties of history. Henry Charles Lea of Philadelphia became the first American medievalist recognized by Europeans as their equal. German methods made a considerable impact upon American historiography. The growing involvement of the United States in European affairs between the Hague Peace Conference of 1907 and the end of World War I generated further interest in the European past, and in 1925 the Mediaeval Academy of America was founded in Cambridge, Massachusetts, for the purpose of supporting the work of medievalists in all fields. The journal of the Academy, *Speculum,* first published in 1926, has often served as a good indicator of the temper of medieval studies in the United States.

In 1929 another journal was founded, this time in France under the guidance of two brilliant historians, Marc Bloch and Lucien Febvre.

Annales d'histoire économique et sociale (since 1946 entitled *Annales: économies, sociétés, civilizations*) represented an all-out attack on the traditional predominance of political and diplomatic history and the narrowness of academic historical research. By insisting upon the equal and often superior importance of economic and social history and, in the work of Febvre, in the reconstruction of "mental worlds" in making coherent longer units of the past (as opposed to the particularistic and event-oriented traditions of political history), French historical theory has displaced the German influence and largely reigned supreme to the present, and has in turn strongly influenced approaches to medieval history. The new, broader frames of inquiry have been very productive, particularly in conjunction with the arrival of many European scholars in the United States during and after World War II, the increasing availability of research support permitting travel and research in European archives, and the growing influence of the techniques of the social sciences. Since 1945, in fact, most aspects of historical inquiry have changed and many medieval historians have extended their interests to the hitherto neglected areas of Islamic and Jewish studies, Byzantine history, interdisciplinary approaches, and the detailed and sophisticated study of small regions. The widened character of historical inquiry and the increasingly interdisciplinary character of research are perhaps the two most striking aspects of the most recent stages in the discovery, rather than the invention, of the Middle Ages.

PART **ONE**

EUROPE AND THE
ANCIENT WORLD

A MAP OF THE MEDIEVAL ENVIRONMENT:
The Geography and Climate
of Mediterranean
and North Temperate Europe

PHYSICAL EUROPE: LANDS AND WATERS

The topographical and climatic changes that produced the physical map of Europe were completed shortly after the last withdrawal of the great glacial ice sheets after 7000 B.C. By then, human societies had already made their first settlements in transalpine Europe and the Mediterranean basin, and, thus, the shaping of Europe involved human activity as well as large-scale physical change. Geological, geographical, and climatic change constitute the largest segments of time within which the human community may be studied, but precisely because they are so large, their role in smaller historical segments is not always clear. Shorter conventional divisions of past time, however, are not the only ones that bear upon the experience of the European peoples, and the characteristics of geography and climatic change exert a set of long-range influences that are best considered at the outset of any longer study.

Physical relief, soil characteristics, vegetation, and climate helped shape the character of agricultural Europe from the earliest societies until the Industrial Revolution in a consistent way. Yet neither geography nor climate pose rigid, deterministic patterns on human life. Mountains, for example, may serve to protect the last remnants of earlier societies in the face of new migrations in the lowlands, as they have in the western and northern highlands of Great Britain, the Massif Central of France, and the Pyrenees. Yet mountains may also constitute sure routes for migration itself, as have the Alps and the Carpathians since the Bronze Age, when

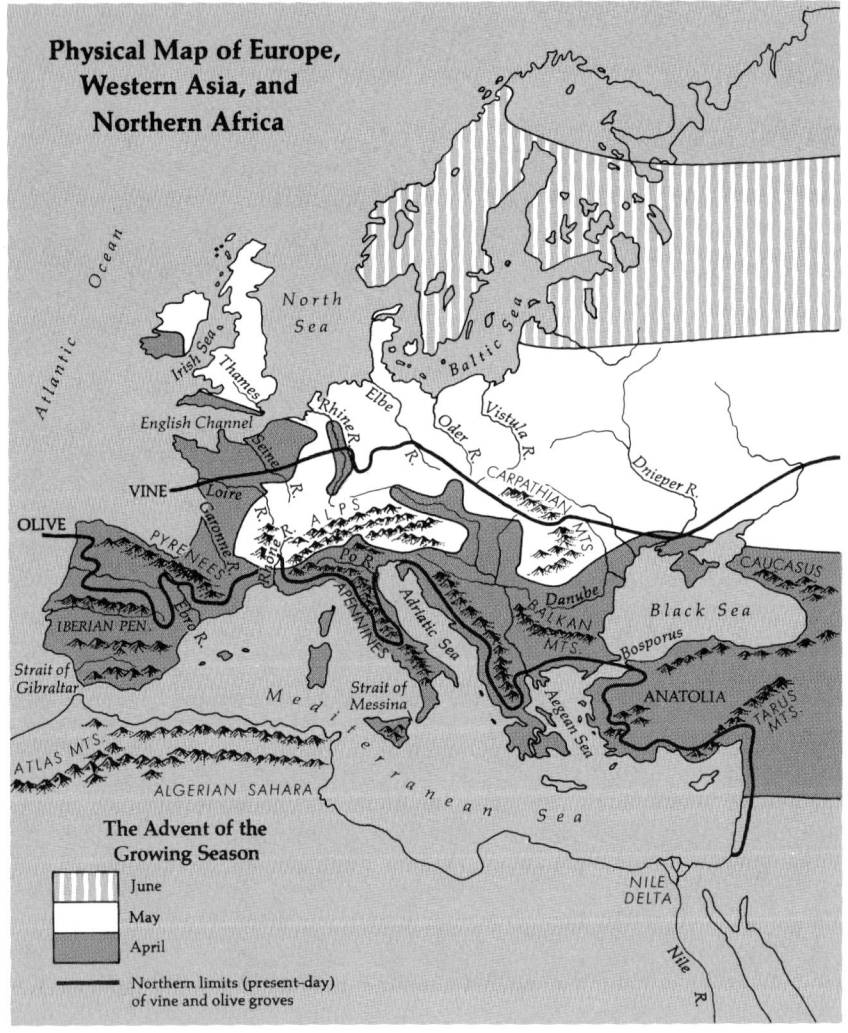

Physical Map of Europe, Western Asia, and Northern Africa

the great passes that are still in use today became roads instead of barriers. Rivers may serve as frontiers or migratory routes, their valleys offering easier communications and passage than the great forests, which, far more than mountains and rivers, offered the most formidable obstacles to early migrating peoples. The orientation of land to river or sea, or to similar kinds of land nearby, influences both settlement and migration patterns, often as much as do the more conventional institutions of linguistic or political unity. The physical environment of human societies has rarely constituted a prison, but, rather, has been a medium for potential growth, cultural change, and communications.

On the physical map of Europe, unencumbered by the familiar but often misleading political, cultural, and linguistic boundaries, three broad areas, each with distinctive characteristics, are prominent: the Mediterranean basin, the mountains and plains of central and eastern Europe, and the western parts of transalpine Europe. These areas constitute the three great geographical and climatic zones of the European world. Considered together, they remind us of the proximity of Europe and the western part of Eurasia generally to the great sweep of the Baltic and North Seas, the Atlantic Ocean, the Mediterranean Sea, and the Black Sea. Few places in Europe are far from one of these bodies of water, and the remarkable systems of navigable rivers that reach out from the deepest parts of the land mass bring much of European society even closer to the sea. Coasts and rivers, valleys, mountains, forests, and plains offer different physical landscapes in each of our three major areas, but the elements they have in common must be kept in mind as we consider their distinctive features.

The Mediterranean basin and the Black Sea have remarkably similar coastal areas, but they link widely diverse hinterlands. Not only does the Mediterranean Sea touch nearly all the early centers of Western civilization, it also joins them. Unlike the Atlantic, with its storms, complex tidal patterns, difficult islands, channels, and headlands, the Mediterranean invites human activity. It has few summer storms, offers generally clear, starry skies for navigation, and is rarely troubled by fog. Its extremely long coastline, interrupted by numerous islands and peninsulas, each with accessible harbors, makes navigation easy. Although the Mediterranean touches very different geographical areas, its immediate coastal regions are much alike, and migrating or colonizing peoples could easily find a physical environment similar to the one they had left, whether they moved to the Levant, North Africa, Southern France, or the eastern coast of Spain. Thus, Mediterranean societies tended to expand northward or southward only as far as a Mediterranean-type terrain and climate prevailed.

Around the sea, mountains and desert often sweep down close to the coastline, and the small societies that lived on coastal plains or possessed a few good harbors were often oriented more toward the sea than toward their inland neighbors a few miles away over the mountains or across the desert. The Mediterranean region, unlike the North, Baltic, and Black Seas, receives few major rivers. Only the Ebro in Spain, the

Rhone in France, the Po in Italy, the Orontes in Syria, and the Nile in Egypt flow into it. Thus, the Mediterranean coastal areas have been more densely populated than the hinterlands and have often formed political units that reflected their geographical orientation. Southern Syria and Palestine, for example, have several times formed a single unit, as have North Africa and southeastern Spain on the one hand, and northeastern Spain and southern France, on the other. The northeastern part of the Mediterranean, including Greece, Asia Minor, and the Black Sea coasts, have also formed cultural and political units on occasion. Finally, certain places in the Mediterranean have frequently served as contact points among different cultures. Sicily, Crete, Malta, the Balearic Islands, Sardinia, and Cyprus have played this role, from the earliest recorded times to the present.

Not only do the Mediterranean Sea and its coastal regions constitute a distinctive area of European geography, but they contain a distinctive variety of soil and vegetation. The Mediterranean region has far less arable land than northern and eastern Europe, and its soil is different from theirs. Mediterranean soil is light and dry, and the warm climate forces ground water to evaporate at a faster rate than rainfall can replace it. Thus, there is little risk of leaching out valuable mineral content, but there is always a very great risk of losing too much of the water that is needed for agriculture. The key to Mediterranean agriculture is the conservation of moisture, usually by careful irrigation, terracing, and water storage. Such agricultural engineering requires extensive labor forces, continual attention to the fabric of agricultural land, and a careful balance between the population that must be supported by the arable land and the population required to work it. The vegetation of the Mediterranean region consists of scrub pines and cypress trees, olive groves and vineyards in the lower altitudes, and a few hardwoods, such as oak, only very high up. The richest soil in the region lies in a few river valleys and coastal plains that lie very low and, when rainfall runoff is particularly heavy, tend to catch standing water and turn into marshy fields. The draining of these marshes has occupied Mediterranean society from the age of the Romans to the twentieth century. Wood that can be used for building is scarce, and stone and brick structures with flat roofs thus characterize the towns and farms on all coasts. The people live much of their lives out of doors. Most societies are small and local.

A second broad area of Europe comprises the lands from just east of the Rhine to the Ural mountains. This area has played perhaps the greatest role in the migration of peoples from western Asia into eastern and western Europe. In the southern parts of this region, the Alps, Carpathians, and Balkans constitute mountain barriers with a few direct routes south into the Mediterranean world. Within these mountain strongholds, and on the great-plains and steppe of South Russia, many primitive societies found relatively easy agricultural and herding conditions that sustained them on their great treks west. North of the line of mountains, the great plains and very low mountain ridges of central and eastern Europe offered easy access to agricultural land and westward migration routes.

In this region, as in western Europe, the soil is different from that of the Mediterranean region. Here, the land is heavy and clayey, and the problem is to dispose of water rather than conserve it. The climate allows less evaporation of ground water, and the heavier rainfall increases the danger of minerals being leached from the heavier, wetter soil. Therefore, the soil must be drained, dried, and, in the south and west, fertilized intensively if it is to regain its lost mineral content. The lands of the lower Danube valley possess soils of easily cultivated *loess,* wind- and flood-deposited rich earth, although in other parts of central Europe there are great areas of sandy, marshy soils interspersed with large coniferous forests. Stretching out just north of the southern mountain and plain region, are the great plains of central Europe and western Russia, where the quick freezing of winter and the high humus content prevent leaching. These lands thus contain some of the best soils in the world for large-scale agriculture.

The South Russian plain and the eastern Balkan region offer several corridors to the Mediterranean south, and the great Danube valley offers a corridor to the western lands of Europe. Rivers in central and eastern Europe are generally easily navigable, and the advantages of soil and migration routes help explain why this region was both a "hearth" of prehistoric and historical migratory cultures and a corridor of transmission north of the Alps and the eastern Mediterranean for the cultures and peoples of western Asia on their way to Europe.

Western Europe, the third geographical region, constituted the end of the long westward migration routes from prehistory until the thirteenth century A.D. It consists generally of a great fan-shaped plain that begins in southern France and opens out north and east all the way to Russia. This great plain is crossed by many navigable rivers and by low mountain ranges rich in minerals. South of the plain, the long ridges of the Pyrenees, Alps, and Balkans lie in an east-west axis that separates western and central Europe from the Mediterranean. The maritime and riverine character of western Europe gave access to the sea and, for sea peoples ranging from Bronze Age migrants to the Vikings, access to the land. Surrounded by the sea, the fan-shaped plain of western and northern Europe extends east to Russia and includes southern England and southern Sweden in its sweep. The rivers that cross it are evenly flowing and suitable for navigation. From the Atlantic coast of France to western Russia, the Garonne, Loire, Seine, Meuse, Thames, Rhine, Weser, Elbe, Oder, Vistula, and Duna systems offer both transportation and agricultural possibilities perhaps unequaled anywhere else in the world. Some of these systems extend even further beyond the western European geographical region, providing transportation routes even greater than those just mentioned. The Rhine-Danube corridor offers virtually unimpeded routes from the North Sea to the Black Sea, and the Duna-Dnieper system nearly constitutes a water route from the Baltic to the Black Sea.

The soil and vegetation of western Europe are also distinctive. Heavy clay soils there tend to leach out mineral content and retain excessive moisture. Unlike the Mediterranean and the Russian plains, drainage and fertilizing are essential elements in soil maintenance. Forests grow thick and usually comprise hardwoods, and the land, although rich, requires a sophisticated technology and dense population settlements in order to produce a large agricultural surplus.

Western Europe was reached from the east through the Danube valley, the Carpathians, and, less frequently, the wide northern plains. From the Mediterranean, peoples and influences could travel north over the Alps, and up the Rhone-Saône and Narbonne-Garonne valleys in southern France. Northern peoples could use these routes, as well as the Belfort and Saverne Gaps in what is now southwestern Germany and the southward routes through Yugoslavia in the Dinaric Alps and through the eastern Balkans.

Settlement and migration, survival and starvation, and differences in topography and climate all constitute the fundamental basis for the settlement of Europe and the relations among the cultures that grew up in each of its parts.

THE CLIMATE OF NORTH TEMPERATE AND MEDITERRANEAN EUROPE, 500 B.C.–1850 A.D.

Neither geographic nor climatic characteristics constitute a determinist physical universe. Humans are no more prisoners or victims of the climate in which they live than they are of the lands, rivers, seas, and mountains among which they sustain themselves and create their cultures. Climatic changes, however, particularly when they occur among societies of limited or undeveloped material culture, may create conditions in which the habits of hunting, pastoral, or agricultural societies are altered substantially. Although it is often difficult and sometimes pointless to attempt to relate climatic change to social change in terms of specific years or events, climatic characteristics over long periods of time must be taken into account in considering the history of societies whose means of responding to climatic change are limited. Climate, like geography, is an important part of the physical environment of all human societies, but the long periods of time that constitute the divisions of the paleoclimatologist's "clock" suggest a separate discussion of the climate of North Temperate and Mediterranean Europe, one that must deal necessarily with different divisions of history from those that historians conventionally use.

Before 1750 A.D. or so, the evidence of continuous and minute meteorological observations upon which the modern study of climate is based are either infrequent and inaccurate or completely nonexistent. The modern discipline of paleoclimatology, however, by piecing together

A Map of the Medieval Environment 17

records from widely differing and variously reliable sources and by exploiting newer methods of scientific analysis of historical climatic conditions and changes, has tentatively been able to reconstruct much of the climatic history of Europe and other parts of the world. The broad divisions of the climate of Europe that have been so reconstructed are the Decline of the Post-Glacial Climatic Optimum, 1000 B.C.–100 B.C.; a period of gradual drying and warming that followed, culminating in the Secondary Optimum of Climate, 400 A.D.–1200 A.D.; another decline between 1200 and 1400, followed by a partial recovery between 1400 and 1550; and the so-called Little Ice Age, 1550–1850. The characteristic features of these periods and the names that climatologists give them may at first seem forbidding and recondite, but they become considerably less so if one recalls the long literary and artistic tradition that has preserved some memory of them, however distorted, to the present day. The vivid descriptions of the freezing of the river Thames in England, which sixteenth- and seventeenth-century observers recorded, was marked by the holding of royal courts and pageants on the ice, and the colder English winters of two centuries later are captured memorably in the novels and stories of Charles Dickens. The impenetrable forests and terrifying storms of an earlier period survive in fairy tales and folk legends as well as in the perceptions of medieval chroniclers, in whose works meteorological phenomena are often as important as major political, economic, or religious events.

By 2000 B.C. the Post-Glacial Climatic Optimum had raised temperatures in Europe several degrees higher than they are at present and had permitted the forests to spread north. A subsequent period of heavy and prolonged rainfall transformed much of these forests into bogs and swamps (some of which survive in Ireland, England, Switzerland, and eastern Europe). During a subsequent dryer period, the forests once again circled north. During this period grassland covered much of what is now the Sahara Desert, and people appear to have migrated easily across Northwest Africa. By 1000–500 B.C. the decline of the Post-Glacial Climatic Optimum, the so-called Early Iron Age Cold Epoch, turned the Sahara from grassland to desert and introduced a colder and wetter climate into Europe, one that caused the boundary between forest and steppe grassland to move east. By 500 B.C. the forest had pushed east to the River Don. From this date, the thick, heavy forests of Europe became a fundamental influence upon patterns of migration and settlement. By 100 B.C. the Cold Epoch had begun to ameliorate, and between 400 A.D. and 1200 A.D. Europe once again became considerably warmer and dryer, the Atlantic appears to have been free of great storms and drift ice, and Mediterranean writers observed that the cultivation of the vine and the olive, the characteristic Mediterranean commercial crops, had moved north in Italy into areas that had within living memory been too cold and wet to sustain them.

In western and central Europe vineyards appear to have thrived four to five degrees farther north than they do now, and a mean summer temperature several degrees higher than at present reduced the dangers of

May frosts in northern Europe and resulted in much milder Septembers. In southern Europe and North Africa this period may have produced colder and wetter weather, and rivers flowing into the Mediterranean were probably much broader and deeper than they are now.

After 1200, however, Europe slowly grew colder and wetter. The early period from 1200 to 1600 witnessed considerable climatic instability, flood following upon drought, mild and dry winters upon bitterly cold and wet ones, famine upon plenty. The Northern Hemisphere grew colder, and ice closed around Iceland and Greenland. In some areas land froze that had once been under the plow, and the water temperature in the oceans dropped several degrees below what it is today. Between 1300 and 1600 forest levels declined in Europe, and although the summers north of fifty degrees north latitude were as warm as they are at present, the winters seem to have grown significantly colder, both in northern Europe and in the Mediterranean. The frequency of plague and other epidemic diseases in Europe between 1300 and 1700 may be related to these climatic changes, as may be the significant changes in agricultural activity, the reduction of the amount of arable land, and the marked enlargement of forest and swamp area. From 1550 to 1850, Europe experienced the "Little Ice Age," during which it was consistently beset with colder and wetter weather than it had known for many centuries. Not until the late nineteenth and early twentieth centuries did these conditions begin to change significantly.

The raw data of climatic history do not, however, point inevitably to a single interpretation. Crops and human societies can absorb considerable climatic change without danger. Climatic change is one of a number of long-range variable influences upon the course of human social life. Far more important is to consider the human geography of Europe— the resources with which human societies encountered geographical and climatic phenomena.

SOCIETY AND ENVIRONMENT IN EARLY EUROPE

Neither geographic nor climatic description alone suffices to account for the character of human settlement in particular places at particular times. In general, it is safe enough to say that the small populations armed with crude stone, wooden, or metal tools could make little headway in western and central Europe before the climatic changes and technological innovations of the Iron Age. Geographical and climatic data help explain the precocity in agricultural and social organization of the Tigris-Euphrates and Nile river societies on the one hand, and the commercial cultivation of olive oil and wine by Mediterranean coastal societies on the other hand. But geographical and climatic conditions and their impact upon human communities often depend more upon the size and character of those communities, whether they farm or herd, whether they are migratory or sedentary, whether they consume or trade their produce. The Neolithic Agricultural Revolution occurred between 9000 and 7000 B.C., and by 5500 B.C. human societies had devised irrigation systems in Mesopotamia and had begun to exploit the regular floodings of the Nile to produce large grain harvests that sustained relatively large, well-organized societies. Greece and the Levantine coast, however, had no such rivers nor such possibilities for organizing large societies based upon common mass labor in the fields, because of their poorer soil and drier weather than Egypt or Mesopotamia. Consequently, olive groves and vineyards, which thrive in heat and dry climates, made considerable headway there, the grain being purchased from afar or grown in Black Sea colonies. Fishing and shipping thus played a greater role in these societies' lives, and after 2000 B.C. many Mediterranean peoples began to colonize other parts of the Mediterranean, the greatest movement being generally west, toward North Africa, Italy, and Spain. In such smaller-scale comparisons as these, the relation between geography and climate may become somewhat clearer.

The large populations of ancient Mesopotamia, Egypt, and Rome lived precariously upon the intensive cultivation of particular kinds of land and upon the labor of a preponderantly large portion of their population. Outside these areas, human populations were much smaller and were faced, in terms of geography and climate, with very different conditions. The heavy damp soil and hardwood cover of transalpine Europe had to be turned, drained, and cleared before its wealth could be tapped, and such activity required large numbers of people and sophisticated tools. Small bands of migrants or Iron Age pastoral peoples could not begin to develop the agricultural potential of transalpine Europe until they became adapted to the climate and settled in their new homes.

In this sense, it is possible to conceive a history of the Mediterranean region, or of Egypt or Mesopotamia, over a longer time frame than that of the history of Europe. One of the greatest historians of the twentieth century, Fernand Braudel, wrote his master work, *The Mediterranean and the Mediterranean World in the Age of Philip II,* on the unity of the Mediterranean world in the late sixteenth century, and in so doing drew heavily upon the conditions of geography and climate that had prevailed in that region from Roman times to the seventeenth century.

The expansion and contraction of Mediterranean societies, the Mediterranean contacts with northern peoples, and the settlement of transalpine Europe first by Celtic and later by Germanic migrants thus took place along geographic and climatic frontiers as well as political and cultural ones. One of these frontiers is the track of the prevailing westerly winds that bring rainfall to transalpine Europe, rainfall that the Iberian peninsula prevents the Mediterranean from receiving. Another is the 32° January Isotherm, the line that divides land that freezes in the winter from land that does not. It runs north-south from the eastern Baltic Sea to western Switzerland, and then southeast to the lower Danube basin. Thus, east-west climatic differences can, in certain areas, be more substantial than the conventional north-south differences. Although a characteristic Mediterranean agriculture and society may sustain itself reasonably far north in the western part of Europe, it can be sustained only a little distance to the north of Greece and Asia Minor.

The drying out and exhaustion of Mediterranean soils could be compensated for by a powerful Mediterranean society either by expansion to other, less exhausted areas (for Roman society, both southern France and North Africa provided agricultural substitutes for exhausted Italian soil; for Greece, Asia Minor and the Black Sea region) or by commercial agriculture, in which salable products are sold for essential foodstuffs. As Mediterranean societies expanded west, the position of the January Isotherm afforded an opportunity to expand Mediterranean agriculture, particularly that of the vine and olive, farther north than was possible for eastern Mediterranean society. Mediterranean agriculture, in spite of its enormous skill in caring for and restoring the thin soil available to it, could not continue to sustain an increasing population without expansion and/or argicultural commerce. Italy, like Greece, slowly exhausted its light, easily worked topsoil, and evidence indicates that, for example, between 200 B.C. and 200 A.D.—the period of Rome's rise to universal political power in the Mediterranean—much of Italy appears to have lost between six and sixteen inches of precious topsoil, thereby reducing the effectiveness of its remaining land and reducing equally the land's ability to retain moisture because of the increased runoff of rainfall. It was also during this period that Roman expansion into southern France and, more important agriculturally, Sicily and North Africa, provided Italy with a new source of cereal grains. Of the "bread and circuses" of Roman legend, the circuses were an Italian product but the "bread" came from outside Italy. Indeed, the great African grain fleets constituted the lifeline of Rome's expanded population until their disappearance in the fifth century A.D.

The warming and drying of the Mediterranean coast that reduced the agricultural output of Greece and Rome appears to have increased the productivity of northern Europe and the amount of land under cultivation there, and hence contributed to the population growth in Europe and the increasingly frequent use of iron-edged tools—axes and plows—to encroach upon the hitherto impenetrable forests. If the thinning of dense woodlands in the east drew the steppe peoples closer to western Europe, it also afforded the peoples of Europe agricultural opportunities unequaled anywhere else in the world.

Geographical and climatic features of transalpine Europe gave Europeans considerable incentives for expansion and innovation in agriculture. Nearly all the great labor-saving inventions that have rapidly transformed the character of Western civilization (and presently threaten to help extinguish it) date from the early stages of the 100 B.C.–1400 A.D. "Little Climatic Optimum." The water mill, for example, was probably known to early Mediterranean peoples, but their extensive use of slave labor may have made it unnecessary; a steady supply of slaves could perform its tasks just as well. Moreover, the character of Mediterranean rivers and streams may have made the water mill an unprofitable acquisition. Most Mediterranean rivers are either too small or their flow is too seasonal and irregular for water mills to be of much use. In transalpine Europe, however, where the effects of large-scale slavery were never as extensive as they were in the Mediterranean (slavery was to continue in North Africa and the Middle East long after it virtually disappeared from northern Europe), conditions of geography and climate favored agricultural innovation and the exploitation of nonhuman sources of power. The rivers of Europe, unlike those of the Mediterranean region, flow regularly winter and summer, and summer moisture and coolness increase the effectiveness of summer rains. The prevailing winds in Europe are, like those in Asia and North America, westerly, and hence continually replenish the moisture of Europe. (China and the northeastern United States, in contrast, experience drier westerlies because these reach them over long stretches of land.) In Northwest Europe rainfall occurs much more frequently in the form of showers and drizzles than in that of cloudbursts, and soaks the land far more effectively than in other areas. The European moisture pattern and the character of European rivers are thus two elements that distinguish Europe from other areas.

Of all the physical features of Europe, the last to be adapted to the will and needs of humans was the ocean. Atlantic civilization did not begin to replace Mediterranean civilization until after the sixteenth century. Yet even the Atlantic and the North Sea, far more stormy and capricious bodies of water than the Mediterranean, Black, and Baltic seas, offered Europeans advantages that they were quick to accept. The North and Baltic Seas (like the Grand Banks off Newfoundland) teem with fish, and the European Atlantic coast is not so difficult to sail that maritime cultures from as early as the Bronze Age could not exploit the ocean itself as a means of transportation. The Gulf Stream (which Europeans call the North Atlantic Drift) warms the Atlantic very far north in Europe; even the winter water temperatures off the North Cape of Norway are no lower than those off Boston, Massachusetts (35° F). The Gulf Stream contributes to the cool summers and rarely bitter winters of Europe. When Europeans began to cross the Atlantic, they had two easy corridors. In the tenth century, the warmer North Atlantic and the reduced drift ice allowed Scandinavian sailors to reach and colonize Iceland and Greenland and to touch North America. In the late fifteenth century, Columbus and his successors had only to sail south to meet the easterly trade winds that blow steadily across the Atlantic. For even the best-rigged and manned sailing ships, travel to the east is far more difficult.

Within the framework of geography and climate on the one hand, and available technological resources on the other, Mediterranean and transalpine European societies differed greatly at the beginning of the period with which our study begins, and their exploitation of natural and technological resources in different ways caused them to develop differently. In the north, small migratory or sedentary communities of pastoralists gave way to larger communities that developed means of increasing their agricultural output, thereby creating surplus, and finally turned toward commercial and industrial agriculture. In the south, the Mediterranean societies had little agricultural potential to develop, but their commercial and political organization dominated that of the north for centuries. The Mediterranean world offered little room for new migrants, and its reception of migratory underdeveloped peoples was usually hostile. The open world of the north, however, was both less well guarded and at first less promising. Migration; settlement; population loss, stability, or growth; forms of social and cultural organization—all occurred within these two distinctive physical worlds, each of which possessed different resources. The size of populations, the density of human settlements, and the transformation of societies and cultures all played against the distinctive backgrounds of the physical world. In this sense, the time frame that consists of geographical and climatic conditions is the longest and the most fundamental of the many time frames within which the history of human societies can be considered. The human response to the physical world directs much of the human response to other problems of society and culture.

2

THE FIRST EUROPEANS

THE CELTIC WORLD

From the end of the most recent Ice Age, 7000 B.C., to the sixteenth century A.D., Europe was a sparsely populated open land, consisting, in the words of one recent historian, of "vast, disorganized spaces," the division of which into densely populated modern political states is a very recent phenomenon. Into this open land with its varied physical features and temperate climate, successive groups of immigrants from the Mediterranean and central Europe arrived from the Neolithic period on. Such immigrations numbered at the most in the tens of thousands of people. The control of land, mineral resources, and trade routes constituted a point of difference between older inhabitants and newcomers. However, one of the most characteristic features of the settlement of Europe has been the land's capacity to absorb successive immigrations, and these older inhabitants, whether defeated in battle, simply displaced, or absorbed among new arrivals, could wander still west to the Atlantic coasts of Spain, France, Brittany, England, and Ireland, or move higher into mountainous territory. It is no accident that the last surviving descendants of the earliest Europeans still inhabit precisely those areas of Europe today: the Basques in the Pyrenees and the Celtic fringe of peoples in northwestern Spain, Brittany, Cornwall, Wales, Ireland, and Scotland. If the modern Western world self-consciously proclaims its intellectual and moral ancestry as Judeo-Greco-Roman, its earliest population was central European and Asiatic in origin, and the family of languages that unites most central and western Eurasian peoples, the Indo-European family, was spread by these Bronze Age migrants as they fanned out from central Europe and transformed central and western Eurasia, from India to Ireland and from Russia to Egypt.

Much ink—and blood—has been spilled over the question of race, not just in the nineteenth and twentieth centuries, and also over the question of the superiority—the imagined superiority—of one European "race" over another. Physical anthropology is a relatively new discipline, and the earliest attempts to distinguish among the various physical types of Europeans had largely illusory and tragically misleading results, of which the politically inspired doctrine of "Nordic" supremacy enunciated by Nazi Germany in the mid-twentieth century is only the most ugly example. The physical characteristics of Europeans are the result of continuous contact among peoples who have inhabited Europe, with very few exceptions, since the Iron Age. The contemporary gene pool of Europe contains elements that date from as early as the Neolithic period and as late as the twentieth century. This chapter will deal with the "first Europeans": the Celts, the Mediterranean peoples—particularly the Greeks and Romans—and the early Germanic and Slavic peoples. Collectively, these are the Europeans.

The highly organized and culturally homogeneous societies of Mesopotamia and Egypt contrast sharply with the societies of the first Europeans. The geographical, climatic, and technological conditions of central and western Europe precluded the massive collective agricultural enterprises that laid the foundations for elaborate cultural developments elsewhere. The Europeans thus escaped the cultural rigidity of Middle Eastern and Egyptian civilizations, but they also lacked the collective strength and unified direction necessary for the production of an agricultural surplus, the first condition for social diversification and for civilization itself. Other civilizations developed effective means of mobilizing and diversifying society much earlier than the peoples of Europe, who remained vulnerable to influences from other cultures and had contact with them through migration, war, and trade. Tin, copper, iron, and amber moved from prehistoric Europe into the world of the eastern Mediterranean, and knowledge of metalworking and treasure and food traveled north. Between the eighth and the second centuries B.C., as the frontier between Mediterranean and transalpine societies stretched west to Spain, a highly developed Iron Age society also appeared in the north. These peoples, who had spread from central Europe and the Danube basin west into Europe, east to Asia Minor, and south toward the Mediterranean, were generally known as *Keltoi* and *Galli* to the Greeks and Romans— Celts and Gauls to us. Illiterate, politically fragmented, and culturally distinct from the Mediterranean peoples, Celtic society was nevertheless a wealthy and formidable neighbor to the more developed cultures in the south. Its heroic legends and art continued to exert a strong influence long after it had been absorbed into the Roman and Germanic cultures that displaced it.

Until the period of extensive Celtic contact with the Greeks and Romans, Celtic history is traceable chiefly through physical remains. As the historian H. R. Loyn has remarked, "We know more of the civilized living, more of the barbarian dead." The artifacts found in grave sites, the excavated fortified places, and the traces of agriculture must be exploited by many different disciplines, from aerial photography to anthropology, in order for us to learn about the Celts. Their sole literary remains were not recorded until the Christianization of Ireland in the fifth and sixth centuries, when the heroic tales of the Ulster Cycle opened up what their latest commentator has called "a window on the Iron Age." The picture of Celtic society that emerges from these diverse sources is one of a warrior society that in some respects was not much different from that described by Homer in the *Iliad* and the *Odyssey,* in which kings and warriors ruled from fortified camps over a mixed population in the small surrounding territory. Julius Caesar in his *Gallic Wars* called these camps *oppida,* towns, but they seem to have been rather small-scale centers of power, although many later Roman cities were built on their sites and sometimes took over their names as well. Kings and warriors, free peasants, slaves, and a "middle group" of poets, law-speakers, and craftsmen constituted the general core of Celtic society. Family, clan, and tribal loyalties held these societies together, and a life of endemic petty warfare and raiding occupied the kings and fighters. Wealth was measured in the numbers of cattle and amounts of treasure an individual could amass, and reputation was measured in gifts from rulers, poems of praise, and recognized status. In Celtic society a highly inflammatory notion of personal honor regulated conduct.

At its height, from about 600 to 200 B.C., Celtic heroic society was an impressive and widespread culture. The warriors' artistic patronage influenced not only the heroic songs, but also a distinctive and complex visual art: animals that shift into unfamiliar patterns, vegetation motifs and human figures that become abstractions make Celtic art of the Iron Age far different from the more familiar humanistic visual arts of Greece and Rome. The design and technological levels of Celtic utilitarian products are equally striking. Agricultural technology, the design and decoration of weapons, and the craft of the cartwright reached a level as high as, or higher than, that of the otherwise more developed societies around the Mediterranean. Yet in spite of its grandeur and technological achievement, its profound and mysterious art, and the complex ethical conceptions of its heroic epics, Celtic civilization was utterly destroyed or transformed between 200 B.C. and 500 A.D. The agents of this destruction and transformation were the expanding Mediterranean peoples, particularly the Romans, and the Germanic peoples from eastern and central Europe. By 500 A.D. Celtic culture had been reduced to the "Celtic Fringe"—Ireland, Brittany, Cornwall, Wales, Galicia, and Portugal, where many of its elements remain today. Literacy, the ability to organize and direct the efforts of large-scale societies, the complex kinds of communication within a large area of political stability and economic exchange, and the extensive—and so far little-explored—changes in the individual human personality, all of which are products of the Mediterranean cultures of Greece and Rome, were the specific instruments by which Celtic society was changed. The rise of the Germanic peoples after the second century A.D. (discussed in the third section of this chapter) offered yet another barbarian challenge to Mediterranean society. With that challenge not only the world of the barbarians, but that of the Mediterranean peoples was changed beyond recognition, and the doorway to a different world was finally opened.

MEDITERRANEAN SOCIETIES TO THE SECOND CENTURY A.D.

Between 750 and 550 B.C., as the Celtic world rose to its full geographical extent and cultural development, the societies of the Mediterranean basin began what was—after the domestication of food and animals, the working of metals, and the transformation of tribal society—the fourth great pulse of Western history: the colonial expansion west across the Mediterranean itself. The city-states and kingdoms of Phoenicia and Greece, plagued by a lag between population growth and agricultural production and torn by increased political rivalry, sent out colonies to the West. Phoenicians went to North Africa, Spain, and western Sicily, and the Greeks to southern France, south Italy, the Adriatic, eastern Sicily, and the Black Sea, all areas where the Greek city and its culture have exerted a profound and enduring influence ever since. When a great wave of Greek conquest and cultural expansion began under Alexander the Great in the fourth century B.C., both the eastern and western Mediterranean worlds assumed a veneer of cultural homogeneity. Hellenistic civilization, the term that designates the culture of the Mediterranean between 300 B.C. and 300 A.D., spread throughout the world of homelands, colonies, and conquered territories and constituted the cultural foundation upon which Rome later built its own military, political, and cultural framework.

Greek culture shaped the characteristic social configurations of the Mediterranean world and popularized and spread the remarkable intel-

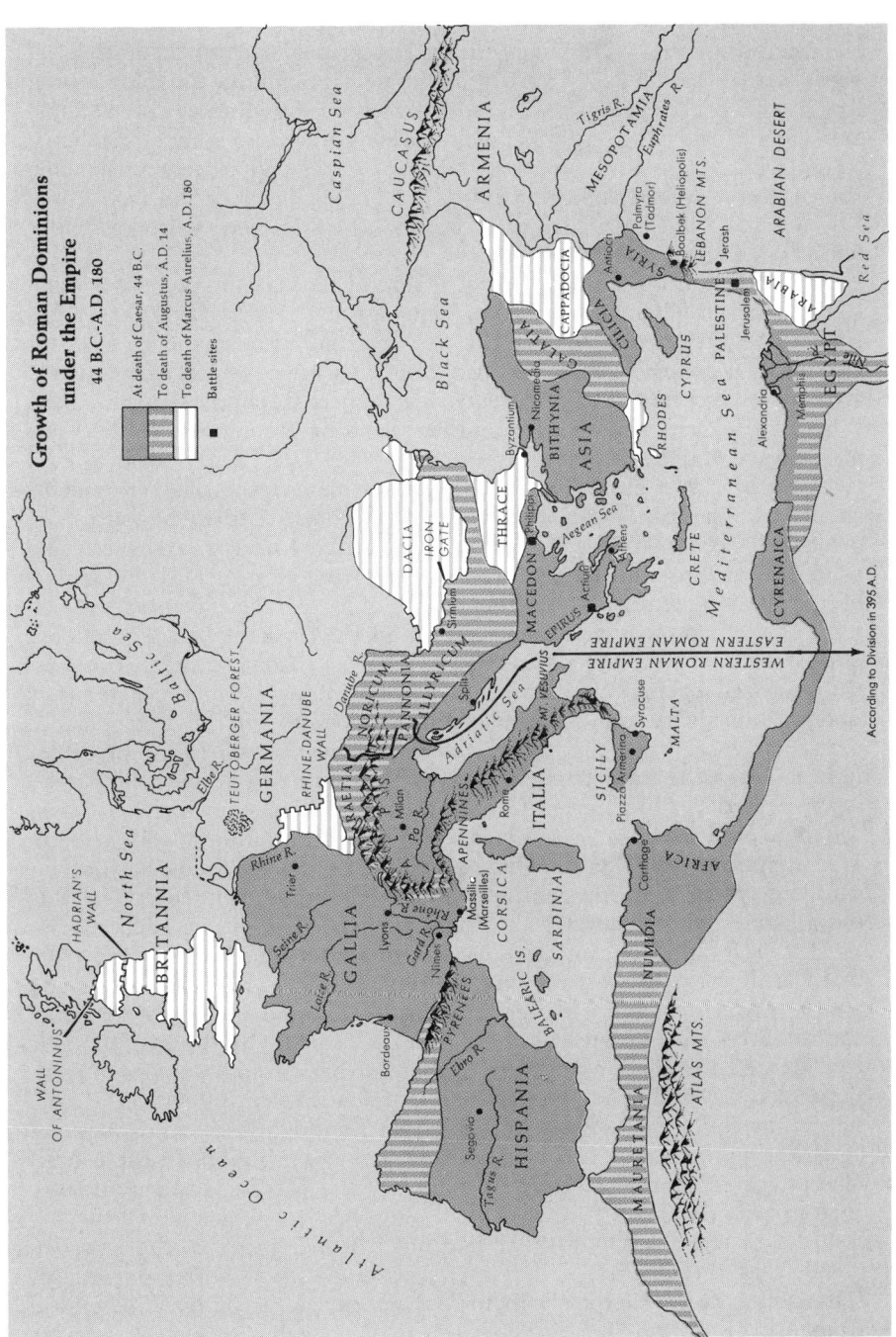

lectual developments of the great age of the Greek city-states. New and extremely influential ideas concerning educational techniques and standards made that culture readily available throughout the Hellenistic world, and encyclopedias and handbooks even offered short cuts to difficult disciplines. The authors included in curricula became "classics," whose works were to be imitated but not developed or extended. The rise of Rome transformed this culturally homogeneous world into a political empire that reached even beyond the Mediterranean and into barbarian Europe and Asia.

Located on the western coastal region of the Italian peninsula, early Rome touched Phoenician, Greek, Etruscan, and Italic cultural worlds. Immediately to the south were the rich colonial cities of the Greeks; to the north were the pre–Indo-European Etruscans, whose agricultural, artistic, and technological achievements were perhaps more advanced than those of the Celts and Greeks; and surrounding Rome were settlements of Iron-Age peoples. Rome in its earliest stages was, then, a kind of cultural frontier post around which peoples of many levels of development circulated. The hilly location of the earliest Roman settlement was easily defended, the Tiber River could easily be bridged nearby, and the trade routes passed through it or close by. Rome rose to power in the center of the Italian peninsula because it was able to take advantage of its natural site and to intervene successfully in the constant struggles among other inhabitants of the peninsula. By 275 B.C., Rome controlled all of the southern part of the peninsula, thus bringing its presence to bear upon Sicily and upon the Mediterranean colonies of the Phoenicians, particularly Carthage, the richest and most powerful city in the Mediterranean. From the third to the mid-second century B.C., Rome and Carthage struggled in a long series of wars—the Punic Wars—in which Carthage was destroyed and Rome assumed control of the southern and western Mediterranean coastal areas. Unlike the Greeks, then, Rome succeeded in assuming control of the entire western Mediterranean coast. In the second and first centuries B.C., Rome was called upon to intervene in Greece itself, and then in Egypt, Asia, and western North Africa. By the first century B.C., Rome had come to exert political and economic dominance throughout the Mediterranean world. Rome inherited not only the resources of that world but its troubles as well. By the first century B.C., Rome's frontiers marched with those of barbarians over the longest perimeter any civilization had yet had to defend. From 100 B.C. on, Rome sought to find a defensible frontier that would allow for expansion, colonization, economic productivity, and firm organization. In the course of that search Rome transformed not only the Mediterranean but also the barbarian world.

Its struggles with Carthage had made Rome aware of the new demands that the defense of her territories made upon her resources. In Italy itself, the Celtic society in the Po Valley had to be brought under Roman control, and the Alpine passes to the north also had to be controlled by Rome. By 200 B.C. Cisalpine Gaul, the Celtic territory from the Alps to Tuscany, was a Roman province colonized by Roman citizens, who built roads, military fortifications, and new towns from the Apennines to the Alps. In Spain, Rome quickly assumed control over the old Carthaginian coastal territories, but the mineral wealth of the interior made that area desirable as well, and the long struggle between the Celtic-Iberian natives and the Roman armies did not end until the late first century B.C. The third territorial consequence of the Punic Wars for Rome was the new importance of southern France as a land bridge between Roman possessions in Spain and Italy. The Greek cities along this coast, notably Massilia (Marseilles), had been friendly toward Rome, and the pressure of Celtic peoples from the north (by way of the Toulouse Gap and the Rhone Valley) and the overland attacks of the Carthaginians (the most famous of which had been the expedition of Hannibal) brought Roman power to the shores of the northern Mediterranean. The continual formation of Celtic confederacies against the Greek coastal cities forced Rome's hand. After defeating one such confederation of Celtic Gauls in 124 B.C., Rome founded Aquae Sextiae (Aix-en-Provence) in 123 B.C., the first Roman foundation in Gaul. In 121 B.C. another Roman army aided a tribe of friendly Gauls against their enemies. Between 121 and 118 B.C., southern Gaul became a Roman province, *Gallia Narbonensis,* and two characteristic Roman institutions were introduced: a city (Narbo Martius, modern Narbonne), founded in 118 B.C., and a road, the *Via Domitia,* connecting Roman Italy with Roman Spain through what was fast becoming Roman Gaul. In the years immediately following, the Romans established garrisons northwest from Narbonne to Toulouse and a string of towns, including Aix and Arelate (modern Arles), along the coastal road. Thus did Rome displace Carthage in the western Mediterranean and reorganize its own defenses and routes of communication throughout its new provincial empire.

Colonizing the provinces of Spain, Cisalpine Gaul, and Transalpine Gaul *(Gallia Narbonensis)* may have solved for Rome the immediate problems raised by its conquest of Carthage and its first contact with the Celtic world, but these three provinces opened up new problems by bringing Rome face to face with a world very different from that of the Greeks and the Carthaginians—the barbarian world of western and central Europe. Just as the need for effective routes of defense and communication had driven Roman power west to Spain, so the new Roman territories presented difficulties of communication and defense that Rome now had to consider. By 100 B.C., Rome was responsible for guarding all the routes, from Spain to the Balkans, that gave access to the Mediterranean world. These were the early routes through which older peoples had migrated, and they now had to be defended by the Romans. The Toulouse Gap, the Rhone Valley, the Alpine passes, and the Balkan Gap now gave access, not to southern Celtic or disorganized Mediterranean cities, but to Roman provinces. Rome had to find a frontier that rendered these routes of access useless to northern barbarians. From the first century B.C. to the end of the Roman Empire in the West in the fifth century A.D., Rome's frontier and provincial policy in the north was determined by these necessities of defense and communication. The story of the final northern frontier of Rome, however, is complicated by several other events in the second and first centuries B.C.: the expansion of Roman power to the eastern Mediterranean, the impact of the Romans upon their new barbarian neighbors and subjects, and the social, economic, and political changes of late republican Rome.

The spread of Roman military power rapidly outdistanced the internal strengths and cultural adaptability of Rome itself. The small Mediterranean city-state on the frontier of Etruscan, Greek, and Latin societies soon faced economic and social problems on a staggering scale. The republican form of government became the focus of most of this discontent, and throughout the second and first centuries B.C. the widespread empire and its troubled capital witnessed much social and political upheaval. Under the leadership of Julius Caesar's adopted son Augustus, a compromise was reached according to which a single ruler controlled the major individual public offices, thus ruling as an emperor in fact and as the "first"—the *princeps*—of the republican magistrates in form. The genius of Augustus, as well as his ruthlessness and power, established for three centuries the particular constitution of the Roman Empire. Subsequent emperors (the question of succession was always a problem, and few candidates could balance with much skill the traditional authority of the Senate, the press of the armies, and the demands of day-to-day policy making) attempted to stabilize the frontiers: under Trajan in 83 A.D. the Rhine-Danube frontier was solidified, and under Claudius in 53 A.D. Britain was added to the empire's territories.

Its sudden exposure to power, wealth, and a world of different cultures took its toll on Rome, and beneath the veneer of a homogeneous society and culture that extended from England to Syria and from Cologne to Carthage there ran deep rifts. The grim morality of traditional Roman culture had never accommodated itself happily to the profundities and extravagances of Hellenistic thought and feeling, and the republican theory of the constitution held up weakly against the pressure from the army and the provinces to turn the emperor into a god. Yet these tensions produced remarkable forces as well: the ability to direct a vast society and its institutions, the adaptability to live in and rule a world whose frontiers included Iron-Age peoples as well as the ancient civilizations of Greece, Egypt, and Persia, the astonishing open-mindedness and the formal toleration of the anthropological differences among its different populations. Moreover, traditional Roman culture insisted upon the institutionalization not only of power and law but of ideals of social, cultural, and ethical values. Such a complex culture often turned oppressive, but it must be said that few civilizations since have managed to do much better. The relation between public power and arbitrariness on the one hand, and public morality, what the Romans called *civilitas,* on the other, still embodies one of the fundamental dilemmas of large-scale societies.

In the first and second centuries A.D., Rome not only influenced the spread and the scope of Mediterranean civilization and determined its first contact with barbarian peoples, it experienced itself the consequences of universal power, foremost among which were internal stresses. It also determined in what ways Mediterranean culture was to spread to the Celtic and Germanic north. The consequences of its influence and determination and weaknesses shaped the first Europe.

THE EARLY GERMANS

Rome's distinct cultural orientation toward the lands and cultures of the eastern Mediterranean and its quest for a defensive frontier for its western Mediterranean territories made it a unique power in Mediterranean history. Its extensive land frontier and its consequent innovations in the conquest and government of land territories were quite in contrast with the maritime orientation of its Mediterranean predecessors, and the concentration of troops on a long frontier, the necessity of settling the lands between the frontier and Italy, and the need for extensive communication systems determined the unique imperial character of Rome's impact on the Mediterranean and on Europe: the centuries of Roman peace upon hitherto unstable barbarian territories, the consumptive demands that Rome made upon her provinces, and the institutions that Rome created in barbarian territory. The Mediterranean city was transplanted in continental Europe; the specialization of agriculture and industry was possible because of protective civil and military administration over an immensely large area; and a great network of roads was thrown up to tie the provinces and Italy together. These achievements brought Romanized Hellenistic civilization to a far wider area of Europe than any earlier civilization had done. Rome left the Mediterranean coast partly for defensive, partly for political reasons, and spread Mediterranean maritime culture throughout all southern Europe. Roman towns, Roman farms, and Roman roads transformed Celtic Gaul and Spain and began the long process of Romanization that was for many centuries to sustain the differences between northern and southern France, between the Romanized Rhine and western Germany, and between the Romano-Greek culture of the southern bank of the Danube and the tribal settlements of Germans, Dacians, and eastern invaders on the northern bank. Rome's settled provinces also offered rich and inviting targets for other barbarian peoples. The most formidable and ultimately the most successful of these were the Germans.

Unlike the Celts, who had expanded outward from central Europe, the German peoples traced their origin to the western Baltic area and the north German coast from the Rhine to the Oder. Although their presence has been identified in that area from 700 B.C., it was not until after 500 B.C. that they began to migrate south and east. By the second century B.C., they had reached what is today western Germany and their forward peoples had encountered the provincial peoples of the Roman

Empire along the Rhine and the borders of Italy. The Germans do not appear to have possessed either the quantities of metal or the artistic skills that made Iron-Age Celtic culture so distinctive and lasting an element in the history of western Europe. Moreover, the Germans, like the Celts, cannot be described in more than a very general way by a single name or label. The confederacies of tribes that constituted large-scale Germanic society broke down constantly and new associations were frequently formed. The various names by which Roman writers from Caesar to Tacitus described the groupings of Germans encountered by Roman forces disappeared and reappeared with great rapidity. Like all Iron-Age societies, that of the early Germans was politically unstable, and the relationship between the characteristics of individual tribes and the larger "peoples" into whom they sometimes assembled themselves is still a matter of scholarly debate. The Germanic peoples who encountered Roman civilization along the Rhine and Danube frontiers entered into a complex relationship with their new neighbors. Military encounters, trading expeditions, settlement near the Roman frontier posts, and even the migration of small groups or individuals into the empire itself, either to fight in the army or to work on the provincial farms of Gaul—all of these elements worked slowly to change the character of Germanic society in the West almost as soon as it encountered the society of Rome and Romanized Gaul.

In the eastern part of Europe, however, other groups of Germans did not experience contact of this kind with the Romans until the second and third centuries A.D. The so-called western Germans were able to practice a more sedentary agriculture and slowly changed their principles of social organization because of the influence of Roman culture so close by. The eastern Germans, usually called the Goths, controlled much more purely barbarian territory and the trade routes that ran through eastern Europe to the eastern Mediterranean. They settled in south Russia, and their society was more pastoral, mobile, smaller, and perhaps more warlike than that of the settled Germans along the Rhine, and was exposed to Iranian as well as Mediterranean influences. These two broad groups, the western and eastern Germans, because of their different kinds of contact with Roman society and culture, responded differently to that contact. Other peoples near them, Iranian and Slavic, lived much the same kind of life.

A few Roman writers left extended discussions of German society in their own times. Although their discussions must be read in the light of their personal and political ideas, Caesar's *Gallic Wars* and Tacitus's *Germania,* written, respectively, around the middle of the first century B.C. and the end of the first century A.D., enable us to see the changes in Germanic society that a century and a half of immediate contact with Rome brought about. Caesar's *Gallic Wars* describes a Germanic society in which groups of kindreds banded together into *pagi,* tribes, and tribes into larger groups, which became less stable the larger they grew. The possession of wealth in a society with few ways of acquiring it or of differentiating among those who possessed it tended to be roughly equal, and the society in many ways resembles a somewhat poorer version of Celtic society in its great age. By 98 A.D., when Tacitus wrote his *Germania*, a work not wholly reliable as historical description, Germanic society appears to have changed greatly. Roman trade, tribute, and influences had introduced economic variation and wider social mobility into the life of the Germans, and this Roman contact contributed further to the incipient instability of tribal and economic life.

By the first century A.D. larger Germanic confederations had assembled, sometimes under a single ruler, such as Maroboduus in the second decade of that century. Differentiations in wealth appeared rapidly in Germanic society, placing new stress on the traditional kindred relationships. New agricultural techniques, not necessarily imported from Rome, also altered the annual redistribution of tribal lands, thereby creating further tensions in traditional society. On the frontiers a new society grew up, one in which the "Germanizing" of the Romans occurred at the same time as the "Romanizing" of the Germans. Under the sustained influence of Roman wealth, manpower needs, and diplomacy (which was often geared to keeping Germanic societies unstable), the early Germans, like some of the colonized peoples of later Africa, Latin America, and Asia, experienced a degree and rapidity of social and cultural shock whose extent and direction was ultimately outside their control. Roman wealth contributed to the disintegration of kindred and tribe, and service in the provinces or in the army of Rome drew individuals and groups into a very different world. Once the Rhine-Danube frontier had been firmly established, Rome saw its mission as one of defense, not of civilization. For civilization too became an element of defense, the means of Romanizing a barbarian people to the point at which, if it was not identical to Roman society, it was at least very different from traditional Germanic society.

From 100 A.D. to the end of the second century, the Roman frontier defenses and frontier policies contained the light Germanic pressure, and life in the Roman provinces of Europe became virtually homogeneous, from Britain to Syria and from North Africa to modern Austria. Neither the provinces nor the frontier, however, remained stabilized for long. After the second century A.D., new population pressures, new migrations from beyond the frontier, the new political world of the Germans, and the political and military transformation of the Roman Empire itself contributed to the large changes that ultimately laid the foundations for a new kind of society in both the old and the new worlds.

3

THE TRANSFORMATION OF THE EURASIAN WORLD, 200-400 A.D.

THE IMPERIAL CRISIS OF THE THIRD CENTURY

By the last quarter of the second century A.D., the Roman world had reached the limits of its expansion. Its military outposts and provincial towns and farms ran from Britain along the Rhine-Danube frontier to the Black Sea, then down through the mountains of Asia Minor through the Tigris-Euphrates Valley, across the Arabian peninsula to the Red Sea, and down the Nile and across North Africa to Mauretania and the Atlantic. Rome's land frontier was the longest in human history. From the third century on, however, the dual process of internal change and crisis within the empire and the increased pressures on larger and larger segments of the frontier transformed Mediterranean society. The vast movements of new peoples outside the frontier represented an equal transformation of the Eurasian world. The changes in both worlds during the period 200–400 A.D. constitute a necessary prelude to the later history of medieval Europe.

Much attention—some historians would say too much—has been paid to that phenomenon known as "The Decline and Fall of the Roman Empire" ever since the English historian Edward Gibbon coined and immortalized that phrase as the title of his multivolume work that appeared in 1776. That the Roman Empire changed is, of course, beyond question. After the fifth century A.D. imperial power ceased to exist in the western part of the empire, approximately from Yugoslavia to Spain. In the east, however, the imperial capital at Constantinople continued to survive in varying circumstances until its capture by the Turks in 1453. The key to Gibbon's picture of these changes is contained in his phrase, "The Triumph of Barbarism and Religion," by which he attributed the disappearance of Roman imperial power and universal culture to, first, the attacks of barbarians and the subsequent effects of barbarization on the settled Roman provinces and, second, the growth of Christianity. These two elements appeared to Gibbon jointly responsible for the end of classical antiquity and the arrival of a period in European history that Gibbon, like many of his predecessors and successors, called the "Dark Ages." As Chapters one and two have attempted to show, the conditions surrounding the nature of the ancient world were somewhat more complicated than this view would have them. "Transformation," rather than "Decline," seems a more objective line of investigation, and the events beyond the world of Rome are at least equally important as the changes within the Roman world for a comprehension of the birth of Europe.

The "constitution" of the early Roman Empire—the exercise of vast personal powers behind the façade of republican office holding—was subject to two perennial dangers: the nature of the imperial office and the changing character of imperial concerns. The fiction of senatorial approval for each succeeding emperor wore thin after the late second century as such forces as the armies, dynasticism, and factionalism grew stronger and stronger. After 200 A.D., new emperors either informed the senate cursorily of their accession or did not bother at all. During the same period each new emperor attempted to install his children or other relatives in the succession, and the armies in the field put forward their own candidates again and again. After the reign of Trajan (98–117), a Spaniard, the imperial office opened out to provincials, and from the reign of Decius (249–251) to that of Valentinian I (363–375) a remarkable series of military figures from the remote provinces of Illyria and Pannonia became emperors.

As the emperors began to display more diverse origins, the imperial concerns began to reflect this. The process of the de-senatorializing and de-Italianizing of the emperors was reflected in the emperors' wider concerns: first, for the support of the armies and, second, for the empire-wide problems that diminished the central position of Rome and Italy in relation to the wider concerns of distant frontiers and troubled provinces. No longer could whole provinces or client states be looted for the benefit of wealthy Roman senatorial families. No longer was Rome necessarily the residence of the emperors. The empire was governed no longer by members of the Roman and Italian aristocracy, but rather by the members of a legal, military, and civil service recruited from widely different social levels throughout the Mediterranean, Balkan, and European provinces. The capital moved with the emperor, and the emperor moved to where there was trouble—to York in northern Britain, to Trier in the Rhineland, to Nicomedia in Greece, and, increasingly after the fourth century, to the new city of Constantinople.

Changes in terminology, public ceremonial, and imperial power were enhanced from the third century on by other reflections of change in the figure of the emperor. Older Roman tradition had implied that the emperor was one of a class of men who shared superiority over other men. This superiority is reflected in the term *princeps,* or first citizen. The relationship of the emperor to the gods was further enhanced by changes in public ceremonial and in the iconography of coins and imperial portraits. Progressively, it became the emperor's personal favor with the gods, not the favor of the Roman people as a whole with the gods that decisively altered the imperial status. Statues, portraits, imperial coinage, and the epithet *maiestas* all implicitly attributed to the emperor physical as well as spiritual qualities that were superior to those of other men. From the third century on, oriental techniques of make-up, costume, and rigid court ceremonial contributed further to highlighting the figure and face of the now-divine emperor, and enhanced the immobility, rigidity, tranquility, and awesome personal power of the ruler. In terms of politics, the old virtues of an exceptional citizen were transformed into the unique virtues of the god-man, whose individual fortune or role as the gods' favorite mattered more than his membership in a ruling patriciate or his birth in Rome. These changes diminished—or even obliterated—the gap between the emperors' remote social or provincial origins and the republican traditions of the senatorial aristocracy. The emperors' concerns were with the universal empire, not with the traditions and privileges of that aristocracy. Hence, the slow process by which the emperor was set apart from the rest of society in a manner different from the ways that had distinguished the leaders of the Roman Republic may be considered one of the consequences of the expansion of the empire. As we will see below, when the emperors became Christians, the ambiguities of imperial status within the framework of Christian political thought created yet further crises in the nature of the imperial office. By the end of the third century, the first citizen of the city of Rome, the *princeps,* had become the *dominus,* the lord of the world. To be fully understood, the new imperial office must be considered against the background of the social and political changes of the period.

No event reflects better the transformation of Rome's character from a city-state ruler of conquered territories to universal empire than the granting of Roman citizenship to most of the empire's inhabitants by the Emperor Caracalla in 212 A.D. By that act the emperor recognized the Mediterranean character of the institution he ruled. Universal citizenship followed by thirteen years the achievement of the fullest extent of the empire with the conquest of Dacia by Caracalla's father, Septimius Severus, in 199 A.D. The social and economic changes of the third and fourth centuries occurred in an empire that acknowledged universal citizenship and divine universal monarchical authority as its constitutional structure.

Yet the fact that through the institutions of citizenship and monarchical authority Rome had become part of its own empire did not mean that the empire became appreciably easier to govern. In fact, during the third century it became more difficult, and only a social and governmental revolution at the end of that century enabled the Roman Empire to thrive again in the fourth century. At the best of times, life in a Mediterranean city-state was comfortable and secure only for a small percentage of the population. Wealthy, governing citizen elites could live as comfortably in Republican Rome as in Periclean Athens, but only at the expense of large numbers of other people whose labor supported them. Not only did the characteristically Mediterranean institution of slavery account for most of the human power necessary for the working of vast estates and mines and for domestic management, but the poverty or marginal subsistence of artisan and laboring classes in towns and agrarian laborers in the countryside surrounding them appears to have been a necessary concomitant of the standard of living of the urban patriciates. As long as that standard of living could be kept reasonably modest, as long as the patriciates even made attempts to live up to their claim of being responsible governing elites, the disparity between rich and poor never became sufficiently great for sudden differential increases of wealth and their resulting oppressive character to inspire rebellions. As long as any city-state retained an advantage in its commercial or military dealings with distant peoples, the successful elite could provide, sometimes generously, for those less wealthy. During the centuries of Rome's vast and unprecedented territorial expansion, however, the opportunity to exploit the resources of new territories increased exponentially the wealth of the aristocracy and of a few fortunate men of lower social origin. This new wealth led in turn to demands for agrarian reform and a new voice in Rome's affairs by both the newly wealthy and the newly oppressed. In the throes of this dissension, the republic collapsed and individual political leaders acquired the backing of aristocrats, newly rich entrepreneurs, and political dissidents in their struggles for power. Julius Caesar had been one such leader. The Roman yearning to live once more under the old republican status quo inspired the political reforms of Augustus and the beginnings of imperial rule.

As long as Roman territory continued to expand, new wealth and new privileges for those not wealthy could continue, as they in fact did through the first and second centuries A.D. Citizens of Rome could be fed, entertained, and amused by public officials having immense personal fortunes, and the figure of the patron—the wealthy man who "looked after" the interests of a large crowd of reputable and disreputable hangers-on, fed them, supported them in their lawsuits, gave them gifts— began to grow more powerful. The senatorial aristocracy had been the first and greatest beneficiary of Roman expansion, but its members' participation in the civil wars of the late republic, their opposition to the early emperors—who were, after all, men of their own class—and the increasing numbers of senators from the provinces weakened this aristocracy appreciably. When senatorial opposition loomed, later emperors were more inclined simply to crush it rather than compromise with it. The imperial rather than purely civic concerns of the emperors after the second century reduced most of the power and much of the wealth of the old senatorial class, and the new universal administrative bureaucracy of the empire and the growing numbers of provincial senators slowly whittled at both Roman and senatorial privilege.

The widespread imperial imitation of Roman building techniques, agricultural institutions, utensils, military equipment, and artistic styles meant that Rome might have continued to thrive economically as a producer of these things for the rest of the empire, but the characteristic Roman distaste for commerce and industry prevented its aristocracy from transforming the economic basis of their class status. Industry, not products, tended to be exported throughout the empire, and Rome missed the opportunity to become the supplier, as well as the ruler, of its new territories. By the third century provincial styles appeared in pottery and decorative motifs, and excavations of third-century archaeological sites in the empire reveal fewer imported goods and far more locally made items. The circumstances of transport, as well as the reluctance of the aristocracy to engage in trade and commerce, contributed to the export of industry. Sea transport was cheap in the Mediterranean, but land transport, as we have seen, was prohibitively expensive and inefficient. Not until the thicker settlement of Europe between the tenth and the thirteenth centuries would road travel improve sufficiently to make a substantial impact upon the economy, and not until the advent of paved road systems and railroads in the nineteenth century would the difficulties of land transport in terms of cost be finally overcome.

The reluctance of the Roman aristocracy to engage in trade derived from tradition and life style. The Roman aristocracy counted its wealth mostly in terms of revenues from agricultural land, and income earned from other sources usually went into the purchase of more land. Even at the height of imperial expansion, the attachment of the Roman aristocracy to the economic productivity of land and to the social status that accrued from the ownership of agricultural land prevented the consideration of a revised status for trade and industry. By the third century, with the empire extended as far as possible, its lands divided into provinces, the modular unit of administration—the Mediterranean city—transplanted to Gaul and the Balkans, the empire experienced a period of stasis. Products were made largely where they were needed, regardless of the quality of local industry, but the homogeneity of the empire reduced substantially the ability of new territories to contribute by their very differences to the transformation of the empire as a whole. Trade consisted chiefly of luxury goods, and the most effective life an aristocrat could attain was public service in a status-defined office, contributions to his native town in the form of buildings and monuments, and a life of leisure surrounded by fellow aristocrats just like himself. In ceasing to grow, the second- and third-century empire also ceased to develop. Town building appears to have declined, the economic vitality of the empire seems to have dwindled, and the aristocracy, now used to its diminished role under an autocratic ruler and his civil service, lost its political role as a governing elite and became an inept conserver of traditions, economically wealthy but politically impotent. The vast aristocratic wealth was, to be sure, conserved, but the price for its conservation was the economic enervation of the empire.

The senatorial aristocracy of the early empire was not only more wealthy than anyone else except the emperor, it also possessed legal and social privileges that differentiated it from the rest of the body of imperial subjects. Senators could not be prosecuted or litigated against in common courts, and even the powerful imperial civil service was reluctant to act vigorously against men whose social rank was far higher than its own. Aristocratic privilege, as well as aristocratic tradition and wealth, separated the upper classes of the empire from those beneath them. Beneath the rank of senator were two broad groups, *honestiores* and *humiliores*. The *honestiores* constituted a "middle" class—but not in the modern sense of "bourgeois"—of professional men, whose numbers included city officials, the army, teachers, doctors, and the civil servants of the imperial administration. They were the salaried managers of society, not entrepreneurs, but when they could, they too bought land and aimed for senatorial rank. Beneath the *honestiores* were the *humiliores,* the merchants and traders, craftsmen, and small farmers. Beneath these two groups were the slaves. Slaves, however, appear to have been used less frequently under the empire than under the republic, partly because the chief source of slaves—the conquest of peoples beyond the border—changed once the empire ceased to expand, and partly because the mines, fields, and industries tended to use more free labor after the second century A.D. Slaves predominated in domestic service, even down to the level of the households of *humiliores.* Barbarians, however, had new careers in the empire after the second century: instead of being made slaves they enrolled in the Roman army or leased agricultural land in the Roman provinces.

The composition of the senatorial class changed in the third and fourth centuries, but the wealth and privilege of that class did not. The financial burdens of the state began to fall more and more upon the *honestiores* and *humiliores,* and the economic decline in the third century must therefore be regarded in terms of its effects upon the lower ranks of society, the men and women whose means to lighten the new economic burdens of taxation and inflation were strictly limited.

The prevailing mental and social attitudes toward science and technology, furthermore, were promulgated chiefly by learned aristocrats who were primarily theoreticians. Hellenistic science had produced remarkable results in those sciences that involved mathematics and measuring—astronomy and musical theory—and virtually none in the so-called experimental sciences—chemistry and physics. The gulf between the scientist and the technician was the social gulf between the aristocrat and the *humilioris,* a gulf that neither science nor society could ever overcome.

Another way for economic development to have taken place would have called for a large amount of capital and easy ways of getting it to whose who needed it. But although the capital was certainly available in the form of the vast wealth of the emperor and the aristocracy, Rome had cumbersome laws and great social reluctance to explore the various ways in which capital could be injected into trade and industry. The laws governing the strict liability of all investors and the legal difficulty of establishing joint-stock ventures, combined with the government's refusal or inability to interfere with individual commercial enterprise, kept Roman capital out of Roman trade and industry.

Power, particularly nonhuman power, has fed the European economy continually from the tenth century to the present. But Rome discovered no new power sources that had not been known to the Mesopotamians two thousand years earlier. The limited Roman use of the water wheel (possibly related to the difficulties of using these devices in Mediterranean rivers and flatlands) does not appear to have altered the distribution of power appreciably. Not until the agricultural and mechanical innovations of the tenth through the fifteenth centuries did substantially new sources of nonhuman power become available to western society. Finally, no economy can thrive unless it is an integral part of the intellectual and perceptual world of its society. The complex parts of any economy touch areas as removed from one another as an interest in the history of science, familiarity with the habits, customs, and laws of distant peoples, a reservoir of statistical information, however crude, and a public faith that these phenomena are on the whole beneficial to society and not inimical to it. The history of any society's economic institutions must consider the culture of that society itself. Roman imperial society's economic profile is encouraging neither to the capitalist nor to the Marxist. Given the attitudes and institutions it possessed, Roman society's economic development was necessarily limited and channeled, and when the demands that were made upon the economy could not be met, a drastic and complete economic transformation took place. To complete the profile of Roman imperial economy in the third and fourth centuries, we must go into some detail.

Three general influences stand out in this study: the unbelievably expensive century and a half of war between 150 and 300 A.D.; the generic limitations of the Roman economy; and the possibility of a decrease in population, at least in the western part of the empire and its consequences in patterns of settlement and urban life. The new migrations and associations of peoples beyond the Roman imperial frontiers, the rivalry among army leaders—and even among members of an imperial dynasty—for the throne, and the increasing use of soldiers in all areas of civil administration imposed a terrific economic strain upon Roman society from the mid-second to the fourth century. As one historian has bluntly remarked, it is pointless to talk of tightening the belt and buckling down to the job when this entails working overtime seven days a week for two hundred years at a steadily decreasing salary. The basis for the Roman imperial economy was agriculture, and as we have seen, Mediterranean agricultural techniques were the human response to a small area of arable land and the constant necessity of renewing that land. Mediterranean agriculture, as we have also seen, could not support an indefinite population growth, nor could it support a growth in the population of animals, particularly those that ravage rather than renew the arable. The deforesting of hills, the overworking of productive land, the overstocking of land with the wrong kinds of animals, and a growth in population beyond the ability of the land to support it all influenced the delicate balance of Mediterranean agriculture, even in its heyday, and the acquisition of new land become one main drive of Roman agriculture. Abandoned, exhausted land could be absorbed only by men who could afford the costly process of renewing it and these men were not the traditional small farmers of Italy, but the owners of *latifundia,* vast estates that came to comprise more and more of the available arable land, not only in Rome and Italy but in the provinces as well. The owners of these estates became not only a ruling agricultural and economic class, but a new level of intervention between the free farmer citizens and the government. "The price of successful agriculture, especially on marginal land," one economic historian has remarked, "is continuous vigilance." Scanty Mediterranean rainfall necessitated careful irrigation, forests had to be retained, so that they would hold the topsoil, and terraced fields had to be repaired, also continually. If such diligence resulted in successful agriculture, the population necessarily increased, but the manpower needs of agriculture were finely balanced: if the population grew too small, land went out of cultivation, and if it grew too large, the land became exhausted. In short, Roman agriculture depended upon too many variables: climate, conservation and renewal, and a manpower supply with very narrow limits. And it always carried within it the seeds of disaster: the inability to recover from severe natural catastrophes, the tendency to waste natural resources, particularly forests, and the tendency to overpopulate. Such an agricultural economy not only could barely produce a surplus, but it depended upon manpower to the extent that slavery was for a long time an integral power source. When the slave population decreased, the total resource of power decreased also. The stress caused by increases and decreases of the slave and free population of the empire not only endangered agriculture but also limited population growth that might have been channeled into industry: men cannot hire those who cannot be fed, and excess manpower experienced first the demands of the army.

    Within the rigid circle of population growth and decrease and the limited use of manpower, the other characteristics of Roman industry also hampered alternatives to dependence on agriculture. Simple industrial tools, the lack of a working technology to improve the process of production and quality control, and the absence of the possibility for either wealth or increased social status through trade and industry continued to depress economic growth. Roman intellectual reliance upon much earlier Near Eastern and Greek science and technology meant that Rome inherited not only its advantages but its limits as well. The gap among scientific thought and technology, and the critical balance between population, agriculture, and industry contributed to the precarious sustenance of Roman economy.

THE WORLD BEYOND THE EMPIRE, 150–375 A.D.

The internal transformation of the Roman Empire took place at the same time as four major, interconnected changes in the life of Eurasia. First were changes among Germanic peoples immediately bordering the empire; second, pressures upon the empire's neighbors by other Germanic tribes who had been displaced by migrations from north to south in central Europe; third, the renewed pressures of Asiatic steppe warriors in central and western Asia pushing west; fourth, the rise of a powerful, unified, and aggressive monarchy after 226 A.D. among the Sasanian rulers of Persia. To a certain extent, both Rome and Persia bore the brunt of the migrations and raids by the Asiatic steppe warriors, but Rome bore the additional burden of pressures from European peoples, and from Persia itself intermittently from the third to the early seventh century.

The Rhine-Danube frontier had drastically transformed the old migration routes across Europe, and the Germanic tribes in the neighborhood of the frontier were caught after the late second century in a political vise: the frontier was closed to them, yet pressure upon their rear from migrating eastern Germanic peoples disrupted their normal patterns of life considerably. The best-known of these migrating peoples were the Goths, who settled upon the banks of the Vistula at the beginning of the first century,. and in Poland somewhat later. The Goths had come originally from the Baltic region. Further migrations from that region had begun to press upon them, and in turn they began to migrate south and east. To the south, they encountered the Vandals and Burgundians, the periphery of the "neighborhood" settled tightly around the Roman frontier. The Goths continued to move south and east toward the Ukraine, but their movements and the pressures of the Gepid people following them disturbed the territorial settlements of other peoples and precipitated the progressive mass movements of still other tribes into territories ever closer to the Roman frontier. In the troubled years 167–174, several large German confederations on the imperial frontiers, led by the Marcomanni, penetrated into northeastern Italy, where a prolonged, costly, and ultimately debilitating campaign of defense led by the emperor Marcus Aurelius resulted in a settlement.

The Marcomanni and their allies were not, however, the only barbarian threats to the empire during these years. The eastern Germanic peoples migrating from north to south encountered a migration from east to west by a number of Asiatic peoples, most notably the Iranian Sarmatians, a large group of peoples of whom the Alans were the best known. At the end of the second century, the Sarmatians had established an empire in South Russia, had developed an extremely effective heavy-cavalry striking force—chiefly through their development of the stirrup and perhaps the spur—and constituted a threat to the Roman provincials and neighboring peoples. Some of the Sarmatians had migrated out of this empire further west, and two of these peoples, the Iazyges and the Roxolani, participated in the Marcomanic confederation that Marcus Aurelius defeated in 174–75. Of these Iranian invaders, only the Alans survived the barbarian wars of the third and fourth centuries and finally penetrated the empire in the fifth. Their activities on the northeastern frontiers of the empire, however, combined with the Germanic threat, marked the beginning of the two centuries of constant border warfare that was to take so many Roman and barbarian lives and exhaust the empire's resources.

Marcus Aurelius's victories, although they temporarily stopped the barbarian penetration of the empire, did nothing about the impulses of that penetration, the pressures of northern peoples upon settled German tribes. That pressure continued until the frontier was permanently breached early in the fifth century. The importance of frontier defense accelerated the process by which the Roman emperors came more and more from the military ranks and their attention, finances, and armies were turned more and more to the defense of the frontiers. Failures in imperial military and domestic policy provoked new revolts among the military leaders of the Roman army, and the new emperors in turn perished from the same difficulties that had caused the downfall of their predecessors. Rome's failure to discover and put into effect a workable program of frontier defense and domestic social and fiscal reform plunged the empire into the destructive civil wars and revolts of the mid to late third century. At this critical point in its history, the empire witnessed yet another new confederation beyond the frontiers. In 238 the Goths arrived in South Russia, mingled with the Sarmatians, and, as a result of Sarmatian influence, transformed both their culture and their military techniques. The growth of the Gothic kingdoms of South Russia shaped the circumstances by which, from 376 to 410, the Rhine-Danube frontier was permanently breached.

The third and fourth centuries witnessed further changes in Germanic society, many of them caused by cross-cultural influences among the eastern and western Germanic peoples and the Iranian Sarmatians, the last themselves influenced by artistic motifs and weapon design and tactics of the Asiatic peoples still further east. Germanic society, plunged into migration, raiding, and prolonged, organized warfare after a period of relative stability, began to organize itself differently. Military leaders participating in the larger confederacies, temporary kings who courted or opposed Rome, the leaders of newly arrived peoples demanding a voice in war plans—all continued the transformation of Germanic society from a loose assembly of free fighting men into a status-defined, military-oriented, mobile society. The acquisition of individual wealth and new agricultural and craft techniques transformed not only internal Germanic culture, but also Germanic relations between confederations of tribes and relations between Germans and Romans. After the early third century, new confederations emerged. Among these, that of the western German Alamanni appears to have been the earliest, that of the Franks somewhat later but ultimately more important. Besides these western Germanic leagues, the eastern Germanic peoples, the Vandals and the Goths, attracted other tribes into their spheres of influence, and still more Germanic peoples migrated into northern and eastern Europe in the wake of these south- and east-migrating peoples. Among the latter appeared the Venetii, probably one of the ancestral groups of the Slavs, a people that first emerged clearly in the fourth through the sixth centuries.

The pressure and aggressiveness of these new Germanic tribal confederations caused renewed frontier warfare with Rome through the third century and intermittently through the fourth century, and this warfare finally produced the breach of the frontier between 376 and 410. In the late third century, Germanic pressures on Gaul produced a brief (258–274) Gallic "Empire," in which cities became fortresses and provincials dealt with new invasions without resorting to the imperial command. The loss of the *Agri Decumates* (the border lands between the Rhine and the Danube) and the province of Dacia, the vulnerability even of Italy to barbarian invasions (Italy was penetrated three times between 260 and 270), and the civil disturbances that troubled in particular the western imperial provinces contributed to the transformation of Roman attitudes toward barbarians and the structure of the western provinces. The tentative peace settlements reached between the late third-century Roman emperors and the western Germanic peoples resulted in the slow Germanic penetration of Gaul, the increasing enrollment of Germans in the Roman army, and the settling of German farmers, individually and in small groups, in the frontier provinces. The uneasy peace during the early fourth century between Romans and eastern and western Germans could not conceal the continuing turbulence within Germanic society, which was always as great as the Germanic rivalry with Rome. By the mid fourth century, the confederations of Franks, Alamanni, and Burgundians dominated the Rhine frontier, and members and groups of these peoples even lived inside the empire and served in the Roman army. Several of these confederations were enrolled formally as Roman allies. In the Danube-Black Sea area, the Vandals and Alans and the two divisions of the Goths—the Ostrogoths and the Visigoths—constituted the eastern Germanic confederations. Beyond these new configurations of Germanic society, however, there remained yet other peoples further east, who would soon begin even more extensive migrations west.

The Asiatic peoples whose pastoral nomadic confederations were less stable than those of the western barbarians gathered periodically in large tribal confederations and made sudden, savage raids upon the more settled societies to the east, south, and west. The Cimmerians and Scyths in classical times and the Sarmatians during the second and third centuries A.D. appear again and again in the records of both Persia and Rome, as well as those of China and India. These migrating empires disturbed the populations around them, absorbing some peoples and driving others away in terror. The Asiatic barbarians whose impact was felt most severely in the east and west were usually peoples who had been driven out of their central Asian homelands by the rise of such empires and forced to migrate—either from threats or terror, or both—beyond the reach of their new masters and enemies. In the course of their movements east and west, these migrating empires and the peoples they drove ahead of them or took along with them lived a precarious existence on tribute and pillage; they did not have the time, numbers, or techniques to settle and completely occupy the lands they conquered, and their rule and organization was often highly unstable. They developed new military tactics and weapons, and these often influenced both other barbarian peoples and the more stable empires of China, Persia, and Rome. Not until the Mongol invasions of the thirteenth century, however, did one of these steppe empires grow strong enough to rule all of Eurasia by itself. Although the Asiatic steppe-invaders of Persia and Europe in the period under discussion were generally the victims of still more powerful central Asian peoples, they seemed incredibly fierce and demonic to their Chinese, Persian, and European—both Germanic and Roman—victims. The most powerful and important of these Asiatic invaders were the Huns. First mentioned in the third quarter of the second century A.D. by Roman writers, they appear to have been a Turkic people, possibly with some Mongoloid blood, whose fierce raids and barbaric customs seemed, even to other barbarians, incredibly ferocious and fearsome. By the beginning of the third century, the Huns occupied the steppe north of the Caucasus, where they were close to the Sarmatians and not far from the new lands of the Goths. Their history during the late third and early fourth centuries is obscure, but suddenly, around 374–375, the Huns fell upon their Sarmatian and Gothic neighbors to the west and destroyed the Gothic empire ruled by Ermanaric. The Hunnic invasion precipitated the greatest and most lasting of all the Germanic migrations: the Goths moved quickly to the Danube and demanded to be allowed to enter the Roman Empire to save themselves from the new invaders. The Huns, pushing other Goths and Alans in front of them, followed close behind. By 376, the last and greatest of the mass-migration periods of the Germanic and Asiatic peoples had begun. This movement transformed Roman society irrevocably, threatened Persia, and ultimately launched the resettlement of Europe.

  The economic, military, and social changes among Germanic and Asiatic barbarians between the second and fourth centuries constituted, then, one of the major transformations in world history and was to have great consequences for the survival of Mediterranean society and Roman power. Rome was threatened by changes not only in the barbarian world of Eurasia, however, but in its neighbor empire of Persia from the early third to the early seventh century. The Parthian Empire of Persia, which had succeeded the rule of the Seleucid successors of Alexander the Great, had remained through much of Roman imperial history a relatively stable neighbor. The Parthian aristocracy held considerable power, and thus Parthia continually experienced fragmentation and a weak central power. During the Parthian period, Persian civilization was subject to both Indian and Hellenistic influences in art and religion, and in spite of its tendency toward central weakness Parthia remained a formidable opponent of Rome in the Tigris-Euphrates valley and the surrounding area. Mounted Parthian bowmen were formidable warriors, and Parthian trade extended east to China and India as well as west to Rome. Around the year 226, however, the Parthian ruler was overthrown by a provincial family, which established a new ruling dynasty in Persia, that of the Sasanids. For the next several decades the Sasanids strengthened and centralized their rule, and by the middle of the third century, they had created a powerful, centralized state whose cultural and military institutions were to affect the Middle East long after the Sasanid Empire itself had passed away. Sasanid culture was to revitalize Persian traditions and make them powerful influences not only in India and Armenia but in the later world of Islam and the even later Ottoman Empire.

The Sasanian dynasty, from Shapur I (222–226) to Khosroes II (590–628) gave great impetus not only to Persian political development but to religion, literature, and the arts as well. Under Shapur I, a new revival and consolidation of Zoroastrianism became the Persian state religion, influenced in its development by Persian religious traditions and by the pressures of Manicheism, a gnostic dualist religion deriving from both Christianity and eastern dualism that flourished in Persia and Rome after the mid third century. Persian rivalry with Rome was sharpened under the centralizing, nationalistic Sasanids, and in 260 Shapur II captured the Roman emperor Valerian, a triumph mourned in Rome and commemorated in Persian relief sculptures that were widely copied and circulated. The crisis in Rome's eastern affairs precipitated by the defeat and capture of Valerian afforded one of Rome's eastern allies, the trading city of Palmyra, the opportunity to assume an important defensive role in the contest against Persia, and from the late 260s to 272 this interesting city, under its rulers Odenathus and his widow Queen Zenobia, maintained a formidable independence from both Persia and Rome. The Roman frontier recovery of the late third century ended Palmyra's independence, just as it did that of the Gallic Empire in the north. The Roman imperial recovery also strengthened Rome's eastern frontier with Persia, and during the fourth century, until the reign of Julian, the Romano-Persian frontier remained reasonably peaceful. With the revival of Persian military strength against barbarian invaders in the fifth and sixth centuries, however, and with the further weakening of the power of Rome, the conflict between the two empires rose to a head in the late sixth and early seventh centuries.

"The Central Asian frontier," writes a recent historian, "was the military laboratory of the Late Antique world." Cavalry and archery tactics, military equipment, and military organization transformed the fighting capabilities of the eastern (and later western) Mediterranean world and Persia, as well as those of the Germanic, Iranian, and Asiatic peoples beyond their frontiers. This transformation of techniques of warfare paralleled similar changes in social, religious, and political organization. Thus, third- and fourth-century changes in the Roman world must not be considered in a vacuum; the rest of western Eurasia changed too. The new Germanic confederations in the west, the Gothic-Iranian cultures of South Russia, the appearance of the Huns, and the culmination of old and new Persian traditions under the Sassanids constitute truly a transformation of the Eurasian world, a transformation whose consequences contributed not only to the later history of western Europe, but to that of eastern Europe and the Middle East as well. The transformation of the Roman Empire was a single aspect of a powerfully and continually changing Eurasian world.

THE INTELLECTUAL AND SPIRITUAL WORLDS OF LATE ANTIQUITY

In the fourth century B.C., the Greek historian Herodotus quoted a reply from the citizens of Athens to the King of Macedonia, who had encouraged them to desert the Hellenic side in the war against Persia.

> It is not well that the Athenians should be traitors to the Greek nation, which is of like blood and like speech, and has common buildings to the gods and common sacrifices, and manners of the same kind.

Having progressed from the bonds of the kindred and the tribe to those of the city-state and, finally, as in the passage just cited, to an ideal of the larger linguistic, religious, and social world of "the Greek nation," a new idea of community and culture radiated from the small Greek world to the larger Mediterranean one. By the third century B.C., Stoic philosophy was already criticizing the narrowness of the Greek *polis,* the city-state, and the parochialism of its world view. Stoicism recognized a universal human capacity for reason, possessed equally by Greeks and other peoples. The development of Hellenistic educational theories accompanied this new belief, and Mediterranean society included by the time of the Roman Empire a homogeneous intellectual elite scattered throughout its world, speaking Greek but sharing the wider vision of a world culture. The Romans first encountered this intellectual and spiritual culture as an undeveloped, unsophisticated, provincial group of military conquerors, but they soon participated in it in a distinctive way. In the first century B.C. the poet Vergil, a Romanized Celt from northern

Italy, rationalized the empire's place in this cosmos in his epic poem, the *Aeneid*. The moralizing of the political order represented Rome's first entry into the world of Hellenistic culture, but Rome never accepted "foreign" learning and spirituality willingly or completely. Even in the works of Cicero in the first century B.C., in which much of Stoic thought is transformed into a program of Roman *civilitas*, public morality, the sturdy traditions of Roman household gods and early Roman political thought endured. The public religion of Rome dealt with the city as a collective and with the city's relations with the gods rather than the individual's relations with the gods. Public religion and public morality reinforced each other. Even Cicero, a skeptical and shrewd politician, urged the continuation of public rites on the ground that even unbelievers had to agree that religion enhanced the individual and collective moral qualities of citizens.

Among the older collective pantheons, particularly that of the Olympian gods and their Roman counterparts, new religious ideas grew up in the first and second centuries A.D. Roman public religion centered more and more in the figure of the divine emperor. From North Africa and the east came "mystery" religions, in which the initiate was promised favor of the god and the revelation of a higher secret truth after passing through a series of actual or ceremonial ordeals and participating with other initiates in the god's rites. The growth of mystery religions was not prohibited in Rome, because participation in them did not prevent their devotees from paying homage either to the Olympian gods or to the divine emperor. Nor, for that matter, did it prevent them from becoming devotees of other mystery cults as well. Publicly, Roman law insisted that rites and customs that violated the Roman sense of propriety had to be modified if their cults were to flourish, and Rome forbade—with few exceptions—religious rites that prohibited their members from participating in the necessary worship of the emperor. Of the religions that came to Rome from the provinces or beyond the frontiers, only druidism and Christianity came to be persecuted violently. Judaism was allowed the status of a *religio licita*, a legal religion, and was allowed to exist without having its Jewish rites profaned by the inclusion of emperor worship in them.

Both the philosophy and the new religions of the late Roman world strongly fostered the connection between religion and morality, and the ideas of a personal relation to a god and life after death—the rewards or punishments there contingent upon one's morality in this life—came more and more to color the traditional religious beliefs of the older Mediterranean world during the first and second centuries A.D. The developments in Platonic philosophy that are commonly called Neo-Platonism also worked toward understanding the world as a series of more or less illusory manifestations of a single ground of reality, and in some cases of a single Being, whom the true philosopher might discover after a life of preparation and study.

Among the religions and philosophical schools of late antiquity, Judaism attracted the curiosity of many. The Jewish state in Palestine had been crushed and the Temple of Solomon destroyed in 67–70 A.D., and the last Jewish revolt had been crushed ruthlessly in 135. Yet Judaism provided the setting for a religious change that transformed Western religious thought forever. Judaism is based upon a series of specific revelations made to the Jewish people by a god who is the only God, revelations concerning Himself and His moral teaching and the covenant between God and His people. After the career of Moses, when the Jews were in constant contact with other peoples and religions of the Near East, there were tendencies to merge Judaism with other, similar religions, but the Prophets hammered at the concept of the Jews as a chosen people of Yahweh and reemphasized both the collective and individual responsibility for fulfilling the terms of the Mosaic Convenant. In spite of the captivity of the Jews in Babylon, the spread and persuasiveness of Hellenism, and the cosmopolitan influences at work in scattered Jewish communities of the Diaspora, Judaism remained a single religion, although many diverse strands made themselves felt in the first century B.C. and the first century A.D. The principal currents in Judaism were, on the one hand, a strong emphasis on the Mosaic Law and the increasing insistence upon its intricacy, and, on the other hand, a cult of personal holiness, individual devotion to God, and an emphasis on the mystical interpretation of the Psalms rather than strict observance of the Law. The two main groups that emerged in Judaism during this period were the Sadducees, who were inclined to rationalize old beliefs in the face of Hellenistic thought and deemphasized the rigor of the Law, and the Pharisees, who urged strict observance of the Law and feared the corrupting effects of Hellenism and other religious beliefs. Also, a large and important Jewish community in Alexandria attempted to rejoin philosophical speculation and observance of the Law within the framework of Greek philosophy. This school of thought, whose greatest representative was Philo Judaeus (25 B.C.–41 AD.), devised a complex system of interpreting the texts of the Old Testament, according to which the stories contained therein were to be recognized as possessing different levels of meaning; the higher levels of interpretation called for learned scholars versed in Hellenistic philosophy.

The Sadducees and Pharisees in Jerusalem, the Alexandrian Hellenizing Jews, and the isolated Jewish communities of the Diaspora constituted a turbulence in Judaism of the first century A.D., and their conflicts, plus the pressures of Hellenistic culture and Roman politics, inspired a number of movements within the Jewish communities, some of which were directed against Rome and the Hellenizing Jews, and others against the literal interpretation of the Law and the rigorous administration of the High Priests of the Temple at Jerusalem. Some of these movements proclaimed the imminent coming of a messenger from God—a Messiah—but the meaning of "Messiah" in Jewish thought in this period is ambiguous. From this theological and social turbulence, there emerged in the first century A.D. a group of men who claimed that their master, Jesus of Nazareth, who had been tried and executed by the Romans, had brought a new law to the Jews and all other men and was in fact the Son of God. The earliest Christians thus adopted one aspect of Jewish Messianic thought, and for most of the first century, the Christians were tolerated and in fact remained members of the Jewish communities of the Roman Empire. Conflicting Jewish and Christian-Jewish interpretation of Scripture, however, differing attitudes toward observance of the Law, and an increasing emphasis upon Jesus' divine nature steadily divided Jewish and Christian-Jewish members of these communities, and after the middle of the first century A.D. a number of Christian teachers appeared who widened that gap further. One such teacher was Paul, a Jew of Tarsus in Silicia, who converted to Christian belief after a career as a persecutor of Christian sects in Jewish communities. From 46 A.D. on, Paul traveled the Roman world instructing Christian communities in their duties, in their relations with their Jewish neighbors, and in sound doctrine. His letters to the communities he had visited or was going to visit—the Epistles—became the single most influential body of dogmatic literature in Christian history. Paul's Epistles are also the earliest body of Christian literature. Shortly after 66 A.D. several texts recounting selected incidents in the life of Jesus appeared. The four surviving Gospels—those of Matthew, Mark, Luke, and John—were not the only ones written (there were at least three others, traditionally designated Q, L, and M). Of the relatively large body of later literature only a few other epistles, a history known as the Acts of the Apostles (86 A.D.), and a prophetic account of the end of the world and the Last Judgment that was deeply colored by contemporary Jewish revolutionary imagery and was violently anti-Roman, the book of Revelations, became accepted and formalized at the Council of Carthage in 397.

Christian communities, even as they separated from the Jewish circles in which they had first arisen, were modeled upon Jewish institutions. The leaders of these new communities were teachers, interpreters of the law, and liturgical officers—in short, Christian rabbis. By 49 A.D. there appears to have been a community of Christians within the Jewish community in Rome. By 59, when Paul wrote his Epistle to the Romans, that community was sufficiently large to attract his missionary efforts.

The first century is a key century in the history of Christianity, yet it is the period of Christianity about which the least is known with any certainty. During the course of that century, the Christian communities slowly broke with the Jewish communities in which they had grown, rejected the Jewish Law and liturgy, and actively proselytized among non-Jews. Although the synagogue left a permanent imprint upon these Christian communities, the division between Christian and Jew was complete by the end of the second century A.D. Then, the full impact of Pauline Christianity made itself felt throughout the Roman world.

Christianity was essentially a personal religion, and conversion, a necessary turning to God, was an essential part of the individual's development. The conversion story became a powerful theme in early

Christian literature, and the two most famous of them—those of St. Paul in the first century and St. Augustine in the fourth—became models for later Christian psychology. The Christian was converted by the Holy Spirit, but the role of the teacher with a valid commission from God was often instrumental in that conversion and in maintaining order in communities of Christians. "Wisdom"—the legal meticulousness of the Pharisees as well as the philosophizing of the Hellenes, was synonymous with the rejection of God, and the "true Christian," like the "true Jew," was essentially the inward man. God was the same for Jews and Gentiles. God gave grace to the Christian, and the Christian was "dead" to the old and now "outmoded" Mosaic Law. The new law was embodied in Jesus, and those who followed it were the "new children of Abraham," a new "chosen people," a "true Israel," *"verus Israel."*

At first, the Christians were neither numerous nor vociferous enough to threaten the Roman state, and the Romans vaguely associated Christianity with Judaism. The split in the Jewish communities that led the Christians to form their own communities, however, deprived the Christians of the protection that the privileged legal status of the Jews had given them, and after the first century intermittent persecution followed. First, the Christian religion, by separating itself from Judaism, had claimed independent status, but it had not received permission from the Roman authorities to do so, and consequently it was an illegal religion (*religio illicita*). Moreover, Christianty experienced some of the same slanders that Judaism had: it was secretive, and it possessed no clearly explained ritual. But, unlike Judaism, it possessed no body of literature that might explain its beliefs. As we have seen, early Christian literature was occasional, dealing with problems that arose in the life of the early Christian communities and relating stories of the life of Jesus and the travels and persecutions of the Apostles, as well as conversion accounts. Romans listened to stories of perverse rites in Christian houses (there were no churches) in which licentious acts and the worship of beasts were performed. The writings of Tacitus portray the Christians as being possessed of an *odium humani generis*—a hatred of humanity—because of these stories of Christian rites and because Christians refused to participate in public rites of emperor worship. The early persecutions were sporadic, however; not until the crisis of the third century and the subsequent revival of the ancient gods did the persecution of Christians reach large proportions. By the third century, however, Christian communities were firmly established, and Christian doctrine had developed sufficiently to attract ever increasing numbers of Jews and Gentiles to it. In fact, the greatest wave of persecutions, those of 303 A.D., took place just ten years before Christianity received legal status as a religion, thirty years before the first emperor was converted to Christianity, and less than a century before Christianity was made the only official religion of the Roman state.

The third century saw intense religious persecutions, but it also witnessed widespread religious experimentalism, an eager seeking for religious satisfaction in a world whose traditional modes of thought and perception had become deracinated. The dynasty of Septimius Severus had brought the Syrian sun god Elgabal to Rome, and throughout the third century the cults of other eastern gods also appeared. Two of these cults, those of the Persian Mithras and the Unconquered Sun— *Sol Invictus*—appealed especially to the army and to the emperors. In addition to the traditional gods, the official cult of the emperors, and the new gods from the east, the third century also witnessed the deification of abstractions—Fortune, Providence, and Victory—and the increasingly widespread conviction in the existence of subdivine powers, *daimones,* who filled the air unseen and who were controlled by the greater gods and propitiated by magical rites and charms. The third century, in fact, witnessed an increase in the numbers of magicians, soothsayers, and sorcerers, and at the same time the old oracles of classical Greece revived in popularity. The spiritual side of physical existence made its presence felt, then, not only among Christians and Jews, but throughout the empire. Believers of the official cult of the emperors could belong to mystery religions, join the cult of Mithras, and patronize astrologers, magicians, and prophets in an unending quest for spiritual certainty and elusive power.

The increasing political, social, and economic instability of the third-century empire inspired several of its rulers to tighten official control over religious activities. The old idea that the well-being of the state depended upon the piety of its people revived during this period of crisis, and the late third-century emperors, particularly Diocletian, insisted upon a public revival of Roman religion and acted ruthlessly against those who resisted. Yet Christianity had spread widely precisely because of this social turmoil. The Christian communities offered to all who joined them the fellowship that an increasingly impersonal and economically oppressive empire did not. Communal charity, fellowship, prayers for the dead, and protection of fellow Christians offered many groups in Roman society an amelioration of their present life while promising them a life after death. The communal spirit of third-century Christians attracted many of the poor and the exploited professional classes, and the progressive intellectualization of Christian doctrine began to attract the learned classes as well. The humble and diverse literature of early Christianity had originally as difficult a time attracting the Mediterranean intelligentsia as had the Old Testament texts before Philo's allegorizing of them. The attraction of this intelligentsia to Christian belief was as important a change in the history of Christianity as was the later Christianization of the empire. Christianity had begun as a religion of the religiously and socially disenfranchised. Its earliest image of itself was that of a separate people, "the true Israel," which was alien to this world, and its members were pilgrims and strangers passing through a world of evil to a better world prepared for them by God. Yet Christianity could not have succeeded in spreading so far so quickly if it had not offered other attractions as well. To those provincials whose place in the empire was defined by no local traditions, by no ancestral contribution to the greatness of Rome, by no clearly defined social or legal status, Christianity offered a coherent sense of belonging, which both satisfied people's inner spiritual needs and eased their sense of displacement in a rapidly changing and threatening world. The provincials from the fringes of the empire in the East first participated in Roman civilization as Christians, just as the Irish were to do in the fifth century. The lack of educational traditions among these provincials, their mental separation from the "high" literary culture being revived around them, and their sense of organization and efficiency turned them not only to Christian beliefs but to transforming the organization of the Church into a clear hierarchy, with different officials responsible for different aspects of community life. Not the least attractive feature of third-century Christianity was its efficient organization, freely operative at precisely the time when the state organization was conspicuously failing.

The oppressed citizen and the déclassé provincial were not the only converts to Christianity. The Roman intelligentsia constituted perhaps the most important group to join the new faith. Their conversion brought to Christianity not the loyalty and gratitude of the socially and economically oppressed, but the full influence of antique thought in its highest forms. To understand this complex phenomenon, something must be said of the conditions of late antique thought itself. One of the most striking aspects of third-century culture is its conscious revival of older classical traditions. Schools and lecture halls, archaic Greek speech, and a detailed antiquarianism grew up precisely at the time when the classical world was on the verge of disappearing. Not only did the third-century emperors revive the stern public piety of the state religion, but the third-century intelligentsia established authoritative texts of classical Greek literature, renewed emphasis on the elaborate literary and rhetorical character of an elite educational system, and began the antiquarian researches into older Greek and Roman history, language, and religion that characterized much of the scholarship of the fourth and fifth centuries and that firmly set forth the classical literary tradition as the basis for a world culture. This "high" learning in letters and philosophy, however, was accompanied by an increasing amount of half-education, digests, extracts of quotations, short popular biographies of emperors and philosophers, and shortcuts to understanding philosophical systems. The rigorous and prolonged training offered by late antique schools contrasted with the "instant learning" offered by charlatan philosophers, popular writers, and quack religious cults. Thus, the gulf between the respected traditions of literary culture and the bastardized versions of that culture available to most people separated the language, thought, and habits of a mandarin elite from those of the rest of the population. If the learned Neo-Platonists could postulate a single ground of Being, which radiated its manifestations through progressively more material things, from the harmony of the stars and planets to the spirits and demons of the air and finally to the physical world, popular belief turned grossly to astrology, demonology, magic, and fortune telling to acquire instantly the results of what would otherwise require a lifetime of discipline and thought. With this intellectual division of the Mediterranean cultural world, Christianity sensibly had little to do. Christian literature offered a religious and ethical system contained in parables and moral stories of striking literary simplicity, whose ethical level claimed to be as high as that of the best pagan thought. The element of conversion in the Christian consciousness meant a literal and symbolic rejection of one's past, and the Christian doctrine of an afterlife did not need the popular devices to which other cults turned.

No intellectual change reflects the early relations between Christian and pagan thought better than the influence of Neo-Platonism on early Christianity. Neo-Platonism emerged in the second and third centuries as the distillation of antique philosophy. Its spiritual dimension already reflected a turning away from the physical world of Aristotelian philosophy, and its rigorous program of mental discipline over a prolonged life of study hardened the minds of its adherents. Instead of emphasizing the gap between the unreachable reality of the spirit and the ugly corruptibility of the material world and the body, however, Neo-Platonism performed the invaluable service of guarding men's perception of this division from the sharply dualistic theories of Gnosticism and Manicheism. The Neo-Platonists postulated a system of thought and mental discipline that led the student to perceive the harmony of the links between the spiritual and material worlds and thus to avoid condemning material creation outright. In this respect, Neo-Platonism played a crucial role in the christological controversies within Christianity, during which the problem of the relation between Christ and God the Father brought the potentially destructive features of pagan dualistic thought directly to bear upon the nature of Christianity. Neo-Platonism reached its height in the third century, and its greatest pagan representatives, Plotinus, Porphyry, and Iamblichus, and its greatest Christian representatives, Origen and St. Augustine, shaped the philosophical terminology of most later Western thought before the seventeenth century. The relation of man to his soul, the relation of the physical universe to the spiritual reality that constantly sought expression through it, the "chain of being" that linked the lowest material creation to the highest spiritual reality— these constituted the "brake" that Neo-Platonism applied to the increasingly rapid and compelling tendency to regard the universe as a perpetual battleground between spirit and matter, the one ineffably good and unreachable, the other a creation of evil powers designed to imprison the spirit forever.

By the late third century, then, not only had Christianity an increasingly broad social appeal, it had also begun to penetrate the stronghold of late antique thought, access to which was denied even to most pagans. Third-century art, in which the inner spirit illuminates and molds the physical character of the subject, in which material objects constantly signify spiritual truths, and in which the eyes, the "windows of the soul," predominate in the human face, is a manifestation of this side of late antique thought. The characteristic form of this art is not the public building or the temple or the triumphal arch, but the painted or sculpted individual human figure—the philosopher, the scholar, and the saint.

By the beginning of the fourth century, classical religion as well as classical culture had changed irreversibly. Christianity and other religions that spread rapidly in the third century had also changed from their earliest origins. Syncretism—the absorbing of some religions and cults by others, resulting in a hybrid religion—on the one hand, and the isolation of several exclusive faiths, on the other hand, competed for people's attention and loyalty. In the midst of these changes, the Roman state also renewed its claim to loyalty, and the late third and fourth centuries witnessed not only a renewal of Roman society, but the adoption of Christianity as the official religion of that society.

4

THE FOURTH CENTURY

THE EMPIRE AND THE TRIUMPH OF CHRISTIANITY

The imperial, social, and economic crises of the third century and the new forces at work among the peoples of western Eurasia transformed the life of the empire but did not destroy it. From the late third century on, a series of able military emperors from the provinces of Illyria and Pannonia and the officials they brought to power with them transformed and streamlined the armies, fortified Roman cities—including, in 276, Rome itself—and attempted, largely through the bureaucratization of the government and the law courts, to overcome some of the economic difficulties that had appeared in the late second and early third centuries.

The reform of the army produced a new and large force of around 600,000 men, which was divided into smaller groups. The *limitanei*, stationed permanently along the frontiers, were backed up by a mobile, powerful cavalry and infantry force—the *comitatenses*—who were stationed at critical central points behind the frontiers. Citizens from remote provinces, and eventually barbarians were enrolled in the army. Within two decades, between 258 and 296, the new army successfully beat back threats against all frontiers. Beginning with the reign of Diocletian (284–305), the maintenance of this army became the emperor's chief concern, and social and economic reforms were increasingly geared to this end. New taxes, attempts at vast projects of social engineering—including "freezing" laborers and their descendants in essential fields of work—price regulation, increasing bureaucratization, and the increasing administrative supervision of the law courts extended imperial governance further and further into daily life, and the increasingly obvious presence of government officials widened further the distance between government and subjects. The new ruthlessness of imperial officials incited more and more free people to turn to wealthy patrons—*potentes,* "big shots"—who alone could stand between them and the government officials. These great landowners and high officeholders absorbed the rights of free citizens precisely because they were the only recourse available to individuals who could no longer deal with the government in traditional ways.

The cities in the western part of the empire were perhaps hit hardest by the new forms of government, but rural areas also suffered, and larger estates, the *latifundia,* sheltered more and more people. Between the new power of the patrons and the pervasiveness of the civil service, the imperial government attempted to adjust its form to the needs of the fourth century.

One major adjustment had lasting consequences. Diocletian created a second Augustus, a partner-emperor for himself, and announced the division of the empire into two halves, the *pars orientalis,* or eastern half, and the *pars occidentalis,* or western half. One Augustus was to rule in each. Each *pars* was in turn broken into two parts; in one the Augustus predominated, and in the other a *Caesar,* the Augustus's assistant and prospective successor. The tetrarchy, or rule of four—two *Augusti* and two *Caesares*—proposed to solve the two perennial problems of Roman imperial rule, the question of succession and the needs of government and defense. Each Augustus was to rule for twenty years, and in 305 Diocletian retired to Split (in modern Yugoslavia), having arranged, or so he thought, the appointment of the next four rulers. Diocletian's arrangements, however, foundered upon the equally perennial problem of dynasticism. Maxentius and Constantine, the sons of the first two Caesars, had been passed over in the succession, and their armies revolted and proclaimed them emperors. In a series of bitter civil wars, Constantine eliminated Maxentius in 312 and systematically eliminated his other rivals, and a large part of his own family, over the next twenty years. Diocletian's reforms, which had been partially discontinued during the wars, survived, however, in Constantine's redivision of the empire and in his creation of a new army and civil service.

Constantine continued the administrative redivisions of the Empire. Each of the main *partes* was subdivided into prefectures. The four imperial prefectures were those of the east and Illyricum (for the *pars orientalis*) and those of the Gauls (Britain, Gaul, and Spain) and Italy (Italy and Africa) for the *pars occidentalis*. Rome and Constantinople each had its own urban prefect. Constantine also transformed the army high command, creating a master of infantry *(magister peditum)* and a master of cavalry *(magister equitum)*. The highest command levels were now opened to barbarians as well as provincials, and by the mid fourth century barbarian *magistri* commanded Roman armies.

Finally, Constantine continued and completed Diocletian's restructuring of society. Members of the class of municipal officials were forbidden to leave their towns for the countryside or the army; free farmers were legally tied to the soil they cultivated; membership in the trade corporations in the towns was made hereditary. Diocletian's and Constantine's reforms have been called the earliest and most complete form of state socialism the West has even seen. Certainly, the price that most of Roman society had to pay for protection and government was excessive; Diocletian and Constantine had succeeded in turning each class in society into an instrument for the survival of the apparatus of government and defense. If these changes pressed most severely on the lower classes of society, they did not leave the aristocracy untouched. Increased government efficiency began to encroach even upon aristocratic privilege and corruption in government. Although the Roman aristocracy remained immensely wealthy and largely untouched by the demands of taxation, it faced the threat of a flood of "new aristocrats" in the imperial service and the willingness of even the most respectful emperors to take drastic steps to preserve the life of the state. As long as the peace of the frontiers and the inner world of the empire was maintained, however, the emperor and the aristocracy could avoid coming to blows. Before the third quarter of the fourth century, though, that relationship was subjected to a strain that it was not to survive in the west.

Constantine's military, administrative, social, and economic reforms have been dwarfed unjustly by another change he made in the Roman state: the legalization of, and his own later conversion to, the Christian faith. The attempts of Diocletian to bolster his own reforms by a renewed emphasis upon traditional Roman religious beliefs had brought about a new persecution of the Christians, one more savage than any other in the empire's history. Mass trials and executions, the willingness of many Christians to perform the perfunctory rites of emperor worship (which could consist of as little as casting a pinch of incense on a brazier before the emperor's image or simply handing over to Roman officials the sacred books of the community), and the intensity of Christian–hunting and persecuting, however, failed to reduce appreciably the attraction of Christianity. Moreover, the images of Christian heroism attracted many pagans to the despised faith, and the stories of the martyrs and the miracles that were frequently said to have attended their execution often served to strengthen the faith of those who survived. Finally, the new imperial aristocracy, however much it might attempt to imitate the conduct and beliefs of the older aristocracy, consisted essentially of new men who attached themselves loyally to the emperor and his policies rather than to the gods of the empire. Following this shift in loyalty, the new aristocrats felt little traditional attraction to an older and archaic paganism. Constantine, the enemy of Diocletian's designated successors, was a worshipper of *Sol Invictus,* the unconquered sun, and was not committed to a policy of persecuting the Christians. On the eve of his battle with his rival Maxentius at the Milvian Bridge outside Rome in 312, Constantine claimed to have experienced a vision in which he was directed to place a sign—a Christian sign—on the shields of his soldiers. Constantine did so, and his force was victorious. In gratitude for this victory, Constantine ceased the persecutions and declared Christianity a *religio licita,* a legal religion. For the first time since its break with Judaism, Christianity was permitted to exist by the Roman state. Constantine, impressed by his victory, turned with sympathy to the Christians, some of whom in turn reversed their attitude toward the Roman Empire.

From the revolutionary elements in first- and early second-century Judaism through the imagery of the book of Revelations, a large segment of Christians had come to regard the Roman Empire as the last of the great persecuting regimes that would precede the final judgment. From the second century on, however, the eschatology of Christianity became less powerful, and within the religion grew a body of apologetic literature whose purpose was to explain Christianity to pagan Romans. This literature and the zeal of Christian communities had converted many pagans. Moreover, before the persecutions of Diocletian there existed a predisposition among Christians to recognize the legitimacy of the Roman Empire as part of God's plan for the world. The new imperial favor shown by Constantine thus met a favorable response from many Christians, and the emperor's favor induced still more conversions once Christianity was free to proselytize openly. Some Christians, however, realized that a new problem had emerged. As in the case of Judaism in the first centuries B.C. and A.D., would Roman imperial favor turn Christianity from its spiritual mission? Would there be "imperializing Christians," just as there had been Hellenizing Jews? Could Christianity survive intact the welcoming embraces of the Roman Empire?

THE STRUCTURE OF THE CHURCH IN THE FOURTH CENTURY

Constantine's legalization of Christianity and the subsequent favor that he showed the Christian Church vastly expanded the attractions of Christianity and opened it to a wider number of influences from the pagan Greco-Roman world. Legalization also made Christianity the object of official imperial concern, and the Christian emperors' conception of their role in church affairs became inseparable from their conception of their imperial duties. The social, political, and economic reforms of the late third- and early fourth-century emperors were, in a sense, capped by the emperors' new religious role in the fourth century. The new Christian Roman Empire influenced the structure of religious doctrine and liturgy, and religion altered the conception of the empire. This mutual influence, of religious institutions and forms of government and culture, was so strong, and the consequent ecclesiastical and political structures so enduring, lasting in some cases until the twentieth century, that this section must deal with these last, and in some ways most powerful, influences that shaped the late antique world.

From 313 to 455 three remarkable dynasties, the Constantinian, Valentinian, and Theodosian, ruled the empire and oversaw its conversion to Christianity and its last stand in the west against outside invaders. They also created a new capital for the eastern part of the empire, Constantinople, and their successors ruled what was left of the Roman Empire from that city until its capture by the Turks in 1453. In the course of this century and a quarter, the emperors retained their image of supreme and remote rulers, although their conversion to Christianity meant that they served as the representatives of God on earth, not as gods themselves. The privileges and wealth that they bestowed upon the Church and the extensive influence that they exerted upon the Church's structure radically altered the character of Christianity, as well as the Mediterranean concept of the relation between religion and government. Under the influence of Christianity, Roman cultural elements reached out and touched peoples beyond the edges of the empire, thereby transforming barbarian culture and determining the cultural world of early Europe.

The Christian communities of the third and fourth centuries had long since begun to grow out of the worship groups that met in private homes under the informal leadership of an elder, who was called *episkopos* or *presbyter*. New forms of ecclesiastical organization in the third century and the writings of influential administrators such as St. Cyprian of Carthage and Tertullian had enhanced both the concept of the Christians as a "new people" and the authority of the leaders of that people. In the course of the third century the term *episkopos*—bishop—came to designate the rulers of each community, and *presbyter*—elder, or priest—came to designate lesser ecclesiastical officials. By the early fourth century, Christian churches were built for public worship, but in the persecutions of 298–313 many of these were destroyed and their congregations scattered. The tendency of small isolated groups of Christians to develop heterodox beliefs also pointed to the need for a group with sufficient authority to define orthodox belief. At the end of the second century, several western Christian writers narrowed the centers of orthodoxy to those churches that had been founded by the Apostles, and the episcopal order came to be considered principally as the body of successors to the Apostles. There were many apostolic churches in the eastern part of the empire, the most prestigious being that of Antioch, where the name "Christians" was first given to the followers of Jesus. But there was only one church in the western part of the empire that could claim apostolic foundation—the church at Rome, allegedly established by St. Peter and also associated with the missionary activities of St. Paul. From about 220, St. Peter was referred to as the first "bishop" of Rome, and although the authority of the Roman bishop was by no means universally recognized by the fourth century, a distinct quality of prestige and importance, particularly in the west, surrounded the "throne of St. Peter."

The order of bishops, however, clearly retained the highest degree of collective authority in the Church in the late third and the fourth centuries. Meetings of local groups of bishops (synods) determined policy and orthodoxy, and the most influential Christian writers and figures during this period were, more often than not, bishops. The reforms of Diocletian before the great persecutions had subdivided the prefectures of the empire into smaller, more manageable units, and these units—*civitates* and *dioceses*—influenced the further growth of the Christian faith. By the time the persecutions ended, with the accession of Constantine in 312, ecclesiastical organization had already become articulated throughout the reformed provinces. Once imperial favor began to flow toward the Christian communities, the parallel structure of ecclesiastical administration and civil administration drew even closer together. Just before the outbreak of Diocletian's great persecution, in fact, a synod of Spanish bishops had worked out the rules that permitted Christians to hold office in the civil government without compromising their faith. Throughout the late third century, then, ecclesiastical organization and the place of Christians in the Roman state had already begun to relax the older hostility and suspicion. That hostility and suspicion had existed on both sides. Christians stayed away from the most important public festivals of the empire and away from their non-Christian neighbors. They refused to eat meat that had once been offered to the gods or food that had been purified by pagan priests before being served. They refused to practice trades associated with pagan religious ceremonies, interfered with pagan temple revenues, and appeared to scorn the very institutions that seemed to the late Romans the essence of Roman—that is, human—civilization. According to their enemies—and some of their friends—the mere presence of a baptized Christian at the ceremonial reading of the portents for the future from the livers of animals or the flights of birds could render the oracles silent. Some Christians refused to join the army because they might come into contact with pagan ceremonies. The intense and articulate character of Christians as aliens and pilgrims in this world had reinforced these aspects of early Christianity, and the religious fervor of late antiquity easily saw in this alienation a fearsome and dangerous rejection of the very gods whose favor supported the empire. To this basic distrust of the close-knit and secretive Christian communities were added accusations of depraved sexual acts and ritual cannibalism, precisely those features of any religion that were most abhorrent to Romans. The intense religious conservatism of Diocletian and his successors Galerius and Maximinus Daia saw Christianity, furthermore, as traitorous to Rome itself, and the great persecutions of 298–313 were thus political as well as religious.

Constantine's official proclamation of legal toleration in the empire transformed the status of Christianity from a politically persecuted and culturally despised religion to a publicly approved one. To show his gratitude for the miracle that had given him victory at the Milvian Bridge in 312, Constantine appears to have insisted that the colossal statue of himself that the Roman Senate erected in the great basilica of Maxentius be decorated with the Christian signs that were responsible for his victory. The head of this statue, nine times life size, remains a remarkable example of late imperial portraiture and emphasizes the physical and spiritual greatness of its subject. The official placing of Christian signs on a public monument was only the first of Constantine's actions that reinforced his new interest in Christianity. Sometime in 312, he gave the great palace of the Laterani family to the bishop of Rome, and sometime in 313 he began erecting an immense basilica next to it, the first Christian church in Rome. The choice of the basilica form for a Christian church was portentous. The basilica was the characteristic late Roman official state building: three aisles ran the length of a rectangular building toward an apse at one end, where imperial officials conducted their audiences. This adaptation of the Roman official architecture for Christian worship strengthened the association between civil and ecclesiastical images, and the image of Christ the king and judge that came to hold the place of honor in the apse is thematically and iconographically descended from the similar positioning of the portrait of the ruling emperor. Other elements of public ceremonial also contributed to the physical transformation of church buildings: the imperial audience chamber became the divine audience chamber; the sacred presence of the emperor became the sacred presence of God, mediated by a priest who faced the congregation assembled in the nave; and imperial motifs of victory, justice, and eternity came to describe the attributes of Jesus, the Apostles, and the saints on the walls of the new imperial basilical churches. From private house to imperial hall, the buildings of worship of the Christians reflected the extent and direction of imperial influence during the fourth and fifth centuries. Other basilicas were erected over the tombs of the martyrs in Rome and, later, in other imperial provincial capitals. In 325 Constantine began the construction of a great basilica over the grave of St. Peter in the *Ager Vaticanus* in Rome, a church that was to be the center of Christianity until its replacement by the present church of St. Peter in the sixteenth century. Constantine's mother, St. Helena, who had discovered what was thought to be the true cross in Palestine, also erected a church, that of Santa Croce in Gerusallemme, close to the Lateran. Moreover, these churches were built directly on the sites of martyrs' graves, in opposition to pagan taboos against covering the graves of eminent men. The physical presence of the saint became a characteristic of Christian churches from the fourth century on.

Just as the buildings the Christians used for worship were transformed during the fourth century by the borrowing of structural and iconographic elements from imperial ceremonial and iconography, so was the form of Christian worship itself and the organization of the Church. The main phases of Christian worship derived from late Jewish practices and from elements of Greco-Roman mystery worship. Scriptural readings, psalms, and the sermon, hymns of praise and thanksgiving, the cult of martyrs, the formal division of the day and year into specific times for prayer, and the "paradigmatic prayers"—which called for help from God by recalling from history earlier examples of divine assistance—all came from late Judaism and the services of the synagogue. Rites of initiation, baptism, exorcism, the practice of keeping secret the heart of ritual and its meaning, and the geographical orientation of churches from east to west came from Hellenistic religion. Such common terms as "eucharist," "mystery," "canon," "epiphany," "vigil," "hymn," and "agape" all derive from the technical vocabulary of the pagan mystery religions. The earliest Christian services were timed to coincide with traditional Jewish services, and they derived many elements from the synagogue. In the fourth century, the spiritualized Eucharistic service was joined to a series of readings, resulting in the earliest form of what the century began to call the *Missa*—the Mass. The key festival for Christians was Easter, and Sunday services were in a sense repetitions of the Easter service, as they are in Orthodox congregations today. In the third and fourth centuries, other liturgical feasts appeared: Christmas and Epiphany and the feasts of early martyrs. The proliferation of feasts and civil recognition increased the bishops' sense of their own authority and also produced the first books of services. These sacred books were so well known by the time of the great persecution of 298–313 that simply handing them over to a Roman official was considered sufficient evidence of emperor worship. In the fourth century, service books appeared again, and these Sacramentaries became especially influential in spreading Christianity throughout the Roman Empire and beyond.

About the middle of the third century, Latin began to replace Greek in services in the western part of the empire, especially in Rome. This change of liturgical language reflects a broader change: the increasing unfamiliarity with Greek in the western parts of the empire during the third and fourth centuries, a symptom of the process by which the eastern and western parts of the empire drew apart from each other between 250 and 550. The substitution of Latin for Greek meant that the semantic structure of Latin shaped not only the prayers but the ideas of Christians in the west. The doctrinal controversies that took place in the fourth and fifth centuries, usually in the Greek-speaking parts of the Empire, were to become intelligible to western ecclesiastics only through translation—always a dangerous medium for the discussion of complex ideas and verbal connotations. And when the Old and New Testaments were finally translated into a generally recognized Latin version by St. Jerome in the fifth century, the subtle overtones and associations of the Hebrew and Greek words were transformed by those of the Latin terms Jerome chose. Thus, separate Jewish, Greek, and Latin scriptural styles of interpretation continued for twelve centuries, until Biblical scholarship rejoined them between the seventeenth and the twentieth centuries.

From Constantine's reign on, bishops acquired new civil powers: jurisdiction in civil proceedings between Christians, the power to legalize the freeing of slaves done in a church, immunity from the civil obligations of the ruling class in cities, and the freedom to expend vastly increased church wealth on charitable enterprises. To correspond with their new civil privileges, the bishops and other clergy were also given appropriate civil ranks. Bishops officially corresponded to *illustres,* the highest civil rank of the empire, and they were entitled to use the costume, forms of address, and insignia of this rank: the *pallium,* distinctive robes and shoes, a gold ring, and the ceremonial throne that became the characteristic feature of episcopal rank, the *cathedra,* whence comes the designation of a bishop's own church as a cathedral. The new public status of bishops, churches, charitable funds, and legal transactions of Christians had an important dual aspect that must not be forgotten: the Church became an integral part of the very world that it had, until very recently, abhorred—an arm, as it were, of the state itself. Second, it acquired new converts whose attachment to it was not nearly as thorough as that of earlier converts, and thus opened itself to new varieties of belief and worship. The disadvantages of this double experience were clear to Christians of the fourth century, just as they are clear now: the Church ran the risk of being "watered down" by its new official public status and its new members. On the other hand, the advantages are equally clear: the Church could now proselytize, organize itself, and expand its charitable works. If the fourth-century Church sacrificed its exclusivity for greater visibility, it also made itself accessible to many more people, not only inside the empire but beyond its borders as well. And these fourth-century changes were not passing fashions. From the fourth century to the twentieth, the authority, insignia, and character of bishops, the structure of Christian congregations, and the language and conceptualization of the most sacred dogmas and ceremonial prayers may be seen to have had their roots in the experience of the late third- and fourth-century Church.

Yet the Church was not controlled by the bishops alone. The Emperor, although no longer a god, had become God's vicar, and imperial intervention often influenced ecclesiastical policy, particularly in the fourth and fifth centuries, in the question of orthodox versus heterodox beliefs. The earliest Christian literature reflects differences of opinion within ecclesiastical communities. During the persecutions of the third and early fourth centuries, further divisive influences worked within Christian communities. The first heterodox problem that attracted imperial attention was that of Donatism, a belief that emerged in North Africa and that claimed that Christians who had submitted to imperial persecution and threats had to be rebaptized before being accepted again into the Christian community. By extension, Donatism proposed the larger question of the relation between the moral character of individuals, priests or laypersons and the indelibility of sacraments. How could a community be absolutely certain of the moral worth of its clergy and members? A secret sin by a priest might wipe away his sacramental power and plunge his entire congregation into damnation. The orthodox response to Donatism became a fundamental ecclesiological doctrine of the Christian community until the sixteenth century: the efficacy of the sacraments depends only upon the canonical ordination of a cleric, not upon his personal state of grace. With a little help from Roman law, one of the fundamental premises of ecclesiology took shape in the fourth-century Donatist experience.

The Donatist schism was resolved formally by a council of clergy under imperial direction. This institution dealt with many similar crises in the ensuing two centuries, and this first great age of Church councils had a major influence upon the shape of Christian belief and life. Struggles between orthodox and heterodox beliefs, often with "orthodoxy" becoming sharply defined after the fact, also centered in Christology—the problem of the divine and human natures of Christ— and trinitarianism—the character of the three persons in the Trinity. The most significant heresy in trinitarian history was that of Arius, a priest of Alexandria who maintained that Christ had been created by God and hence was inferior to the Father, a doctrine that had wide appeal and wide consequences. Christ-founded institutions, for example, the Church and the sacraments, could be considered inferior to the power of the Father, or the Emperor. The ensuing quarrels brought into Christian theology the full force of the Greek philosophical vocabulary, and the quarrel raged for more than two centuries. The Council of Nicaea of 325 laid down what ultimately became the orthodox dogma, that Christ and the Father were *homoousios,* "of the same essence." Nevertheless, the divisions among the clergy, the contrary opinions of successive emperors, and the philosophical arena that had been opened by the free discussions of learned bishops heralded many of the future difficulties in the definition of theological orthodoxy. The imperial Christianity of the fourth century transformed both the empire and the Church.

PAGANISM AND CHRISTIANITY IN THE FOURTH CENTURY: LEARNED AND POPULAR CULTURE

The ability of the reformed empire of the fourth century to absorb and influence Christianity is a sign of the resiliency that the reforms of Claudius II, Aurelian, Diocletian, and Constantine and their supporters had given to the troubled empire of the third century. The willingness of most Christians to be absorbed indicates Christianity's deep roots in the late antique world and its own ability to undertake the conversion and maintenance of that world. The mutual accommodation of Christian institutions and the empire, however, was not universally regarded as a benefit to either. Learned pagans and learned Christians, as well as members of the lower rural classes and the proletariat in cities—pagan and Christian alike—all disputed the value of the empire's slow but inexorable conversion to Christian belief, on the one hand, and Christianity's slow but equally inexorable coming to terms with the empire, on the other. Pagan opposition took two forms: among the learned and the wealthy classes, a self-conscious revival of pagan antiquarianism and consequent outrage at Christian incursions into what had been hitherto the most sacred aspects of Roman culture; among the rural peasants, a stubborn agrarian paganism that city-oriented Christians were slow to eradicate. Christian opposition to the residual pagan beliefs and institutions took two forms as well. Among the learned and the politically powerful there emerged a large body of Christian literature that developed an alternate conception of history and politics and refined Christian dogma into the philosophical language of late antique metaphysics—but not, as we have seen, without raising doctrinal questions that drove serious rifts into the Christian community itself. Other Christians, however, suspicious of both paganism and the new imperial Christianity, withdrew from the worlds of both and retired either into personal mysticism or withdrawn communal religious life, free to deal with the temptations of the devil, whether they came in the form of hostile pagans or too-worldly Christian bishops. Both pagan and Christian reaction to the success and character of the imperial church form as important an aspect of fourth-century life as does the success of the imperial church itself.

The senatorial class of Rome had long been the repository of what was considered the best of Roman tradition. When Constantine and his successors first tolerated, then joined, Christianity, the senate and the aristocracy long embodied the strongest articulate resistance to it. At first, the senate simply pretended that the imperial Christian belief did not exist, and Constantine and his sons allowed essential pagan ceremonies to continue, making only the change that burnt offerings to the divine emperors were no longer tolerated and delegating their traditional pagan priesthoods to substitutes. The aristocracy, wealthy as it was, still had to be accommodated, even by the most autocratic and determined of emperors, and any policy of imperial domestic reform was bound to conflict with the interests of this group. Hence, the aristocratic pagan opposition to the Christianizing policies of the emperors drew strength both from traditional Roman religious beliefs and the class interests of a privileged aristocracy that felt itself—and properly so—threatened in its pocketbook as well as in its spirit by imperial reforms. In a short time, however, Constantine's reluctance to allow all of the traditional ceremonies to occur, his obvious favoring of the Christians, and his infringement upon the finances and the privileges of pagan religious institutions generated a quiet but determined body of pagan opposition to him. The third century had seen the elimination of senators from many important offices of state and the end of imperial favor to the equestrian class. During and after the reign of Constantine, however, senatorial rank was not only hereditary, but accessible through a broad series of civil and military offices. Not only could officeholding bring aristocratic status to an ambitious man, but offices could often be purchased. Thus senatorial rank was opened to those wealthy enough to buy their way out of lower social grades or able enough to work their way up through the civil or military services. Not only soldiers and minor officials, but lawyers, notaries, and lowly clerks might be appointed to—or buy—offices of sufficiently high rank to entitle their holders to senatorial privileges. Libanius, a fourth-century rhetorician and philosopher, acidly described some of the high officials of Constantine and his sons: stenographers, the son of a cloakroom attendant at the baths, the son of a sausage maker, the son of peasants. Moreover, many new senators came from the provinces, especially those recently Romanized—Pannonia and the Balkans—and some were barbarians. This increase in the number of men of senatorial rank had different consequences in the eastern and western parts of the empire. Traditional Roman families, who were very few in number and imbued both with clan loyalty and old pagan beliefs, predominated in the West, particularly in Rome, which the emperors rarely visited. In the East there were more "new" senators, who had risen from lower grades and, consequently, were less hostile to Christian beliefs. Although some vestiges of paganism, particularly in the philosophical and rhetorical schools, re-remained among the aristocracy of the east, it appears that this aristocracy was predominantly Christian and of recent origin, whereas the western aristocracy was strongly pagan and proud of its family traditions and heritage.

After the death of Constantius II in 361, however, a philosophical paganism was revived under Constantine's nephew, Julian, emperor from 361 to 363 and a convert from Christianity to paganism under the influence of his teachers and friends among the pagan aristocracy. Julian declared a policy of religious toleration and gave equal support to doctrinally opposed factions among Christians, hoping that internal quarrels would prevent a unified Christian reaction to his pagan sympathies and that, ultimately, Christianity would simply become one of the many religions in the empire, all subordinate to Julian's own hybrid brand of intellectualized paganism. The senatorial refuge in traditionalism—both in religion and privilege—gathered strength and came to a head in the second half of the fourth century. The short and promising reign of Julian was followed by the brief and conciliatory reign of Jovian, and then, in 365, the military acclamation of Valentinian, "the last of the great Pannonian emperors" and the son of a soldier who had worked his way up through the military from very low to the highest rank. Valentinian himself had been an army officer, and his tenacity in maintaining Christian beliefs had prevented his promotion under the pagan Julian. Valentinian's accession was the result of a unique agreement between different factions in the imperial court, and it was hoped that his moderation would allow for continued exploration of ways in which pagans and Christians could share the empire for a longer time. Valentinian, however, proved equally resolute as a Christian and an emperor. His officials fought aristocratic corruption vigorously, but the causes of that corruption were complex. The aristocracy was living the consequences of exclusion from meaningful political roles after the second century, as well as the myth of guardians of tradition, which had been substituted for real political power. The fourth-century pagan aristocratic opposition to imperial policies had roots in economics and social status as well as in religion, and it had been created by the third-century emperors as well as the senators. In a sense, the opposition between Valentinian and the aristocracy was the fruit of both imperial policies and senatorial short-sightedness. The senators had become the pampered darlings of the empire after their political role had been relaxed. It was no wonder that the attacking of their privileged status drove them back into politics. They were corrupt, ruthless, and unfeeling because no one had ever taken the trouble to urge them to be otherwise. The complex political and economic status of the western aristocracy must be kept in mind in assessing its strength and tenacity in the pagan reaction that occurred during the later years of Constantine's reign and continued to the end of the fourth century.

Paganism, as it flourished in the mid to late fourth century, may be said in fact to have been a creation of these aristocrats and the philosophical writers who were their allies. The gods they worshiped, their religious metaphysics, and their studied attempts to reconstruct the old Roman religious aristocratic culture constituted as much a distinctive phenomenon of the fourth century as a continuation of earlier pagan thought.

No episode characterizes the opposition between Christianity and paganism better than that of the Altar of Victory. The Altar stood in the Roman Senate chamber and was lit anew at each meeting of the senate. Far more than emperor worship or the Olympian gods, the Altar represented the deepest roots of pagan belief, the quiet assurance that the favor of the gods depended upon this subtle, dignified, and ancient ritual. In 357 Constantius II ordered the Altar removed, but it was restored to its place under his successor Julian. Then in 382, the emperor Gratian, the son of Valentinian I, struck a double blow at pagan belief and practice. He withdrew the funds supporting the public pagan cults, and he removed the Altar of Victory from the senate. The ensuing debates brought forth two great spokesmen, St. Ambrose, Bishop of Milan, who argued against its restoration, and Symmachus, prefect of the city of Rome, who argued for it. These two men illustrate the character of the opposition between Christianity and learned paganism better than any others. Ambrose had been born in Spain, and since he came from a noble family, he was posted to a career in the civil administration, which progressed brilliantly. Sent to Milan as its governor, Ambrose was soon acclaimed by the population as its candidate for bishop. Reluctantly, and with much searching of conscience, Ambrose accepted the episcopate in

374, and from then until his death he was the most articulate and influential spokesman for Christianity in the west. Quintus Aurelius Symmachus descended from one of the oldest and most distinguished aristocratic families in the empire. His upright life and unimpeachable morals made him the embodiment of the best in the senatorial cause, and in his capacity as prefect of the city of Rome he had occasion to send official reports, *relationes,* to the emperors. Symmachus's third *relatio* is one of the most memorable documents of pagan antiquity, an articulate and moving appeal for the restoration of the Altar of Victory to its proper place in the senate, couched in faultless antique rhetoric and expressing an appeal for religious toleration in terms that still move those who read it. Rome, personified as an old and honorable woman, appeals to the emperor on the grounds of honored tradition, on the effectiveness of the cult of Victory in Roman history, and upon the essential harmlessness of its continuation. She then broadens her appeal to the question of the basic relation between man and the gods—"everyone has his own customs, his own religion . . . one cannot reach so vast a mystery by one way alone"—and then appeals that she be left to live the rest of her life according to her ancient ways, for she is too old to repent of them. Symmachus's appeal reportedly moved Gratian's successor, Valentinian II, considerably, but St. Ambrose's response was ultimately the most persuasive. It is not a response that appeals to many readers today, but in the intensity and heat of the argument it is at least understandable. Pagan rituals, being wrong, have done nothing for Rome. What good is a custom, however old, if it has no meaning? The compelling reality of the Christian God and His explicit instructions regarding the conduct of men in this world leave no room for pagan ritual, however ancient, however harmless. Ambrose respects his opponent but he hates the cause, and his response is an impassioned but unprejudiced statement of orthodox belief. In a sense, the difference in tone of the two works reflects the character of the opponents. Symmachus's work is clear, moving, learned, and based on the widest possible concepts of humanity and civilization— but it is an appeal; Ambrose's work is a statement possessed of a force and certainty that Symmachus, with all his eloquence and humanity, cannot match.

The permanent loss of the Altar of Victory and the withdrawal of temple funds constituted the death blow to pagan opposition. But the death of that opposition was prolonged by yet another element in paganism, that of the literary opposition to Christian culture. The greatest historian in Roman literature since Tacitus in the second century was the late fourth-century Ammianus Marcellinus. Ammianus's history, of which that part covering the years 353–371 still survives, is an articulate defense of aristocratic paganism against the political and economic moves of the Christian emperors. Although Ammianus scored senatorial corruption and the vast disregard of human misery that characterized the wealthy classes of the fourth-century empire, his sympathy remained with the cause defended so eloquently by Symmachus. Other fourth-century literary figures, some of them Christian, persisted in regarding pagan culture highly. The professor of rhetoric from Bordeaux, Ausonius, was tutor to Gratian and later held the highest governmental posts in the western part of the empire. Another literary man, Flavius Eugenius, attempted to usurp imperial rank in the west in 392, and with the aid of two influential members of the aristocracy, Virius and Nichomachus Flavianus, he revived for the last time the old pagan cause. In 394 the Emperor Theodosius moved against them, and on September 6, 394, the last pagan army of the ancient world was defeated by the greatest Christian emperor. In 391 and 392 Theodosius had finally outlawed pagan religion in the empire, and the destruction of Eugenius and the Flaviani in 394 signaled the formal death of pagan institutions and culture.

Ironically, the last pagans in the ancient world were not those who represented the flowering of pagan literature, arts, and thought or the flowering of pagan aristocratic society, but the humble rural farming people who shared with their fellow believers only the belief in the magical efficacy of the myriad pagan spirits into whom the once mighty Olympian gods had degenerated by the fourth century. Belief in magic, in the world of spirits of varying powers and dispositions, and in the inchoate but ubiquitous attempts of fortunetellers, astrologers, soothsayers, and magicians to harness the invisible powers of these spirits for the good of men—or for their harm—permeated late pagan society, and appealed even to Christians. The fourth-century imperial legislation against magic and allied practices and beliefs was ferocious and compelling. In the cities particularly, anyone caught wearing even an amulet to prevent disease could be tried and executed on the spot. The widespread belief in pagan gods and spirits was sharpened by the Christian belief that the old pagan gods were really demons, and that recourse to them in any rite, however apparently legitimate, constituted idolatry: the attribution to demons of those powers rightly possessed only by God. Thus, for some Christians paganism took on the aspect of demon worship, and the stubborn rural conventions toward the agrarian deities of hearth and field came to be regarded as identical with both the learned philosophical spiritualism of the pagan philosophers and the popular appeal of white and black magic among the unlearned masses of the cities. Of all these manifestations of pagan beliefs, that of the country folk lasted the longest, retaining its pagan character well into the era of universal Christianity. The city-oriented religion of the Christians succeeded best in the cities of the late empire; only much more slowly did it reach the rural folk. By the end of the fourth century that process was just beginning, although the conversion of the towns and the aristocracy and learned pagans had proceeded vigorously throughout that century. The transformation of rural religion from the late empire to the Industrial Revolution is one of the most difficult historical problems in the history of those centuries. Certainly, many aspects of late imperial rural paganism lasted for a long time in the Christianized Middle Ages, for the beliefs and devotional forms of the countryside changed slowest of all. The problems of explaining Christianity to rural laborers and farmers were ameliorated, of course, by Christianity's development of a simplified literary style, which was already successful among the uneducated lower classes of the towns. The preoccupation of bishops with the towns in which they lived, the indifference of landowners to the spiritual life of their laborers and slaves, and the deep-rooted peasant belief in the spirits of springs, fields, and forests constituted an impediment to Christianity in the countryside that remained very strong until the sixth and seventh centuries.

Pagan learning and the sense of tradition, on the one hand, and the stubborn beliefs of those unlearned pagans who subscribed to magic and soothsaying or rural pagan spirits, on the other, were not the only opponents of the new imperial church in the fourth and fifth centuries. Ever since the toleration acts of Constantine, powerful and articulate voices among Christians had rejected the possibility of a fully Christianized empire, and the pro-Arian sentiments of some of Constantine's successors, notably Constantius II, further alienated those who believed that the favor of the emperor could only bode ill for the Church. Although large numbers of Christians—including most of the Church's ablest leaders, such as St. Ambrose—were devoted to Christianity's role in the Roman state, other Christians fled—figuratively and literally—from the embraces of the world, the *saeculum,* to a life of individual devotion or communal living away from the imperial officials and bishops, the great new basilicas, and official Christianity. These were the hermits and mystics of Egypt and Syria, and the isolated religious communities that grew up around them and formed the heart of the monastic movement that was to play so important a role in the history of Europe between the fifth and the sixteenth centuries.

Although Christianity had rapidly developed an intellectual framework for expounding the metaphysical truths of its beliefs, and although Christian intellectuals were as renowned as their learned pagan opponents by the end of the fourth century, Christianity had not renounced the simplicity of its earliest literature or forgotten the humble unlettered people among whom it had first spread so widely. To be sure, often only a veneer of Christianity covered the minds of converted philosophers and aristocrats, but scriptural injunctions to serve the poor, to flee the corrupting world, and to seek values only in personal devotion continued to anchor Christianity deep in the lower levels of society. Tertullian had rejected classical learning with the savage question, "What has Athens to do with Jerusalem?" And St. Paul's remark that the wisdom of men was foolishness in the eyes of God often served to remind Christians that higher learning and social acceptance carried with them tinges of despised paganism and that Christians ought rightly to be suspicious of them. The long process by which Christianity came to terms with pagan learning, ultimately to use the roots of pagan literary education as the basis of Christian education, was filled with many hesitant steps. Christian writers prided themselves on the *sermo humilis,* the "simple style" of the gospels that enabled them to explain truths of great complexity to simple folk, and the fourth- and fifth-century bishops constantly reminded their wealthy congregations of the Christian responsibility for the spiritual well-being of the lower orders of society. Although such writers as St. Ambrose could use the language and logical techniques of Neo-Platonism, they also wrote much on the care of souls, and next to St. Ambrose's theological writings must be placed his hymns, ecclesiastical songs to be sung by the whole congregation, songs whose clarity and language reveals the best of late Latin poetry. Some Christian intellectuals attempted to take over pagan learning wholesale, sometimes with admirable, sometimes with ludicrous results. Next to the moving philosophical treatises of Origen and the rhetorical genius of St. Augustine and the immense, encyclopedic learning of St. Jerome, one must count in this respect the attempts to turn the Gospels into heroic Latin verse, the attempts to allegorize away those elements of the Old and New Testaments that might be considered offensive to the refined sensibilities of learned pagans, and the selecting from pagan poetry of individual lines and phrases that, when reassembled, turned magically into cryptic "Christian" documents. "New learning," as the literary historian C. S. Lewis remarked some years ago, often brings with it "new ignorance."

About the year 269, a young man from a prosperous peasant family in Egypt, moved by Christ's injunction to "go, sell all you have and give to the poor and follow me," left his family and the narrow agriculturalized belt of the Nile valley and went out into the desert to live a life of devotion. From the time of earliest Egyptian civilization, the desert had symbolized the emptiness of the world and the habitation of demons *par excellence.* To Egyptians, the desert represented the annihilation of everything remotely connected with civilization, and Anthony's self-imposed exile was a literal and figurative rejection of both the imperial church and the ancient, deep-rooted Egyptian terror of the waste. The name that Egyptians gave to St. Anthony and those who followed him was a Greek word, *anachoresis,* which traditionally described those who had fled from the pressures of civilization into the hostile wilderness. The first anchorites were thus thought of as rejecting both the dangers of a secularized church *and* the social roots of civilization itself. St. Anthony attracted a number of followers, although he moved several times further away from civilization. His struggles with the demons of the desert, themselves a combination of Christian belief and traditional Egyptian peasant folklore, attracted the admiration of many, and in the mid fourth century the image of the isolated holy man reverted to the more dramatic ideal of an earlier Christian age—that of martyrdom and persecution suffered for the faith.

The *Life of St. Anthony,* written by St. Athanasius, the pugnacious Alexandrian defender of orthodoxy against Arianism, was translated into Latin before 386 and started a new genre of Christian literature. The lives and passions of the early martyrs had constituted the most popular literature in the third- and early fourth-century church. In the era of religious persecutions of 298–313, martyrdom came to be considered the highest stage of the life of the spirit, one that brought man to the very threshold of Heaven. St. Anthony and the other hermits of Egypt and Syria offered a new kind of religious ideal, the monk—a "martyr" whose martyrdom consisted in making himself "dead" to the world and achieving in the desert through rigorous self-discipline, contemplation, combats with demons, and, ultimately, mystical experience that stage of the spiritual life that the martyrs had reached in so different a way and in so different a world. The spiritual biographies of early monks, inspired by the vast popularity of St. Athanasius' *Life of St. Anthony*, became the new literature of piety and the guide to the new spiritual life. Ironically, the spread of monastic popularity attracted the interest of the very world that the monks had rejected so dramatically. Lives of the "desert fathers" were widely read, and Christians thronged into the desert to consult the holy men just as they had once made pilgrimages to the sites of earlier martyrdoms, some taking up the monastic life themselves and some returning to the corrupting world invigorated by their brief contact with the monastic ideal.

The variety of forms of monasticism was great during the fourth century. Some men retired to caves in the desert, some, especially the Syrians, took to living atop tall pillars for decades, some subjected themselves to extreme bodily tortures and privations. In the late fourth and early fifth centuries monasticism began to change. Instead of isolated holy men fighting the demons by themselves, small communities grew up around famous hermits, and these began to become organized. Under the influence of St. Pachomius (286–346), a former soldier in the army of Constantine, an organized monastic life appeared in Egypt; later, under the influence of St. Basil of Caesarea (329–379), this life style evolved in the east as well. These monastic communities, along with diocesan episcopal organization and the collectives of unfree people on great estates, were the unique contribution of late antique social organization to the later Western world. By constituting a model, or "perfect," Christian society, these communities offered a moral pattern whose elements might be absorbed slowly by the broader society around them. People considered the monastery, untroubled by the upheavals of the world around it, the paradigm of ideal Christian society, a copy of Heaven. Monasteries flourished in Gaul and Italy as well as in North Africa, Egypt, Syria, and Greece by the beginning of the fifth century. The monks, the new culture heroes of Christianity, represented the tradition of rejecting the secularization of Christianity, which the martyrs had originated. The appeal of the monks, like that of the martyrs, transcended the bounds of learning, philosophy, and social class. In monasticism, the devotion of the humble man to God was raised to the highest level of Christian life and therefore militated against the increasing secularization of the Church.

Monasticism in a sense balanced the secular success of the Church in the fourth and fifth centuries and thus retained its deep roots in the lower orders of society and in its concept of the relation between the individual, however lowly, and God. Henceforth, Christian adaptations of pagan learning and Christian monasticism were to be the twin supports of the spread of Christian belief—both inside Roman imperial society and outside, in the world of the barbarians, a world more important ultimately than the demon-infested deserts or the book-stocked libraries of the urban fathers.

THE SECOND ROME AND THE OLD EMPIRE, 330–395

To solidify the division of the empire, Constantine created a new city in the east, a city to balance Rome. Diocletian had favored Nicomedia in Asia Minor as the center of his activities when he was the Augustus of the east, but Constantine had no such preference for that city. At his accession, the question of an eastern center for his activities remained open. In 324, Constantine defeated his imperial rival Licinius in a sea battle, and like other conquerors in the classical world decided to found a city to commemorate the event—the classical act of self-expression: city founding. He ultimately chose the small fishing town of Byzantium, located on a triangularly shaped peninsula between the Bosporus and the Sea of Marmora, whose location on the very edge of continental Europe gave it potentially strategic value in controlling traffic from the Black Sea to the Adriatic. Moreover, being located at the southern tip of the Balkan peninsula, it served as a good defense against invaders of either the lower Danube or the Asiatic frontiers. Between 324 and 330, Constantine supplied vast funds and materials for the renovation of the old town, but there is little evidence during this period that he conceived the city to be anything more than a particularly favored imperial residence. He ransacked pagan temples and other cities to decorate his new city, and he gave its inhabitants unique privileges, which were not, however, equal at first to those of the inhabitants of Rome. Like Rome, Constantinople was to be ruled not by one of the great praetorian prefects as part of a prefecture, but by its own administrative ruler; in Rome this was the prefect of the city, a post that the pagan Symmachus held in the late fourth century, as we have seen. Like the population of Rome, the population of Constantinople received a free ration of bread, shipped from Africa. The splendor of the city soon made it greater in both appearance and privileges than any other former imperial residence except Rome itself. Yet, other aspects of Constantinople were destined to give it a place equal to that of Rome. Constantine, conscious of the favor of the Christian God, refused to permit pagan ceremonies to take place in his city; he is reported to have remarked in later life that he founded Constantinople under divine inspiration. Within ten years after his conversion to Christianity, Constantinople began to appear in official documents and in art as a new capital. By 339, the personification of Constantinople on coins had lost the cornucopia of prosperity and began to be depicted holding the sceptre of sovereignty, and continued imperial residence over several generations gave the city the character more and more of a capital. Soon, men spoke of Constantinople as the "Second Rome," and the privileges of its inhabitants were made equal to those of inhabitants of Rome. During the revival of paganism in the late fourth century, Constantinople's role as a center of Christian orthodoxy increased, and by the third quarter of the fourth century, its control of the wealthy eastern provinces and its identification with the increasing prestige of the emperor Constantine the Great gave it a status equal to that of Rome and superior to that of any of the other imperial residences in the west. Its strategic location soon increased its importance even further.

The migration of the eastern Germanic peoples brought them to the area bounded by the Danube on the south and west and by western Asia on the east. There, they had established two major confederations, that of the Visigoths just across the Danube frontier and that of the Ostrogoths in South Russia. The appearance of the Huns in western Asia in the middle of the fourth century had caused great changes in the Gothic kingdoms. The pressure of the Huns on the Ostrogothic kingdom in South Russia caused Ostrogothic pressure on the kingdom of the Visigoths close to the frontier of Rome. The Visigoths, faced with these pressures and fearful of internal collapse and outside invasion, appealed to the emperor Valens for permission to enter the empire. In 376 that fateful permission was given, but the oppression of Roman officials soon generated substantial resentment among the Visigoths, and they revolted against their Roman hosts. In 378 Valens was defeated and killed by the Visigoths at Adrianople, and in 379 his nephew Gratian appointed a retired Spanish general, Theodosius, Augustus of the east. In 383 the revolt of the Spaniard Maximus resulted in the death of Gratian, and from that date until his own death in 395, Theodosius ruled the empire single-handedly.

The invasion of the Visigoths posed a problem that strained the resources of the empire to the utmost. Theodosius' final solution was unprecedented: the Visigoths were to be allowed to settle in the empire as a whole people under their own leaders—constituting a movable kingdom, as it were, inside the empire but not under the jurisdiction of the empire and its officials. In return, the Visigoths were to help the imperial armies as *federati*. Yet the precedent set by Theodosius ultimately opened the door of the empire to more and more peoples who claimed the same—or greater—privileges. The Visigoths posed other problems to Rome, and to understand these we must remember that after the death of Gratian, only the weak Valentinian II remained in the west. After the death of Theodosius, his son Honorius, an equally ineffective emperor, ruled in the west. The weakness of Valentinian II and Honorius permitted a number of generals to come to power although without the official titles of Caesar or Augustus. The military reforms of Diocletian and Constantine had made the army and the Church the repositories of talented and able men, and the reforms of the fourth century had opened army careers to wider and wider ranks of the population of the empire and to barbarians as well.

Constantine's division of the empire into two parts had made Rome and Constantinople twin capitals. Under the Augustus of the west were two praetorian prefectures—that of the Gauls and that of Italy—each of which was divided into dioceses. The prefecture of Gaul consisted of Gaul, Britain, Spain, and Morocco; its dioceses were Britain, Gallia I, Gallia II, Spain, and Morocco; these in turn were subdivided into provinces. Dioceses were ruled by vicars, and provinces by provincial governors, and these officials were responsible to the praetorian prefect of the

Gauls. The Prefecture of Italy consisted of Italy, Switzerland, the Danube area around modern Austria, and North Africa. The urban prefect of Rome was independent of these praetorian prefects. The Augustus of the east ruled over two praetorian prefectures—Illyricum and the Orient. Illyricum included the Balkans and the troublesome Danube frontier; the Orient included Thrace, Egypt, and Asia. The urban prefect of Constantinople, like his counterpart in Rome, stood outside the system of praetorian prefectures.

The army, too, had been reformed. But the symmetry between the eastern and the western parts of the empire did not extend to the military reforms of the fourth century. In the west, there were two masters of soldiers (*magistri militum*), one for cavalry and one for infantry. One able master of soldiers could easily dispose of a single rival and thus exert a preponderant influence over a weak imperial government and a child emperor. In the east, however, there were five masters of soldiers, and never the opportunity for a single general to assume absolute influence over the government. The youth and inexperience of Valentinian II, the youth of Honorius, and Theodosius' preoccupation with the east allowed military men to extend their personal authority considerably in the west, not by usurping the throne, but by standing behind it.

Thus, the accession of Theodosius occurred in an empire whose century-old administrative divisions had been reflected in linguistic, religious, social, and military divisions. Expediency, rather than long-range planning, had opened military and civil ranks to men of all origins and had closed them only to pagans. It was an empire with two capitals, two emperors, and one religion. But it was no longer the classical world of Augustan Rome. It was no longer even the world of Constantine.

PART **TWO**

THE LEGACY OF MEDITERRANEAN ANTIQUITY, 395-650

5

EAST AND WEST ROME AND THE INVASIONS, 395-530

EMPERORS AND CHURCHMEN

The transformation of imperial rule and the division of the empire into eastern and western parts were only two of the legacies of the late fourth century. Two others, equally important, contributed to the character of the Roman Empire in the fifth century. The first of these, already noted, was the massive assault on paganism by churchmen and emperors after 379, a movement that was completed by Theodosius' outlawing of pagan practices in 392. The second was the appearance of new, militant, learned churchmen in the imperial world.

In Africa, Cappadocia, Italy, Gaul, and Spain, the fourth century had witnessed the rise of powerful churchmen and of a new militant

Plate 1 courtesy Thames and Hudson Ltd., London.

Plate 2 courtesy Hirmer Fotoarchiv, München.

THE BYZANTINE IMAGE. From the fifth to the fifteenth centuries the great city of Constantinople inspired both inhabitants and strangers with its elaborate material culture and its aesthetic appeal to the senses. The reconstruction of the city of Constantinople made by the artist Alan Sorrell (Plate 1) shows the city as it may have looked around the year 1000. The city, with a population of around 350,000, is bordered by the Golden Horn at the top of the picture and the Sea of Marmara at the bottom and the right. The city was under the particular protection of the Virgin, shown here in a mosaic from Haghia Sophia, in which the Emperor Constantine, on the right, presents the city to the Virgin and Child, while the Emperor Justinian presents Haghia Sophia itself (Plate 2).

Plate 3 courtesy of Dumbarton Oaks Center for Byzantine Studies, Washington, D.C.

The interior of Haghia Sophia (Plate 3), shown with later Islamic additions, gives some sense of the awe and majesty inspired by the great church.

Plate 4 courtesy Skira, Geneva.

Plate 5 courtesy Bildarchiv Foto-Marburg.

The portrait of Justinian's empress Theodora (Plate 4) from the Church of San Vitale at Ravenna suggests both the majesty of imperial court ceremonial and the projection of this majesty through the use of the art of mosaics to the distant corners of the Empire. The fifth-century ivory carving (Plate 5) depicts a procession bearing relics and led by the emperor. The harmony of city life and the unity of emperor and churchmen is one of the constant and most effective themes of Byzantine history.

church spirit, increased by the late fourth-century revival of paganism. New institutions such as monasticism had succeeded in spreading Christianity widely throughout the empire, and a new generation of imperial bishops became the spokesmen for a more numerous and privileged Christianity. St. Ambrose, the great bishop of Milan, had become the model of a Roman Christian bishop, his pastoral rule and his theological and liturgical writings revealing not only the influence of late antique Neo-Platonist philosophy but that of traditional Roman concepts of public responsibility and civic morality in the vein of Cicero. In Theodosius, Ambrose met an emperor after his own heart. This devout but volatile emperor, although he resembled Constantine in many ways, was far more thoroughly a Christian than his great predecessor. When Theodosius became emperor in 379, for example, he became the first emperor to refuse the title of *Pontifex Maximus,* the chief priest of the pagan state religion, a title retained even by Constantine and his successors. Theodosius' example inspired his imperial colleague Gratian to renounce the same title, and in 380 Theodosius' constitution against all heretics launched one of the major phases of Christian history. Theodosius' reign witnessed a concerted attack not only on paganism but on heretical Christianity and Judaism as well. In 382 Gratian deprived the vestal virgins of their privileges, withdrew the revenues of pagan temples, and, as we have seen, removed the Altar of Victory from the curia. Throughout his reign, Theodosius deferred to St. Ambrose, even to the extent of submitting himself to public penitence at the order of the bishop because he had massacred the population of Thessalonica in retaliation for the murder of his military governor.

St. Ambrose and Theodosius were not the only remarkable ecclesiastical-political figures of the late fourth century. The long pontificate of Damasus (366–384) as bishop of Rome helped increase the prestige of that see by renewing the Christian history of Rome, turning the catacombs into shrines, and patronizing the martyr cults of the city. Damasus also cooperated with Theodosius' ecclesiastical pronouncements concerning orthodoxy, and in return Theodosius recognized formally the preeminence of the bishop of Rome as successor to St. Peter. Damasus was one of the first of a series of dynamic popes whose efforts to elevate the see of Rome over other churches laid the foundations of the medieval and modern papacy. Angered by Theodosius' elevation of the patriarch of Constantinople, "the new Rome," to a position of personal authority second only to that of Rome, Damasus became the first pope to use the title "apostolic" in connection with his see and began addressing other bishops as "sons" instead of "brothers" in his correspondence. Damasus' fifth-century successors as bishop of Rome continued the struggle for ecclesiastical primacy. Siricius (384–399) was the first person to use the title *papa,* or pope, for the bishop of Rome, and Innocent I (401–417) claimed that important cases should be judged only by the pope. By the time of Pope Leo I (440–461), the greatest of the popes that held office before the end of the sixth century, the bishop of Rome clearly emerged as the successor of the senatorial guardians of imperial tradition and as the highest churchman in Christendom.

The prestige of individual bishops such as St. Ambrose and the slow rise of the bishop of Rome were two of the forces that contributed to the remarkable success of Christianity between 350 and 450. The devotion of Theodosius and its consequences for paganism, Judaism, and sects of heretical Christians shaped further the structure of imperial Christianity, and the emergence of a series of truly remarkable theologians between 350 and 450 marked the Christian absorption of pagan culture and its consequent transformation. Although far from the most politically powerful, the most enduringly articulate spokesman for Christianity during this period was the African St. Augustine. Augustine was one of the "new provincials" whose secular and ecclesiastical career revealed much not only about Christianity but about Roman society as well. The great Cappadocian Fathers of the mid and late fourth century—St. Basil of Caesarea, St. Gregory of Nyssa, and St. Gregory Nazianzus—also represented the intellectual and spiritual vigor of what had hitherto been remote and backward provinces on the fringe of the empire, and their influence extended not only to monasticism and the eastern churches but to the arch-Roman, St. Ambrose, himself. The career of St. Augustine offers a western counter-example to those of the Cappadocian Fathers.

Born at Thagaste in North Africa in 354, the son of poor, free peasants, Augustine was baptized a Christian but during his youth was raised with little spiritual guidance except for the prayers of his Christian mother, Monica. Augustine's parents were unable to afford more than minimal schooling for their precocious son, but a wealthy fellow citizen undertook the expense of his continuing education at Carthage. From Carthage, Augustine's success as a teacher of rhetoric brought him to Rome, and thence, in 384—under the sponsorship of the great pagan noble Symmachus—to the professorship of rhetoric at Milan, then the greatest city in Italy and an imperial capital. Until Augustine was thirty, his career as a successful intellectual had been a classical illustration of "making it" within an open and receptive social system. From his professorship at Milan, Augustine, not unlike some modern professors, was eligible for marriage into an aristocratic and wealthy family, and with these credentials he could obtain a high administrative post in the empire, possibly a provincial governorship or the position of tutor to a future emperor. A generation earlier, the Bordeaux professor Ausonius had parlayed his own status into a praetorian prefecture and a position of power behind the throne of Gratian. There was no reason, save one, why Augustine's career should not have followed a similar path. That reason was Augustine's restless spirit. In the course of his education and social success, Augustine had encountered intellectually the rich spectrum of spiritual experience that the fourth-century Roman world had to offer. He had embraced Neo-Platonism and several Christian heresies, and he had flirted with mystery religions. Two hundred years before, the brilliant North African, Lucius Apuleius, had embraced the mystery religion of Isis and left a remarkable novel, *The Golden Ass,* which paints a vivid picture of late imperial life and the attraction of such mystery religions. Augustine, however, if he was not to be another Ausonius, was not to be another Apuleius either. The pressures from his mother had followed him to Italy, and the emptiness in his own heart, as he was later to say, made the varieties of spiritualism he had experienced so far only dim and faulty shadows. In Milan, however, Augustine met St. Ambrose, and the influence of the older man began to turn the professor's mind back to the Christianity that he had ignored for so long. After a moving personal religious experience, Augustine returned to Christianity in 386, renounced his professorship, and returned to Africa, there to become the bishop of the coastal city of Hippo Regius.

Augustine left one of the most remarkable documents in literary history—his *Confessions,* written in 397. This work is the first intellectual self-portrait in history, and in it Augustine offered not the external events of his life but the "history of a heart," the story of his own religious experience told from the viewpoint of a middle-aged bishop. In his *Confessions,* Augustine transformed the traditional conversion story into the scheme of a whole life of individual struggle to come to terms with the traces of God—the *vestigia Dei*—in the human soul. For Augustine, the discovery of the will of God, the conversion, was the climax of human life. But Augustine's work was not one of saccharine spiritualism; conversion did not lift the human burden from his shoulders, and the *Confessions* read more like "the account of a great spiritual disease and its convalescence" than like the heroic martyr or conversion stories of old. Augustine keeps constantly before his and the reader's eyes the full complexity of human feeling and habit. Nowhere does Augustine betray that complexity, nowhere does he offer an easy life as a result of his experience. Augustine was perhaps the first writer to reveal his own personality as the only means of describing accurately not only the spiritual disorder that pervades the life of the man who ignores God, but the continuing burden of the human condition *after* conversion, even during the episcopate. During his period as bishop of Hippo, from 389 to 430, Augustine witnessed the great ecclesiastical reforms of Theodosius and his successors, but his role was not the public one of St. Ambrose. Augustine ruled his city and wrote commentaries on scripture, treatises on dogma, sermons, and letters—270 of them—on all aspects of Christian belief and thought. More than any other Church father, Augustine shaped the future intellectual development of Western Christianity.

Another Roman provincial also became one of the great fourth-century fathers. St. Jerome, born in what is now Yugoslavia, attained a scholarly eminence greater even than that of St. Augustine, and became the greatest scholar among the early churchmen. Jerome's standing in Roman society, his friendships with Damasus and others, his vast scholarly labors, and the model of his own life—he retired to a monastery in Bethlehem—gave him an eminence that has persisted to this day. Of the four fathers of the Latin Church, Ambrose was the ideal official, Pope Gregory I the most simple and straightforward, St. Augustine the most intense and personal, and Jerome the most learned. The Latin Vulgate text of the Bible came from Jerome's hand, as did several important works of Christian history.

The divisions of the empire and the new civilian character of the Theodosian dynasty joined with the new vigor of two generations of remarkable churchmen to deal classical paganism a death blow from which it was never to recover and to shape both ecclesiastical institutions and ecclesiastical thought. These achievements, on the very eve of the new invasions from beyond the frontiers of the Roman empire, survived to exert an influence both on the kingdoms that were to supplant the Empire in the west and on most of the forms of Western thought until modern times.

THE WORLD OF GALLA PLACIDIA: VISIGOTHS AND ROMANS IN THE WEST

The courts of the young emperors Honorius and Arcadius, at Ravenna and Constantinople, respectively, consisted of circles of relatives, advisors, nobles, and generals whose rivalries with one another for imperial favor—sometimes even for control of the emperor—limited the emperor's ability to deal with large-scale crises and to form consistent policies. Moreover, the aims of the military advisers with whom Theodosius had surrounded his sons often conflicted violently with the ideas of the civilian courtiers. It is in the light of intracourt rivalries such as these that the fifth-century barbarian threats to the western part of the empire must be understood. The history of the relations between the western imperial court and the Visigoths is not one of directionless barbarian hordes sacking the entire west, but of a string of tentative agreements and broken promises, of bravery, family advancement, betrayal, and assassination. The absence of imperial consistency in facing these threats had consequences not only in the reaction of Romans to the Visigoths between 378 and 621, but in the other invasions of the empire in the east and west that began to occur with greater frequency after 406 and had, by 600, completely transformed the political and cultural life of the empire in the west.

The Visigothic defeat of the Emperor Valens at Adrianople in 378 did not precipitate an immediate barbaric inundation of Rome. The Visigoths, driven from their homes on the Black Sea, still demanded the terms of their original crossing of the frontier: land, food, and some form of imperial military recognition for their leaders. The reign of Theodosius witnessed delicate imperial handling of the Visigoths, who remained in Pannonia. During the reigns of Honorius and Arcadius, however, the Visigoths were drawn into the court struggles surrounding the young emperors, and the imperial treatment of the Visigoths often reflected not awareness of the Goths' needs, but the policies of the moment of one court faction or another. Generally, the great barbarian master of soldiers, Stilicho, favored Gothic demands, and the Roman aristocracy and the imperial family opposed them. In 396 the Visigoths elected Alaric their leader, and under his rule they began to expand into Greece and Dalmatia, the opposition of Stilicho not constituting a major block to them. Among the sequence of promises and broken agreements that occupied the years 400–408, Stilicho was assassinated by imperial order, and the Roman imperial court declined to deal further with Alaric. The Visigothic king, his supporters at court dead or silent, moved into Italy, circled Rome several times between 408 and 410, and finally sacked the city in 410. The Visigoths' stay in Rome lasted only a few days, however. Alaric began to lead his people south, probably intending to cross to Sicily and then to Africa. Finding no ships, Alaric turned north at which point he suddenly died. His brother Athaulf succeeded him, and on their route north the Visigoths passed close to Rome once more. The shock of the Visigothic sacking of Rome echoed throughout the Roman world. If the Romans had been unwilling or unable to defend themselves against a numerically inferior band of dissatisfied former allies, they were prepared to lament eloquently the results of their inability. A great amount of literature—much of it extremely moving—arose in the east and in the provinces lamenting the fate of the city. The court of the reigning emperor Honorius, driven to the hidden city of Ravenna, was unable to act against the Visigoths, who began to leave Italy for Gaul under their new king. In leaving Italy, however, the Visigoths took with them a prisoner, Galla Placidia, daughter of Theodosius and sister of Honorius. Athaulf took Galla Placidia and later made her his wife as a hostage against Roman retribution. With her in his train, he led the Visigoths into western Gaul.

Roman history, far more than Greek, is filled with remarkable women whose public role and literary depiction illuminate a history that is otherwise superficially too purely military and political. The life of Galla Placidia illuminates both the world of the imperial court in the first half of the fifth century and the world of the barbarian settlements in the western part of the empire. Galla Placidia stands at the end of a train of particularly remarkable Roman women whose prominence in the fourth-century sources is striking and not readily explicable. The rise of martyr cults had, of course, included Christian female martyrs, and the status of Christianity in the imperial houses of the fourth century, particularly the Constantinian and Theodosian, had included greater power for Christian women. Constantine's mother, St. Helena, not only was alleged to have discovered the true cross, but also founded a number of churches, including Santa Croce in Gerusallemme in Rome. St. Augustine's mother, St. Monica, is recalled throughout her son's *Confessions;* her portrayal there is the first comprehensive psychological portrait of a mother in Western literature. As successful military adventurers turned their families into imperial dynasties, the careers of the female members became politically as well as religiously important. By the early fifth century, the female relatives of emperors had become eminent figures, holding considerable personal influence and serving as marriage partners for imperial allies. In this respect, Galla Placidia was the first of a long line of imperial women who served the religious and diplomatic interests of the Roman Empire.

Galla Placidia was the daughter of the second marriage of Theodosius, and spent her early life at Constantinople and Rome, where she was probably educated in traditional Greek and Roman literature, trained in Christian morality, and given the stylized domestic education traditionally offered to aristocratic female children. Her early life may have been dominated by Serena, the niece of Theodosius and the wife of Stilicho, and she remained unmarried far longer than was usual among imperial children. After being captured in Rome in 409 by the Goths, who kept her in respectful captivity, she witnessed the sack of Rome in 410 and accompanied the Goths north on their exodus from Italy. In 412 Athaulf temporarily settled the Goths in western Gaul, around Bordeaux and Toulouse, and in 414, the year before he entered into a treaty with the Roman emperor in order to maintain a kind of order in the lands in which he and his people were now settled, he married Galla Placidia.

Athaulf is an ambiguous figure in the early history of Europe. The Spanish historian Paulus Orosius, who had been driven from his home in Spain by the events of 406–413, recounts a story in which Athaulf is alleged to have once planned to replace "Romania" with "Gothia," but found that his disorganized people could best be used for preserving Roman glory and restoring Roman power by Gothic arms. Athaulf's alleged observation concerning the new role of the Goths as the defenders of Roman culture was to have an interesting future and to serve as a rationale for later barbarian masters of provinces of the empire. Together with his marriage to Galla Placidia, his remark has often been interpreted as a rationale for a complete integration of barbarian and Roman in the new world of the early fifth century. In fact, neither of these actions was to have much issue. Athaulf died in 415, having moved his people into northern Spain.

The continued harassment of the Goths by Roman forces, the blockading of the ports on which the Goths depended for the importation of food, and the Goths' lack of success in sailing to Africa forced the successors of Athaulf to come to some sort of terms with the Romans, who, in spite of Athaulf's proclamation of himself as a protector of Roman culture and his obvious affection and respect for Galla Placidia, had never ceased their hostility toward the Goths. Galla Placidia was returned to her brother Honorius in 416, and as a result the Goths received a commission from the Romans to attack other barbarians. In 417, Galla Placidia was married at her brother's order to Constantius, an able general and a Roman nobleman who had emerged as Honorius' most influential adviser. Through Constantius, Honorius managed to restore imperial influence among the barbarian invaders of the western part of the empire. At the death of Constantius in 421, Italy was free of barbarians and its invaders had been either destroyed or recruited as Roman allies. From 424 to 437, Galla Placidia reigned in the western part of the empire as regent for her son by Constantius, Valentinian III. Revolts, new barbarian threats, and the reestablishment of imperial authority in the person of her son occupied her time. After their frustrating experiences in Italy and Spain, the Visigoths finally received imperial permission to settle in Aquitaine (southwestern Gaul), where they remained as confederates of Rome for the next century.

THE BREACHING OF THE RHINE FRONTIER: VANDALS, BURGUNDIANS, AND HUNS

In 405 and 406 large barbarian armies crossed the Rhine and poured suddenly into Gaul. In 405 Stilicho was able to disperse the invaders, but in 406 the invaders ravaged the countryside virtually unopposed. During the next year a series of uprisings led by the *Bagaudae,* bands of renegade peasants and soldiers, occurred in Gaul. The year 407 also witnessed a pretender to the imperial throne, Constantine, remove the Roman troops from Britain in order to establish himself in Gaul. The consequences of these events have, in part, already been seen. Stilicho was assassinated in 408, relations between the court and the Visigoths broke down in 409, and the Visigoths kidnapped Galla Placidia in 409 and sacked Rome in 410. Constantine's revolt was put down and the *Bagaudae* were controlled temporarily, but for two years the new invaders sacked Gaul and in 408 they crossed the Pyrenees for Spain. In 416 the Visigoths themselves received an imperial commission to exterminate the Sueves, Vandals, and Alans, the most distinctive of the peoples who had crossed the Rhine in 406.

The death of Constantius, Galla Placidia's second husband, in 421 left Galla Placidia virtually alone to govern the western part of the empire. To defend her son's title, she had to cooperate with a number of ambitious military leaders, particularly Aetius, a noble who had spent much time among the Huns, and Boniface, Count of Africa. In the ensuing court rivalries, Boniface was killed and Aetius became more powerful than ever. In Gaul and Spain, the Visigoths exerted pressure on the invaders of Spain. In 428 the Vandals crossed successfully to Africa, and within the next decade, under their king Gaiseric, they removed North Africa from the Roman "circle of the lands" around the Mediterranean and for the first time cut the grain supply line that extended from Africa to Italy. In 435 another Germanic people, the Burgundians, rose up against the Romans, and Aetius, with his Hun allies, wiped them out— a destruction so complete that the legends of the annihilation remained in the Germanic memory forever. The annihilation was revived in the thirteenth-century epic poem the *Niebelungenlied,* which in turn became the basis for Wagner's *Ring* cycle of operas in the nineteenth century.

From 425 to 455, a further series of military crises befell the western part of the Roman Empire. The rise of Aetius divided the imperial court at Ravenna into factions, their activities always colored by the personal attachment of Aetius to the Huns and the potential danger the Huns posed to both the east and the west. But the Huns, although they were the most formidable threat to stability, were not the only one: in 446 a mixed horde of Picts, Irish, and Saxons invaded the province of Britain; in 455 Gaiseric, king of the Vandals, sacked Rome and threatened a Vandal seizure of all of Italy; in 452 the Huns finally turned against Aetius and their earlier role as confederates of Rome and struck in Gaul and then in Italy. After Galla Placidia's death in 450, her son, the emperor Valentinian III, had Aetius killed. Later in the same year (455) he was himself assassinated, and thus ended the Theodosian imperial house, the last imperial dynasty in the western part of the empire.

Nor was the west the only area of crisis: much of the west's difficulties had been caused by the skill and policy of the eastern imperial court at Constantinople in directing invading barbarians west, away from the western coast of the Black Sea, the Balkans, and Greece and toward Illyricum, Italy, and Gaul. From the time of the first breakthrough of the Visigoths to that of the other peoples who fled the Huns and finally to the advent of the Huns themselves, eastern diplomacy averted disaster in the east, but at the terrible price of the virtual destruction of the west. The eastern court showed itself reluctant to join with the west in combined action against the barbarians. Most important, however, was the growing internal estrangement of the eastern and western imperial courts. The most striking instance of this estrangement occurred at the death of Theodosius II, Augustus of the east and the son and successor of Arcadius, in 450. Theodosius left only a sister, Pulcheria, who married the nobleman Marcian and raised him to the imperial purple in the East utterly without the consent or the knowledge of her cousin Valentinian III, by law and tradition the sole surviving Augustus and the sole authority to create another emperor. This indifference on the part of the eastern imperial circle to the authority of the west underlines further the rift between the two halves of the Roman world.

In 445 the succession of Attila to the sole leadership of the Huns brought the greatest ruler of the steppe peoples before Genghis Khan to the forefront of western Roman politics and diplomacy. Attila's growing independence of Aetius and Rome during the years 445–450, his increasing demands for an imperial bride—demands that the proposed bride, Galla Placidia's daughter Justa Honoria Gratia, cannot be said to have opposed entirely—and the results of eastern imperial diplomacy in the Hun camp induced him to attack the reduced forces of Aetius in the area near modern Champagne in 451. Perhaps it was only the intervention of the Visigoths on the side of the Roman army that turned the tide, but the famous battle of Chalons succeeded in halting Attila's advance into Gaul, although it did not significantly weaken his forces, which he now turned towards Italy. Attila's progress into Italy has been the subject of much scholarly curiosity, widespread speculation, and any number of bad historical films. Italy, plagued by famine and defenseless, its sole army still in Gaul, seemed to lay open to the Huns' advance.

Only a deputation of Roman nobles, including Pope Leo I, succeeded —although we know neither why nor how—in turning Attila back to the north, where he died suddenly in 453. The personality of Attila had been the sole bond of the Huns, and the ensuing struggle for leadership among his successors and an uprising of several subject Germanic peoples in 454 led to the final destruction of the Huns at the battle of Nedao. This battle, from the little we know of it, appears to have been far more significant in western history than the more famous one at Chalons three years earlier. The remainder of the Huns either were absorbed into the local Balkan population or migrated elsewhere, possibly joining the people known as the Bulgars much later. In any case, in 454 the Huns disappeared from history.

Gaiseric's sack of Italy and the Vandal domination of Africa from 455 to 530, the death of Theodosius II in 450, and the death of Valentinian III in 455 marked the extinction of the Theodosian house and the ensuing domination of both eastern and western imperial courts by the barbarian masters of soldiers, against whose influence Roman aristocrats and generals had struggled so successfully since the fall of Stilicho in 408. This domination of puppet emperors by barbarian masters of soldiers resulted in the disappearance of a western emperor after 476 and the restoration of able imperial dynasties in the east. Between 455 and 626, what remained of the Roman Empire was only whatever territories the emperor ruling at Constantinople could defend and govern. That area consisted more and more of the east: Greece, the Balkans, the Black Sea, and Asia Minor. These years witnessed the slow transformation of the eastern part of the Roman Empire into the Byzantine Empire, which survived, sometimes precariously, sometimes gloriously, until 1453, forty years before Columbus reached North America.

ROMANIA: THE IMPACT OF THE INVASIONS ON EAST AND WEST ROME

In the nonclassical, imprecise, but lively and revealing linguistic usage of the fourth century, lands were roughly designated according to the name of the peoples who inhabited them. *Germania, Gothia, Barbaria* served Romans well enough when they needed to talk about military geography. By analogy, the term *Romania*, "the lands of the Romans," also appeared in the fourth century, suggesting a semantic equality between Roman and non-Roman worlds. The empire had become "the place where the Romans live." In linguistic usage and in formal literary works we can trace some of the effects of the invasions. Some Romans invoked the old glories of the fading empire, and others remained largely indifferent to events in the material world. No single work reflects better the complexity of such attitudes than St. Augustine's *The City of God,* a long study of society and history composed during his last years as bishop of Hippo. There are two cities, Augustine says, the City of God and the City of Man. The true Christian belongs to the City of God, although it is not located in space or time and cannot be identified with any temporal society, not even that of Rome. The Romans, when they were pagans, built for their own glory, gave the world a temporary peace, and received their reward. The citizens of the City of God place little faith in temporal institutions, and they live as strangers and pilgrims in the temporal world. Much less complex than the *City of God* were the blunt views of the fifth-century writer Orientius, who asked:

> But why should I recount the deaths of a world which is dying by the law of all that perishes? Why should I repeat the number of those dying in the world when you yourself see your last day is hurrying on? I pass over how many die by the sword, how many by falling buildings, by fire, by poison, by flood, how many war, famine, and plague carry away. Death, by different ways, is the same for all. . . . Blessed is he who, awaiting God's solemn judgement on cities and nations, can do so with a constant mind, calmly sure of the innocence of his life.

Traditional cultural resources, the complex vision of an Augustine, and the pointed indifference of an Orientius suggest different facets of both the character and the temper of *Romania*.

Although both east and west Rome faced similar crises, the east possessed a greater resiliency, a greater self-confidence, and a degree of detachment from the misfortunes of the West that served it well in the fifth and sixth centuries. Economic and social resources, the fifth-century emperors' ability to withstand barbarian pressure, and a confidence in divine favor that was very different from that in the West laid the foundations of the Byzantine Empire and its distinctive culture in the fifth century.

Problems of collective and individual response to the crises of the first half of the fifth century were obviously shaped by the aristocratic or nonaristocratic, pagan or Christian, worldly or other-worldly attitudes of those who perceived and attempted to solve them. Any legitimate emperor could in the future extend his claim of legitimacy to the whole of the old empire, and after 476 the only emperor left was the Augustus of the east. Behind the façade of imperial claims, however, lay real resources. The east was urbanized more thoroughly than the west and had always enjoyed a preponderance of commerce. These strengths were virtually untouched by the crises of the fifth century. The eastern aristocracy was more numerous and less wealthy than the few great families of the west, and its members were tied more closely to imperial fortune and favor. The growing mythology of Constantinople as a purely Christian and divinely favored city, coupled with the success of the Church of Constantinople in curbing the ferocious religious energies of Greece, Asia Minor, the Balkans, Syria, Palestine, and Egypt, focused attention on the capital and the emperor and his clergy. Resources in population, agricultural and commercial production, and diplomatic and military strength spared the east of much of the consequences of both the invasions and the internal crises of the west.

If the eastern half of the empire had succeeded in deflecting the most substantial of the barbarian threats toward the west, it faced other threats to its unity that were different from those that confronted the west. The power and intermittent hostility of the Sassanid empire of Persia loomed particularly large over Constantinople between the fifth century and the extinction of the Persian empire early in the seventh century. In addition to the existence of a powerful, civilized, and well-organized external enemy, the eastern part of the empire paid the price for its higher degree of urbanization, learning, and religious fervor by being subjected to more frequent and more intense religious dissensions. In fact, religious dissension became so fierce in the fifth century that it often seems to have served as a focus for other kinds of local resentment against imperial rule. Problems involving regional customs, native languages—such as Coptic in Egypt—and social discontent often seem inseparable from heretical challenges to Constantinopolitan orthodoxy. In the dramatic series of church councils held in the eastern empire between 325 and 451, the framework for orthodox belief had been laid down, often very roughly and often to the discontent of provincials—such as the vocal and numerous Egyptian supporters of the patriarchs of Alexandria—and in consequence raised the prestige of the patriarch of Constantinople, the only major churchman whose see could not boast apostolic foundation, but benefited from the see's proximity to the imperial court and imperial favor. The Council of Constantinople in 381 decreed that "the Bishop of Constantinople shall have the primacy of honor after the bishop of Rome because the same is New Rome." The bishop of Rome was not the only prelate who objected to this elevation of Constantinople to such high status. Both of these threats—the power of Persia and internal religious dissension—formed the background for the restoration of imperial power associated with the emperor Leo I (457–474).

A succession of barbarian generals in command of the western armies of the empire had succeeded the extinct Theodosian house, not as emperors themselves but as formidable emperor makers. Such figures as Ricimer (d. 472) in the west and Aspar (d. 471) in the east succeeded briefly in placing imperial candidates of their own choosing on the thrones of the east and the west, but the western emperor-makers were constantly plagued by revolts and eastern opposition, and the installation of the strong Leo I in the east restored dynastic stability at a critical time.

Leo, a general from Dacia, became emperor, as had his predecessor Marcian, through the barbarian kingmaker, the Alan general Aspar. It appeared briefly that Aspar, like Ricimer in the west, intended to establish a string of ineffectual puppet emperors, being barred by his barbarian birth and his heretical Arian beliefs from assuming the throne himself. Leo, however, staged his own revolution in 471 and, basing his strength on the loyalty of the Isaurian troops from Asia Minor, overthrew Aspar and reigned independently. The commander of the Isaurian troops was rechristened Zeno and married Leo's daughter, thus becoming the second member of the "Isaurian" dynasty. Zeno (474–475 and 476–491) was reigning when the western successor to Ricimer, Odovacar, deposed the last emperor of the west in 476 and returned the imperial regalia to Constantinople, remarking that there was a need for only one emperor, Zeno. Odovacar appointed himself Zeno's regent in Italy, and was anointed king by his own troops, thus playing a double role among the Roman population and the barbarian soldiery. Zeno was incapable of acting directly against Odovacar, but he did possess other resources and could use the same device Odovacar had used. In 481, another Gothic people who had followed the Visigoths into Dacia and Macedonia, the Ostrogoths, began to threaten Constantinople. Zeno appealed to the Ostrogothic king, Theoderic, to move to Italy and destroy the usurper Odovacar, replacing him as the imperial regent. Possibly Zeno had hoped for the mutual destruction of his two enemies, but Theoderic proved him wrong. Moving with his people to Italy, Theoderic destroyed Odovacar and established himself securely in his place, reigning as king of the Ostrogoths and as patrician and master of the soldiers over the Romans. Zeno had succeeded only in replacing a barbarian military adventurer with one of the most remarkable rulers in the history of the ancient world. Zeno's successor, Anastasius (491–518), concentrated upon reorganizing imperial finances, and when he died he left the imperial treasury full and the empire with a sound, nonextortionate tax system. Anastasius' successor was a Pannonian soldier named Justin (518–530), who continued the recent imperial policy of soft-treading difficult religious issues, strengthening the army and the public finances, and making secure the imperial authority in the eastern part of the empire. The success of the eastern emperors from Leo I to Justin left the eastern part of the empire economically, politically, and socially stronger than it had been since the death of Theodosius I, and it set the stage for the most remarkable emperor since Theodosius, Justin's nephew Justinian, whose use of the restored resources of the eastern empire to restore the old empire in its entirety sharpened the rift between east and west and left the exhausted empire prey to new assaults from Persia and new threats from other barbarian groups in the late sixth century.

Beneath the shadow play and real power involved in imperial succession politics, the rest of the political structure of the Roman west was altered substantially. From Alaric on, barbarian leaders had assumed the title of king among their own people, although their "kingship" implied no territoriality within the empire. By the late fifth century, there were Visigothic "kingdoms" in Gaul, a Vandal "kingdom" in Africa, a Burgundian "kingdom" in the Rhone valley, and a number of much smaller "kingdoms" among the Franks in what is modern Belgium and among the Germanic invaders of Britain, although neither of these last two peoples had yet extended their power over the area it would cover by the sixth and seventh centuries. With the creation of these barbarian kingdoms, the old imperial administrative divisions had become virtually meaningless. Dioceses and provinces retained some of their old institutions and some memory of their former unity, but there was no one to rule them and no effective emperors to appoint rulers. The barbarian kings began to issue laws for their own Roman subjects, based upon the widespread Roman "vulgar" law. Formerly clear-cut administrative divisions became fragmented Roman societies devoid of contact with the imperial court. One such society, centered in Soissons, was ruled by a father and son, Syagrius and Aegidius, and was called a "kingdom of the Romans" by its barbarian neighbors. Of all the civil officials, only the Christian bishops and the lay rulers of some regions and cities remained to direct what was left of the most efficient and impressive administrative system the world had ever seen. When the barbarian kingdoms expanded, some memories of these old Roman provincial and diocesan divisions became incorporated into them, and the barbarian rulers assumed some of the characteristics of the earlier Roman provincial rulers.

At Rome, however, the senate still sat and circuses were given—although both institutions were in reduced circumstances. Provincial aristocrats, especially those in Gaul, became aristocratic bishops (Sidonius Apollinaris is an example), and aristocratic culture maintained its intricate literary learning and its political antiquarianism, waiting for a revival of imperial power and detesting the new barbarian masters, as much for their heretical Arian beliefs as for their political power. The old Mediterranean cities in the south of Gaul—Arles, Narbonne, Marseilles—still maintained contact with the eastern Mediterranean, but the economic decline of the cities, which itself had preceded the barbarian invasions, prevented any revival of their power or substantial resistance to the invaders. The vast structure of public works that had marked the thriving empire came to a halt in the fifth century.

Trade appears to have continued, and the east, with its navy and commercial maritime interests, still maintained contact with the west. The western capital, Ravenna, and the most prosperous western towns were all seaports. If the western economy by no means collapsed as a direct result of these first invasions, it became more clearly dependent on the economic vitality—and interest—of the east. Even the seaborne Vandals were traders, and the life rhythms of the vast agricultural estate complexes in the provinces seem hardly to have been altered by the presence of new barbarian neighbors and masters.

6

THE BARBARIAN WEST

THE TRAGEDY OF THE "GOOD" BARBARIANS: OSTROGOTHIC ITALY

Like the Visigoths and Burgundians before them, Theoderic's Ostrogoths had few precedents to which they might turn in order to solve the problems attending the settlement of an entire barbarian people inside the borders of the Roman Empire. The experience of the preceding century had, of course, offered some models, and the old legal technicality *Hospitalitas/hospitium,* sharing existing lands with discharged soldiers (or, in this case, newly-arrived barbarians), offered another. Yet the real problem devolved upon one Roman "official," the patrician Theoderic, and about 50,000 Ostrogoths whom he ruled, not as a patrician but as their king. Theoderic was determined to make in the west an effort that had been impossible in the more thickly settled and closely administered east: the peaceful establishment of his people in a kind of economic and political symbiosis with the native Roman inhabitants. The resulting political structure, as ungainly as it may have seemed at first, came very close to succeeding.

The institutions of the western Roman world at the end of the fifth century were a far cry from those of the first and second centuries. The decline of the *curialis* class of urban administrators had caused many of the local building programs and public services to be discontinued, and the removal of large sections of the provinces from imperial administration had weakened the loyalty even of those provincials still under imperial rule. The theories of public authority that held the empire together were far too complex for many barbarians to understand, and, certainly, nothing in earlier barbarian life had inclined any Germanic people to undertake the necessary social and intellectual transformations that they had to make in order to become fully Romanized. The enormous, intricate, and highly sophisticated complex of Roman law had for the last few centuries confused even Roman citizens in its bulk, detail, and intellectual diffuseness. One of the reforms of Theodosius II (408–450) had been to pare down and reorganize much of this early confusion of law, and the resulting *Theodosian Code* constituted a useful basis for the public and private law of the empire and the foundation for the even more extensive reforms of Justinian in the next century. But even the *Theodosian Code* meant little to the barbarians, who lived under a personal law applicable to them as individuals and who had, on the whole, little experience that could have prepared them to live under a legal system like Rome's. Barbarian law was essentially tort law, a system accepted by everyone within a tribe for the purpose of allaying the disastrous blood feuds that ravaged tribal societies. Each personal injury had its price, even the killing of an individual: in such an instance, the *wergeld,* "man-money" had to be paid by the killers to relatives of the victim. The scale of payments differed among different peoples. Romans were allowed to live under their own laws, however. This confusion of laws was one of the first problems to be regulated by barbarian kings in the sixth and seventh centuries. While the empire remained in the west, however, the sophisticated Roman law and the barbarian Germanic law reflected in their contrasts the different social principles of Roman society and its new masters.

Theoderic's Ostrogothic people was not a particularly large group. Numbering 50,000 at the most, the entire Ostrogothic population and its possessions were once sheltered inside the walls of Roman Pavia, a comparatively small city, during the conflict with Odovacar. The Ostrogoths did not rule in Italy by their numbers, nor could they "occupy" the peninsula in any modern military sense. Theoderic's imperial commission as patrician and master of soldiers was one sort of legitimation. The support of a segment of the native Roman aristocracy, from among whom Theoderic drew his most important advisors, was another. Theoderic's frequently stated admiration for Roman custom and tradition—*vetustas*—was a third, and his political and diplomatic genius was a fourth. Weighing against these forces were the perennial suspicions of the eastern imperial court, the opposition of other groups of Roman nobles, the religious differences between the Arian Ostrogoths and the orthodox Christian Romans, and the problems arising from the settling of the Goths on Roman land in the heart of the old empire.

Theoderic's Ostrogothic-Roman state was destroyed by Justinian in the mid-sixth century. But for forty years, the Ostrogothic compromise worked out by Theoderic and his Roman allies constituted a truly remarkable attempt to integrate barbarian and Roman cultures behind a strong defensive military power and a retrenching of social institutions. Of all the forms of barbarian settlement in the western empire, and of all of the changes that barbarian societies underwent in the critical period 250–600 A.D., the Ostrogothic state in Italy attempted to absorb more of traditional Roman culture than any other barbarian state and inaugurated a new respect for traditional Roman culture that was more productive than any similar European attempt before the Italian Renaissance in the fifteenth and sixteenth centuries.

The principles of Theoderic's state were simple. The Germanic warriors were the only military force in Italy and were separate from the Roman senatorial class and bureaucrats. The settlement of Goths on Roman land was conducted according to the revived principle of *hospitium*, and in affairs of law, taxes, coinage, and administrative institutions, Goths and Romans were each under separate systems of rule. For the Romans, however, the old imperial institutions remained largely intact. Civil posts were restricted to Romans, the senate continued to sit at Rome, public festivals and entertainments continued, and Theoderic's official proclamations were properly called Edicts, that is, administrative pronouncements issued by a Roman official subordinate to the emperor. The emperor's image continued to grace the coins struck in Ostrogothic Italy, and his foreign policy was designed to maintain different barbarian peoples in the provinces without permitting any one group to become too strong.

In terms of the delicate cultural conflicts between barbarian masters and Roman subjects, the greatest contribution of Theoderic was nearly forty years of peace in Italy, which contributed to the stabilization of social and economic problems and even mitigated the inveterate hostility between Arians and Christians. Theoderic protected orthodox Christian churches, at least during the first part of his reign, lowered taxes slightly, and simplified effectively the complex system of Roman public administration. But Theoderic was not content merely to improve the general quality of life in Italy. Under his reign the city of Ravenna became decorated with the great mosaics in the churches of San Vitale and San Zeno, and the city itself became an iconographic symbol of Ostrogothic power and Arian religion. Gothic Arianism, with its emphasis upon God the Father rather than Christ and upon the secular rule of the king rather than the authority of ecclesiastical institutions, remained a point of contention throughout the Ostrogothic occupation of Italy. Its great monuments in art did not soften the animosity felt by orthodox Christians, and the revival from 518 to 527 of imperial persecution of variant sects, including Arians, in the eastern part of the empire under Justin aroused strong Ostrogothic resentment in Italy. Theoderic began to act against Orthodox privileges, but only after he had been provoked by the eastern emperor. The flaring up of religious controversy was the first sign of the renewed Roman attack upon the heretical barbarian overlords of its western provinces.

Nowhere is the complex interdependence of Ostrogoth and Roman more in evidence than in the lives of two Romans who were closely associated with Theoderic throughout much of his reign: Boethius and Cassiodorus. Anicius Manlius Severinus Boethius was a descendant of the highest senatorial aristocracy. Born about 480, he was raised in the family of another representative of the oldest traditions of the senatorial order, Quintus Aurelius Symmachus. Having been trained in the still elaborate Roman aristocratic education, Boethius met Theoderic around 505, and from that date until his death in 525 he became an important figure in the royal court. First an adviser on what seem to have been purely technical matters—he designed, among other things, a water clock that Theoderic presented to Gundobad, king of the Burgundians, and his brother-in-law—Boethius soon acquired a series of public offices, which culminated in the consulship in 510 and the important post of master of offices in 523. Boethius's tasks made him the most important civil official in Italy, a constant companion of Theoderic, and, in another sense, a symbol of the extraordinary wealth of willing Roman talent available to the Ostrogothic king.

The public service of Boethius, as important as it was, was not the only side of this remarkable man. Like many of the Italian and Gallic aristocracy, Boethius had considerable learning and certainly worked at scholarship during his public career. His greatest ambition was to translate both Plato and Aristotle into Latin, and with that end in view he produced several works that were to serve for the next seven centuries as the introduction to philosophical and logical thought for all Europeans. One of his first works was a translation of and commentary on Porphyry's *Introduction to the Categories of Aristotle*. Later, he did the same with some of Aristotle's other works on logic, primarily the *De Interpretatione*. The importance of this body of work is immeasurable. By beginning with broad questions dealing with the art of classifying objects external to the mind, by classifying the remarks that can be made about these objects, and by classifying further all remarks that can be made on any subject, Boethius left one of the greatest legacies of late antiquity. The nature of that legacy is often difficult for modern readers to appreciate. Essentially, it involved devising in Latin a vocabulary capable of discussing the intricate mental processes that had hitherto been written about in Greek. By systematizing a Latin philosophical and logical vocabulary that could be applied effectively to the analysis of mental processes, the classification of valid arguments, the detection of logical errors, and the accurate description of the world around him, Boethius left to the European West the tools for the elaboration of theology, law, logic, and metaphysics. St. Thomas Aquinas and Descartes are in this sense his direct heirs, but the entire West used these works of Boethius as its own introduction to logical thought, and in the great revival of logic that occurred in the eleventh century, the work of Boethius played the most important role. There are no more important legacies in terms of vocabulary and critical language than St. Jerome's translation of the Bible into Latin early in the fifth century and Boethius's translation of Aristotelian logical works into Latin a century later.

Nor was formal philosophical scholarship Boethius's only other contribution to the early sixth century and to history. He never finished—indeed, he hardly began—his vast plan of translation. But he composed other works, works that differed from both public service and philosophy. He wrote a number of treatises on Christianity that constitute one of the first attempts to apply the logic of Aristotle to the theological ideas of Cristianity, an attempt that played a crucial role in the shaping of later Christian thought.

Yet Boethius's most famous work really falls into none of these categories. To see it in its proper context, we must turn briefly to the problems of the last years of Theoderic's reign. Continuing eastern resentment of the Ostrogothic domination of Italy was sharpened, as we have seen, by the renewal of the persecution of Arian heretics in the east early in the sixth century. Other eastern attempts to undermine Theoderic's rule appear to have occurred at the same time. One such attempt may well have been an appeal to Roman antiquity that was designed to break the loyalty of the Roman senatorial class to their barbarian master. In any case, secret communications between Constantinople and Rome appear to have taken place, and in 524 both Boethius and his father-in-law Symmachus were accused by Theoderic of treason and imprisoned. Boethius remained in prison for a year and was summarily executed in 525. The executions of Boethius and Symmachus (in 526) suggest how effective eastern imperial opposition to Theoderic had been. It was during his year in prison that Boethius wrote his most famous work, a dialogue called *On the Consolation of Philosophy*. The setting of the dialogue is Boethius's prison, where he has been seeking means to console himself for the undeserved fate that has befallen him. Philosophy enters, personified as a woman, and the remainder of the work is a dialogue between the two in prose, with moving verse interludes, written in a clear, simple Latin. In the course of the dialogue, Philosophy leads Boethius through various logical steps to a consideration of the nature of true happiness and the highest good, which Philosophy identifies with God, although not with any specifically Christian aspects of God. This apparent avoidance of Christianity has raised the idea in the minds of many scholars that Boethius was only a surface Christian and that in time of trouble he reverted to an older and deeper-rooted philosophical paganism. It seems, however, that Boethius is attempting to resolve the problems of misfortune and justice, good and evil, within a philosophic framework. The dialogue culminates in a description of the philosopher's obligation to accept the essential justice of the divine plan and to interpret the fragments of experience accordingly. The work became so popular that it was translated in the ninth century by no less a person than King Alfred of England, and in the sixteenth century by no less a scholar than Queen Elizabeth I. Certainly, Boethius was the most popular—with Vergil and Ovid—of all Roman writers in the Middle Ages, even finding a local cult of sainthood and a place in Paradise in Dante's *Divine Comedy*. As late as the eighteenth century, Boethius was described by Catholic hagiographers as St. Severinus.

The destruction of Boethius and Symmachus and its implications for the stability of Ostrogothic Italy loom over the unhappy last years of Theoderic and the regime he founded. It is in the career of Boethius's successor at Theoderic's court, Cassiodorus Senator, that these implications were felt most fully. Cassiodorus did not come from the same high aristocratic circles of Symmachus and Boethius. He was a noble holding extensive lands around Squillace in Calabria, and he entered Theoderic's service with none of the sociological overtones that Boethius's service had. He had studied under Dionysius Exiguus, one of many Greek-speaking scholars who worked on Latin translations and a person who became an influential figure in the later history of western law. Cassiodorus's work for the Gothic king Theoderic was of a different kind from that of Boethius. The aristocratic philosopher left a body of work that was the legitimate occupation of a learned Roman nobleman of the sixth century—philosophy, translations, poetry, and high theology. Cassiodorus was far more concerned with the historical phenomenon that he saw before him in sixth-century Italy—not philosophical verities, but the day-to-day problems of explaining Roman culture to the Goths and the Gothic character to the Romans. Boethius's major works, as described above, required no knowledge of the Goths in order to be understood, but Cassiodorus's major work is wholly inexplicable without an acquaintance with the Gothic kingdom. When he succeeded Boethius as master of offices in 525, Cassiodorus undertook, in the official correspondence that he wrote in Theoderic's name, to rationalize among other things the Gothic role in preserving Roman *vetustas*—tradition— and in guarding what Cassiodorus called *civilitas*—the essence of traditional Roman civic culture. These letters, the *Variae,* are an amazing wealth of information, digressions, learned ramblings about hopelessly obscure points, and learning paraded for its own sake, some of it pompous and much of it infinitely interesting. Cassiodorus also wrote several histories, and in these his concern for a proper understanding of the Goths became even more explicit. In several chronicles, most notably in the lost *Gothic History,* Cassiodorus extended the history of the Ostrogoths back in time until it became as ancient—and heroic—as Roman history. Cassiodorus made an impressive attempt to reconcile Goths and Romans by showing that each was of equal antiquity and that each was created to collaborate with the other in preserving civilization. In a sense, Cassiodorus's *Gothic History*—which survives only in the epitome made by Jordanes—carried to fruition the alleged ambitions of Athaulf: to make the Goths the shield and defender of Roman civilization.

The last years of Cassiodorus's life, however, witnessed the destruction of his dream of Romano-Gothic collaboration and the destruction of the Ostrogothic kingdom in Italy. The deterioration of relations between the empire and the Goths over the question of religion was hastened by the imperial propaganda among the already disloyal Roman aristocracy and by the end of Theoderic's dynasty in Italy. When Theoderic died in 526, he was succeeded by his daughter Amalasuntha (the root *Amal-* was the family name of the dynasty), who encountered a sharp division among the leading Ostrogoths regarding the Gothic attitude towards native Romans and the imperial court in Constantinople. Sharp pro- and anti-Roman voices spoke out, and Amalasuntha was finally confined in a convent and later murdered. The successors of Amalasuntha had no choice in their attitudes, for in 533, the emperor Justinian launched his massive attempt to reconquer the western part of the empire from its new Germanic masters. Between 533 and 565, the western Romano-Germanic world was transformed considerably, the powers of the emperor redefined, and a new and vigorous movement of spiritual life begun. These events, and the important last years of Cassiodorus, however, belong to Chapter 7. It remains to survey the western part of the empire on the eve of Justinian's attempts at reconquest between 533 and 565.

THE FRANKS IN GAUL

Unlike several other Germanic peoples, such as the Visigoths, Ostrogoths, and Vandals, the Franks did not enter the empire suddenly and did not retain the integrity of their name and customs as they wandered throughout the imperial provinces and heartlands. The Franks appear to have been, rather, one of those temporary conglomerations of different Germanic peoples who migrated south along the North Sea coast in the third century and crossed in small groups into what is now the Netherlands and Belgium, some settling as farmers and some, individually or in groups, serving in the Roman army. Some of the latter, for example, served the Emperor Julian, and throughout the later fourth century imperial generals retained groups of Franks as *federati*, serving against other, more hostile Germanic peoples. In the course of the late fourth century, two groups of Franks become identifiable, at least in Roman sources: the Salian Franks, so called because of their settlements near the mouth of the Rhine, and the Ripuarian Franks, named for their settlements further up the Rhine near Cologne. Throughout this period, pressure from other peoples in their rear drove the Salians down the valleys of the Scheldt and Lys into the richer agricultural lands further south, and several groups of them settled in the vicinity of the towns strung out along the Roman road from Boulogne to Cologne, most notably Tournai. By the first quarter of the fifth century, several groups of Salian Franks had formed under a new kind of leader. This person was perhaps originally a war leader, but after the experience of dealing with Roman military officials and finding settlement lands for his people, he certainly developed some of the authority and responsibilities that were characteristic of new kinds of Germanic rulership elsewhere.

One such leader of the Franks at Tournai was Childeric, who ruled around the middle of the fifth century. After a career of leading his warriors against other raiding peoples, and in the process achieving great personal wealth, Childeric died and was buried at Tournai in 482. In 1653, Childeric's tomb was opened and its contents described. Weapons, jewelry, hoards of coins and the head of the king's war-horse were found in the tomb, along with an elaborately brocaded and jeweled cloak. The wealth of the ruler, the evidence of contact with Rome, and his death and ceremonial entombment in "his own" town of Tournai all indicate that serving as a Roman mercenary could be not only a profitable way of life for an ambitious chieftain, but also perhaps the basis for a new kind of rulership over a group of warriors and settled farmers.

Although Childeric's is the richest Frankish grave, it is certainly not the only one. Germanic cemeteries known as *Reihengräber,* "row graves," provide much of what is known of Frankish costume and custom before their literary records began in the sixth century. Bronze, iron, gold, and silver weapons, buckles, and brooches reflect barbarian adaptations of Roman design influences, suggesting that the fifth century witnessed, not the arrival of a distinctive barbarian art with the Franks, but the prolonged interaction among Roman, oriental, and Germanic motifs in a fluid milieu, which was influenced by changing design and craftsmanship and only later developed into the sure and distinctive Germanic styles of the sixth and seventh centuries.

Later sources of Frankish history indicate a rapid settlement by the Franks of their new lands in the north of Gaul. The character of Franks as settling farmers as well as warriors expanding their small kingdom throughout northern Gaul should be kept firmly in mind. Unlike many other Germanic peoples, the Franks settled in their first homes within the empire and remained where they had settled. The Frankish kingdom established by the successors of Childeric became the most stable and the strongest of Germanic monarchies.

After his death in 482, Childeric was succeeded by his fifteen-year-old son Clovis as ruler of the Franks around Tournai. In a world in which there was no longer an emperor in the Roman west, the military-provincial rulers of Gaul had tended more and more toward independent action. One of these rulers, Syagrius, controlled the important city of Soissons, and was called, at least by his German neighbors and soldiers, *rex Romanorum*—"king" of the Romans—although that very un-Roman title probably indicates the virtual independence of a Gallo-Roman governor and the way in which he chose to be known to the war bands he employed. In 486 Clovis attacked the forces of Syagrius and defeated them, thus adding to his personal status as a successful war leader and taking over the imperial lands and personal wealth of the defeated Syagrius. Clovis probably spent the next few years establishing himself in his newly expanded territories, rewarding his followers, and developing a relationship with one of the most influential forces of the Gallo-Roman world, the Christian bishops of Gaul. When he succeeded his father in 482, Clovis had received a letter from St. Remigius, Bishop of Reims, urging him to respect the Church, protect the rights of the defenseless, and rule with as little rapaciousness as possible. The interest of the Gallo-Roman episcopacy in Clovis and his descendants is a striking example of Roman aristocratic attitudes toward barbarian rulers. Not only St. Remigius but other bishops, including the great sixth-century historian of Clovis and his successors, Bishop Gregory of Tours, clearly regarded the establishment of a Frankish kingdom in *Belgica Secunda* as a not unattractive prospect, and their later correspondence with Clovis indicates the surprisingly high estimation that Roman bishops could assign to a cooperative, orthodox, Christian barbarian chieftain.

Clovis's marriage to a Catholic Burgundian princess resulted in Frankish intervention in Burgundian affairs, and the new territories of Clovis, threatened by the more primitive Alamanni on the east, brought the Ripuarian Franks under his rulership sometime before 500. Clovis's wife's orthodox Christianity and the influence of the Gallo-Roman episcopate resulted in Clovis's conversion to Christianity, probably sometime around 500. Unlike the conversions of other barbarian rulers to Arian Christianity, Clovis converted to orthodox Christianity, thus emerging as a champion of Catholic Gallo-Roman society against the heretical—usually Arian—Christianity of other barbarian rulers. Accepting Christianity made Clovis seem more acceptable to the Gallo-Romans, and accepting orthodox Christianity made him seem like a gift from God. The sensitivity of orthodox Christians to the dangers of heresy has been noted above, but in the west, where heretical barbarian rulers seemed to carry the day—the Ostrogoths were Arians, and toward the end of their stay in Italy Arian and Orthodox Christianity heightened Roman and Gothic rivalry, and the Visigoths were not to become orthodox Christians until 587—the attractiveness of an orthodox Christian barbarian ruler to the orthodox Gallo-Romans should not be underestimated. Thus, something more than rhetoric inspired the letter that Bishop Avitus of Vienne wrote to Clovis shortly after the king's baptism.

> We saw (with the eyes of the spirit) that great sight, when, a crowd of bishops around you, in the ardor of their holy ministry, poured over your royal limbs the waters of life; when that head feared by the peoples bowed down before the servants of God; when your royal locks, hidden under a

helmet, were steeped in holy oil; when your breast, relieved of its cuirass, shone with the same whiteness as your baptismal robes. Do not doubt, most flourishing of kings, that this soft clothing will give more force to your arms: whatever Fortune has given up to now, this Sanctity will bestow.

The transformation of Clovis's success from fortune to sanctity, indicating as much the unreserved cooperation of the episcopate as spiritual benefits, goes far to account for Clovis's image in the eyes of later generations. Of all the barbarian rulers, only he had become an orthodox Christian—and of all the barbarian rulers, only he had met with unmitigated success. Legends circulated quickly around Clovis's baptism, the most persistent and influential being that the Holy Spirit had descended from Heaven with the baptismal chrism, a legend fleshed out by later claims of French kings to be anointed at their coronations with the same oil and to possess alone the title of "Most Christian King."

In 506 Clovis led the Frankish armies against the Alamanni at Tolbiac and destroyed them, taking the defeated enemies as his subjects. In Aquitaine, the Visigoths, perhaps now intensely concerned at Clovis's success and surprised by the sudden rise to power of a petty Frankish warlord, were probably not impressed so much by the Frankish king's sanctity as they were by his remarkable fortune. That fortune, and Clovis's skill, persisted. Seeing clearly the necessity of protecting the Loire Valley, Clovis marched against the Visigoths in 507 and defeated them at Vouillé. In the following year Clovis was recognized by the emperor at Byzantium, Anastasius, who bestowed upon him the rank of consul, thus giving Clovis an obvious, though not specific, place in the governing structure of the empire. On his homeward journey from Vouillé, Clovis stopped at the shrine of St. Martin at Tours and made public homage and reward to the saint, who was later adopted as a patron by Clovis's Merovingian dynasty.

By 508 Clovis had consolidated his kingdom in the north of Gaul, defeated his two most likely and dangerous enemies, the Alamanni and Visigoths, and begun the intervention in the affairs of the Burgundians that led to the annexation of Burgundy by the Franks. He had become an orthodox Christian and thus won the not inconsiderable support of the Gallo-Roman population and clergy, and he had received recognition from the Roman emperor. Clovis had raised the fears of Theoderic the Ostrogoth, whose control of Provence forbade the Franks further conquests in the southeast of Gaul. It is doubtful, however, how far Clovis's ambitions ran. He does not appear to have contemplated either a push into Provence or a drive to the Mediterranean coast. Immediately after Vouillé he returned to Tours, and then he proceeded to Paris, the leading city in his newly conquered territory. There, after patronizing the cult of the alleged third-century martyr St. Denis, and the greatest proponent of that cult, Ste. Geneviève, Clovis died in 511, leaving behind him a new kind of Frankish—and barbarian—kingdom, far enough away from the Mediterranean centers of political strife to retain its independence and vigor, and orthodox enough in its faith, or at least in the reputed faith of its ruler, to leave not only a memory but a legend of Clovis as the "new Constantine," a great Christian king.

FROM FRONTIER PROVINCES TO BARBARIAN KINGDOMS: BRITAIN, SPAIN, AND AFRICA, 450-530

The establishment of a temporarily strong and quasi-official Ostrogothic kingdom in Italy, the restoration of a reduced Burgundian kingdom in the region west of the Rhone valley, and the collection of various Frankish, Alamannic, and Gallo-Roman peoples under the new line of strong Frankish rulers in Gaul constituted a major phase of the consolidation of the impact of the Germanic peoples upon the oldest provinces and heartlands of the western part of the Roman Empire. In the more remote provinces of Britain, Spain, and Africa, other barbarian peoples made deep inroads into the structure of Roman provincial society and culture. In Britain the waves of Germanic invaders took root and de-Romanized that province so thoroughly that only new contacts with Christian Ireland and Rome in the late sixth century restored Roman influence on the island. In Spain the Visigoths, driven from southern Gaul by Clovis's victory at Vouillé in 507, founded a precarious Arian kingdom that lasted until the victories of Islam in the early eighth century. In Africa the Vandals, the only Germanic peoples to succeed in crossing the Mediterranean and in developing an effective seaborne power, ruled until their fall under the eastern Roman imperial reconquest in the mid sixth century.

Provincial Britain was one of the occidental dioceses of the reorganized fourth-century empire. It was subdivided into five provinces and was, with Gaul, ruled by the praetorian prefect of the Gauls, who resided in the great Rhineland city of Trier. Britain contained a provincial army, and throughout the fourth and fifth centuries that army had its hands full guarding the island province from attacks by the barbarian Irish from the west, the Picts from the north, and the seafaring barbarian peoples of Jutland and Frisia from the east. After the usurper Constantine removed what may have been the last Roman army from Britain in 407, literary and archaeological sources become vague as to the extent of the new threats to the island and the extent—if any—of imperial assistance to the remote province. In 410 the Emperor Honorius wrote to the Britons that they would henceforth have to defend themselves, but there are some indications of the continuity of imperial defenses, although doubtless on a much reduced scale and composed largely of non-Roman mercenaries throughout the first half of the fifth century. Certainly, archaeological sources reveal some degree of continuity in terms of the continuing habitation of Roman villa and town sites and the continuing, if diminished, circulation of fifth-century imperial coins. Yet without doubt, the fifth century witnessed the breakup of the imperial administrative structure of Britain, the increasing independence of formerly well-organized and well-connected regions, the rise of regional chieftains, and the gradual shift in spoken language from Latin to a revived Celtic British vernacular.

The new rulers of pieces of Roman Britain were faced with problems of defense, and they appear to have resorted to the same measure that Roman governors in more organized provinces used, the hiring of barbarian Germanic peoples as mercenaries—*federati*—against the old Celtic enemies in the west and north. The name of one mid fifth-century local British ruler who called in such allies is known—Vortigern—and from the mid fifth-century on, the Saxon and Jutish mercenaries appear to have begun to settle in the southern and eastern parts of Britain. The transitions of these Germanic peoples from confederates to settlers, immigrants, and invaders appears not very dissimilar to the Continental experience, except for the probability that fewer Roman institutions survived in Britain than on the Continent and that the Romanizing of the Saxons and other Germanic peoples in Britain took a different and longer course than the same process for other barbarian settlers on the Continent. Certainly, the advance of the new peoples in Britain was not swift. There is persuasive evidence that once the mercenaries became invaders, British resistance, at least until the end of the fifth century, remained effective. Around 500, there is good evidence for a remarkable British victory over the invaders at a place called Mount Badon—now tentatively identified as the Iron Age hill fort at Badbury Rings in Dorset. As a result of this victory, a British leader, later identified with the legendary King Arthur, may have succeeded in holding up a substantial Saxon advance for nearly half a century. In the course of the sixth century, it is impossible to trace with any accuracy the changing lines of Saxon and British territories, except to note the inevitable westward push of Germanic immigrants and to note that by 550 the fate of Roman Britain was sealed. Not only is there evidence of new Germanic migration to the island, there is substantial evidence of Germanic absorption of the British people and of a British flight from the island—to Brittany, perhaps to the Continent, and, as recent evidence indicates, even to the northwest coast of Spain. From 550 on, Roman Britain became Anglo-Saxon England.

The British emigrants who left the island in the early sixth century found very little that might be recognizable—or particularly Roman—in the places they went to, but perhaps they were no longer looking for a particularly Roman province at all. Certainly, Spain and Gaul, although they maintained substantial Gallo-Roman and Hispano-Roman populations, had begun to enter that Romano-Germanic period of their history that historians now call sub-Roman. Spain, one of the oldest of Rome's European provinces, was entered in 408 by the invading force that had crossed the Rhine in 406 and spent two years pillaging Gaul. Among this force were the Asding and Siling Vandals, the Iranian Alans, and the Suevi. By 410, the provincial administration had recovered sufficiently to settle these people in different parts of the Iberian peninsula, and in 416 the Romans, following their custom of employing one barbarian people against another, invited the Visigoths to attack the invaders of Spain. The following decade witnessed further Roman attempts to reduce the Vandals, Alans, and Suevi, and until around 420 Roman policy succeeded. The remnants of the invading force of 410 were driven into southern Spain, where they took and held a number of important coastal cities, including Seville and Cartagena.

In 428 Gaiseric became king of the now-amalgamated Alans and Vandals, and in 429 he launched the Vandal attack on imperial Africa. Although the cities held out for a time, Gaiseric was successful everywhere in the countryside, and by 442 the Vandal kingdom received recognition from the imperial court at Ravenna. Unlike other barbarian kingdoms that existed with vague imperial approval in the provinces and heartlands of the western parts of the empire, Vandal Africa posed enormous threats. The Vandal skill at seamanship rendered the central Mediterranean unsafe, and the capricious policy of Vandal rulers could at any moment cut off Italy's grain supply, which originated in Africa and Sicily. Moreover, the intense Arianism of the Vandals rendered them formidable overlords of the heresy-torn African provinces, since their great hostility toward orthodox Christianity caused further destruction to the African church, itself already weary with the fourth- and fifth-century heretical struggles between orthodoxy and Donatism and other heresies. Arian clergy now ruled the African ecclesiastical provinces, and the thorough confiscation of Roman estates by the Vandal overlords increased the animosity between Vandals and Romans. The Vandal fleets, carrying their lords throughout the Mediterranean, controlled Sardinia, Corsica, part of Sicily, and the Balearic islands and harried the coasts the Spain and Italy. Gaiseric was strong enough in 455 to besiege and sack the city of Rome in purported revenge for the assassination of the Emperor Valentinian III. From 440 to Gaiseric's death in 477, the expanding Vandal power posed perhaps the single greatest barbarian threat to the empire.

Gaiseric's successors, some of them able rulers, could not prevent the weakening of Vandal militarism under the attractions of Roman provincial culture. The Vandal talent for conquest was not matched by an equal talent for resisting the unguarded assimilation of that culture. The Vandals were able to sustain their kingdom until the early sixth century. Then, along with Ostrogothic Italy and part of Spain, the greatest of the barbarian provincial kingdoms collapsed before the onslaught of the Roman emperor Justinian.

The successful Roman attempt to reduce the strength of the Vandals, Alans, and Suevi in Spain left that province relatively peaceful between 429 and 507. The Suevi, settled in the northwest corner of the peninsula, converted first to Arian Christianity and then, in the 560s, to orthodox Christianity. Their kings ruled from the capital of Braga in Galicia, and after 440 they appear to have come to agreeable terms with their Hispano-Roman neighbors. After their conversion to orthodox

Christianity, under the influence of St. Martin, Bishop of Braga, the Suevi ruled Galicia. Occupying Galicia throughout most of the sixth century, the Suevic kingdom collapsed before the last invaders of the peninsula, the Visigoths, in 585.

The Visigoths established themselves as Roman *federati* in southwestern Aquitaine, intervened briefly in Spain in 416 on behalf of Rome, and in 418 settled again in Aquitaine. By 475, the Visigothic king Euric (466–484) felt strong enough to declare his independence from Roman imperial authority and to begin to extend Visigothic power east to the Rhone valley and south into Spain. Euric's son, Alaric II (484–507), nearly an exact contemporary of the Frankish Clovis, consolidated his father's conquests and ruled a vast Visigothic kingdom extending from the Loire to the southern tip of Spain and from the Atlantic to the Rhone, bridging the formidable Pyrenees and excluding from direct rule only the Suevic kingdom in Galicia and the Basque enclaves in the mountains of northern Spain.

Such aristocratic bishops as Sidonius Apollinaris, St. Remigius, and Avitus of Vienne remained influential men, the leaders of an otherwise leaderless Roman provincial society. They complained occasionally about the uncouthness of barbarians but were apparently well thought of by the Visigothic kings, whose meticulous care for the legal rights of their Roman as well as their Visigothic subjects produced a number of legal codes designed for the use of Romans living in barbarian kingdoms. The most famous of these is the *Breviary of Alaric,* compiled in 506 by Alaric II. The *Breviary,* possibly compiled to restore the wavering loyalties of Alaric's Roman subjects, may be considered in terms of another concession made by Alaric around the same time—the calling of the ecclesiastical Council of Agde (506), a rare example of an Arian king permitting the Catholic clergy of his kingdom to enact ecclesiastical legislation for their orthodox co-religionists. The *Breviary* and the work of the Council, the archaelogical and literary evidence, particularly in the letters of Sidonius Apollinaris, and the evidence from Roman and Byzantine sources all indicate not only a continuity of provincial Roman culture through the fifth century, but some improvement in communication between the Roman subjects of barbarian kings and the ruling imperial factions in Italy and the imperial court at Constantinople. The Gallo-Romans were probably not as oppressed and were probably more in touch with the rest of the Roman world than many, including themselves, would have us believe, and it is possible that without an emperor in the western part of the empire, the barbarian rulers of provincial kingdoms were as unsettled as the Romans professed themselves to be.

After the stunning defeat of Alaric II and the Visigothic army by Clovis's Franks at Vouillé in 507, the Visigothic kingdom in Aquitaine collapsed and the Visigoths withdrew into Narbonne and Spain. There, under the protection of Theoderic's Ostrogoths, who had adopted the policy of attempting to balance the strength of barbarian kingdoms in Gaul and who had prevented the Franks from following the Visigoths into Spain, the Visigoths established a kingdom that lasted until the second decade of the eighth century. Still Arian, outnumbered by the native Hispano-Roman population, and dependent upon the Ostrogoths of Theoderic, the Visigoths developed a kingdom that was centrally weak, generally tolerant of orthodox Catholics, and ruled for its first forty years in Spain by kings who were not even of Visigothic stock. Early Visigothic Spain appears to have maintained better contact with Italy, Africa, and even Constantinople than with France, although its rulers followed a policy of nonintervention in Mediterranean affairs.

MONASTICISM AND CULTURE IN THE BARBARIAN WEST

The Germanic kingdoms in the old western provinces of the Roman Empire continued through the fifth and sixth centuries to come to terms with their new territorial acquisitions and the peoples who inhabited them. Some kingdoms, like that of the Vandals, were completely unable to form any other social basis for their rule than appropriation and exploitation of Roman public and private property. Others, like that of the Visigoths in Spain, established a means of living with their Roman "hosts" and suffered instead from political difficulties—that is, the problem of the relative powers of king and aristocracy, and the vexing question of royal succession. Still others, like that of the Ostrogoths, attempted to appropriate not Roman property, but particular functions of the Roman imperial government, specifically the roles of tax collectors and military defenders of Roman aristocratic society. The broad variety of Germanic experiences in the imperial west makes generalizations about "Barbarian occupation" very difficult unless they are restricted to specific groups and downright misleading in their implication that there was anything like a common Germanic experience in the Roman west.

Moreover, the barbarian Germanic kingdoms were not the only new kinds of social organization that the west witnessed in the fifth and sixth centuries. From the east came not only the authentic documents and messengers of a surviving Roman emperor, but forms of devotion and ecclesiastical life as well. The rich variety of spiritual experience in the eastern imperial provinces created a constant state of social and political turmoil among the eastern Christians. Varieties of religious thought from Egypt, Palestine, and Syria flooded the capital at Constantinople, and the imperial policies of the capital excited religious opposition among the provinces. In spite of this never ending sequence of religious differences turning into social and political opposition, some immensely important and influential devotional forms made their way into both the eastern and western parts of the empire. From the Coptic Christianity of Egypt, for example, came the devotion to the Virgin Mary, possibly derived from the preserved images of Isis and Horus in

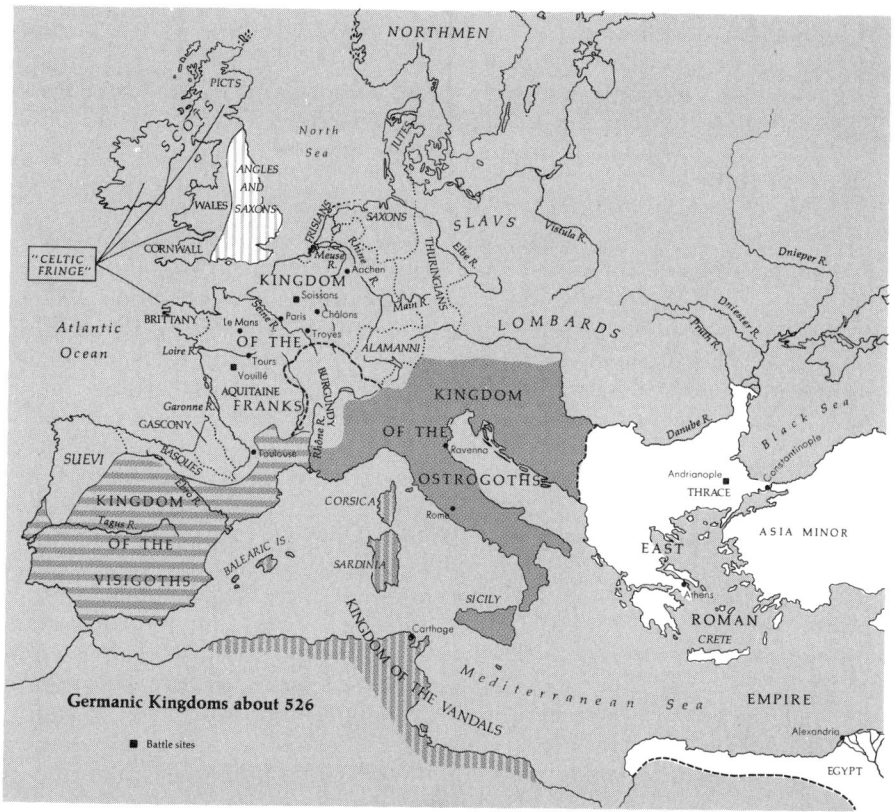

Germanic Kingdoms about 526

native Egyptian religion. From Coptic Egypt, too, came the painted portraits of holy men and divine figures, the contemplation of which was supposed to release the senses to higher spiritual experience. These portraits were the ancestors of the icon, the sacred religious picture that played so prominent a role in Byzantine and, later, Russian religious experience. From Syria came the concept of the holy man, the man close to God who had earned through trials and temptations a prominence nearly equal to that of the emperor himself, and music, the greatest Syrian contribution to Byzantine culture. From the east also came the idea of the organized religious community—first, the anchorites, individual holy men who had fled from the temptations of this world, and later the cenobites, groups of men living together in constant prayer and meditation. Originating in Egypt these groups influenced men and women elsewhere, and in the fourth century such prominent eastern Christians as St. Basil adapted the idea to form religious communities in the major cities of the empire, including Constantinople itself. Thus, in the eastern parts of the empire, the Egyptian concept of isolated religious societies also became a part of the consciousness of eastern imperial Christianity and was adapted not only to the rural areas but into the heart of the Near Eastern city as well. From the fifth century on, the monks of Constantinople, Antioch, and Jerusalem constituted a continuing and vocal part of the religious and social community.

Monasticism also came to the west, although its original circumstances there were different. By 500, the old western parts of the empire resembled the "deserts" of original monasticism far more than did the urbanized east.

In the west, church organization had already begun to feel the inroads of the culture of Germanic Christians. The "secularization" of ecclesiastical organization in the two centuries following Constantine occurred in terms of Roman conceptions of territorial administration. The bishop presided both spiritually and judicially over a *civitas*, the same unit that had a provincial administrator. Like his secular governor, the bishop was conceived as maintaining an office, not a personal possession, and he was subject to the Roman rules of officeholders. The bishops of a province were subject to the metropolitan, the chief bishop—or, rather, the bishop of the chief *civitas* in the province, and some episcopal sees, because of tradition or a particularly energetic incumbent of the episcopal throne, managed to create occasional episcopal "empires" wherein one diocese would dominate several others. By the fifth century, particularly in Africa and Gaul, the bishop's authority might extend over other churches, either lesser churches financed by part of the bishop's income or churches called *parochiae*, which usually had their own financial resources. The resources of churches came from offerings and from endowments, which were given as acts of charity in anticipation of spiritual benefit. In the course of the sixth century, the distribution of ecclesiastical income became the subject of legislation. Sometimes the income was divided among the bishop, his clergy, the upkeep of the physical plants of the episcopal churches, and the poor; sometimes it was divided otherwise, with occasionally a share for the man who endowed (and, according to Germanic law, could be said to "own") a particular church. The predictable unevenness of different episcopal incomes remained a problem through the Reformation, and questions concerning the financing essential to ecclesiastical enterprises played an important role in the social history of the Church.

In the lower ecclesiastical ranks, priests and others in minor orders came mostly from the same segment of the population that they served— peasants and half-free farmers. The most thorough Christianization had taken place in the great cities of the east and west in the third through the fifth centuries. In the rural areas of the empire, more in the west than the east, the process of Christianization had not been thorough or rapid. *Paganus*, a farmer, came to mean pagan, a non-Christian, just as later, in Old English, a dweller of the heath, outside the human pale, a *hæpen*, became the non-Christian, the heathen. By 450 the Christianization of the rural population of the west was barely underway, and the church in the west was beginning to reflect, as a result of the weakening of the hold of the cities over the countryside, the dissolution of the administrative character of post-Constantinian Christianity. The monasticism introduced into the west encountered a different society from that of the east.

The earliest evidence of monastic communities in the Roman west comes from the late fourth century, when St. Ambrose of Milan, St. Jerome, and St. Augustine founded semimonastic communities within the secure framework of the imperial Christian church. Also in the late fourth century, St. Martin of Tours, a Pannonian soldier, settled in southern Gaul and began to establish monastic communities on a small scale, intending to convert the rural population to Christianity. Then, in the early years of the fifth century, a Gallic Roman named John Cassian (385–440) returned from the east and imported not only the idea of monasticism but a substantial monastic literature, some of it original writings of his own, which had an enduring impact on Western society. Cassian brought to the west an attempt to systematize the always individualistic and sometimes eccentric forms of the eremitical life that had already come to Gaul from the east. The fifth century was a time of extraordinarily varied religious experiences, and the absence of any systematic means of discriminating among different aspects of religious life led not to a firm monasticism, but to the wholesale adoption of Egyptian practices based upon rumor, hearsay, and outright fiction. Cassian's *Institutes* attempted to offer a selective description of monastic purposes and institutions culled not only from Egypt, but from Syria and Constantinople.

John Cassian's monastic community at Marseilles, Honoratus's community on the island of Lérins, off the southern coast of Provence, and the remnants of idiosyncratic eremitism in Gaul from the days of St. Martin constituted the basis of western monasticism outside of Italy. In Italy itself, there continued the remains of the established monasticism of St. Ambrose, and the novel approaches of Cassiodorus, who, after the end of his service with the Ostrogothic kings, retired to his estates in Calabria and founded a religious community of his own. Cassiodorus's community, unlike all the others, strongly emphasized the monk's responsibility for learning, and the *Vivarium,* as the religious community was called, remained a center of learning as well as devotion. The most substantial Italian contribution to monastic and social history, however, was the community founded by St. Benedict of Nursia (480–547) at Monte Cassino, just south of Rome. Of all the various "rules" that different monastic communities followed in the fifth and sixth centuries, only Benedict's rule gained something resembling a universal ascendancy. The chief virtue of the Benedictine rule is its emphasis on monastic discipline as a preparation for the receiving of grace; hence, Benedict insisted upon a temperate mode of life, one that mingled contemplation, prayer, and manual labor and avoided the extremes of eccentric behavior that were sometimes encouraged by other rules. The *Rule* of St. Benedict is as important a document in the history of psychology as in the history of religion. It shows considerable concern for what we would today call the monk's personality and temperament, and its main thrust is toward a kind of psychological conditioning, dependent on the balance and proportion of spiritual, intellectual, and manual effort, extensive—but not ferocious— dietary regulations, and concern for the continuity of monastic experience through every waking hour of every day. Regularity, consistency, order—these are the keys of Benedictine monasticism. The earliest use of the concept of revolution in modern Western thought, in fact, comes from this monastic environment, in which it meant, not social disorder or reversal, but the repetition day after day of the same patterns of monastic devotional life. One reason for the later success of the Benedictine rule may have been, in fact, that it helped create the most stable psychological personalities in the west between the sixth and the eighth centuries. Not before the ninth century, however, would Benedictine monasticism leave its imprint on the west. Between 400 and 800 a large variety of monastic rules flourished side by side in Europe, and some of them even reached out to change the ecclesiastical life of Gaul and, later, lands beyond the old imperial frontiers.

Thus, the church in Gaul in the fifth and sixth centuries was a mingling of the aristocratic Gallo-Roman episcopacy, the rural proselytizing of St. Martin, and the spiritual energy of the monastic communities, first at Marseilles and Lérins, then throughout Gaul and into Britain and Ireland. One prominent historian of this period has suggested that it was precisely this variety of religious structures that enabled the Gallo-Roman Church (1) to adopt a deferential attitude both to the bishops of Rome and to the new barbarian rulers, particularly the Frankish successors of Clovis, and (2), having lost the old imperial divisions of the western provinces, to focus on a new idea of Christian society, one in which the spiritual traditions of Rome stood out more sharply than the political and cultural traces. Monks went out from Gallic monasteries to become bishops and brought with them the new forms of devotion to older ecclesiastical institutions. Monasticism, in its varieties, extravagances, and the beginnings of its systematic regulation of the collective religious life, thus made considerable headway among the barbarians and Romans of Gaul and Italy in the period 385–450.

The roots of western monasticism in Gaul and Italy do not, however, exhaust the importance of the work of St. Martin, John Cassian, Cassidorus, St. Benedict, and others. Monasticism was also the first form in which orthodox Christianity in the west reached beyond the old frontiers of the Roman Empire into new lands and new peoples. The earliest example of this was the conversion of Ireland. Its latest example was the reform of the Church in Gaul and Italy and Germany by later monastic missionaries trained in the Irish, Anglo-Saxon, and Roman traditions. With the introduction of monasticism, Ireland steps onto the stage of modern history.

The last unassimilated Celtic peoples of the west lived in the north and west of Britain, in Ireland, and in northwestern Spain. As we have seen, the assimilation of many Celts accompanied the creation of the Roman provinces of Gaul and Britain, and with their absorption into the Roman Empire came literacy, new forms of social organization, and the disappearance of Celtic tradition. In the unassimilated areas, however, many of the old conservative barbarian Celtic traditions survived, and one historian has called Irish society of the fourth and fifth centuries A.D. "a window on the Iron Age." In Ireland, Celtic tribal society still flourished in the fourth century. Never having been a part of the Roman Empire, the Irish had not taken to living in cities and towns, never acquired literacy, and lived a life of stock raising without the stimulus to practice more complex agricultural forms and to adopt trade that had characterized the continental Celtic experience. Irish society was one of clan and tribe, tribal leaders being the most powerful men in the kingdoms. Celtic law and culture were preserved by groups of law-speakers, *brehons,* and groups of poetry reciters, *fili.* The former memorized the laws of Irish society and gave statements of the law when asked, and the latter immortalized the military tribal leaders and preserved the religious lore of the prehistoric Celts. As Kenneth Jackson has said, these two groups were the Nestors and Homers of Iron Age Celtic society.

In spite of its geographical proximity to Roman Britain, Ireland appears to have had little contact with Britain before the sixth century. Roman Christianity in provincial Britain, and Celtic Christianity among the peoples living beyond the Roman frontier appear to have had no influence upon the first Irish Christians. The earliest association of Christianity with the northern British highlands centers in the obscure figure of St. Ninian, who in the early fifth century was said to have built a church, the *Candida Casa* at Whithorn, near modern Galloway. In non-Roman Wales, Christian origins are again obscure; they may have infiltrated from Roman Britain in the fifth century. The earliest reliable evidence of the Christianizing of the non-Roman Celts, however, comes from St. Patrick, the son of Romano-British Christian priests, who was captured by Irish raiders in his youth and kept as a slave in Ireland for six years before escaping and returning to England. Patrick's own spiritual autobiography, his *Confession,* describes, often in obscure fashion, his conversion to active Christianity, his vision in which he heard the Irish calling for him to return, his sketchy ecclesiastical training, and his journey to Ireland. There, in spite of many dangers, Patrick claimed to have won many souls to Christianity. By the seventh century, St. Patrick was being claimed as the founder of Irish Christianity, and his legendary popularity has not declined since.

The place of Patrick in the conversion of Ireland is not, however, always as clear as legend makes it. There is evidence that there were Christians in Ireland before Patrick, and there is convincing evidence that in 431 a cleric named Palladius was sent to minister to them. Moreover, Patrick's ecclesiastical status was irregular, and evidence survives of general hostility to his Irish mission. Certainly, his learning and his command of Latin were only rudimentary, in an age when British and Gaulish ecclesiastics still maintained reasonably high linguistic and literary standards. Patrick's irregular status, the novel conditions that Christianity found in Ireland, and the scarcity of sources makes the history of fifth- and sixth-century Irish Christianity obscure. It is certain that the most distinctive characteristic of Irish Christianity was the absence of the vast and articulate civil foundations that assisted the spread of Christian organization in the Roman Empire. Ireland possessed no central authority, no towns, no provincial subdivisions to which the structure of the Church could be adjusted conveniently. Although the first form of Christianity in Ireland was probably the same as that on the Continent and in Britain, the assimilation of Christianity by Irish tribal life soon produced a distinctive kind of Christianity, one as idiosyncratic and ultimately as influential as Syrian and Egyptian Christianity.

Like Syrian and Egyptian Christianity, Irish Christianity soon developed a highly ascetic tradition, one that seemed capable of sustenance in a monastic setting. Moreover, the technical difficulties of Irish land law made the establishment of family monasteries possible. In the second half of the sixth century, Irish monasticism received new impetus from a sudden series of monastic foundations: Clonmacnoise on the River Shannon was founded around 550, Bangor in the North around 560, and Clonfert around 570. Irish monasticism quickly absorbed Irish asceticism, and around 565, Columba left Ireland and founded a monastery on the Island of Iona, off the northwest coast of Scotland. Irish monasticism quickly developed its two most characteristic features: an intense missionary activity and a love of literary and sacred learning. St. Columba's monastery on Iona was the first Irish missionary monastery, and from it began the conversion of northern Britain. In the monasteries themselves —whether set in old Irish territories or on the barren rocks off the south coast, as was the grim, isolated, rock monastery of Skellig Michael—Irish monastic asceticism encouraged literacy and intense devotion. The ornate, abstract traditions of Irish art began to illuminate ecclesiastical documents, and Irish learning, never having struggled with the pagan origins of the literary culture of pagan Rome, absorbed that culture with zest. The flowering of Irish ecclesiastical institutions and Irish art and learning provided the Continent with a distinctively modified version of Christian culture, which influenced much of the Christian world.

The influence of monasticism on the West thus manifested a variety of forms and changed the religious life of both old Roman provinces and new barbarian kingdoms, reaching out to those remaining pagans beyond the old Roman world.

7

THE MAKING OF BYZANTIUM

THE EMPEROR WHO NEVER SLEEPS

Flavius Petrus Sabbatius Justinianus succeeded his uncle Justin I in 527. Upon his accession to the imperial title, the Roman Empire appeared to have survived two of the greatest threats to its continuity in the fifth century, the pressures of Germanic peoples and the financial difficulties of the mid fifth century. The Emperor Zeno (474–491), in directing Theoderic and the Ostrogoths to Italy, had succeeded in drawing off the last major barbarian threat before the 540s. Zeno's successor, Anastasius I (491–518), a former civil administrator, undertook the immense problem of rearranging the imperial finances, removing some of the most onerous commercial taxes, and making agriculture more prosperous. Reforms of the coinage and of imperial expenses put the economy on a much sounder footing, and at Anastasius's death the treasury held a vast surplus, probably greater than at any time since the fourth century. Military and economic reforms, although they strengthened imperial society in the east considerably, did not obliterate all of the problems threatening the empire's survival. Religious controversy, internal political dissatisfaction, and the beginnings of new barbarian raids into the Balkans and Thrace by Hun-related and, later, Slavic peoples remained endemic. Of these threats, that of religious dissension was probably the most important. More cultivated and used to philosophical disputation than the west, the east paid the price for the fertility of its religious genius by the range and social consequences of its religious dissent. In the fourth century St. Gregory of Nyssa had complained bitterly that dogmatic opinions pervaded even the transactions of everyday life. Trinitarian and christological heresies thus played an extremely important role in East Roman society, and they are perhaps the most difficult aspects of East Roman culture for the modern student and reader to understand.

Of all the dissident religious doctrines of the fourth through the seventh centuries, christological disputes, those dealing with the natures of Christ came to predominate. Of all the christological heresies, that of Monophysitism was the most dangerous. Monophysitism argued that Christ possessed one nature (*mono-physis*), a divine one. After a stormy series of disputes, the Council of Chalcedon in 451 condemned Monophysitism, stating what then became and has since remained the orthodox dogma, that Christ had a completely human and a completely divine nature:

> Following the holy Fathers, we teach with one voice that the Son of God and Our Lord Jesus Christ is to be confessed as one and the same person, that He is perfect in Godhead and perfect in manhood, very God and very man, of a reasonable soul and a human body consisting, consubstantial with the Father as touching his Godhead, and consubstantial with us touching his manhood; made in all things like unto us, sin only excepted. . . . This one and the same Jesus Christ, the only-begotten son of God must be confessed to be in two natures, unconfusedly, immutably, indivisibly, inseparably united, and that without the distinction of natures being taken away by such union, but rather the peculiar property of each nature being preserved and being united in one Person and subsistence, not separated or divided into two persons, but one and the same Son and only-begotten, God the Word, our Lord Jesus Christ, as the prophets of old time have spoken concerning him, and as the Lord Jesus Christ hath taught us, and as the creed of the Fathers hath delivered to us.

The ringing definition of othodox christology by the Council of Chalcedon attacked and denounced a large number of rival beliefs and made clear certain implications of orthodoxy. The Virgin, for example, was thus clearly *Theotokos,* the Mother of God, not *Christotokos,* the mother of Christ. Given the traditional philosophical and theological conceptualizations available to them, the intricate subtleties of "nature, person, substance, will, and energy" the achievement of the fathers at

Chalcedon was remarkable. On the one hand, by insisting upon the inseparability of the two natures, Divine and human, of Christ, they avoided the oriental tendency to reject the material world; on the other hand, they elevated human nature itself, in the Greek philosophical tradition, so that it was capable of sharing a single person and substance with the godhead.

The decision of Chalcedon did not, however, end the disputes satisfactorily. Throughout their reigns Zeno and Anastasius were forced to try to compromise with both sides, and the bishops of Rome, particularly Leo I (440–461) and Gelasius (492–496), took up strongly pro-Chalcedon and anti-Monophysite positions. Moreover, the arena of religious dispute was not confined to the august (and sometimes not so august) sessions of ecclesiastical councils, or to the learned (and sometimes physically violent) arguments of ecclesiastical figures. Strongly held heterodox beliefs were stoutly maintained in the provinces, particularly Syria and Egypt, and in the capital city of the empire, Constantinople itself. The intensity of religious discussion recorded by St. Gregory of Nyssa in the fourth century was echoed in the Constantinople of the late fifth and sixth centuries. There, religious opinion centered in the factions formed by various groups within the city's population, and found its focus where all broad popular disputes were aired, in the games and chariot races held in the great Hippodrome.

The ancient Roman tradition of factional support of various racing teams took in Constantinople the shape of two major factions, the Blues and the Greens. Around these opponents were formed divisions of civic organizations and, ultimately, something resembling the divisions of political, social, and religious opinion. The supporters of these two factions took their differences to the streets as well as the Hippodrome, and riots broke out in 496, 498, and 501. Dissent spread beyond the cities to the armies in the field, and much of the imperial efforts in the second and third decades of the sixth century were directed at finding a compromise solution to this doctrinal rivalry that seriously threatened to tear Constantinople and the empire apart. The reign of Justin I (518–527) witnessed further imperial attempts to pacify both factions.

Justin I was childless, and nearly seventy when he became emperor. He had, however, several nephews, whom he brought to the capital and educated, one of whom, Flavius Petrus Sabbatius, he adopted as his son, giving him the name Justinianus, after himself. In 525 Justinian, already a powerful figure in his own right and possessing considerable influential support, was named Caesar. Upon Justin's death in 527, he was hailed as Augustus. Not only did Justinian have the opportunity of observing closely the machinery of imperial government during his young manhood and developing his own considerable intellectual skills in the fields of law and theology, he also married one of the most remarkable women in history, Theodora. Much of the early history of Justinian's reign is in fact, the history of Justinian and Theodora.

Theodora was born, not into the Roman aristocracy, but into the family of a bear trainer in the circus. She was strikingly beautiful and possessed an unquestionably commanding presence. She grew up in the early sixth-century entertainment industry, an industry so broadly defined, however, that it included prostitution and a wide range of other erotic as well as artistic endeavors. Much of our knowledge of Theodora's early life is contained in *The Secret History*, by Procopius, a bitter and abusive attack on Justinian and Theodora by a man who also, more publicly, wrote several important historical works in praise of the imperial pair. The portrait of Theodora that emerges from Procopius's *History* has rightly been called "probably the most infamous and scurrilous piece of sustained character assassination in all of literature." Yet in spite of Procopius's known bias against her, Theodora's early life was probably not very different—except, perhaps, for some of Procopius's most picturesque charges, dealing with bestiality and other extreme forms of sexual license —from Procopius's description. After a life of various adventures in different cities of the Empire, Theodora met Justinian, probably in the early 520s, and he married her. Thus, when he ascended the imperial throne in 527, Justinian had for a consort the most remarkable woman ever to rule in the ancient world. Intelligent and perceptive, strong-willed and ruthless, she sustained Justinian in times of crisis, and she often designed imperial policies herself and possessed the power and influence to carry them out.

The importance of Theodora's presence became dramatically evident during the first great crisis of Justinian's reign, the famous Nika riot of 532. The factions supporting the Blues and the Greens in the Hippodrome had continued their internecine conflict through the years of Justin's reign, a conflict rendered more serious because the factions had been armed and made into an urban militia some years earlier. In 532, for once disregarding their opposition toward each other, the Blues and Greens erupted in a riot in the Hippodrome directed against Justinian. The riot spread from the arena into the city, destroying most of the old town and killing thousands. Justinian, having fled from the Hippodrome, is said to have contemplated abdication and flight and to have been restrained only by Theodora's firmness, embodied in her alleged remark that "the purple makes a glorious winding-sheet." Justinian regrouped his scattered forces and quelled the riot with a force and thoroughness previously unsuspected. Against the aristocrats and their followers he unleashed reprisals that may have killed as many as 30,000 people.

Immediately after the Nika riot (so-called because of the rioters' cry of the Greek word for Victory) Justinian began firmly to establish his own, the imperial, authority against the traditional powers of the aristocracy and the urban population. By the middle of his reign, he had destroyed most of the traditional powers in the empire and had left himself supreme, basing his strength upon the vast fiscal resources of his predecessors and the support of the Christian provincial population of the empire. The necessity of rebuilding the shattered city of Constantinople and the need to reassert the political prestige of the emperor gave Justinian his opportunity.

In rebuilding Constantinople, Justinian gave it the shape it was to have throughout its long history. His triumph was the reconstruction of the great Hagia Sophia (Church of Holy Wisdom), in which the boundless architectural and engineering talent available in Constantinople created one of the greatest buildings in history. Justinian's architects, Anthemius of Tralles and Isidore of Miletus, created an immense quadrilateral of four arches, on the top of which was set a vast dome that seemed to hover lightly over the heads of those far below.

> The great door of the new-built temple groaned on its opening hinges, inviting Emperor and people to enter; and when the inner part was seen, sorrow fled from the hearts of all, as the sun lit the glories of the temple. And when the first gleam of light, rosy-armed driving away the dark shadows, leapt from arch to arch, then all the princes and peoples with one voice hymned their songs of prayer and praise; and as they came to the sacred courts, it seemed to them as if the mighty arches were set in heaven.

The impression of vast interior dimensions culminating in the great dome was heightened by intricate marble paving of a great variety of colors and designs, and completed in the great eastern and western apses and in the rows of pillars that supported the north and south galleries, which in turn led the eye upward toward the four great arches. In the pendentives, the spaces where the arches join, groups of six great angels appeared to loom over the floor far below; and with the row of clear glass windows at the base of the dome, the effect created is that the great dome is not supported by the arches, but is suspended delicately from heaven. No other achievement of Justinian captured both the variety of resources and talents available to the emperor and the emperor's intelligence in using them. Procopius also summed up the impression the church made upon the people of the city and the empire:

> Whenever anyone enters the church to pray, he realizes at once that it is not by any human power or skill, but by the influence of God that it has been built. And so his mind is lifted up to God, and he feels that He cannot be far away, but must love to dwell in this place He has chosen. And this does not happen only to one who sees the church for the first time, but the same thing occurs at each successive visit, as though the sight were each time a new one. No one has ever had enough of this spectacle, but when present in the church men rejoice in what they see, and when they are away from it they love to talk about it.

The impression thus described was surely not unanticipated by Justinian, nor was it limited to the sixth century. When, in the tenth century, Vladimir of Kiev was negotiating with Constantinople for an alliance, his envoys were shown the glories of the city's ecclesiastical centers and were apparently swayed by them toward Contantinople:

> The Greeks led us to the edifices where they worship their God and we knew not whether we were in heaven or on earth. For on earth there is no such splendor or such beauty, and we are at a loss how to describe it. We only know that God dwells there among men and their service is fairer than the ceremonies of other nations. For we cannot forget that beauty.

The later strengths of Constantinople lay with her economy, her new armies of the eighth through the tenth centuries, and a sequence of able, dedicated soldier-emperors. But when Constantinople reached out, from the sixth century on, to Slavs, Armenians, and Bulgars, it was the spiritual grandeur of such churches as Hagia Sophia that caught and held the hearts of these peoples in bonds as strong and enduring as the diplomacy of emperors, the wealth of the empire, or the might of her armies.

The need to impose imperial authority firmly, the resources of money and talented men, and the ability to select the appropriate men for a variety of different tasks characterizes Justinian's entire reign. Just as Anthemius and Isidore were but two master builders selected out of many, so were Justinian's other great servants. Tribonian and Dorotheus, for example, were commissioned by the emperor to revise the unwieldy and hopelessly intricate law of Rome, which had first been codified in part by Theodosius II in 438. The work completed by these two men and their aides represents an achievement as striking in its clarity, order, and economy as Hagia Sophia. The first part of the *Corpus Iuris Civilis*, the *Institutes (The Body of Civil Law)* is a scholarly and lucid introduction to the law itself and its place in the Roman world. The *Institutes* were followed by the *Digest*, systematic extracts from the great Roman philosophical jurists of the second through the fourth centuries, whose writings had been instrumental in revising the earlier rudimentary religious law of the Roman Republic into the civil law of the empire, and who were strongly influenced by Stoic ethical thought and Hellenistic ideas of equity and justice. The third part of the *Corpus* was the *Code*, in which the laws promulgated personally by the emperors were contained. A fourth section, the *Novels*, which contained subsequent imperial legislation, was added later. Together, the parts of *Corpus Iuris Civilis* constituted the most thorough body of legislation, jurisprudence, and systematic scholarly instruction in the law the world had ever known. The whole was issued in Latin, and all other collections were forbidden. Although Justinian's *Corpus* did not make much headway in the west and gave way in the east to later Greek abbreviations and alternatives, it remained a model for western jurisprudence. After western scholars read and studied it in the twelfth century, it became an immensely influential model not only for the later revival of Roman law and the law of the Church that is modeled directly upon it, but for the various laws of the later kingdoms of Europe. No legal system now in use in the Western world is free from at least some influence of the *Corpus Iuris Civilis*.

Architecture, city planning, and law represent Justinian's greatest and ultimately most enduring contributions to the history of the Western world, but his energies were not totally absorbed in them. Justinian's great assertion of absolute imperial authority also extended outward into the empire, those parts that had long been lost as well as those remaining under imperial rule. Justinian's knack for utilizing talented men held true in military and administrative affairs, just as it did in other areas of imperial activity: Justinian gathered around him a series of vigorous, able generals and administrators, with whom he made imperial rule a reality not only in the riot-torn city itself but in the distant west. The military strength of the empire, restored by the respite from serious barbarian attack and freed from the eastern frontiers by a truce with Persia, was turned west in Justinian's most costly, and ultimately most destructive attempt to restore imperial grandeur. Under his great general Belisarius, Justinian launched an attack upon the Vandal kingdom of Africa in 533. That kingdom, weakened by its own failure to retain cultural cohesion and political stability, collapsed instantly, and imperial North Africa was restored to the east, the Vandal king, Gelimir, being brought captive to Constantinople and forced to walk in chains in Belisarius's triumphal procession in the Hippodrome. Thus, a brief two years after the Nika riots, the emperor used this traditional public place where he met his subjects to demonstrate his awesome might. In 535 Justinian once again sent Belisarius west, this time committing him to the formidable task of destroying the Ostrogothic kingdom of Italy.

The relations between Constantinople and the Ostrogothic kingdom, never stable, had deteriorated rapidly in the last years of Theoderic's reign. The increased eastern orthodox persecution of all heresies included attacks on Arianism, and in return, Theoderic adopted a harsher policy against orthodox Christianity in Italy. The claims of Constantinople to exercise the imperial Roman inheritance in spite of Theoderic's power appealed to the Roman Senatorial aristocracy, many of whom had never converted to the policies of collaboration with the Ostrogoths that Boethius and Cassiodorus embodied. Finally, the complex diplomatic ties that Theoderic had constructed in order to bind himself to other barbarian kingdoms in the west were all dissolving in the shifting power structures of Burgundy, Gaul, and Spain. The imperial condemnation of Monophysitism in 519 restored cordial relations between the emperors and the bishops of Rome, and the increased polarization of Ostrogothic society after Theoderic's death left pro- and anti-Byzantine factions struggling with each other. Theoderic's daughter, Amalasuntha, was an ally of Justinian, and many, including Cassiodorus, hoped that a pro–imperial policy would continue to guide Ostrogothic rule. The murder of Amalasuntha and Justinian's military expedition of 535 destroyed those hopes.

Once again Justinian turned to his great general Belisarius. With an army of 8,000 men, Belisarius began the reduction of Ostrogothic Italy, a task that lasted over twenty years. The Gothic wars of Justinian, whose history is also told by Procopius, devastated Italy far more seriously and more extensively than any previous barbarian invasion or Roman resistance. Hampered by a lack of men and by imperial indecision, Belisarius waged war on a frequently shifting front, the city of Rome passing back and forth between imperial and Ostrogothic forces several times, and encountered prolonged and fierce resistance. Late in the war, the Ostrogoths, under the leadership of Totila, even made an appeal to unfree Italian subjects: they might receive their freedom if they fought in the Ostrogothic army. The appeal to the oppressed peasantry and the end of the Ostrogothic attempt to ally itself with the Roman aristocracy came too late. By 552 Italy had been restored to the Emperor's control and the Ostrogothic kingdom and people had been utterly destroyed.

The reconquest of Africa and Italy, the rebuilding of Constantinople, the exaltation of the powers of the emperor over those of the eastern Roman aristocracy, and the new weight of imperial religious orthodoxy were remarkable achievements. The weight of these successes was proclaimed throughout the empire by a great wave of building, decoration, and ecclesiastical and administrative pronouncements that echoed the old uniformity of imperial culture and the might of imperial patronage. The culture to which Justinian gave a physical shape and an imperial stamp was that of the oldest and most persistent ideal of antiquity—that of the *polis*, the city-state—and some of the ideals he proclaimed had deep roots in ancient Romano-Greek culture. When Justinian revised the Roman law, for example, he claimed that he did so out of *philanthropia*, a love for his fellow men. This concept had a long Greek and Christian history behind it and took on in East Roman society the deep-rooted character of a social bond, being universally recognized and implemented in all ranks of society, from charitable institutions to the splendor of imperial court ceremonial and diplomacy. Under Justinian, some of the former grandeur of the empire was self-consciously restored. The imperial bureaucracy, a legacy from Anastasius, continued to function. The income from public taxation continued to flow in, and in return the state provided complex and extensive services. The imperial government acted reasonably quickly to correct economic and social disorders. In contrast with the west, the Church had no necessity or opportunity to arrogate to itself the civil functions of the empire. In the restored empire, imperial tradition and Greco-Roman learning continued to flourish, and Procopius's histories of Justinian's reign stand in the direct literary tradition of Herodotus and Thucydides. Between the death of Theodora in 548 and his own death in 565, Justinian worked out the consequences of restored imperialism, in politics, diplomacy, religion, and art.

After the great triumphs of the first fifteen years of his reign, Justinian witnessed new threats and disasters and spent the last twenty-three years doggedly trying to cope with them. In 540 the king of Persia broke the long truce that Justinian had so painfully arranged, and the eastern frontier once again became a troubled land—a land, moreover, with few soldiers left to defend it. From 540 until the critical years 613–628, the threat of Persia loomed large in imperial policies. In 542 a devastating plague struck the empire, weakening the population and dealing the economy a severe blow. In the 540s also, new immigrants to the Danube and the Black Sea began probing the frontiers and making tentative raids into Thrace and the Balkans. These peoples, Bulgars, Avars, and Slavs, plagued the northern frontier and occupied much of the time, money, and energy of Justinian and his succesors.

The emperor's efforts to stem these new disasters and yet preserve something of the triumphs of the 530s shaped the contemporary image of his last years. To the chroniclers, he became "The emperor who never sleeps," all day and night directing the vast and intricate process of salvaging an empire, constantly vigilant, eternally deceptive. Justinian gained this reputation by cutting costs, exhausting the treasury left by his predecessors, keeping the western armies small and experimenting constantly with new military organization and new techniques of diplomacy, restructuring the imperial civil service, and drawing the provincial cities more tightly to the imperial fiscal system. At his death in 565, Justinian witnessed many of his greatest achievements still intact. Constantinople stood, the greatest city in the world, and from it the emperor ruled Thrace and Asia Minor, Syria, Palestine, Egypt, and North Africa. Imperial rule was restored in Italy, and from the old imperial and Ostrogothic capital of Ravenna, a window on the east and the end of the sea route from Constantinople, a restored imperial Christianity glittered in the mosaics of imperial churches, and the aristocracy and churchmen turned once again to the emperor.

CONSTANTINOPLE: THE EYE OF THE WORLD

The city founded by Constantine, expanded by Theodosius II, completely rebuilt by Justinian, and preserved by Justinian's successors until its fall to the Latins in the Fourth Crusade in 1204 and its capture by the Ottoman Turks in 1453, remained the heart of the surviving Roman Empire. Frequently isolated and besieged, subject to dramatic outbursts of political and religious passion, governing an empire that expanded throughout the eastern Mediterranean and contracted sometimes to the walls of the city itself, it aroused the feelings of aliens and citizens alike. Constantinople was the greatest Christian European city until its decline in the fourteenth century. Its presence fills Byzantine history, and it is the setting for the glories and disasters of the Byzantine Empire, its religious crises, and the secret of its appeal to the Balkan and Anatolian peoples on whose culture and religious life it left so strong an imprint. Although the city was to change between the sixth and the fifteenth centuries, a description of it as it came from the hand of Justinian in the middle of the sixth century may convey an impression of the role it played in the lives of its own citizens and in the imaginations of those who viewed it from afar.

The fishing village of Byzantium, upon which Constantine founded his new city in 333, was located on a point of land between the Sea of Marmara and the Bosporus, the narrow stretch of water that connects the Sea of Marmara with the Black Sea. Constantine's city filled a triangle-shaped point of land whose southern and eastern sides looked out on the Sea of Marmara and whose northern edge was flanked by an inlet

Plate 6 courtesy Musées Royaux d'Art et d'Histoire, Brussels.

Plate 7 courtesy Suermondt Museum, Aachen.

THE CAROLINGIAN WORLD. The archaeologists' reconstruction of a Merovingian villa of the eighth century (Plate 6) suggests the limits of material culture of the Frankish monarchy, while the palace complex built by Charlemagne at Aachen (Plate 7) suggests the influence both of more accomplished building techniques and the appeal of late antique forms. Charlemagne's great hall (now destroyed) is at the top of the picture, while his chapel, the octagonal building in the left of center (now part of Aachen cathedral) became an important part of imperial tradition for several centuries. In spite of the idealisation of Charlemagne by later artists, this early manuscript illumination, the first known representation of the emperor (Plate 8), catches something of the traditional Frankish dress he wore and conveys an impression closer to the reality of the ninth century.

Plate 8 courtesy Radio Times Hulton Picture Library.

of the Sea of Marmara, a long arm of water called the Golden Horn. Only along its western edge did the city face open land, and it is along this western side, which connects the Sea of Marmara with the Golden Horn, that Constantine built his walls in the fourth century. In 439 Theodosius II constructed a great triple wall several miles farther west, which was to be the city's main land defense against all invaders until it was breached by the artillery of the Ottoman sultan Mohammed II in 1453. Protected by excellent water fortifications and the greatest land walls in the Western Hemisphere, Constantine's city formed a vast triangle, at whose eastern tip was located the heart of the empire: the emperor's palace complex, the Hippodrome—the only place where the emperor and the mass of subjects ever met face to face—and the great church of Hagia Sophia, the jewel of the Empire and of Christendom. Its easy access to the Black Sea gave Constantinople the great majority of all trade west of the Caucasus, particularly in later centuries the grain, furs, gold, and slaves of the vast Russian lands sweeping away to the north. Across the Bosporus lay Asia Minor, and at the western end of the Sea of Marmara the Hellespont opened out into the Aegean Sea and Greece, the Aegean islands, and the Balkans. From Constantinople across Thrace and the Balkans into Yugoslavia ran a chain of defense works and frontier forts, and across Asia Minor ran the great road to the eastern frontier, the one road that Justinian insisted on preserving in his last troubled years. Constantinople drew to itself the great trade routes from China and India across northern Persia and Armenia, and it possessed easy contact by land and sea with the provinces of Syria, Egypt, North Africa, and Italy. Constantinople itself was surrounded by fertile lands, and the rich fishing grounds of the Black Sea and the Sea of Marmara easily provisioned the capital.

Like all truly Mediterranean cities, Constantinople was a great port, and at one time or another much of the world's shipping found berths in its many harbors, commercial mooring facilities, and innumerable private docks for pleasure yachts. Inside the sea walls (for Constantinople was impregnable from the sea as well as the land) houses crowded the streets. Most houses were wooden with several stories, yet there were many brick mansions, faced with marble and built around a courtyard. The two main avenues of Constantinople were dotted with bazaars, covered markets, the centers of the craft organizations, hundreds of churches, great and small, great commemorative pillars bearing the statues of emperors and empresses, and the innumerable monasteries, islands of prayer that were generally sealed off from the population but sometimes disgorged their monks in order that they might take active part in the religious or political disputes of the city.

The ruler of the city proper was the prefect, who was appointed by the Emperor and was in charge of the urban militia and the vast guild organizations into which all trades and crafts were structured. The city also provided the means of sustenance to its inhabitants, there being close imperial control over the markets and over the construction of the great aqueduct of Valens, which carried water into the city from over thirty miles away. The water was caught and preserved in great cisterns, themselves architectural triumphs.

The great *Meses* drew the long roads of the empire into the city and to the Augusteon, a great square that contained the Milion, the marker from which all distance in the empire was measured, the imperial palace, and Hagia Sophia. The Hippodrome, also located close to the palace complex, seated as many as 60,000 spectators, and the imperial box, not accessible from the Hippodrome itself, was connected directly with the imperial palace. From the vast palace complex the emperor, guarded by an elaborate court ceremonial, ruled the East Roman world. In his own city, he watched the brilliant urban life of the empire at its most complete and varied.

AFTER JUSTINIAN: AVARS, SLAVS, AND THE FLOWERING OF SASANID PERSIA

The price that Justinian had paid for rebuilding the capital and reestablishing imperial government in the west was the neglect of the important Balkan and Asiatic frontiers. The financial prosperity that Anastasius had carefully husbanded and Justinian so determinedly spent was based upon the solid agricultural and commercial economy of Constantinople, a strong and stable gold coinage, and an efficient and often ruthless system of taxation. The imperial government, which was well financed, maintained a high level of civil and social services and at the same time paid its armies and used money as part of its complex diplomatic relations with the powers adjoining its borders. The expenses of militarism and diplomacy, however, became heavier and heavier as the sixth century wore on. To fill out his small western armies, Justinian removed troops from the Balkan frontier, thus weakening that frontier and opening to the Slavs and Bulgars a way into the Balkans and Greece. The fiscal risks Justinian had taken assumed a stability of Near Eastern affairs, particularly a continuation of the stalemate between the empire and Persia. The revival of an ambitious Persian monarchy in the last years of the sixth century, however, raised once again the threat of a Persian invasion. Thus the empire was pressed on precisely the two frontiers that Justinian had failed to defend. Moreover, the extraordinarily heavy hand of imperial taxation on an exhausted Italy, which had been ravaged beyond recovery by the thirty years of Justinian's Gothic wars, reduced severely the value of Italy as a productive province. In 568, when yet another Germanic people, the Lombards, descended onto the Italian peninsula, imperial power there was reduced to a strip of land running from Ostia, in the west of Italy, through Rome to Ravenna, which was once again a remote outpost of imperial power. Finally, for all of his theological and political skill, Justinian had not solved completely the problem of orthodoxy and heresy in Christian belief. In Syria, Egypt, and North Africa, heretical Monophysite beliefs lingered, their proponents bitterly resentful of imperial attempts to force a compromise. In orthodox Italy, the oppression of heretical sects by imperial governors and churchmen once again threatened to reopen old political and ecclesiastical wounds.

The crises of the mid sixth century, from the great plague to the threats of Persia and the Slavs and Bulgars, forced a drastic overhauling of imperial strength. In that process, the half-Roman, half-oriental character of Byzantium was shaped. Sharing a common classical and Christian heritage with the despised barbarian west, sharing a common economic and urban culture with the Near East, Byzantium survived as a great Christian power to which many western Christians were hostile and as a great Near Eastern power rooted in the economic and political world of the eastern Mediterranean.

In addition to massive immigration in the Balkans, Thrace, and the Greek Peninsula, the emperors who followed Justinian were faced with the increasing threat posed by the Sasanid kingdom of Persia. The enormous commitment of men and money to the defense of the northern and eastern frontiers produced a new society in the empire, one geared for continual war, whose success lay in drawing upon the vast reserves of the populations of Thrace and Asia Minor and maintaining close control over the armies by means of an effective bureaucracy in the capital, a bureaucracy financed by new forms of social organization and taxes. Throughout the late sixth and early seventh centuries, the Roman Empire, reduced in territory and threatened on two sides, rearmed itself, geared for war, and concentrated its full energies on defending itself and the areas immediately surrounding it.

The origins of the Slavic peoples, like those of the Germans, are utimately unknown. In the first century A.D., some Roman writers described barbarian peoples living in the river valleys of the Vistula and Pripet. By the beginning of the sixth century, the Slavs had reached the Danube and had fanned out to the north of that river into lands that have remained Slavic since. Like the Germans, the Slavs were composed of numerous different peoples, and nothing like a common "Slavic" culture united these localized groups. The Slavs entered the empire, beginning in 547, under circumstances approximately similar to those under which the Franks entered. Initial raiding parties, serving occasionally as military confederates, sometimes allied themselves with other peoples. The Slavic peoples moved west along the Danube and into the eastern Alps in the early sixth century, establishing settlements on both sides of this great frontier river. In the mid sixth century, possibly fearing Slavic pressure on the frontier, the Byzantine emperors invited an Asiatic people, the Avars, to attack the Slavs. The Avars, related to the Huns, moved west, exerted pressure on the Slavs, and drove a territorial wedge between the Slavs of the northwest and those of the south and east. In the third quarter of the century, Avar armies with large Slav components penetrated imperial territory, as did Slav forces alone, the latter possibly fleeing the Avars. In 583 the Avars destroyed the city of Sirmium. The Avar pressure forced the Slavs north as well, and Bavaria and Moravia may have received their Slav populations at this time. By the end of the sixth century, the Slavs exerted steady pressure on Macedonia and Greece, particularly the northern and western parts of the peninsula. In the early years of the seventh century, Thessalonica, the second largest city in the Byzantine Empire, was frequently under Slavic, and sometimes Avar, siege. By 617, a combined Slavic and Avar force assaulted Constantinople.

The seventh century, crucial in the history of Slavic settlement in Greece, witnessed the movement of Byzantine forces to the eastern frontier, where they dealt with threats first from Persia, then from Islam. Thus, Byzantine resistance in Greece was particularly weak at this time, and in the course of the seventh century much of the inland part of the Greek peninsula was Slavicized. The Slavic war bands that penetrated the Empire were not, however, merely raiders and tribute collectors, as had been, for example. the Huns and Avars. Before the Avars attacked them, the Slavs had already begun to settle along the Danube, and except for the disruption of social institutions caused by the Slavic raids into Macedonia and Greece, the Slavs quickly resettled themselves. Thus, the Slavic peoples of the Balkans and Greece became a potential source of new Byzantine subjects. The Avars, ruling western Hungary and Yugoslavia, remained a powerful influence upon Slavic life until their annihilation by the armies of Charlemagne in 795.

To the north of the Avar kingdom, the Slavs settled in eastern Bavaria, in Moravia, and in Bohemia, where they came under the influence of the growing eastward thrust of Frankish power and Christian culture. Further north, Slavic tribes such as the Wends, Sorbs, and Obodrites extended along the shores of the Elbe, facing the sparsely settled Germanic peoples to the west and other pagan Slavic and Baltic peoples to the east.

The kingdom of Persia had marched with the frontiers of, first, the Levantine Mediterranean peoples, then the Greeks, and finally the Romans, for over a thousand years. Centered in the Tigris-Euphrates river system and the vast Iranian plateau to the east, Persia was a major civilization, one with different aims and values from the Greco-Roman, and reached much further east, to China and India. Persia was, in fact, the great central Eurasian civilization, bordering China on the east and Rome on the west, having contact with both, transmitting eastern knowledge and ideas to the West, and defending itself, as Rome and China also did, against the barbarian nomadic hordes of the Asian steppes. Across Persian-dominated lands, knowledge of glassmaking passed from Rome to China, and knowledge of silk production passed from China to Byzantium. The two major areas of Persia, the Iranian plateau and the Mesopotamian river valleys, were very different from each other, however. In Mesopotamia, Mediterranean and Iranian influences competed with Levantine, and religious differences were disputed among orthodox and heretical Christians, articulate Jews, and Persian orthodox Zoroastrians and heretical Manicheans. In the Iranian plateau and in south Persia this cosmopolitanism was regarded with distaste.

The importance of the military and agricultural reserves of Iran declined rapidly in the fifth century, when, like Rome, it came under heavy attack from Asiatic barbarians. The revival of the Persian monarchy under Khosroes I in the last years of the fifth century depended upon the resources of Mesopotamia, not Iran, and a governing elite of courtiers built a powerful monarchic state on the ruins of the ancient Persian monarchy. Under the forceful rule of Khosroes II (591–628), the Mesopotamia-centered Persian monarchy found itself drawn into the economic and political world of the eastern Mediterranean and into a prolonged rivalry with Byzantium. In the early years of the sixth century, Khosroes II, backed by the restored economy of Mesopotamian Persia, launched a series of military campaigns aimed at establishing his rule throughout a united Near East. In a series of quick and thorough campaigns, Khosroes conquered Antioch in 613, Jerusalem in 614, and Egypt in 619, and from 620 on, he assaulted Constantinople directly.

The new orientation of Persia toward the west, the onslaughts of the Slavs and Avars in the north, and the weakness of Byzantine imperial power in the first years of the seventh century constituted the greatest threat Constantinople had ever faced. Persia made contact with the Slavs and Avars, and in the crucial years 626–628, combined with them to begin an assault on Constantinople. All that was left of the Roman Empire was the land within the city walls.

HERACLIUS AND THE DEFENSE OF THE EMPIRE

The success or failure of the defense of Constantinople rested squarely upon the reforms of Justinian's successors, particularly the Emperor Maurice (582–602). Having inherited a near-bankrupt empire, Maurice engineered the restructuring of Byzantine provincial society and began to mobilize Byzantine society on a permanent war footing. The threats in imperial provinces had already urged the creation of special military and civil commands, in which the power in both spheres, traditionally separate in Roman history, was put into the hands of a single man, the *exarch*. Against the Lombard invaders of Italy there was created the Exarchate of Ravenna, a militarized command that included all imperial territory in Italy. Against the Berber invaders of Africa there emerged the similar Exarchate of Carthage. The exarchates were subdivided into lesser military commands, and the civilian population of these districts became the army. In these two provinces, Roman society became the Roman army, and military needs and military government characterized their way of life.

The economic straits of the late sixth century reduced severely the capacity of Constantinople to deal with external threats. The drastic economies practiced by Maurice only produced an intense dislike of him, and in 602 he and his family were assassinated. Phocas (602–610), who replaced the assassinated Maurice, was undoubtedly the least talented emperor ever to rule, and the years of his reign were among the most disastrous in Byzantine history. His ferocity was directed against real or imagined threats to his own rule, and none of his actions indicate any awareness of the difficulties mounting around the city or any glimmer of a solution to the empire's profound problems.

In 610, Heraclius, the son of the exarch of Carthage, revolted against Phocas, leading a fleet supplied by the last prosperous province in the empire. Heraclius executed Phocas and was proclaimed emperor. The first years of Heraclius's reign were, if anything, worse than the reign of Phocas. The sweeping victories of Persia between 613 and 620 swallowed up the east and Asia Minor. The Avar and Slav threat grew greater daily, and by 618 Heraclius was seriously contemplating the removal of the imperial capital to Carthage. The population of Constantinople, however, refused to abandon its city. The church turned over its vast resources in wealth and plate to the emperor, the citizens submitted voluntarily to even more stringent economic measures, and the reorganization of the surviving provinces into *themes*—areas of military-civil command populated by a soldier-peasantry and governed by landlord-generals—extended to Armenia.

The growing menace of the barbarians in the north and Persia in the east finally culminated in the great Avar-Slav siege of the city in 626 and 627. Heraclius, however, was not present at the siege. In 626 he had disappeared into Asia Minor with his new, small, but superbly trained and disciplined army and all the treasure he could lay his hands on. Buying allies in the north, Heraclius struck south, straight at the heart of Mesopotamian Persia. His army carried all before it. His victories in Persia culminated in the defeat of the last Persian army near Nineveh and the destruction of the king's palace at Dastgerd. Khosroes II, humiliated by the unexpected reversal of force, was assassinated in 628, and the collapse of the Persian empire was complete. As Heraclius fought his way through Persia in 627, the citizens of Constantinople destroyed the barbarian fleet that lay before the city. Thus the two major threats to the Empire's survival were eliminated within a few months of each other.

The victories against the barbarians and Persians left Byzantium secure, but exhausted. Not only had the defense forces in the provinces of the Near East been stripped to provide a striking force for the emperor, but the economic crisis of the period caused Heraclius to stop paying tribute to his Near Eastern allies, the rulers of the Arabic kingdom of the Ghassanids. Any attempt to reconquer Greece from the Slavs had to be delayed until the economy recovered and the army rebuilt itself.

The last years of Heraclius's reign witnessed the beginnings of the reconstruction of the empire, but on a very different basis from the reconstructions effected by Augustus, Diocletian, and Constantine. The situation facing Heraclius was not promising. The westernmost provinces were drastically reduced in strength, and this endangered the Byzantine enclaves that occupied them. The prosperity of the Levantine Near East appears to have received a blow from which it did recover for several centuries. In much of Greece and the Balkans, the inroads of Slavic and Bulgar peoples had removed virtually all traces of imperial rule, and in some cases, of Christianity. The severely depleted economy of the empire forced the continued expansion of the *thematic* system, first through Anatolia and later throughout the empire. The separation of the capital from the western parts of the empire accelerated the decline of Latin, and from Heraclius's reign on, Greek became the official language of Constantinople. Finally, the enormous military threats, economic disasters, and unstable imperial rule of the early seventh century had no effect at all upon the ferocious religious disputes that had swept and torn the empire since the days of Constantine.

Facing a general crisis of this magnitude, Heraclius and his successors slowly reconstructed a new empire in the ruins of the old. The immediate needs of Constantinople forced these emperors to turn to the most productive, well-populated areas nearby for men. From this period dates the close association between Byzantium and Asia Minor, from which most later armies and many later emperors were to come. Turning by necessity away from the west, using Greek instead of Latin, converting the peasantry of Asia Minor and Thrace into a citizen-army, and attempting to reduce the danger of religious disputes completed the transformation of the Roman Empire to the Byzantine Empire of the Middle Ages.

8

GERMANIC KINGDOMS AND THE CHURCH IN THE WEST, 565-700

LOMBARD ITALY AND THE FIRST ROME

The westward thrust of the Asiatic Avar peoples between the northern and southern Slavs brought them into contact with Germanic peoples still living outside the old Danube frontier of the Roman Empire. The establishment of an Avar center of power exerted great pressure on some of these peoples and attracted others to the idea of an alliance with the powerful new invaders from the east. The Lombards were one such group. Originally from the region of the lower Elbe in northern Germany, they were drawn, like other Germanic peoples, into the south after the great migrations of the fourth and fifth centuries. The Lombards had served as mercenaries in the Roman imperial armies, had participated in Justinian's Gothic wars in Italy on the imperial side, and had entered into contact with imperial diplomacy by receiving subsidies. Roman diplomacy however, instead of making life pleasant for barbarians, was designed to make it insecure and unstable. Roman favor shifted back and forth between the Lombards and the Gepids, another formidable Germanic people, until the Lombards offered to ally themselves with the Avars against the Gepids. In 567 the combined Lombard and Avar armies annihilated the Gepids, and the Avars settled in the Gepid lands in what is now Hungary and launched from their new center numerous raids against Byzantine frontiers in the Balkans. The Avars used their power to force other neighboring peoples—for instance, the Slavs in the Balkans—into their armies. Perhaps it was this fear of being swallowed by the Avar war machine that inspired the Lombards under their chief Alboin to migrate to Italy. There, there were no Avars, but a Byzantine expeditionary force. Some of the Lombards knew it well: they had helped it to defeat the last Ostrogothic resistance in 552.

In 568 the Lombards invaded Italy. The weakened condition of that land after the Gothic wars, the small occupying army, and the fierce thrust of the Lombard invasion resulted in the main Lombard army driving down into Tuscany, while individual raiding groups struck even further south to Benevento and Spoleto. Their assaults were least successful against the fortified cities and the coastal areas defended from the sea. The Byzantine forces managed to hold Ravenna and Rome and a small central and coastal section along the Adriatic. The Lombards roved freely, and after the death of Alboin in 572, disposed to live without a king under local strongmen, thirty-five "dukes," each ruling from the area of one of the Roman cities. The Lombards were held together by clan loyalties, themselves regulated by the blood feud. Not farmers of particular distinction, they retained for a long period their character of plunderers of Italy and lived on the results of confiscated Roman and Gothic properties and slave labor. In the course of the sixth and seventh centuries, however, the fragmented Lombard territories began to exert a territorial bond that to some extent replaced the clan bond. After the election of Authari (584–590) as king, the Lombards appear to have made attempts to placate the Romans and at the same time to have encroached slowly upon the territories still in Byzantine hands.

The smallness of the Lombard forces attracted the attention of the Franks, who attempted to invade Italy several times in the late sixth and early seventh centuries, but the Franks, like the Lombards and the Byzantines, did not possess sufficient resources to mount a successful assault on the others. The weak Byzantine force at Rome and Ravenna held out against Lombard pressure until 751, but it did so by drastically reordering Roman society, converting the governor of Ravenna into an exarch with combined civil and military powers, and arming a militia of citizens to serve under him. The rich mosaics on the walls of San Vitale at Ravenna revealed the elaborate and stately court life under Justinian, a reminder to the people of the presence of the emperor and his power just a few decades earlier; now, there was no imperial power prepared to relieve Byzantine Italy. The military structure of the exarchate was the structure of a Byzantine frontier province, and the First Rome had finally become a province of the Second. Yet even after the fall of Ravenna in the middle of the eighth century, Byzantine influence remained in the southern part of the Italian peninsula, and the northeastern coast of Italy never forgot its Byzantine heritage. Byzantine and Syrian governors, popes, bishops, and saints influenced the later development of such cities as Venice, with its close maritime ties with Constantinople, and the penetration of the Greek peninsula by the Slavs in the late sixth century sent many Greeks to southern Italy. The Lombard invasion and ultimate conquest of northern Italy created an intermission, not an end, to the Byzantine influence on medieval Italian culture and society.

When the Lombards entered Italy they were, like other Germanic people before them, already Christians, but heterodox Arians. Similar in custom and in their meager interest in Romanization to the Anglo-Saxon conquerors of Britain, the Lombards did not share the desire of the Ostrogoths to come to some kind of terms with the Romans. Italy was a territory the Lombards had conquered, not one they had been sent to defend, and whatever they could take of it was theirs; they did not pretend to share their conquest with the native Romans. Arian Christians and fierce enemies of Byzantium from their days in Pannonia, the Lombards refused to deal with Byzantine military governors and chose instead to regard the bishop of Rome as the appropriate contact with the Byzantine Empire. The Lombard affection for the popes of the sixth and seventh centuries not only perplexed the popes, but raised the suspicions of the Byzantine emperors toward the bishops of Rome. The Lombard insistence on dealing respectfully with the pope and with no one else with imperial affiliations contributed to the growing alienation of the bishops of Rome from the imperial government at Byzantium and the Christian emperors. However, papal relations with the Lombards were never stable, nor were the popes able to come to terms with them.

Unlike the Anglo-Saxons, however, and in spite of their fierce and unyielding hosility to Byzantium, the Lombards did ultimately experience the influence of Roman social forms and something of Latin Christian culture. Lombard documents—charters and law codes—were written in Latin and not, as in England, in a native Germanic language. Unlike other barbarians, the Lombards adapted quickly to town life, although they despised trade and manual labor. The Roman cities survived as meeting places for the Lombard landowners and warriors, and craftsmanship and agriculture were preserved by native Romans, many of whom had declined drastically in status and degree of personal freedom, and by Greeks. The presence of the uncultivated Lombards, however, had profound effects on Roman culture in Italy. The disasters of the Gothic wars, the harsh Byzantine occupation, and the Lombard invasions had reduced Roman society to its lowest level. Literacy declined, although it did not vanish completely, even among laymen. On the other hand, the slow penetration of Roman servants into Lombard government guaranteed the preservation of some of the old Roman culture.

Lombard Arian Christianity, unlike that of the Visigoths, did not possess a particularly strong or articulate clergy, and the enormous spiritual attraction of Christian Rome must have worked slowly but steadily upon the Lombards. Theodelinda, the wife of King Authari, was an orthodox Christian, and in spite of the Arian reaction under Rothari (636–652), the fragmented Lombard areas of the late seventh and early eighth centuries converted quietly to orthodox Christianity. By the reign of Liutprand (712–744), the greatest of the Lombard kings, both the central authority of the Lombard king and orthodox Christianity became important parts of Lombard life.

The attempts to restore the monarchy under Authari, Rothari, and Liutprand produced one of the most remarkable achievements of any Germanic people, a code of law that was extremely sophisticated. The first part of the Lombard law to be written down was the *Edict* of Rothari in 643. The *Edict*, in spite of its Roman title, is really a compilation of nearly pure Germanic custom, but the additions made to Rothari's law in 688, the many laws of Liutprand between 713 and 735, and the few laws of Liutprand's successors in the 740s and 750s reveal an increasing legal sophistication. Crimes came to have a force against the king and people as well as against the immediate victim; fines and compositions still resembled the old Germanic *wergeld*, the "price of a man," but now part of the *wergeld* was paid to the court and part to the victims. The procedure in Lombard courts was the familiar Germanic one of compurgation, in which the accused had to swear his innocence of the charge and had to bring to court a certain number of free Lombard citizens who would also swear to his innocence. Meticulous observance of the form of the oath and severe penalties for perjury were also part of the law. Although the Lombards made no specific law for the Romans who lived under their rule, as did, for example, the Burgundians and the Visigoths, there are sufficient references in the Lombard laws to indicate that a form of Roman law continued in Italy, although it was most likely the vigorous, uncodified vulgar law rather than the *Corpus Iuris Civilis* of Justinian. The influence of Roman on Lombard law was more than simply that of a helpless and impoverished neighbor. The increasingly complex economic relationships between Lombards and Romans and between Lombards themselves frequently produced problems for which Lombard law offered no solutions. Thus, formulas for drawing up contracts, as well as the increasing tendency shown in later Lombard laws to demonstrate the legal reasoning that led to the decision in a given edict, both reflect the influence of the more complex and reasoned Roman law upon the invaders of Italy.

In the shifting political world of the Lombards, a number of institutions and offices stand out clearly. The king of the Lombards was simply one of the many dukes who insisted on dividing power rather than sharing it with a successful ruling dynasty. During the reestablishments of the Lombard monarchy, however, each duke gave up half of his *civitas* to the king, and the king appointed an official of his own, a *gastaldus*, to manage it. Yet the Lombard king lived in a very different world from that of the kings of the later middle ages. He could not tax his free Lombard subjects, who regarded the paying of taxes as a sign of servitude, and he could retain only as much income from the surviving Roman taxes as the dukes chose to give him. The king, like other landowners, lived off the land he owned. He provided no public services, some of the previous ones having disappeared and others having been undertaken by the Church. The courts and the armies paid their own way: the former, out of the court fines, and the latter, out of their own pockets. Finally, like other Germanic leaders, the Lombard kings developed a group of faithful retainers, the *gasindi,* whose loyalty was rewarded by outright grants of land from the king's personal possession.

Unlike their barbarian predecessors in Italy, the Lombards left longstanding traces of their earliest occupation of the peninsula. Even after their defeat by the Franks late in the eighth century, the Lombards continued to live in northern Italy, and until the eleventh century their preserves in the south of Italy increased at the expense of those of the Byzantines. Their law lasted even longer: it survived the Frankish conquest, and even the revival of Roman law in the twelfth century; as late as the fourteenth century it was being taught at the law schools of northern Italy; and a copy of it was among the first printed Italian books. Lombard Italy, with its Byzantine enclaves and papal Rome, is the beginning of medieval Italy. Officially still a province of Byzantium, its pope still writing deferentially to the emperor in the eighth century, Lombard Italy nevertheless completed the dissolution of western Roman imperial institutions and the establishment of a Germanic-Roman kingdom.

GOD'S CONSUL

The bishop of Rome to whom the Lombards turned in their indirect dealings with the emperor at Constantinople was Pope Gregory I (590–604). Gregory, perhaps more than any other figure in the west, represents the character of sixth-century Italy in its double existence as Byzantine frontier province and spiritual center of a new Latin Christianity. Gregory was born around 540 into a wealthy aristocratic Roman family that owned much property in Rome, including a large palace on the Caelian Hill, and extensive estates in Sicily. Gregory's earliest years were spent in his family's attempt to evade the worst consequences of the Gothic war of Justinian. Moving from Rome to Sicily and back again, Gregory and his family witnessed the ravaging of the city of Rome and the devastation of the countryside. Gregory's education also suffered from the ravages of the wars. At the beginning of the sixth century the great imperial university of Rome was still functioning, supported by Theoderic. Cassiodorus even attempted to found a school of theological studies in the city. By the 560s, however, the schooling to be had in Rome was far inferior to that available in Constantinople or Beirut. Gregory's studies in literary technique and logic mark another great change in the ancient world. In the west, philosophy, law, and advanced literature were no longer taught beyond the rudimentary level. The "liberal arts" were taking on the shape they would have until the twelfth century: the study of grammar and rhetoric predominated; logic and mathematical subjects were available only in a few places, and even there they were taught from compendiums and late texts. Boethius, dead for twenty-five years, was becoming the "schoolmaster of the West," and Cassiodorus, the last Roman to know and admire the classics, had retired to his religious community at Squillace, there to preserve the learning he had acquired and to write his *Divine Institutes,* the curriculum guide for a thousand years of Western education.

In 573 Gregory was prefect of the city of Rome, a once-glorious office by then reduced to supervising the civil government of the city, and cooperating with the master of soldiers in its defense and with the Pope in distributing the grain and alms that constituted the social welfare that the church had gradually taken over from the imperial government. Shortly after his term of office, Gregory, by then having inherited his family's wealth and become one of the richest men in Rome, converted his family estates in Rome and Sicily into monastic houses, gave the rest of his vast fortune away to the poor, and converted his own palace in Rome into the monastery of St. Andrew, which he himself entered as a novice. Throughout his life as a monk, Gregory displayed an asceticism and self-discipline that carried beyond the monastery into the later stages of his life. Gregory remained in the monastery of St. Andrew only three years. In 578 he was made one of the seven deacons of Rome, papal assistants who supervised the ecclesiastical and charitable life of the city. The next year, Gregory was made *apocrisiarius,* ambassador of the pope at the imperial court in Constantinople.

The papal mission in Constantinople focused on the need for imperial troops to defend the Byzantine territories from the Lombards, who had once again begun to approach Rome. Gregory's six-year stay in Constantinople, however, brought no results; Gregory never even learned Greek. In 585 he returned to Rome. Upon his return Gregory was elected abbot of St. Andrew's monastery, where he completed his exposition of the Book of Job, the *Moralia in Job,* a major document in the history of scriptural exegesis. Gregory's expository technique culminated in the complete allegorizing of the events described in the text, and passed on to the later Middle Ages the late Roman literary technique of reading philosophical or theological meanings into documents whose literal meaning does not readily suggest such other levels. With Boethius's *Consolation of Philosophy* and introductory works to Aristotle, and Cassiodorus's *Divine Institutes,* Gregory's *Moralia* constitutes the chief sixth-century legacy to the next ten centuries of Christian learning.

In 590 a recurrence of the great plague of 542–543 struck Rome, taking with it Pope Pelagius II. The city immediately elected Gregory pope on September 3. The importance of Gregory's pontificate lies in the increasing responsibility of the pope for the civil as well as the religious welfare of Rome, in the restoration of contact between Rome and the churches in barbarian kingdoms, and in the steps he took to reorganize the structure of the church in the west.

In realizing that the west had to survive as a group of barbarian Christian kingdoms, Gregory ran counter to the official view of Byzantium, and the emperors looked askance at his efforts to make peace with the Lombards. Yet not only did Gregory establish continual contact with the Lombards, he sent hundreds of letters to other barbarian kingdoms in Spain, Gaul, and Illyricum. The *Register* of Gregory's letters is one of only two (the other is that of Pope Leo I) that survive from before the eleventh century. In letters to bishops, kings, queens, clerics, and laymen, Gregory expounded his principles of personal and institutional Christianity. In the letters, as in his sermons, he used a simplified direct discourse, included anecdotes and puns, and dealt with matters of both theology and day-to-day administration. He wrote to Desiderius, bishop of Vienne, scolding the prelate for teaching letters instead of scripture. To Etherius, bishop of Lyons, he described the steps to be taken in the case of a chronically ill or insane bishop. He wrote to Augustine, leader of the mission that Gregory had sent to pagan Anglo-Saxon England, advising him to adapt pagan festival days and shrines to Christian uses in order that the conversion of the pagans might be facilitated. Gregory wrote diplomatic letters as well—for instance, to the terrible queen of the Franks, Brunhild, and to the even more terrible Emperor Phocas.

Besides his letters, Gregory began a systematic policy of converting pagan barbarians and reforming Christianity in the lands of the Germanic rulers in which Christianity already existed. Gregory's best-known missionary endeavor was the conversion of Britain. Although the story of the origins of the mission to England has long been surrounded by a great deal of pious fiction, what can at least be ascertained is that this mission was part of Gregory's larger vision of reorganizing the Church and bringing the old Roman provincial administrative organization, which had also been the ecclesiastical organization of the empire since the fourth century, directly under papal control. Among his reforms in this area, Gregory instituted the custom of giving to an archbishop the *pallium,* the stole of white wool that had once been simply a mark of singular imperial favor. This practice, instituted in England and later elsewhere throughout the newly converted parts of Europe, became one of the ways in which new metropolitans acknowledged papal supremacy.

For the conversion of England Gregory chose Augustine, the prior of the monastery of St. Andrew in Rome. Dispatched in 596, Augustine and his companions traveled through Gaul and arrived at Kent in 597. Kent, in the southeastern part of England, was ruled by the Anglo-Saxon king Aethelbert, who was married to Bertha, a Christian Frankish princess. Permitted to settle and preach, St. Augustine and his companions soon converted the king and a large part of his following. In several letters written in 601, Gregory announced that he was sending more assistance to St. Augustine's mission, wrote to Aethelbert concerning the duties of a newly converted Christian king, and described for St. Augustine the organizational principles according to which the church in England ought to be expanded when the time was ripe.

The organizational principles, the influence of Rome directly upon a newly converted former pagan land, and Pope Gregory's close supervision of the mission characterize his concept of papal responsibility for the conversion of the barbarian kingdoms as well as the survival of old Roman organizational and administrative principles, no longer in the western imperial world, but in the organization of the Church. The epithet given Gregory by contemporaries, "God's Consul," is an accurate designation of the utilization of Roman concepts of office and organization by a religious society with the pope at its head.

Gregory's administrative concerns were not restricted only to his planning and execution of the English mission. One of his most popular works, the *Liber regulae Pastoralis,* was a guidebook for those holding ecclesiastical office, written directly in the tradition of Cicero's *De officiis* and St. Ambrose's *De officiis.* Gregory's work, straightforward and practical, enunciates his favorite maxim: the authority and responsibility of priests for the souls of those in their care is the greatest of responsibilities, and "the care of souls is the art of all arts." The work deals with the ethical responsibilities of priests and bishops as well as their practical duties, and throughout many later centuries it served as the standard introduction to clerical conduct and clerical concepts of ecclesiastical office.

Gregory's practical concept of ecclesiastical administration found avenues for expression in yet other areas. The vast territories of the Church, increased by imperial gifts, the donations of the pious and intestate, and the personal wealth of prelates such as Gregory himself, had increased considerably during and after the period of the Gothic wars. All the possessions of the Church, stretching from Africa to Gaul and the Balkans to Italy, were called patrimonies, and the entire body of Church possessions was termed the Patrimony of St. Peter. The income from these properties was used for the upkeep of churches and clergy, the dispensing of charity and other forms of social welfare, and the redemption of captives from barbarians. Gregory once wrote to the rector of some estates in Gaul, for example, that revenues from those estates, because Gallic money was not acceptable currency in Italy, should be spent on purchasing captives and slaves, and that in some cases the persons thus purchased should be returned to their homelands accompanied by priests, who might convert them or those to whom they were returned. Thus, in one light Gregory stands at the end of a long line of capable and conscientious Roman administrators, pagan and Christian, in his solicitude for his office and his high conception of the ethical responsibilities of his position. In another light he stands as a new man, concerned less for the survival of the empire than for the conversion of the barbarians who, in his eyes, had come to stay. In no other figure may we see as clearly the often delicate and hardly perceptible shift of sensibility that pointed the way, not to a restoration of the old world, but to the creation of a legacy for a new world.

In yet one other aspect of his pontificate Gregory reflected the new world even more strongly and directly. We have already noted his contribution to the tradition of allegorical interpretation of scriptural texts derived from Hellenistic Jewish thought and late Roman neo-Platonism. As late as the days of St. Augustine and the pagan Macrobius, such techniques were well under the control of the rigid and demanding intellectual standards of a highly literate society. By Gregory's day, the intellectual vigor of that earlier tradition was fast weakening, and Gregory's own interpretations of Job are both much freer and less disciplined intellectually than the work of his predecessors. The interpretations of Gregory and others were often based on fanciful etymologies, an extensive number symbolism, and a conviction that Scripture, not formal classical learning, contains all that man needs to know, not only about how to be saved, but about how to understand the world. From Gregory's *Moralia in Job* derive the later traditions of medieval bestiaries, the allegorizing of pagan as well as Christian literature, and the vast biblical commentaries in which are to be found so much of the changing intellectual style of the later Middle Ages.

Gregory's Rome was the Rome of St. Peter rather than that of Augustus or Constantine. In this respect as well, Gregory shared the Christian tradition of admiring the saints and looking upon their lives as sources of inspiration. Traditions of sainthood, from the martyrs of the time of the persecutions to the well-known church fathers and the holy hermits in the Egyptian and Syrian deserts reached out in the sixth century even to small localities, and from the fifth to the eleventh centuries sainthood was conferred by local inhabitants on deceased holy men and women. Some saints, of course, achieved a much more widespread popularity: their cults were brought by missionaries to new lands (as were those of some Italian saints by Augustine's mission to England in 597), they were adopted by powerful lay or ecclesiastical figures as patrons (as was St. Martin of Tours by Clovis and his successors), or their lives became familiar to many, usually through the brief biographies that constitute so much of early Christian literature. In 593–594, Gregory wrote a long work called the *Dialogues,* conversations between himself and the Deacon Peter about the lives of some saints. Gregory's *Dialogues* and the accounts of other saints' lives are important to the historian, of course, for purposes other than devotional. They reflect the interests, values, and sometimes even the social institutions of the saint's world. And they constitute nearly the only sources that we possess for some periods and places. Heaven, too, has a social history that tells a great deal about the earth.

Sometimes, a saint's life assumed an importance beyond all proportion to the saint's literary or inspirational abilities. Such was the *Life of St. Anthony* by St. Athanasius, a description of the first of the desert fathers, and a work that was prominent among the influences that led St. Augustine to convert to Christianity in the fourth century. Such also was Book II of Gregory's *Dialogues,* which was devoted entirely to the life of one saint, Benedict of Nursia. St. Benedict (480–550) retired from worldly life as a young man, tried the solitary life of the hermit, and then attempted unsuccessfully to organize a monastic community at Vicovaro. Finally, after several other attempts, he settled at Monte Cassino, to the south of Rome, where he built a monastery and formed a monastic community. This community was neither the first nor the best-known western monastic community. The foundations of St. Martin at Tours, St. Honoratus at Lérins, and of John Cassian at Marseilles were three among many older communities as were some of the Celtic communities in Christian Ireland. Nor was Benedict's Rule particularly well known or widely followed. The Benedictine Rule ultimately became the "constitution" of all western monasticism, though its influence did not begin to spread widely until the eighth century, and it was the criterion of intensive monastic reform movement, chiefly in the tenth, eleventh, and twelfth centuries.

Unlike the monastery of Cassiodorus, however, the community at Monte Cassino was not specifically enjoined to become learned in secular matters. Although the Benedictine Rule presupposes a necessary amount of monastic skill in reading and writing the *sacra pagina*—the Scriptures—it contains no thrust toward what became in Ireland, England, and, later, in Monte Cassino itself, a high level of monastic scholarship. Literacy, in the Rule, was one more tool, as were obedience, manual labor, continuing rounds of devotions, and clothing and dietary regulations, that prepared the soul of the monk for the "hard road" of discipline and penitence that led to God.

The significance of Gregory's life of St. Benedict in the later history of European society cannot be overestimated. For the pope to place his own enormous personal prestige behind the founder of Monte Cassino meant not only that Benedict and the Benedictine Rule were to possess great weight in the later development of monasticism, but that monasticism as an institution was to have a place in the community of the faithful that was guaranteed by this great pope. The cultural history of the West in the six centuries after Benedict and Gregory can be said to have taken its shape and direction from the spirit and the institution created by the first and its diffusion and praise in the work of the second.

The life of St. Benedict received the lengthiest treatment in the *Dialogues*. The accounts of the other saints' lives relate visions, prophecies, and miracles, depict scenes from the lives of the great and the humble, and contribute to the literary traditions of Europe much of the psychological coloring and epistemology of the next ten centuries. It is in the *Dialogues* that demons actively and horribly persecute the faithful, that the dead reveal their eternal rewards and punishments for the edification of the living, that the Apostles and patron saints of churches become visible to the eyes of living men. In them, the visible yet real spiritual population of the Christian universe appears in all its variety in stories whose simplicity and directness appeal to all ranges of culture. Here, in what an anthropologist has recently called "the magic of the medieval church," the complex process of combining folklore, moral tales, saints' lives, and miracle stories is launched into the European consciousness. It is no accident that Gregory himself became the subject of a vast and elaborate folklore in later centuries: he had succeeded in framing Christian doctrine in a form acceptable and easily assimilable by all levels of society.

In his allegorical interpretations of Scripture, his miracle stories, and his instructions for the conversion of pagan peoples, Gregory showed a vast and flexible resourcefulness, and at the same time—recognizing, perhaps, that he could not abolish the variety of beliefs concerning the supernatural and its effects on the material world—he attempted to edify the entire spiritual consciousness of the seventh century. If he could not do away with the demons, he could at least show them always defeated. In the fifteenth and sixteenth centuries, when people's faith in the power of monks and in the Church in general grew weak, the unleashed science of demonology led to the great witch persecutions that did not end until 1700. The demons were a vivid part of Gregory's universe, but they were kept firmly under control, and when the souls of the dead or the saints appeared, it was to inspire, not terrify, the living.

Gregory taught not only by his actions and writings, but by his instructions in other matters as well. At his urging, the visual depiction of scriptural scenes on church walls (and, much later, on windows) took on a new role; these scenes were to be "the Scriptures of the unlettered," and the motifs of Romano-Christian antique visual art, like the principles of late Roman administration, were transformed into instructional materials for the European world, whose birth Gregory may truly be said to have witnessed. By his death in 604, at the end of a life wracked by physical illness as well as spiritual concern for the Christian world, Gregory had succeeded in reorienting the western Church to the existence of its new rulers, taken steps to guide the long process of conversion, reestablished papal contact with far-flung churches from Spain to Britain and from Italy to Alexandria, and shaped the mold of Christian devotion in forms that lasted for a thousand years.

ROMAN AND CELTIC CHRISTIANITY IN ANGLO-SAXON ENGLAND

The mission of St. Augustine of Canterbury that Gregory sent to England in 597 arrived in a land in which pagan Germanic invaders had obliterated most traces of surviving Roman Christianity and had driven the remaining Celtic Christians into the borderlands of Wales and the north of Britain. There, partly through the assistance of Celtic missionaries from Ireland, they survived, maintaining come contact with the church on the Continent.

With the reign of Aethelfrith (c. 593–616), the history of the English kingdoms in the north comes into focus. Around 603 Aethelfrith joined the kingdoms of Bernicia and Deira by marrying the daughter of Aelle, king of Deira. The combined kingdom was Northumbria ("the kingdom north of the River Humber"). Aethelfrith was succeeded by Edwin (616–632), who defeated and killed him with the aid of Raedwald, an English king of East Anglia, to the south. Aethelfrith's sons, Oswald and Oswy, fled to exile in the north among the Picts and Scots.

The shaping of Northumbria in the first years of the seventh century marks the establishment of English power in northern Britain. To the south of Northumbria lay the kingdom of Mercia in the Midlands and the smaller kingdom of Lindsey, to the east of Mercia. South of Mercia and Lindsey were a number of English kingdoms, of which the most commonly known are East Anglia, Wessex, and Kent. The extent of these kingdoms had been determined as much by the skill and fortune of their leaders as by any "natural" political combinations, and they should be considered analogous to similar Germanic and Slavic settlements on the edge or just outside of the old Roman frontier.

It was to Kent that Pope Gregory sent St. Augustine in 596, and it was from the Kentish base that the first stage of the conversion of England was undertaken by Augustine and his followers. The second stage of the conversion occurred when King Edwin of Deira was baptized in 627. His reign for the next five years was said to have ushered in a time so peaceful that "if a woman with her newborn babe chose to wander throughout the island from sea to sea she could do so without molestation," as Bede was to describe it when he wrote the history of the conversion of England a century later. In 632, however, the Christian Edwin was killed in battle.

Edwin's successor in Northumbria was Oswald (633–641), whose description in Bede's *Ecclesiastical History of the English People* is one of the most successful and moving portraits of an ideal Christian king. Oswald was the son of Aethelfrith, whom Edwin had defeated, and was raised in the Celtic north of Britain, where he was baptized a Christian by Celtic clergy. Oswald's successful reoccupation of Northumbria enabled the Celtic Christian clergy from the far north of Britain to enter Northumbria, and it was there that the first signs of a settlement between Britons and English appeared and that Celtic Christianity confronted the Roman Christianity of the successors of St. Augustine.

Throughout the fifth and sixth centuries, contacts among the Celtic Christians of Northern Britain, Wales, and Ireland greatly aided the development of Irish monasteries and strengthened the homogeneity of Celtic Christian beliefs. Two distinctive characteristics of Celtic monasticism were its widespread use of the notion of individual, rather than public confession of sins, and penitentials—the meticulous lists of penances for various sins. The solicitude of the Irish for penance may explain the most distinctive of all characteristics of Irish Christianity, the concept of "exile for the love of God." For many Irish monks, the departure from their homeland to wander far from Ireland in attempts to convert pagans was an attractive idea. Whether these journeys were undertaken as penances or as an exuberant devotional form, it is difficult to say. Nevertheless, the most famous of the Irish monastic exiles, Columba (521–597), or Colum Cille ("Colum of the Church"), a slightly older contemporary of Pope Gregory I, left Ireland in 565 and founded a monastic retreat on the island of Hy, later Iona, off the Scottish coast. A monastic community developed around him, and from it the monks penetrated western Scotland.

When Oswald was in exile in the north, he was converted to Celtic Christianity, and when he returned to Northumbria he sent to Iona for monks to help him restore Christianity. Under the leadership of St. Aidan, a monastery was founded at Lindisfarne, off the eastern coast of Northumbria, and Celtic monks began to disseminate their form of Christianity in the wake of the reduced strength of the Roman mission. Under Oswald's brother and successor, Oswy (641–670), matters came to a head. Oswy, a Celtic Christian, and his wife, a Roman Christian, celebrated different rites and, as Bede tells us, even celebrated Easter at different times. In a synod held at Whitby in Northumbria in 663, the leaders of Celtic and Roman Christianity in Northumbria argued their cases. Rome won the day when Wilfrid of Ripon convinced Oswy of the greater authority of St. Peter. From 663 until the early eighth century, the fusion of Roman and Celtic Christianity under the guidance of the Roman ecclesiastical organization produced a church that was thoroughly loyal to Rome yet retained many of its distinctive Celtic characteristics. In its art, its missionary zeal, and its intricate devotional forms, the English Church strongly influenced the rest of the continent in the eighth and ninth centuries.

The third quarter of the seventh century witnessed important political changes in England. The growing power of Mercia under its pagan king Penda (d. 654) and his Christian successors Aethelbald (716–757) and Offa (c. 760–796), prevented the southward expansion of Northumbria, and the resumption of hostilities between the Northumbrians and the Picts drew Northumbria's attention away from southern political matters after 678. Yet Northumbria produced, out of its rich Celtic and Roman heritage, a distinctive culture whose high level in both art and literature dominated the intellectual and spiritual life of England in the late seventh and eighth centuries. With the rise of Northumbrian cultural predominance and the conversion of Mercia and the south to Christianity, the mission of Augustine in 597 was completed. The results were probably those for which Pope Gregory I had hoped, but they occurred in the wake of difficulties he could not possibly have foreseen. The amorphous political condition of England in the late sixth century produced the rise of Northumbria and Mercia in succession, and the slow penetration of Christianity in the heavily pagan south was further hampered by the political instability of the island. The great confrontation between Celtic and Roman Christianity guaranteed the eventual orthodoxy of the island, but the uniformity of English Christianity did not stabilize the shifting political structures of eighth century England.

VISIGOTHIC SPAIN

The vast Visigothic empire of Euric in the late fifth century extended, as we have seen, from the Loire to Seville, and from the Atlantic Ocean to the Rhone river. The successful expansion of the Franks to the south and their defeat of the Visigoths at Vouillé in 507 reduced the Gallic kingdom of the Visigoths and threw them under the protection of Theoderic the Ostrogoth, who preserved Visigothic independence in Spain until the reestablishment of the Visigothic monarchy in the middle of the sixth century. The Visigoths survived the terrible fate of the Ostrogoths at the hands of Justinian, and the Byzantine reconquest succeeded in establishing only a small foothold in Visigothic Spain—in the old imperial province of Tarraconensis, in the southeastern part of the Iberian peninsula. The factionalism among the Frankish successors of Clovis prevented extensive Frankish assaults on the Visigoths, and from the mid sixth to the early eighth centuries Visigothic Spain remained independent, as did Frankish Gaul, Lombard Italy, and the English kingdoms of Northumbria, Mercia, Wessex, and Kent. Coexisting with a population of Hispano-Romans that greatly outnumbered them, exceeded them by far in the development of material and intellectual culture, and opposed them in the matter of religion, the Visigoths lived apart from their Roman subjects but granted the Roman aristocracy a degree of freedom unequaled anywhere else in the old imperial west. The Arianism of the Visigoths continued to the reign of Reccared (586–601), a contemporary of Pope Gregory I.

The turbulence of mid sixth-century Visigothic Spain—the rebellions in the south and northwest, and the threat of the Byzantine forces in the southeast—was slowly brought under royal control during the reign of Leovigild (578–586). Ruling the kingdom from the city of Toledo, which had become the royal city shortly before he ascended the throne, Leovigild established the power of the Visigothic kings. Trade with the east, Byzantium, the Franks across the Pyrenees, and, until the fall of the Ostrogothic Kingdom, Italy, maintained Spanish connections with the western and eastern parts of the empire, and churchmen and merchants both appear to have had easy access from Gaul, Italy, and Byzantium to Spain, and even Ireland, throughout the seventh century.

The peaceful succession to the throne in 586 of Leovigild's son Reccared (586–601) suggests both the security of the kingdom under Leovigild and the prestige that Reccared brought to the throne with him. The reign of Reccared is significant for the momentous conversion of the king and the kingdom to orthodox Catholicism, and for the subsequent changes in Visigothic life that the conversion brought.

In 587, Reccared convened the Third Council of Toledo in order to arrange the conversion of the kingdom. In his address to the council in 589, Reccared may be seen reflecting what later became a distinctive aspect of Visigothic Catholic kingship—the elevated notion of the Christian king, who is responsible to God for his people, a defender of the Church similar to the Byzantine emperor:

> Although Omnipotent God has given us charge of the kingdom for the profit of its peoples, and has entrusted the rule of not a few races to Our Royal Care, however, We remember Our mortal condition, and that We cannot merit future beatitude unless We devote ourselves to the cult of the true faith and please Our Creator with at least the confession which He deserves. . . .

The Spain of Reccared was witnessing the slow disappearance of the differences between the Gothic and Hispano-Roman populations, possibly, as had been the case in Vandal Africa a century before, a slow process of the assimilation of the Goths by the provincial Romans. The Gothic language seems to have disappeared in the seventh century; the Goths adopted Roman dress, and in the seventh century the laws forbidding marriage between Goths and Romans were abolished. With the publication of the legal code of King Reccesswinth in 654, the *Leges Visigothorum*, a single code for all subjects of the king replaced two separate sets of laws, one for the Visigoths and one, the *Breviary of Alaric* (506), for Romans. The *Breviary* survived, however, in southwestern Gaul for several centuries thereafter. The *Leges Visigothorum* of Reccesswinth had an even longer life: translated into Spanish in the thirteenth century as the *Fuero Juzgo*, it was incorporated in the great thirteenth-century Spanish law collection, *Las Siete Partidas*, and underlay all subsequent Spanish law, including that of the New World.

Under the Visigoths, the Roman provincial population of Spain had survived to a much greater degree as a whole than elsewhere in the old western parts of the empire. The *curialis* class still governed the cities, great Roman landowners still held vast estates, and Roman provincial governors still judged according to Roman law in Roman courts and also collected several of the old Roman taxes on behalf of the Visigothic king. This survival of Roman life and institutions and the continuation of other kinds of contact with the Roman imperial world—whether from Italy or Byzantium or from Byzantine southeastern Spain—slowly influenced Visigothic custom and habit. The reign of King Sisebut (612–621), however, reflects other distinctive characteristics of Visigothic Spain. Sisebut, a poet and scholar of no mean achievements, instituted a ferocious persecution of the Jews, far more thorough and savage than any earlier persecution and with far more disastrous results, not only for the Jews of Spain but for the internal stability of the monarchy itself.

Visigothic Spain in the mid seventh century witnessed the continuation of the Jewish persecutions, the growing tendency of its kings to utilize the councils of Toledo to handle both the secular as well as the religious affairs of the kingdom, and the increasing unruliness of the aristocracy, particularly in regard to the question of royal succession, which the aristocracy stubbornly forced to remain elective rather than basing it on inheritance. Under King Reccesswinth (649–672), persecution of the Jews increased, and witnessing Jewish ceremonies became a capital crime. The Visigothic persecution of the Jews—far more violent and thorough than any similar persecutions in Europe until the eleventh century, and enshrined in a legal system in a way not to be repeated until the fourteenth and fifteenth centuries—is still not completely explicable. There is little evidence that the general population of the kingdom or the clergy shared the royal mania for persecution, and even though the increasingly Christian concept of kingship that appeared in seventh-century Spain may have made the kings more acutely aware of the "otherness" of the Jews, later Christian kingdoms felt no such pressing need to annihilate a body of people who were, after all, Roman citizens, identical in speech and manner to the rest of the population, and hardly as yet the victims of the vast, diseased, anti-Semitic folklore that obsessed and polluted the European mind from the twelfth through the twentieth centuries.

From the seventh century on, the Visigothic kings began to imitate consciously the Byzantine emperor in the structure of their courts, their dress, and their relation to God. The king, through the councils of Toledo, ruled the church, proclaimed himself a *novus Constantinus,* a "new Constantine," and borrowed from the Old Testament descriptions of the Hebrew kings the practice of being anointed with holy oil. This fusion of Germanic, western Roman, Byzantine, and Old Testament elements influenced not only the outward protocol of later Anglo-Saxon and Frankish kingship, but raised for the first time in the west a Germanic king who claimed Christian kingship of the same kind as that of the emperor—a "new David" and a "new Constantine." The rituals devised by the Visigothic court were echoed and repeated in England in the tenth century and among the Franks in the eighth century and beyond.

The sources for the later seventh and early eighth centuries reveal acutely that in spite of the reigns during that period of a number of vigorous and intelligent rulers, not all of whom repeated the Jewish persecutions of Sisebut and Recceswinth, the kingdom experienced severe political difficulties. By the end of the seventh century, Visigothic kings had trouble raising an army. Legislation against escaping slaves increased, indicating a breakdown in the organization of landholding as well as in the army. The last Visigothic army of Spain fell to an Arab and Berber army at the battle of Medina Sidonia in 711. For all of their remarkable experimenting with a new form of kingship, for all of the implications of that kingship for Germanic society, for all of the continuity of Roman institutions into the late seventh century, and for all of the assistance of the episcopal councils of Toledo in the governing of the kingdom, the Visigoths seem not to have found a means of political survival. The bizarre eccentricities of the royal persecution of the Jews and the collapse of the kingdom well before the invasion of al-Tarik in 711 still pose vexing questions. Like the Ostrogoths in Italy, the Visigoths virtually disappear from history after the mid eighth century. Their successors, who came from the tiny mountain kingdoms of Asturias and Navarre far to the north, claimed that their own campaigns against the Arabs were a *reconquista,* a reconquering of old Christian Spain. But no Visigothic monarchy ever succeeded the rule of the Arabs.

The distinctive qualities of Visigothic Spain also include important cultural achievements, for Spain was a communications route for eastern and Italian ideas as well as for merchants and churchmen, and the contribution of seventh-century Spain to the intellectual life of later Christian Europe was substantial. St. Martin, Bishop of Braga (c. 550–579), produced a number of ecclesiastical works, several of which, including a remarkable and informative sermon against pagan superstitions, were used later by churchmen and missionaries in Germany in their own conversion efforts. Two remarkable chroniclers, John of Biclaro (c. 573–620) and Julian of Toledo (fl. 720), left us vivid, remarkably reliable portraits of their age. All three of these men reflect a vigorous Spanish ecclesiastical culture and the evidence from legend and archaeology indicates that Spanish ecclesiastical influences reached England and Ireland in the seventh century and possibly became the vehicle for much of the eastern, particularly Syriac, influences long associated with the Irish church.

The most influential Spanish writer of the Visigothic kingdom was St. Isidore, bishop of Seville, (c. 600–636). Seville, close to the Byzantine frontier and to the sea routes to the north, was a center of intellectual and devotional activity. Isidore's numerous works reflect that culture. They include expositions of Scripture, short treatises on Christian ethics and obligations, and works on ecclesiastical government and law (a field in which Spanish churchmen were preeminent in the seventh and eighth cenuturies). Isidore was something of a historian as well, and his *History of the Goths, Vandals, and Suevi,* though not particularly accurate or informative, is interesting evidence of his concern for the continuity of Christian histories of barbarian peoples.

Isidore's masterpiece, however, and one of the half dozen most influential works of late antiquity, was his *Etymologiae,* a vast encyclopedia in twenty books comprising information on topics ranging from the liberal arts, treated in the first three books, to food, drink, and furniture, discussed in the twentieth. Each entry is introduced by an enthusiastic study of the etymology of the object's name, an etymology no more accurate than Pope Gregory's interpretations of the Book of Job. Yet the magnitude of Isidore's attempt and the vast amounts of accurate information the *Etymologies* do contain, made it a standard reference work from its own day until the fifteenth century.

FRANKISH GAUL UNDER THE SUCCESSORS OF CLOVIS, 511–683

Upon Clovis's death in 511, his single kingdom was divided among his four sons, each of whom became a king, possessed a capital, and drew an equal share in his father's possessions, including his political possessions. Yet some of these possessions stubbornly resisted the tidy division required by Frankish law. Gaul, completely conquered as it was, was not a patch of Toxandrian forest or underpopulated Roman outpost province, as was Cambrai. It was the oldest, the most Romanized of all the empire's provinces, and its internal divisions, the lines between old Celtic regions and administrative *civitates* soon made the boundaries of royal authority among Clovis's four successors irregular and variable. Some regions, such as Aquitaine and Brittany, maintained a stubborn independence, one that sometimes yielded to Frankish power, but more often did not. Aquitaine, from the fall of the western imperial provinces, managed to remain intractable to its new rulers, and often successfully, if never permanently, reasserted its separateness from the other compact Frankish kingdoms.

Clovis's sons ruled their kingdoms from four capitals that, to a modern reader, seem surprisingly close together considering the vast lands they controlled. The four cities, Paris (Childebert's kingdom, 511–558), Soissons (Clothar I's kingdom, 511–561), Orleans (Chlodomir's kingdom, 511–524), and Reims (Theoderic's kingdom, 511–534), were all located close to one another in the Parisian basin, and this gave their rulers mutual opportunities for assistance in times of danger, as well as a dangerous proximity in the deadly family quarrels and wars that came to characterize late sixth-century Frankish Gaul.

The expansionist character of Clovis's monarchy continued throughout the careers of his sons, most notably in the thrust into the Burgundian kingdom and the defeat of the Thuringians, a Germanic people east of the Rhine. These actions extended Frankish power east into the old Germanic lands outside the Roman Empire. Moreover, the removal of the Thuringians brought the Franks face to face with the Saxons and the Slavs, two peoples whose presence dominated Frankish policies toward the immediate east for the next two centuries.

Of the lines established by Clovis's four sons, the most immediately remarkable was that of Theoderic at Reims. Theodebert I, Theoderic's son, registered immediate military success in the east and even participated in the Gothic wars in Italy. The kings of Reims were extraordinarily conscious of the possibilities that Christian kingship offered, and Theodebert's coins and adventurous policies reveal an exalted concept of his rulership as well as a self-conscious sense of rivalry with the emperor at Constantinople.

Dynastic accident, which had divided the kingdom of Clovis into four parts upon his death, welded it together again between 558 and 561, the last years of the reign of Clovis's last surviving son, Chlothar. Clothar consolidated the gains of his brothers and nephews since Clovis's death, and extended his own kingdom into northern Italy, the German Rhineland, and the Mediterranean south. At his death in 561, however, the kingdom once again had to be divided among his sons, and again by dynastic accident, four kings, Clothar's sons, divided the kingdom among themselves. Under Clothar's sons, however, family rivalry and the inherent instability of the Frankish kingdoms began to play a stronger part in social and political life. The furious rivalry between two of these sons, Sigebert I (king at Reims, 561–575) and Chilperic (king at Soissons, 561–584), plunged the kingdoms into internal warfare, in spite of the wealth and increasingly complex ideas of kingship that each maintained. (The other two brothers were Charibert, king at Paris, from 561 to 568, and Guntram, king at Burgundy from 561 to 592.) This destructive feud between Sigebert and Chilperic, involving their remarkable queens Fredegund and Brunhild, drew other Germanic peoples from across the Rhine into Frankish affairs. After the first decade of the seventh century, all the Frankish kingdoms once again came into the hands of a single ruler, Clothar II (584–629), the son of Sigebert of Reims.

Thus, in 511 and 561 (and also in 567 and 595), Clovis's kingdom was partitioned according to Frankish customary law; only under the brief reign of Clothar I (558–561) in the sixth century and the longer reigns of Clothar II (613–629) and his son Dagobert (629–639) did the kingdoms unite under a single ruler. Not only did dynastic fortune play an obviously important role in the history of the Frankish rule of Gaul, but a century of Frankish political expansionism transformed the later Frankish conquests into something very different from the Frankish conquests of the late fifth and early sixth centuries.

First, the regularity of the partitions after 511 began to impart a regional character to several of these kingdoms, which alternately merged and reconstituted throughout the sixth century. Of these, Paris tended to become neutral, partly through dynastic accident and partly by its central role in the circle of Frankish royal towns. Predominance in the western part of Gaul passed into the hands of the rulers of Soissons, who extended their power west to the sea under Chilperic and had begun to refer to their territories as Neustria by the seventh century. The kings at Orleans became more and more involved with the absorbed kingdom of Burgundy, and increased their territory through sixth-century expansion to include the Saône and Rhone valleys, the lands between the Alps and the Jura, and part of Provence. Under Guntram, the capital of the kingdom was moved from Orleans to Châlons-sur-Saône, and Burgundy emerged briefly as a third part of the Frankish kingdom. The old kingdom centered in Reims, profiting from the eastward expansionist aims of Theoderic and Theudebert, became centered in Metz in the late sixth century under Sigebert I, and before 600 was being referred to as Austrasia. Besides its new eastern territories, it included Auvergne in the south center of Gaul as well as the Mediterranean cities of Marseilles and Avignon. From 600 to the early eighth century, Neustria, Austrasia, and Burgundy became three distinct, self-conscious parts of the Frankish kingdom, and as they became rivals of one another, Aquitaine, Brittany, Gascony, and Septimania gained some measure of independence. The neutralized part of the kingdom centered in Paris served intermittently as the capital of the kings Clothar II and Dagobert, each of whom briefly reigned over all Frankish kingdoms.

The wave of Frankish royal and aristocratic prosperity that accompanied the first flush of Clovis's victories did not abate during the sixth century. The increased control of the Frankish kings over the south and east, their occasionally successful intervention in the affairs of Italy and the Iberian peninsula, and their ruthless searches for war booty increased the wealth of Clovis's successors and their followers. The Frankish kings of the sixth century were ambitious, cruel, and rapacious, however, and surviving fiscal institutions and commerce in Gaul, as well as imperial lands and those territories of neighboring peoples, all paid the enormous price for that rapacity.

The redistribution of provincial wealth throughout the sixth century and the continuity of Mediterranean trade made Clovis's successors powerful and wealthy men. Gold coins struck in the Roman imperial fashion bore Frankish kings' likenesses and names. Royal documents, of which a few survive, and the collections of sample documents for official business reveal in their use of the royal titles an ambitious monarchy modeling itself upon both war leadership and Byzantine and Visigothic ceremonial. The letters of the Gallic clergy addressed homiletic descriptions of ideal Christian kingship to the sixth-century Frankish kings, and there is evidence that several of these rulers conceived a high place for themselves among the Christian peoples of whose existence they were aware.

No descriptive evidence, however, can rival the *History of the Franks*, composed by Gregory, bishop of Tours, between 573 and his death in 594. Of Gallo-Roman lineage, a member of the family that had earlier produced bishops of Tours, Langres, and Lyons, Gregory lived between the Gallo-Roman and Frankish worlds, the city of Tours being a natural crossroads between northern and southern Gaul as well as the site of the monastery of St. Martin, founder of Gallic monasticism and the patron of Clovis. Gregory wrote for his contemporaries, Clovis's grandchildren and their families, and his *History* is a moral lesson in edification as well as an account of Frankish history. Yet there is much more to Gregory's work than edification and prophecy. Lacking the classical Latin prose style, the rhetorical obligations, and the epistemological forms of classical Roman historiography, Gregory was able to draw vivid portraits from the life around him, portraits that were enhanced by his own imagination in the creation of dramatic scenes and gestures, the addition of dialogue, and the limited directness of his own Latin literary skills. Gregory shows the reader both groups of people, Franks and Gallo-Romans, in their daily lives and arguments as well as in political affairs. His portraits of the successors of Clovis are both fulsomely praising and savagely condemning. For few periods of early European history do we possess a work as informative and illustrative of the varieties of contemporary life as the *History of the Franks*. It is from such literary works as Gregory's *History* and the seventh-century *Book of Chronicles* of Fredegar, Marculf's seventh-century collection of sample official documents, and the few surviving Merovingian royal charters that it is possible for us to reconstruct some aspects of Frankish life in the sixth and seventh centuries. Sixth-century Gaul, like the rest of the Western world of that time, was primarily agricultural, the vast *latifundia* of the late empire adjoining the small villages of independent farmers, the *vici*. Rural farming settlements, worked by both slaves and free peasants, constituted during these centuries the agrarian profile that remained characteristic of western Europe for a thousand years. Different regions in Gaul formed different agricultural techniques and different types of agricultural settlements. The latter ranged from loosely scattered farmsteads to clustered houses in a village, but most had inalienable fields surrounding the *mansus,* or farm building proper, a term that later came to designate the buildings and lands necessary to support a family. *Mansus,* with its cognate terms, represented, in short, the small farm. This institution, strengthened by the Frankish interest in private ownership of land, became the agricultural module of Frankish society. The great estates, *villae,* either survived on a reduced scale or were administratively broken up so that groups of farmers might work parts of them in return for contributing labor and produce to the owner. Agricultural land was not only the primary income-producing source for most of the Franks, it was also virtually the only reward that kings and lords possessed with which to pay their followers. Hence, farming and farmlands, whether centered in small households or great monastic or aristocratic villas, whether providing the income of a priest who served a remote church or a soldier in the royal service, constituted the physical surroundings of Frankish daily life, and it is as a society of farmhouses and hunting lodges, villages and great estates, small churches and provincialized, shrunken cities that we may visualize the physical character of Frankish life.

By the end of the reign of Dagobert (639), the frontier of Frankish expansion had begun to close up. Not only were there fewer available new territories to conquer, but much of the enormous royal wealth of the fifth and sixth centuries had been given out by the kings even faster than their rapacious acquisition of new lands and incomes. The increasingly regionalized aristocracy settled on their large estates enjoyed their patronage of whole regions and their opportunities to expand their wealth by marriage and by participating in the shifting rivalries around the Frankish thrones and serving as functionaries to different kings. These men—*nobiles*—were not an aristocracy in the later sense of a legally privileged caste designated by blood, but rather privileged landholders who had experienced several generations of royal generosity, received *immunities*—that is, privileged status in the face of royal instruments of government—and risen to positions of regional prominence in lands that had witnessed and contributed to their family prosperity for many years. Although their status lacked regularity and is difficult to define for all parts of the Frankish kingdoms, the seventh-century landholding warlords began to eclipse the seventh-century impoverished kings in power.

By the reign of Dagobert, each of the kingdoms maintained separate royal institutions inside its boundaries. Dagobert appointed high officials—*mayors*—of the royal palace in each kingdom, and these mayors gradually came to control more and more of the royal activity in each kingdom. Understandably, the power of the weaker kings of the late seventh century diminished before the wealth, power, and political dependencies of the mayors. From the death of Dagobert in 639 until 677, Dagobert's original kingdom, Neustria, remained predominant over Burgundy and Austrasia. Under the mayorship of the mighty Ebroin (657–683), the palace of Neustria overcame powerful rivals in Burgundy and Austrasia. The problems raised by the minority of several of Dagobert's successors, the opportunities for others to dominate royal activity, the lack of royal success in battles against enemies, and the rising fortunes of aristocrats—particularly the mayors of the palace, who dispensed royal largesse in their own as well as the king's name—all contributed, not necessarily to the end of the Merovingian monarchy, but to a prolonged period of monarchical weakness—both institutional and personal—a period that coincided with a new flush of prosperity among several of the most powerful regional aristocratic families.

The rise of Ebroin is an early example of this new aristocratic power, but the most successful story takes place not in Ebroin's Neustria but in Austrasia, where by the seventh century the office of mayor of the palace had come into the family of the Arnulfings. The immense wealth and prestige of this line passed on to Pepin II of Herstal, who, after the death of Ebroin, asserted his military supremacy over Neustria at the Battle of Tertry in 687, installed yet another weak Merovingian king, Theoderic III, as the single ruler of the three kingdoms, and established himself mayor of the palace. The Frankish kingdom of Theoderic III and his successors had lost much since the reign of Dagobert. Gascony, Aquitaine, Provence, Frisia, and other territories had slipped from the kings' direct rule, and the trans-Rhenish population of German tribes was growing more and more restive. Moreover, the problem of establishing royal and mayoral power within the diminished kingdom occupied much of Pepin's time and energies during the first years of his term as mayor. When Pepin died in 714, he left only an illegitimate son, Charles, to succeed him, and the possibility of renewed particularism reappeared. Neustria, Aquitaine, and the Saxons all threatened the kingdom once again, and only a remarkable series of victories between 716 and 719 gave Charles control over Neustria and Austrasia. But during this time, much of the south had slipped from royal and mayoral control, and the Islamic incursion into the northern parts of the Iberian Peninsula had further disordered the political life of Aquitaine. Charles's expeditions against the Duke of Aquitaine were interrupted by the first great Islamic incursion into Gaul, which Charles encountered with a hastily assembled northern army and defeated at the Battle of Poitiers in 733. In the following years Charles, now called Charles the Hammer, or Charles Martel, enforced his own political control in the south. During his reign as mayor of the palace (719–741), Charles Martel reasserted his personal ascendancy over the kingdom of the Franks even more successfully than his father had. His powerful army, which included a much higher proportion of cavalry than had formerly been customary, was successful everywhere, and his destruction of political opposition demonstrates that he knew how to use it. To reward his successful and loyal followers, Charles presented them with gifts of land and money, but in order to do this he began a systematic depletion of the wealth and lands of the Frankish Church. Upon his death in 741, Charles left his wealth, dependents, and power to his two sons, Carolman and Pepin III, thereby assuring the continuity of the power of the mayors of the palace and continuing the transformation of the Frankish kingdom in Gaul.

9

THE NEW MEDITERRANEAN WORLD:
The Rise of Islam

THE IMPERIAL AFRICAN PROVINCES

Justinian's destruction of the Vandal kingdom of Africa in 533 restored both prestige and the burdens of imperial government to one of the empire's oldest provinces. Once again, African grain fleets sailed to the empire's capital—now at Constantinople. Once again, imperial military and civil governors ruled a province whose wealth was in the hands of Roman aristocrats. The spiritual life of the province, which had been reduced considerably as a result of the ferocity of Vandal heterodoxy, was renewed in the great North African cities, and contact resumed with the Church in Italy as well as the east. During the century 533–633, Carthage was probably the most secure and peaceful city in the empire, and the Emperor Heraclius, during the crisis of 618–624, seriously considered moving the imperial capital there. Once back in imperial hands, the African provinces began again to pump wealth and vigor into the changed empire.

But the reimposition of imperial rule also meant the reimposition of imperially dictated religious orthodoxy. The varieties of African, Egyptian, and Syrian religious beliefs had troubled the empire from the fourth century on, and the pressures of imperial statements concerning dogma, the power of the patriarchs of Alexandria, and the furious religious energies of the Roman provincials created a climate of religious tension. The power of dissident groups had grown during the life of the Arian Vandal kingdom, whose rulers had tolerated varieties of heresy in order to weaken the resistance of orthodox churchmen to their rule. The problem of Monophysitism in Egypt and Syria marked a sharp division between the native Monophysite Christians and their imperial, orthodox Christian rulers. Besides the perpetuation of religious and political opposition, the vast difficulties involved in restoring the heirs of provincials dispossessed by the Vandals created social and legal conflicts in provincial Africa, and these had a distinctly unsettling effect. The difficulties of Byzantine rule in Africa are indicated by the creation of a new post of master of soldiers in the province. The men who held this office gradually began to assimilate all civil and military power in their own hands, and, ultimately, the master of soldiers became another Byzantine frontier governor, like the exarch of Ravenna—another sign that provinces, even restored provinces, were also troubled frontiers.

Imperial Africa soon found that it had the problems of a frontier. The problem of maintaining control over the Roman army, a problem complicated by a series of inept Roman commanders, was a major factor in a renewed series of attacks by the desert peoples on Roman territory. Difficulties with the small Roman army in Africa would have been sufficiently troublesome in any period, but the nature of the army's service in Africa made such disaffection critical. Traditionally the Roman armies in Africa had never needed to worry about the desert nomads, and, consequently, the military force had been small and strictly defensive. Since the desert nomads were unable to mass the numbers sufficient for a major assault on the civilized centers, and since their mobility was limited, minimal defenses guarded the southern border of the empire. From the third century A.D. on, however, a new element entered the world of the desert nomads—the one-humped Arabian camel. Not until the fourth century did the camel—long restricted to Egypt—became domesticated in North Africa. It gave the desert nomads a prodigious mobility and a force that substantially threatened any defense the Romans might put up. Moors, disaffected provincials, and rebellious soldiers made imperial Africa a potentially unstable province and a vulnerable frontier, attractive to outside invaders and potentially sympathetic to other kinds of rule that might relieve the weight of imperial administration and offer a broader religious tolerance than imperial orthodoxy permitted.

THE ARAB WORLD AND THE REVELATIONS OF MOHAMMED

Far to the south of provincial Roman Africa there lived other peoples, who possessed differing levels of culture and civilization. Among these were the old Semitic inhabitants of the Arabian peninsula, desert nomads and intermittent town dwellers had long played a role in Near Eastern history. The South Arabian kingdom of Saba, which flourished around 1000 B.C., was the Sheba of the Old Testament. Its wealth drew trade to it from the east and influenced Ethiopia to the west and Persia to the north. Saba declined, however, during the centuries of the rise of the Roman Empire, and most of Arabia came to be ruled by the nomadic tribesmen of the desert. Unlike the Arabs of the south, the northern Arabs had been drawn intermittently into the orbits of Rome and Persia, and on occasion prosperous mercantile and mercenary Arab kingdoms appeared on the Roman frontier. Such, for example, were the short-lived kingdoms of Nabatea and Palmyra in the third century A.D. The declining prosperity of South Arabia and the instability of frontier kingdoms during the struggles between Rome and Persia, however, resulted in what some historians called a rebedouinization of the Arab peoples between the fourth and the sixth centuries. The nomadic tribe, under its elected *shaikh,* became the module of Arabic society, as it had often been in the past. New kingdoms were assembled periodically during the sixth century, usually for the purposes of mercenary defense of the Roman and Persian frontiers. Thus, the kingdoms of the Ghassanids and the Lakhmids, serving Rome and Persia respectively, continued on a limited basis to transmit cultural elements from these two great empires down into the more loosely organized, fiercely independent nomadic tribes that constituted the majority of Arabs.

In addition to the precarious existence of the Ghassanid and Lakhmid kingdoms in the north of Arabia, the sixth century also witnessed profound economic changes in the Arabian peninsula. The trade routes of Persia, made dangerous by its continuing wars with Rome, and the trade routes of Egypt, made difficult because of religious and political unrest and nomad attacks, declined in importance. The third major route of southern trade from the Mediterranean, one that ran down the western edge of Arabia to the Yemen, increased in importance, and the central towns of western Arabia, Medina and Mecca, grew in wealth and prominence, attracting even desert tribes to settle in them and maintaining close contacts with the desert peoples. The tribes that moved to these cities brought their desert independence with them, and their sudden increase of wealth and the indisposition toward authority created a population in the towns that became economically productive, highly organized for commercial purposes, but also uncontrolled in its civil life.

The commercial and tribal life of the Arabian cities and the nomadic tribal independence of the desert people, the transmission of ideas and beliefs down caravan routes and through mercenary kingdoms, and the enormous religious fertility of Mesopotamia and Syria all exerted influences on the emerging Arabian trading cities and sharpened the growing gulf between the city dwellers and the Bedouins of the desert. In the early years of the seventh century, a middle-aged Meccan entrepreneur, Mohammed, began to receive visions and commands from Heaven. In the years after 610, following the instructions he received, he began to write down his "recitations," his *Qur'an,* and proclaimed that his inspiration was the single god Allah and that the substance of his revelations was a body of instructions concerning the proper life—indeed, the only acceptable life—for a subject of Allah to live. Born around 570, Mohammed was orphaned at the age of six and brought up in modest but not impoverished circumstances by his grandfather and uncle. As a young man Mohammed was a successful caravan manager, and later married a wealthy widow, Khadija. During the first forty years of his life, Mohammed witnessed the growing prosperity of Mecca, the weakening of traditional ethical patterns in the changing life of the city tribes, and the growing contrast between the settled life of the towns and the nomadic life of the Bedouins.

The revelations set down in the *Qur'an* declared Allah the only God, to whom man must subject himself and worship; the duty of man was to follow the ethical instructions of God. Mohammed was a prophet, the last prophet, to whom the final revelations of Allah had been given. For Allah had spoken before. To the Jews and to the Christians He had sent prophets—Abraham, Moses, and Jesus—but these had borne only a partial revelation, and their followers had perverted or misunderstood it. To Mohammed, *Islam,* "submission to the will of Allah," was the ultimate revelation. Like Moslems, Jews and Christians were to be considered People of the Book, but only Moslems were the true followers and worshipers of Allah. The injunctions contained in the *Qur'an* attacked the ills of contemporary Arabic society and attempted to forge all believers into an *'Umma,* an expanded conception of the Arabic tribe, to which all the faithful would belong regardless of former ties and allegiances.

At first Mohammed gathered about him a few followers from his family and tribe, but subsequently he encountered opposition from the ruling patriciate of Mecca. Possibly fearful of the decline of Mecca as a pagan religious center, and certainly disapproving of Mohammed's relatively low social origins, the Meccan rulers at first remained indifferent to the new faith, but then became actively hostile to it. In 622 Mohammed and his followers had to flee the city. From Mecca they went to Medina, a city to which Mohammed had been invited as a kind of outside judge and arbitrator of the city's internal difficulties. It was in Medina that Mohammed was able to give the *'Umma* a practical form and to ally his followers with the desert tribes, and from Medina Mohammed returned to Mecca as a powerful religious leader in 630.

Although it responded to social, cultural, and political needs of the Arabs, Islam was first and foremost a religious revolution, and like other religious revolutions its most enduring effect was the establishment of a new role for religion in the individual lives of its followers. The tribal pagan gods, whether worshiped by Bedouin tribes or in such sanctuaries as the *Ka'ba* in Mecca, either disappeared or were transformed into *djinn*, the spirits of the air. The varieties of religious ritual and custom were obliterated, and in their place stood a unified theological and ethical system whose influence reached out from the individual soul to the entire community of believers. Unlike Christianity, however, Islam offered no complex theological ideas, such as the Trinity or the relation of the two natures of Christ, to detract from the absolute single majesty of Allah. Unlike Judaism, Islam possessed no history of complex theological and eschatological movements, nor was it practiced only at the sufferance of Christian masters in strictly prescribed forms. The intensity and directness of Islamic beliefs, its specific commands from God to man, and its firm rooting in the desert mind gave it a persuasive power that appealed to peoples at all levels of theological and social development, from the ferocious Berbers of Northwest Africa to the subtle theologians and country gentlemen of Persia.

At the core of Islam is the single truth that Allah is God and Mohammed is His Prophet. Radiating from that core is the dramatically simple ethical law of Islam, the *Shari'a*, a code of law and theology at the same time. The demands of that law were, first, the acknowledgment of Allah and of Mohammed's authentic prophetic role. The ritual prayer said five times a day, with the great public prayer at midday on Friday, was the second element. The necessity of observing the holy month of *Ramadan* by fasting from dawn to sunset was a third. The obligation to visit Mecca once in a lifetime, if possible, was the fourth. The obligation of almsgiving was the fifth. These elements are the same for Moslems today as they were in the seventh century, and the moving passage in *The Autobiography of Malcolm X* describing Malcolm's pilgrimage to Mecca is in the direct tradition of the earliest recorded Arabic pilgrimages. Faithful observance of the law gave the Moslem a place in paradise. Throughout the Middle Ages—in fact, to the present day—Islam has been much misunderstood—and maligned—in the West. In particular, the elements of Islamic law that reflect directly the customs of the seventh-century desert tribesmen—especially the predominance of the male, the abstention from pork and alcohol, and the surprisingly fleshly delights of the Moslem paradise, have detracted attention from other, ultimately far more influential, Moslem beliefs. For the Moslem, no priest intervenes between man and God; there is no Islamic liturgy; the visual representation of living things is forbidden; knowledge of the *Qur'an*—even the memorization of the entire text—is praiseworthy; and the *Qur'an* regulates personal and social life.

After reestablishing himself and his followers at Mecca, Mohammed began the long process of converting the city and the desert tribesmen, and both these aims were well underway when the Prophet died in 632. Mohammed had left no instructions for his successor, and many of the tribes that had allied themselves with him considered his death the

The New Mediterranean World: The Rise of Islam 163

severance of their bond with him. Among the delicate problems of Arab diplomacy, the question of the nature of Mohammed's successor became extremely important. He could not be a Prophet because that title always designated Mohammed alone, nor could he be a *shaikh,* which was a title of tribal particularism. The problem was solved by declaring one of Mohammed's followers, Abu Bakr, "representative," or "deputy," of Mohammed; his title was *khalifa,* caliph. Technically, the *khalifa* was a protector of the faith, and the successors of Mohammed faced the task of spreading Islam throughout Arabia and then throughout the world.

MOHAMMED'S SUCCESSORS AND THE SPREAD OF ISLAM TO 750

The successors of Mohammed constituted one of the most talented and energetic groups of rulers the Mediterranean world had ever seen. Trained in the most highly developed military tactics, capable of drawing upon the fanatic loyalty of the desert tribes and the resources of the town dwellers, and willing to take infinite pains in negotiating with cities under Arab attack, Abu Bakr (632–634) and his colleagues launched Islam on a program of territorial expansion that did not stop until it reached, in the west, the plains of central France, and, in the east, the borders of China. Cadres of Moslem officers led the still-pagan Bedouin armies out of the Arabian peninsula into the old territories of the Byzantine and Persian Empires. The exhausted border provinces and the disaffected provincials of Africa and Syria fell quickly to Moslem armies: Jerusalem in 638, Egypt in 642, and the once great Sasanid Empire of Persia in 643. Not only the caliphs, but their remarkable generals soon turned Arab expansion into a systematic assault upon the old territories of Rome and Persia. Under Abu Bakr's successor, Umar (634–644), the greatest thrust of Arabic conquests began, and under Umar's successor, Uthman (644–656), a dynasty of caliphs was founded, the Ummayad, which directed the expansion of Islam until its fall in 750.

In 647 the military governor of Arabic Syria, Moawiya, began the regular ravaging of Asia Minor and at the same time inaugurated the creation of an Arab fleet so that Byzantium might be assaulted by sea as well as by land. In 636 a powerful Byzantine army had been routed at the Battle of Yarmuk, and by 678 the first major Islamic assault struck Constantinople. The defense of the city, led by Emperor Constantine IV, managed to repel the attackers, but the Arabs struck again, again unsuccessfully, in 718. The defense of Constantinople, far more than other Christian victories over the Arabs in the west, guaranteed the survival of Christian Europe. As the history of the thirteenth through the seventeenth centuries would show, the real gateway to Europe was its eastern frontier. And in the crucial years between 678 and 718, Constantinople withstood the Arab advance and thereby prevented further Arab expansion into western Europe. The boundary between the Byzantine Empire and the caliphate in Damascus, became localized in southern Asia Minor, and a centuries-long frontier culture developed between the Greek and Moslem parts of the east.

After the early eighth century, the native populations of the newly conquered territories, particularly Persia, began to exert the force of their own culture upon their masters. Damascus, the new capital of the Arab empire, quickly fell under the influence of Byzantine civilization. Greek learning, Syrian artists, and the energetic commercial resources of Egypt, North Africa, Palestine, and Syria supported the new rulers. The native populations were encouraged to continue their normal life, paying taxes, including a new tax that all non-Moslems now had to pay, and being defended from all enemies by the Arabs. For the years of the Ummayad caliphate were specifically the years of Arabic supremacy.

For the first century of the Arab empire, however, Arab-led armies and Arab caliphs, viceroys, and generals removed the legacy of Mohammed from the desert and imposed their own elitist supremacy on a conquered world. Arab warriors speaking Arabic lived in fort-cities away from the old urban centers of Near Eastern life. Conversions to Islam were not encouraged, and the still-recent memories of life among the tribes of the desert, with its culture, poetry, and intense loyalty to fellow tribesmen, preserved the culture of the native Arabs in a new and confusing world. One consequence of this first phase of Arab expansion was the continuity of antique forms of society and culture. As the most recent historian of this period has observed, Arabic isolation and elitism required the continued functioning of social and economic life. In Byzantium and the west, drastic changes had been necessary, partly because of the reduced resources of these heirs of the Roman world, and partly in response to the Arabic threat. Only under the rule of Islam did the ancient world survive relatively intact. Not only economic and social tolerance, but a broad religious tolerance toward Christians and Jews (and toward heretical as well as orthodox Christians) characterized this phase of Arab expansion.

If the confrontation with Byzantium is the critical element in the history of the Ummayad dynasty and the expansion of Islam, the rapid spread of Islam elsewhere must also be considered. Spreading quickly across North Africa, slowly beginning the process of converting the Berbers, and spreading to the Iranian Plateau and to the borders of India and China, the remarkable success of the Arabs faced them also with a dilemma: how could a people limited in numbers, vastly outnumbered by the populations of the worlds they had conquered, and committed both to Arabic cultural traditions and Arabic ethnic supremacy in the empire survive intact among the pulls of so many other cultures and religions? Would Islam remain an Arab prerogative, or would the Arab rulers eventually have to come to terms with their newly conquered domains?

The New Mediterranean World: The Rise of Islam   165

THE ABBASID DYNASTY AND THE
DIVISIONS OF THE ISLAMIC WORLD

The impetus of Arabic expansion frequently resulted in indiscriminate overreaching by the energetic but undisciplined military leaders. One such leader in Northwest Africa, Tarik, was sounded out by one of several rival factions among the Visigothic and Byzantine aristocracy of Spain on the matter of providing mercenaries for one of the Visigoths' innumerable civil wars. Crossing to Spain, Tarik decided to launch his own unauthorized campaign of conquest, and between 711 and 719 he managed to destroy forever the Visigothic kingdom and to establish an Islamic state in its place. The route by which he crossed has immortalized his name, for Gibraltar means *Gebel-Tarik,* the Hill of Tarik. The rapid Moslem conquest of Spain drove what few Christian rulers were left far to the north, where the tiny kingdom of Asturias and the independent Basques held out for centuries. From Spain, Arab raids were launched into southern Gaul, and only the exhaustion of the Arab drive from North Africa into Spain prevented a major permanent settlement of Arabs in France. In 733 the mayor of the palace of Austrasia, Charles Martel, defeated a weak Arab raiding force near Poitiers. Although the Battle of Poitiers has long occupied a prominent place in western histories, its role was far greater in increasing Charles Martel's personal prestige and power than in preventing the Arabs from conquering France. In the latter respect, the defense of Constantinople in 678 and 718 was far more important for Christian Europe. Moreover, Arab raiders continued to dominate southern France, penetrating as far as the Swiss Alps and the coastal and inland river towns until well into the tenth century.

The conquest of Spain is more a dramatic example of Arabic expansion than a strategic one. Spain was far from Damascus, separated not only by the Mediterranean Sea, but by the deserts of North Africa. Although early Arabic supremacy influenced the shaping of Islamic Spain, *Al-Andalus* to the Arabs, Spain remained a partially independent Arabic state, very different from the scattered territories of North Africa, the home of a flourishing agricultural and commercial civilization.

In the east, the stalemate between the Arab caliphate of Damascus and the Byzantine Empire brought great pressure to bear on the Ummayads. Heterodox sects within Islam, the growing numbers of non-Arab Moslems and their demands for recognition, and the instability of the Arab elite all contributed to this unrest. In 750 a revolt took place in Iran against the Ummayad caliph, and within the next few years a new dynasty, the Abassids, assumed the rulership of the Islamic empire. The Abassids, depending heavily upon the non-Arab Moslems and drawn more and more into the orbit of old Persian culture, moved the seat of their power further east, founding the city of Baghdad in 762 and abandoning the frontier-capital of Damascus, with its memories of Byzantine influence and Ummayad rule. At Baghdad, the Islamic world

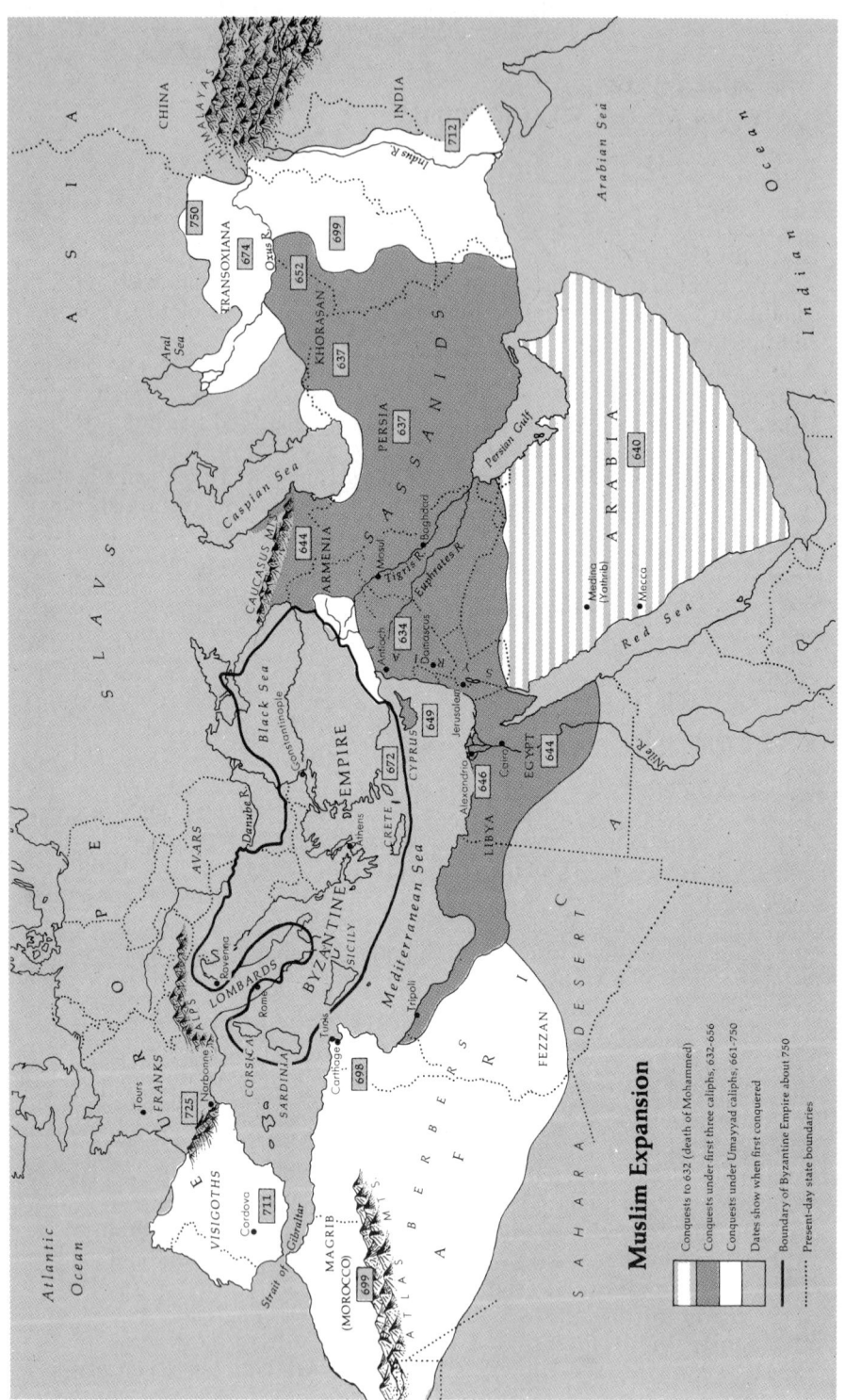

Muslim Expansion

established a new base of power in the old Sasanid Kingdom of Persia. There, the rich native Persian culture lent to Islam its centuries-old intellectual and literary traditions and provided a new non-Arab elite, the Persian country gentlemen, as an administrative and ruling class. The traditions of pre-Islamic Arabia had contributed much of the original impetus to Arab expansion, and Arabic language and culture were adopted by many of the peoples conquered by the forces of Islam. But Arabic culture and the Arabic language survived only as a veneer after the eighth century, whereas native traditions reasserted themselves and the institutions of the ancient world kept operating.

The eastward shift of Moslem power had immense consequences for the old unity of the Mediterranean world. The reduced forces of Byzantium maintained defensive frontiers in Asia Minor and in Thrace and the Balkans; Germanic Europe retained little from its Roman heritage in the way of culture, and little but diminished towns and atrophied Roman institutions from imperial governance. Only in the Islamic world did an ancient culture—that of Persia—rise up again and capture its captors. As a consequence, the orientation of Islam turned to the east, away from the Mediterranean. Islamic states in North Africa became independent, and the last Ummayad caliph found a home in faraway Spain. The attraction of the Persian east, combined with the overreaching Islamic expansion throughout the Mediterranean world, weakened the power of the caliph in the west and drew Islamic economic and cultural concentration to Persia and the east. As a consequence of the eastward drift of Islam, pressure upon Byzantium and upon Christian Europe relaxed, and the threat of their absorption by Islam passed. In the deserted Mediterranean world, local tradition, the Byzantine enclave in the northeast, and the north-turning Frankish kingdom were able to survive and create a new cultural world without the threat of imminent invasion and conquest. But the old unity of the Mediterranean world had disappeared forever.

PART  THREE

THE BOOK AND THE SWORD, 650-950

10

THE WORLD OF BEDE AND BONIFACE, 650-750

BEDE: "THE LIGHT WITHIN THE CHURCH"

The mutual influences of Celtic and Roman Christianity in seventh century England, particularly in Kent and Northumbria, produced a remarkably developed ecclesiastical culture. In the careers of several individuals and institutions—notably Benedict Biscop, Wilfrid of Ripon, and Bede of Jarrow and the schools of Canterbury and Wearmouth–Jarrow—there was shaped and consolidated a system of learning and devotion that influenced European culture intensely for two centuries and created a framework for the achievements of Charlemagne a century later.

The circle of monastic and cathedral schools centered in the small stone churches decorated with Continental motifs produced in Bede and Boniface, as well as in many others, able, educated men who were eager to convey their learning, so different from that of the fourth- and fifth-century learned ecclesiastics of Gaul, to others. In the sixth century, Columba and Columbanus had carried Irish Christianity and learning to England and the Continent. In the eighth and ninth centuries a stream of English missionaries carried the Romano-Irish learning and devotion from England to the Continent. The results of that mission included the thorough reform of the Frankish church, new communications between Rome and Gaul on the one hand, and new conversions for Rome in Germany, on the other, and the regeneration of the idea of a universal Christian society that embraced all of the particularistic kingdoms and tribal societies in the eighth- and ninth-century West. With the eighth-century English missions to the Continent, a new phase of European history begins.

Benedict Biscop, a Northumbrian noble who traveled widely in the seventh century, founded several monasteries in Northumbria with what Bede later called "the best-established rules of the ancient monasteries which he had learnt on his pilgrimage." Benedict had made at least five trips to Rome, had seen many other monasteries, including Lérins, and had made it a point to acquire copies of the best books known to the inhabitants of the churches and monasteries he visited. Thus, his monasteries at Wearmouth and Jarrow were able, soon after their foundation, to serve as a twin center of ecclesiastical learning that rivaled Canterbury, the center of English Christianity, and to claim equality with the Irish monastic schools. This double Mediterranean tradition—represented by Theodore and Hadrian at Canterbury, and by Benedict Biscop at Wearmouth-Jarrow—thus infused new life into older English Christianity and into Irish learning as well. In addition to these lines of influence, one other should be mentioned. Accompanying Benedict Biscop on one of his prilgrimages to Rome was Wilfrid, a Northumbrian youth of aristocratic lineage who also later returned to England bearing Continental influences—chiefly, his determination to found monastic settlements using the rule of St. Benedict exclusively, and his desire to transform the humble churches of England into buildings of greater size and beauty, along the lines of basilican architecture he had seen in his travels on the Continent. In his responsibility for bringing the Benedictine rule to England, his church design, and his powerful role in the dispute between Celtic and Roman Christianity at the Synod of Whitby in 664, Wilfrid represents yet a third example of the influences that bound English ecclesiastical life and institutions so much more closely to Rome than was the case with any northern Continental institutions or those of Ireland. This unique English affinity with the churches of the Continent, particularly Rome, became a very important element in Continental history during the eighth and ninth centuries. Then, when English missionaries moved to the Continent to pursue their efforts of conversion, they brought with them not only superior learning and a more regular religious life, but the loyalty to the Roman church and to the pope that shaped the future religious and political development of Europe.

The books, the Roman tradition, and the atmosphere of learning that flourished in Wearmouth–Jarrow in the late seventh century shaped the mind of the young monk Bede and influenced his interests as he ascended in orders and became the chief teacher at Jarrow. It also influenced his own body of brilliant scholarship and the shape he gave to the Christian legacy of antique classical culture. Yet Bede's own genuine intellectual distinction must not overshadow what for him was the chief function of his life as a monk, the *opus Dei,* the round of liturgical services, daily readings, and manual labor that constituted the subtle and regular rhythm of the Benedictine monastic life. "Seven times a day do I praise thee," said the Psalms, and the seven ritual prayers of the monastic day came to acquire the shape that Benedict had given them. Adding to these seven hours (Matins/Lauds, Prime, Terce, Sext, Nones, Vespers, and Compline) the evening service (Nocturns/Matins), Benedictine monasticism shaped a daily revolution of prayers that still constitutes the monastic office and, with reading and labor, constituted the essential life of a monk, spreading in influence as the Benedictine rule itself spread throughout Europe between the seventh and the twelfth centuries. Within this daily round, other works were produced, as it were, in the interstices between scheduled activities. Among these works were Bede's scholarly labors. Before describing them, it may be well to consider the character of learning around the year 700, just as Bede had grown into manhood.

By Bede's day, Christian literature, particularly Scripture, had worked its way firmly into the earliest reading courses, although the classics still taught the advanced students. Learning itself, however, no longer had as its object the formation of an elite, mandarin governing class that would be, at least in its devotion to letters and class interests, homogeneous throughout the empire. All learning, from barest literacy to the ornate, classical, and occasionally willfully obscure, aimed at a better understanding of the *sacra pagina,* Scripture. The liberal arts, or as many of them as were likely to be taught in a given school or monastery, were subordinated, or redirected, to the understanding of Scripture and other sacred texts. Logic, arithmetic, music, and rhetoric became tools for understanding Scripture better and learning to expound that understanding better. History, geography, and other disciplines were also tools designed to improve the understanding of Scripture. The need for the appropriate literary skills to study Scripture thus became not only a social and cultural requirement among the clergy, but a sacred duty for those who were able to pursue it. Under the new form of learning, classical literature achieved an increasingly secure niche, although it lost its primacy.

What were the *sacra pagina?* Why did an understanding of Scripture require the preservation of an originally pagan and spiritually risky body of letters? The Old Testament, written originally in Hebrew and Aramaic, the New Testament, written originally in Greek, and the apocryphal books, written in all three languages, rarely existed together in one volume before the seventh century. The *Septuagint,* a first-century B.C. Greek translation of the Old Testament, found favor among the Jewish communities of the Diaspora, but not at Jerusalem. Throughout the first four centuries of the Christian era, individual books were translated into Latin by different scholars, the whole work, although it probably did not exist in single complete copies, was called the Old Latin Bible, and its texts survived through the following centuries, although St. Jerome's new translation from the Greek and Hebrew, made in the early fifth century, ultimately became the orthodox Christian text. The Vulgate, as St. Jerome's version was called, included the books that the Council of Carthage of 397 had defined as canonical—that is, official divinely inspired sacred texts. Jerome's work, however, was done in several stages over twenty-three years and involved several revisions of individual books of the Bible. With the Old Latin Bible, Jerome's Vulgate, and earlier stages of Jerome's work available, the "Bible" of the fifth, sixth, seventh, and eighth centuries was really a collection of different translations consisting frequently of quite different versions of the same text. Moreover, some parts of the Bible were often copied separately into individual volumes. The Gospels, the Psalter (the Book of Psalms), the varied liturgical materials associated with these, and individual books of the Bible with commentaries by churchmen also existed in single manuscripts. Thus, it should be no surprise that the oldest known surviving copy of the whole Latin Bible, the famous *Codex Amiatinus,* now in Florence, was copied at Wearmouth under the direction of Abbot Ceolfrith around the year 700. The production of a whole Latin Bible was a prodigious and unusual undertaking, even in the seventh century, and in the characteristic pictures of the evangelists that often accompanied the Gospels, the reader can still see the respect for the act of writing that flourished during this period and after and can guess from the portraits of Matthew, Mark, Luke, and John what a seventh- or eighth-century English or Continental scribe might have looked like. From the seventh century on, there also appear the increasingly ornate Gospel books, such as the *Lindisfarne Gospels,* that were produced in monasteries and reflect, in the changing styles of illumination and decoration, changing visual imaginations and new concepts of the relation between the sacred script and the visual setting in which it should be produced.

    The individual skills, whether those of patron, copyist or illuminator, required to produce such works as the *Codex Amiatinus* and the *Lindisfarne Gospels* presuppose a reasonably sufficient number of capable personnel, a sufficient interest in the careful production of books, and a demand for the books. They also presuppose a quality of learning, and enough time for teachers to teach and students to produce work. Several of Bede's early works, dealing with Latin meters and figures of speech, indicate some of the intermediate stages of literary education in the monastic schools. But literary skills were not the only ones required, either for the monastic life or for competent biblical scholarship. The monastery also required some knowledge of mathematics, which was used to meet the practical need for reasonably accurate means of telling the hours of prayer, particularly at night, to explain the number symbolism of Scripture, and to compute the dates of important liturgical feasts that are called movable because they depend upon a lunar rather than a solar reckoning. The Julian calendar, a solar calendar, was of no use in determining the proper reckoning of such movable feasts as Easter, and one of the most serious problems facing thinkers from the fifth through the eighth centuries was the proliferation of new means of computing the lunar calendar.

The rich materials of hagiography, the writing of the lives of saints, also provided a need and an occasion for scholarship. Martyrs, holy men, and monks were the cultural heroes of the Christian world, and their feasts, sacred places, relics, and recorded deeds played immensely important roles in the life of Europe. The saints were believed to be actually present in their shrines and relics, and this trait of the firm belief in the possible intervention of the supernatural survived from the world of late antiquity into the early European world. The acquisition of relics was an occasion for liturgical and civic ritual splendor; dwelling in the "midst of a legion of saints," as one sermon says, thus helped peoples who were no longer dwelling in the midst of the Roman military legions. Thus, the writing of saints' lives, descriptions of their miracles, and the honor paid to their churches constituted a large cult, out of which came not only a new kind of literature but a new kind of biography. In the following centuries, this literature influenced narrative prose. Bede wrote a series of the *Lives of the Abbots* of his own monastery, and contributed to yet another manifestation of literary culture in the early eighth century.

Bede's greatest work was his *Ecclesiastical History of the English People,* completed in 731. In this work, which shows traces of the influence of Gregory of Tours's *History of the Franks,* written a century and a half earlier, Bede shaped a consciously unified history of Anglo-Saxon England within the framework of the story of England's conversion to Christianity. Scornful toward the Celtic Christians, who made no attempts to convert the newcomers, Bede's praise of Gregory I is boundless. The story of early martyrs, the mission of St. Augustine to Canterbury, and in particular the portrayal of Oswald of Northumbria as a paradigm of the ideal Christian king—all included in a historical work based upon Bede's study and inclusion of documents, his questions of others, and his careful annotation of his own uncertainties—make Bede's *History* not only one of the highest points of early European literary and intellectual culture, but one of the greatest of all histories.

At Bede's death in 735, he was still working on the biblical commentaries that had occupied much of his life. The level of education and ecclesiastical culture achieved by Bede supremely and by other representatives of monastic learning elsewhere in England by the first half of the eighth century—Hexham, Ripon, Canterbury, and the growing school at York—are reflected in the epithet applied to Bede by St. Boniface, one of the greatest of the bearers of this English cultural and ecclesiastical tradition to the Continent later in the century; *candela ecclesiae,* "the light within the church."

THE ENGLISH CONTINENTAL MISSION AND
ST. BONIFACE, *EXUL GERMANICUS*

The missions of the eighth century were new only in terms of the kind of men who conducted them and their pronounced and enduring loyalty to Rome. English and Irish pilgrims had traveled freely on pilgrimages throughout the seventh century; Benedict Biscop traveled to Rome five times, Wilfrid of Ripon made the same trip several times, and Bede was occasionally informed by pilgrims returning from Rome via the Continent. The customary route for such pilgrimages began at the port of Quentovic (near modern Boulogne) and continued overland to Lyons, then down the Rhone valley to the Mediterranean, and then overland to Italy. To circumvent the Frankish kingdom, as this route did not do, Columbanus and his disciples had gone north and then up the Rhine into what is now Switzerland, where they founded the monasteries of Luxeuil, St. Gall, and Reichenau. One English missionary, Wilfrid, had gone directly to Frisia, much to the north of Quentovic, and in 690 another English mission led by Willibrord also went into pagan Frisia. In 692 and 695 Willibrord made trips to Rome, on the last of which he received consecration as an archbishop and the name of Clement. In 718 a monk from Wessex, Winfrid, also undertook the task of converting the pagans of Frisia, and in 719 he also went to Rome to receive a missionary commission, receiving at the same time the name of Boniface, by which he has since become best known. Between 719 and 722, Boniface worked in Frisia, Bavaria, and Saxony. In 722 he went once more to Rome, where he was consecrated bishop, placed directly under the pope, and sent back into the lands of pagans. From 723 on, Boniface acted as missionary bishop (after 739 as archbishop), and upon papal recommendation, he received the protection of Charles Martel. Boniface's next ten years, beginning in 723, were spent on the fringes of Frankish territory in the work of conversion, which was highlighted in 723 by his destruction of the sacred oak tree of the pagans at Geismar. During these years, however, Boniface's independence and the hostility of the Frankish bishops often blocked his attempts to organize programs of ecclesiastical reform. Charles Martel's lack of interest in the Anglo-Saxon conversion project deprived Boniface of the aid necessary to strengthen his position.

Under Charles Martel's sons, particularly Carloman, contact was renewed between the rulers of the Franks and the Anglo-Saxon missionaries. At the first reform councils held in 743 and 744, the first influences of English reform principles were felt by the Frankish church. Boniface went on to found new bishoprics, to involve Carloman and

Pepin III in regulating the life of the clergy, and to guarantee the authority behind these reforms by having them issued by the new rulers of the Franks. By 740, Boniface had become the most prominent churchman among the Franks and had laid the foundations for Frankish ecclesiastical expansion to the east. His monastery at Fulda was the focal point of this extension. Focusing in his last years upon his Frisian mission once more, Boniface was killed by pagan Frisians in 753. Later he was revered as the apostle to the Germans, the *Exul Germanicus*. Boniface was one of the last and one of the greatest of the islanders who brought back to the continent a sense of ecclesiastical order and secular religious responsibility that contributed so much to the shaping of the kingdom of the Franks under Pepin III and Charlemagne.

ECCLESIASTICAL REFORM AND THE NEW RULERS OF THE FRANKS

The success or failure of Willibrord and Boniface often depended on whether the house of Charles Martel and Pepin of Herstal gave or withheld its support. Political and ecclesiastical reasons caused this support to fluctuate between 690 and 750, but at particularly important moments, the new Frankish rulers derived great benefits from the reformers' presence. Carloman's support of Boniface in the early 740s precipitated a continuing movement of Frankish ecclesiastical reform, and Boniface's later reputation for sanctity and his martyrdom gave him a prestige that became extremely useful to the ruling house of Pepin III. For at midcentury, the house of the Arnulfings engineered a momentous change in its status. The mayors of the palace made themselves the kings of the Franks, and under their kingship the character of Frankish monarchy and the Frankish conception of the kingdom changed considerably. The association between the new Frankish rulers and the English missionaries —brief as it had been, and intermittent as well—contributed several momentous elements to that new conception of kingship. Not only the power, wealth, and daring of Pepin, then, but the concept of Christian kingship delineated in Bede's *Ecclesiastical History of the English People* and the mastering idea of ecclesiastical homogeneity and regularity that was one of the consequences of the close English association with the Church of Rome—all these together shaped the theories, institutions, and rationales of governance and the new concepts of legitimate political authority that the house of Pepin brought to the rulership of a barbarian Christian people. The fecundity of these influences inspired in Frankish kingship from 750 to 900 an administrative and ideological precocity unknown to any other barbarian kingdom, and the political skill of a series of rulers from Pepin III to Charles the Bald in the ninth century gave precocious shape and material reality to many of those theories. In a century and a half, the new Christian kingship of the

Frankish rulers transformed forever both the old Roman idea of power and the barbarian practice of kingship.

The letters of the Gallo-Roman bishops to Clovis, the traits of good and bad kings outlined, and sometimes stated explicitly by Gregory of Tours in his *History of the Franks,* and the letters of Pope Gregory I all suggest many different kinds of influences—to which others can certainly be added—that shaped not only the conversion of peoples to Christianity, but the moral and political expectations of Christian societies as these were described in letters, saints' lives, and histories. Particularly influential was the Old Testament, with its portraits of kings whose power and success depended upon their obedience to God, kings who were anointed ceremonially by prophets and judges, kings whose transgressions frequently entailed swift and terrible retribution.

In 589 Reccared, the Visigothic king of Spain, presented to the ecclesiastical Council of Toledo a concise statement of the principles of Christian kingship as these had developed during the fifth and sixth centuries:

> Although Omnipotent God has given Us charge of the kingdom for the profit of its peoples, and has entrusted the rule of not a few Races to Our Royal Care, however We remember Our mortal condition, and that We cannot merit future beatitude unless We devote Ourselves to the cult of the True Faith and please Our Creator at least with the confession which He deserves. As we are raised in Royal Glory far above our subjects, by so much We should provide for those things which are God's, and increase Our hope and take care of the races God has given Us.

Specific royal liturgies, dynastic patron saints, and the increasingly frequent description of individual reigns in terms of the moral virtues most practiced in them characterize writings about Frankish kingship in the seventh century. The precocious Visigothic monarchy, with its anointing, votive crowns, and elaborately described relations between the king and God in the works of Isidore of Seville, influenced both Frankish and English ideas of monarchy in the seventh and eighth centuries.

In Bede's *Ecclesiastical History of the English People,* the process of christianizing kings and of Christian kings protecting the Christian faith, defending its priests, and spreading Christianity to neighboring peoples became the main rationale for the making of an English people. Thus, from literary sources as well as documents emanating from rulers, Christian thought directed new ideas of community and society toward the identification of the king with the community on ecclesiastical and theological principles. Such criteria, however, were not always to the advantage of the kings. Along with new theories of royal legitimacy and new justifications for new manifestations of royal power, there emerged, sketchily at first and for a long time afterwards, new theories of legitimate resistance to a bad king, and the earliest European writings upon this topic appear in the wake of the changing ideas we have just considered. Kings could indeed, after the sixth century, increasingly sur-round themselves with an aura of Christian legitimacy and use that aura to expand their power and even to continue to act in an unexceptionally traditional manner, but kings' enemies also acquired in this process a new kind of moral criticism, one that could be, and later became, a powerful weapon in the hands of churchmen and laymen alike. When religious and moral criticism was added to traditional Germanic theories of legitimate resistance, the shaping of a new typology of Christian kingship was complete. The descendants of Charles Martel and Pepin III were the first to exploit it fully.

Political theory, however closely connected with political action, cannot by itself explain wholly the changes in the character of political authority over a century of Frankish history. We have already seen some of these changes: the murderous domestic rivalry among Clovis's successors; the institution of mayors of the palace; continual depletion of royal wealth and hence the royal ability to bind followers closely; the separatism among formerly attached provinces and across the Rhine in Germany; Charles Martel's confiscation of ecclesiastical properties to reward his own followers. To these may be added a distinct decline in the quality of Frankish higher clergy and a diminishing of the quality of religious life, a diminution that the Frankish Church could ill afford. The weakening of the Frankish Church contributed further to the weakening of the Merovingian kings, who were associated closely with the Church. The increasing number of ecclesiastical gifts made by Pepin III indicates that the mayor of the palace was replacing the Frankish king as the protector of the Church. This relationship, followed within a few years by the new energy and ideas of the English missionaries and their concept of effective kingship based upon protection of the Church and furtherance of the faith constituted one of the firmest bases for Pepin's successful removal of the Merovingian dynasty and its replacement by his own. The support of the Frankish aristocracy, particularly those east Franks closely associated with Pepin's house, constituted another base of Pepin's support.

The ways in which people made and unmade their kings between the eighth and the eighteenth centuries are often far more informative about their true ideas of legitimate authority and governance than are their formal works of political philosophy. The liturgical and other ceremonial aspects of public events, as anthropologists and historians have both come to learn, are highly illuminating, and for the period between the sixth and the ninth centuries particularly, they constitute a rich source of information for changing political ideas. The coronation of Pepin as king of the Franks in 751 and the tonsuring and placing in a monastery of the last Merovingian king, Childeric III, constitute one of the earliest and most important aspects of this process. In 751 Pepin sent two representatives to Rome (the Rome of Wilfrid and Benedict Biscop, of Willibrord and Boniface, as well as the Rome with which the Merovingian Church still maintained tenuous connections), whose mission is described in a somewhat later chronicle:

Burghard, bishop of Worms, and the chaplain Fulrad [of St. Denis] were sent to Pope Zachary to ask him about the kings in France, who at that time had no royal power. Was this right or not? Pope Zachary replied to Pepin that it was better for the man who had power to be called king rather than one who remained without royal power, and, to avoid a disturbance of the right ordering of things, he commanded by apostolic authority that Pepin should become king.

There are many problems with this and similar texts that have exercised the skill and wit (and sometimes the imagination) of scholars for several centuries. Why should Pepin ask the pope about the kingdom of the Franks? What principles governed Pope Zacharias's answer? Did Zacharias have any authority at all to "command" that Pepin be made king? Since the source seems to indicate that Childeric III simply was no longer king, because of his own inability and lack of power, was there some formal process of deposition or not? What seems reasonably clear, however, can be summed up briefly. Pepin sent two high-ranking Frankish churchmen to ask the pope a question whose answer Pepin had already decided upon. This act may well reflect some of that strong connection between the Frankish kings and the papacy that appears to have been shaped by both Frankish churchmen and English missionaries during the first half of the eighth century. The pope, basing his response (which may be considered as a lawyer's advice) upon a concept of the "right order of things," gave the answer Pepin wanted and "commanded" that Pepin be made king. The concept of "right order" is an important one, and it echoes ecclesiastical and not political thought of the fourth through the eighth centuries. The "right order" referred to by Zacharias is the order imposed by God in the world, the order that sets everything in its proper place and gives everything the attributes it requires for that place. Isidore of Seville put the concept bluntly: "The name king comes from reigning; he is no king who does not correct abuses." Thus, according to this view, the name and power of king must not be separated. If they are, then the title alone is an anomaly and does not indicate legitimacy. "Commanded" must be interpreted very carefully, so as not to imply any sort of papal "constitutional" authority among the Franks. Pepin would certainly not have recognized such a claim, and Zacharias probably never did either.

Behind Pepin's publicized solicitude for papal approval, there lie other, equally important ideas. Pepin became king of the Franks in a manner different from earlier Frankish kingmaking ceremonies. A liturgy, constructed from Old Testament, Visigothic, and Anglo-Saxon coronation practices, indicated very strongly the divine approval of Pepin that Zacharias's response had hinted at and even implied. Pepin was, according to a near-contemporary account of the ceremony, "a *pious* king . . . raised to the throne by the *authority* and *order* of Pope Zacharias, . . . by *anointing* with the holy chrism at the hands of the blessed bishops [and] by the *choice* of the Franks." This text blends hitherto unknown elements into a single sweeping justification of the authority by which Pepin became king. Ecclesiastical authority and anointing indicate the new aspect of divine approval, and the Frankish "choice" echoes the older public recognition of a new king.

A divinely approved king, protector of the Church and spreader of the faith, ruled a God-favored people. The prologue to the Salic Law, a Frankish law code revised several times between the sixth and the ninth centuries, reflects just such a conception. The Franks were orthodox, powerful, and wise, favored by God—or so it seemed to them, and so it seemed to others who were influenced by the new Frankish rulers, the Anglo-Saxon missionaries, the popes of the late eighth century, and the land-hungry, east-facing Austrasian nobility. To others, who were less favorably disposed toward the Franks, the Franks and their new rulers soon appeared otherwise—ferocious indeed, but also treacherous, aggressive, presumptuous, and illiterate. For two centuries, the fate of the old Roman west lay largely in the hands of Pepin and his descendants.

11

FROM FRANKISH KINGDOM TO CHRISTIAN EMPIRE

FRANKISH KINGSHIP, THE CHURCH, AND THE INSTITUTIONS OF ROYAL GOVERNANCE UNDER PEPIN AND CHARLEMAGNE, 751–800

The adoption of new forms of royal style did not by itself, of course, either obliterate the traditional roles of the Frankish king or guarantee the Carolingians, as Pepin's and Charlemagne's family came to be called, a particularly easy time of ruling. The political dimension of kingship still posed the same intractable problems: the king still had to wield substantial personal and family power; he had to organize the governance of his kingdom according to recognized and accepted formulas and institutions; he had to acquire wealth and reputation and utilize these with a dignity and liberality that was consistent with traditional ideas of

Frankish kingship; he had to secure or enforce loyalty among his officials because one's loyalty was to an individual man not to an abstract institution or office. Most of all, he had to impose his will more often through force than through persuasion, and, thus, the personal character, ability, and energy of the king counted for much. The first years of Pepin's reign were spent largely in suppressing revolts throughout the kingdom and on its fringes, particularly in Aquitaine and Bavaria.

This dual character of the Carolingian monarchy—ecclesiastical concepts of legitimacy and authority, on the one hand, and practical energy, on the other—cannot easily be divided without distorting the image. Considered purely as practical rulers whose sole aim was to increase their power, the first three generations of Carolingians can appear to have been too brutal, grasping, and ultimately wasteful and inefficient. Considered solely as the exponents of a new spiritual concept of Frankish society, they can appear to have been too insensitive to spiritual matters, to have patronized the Church too heavily, and ultimately to have been the victims of the ecclesiastical authorities they did so much to create. In the following pages we will consider, first, the transformation of the church and the royal office in the hands of Pepin and Charlemagne, and then the circumstances that led to the re-creation of the Roman imperial title and the coronation of Charlemagne as emperor of the Romans in 800. The social and economic experience of the Franks in the late eighth and ninth centuries will be taken up in Chapter 12.

The new and insistent articulation of the Frankish king's ecclesiastical mission makes the ecclesiastical reforms under Pepin and Charlemagne an illuminating first step in considering the character of Carolingian kingship. The divisions of ecclesiastical administration that were created in the last years of imperial rule in the Roman west had virtually disappeared by the late seventh century. Episcopal offices were left vacant for long periods or given to royal relatives and favorites without consideration of personal qualifications or the canonicity of elections to ecclesiastical offices. The ecclesiastical reforms urged by St. Boniface changed the course of the Frankish church in the late eighth century, but the power of Pepin and Charlemagne prevented the church's establishment of an autonomous hierarchy. Part of the royal mission was the assumption of responsibility for a Christian people, and the Carolingians retained considerable power in the matter of ecclesiastical appointments. The reorganization of the church, however, was now sponsored powerfully by the kings themselves, and the restoration of the old archbishoprics, the subordination of bishops to their metropolitan and of clergy to bishops, and the frequency of ecclesiastical synods and councils contributed to the restoration of administrative order within the Frankish church and constituted simultaneously a new kind of organized support for the king. Not only were older sees reconstituted, but new ones were founded, some such as Salzburg in 798, being capable of functioning as part of the kingdom's expansion to the east. This vigorous, newly organized episcopate, drawn often from the greatest families of the kingdom, became one of the strongest supports of the monarchy and eventually a nearly independent group in the complex ecclesiastical and political atmosphere of Charlemagne's son and successor, Louis the Pious.

The Carolingian reform of the episcopacy encountered considerable difficulties. The sheer difficulty of overseeing the conduct of bishops complicated the questions of social rank and family loyalty that new appointments raised, and the kings' insistence upon controlling episcopal appointments and keeping the archbishops relatively weak brought problems concerning the higher clergy to the royal court again and again. Carolingian bishops were expected to serve the king while fulfilling their ecclesiastical obligations. Sometimes such service required distinctly uncanonical activities, such as participating in diplomatic and political missions, serving in the army, and inspecting the activities of lesser figures in the royal administration. The achievements of the Carolingians on the administrative side of ecclesiastical reform were, however, impressive. The restoration of the old ecclesiastical divisions of Gaul and the creation of new missionary centers suggest at least a partial attempt to restore some of the metropolitan's authority. The frequent promotion of able men and the repeated royal insistence, embodied in the *Admonitio generalis* to the clergy in 789, upon certain minimum levels of conduct and intellectual achievement represent the beginnings of a process that led ultimately to the restoration of an organized, learned church on the Continent. At the levels of more profound spirituality, however, the Carolingian higher clergy fell distinctly short of even modest reforming goals. Royal service, aristocratic status, and social ties helped make the episcopacy vigorous and able administrators, but they did little to create a more spiritual ecclesiastical hierarchy. With few exceptions, the Carolingian higher clergy made far more effective royal servants and landlords than spiritual directors. Like the kings, their greatest contribution to this aspect of religious life came to be their patronage of scholarship and new forms of devotion, not their invention of them. Above all, Pepin and Charlemagne created a higher clergy that was responsive to their own particular needs and limited by the royal power wielded over them. For the Carolingians, proper organization of the church took precedence over the spiritual qualities of those doing the organizing; they had other things to do.

The reform of the higher clergy, largely limited as it was to clerical discipline and ecclesiastical organization, gave the first two Carolingian kings the rudiments of an administrative system, control of which remained securely in the hands of the king. Yet there were other forms of ecclesiastical life equally prominent in the Frankish kingdom from which the kings could expect other services, and the Carolingian monastic reforms equaled in importance the reforms of the higher clergy; for several centuries to come, the great monasteries played political, intellectual, and social roles as great as or in some cases greater than those of the bishops and archbishops.

The monasteries of the Frankish kingdom were far removed in their social roles from both the cenobitic desert communities of fourth-century Egypt and the original eremitical institutions of southern Gaul and Ireland. Endowed heavily by the landed magnates who founded and often owned them, occupying lands scattered throughout the length and breadth of the kingdom, controlling many parish churches, and drawing upon all levels of Frankish society, the monasteries of the eighth and ninth centuries constituted not only spiritual but political and economic institutions of great importance. The abbots of these monasteries, usually members of aristocratic families, played important roles in the life of both court and countryside. As much as the ecclesiastical hierarchy, the monastic institutions of the Franks constituted a pillar of royal power.

As was the case with the bishopric, the abbacy of a monastery, when it was within the king's power to give, was an attractive way of rewarding royal service. Many of the eighth- and ninth-century abbots ruled their communities by this form of royal appointment, and the spiritual support of monastic communities heightened the king's place as God's regent on earth. The monastery of St. Denis, outside of Paris, had had particularly close connections with the Merovingian dynasty, and it remained close to the Carolingians, just as two centuries later it received the patronage of the Capetian dynasty and remained one of the strongest supports of the medieval French monarchy. The monasteries of Fulda, Lorsch, and St. Martin of Tours were all particularly associated with the royal court and royal patronage.

Aside from their role as cult centers, the greatest functions of the monasteries were agricultural and literary. Labor had been introduced into communal monastic life by the Benedictine rule, and although few monasteries of the eighth century required all monks to perform manual labor, the problems of husbanding monastic resources occupied a large proportion of monastic energy. The practices of monastic estate management contributed immensely to the agricultural reforms of early medieval Europe.

For royal purposes, the intellectual activity of the monasteries was as important as their economic and political support. The state of learning on the part of the Continental clergy had declined considerably, and monasteries emerged as important centers for the restoration of learning. One of the most striking features of Carolingian ecclesiastical legislation is its emphasis upon learning. In official proclamations, public patronage, chronicles, and personal inquiries, the Carolingian kings stressed their dependence upon monastic learning and the literary activities of the monasteries. The productivity of monasteries as centers of learning, however, was not consistent, and several difficulties faced by Pepin and Charlemagne were never really overcome, not even during the energetic reforming period sponsored by Charlemagne's son Louis. First, the proliferation of different rules made the character of monastic life throughout the kingdom remarkably uneven. Moved by his great desire to regularize all aspects of worship and ecclesiastical conduct, Charlemagne urged the adoption of the Benedictine rule in all Carolingian monasteries, but in this he had little success, in spite of the care and effort he exerted in obtaining an accurate and definitive version of the rule, copied at Charlemagne's order at Monte Cassino in 813. The earlier unchecked growth of Frankish monasticism, the confiscation of ecclesiastical lands and the institution of lay abbots by Charles Martel, and the fierce independence of many monasteries doomed Charlemagne's efforts, but the royal consideration of many monasteries, such as St. Martin of Tours, Corbie, and Echternach, at least established the principles of monastic reform, and Charlemagne's and, later, Louis's patronage of the great monastic reformer St. Benedict of Aniane resulted in a monastic synod in the year 817 in which massive legislation was enacted and as a result of which the theory, if not the practice, of monastic reform in terms of the Benedictine rule became an enduring part of western church history.

In spite of the difficulties over questions of reform, royal patronage made the monasteries useful in other, more successful ways. Monasteries became the religious centers of whole regions and an integral part of the expansion of Frankish power into pagan lands east of the Rhine. Thus, the monasteries of Fulda (founded by St. Boniface), Corvey (a monastic community that was an offshoot of the Frankish monastery of Corbie), and Hersfeld played important missionary roles in the late eighth and ninth century, and others, particularly St. Gall, St. Martin of Tours, and Reichenau, became noted centers of intellectual activity. Monastic communities, however checkered their seventh- and eighth-century history, had retained a level of intellectual activity that the Carolingians supported and encouraged. Not all monasteries, of course, considered intellectual work a requisite for their members. Early monasticism had been concerned with the quality of monastic devotion, not the level of monastic learning. In some communities, however, traditions of learning grew up and influenced other monasteries as well. Cassiodorus's monastery as Vivarium, the monastic communities in southern Gaul, and, most spectacularly, the monasteries in Ireland and England had instituted sacred learning as an integral part of monastic life, and the culture that had produced Bede had devoted much energy to providing a literary and intellectual role for the monk. From the requirements of monastic administration and liturgical practices to biblical commentary, chant, and the production of prayer books, eighth-century monasteries possessed both a practical and a theoretical need for learning. The reforms of St. Boniface and other eighth-century reformers spread these practices on the Continent, and the older Irish monasteries such as Luxeuil, St. Gall, and Bobbio, as well as Reichenau, had also preserved a high standard of learning. These insular and Continental influences received extensive patronage from Pepin and Charlemagne, particularly in their zeal to regularize ecclesiastical texts and practices. The same inspiration that commissioned an official copy of the Benedictine rule requested more books from the Frankish monasteries and frequently provided the means by which monastic writers could obtain books to copy.

Charlemagne's growing conception of his divinely ordained mission included a sense of responsibility for the quality of ecclesiastical devotion, and that quality in turn depended upon the clergy's knowledge of Christian doctrine. Thus, Charlemagne's first desire in this respect was for accurate copies of essential Christian literature—the Bible, canon law, a reliable Sacramentary, and, later, a copy of the Benedictine rule. From this essentially pragmatic sponsorship of learning, there quickly grew up active book-producing centers that copied other manuscripts, including the works of classical writers as well as those of church fathers, borrowing books to copy from Spain, Italy, Ireland, and England and in turn circulating copies to other monastic and episcopal centers. If not the intellectual profundity or originality, then certainly the sheer volume of book production in the late eighth and early ninth centuries characterizes the reigns of Charlemagne and Louis as being of critical importance in the intellectual history of Europe.

The Carolingian literary renaissance was marked not only by the increasing circulation and standardization of basic Christian literature, but also by striking changes in the techniques of book production, particularly decoration and handwriting. Book covers of jewels and precious metals adorned the most important sacred writings. A new and much clearer form of handwriting, the Carolingian minuscule, replaced the irregular and difficult-to-read Merovingian script, and durable vellum replaced papyrus. The organization of the writing rooms, the *scriptoria,* of the monasteries included the selection of works to be copied, the assignment of works to copyists, and the training and supervision of new scribes. The head of the monastic *scriptorium* became an important figure in the monastery and, when the abbot himself happened to be a learned man, often produced a treasury of literary work whose importance cannot be overestimated. The Carolingian bishops constituted an administrative and disciplinary kind of support for the new Frankish monarchy, and the monasteries constituted its intellectual and literary complement.

The bishoprics, archbishoprics, and monasteries became permanent local centers for the extension and continuity of royal authority and royal influence. The Carolingian kings were wandering monarchs, moving from estate to estate in the winter to absorb their wealth of produce and services, and they invariably took to the field with the army in late spring on a series of endless military campaigns designed to suppress local revolts, extend royal authority into new territories, or overawe restive subjects. Except for those prelates who were kept close to the king, bishops and abbots fulfilled the function of maintaining stability and order in their own localities. Much of the immediate ecclesiastical advice and assistance that Charlemagne received came from different clergy, the court scholars, and the staff of the palatine chapel. The chapel and its clerical personnel provided for the spiritual needs of the king and his court and guarded the precious collection of relics that the king carried with him, one of the most venerated of which was the cape (*capa*) of St. Martin; hence, the designation of the clerical personnel surrounding the king as the *capella,* or chapel. The head of the chapel, the arch-chaplain, was the king's chief ecclesiastical advisor. Some of the ecclesiastics were occasionally used for the infrequent personal scribal needs of the ruler, for producing the royal diplomas, and for service upon personal missions of the king. The official responsible for the scribal duties of the chapel staff was the chancellor, the *cancellarius*. By resorting to the chapel on matters of day-to-day administrative and spiritual affairs and to the great bishops and abbots on matters of greater importance, the Carolingian kings controlled the Frankish church, and Frankish churchmen reciprocated by constituting a steadfast and energetic body of royal supporters.

We have traced the ecclesiastical side of the activity and interests of the Frankish kings from the ecclesiastical provinces and *civitates* through the monasteries and into the royal palace and chapel. The palace, *palatium*, consisted only in part of clergy. The household of the Carolingian kings, like that of their predecessors, was the real center of royal governance. The households of the Germanic kings should not, however, be considered even remotely comparable to the central administrations of modern governments. To most readers of this book, the term "government" probably implies a carefully and clearly articulated system of offices through which public power is distributed, made effective, and regulated, a system that depends upon clear lines of communication, clear definitions of authority, secure finances, and continuity, both in the form of permanent archives and records and in the employment of service personnel. The governance of Carolingian rulers had none of these characteristics. The king's power was personal, and his right to the title and the kingdom was private; that is, it could pass to his heirs like private property. The king possessed the *bannum*, the power of command and prohibition, and he shared his power with no one; the assemblies, diets, and synods he convened could consult, advise, or urge, but the king was under no obligation, certainly no "constitutional" obligation, to follow their advice. The kingdom was the king's, and it could not be conceived of in any other fashion.

Yet the apparent limitlessness of the royal power did have effective practical limits, and it is important for us to realize these limits before considering the secular administration of the kingdom. Difficulties of communication, slowness of orders and communication generally, the lack of personnel, and the interminable inefficiency of a continually mobile court all imposed understandable brakes upon the unchecked— and otherwise uncheckable—exercise of royal power. In addition to these, the kings continually faced problems involving personnel—in terms of sufficient numbers, personal loyalty, and efficiency—and finance, particularly in finding the means of rewarding dedicated service or in simply supporting the numbers of servants that any effective mobilization of royal power would have demanded.

Perhaps the most conspicuous absence that a modern student of government would notice is the lack of anything resembling an administrative framework at the center of royal power. The Carolingian king ruled by means of the same institution through which he lived—his household staff—and the governance of the kingdom of the Franks was performed by the king's domestic servants carrying out whatever business the king assigned to them. It is in terms of this household staff, then, and not in terms of a closely interconnected network of governmental institutions that the secular aspect of the kingship of the Franks must be considered.

The royal resources that supported these servants were, like the kingdom, private. Most existed in the form of royally owned lands scattered throughout the kingdom, the income that those lands produced, and the slaves and other peasants who worked them. Royal lands, whether farms or forests, constituted the largest and most regular source of royal income. That income, however, was not often translated into money. Much of it was consumed on the spot by the royal court moving from estate to estate; some of it was given to royal servants in return for service and in lieu of other forms of payment; only a very small portion was ever converted into fluid capital. In addition, the king profited irregularly from military success. The king's share in the booty from a successful campaign constituted a kind of income distinctly different from that produced by royal lands. A successful conquest, such as that of the Avars in 795, provided the king with immense amounts of treasure, which gave him far more liquid capital than he usually possessed. This capital was generally given away, sometimes in money grants to individuals, and sometimes in the form of ecclesiastical patronage. In spite of its inherent possibilities, however, this form of income was highly irregular and left royal control almost as quickly as it had come into it.

Profits from coinage, the administration of justice, and the sale of privileges also constituted royal resources, and a series of various forms of indirect taxes, such as tolls, and involuntary "gifts" to the king from individuals constituted the remainder of the royal income. Considerable as much of this income was, it was characterized more often, at least to modern eyes, as unpredictable, sporadic, and uncontrollable. The Carolingian kings of the Franks were without doubt enormously wealthy, but the forms in which their wealth existed limited the uses to which it could be put. Inefficiency, malfeasance, lack of even a rudimentary accounting system, and the general difficulties of hauling the treasury around with the king and the court all constituted equally important aspects of the financial side of royal power. What marked the Carolingian success in the area of exploiting the royal income is, rather, their success in acquiring a larger proportion of the potential wealth in their kingdom and their initial success in dispensing it to servants and institutions who remained loyal. They did not introduce new uses of "public" finance, but they husbanded more successfully than their predecessors the wealth they did possess.

Wealth meant the support of servants, rewards, and patronage, the three areas in which the Carolingian kings made perhaps their most important contribution to royal governance. Liberality, loyalty, and largesse remained aspects of royal governance that were as important as legitimacy, the maintenance of justice, and the protection of the church. The bonds of loyalty were conceived as personal, and they were cemented by very material demonstrations of generosity—or they were not cemented at all. One aspect of traditional Frankish kingship that survived was the expectation that kings would give away their wealth in rewarding their followers, and that their followers would reciprocate by remaining loyal. It is a curious combination of materialistic demonstrations of what the modern world considers usually immaterial bonds, but people in the eighth and ninth centuries saw nothing inconsistent in it. *Magnanimitas*—excessive liberality with personal wealth—was considered an essential sign of good kingship, and one of the bases of the success of the Carolingians is their ability, and good luck, in managing to acquire wealth—for several generations, at least—faster than they could dispense it. When that wealth existed in the form of lands, they devised another expedient, that of giving it in return for continuous service, thus rewarding faithful servants, although this method ran the risk of alienating part of their wealth.

War booty, indirect taxes, and gifts were impressive but unpredictable sources of royal income. Far more stable, and hence far more useful most of the time, were the royally owned lands. Not only did they support the day-to-day needs of the king and his court, but their surplus could be turned into cash and added to the treasury, and some estates could even become partially specialized in terms of agriculture. Besides these essential roles, however, royal lands could be assigned to royal servants for the duration of their service, or they could be awarded to royal servants for past service. These two latter functions, though less spectacular and memorable than the lavish dispensation of recently acquired treasures, constituted a far more fundamental basis of royal power. Scattered throughout the kingdom and consisting largely of agricultural lands, ecclesiastical institutions, hunting preserves, the royally owned lands were used to support the king's regional administrators in much the same way that royal estates were exploited to support the king himself.

The church and the palatine household constituted the most stable and the most regular aspects of Carolingian royal governance. But most of the kingdom was beyond the direct control of these institutions, and to govern most of his subjects the king had to rely upon the loyalty and service of a body of administrative personnel over whom he possessed far less immediate control: the counts, dukes, and marquesses who formed the provincial and regional arm of royal governance. The module of Frankish regional governance was the count (*comes* or *grafio*). Under the Merovingian kings of the Franks, the title of count slowly ceased to designate a provincial Roman military commander and began to designate certain royal followers who administered what survived of civil order in the fifth and sixth centuries. In the provinces of the kingdom that had long been Romanized, the count controlled most of the regional public services and incomes that had become the personal property of the Frankish kings. The count was at once the district judge, district military commander, court clerk, and royal representative. Among the later Merovingians, when dynastic rivalry weakened the surface administration of the rulers, the counts joined the powerful landed families, and as royal power was felt less directly the counts built up their own personal resources, often using their remote "official" origins, titles, and lands to increase their personal wealth until the "public" and "private" resources of comital families became hopelessly blurred. By the late seventh and early eighth centuries, the counts were drawn from that very group of families of landed magnates against whose interests they were supposed to enforce the royal will. They had also begun to serve in areas where their own private wealth lay and to turn their offices into personal property, which was inherited by their descendants. Like other magnates, the early eighth-century counts had to be courted by the kings before they could be prevailed upon to perform any functions in the royal interest.

Under the first Carolingians, the office of count underwent a distinctive transformation. Many of the new counts were Frankish and were systematically appointed to serve in areas in which they had neither wealth nor family connections. Their offices ceased to be heritable, and they were distinguished from the surrounding landed families by a clearly outlined relationship with the king. The *wergeld* (man-price) of the count was lifted above that of other men, no matter how wealthy or powerful, and his duties were spelled out in directive after directive emanating from the royal court: he was to enforce royal authority, prosecute criminals, arrest malefactors, supervise the infliction of punishments and the collection of fines, and raise the segments of the royal army for which his district was responsible. Particularly in the conquered eastern parts of the kingdom, the counts were often the only representatives of Frankish royal authority within hundreds of miles. Under the Merovingians, the counts had grown into great, local, private powers. Under the Carolingians, the counts had to work long days against formidable opposition in order solely to extend the hand of the king into the remoter areas of the kingdom.

By 800 there existed nearly 300 counties, each ruled by a count who not only had to report regularly back to the king, but also had to submit to an annual inspection of his year's work by the touring *missi dominici*, teams of inspectors sent directly from the king to check on the count's activities, a team to whom men could appeal directly against any malpractices they thought the count guilty of. The count's functions can be labeled approximately judicial, fiscal, and military, but they should be considered in greater detail in order to illuminate at least the ideal of Carolingian regional governance. The county court, *mallus*, was a descendant of both the old Roman provincial courts and the Germanic local assemblies. The count himself was the judge—and often the prosecutor when the offender was brought to trial because of his notoriety, his *mala fama*—the court clerk, and the police agent. Sometimes assisting the count in these functions were viscounts (*vicecomes* or *vicomtes*); more usually, this aid was provided by vicars and hundredmen from the district, and in some places by local courts called "hundred courts," remnants of older forms of community justice. The sessions of the county court were *placita;* the district that it served was the *pagus*. Under Charlemagne, the general *placita* for a *pagus* were restricted to three a year, at which the attendance of all the free men of the district was expected. In addition to the count, his staff, and the free men of a district were men called *boni viri* (good men), who knew the law of the district and advised the count on an informal basis. Later, the *boni viri* appear to have given way to the *scabini,* or *judices,* permanently assigned professional judges who could assist the count in person or substitute for him when he was away. Although the count's judicial authority was considered part of the king's authority, it was limited in particular areas: the count could not offer mercy without royal consent; in particular he had to defend the rights of *miserabiles personae* —the poor, widows, and orphans. He sometimes needed a special royal mandate to prosecute particular cases, and the most difficult cases had to be sent to the king himself.

The fiscal duties of the count were equally exhausting. He was responsible for collecting judicial fines and tolls and certain other parts of the royal income. His accounts, such as they were, were carefully scrutinized, and his ability to act independently was limited carefully in all but the most ordinary of circumstances. In addition to these duties, the count was also the regional military commander, responsible for raising and leading that portion of the royal host for which his county was responsible. But the count was not merely a commander; under Charlemagne he was also a quartermaster, responsible for fodder, boats, bridges, and weapons. Finally, the count was also expected to provide lodging, travel facilities, protection, and assistance to the *missi dominici* on their annual inspection trips to his district.

For these services, which would have overtaxed even an energetic Roman civil servant in the heyday of the empire, the count received no salary. He was given instead the use of certain royal lands and incomes located in his county, the whole of which was called the *comitatus* and was roughly equivalent to the similar combination of the use of royal lands and incomes awarded to a bishop, the *episcopatus*. The count did not own these resources, however, and when he was dismissed, or when he died, they immediately reverted to the king, who reassigned them or other resources to the count's successor. Often, the county was coterminous with the diocese of a bishop, and the count and bishop had to cooperate. Finally, it must be noted that the 300 counties were not contiguous, some areas had no count at all, other areas were specifically immune from comital jurisdiction, and sometimes, because of the chronic shortage of personnel, some counts ruled more than one county.

The count was the module for higher commands as well. The

marquesses, rulers of great frontier territories, were technically *comes marchae,* counts of the march, whence the titles marquess, marquis, and *markgraf.* The lords of the marches often ruled many counties and sometimes supervised the activities of counts located closer to the territorial center of the kingdom. The units into which the kingdom was divided each year in order that the *missi dominici* could be assigned their areas of inspection were groups of counties. Under the Carolingians, the counts were controlled more carefully, and the units of governance within the kingdom appear to have been the counties.

Yet the county system too had its drawbacks, and these were largely the same as those that restricted the unchecked use of royal authority. The slowness of communication, the requirement of incessant royal vigilance and force to keep subordinates obedient and efficient, and the sheer difficulties in finding the necessary numbers of appropriately talented individuals were never more than momentarily overcome. The increase in comital status and prestige, which was necessary in order for the count to be on a par with the great landed magnates of his district, sometimes created loyal and powerful servants. Just as often, however, it did not. The counts did not automatically become dedicated government administrators and cut themselves loose from the family and clan interests of traditional Frankish society. Hampered in their duties by poor communication, they might also take advantage of this to sink personal territorial roots in their district, particularly when the prestige of the comital office had been so raised that it attracted members of powerful aristocratic families, whose sense of family loyalty was always at least as strong as their sense of loyalty to the king. In terms of personnel, it has been estimated that Charlemagne's county system required ideally a total administrative staff of between two and three thousand persons, a hopelessly high figure considering the population of the kingdom and its territorial extent. Eventually, the problem of personnel resulted in the counts themselves being pressed into duty as *missi,* sometimes serving as inspectors of their own administration. Some counts conveniently failed to distinguish between lands that belonged to the king and of which they had only a temporary use and lands that belonged to them and could descend to their children. Given the problems of personnel, the Carolingian kings slowly permitted the growth of families in which the comital (count's) office was passed down, further confusing the family property with that of the office that the counts now held almost on a hereditary basis.

All the lay officials of the kingdom, from the palatine household to the *scabini,* faced another handicap: the lack of specific ethical precepts expounded particularly for laymen. The counts, like the rest of Frankish society, were Christians, but of a very different kind from the members of earlier and later Christian societies. Their religion was largely the public observational religion of the bishops and the king; of personal devotion, piety, and guidelines of ethical conduct they generally knew little, and most of them were educated superficially, if at all. Even if their duties looked new and official, their culture was for the most part old and traditionally Frankish. The only extant work on the moral life of laymen written by a cleric—Alcuin's *Book of Vices and Virtues for Count Guido*—was written solely at the request of the count and consisted chiefly of vague and clumsy adaptations of moral precepts that had originally been written for clerics, and monks in particular, and must have been of minimal value for the lay aristocracy of the eighth and ninth centuries. One virtue dominated all others: fidelity. Fidelity, and its opposite, betrayal, dominate the literature of the ninth century, and the limitations of the ethical world of these royal servants is shown nowhere more clearly than in the constant emphasis upon loyalty, personal loyalty, to the king. As late as the thirteenth century, treason was understood chiefly in terms of personal disloyalty to a lord to whom one had taken a personal oath of allegiance.

Out of these limited resources and on the tenuous foundations of personal oaths of loyalty, the Carolingian rulers of the Franks built their extensive kingdom. The church and the palace household, the local courts, the *scabini*, the vicars, and, as the module of all, the count constituted its fabric. The great frontier lords were conceived as a kind of super-count, and the seven marches that they ruled—Spain, Brittany, Bavaria, Pannonia, Friuli, Nordgau, and Swabia—guarded the edges of the expanding but always threatened kingdom. Through these territories traveled the king's *missi*, his household servants, ecclesiastical officials going back and forth to Rome, pilgrims, and strangers. It has been possible to draw a systematic picture of the functioning of royal governance, but that picture has to be modified by the handicaps under which governance operated, handicaps that were occasionally so great as to obliterate local order entirely and that even at their weakest were sufficiently strong to prevent anything resembling government from taking shape under the Carolingians. In the first quarter of the ninth century, Charlemagne's son, Louis the Pious, issued a directive that suggests succinctly the often tenuous relationship between the high ideals of Carolingian political symbolism and pronouncements, on the one hand, and the pressing practical necessity of attempting to control men and institutions, on the other. The command to maintain the church, the public welfare, and justice, says the document, is the king's duty. In fact, however, "the responsibility is divided in such a way that each of you, wherever he lives and in whatever social rank he is placed, may know that he bears part of our burden." This is a statement that would not have been characteristic of Pepin or Charlemagne, but it would not have been untrue as a description of the problems they faced. Thus, behind the rudimentary liturgical vocabulary of Carolingian political statements, we are reminded of the vast actualities that such ideas were being invoked to control. The impressive and eloquent language of Carolingian political theory must be considered in terms of the limited, inefficient, slow, and undependable institutions and resources by means of which the ideas expressed by that vocabulary were put into practice.

THE EXPANSION OF FRANKISH POWER IN THE EIGHTH AND NINTH CENTURIES

It is no coincidence that the fortunes of the Carolingian house, from Pepin II to Louis the Pious, a period of a century and a half, were remarkably stabilized by a succession of individuals who ruled the entire kingdom alone. This situation eliminated the frequent redrawing of boundary lines to accommodate a number of heirs claiming equal shares of the kingdom. Pepin II was succeeded only by his illegitimate son, Charles Martel, who assembled power in his own hands. Charles's two sons, Pepin and Carloman, shared this rule until Carloman retired to

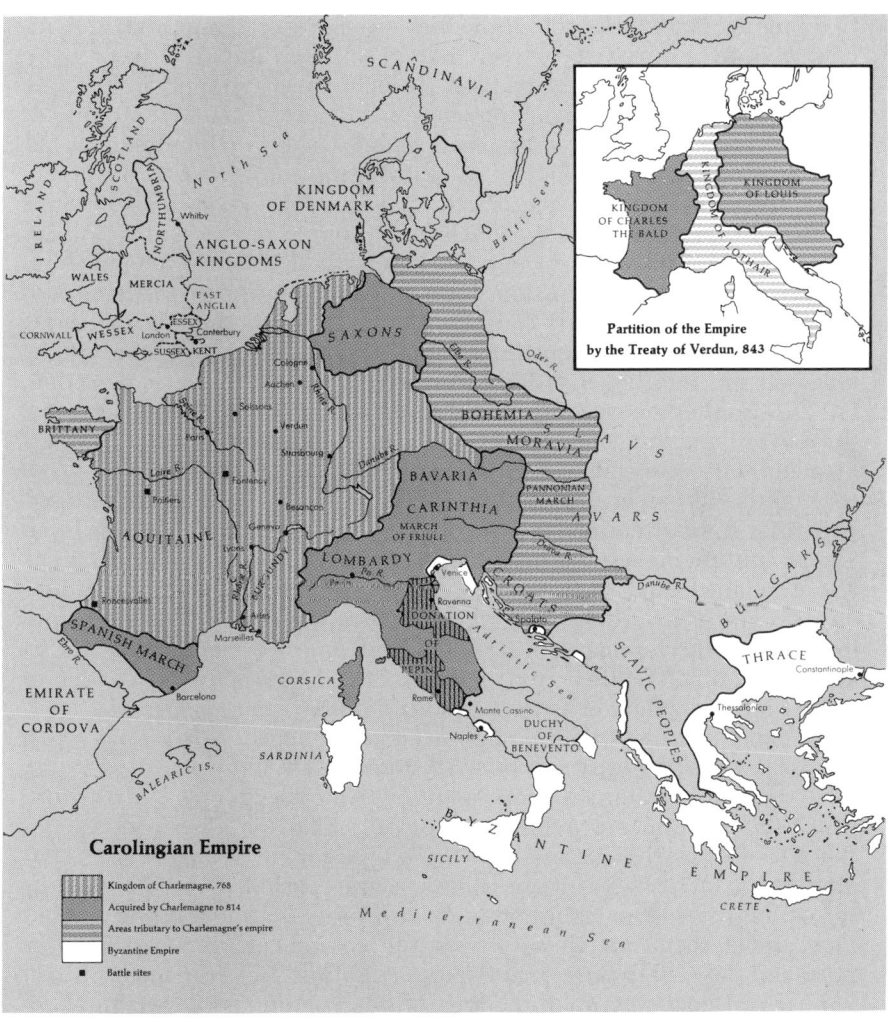

a monastery. Pepin in turn had two sons, Charles and Carloman, between whom he divided his kingdom, giving the inferior portion to Charles. At Carloman's death only three years later, Charles assumed a single rule. Charles had only one son, Louis, who survived him, and the great crisis of the dynasty occurred in the next generation, when Louis had to divide the kingdom and, as we shall see, a new empire, among three sons. For five critical generations, however, with the exception of a dozen or so years, the dangers to centralized royal rule posed by the Frankish laws of the equal division of inheritance were limited: a single ruler sat on the throne of the Franks. Not only the dynastic accidents and the rules of mortality contributed to this rule of individuals, but actuarial statistics as well: the five major Carolingians between Pepin II and Louis the Pious each ruled for at least twenty-five years; Charlemagne ruled for forty-six years. These aspects of the first century of Carolingian power are not negligible; strong, able, long-lived individuals who were survived by men like themselves imposed, if only by habit, the rule of a single man at a single time. Nothing in the law needed to be changed; no "constitutional" novelties were introduced. The later popular images of Charlemagne as a two-hundred-year-old warrior king with a flowing white beard, although inaccurate in nearly every detail and highly anachronistic, may contain a germ of significance for the history of the dynasty, which for a century and a quarter avoided one of the dangers of Merovingian dynasty, the division of the kingdom.

Not only was the kingdom rarely divided, and never for long periods, but it expanded nearly continuously under Pepin and Charlemagne. Not only were regional rebellions suppressed and the governance of the kingdom put into better order, as we have seen in the previous section, but the frontiers moved slowly outward toward Spain, Italy, Germany, the Slavic Lands, and the Netherlands. Territories that had been in the kingdom but continually proved restive whenever crisis troubled the royal authority—areas such as Aquitaine, Bavaria, and Brittany—received particular royal attention, and the commanders of the marches were in an almost continuous state of military preparedness. The Carolingian kings also developed early the ability to conduct different military operations on different fronts at the same time. During the period 752–759, Pepin fought both the Lombards in Italy and the Arabs in Septimania. Later, kings were often recalled from an area of military activity in order to quell a local rebellion or defend another frontier from invaders.

The expansion of the Frankish kingdom depended not only upon the continuous authority of long-lived single rulers, but upon the military force they could call upon in the annual spring assembly of free warriors, which served both as a public assembly at which the king informed his subjects of new decisions and the staging area for the Frankish army. For most of his forty-six-year reign, Charlemagne assembled the army in the spring, notifying counts, bishops, and royal vassals, who in turn notified those under them, prepared soldiers and equipment, arranged for supplies, and traveled to the assembly point established for a summer military campaign. Depending upon the area of campaigning, some sections provided more or fewer men. Free men often banded together to send, and support, one of their number to the army. The infantry were armed with lances, axes, and shields, and later with bows as well. The cavalry carried both long and short swords, and the heavy cavalry often wore mailed coats and helmets as well. The Frankish army, as reorganized by Charles Martel, was the most successful offensive fighting force in the West. Its organization and supply under the close observation of royal officials, its command in the hands of the king, his sons, or proven war leaders, and its area of operations carefully considered, it was the single institution upon which the expansion of the kingdom depended.

Eighth- and ninth-century warfare, as was the case generally with later medieval warfare, usually consisted of infrequent pitched battles that, if the king's forces were successful, reduced military resistance to the kingdom throughout an area. Sustained siege operations, prolonged campaigns, and anything resembling military occupation were extremely rare. Although the eighth and ninth centuries witnessed the increasing use of heavier armored cavalrymen, in Charlemagne's time the infantry still constituted the majority of the host. The increased expense in arming a mounted warrior—specially bred war horses, weapons, mail, and sufficient time to train the warrior in the use of these things—were overcome only slowly, and only when rulers were able to fund such expensive warriors with lands and revenues from their own resources without alienating too much of the royal domain. The host, when assembled, carried its own rations. Discipline was enforced against such offenses as desertion, drunkenness, and betrayal. The king's power to call out the army gave the Carolingian kings an annual force with which to meet invasions or to extend their power into new territories, and their victories must have contributed to the army's cohesiveness, loyalty, and effectiveness.

Aside from the periodic rebellions in Aquitaine, Brittany, and Bavaria, the major thrust of Frankish military power was toward Spain, Italy, and Germany. The turbulent Islamic powers in Spain frequently warred with one another, and in 778 Charlemagne entered northern Spain with an army, failed to capture Saragossa, and lost his rear guard to an ambush by Christian Basques in the Pyrenees. This brief episode became the kernel of later legend, and the epic poem *The Song of Roland,* written around 1100, recalls and transforms this skirmish into a vast battle. In taking Gerona in 785 and Barcelona in 801–803 by an extraordinarily prolonged siege, however, Charlemagne established the Spanish march, a durable enclave of Frankish power south of the Pyrenees, that protected the frontier against Islamic forces to the west.

Charlemagne's limited success in Spain, offset as it was by the securing of the Spanish march and the extension of Carolingian culture into northeastern Spain and southwestern Gaul, had far fewer enduring results than the expansion of the kingdom to the north and east, into the lands controlled by the pagan Frisians and Saxons. Certainly, two groups interested in Frankish expansion into Saxony were the Frankish magnates of Austrasia, who were eager for an opportunity to expand their power into Saxony, and the missionary churches along the eastern border of the Frankish kingdom. The Saxons, a Germanic people who inhabited the lands between the Elbe and the North Sea, had long exchanged hostilities with the Franks across their common border. Raids, brief punitive expeditions, and the attempts of missionaries to convert the Saxons to Christianity had characterized Frankish-Saxon relations until the third quarter of the eighth century. But beginning in 772, Charlemagne directed more substantial military campaigns against Saxony, reducing Saxon strongholds, taking hostages, and patronizing the missionary work of the great eastern churches. Charlemagne and the Frankish army were in Saxony during most of the years from 772 to 785. The great Saxon massacre of the Frankish garrisons in 783 led to fearful reprisals by the Franks, the wholesale slaughter of the Saxons, and their conversion to Christianity at sword's point at what historians have called "the bloodbath at Verden." The final pacification and domination of Saxony was accomplished between 785 and 804. Many Saxons were removed to other parts of the kingdom, missionary churches were created for the purpose of administering ecclesiastical affairs, but not without considerable resentment by the Saxons and some Franks as well, and the county was instituted for the purpose of representing royal rule among the conquered peoples.

The Frisians, whose resistance to Frankish rule had waxed and waned as the Saxon resistance grew strong or weak, had long been the object of English missionaries; St. Boniface had been martyred in 754 in a final attempt to convert the Frisians. The Saxon defeat led to the collapse of Frisian resistance, and in Frisia too, both counts and missionary churches spread Carolingian power along the shores of the North Sea. The conquest of Saxony and Frisia brought Charlemagne's northern frontier to the base of the Jutland peninsula, and his power created a distinct threat to the king of the Danes, whose threatening relations with the Franks came to a crisis in the early ninth century.

To the east, Bavaria proved particularly troublesome to incorporate within the Frankish kingdom. Ruled by its independent duke, ecclesiastically dependent upon the patriarch of Aquilea in northern Italy, and exerting a powerful influence upon the Slavic peoples to its own eastern and southern borders, Bavaria remained outside Frankish control until 787, when Charlemagne invaded the duchy, imprisoned the rebellious duke, Tassilo, and began to incorporate Bavaria within his own dominions. In 798 Salzburg was raised to an archbishopric, and Carolingian power was extended through Bavaria to include the duchy of Carinthia, thereby drawing the Carolingians into the affairs of the Bavarians and Slavs and bringing their frontier face to face with that of the Avars.

The Avars, as we have seen above, entered the Danube valley early in the sixth century, divided the Slavs, incorporated many of them into their kingdom, and participated in the great assault upon Constantinople in 626. Throughout the seventh and eighth centuries, the Avars became settled in the area of modern Hungary and the military threat they constituted was reduced considerably. The agitation along the Bavarian and

Carinthian borders continued, however, and it may have been the desire of the Bavarian magnates, rather than any actual Avar threat, that drew the Frankish army into several campaigns against the Avars, which in 796 resulted in the destruction of the Avar kingdom, the removal of the vast Avar treasure to Charlemagne at Aachen, and the disappearance of the Avars from history. The removal of the Avar kingdom involved the Carolingians in Slavic affairs, and completed the extension of the Carolingian frontier in the north and east.

Some historians have argued that by obliterating many border peoples, the Carolingians were forced to construct more expensive frontier works against such new neighbors as the Danes, the Slavs, and the Arabs. The question of the extent of the realm under Charlemagne and the degree to which the new kingdom was "artificial," "fragile," or "unrealistic" must be assessed in terms of its circumstances of origin. The military reforms of Charles Martel, the political revolution of Pepin, and the succession of Charles, a single ruler for forty-three years after 771 and a remarkably successful organizer and king under any circumstances, all contributed to the development of a new type of power under Charlemagne. The weaknesses of surrounding peoples, the remarkably wide base of support that Charlemagne received from the church and the laity, and the effectiveness of the Carolingian host all contributed to the expansion of the kingdom. The kingdom in turn was held together by the only successful means known—loyalty to a single ruler who was sufficiently powerful to enforce loyalty or submission when they were not voluntarily forthcoming. The kingdom itself, particularly in the newly conquered lands, underwent no governmental revolution, and the common Christianity of the whole kingdom cannot have been expected to constitute the bond that it became only much later. The kingdom of the Franks was still the kingdom of the Franks, but the expanded kingdom was also the kingdom of Charlemagne, and it could only have been ruled, its particular loyalties and local and regional senses of independence only overcome, by a ruler as able, vigorous, and fortunate as Charlemagne. No other such king of the Franks was forthcoming. Even in Charlemagne's old age, the kingdom began to come apart.

BYZANTIUM, LOMBARD ITALY, AND THE PAPACY

The expansion of Carolingian power into Italy touches upon more complex relations within the Mediterranean world, and it must therefore be treated separately, with consideration given to changes in the worlds of Byzantium and the papacy as well as that of the Lombard kingdom in Italy.

The elimination of the Avar and Persian threats to Constantinople between 626 and 629 had cost Byzantium enormously in terms of men and money. The continued turbulence in the Balkans, where Slavs and

Bulgars constantly threatened the north of Greece and besieged its most important city, Thessalonika, several times in the seventh century, posed, along with the expansion of Islamic power, continual new threats to the stability of the Byzantine Empire. In Italy and Africa, the sixth century had witnessed several governmental reforms designed to insure the stability of these newly reconquered provinces. In each of these, supreme military and civil power was placed in the hands of a single authority, the exarch. During the crises of the early seventh century, this process was extended to other frontier districts, particularly Anatolia, where the supreme commander, the *strategos,* also became civil and military governor, and where, moreover, the army was settled within the designated provinces, *themes,* on land of its own, thus further militarizing the frontier districts and rooting a citizen army in the district it had to defend. These drastic social and military reforms created a substantial peasant army commanded in the field by the individual who also held peacetime authority over it. The Anatolian soldier-peasants became the new backbone of Byzantine military strength; the taxes from their farms sustained the government in the face of territorial and financial losses in Syria, North Africa, and Italy; finally, the intense concentration of imperial attention upon the Balkans and Anatolia succeeded in invigorating the compacted but still immensely powerful Byzantine state. Greece, the Balkans, and Anatolia were not only the core but the whole extent of the Byzantine Empire.

This constricted yet successfully strengthened empire was ruled for a century by the dynasty of the remarkable Heraclius, the hero of the defense of Constantinople and the defeat of Persia at the end of the first quarter of the seventh century. Under Heraclius's successors, particularly Constans II (641–668) and Constantine IV (668–685), both the Slavs and the Arabs were held in check and turned back from Greece and Constantinople, particularly during the great Arab assault on the city in 678. Under them too, the ecclesiastical prestige of the patriarch of Constantinople increased greatly, and a firm body of orthodox belief came to characterize the churchmen of the whole empire, chiefly through the patronage and guidance of the later Heraclians and the loss of centers of heterodoxy. The late seventh century ended with relations between east and west still on good terms, eastern clerics finding hospitable homes in the west, the emperor visiting the west in 663, and the pope visiting the east in 710.

The seventh century ended, however, in revolution and turmoil. Justinian II (685–695, 705–711), the last member of the Heraclian dynasty, and in many respects an able ruler, generated resentment against his fiscal policies and was exiled in 695. After many years of exile, chiefly in the Khazar kingdom on the northern and eastern edges of the Black Sea, Justinian returned to power in 705, ruled for five years of brutal reprisals, and was again removed from the throne in 711. The disruption in imperial government caused by these upheavals over a fifteen-year period weakened Byzantine resistance to outside invaders, and the new buildup of Arab strength once again threatened the empire.

In 717, however, Emperor Leo III ascended the imperial throne, and in 718 he turned back the second great Arab assault on the city. Under Leo (717–741) and his son Constantine V (741–775) the military and economic resources of the empire were slowly restored.

This political restoration coincided with yet another great religious crisis among eastern Christians. As we have seen, the Near East was an extraordinarily fertile incubator of religious feeling and thought. The meeting place of Jewish, Christian, Oriental, Persian, and Greek thought, it is the home of most of the heresies and orthodoxies of the religions of the Western and Near Eastern worlds today, and in the period between the fifth and the ninth centuries it gave birth to three heretical movements in particular that threatened the stability of the East Roman Empire. Arianism in the fifth century and Monophysitism in the sixth had been resolved only with great effort and with many irreversible consequences. The emergence of iconoclasm in the eighth century under Leo III and Constantine V struck the empire as forcefully as any earlier heresy. Unlike them, however, it caused serious repercussions with enduring consequences in the west.

The problem of iconoclasm centered in the increasingly widespread popularity of religious images—in mosaic, sculpture, and icons—in the Byzantine Empire during the sixth century. The popularity of these practices grew, particularly during the trying years of the early seventh century, when the appearance of divinely created icons and images and the belief in their magical powers grew under the Heraclians. As early as the sixth century, moreover, non-Christians, such as Jews and pagans, directed substantial criticism against what they considered these idolatrous practices, and in the seventh century even Christians began to object to the extremes of image worship. The use of images, of course, could easily border upon idolatry. Against the oriental reluctance to depict the ineffable divine mysteries in human forms, thereby implicitly limiting them, and the Old Testament prohibition of the worship and building of graven images, there emerged a Neo-Platonic doctrine justifying image veneration as a pious help to the unlettered faithful, a view that was expressed most eloquently and influentially by St. John of Damascus, a seventh-century Chystian Syrian thinker who was employed by the Moslem ruler of Syria.

The origins of the iconoclastic movement are still not a matter of agreement among scholars, and explanations of the rise of iconoclasm vary from positivistic economic ones to the purely political and extremely metaphysical. It is hardly possible that the iconoclast movement did not bring to a head opposition to the cult of images that had been growing among otherwise orthodox Christians for some time. Whether the origins of the movement were ecclesiastical or not, Emperor Leo III appears at first to have proceeded cautiously; not until 730 did he issue an imperial edict abolishing icons. Under Leo's successor, Constantine V, iconoclasm became a church dogma as well. At a church council held in 754, the assembled fathers denounced icons and, backed by the overrich experience of three centuries of complex theological debate, identified iconodules (image–makers) with earlier forms of condemned heresy. By the 760s, extensive persecution had begun, at least partly because several ecclesiastical elements, particularly the monks, had turned on the emperor and urged political resistance to the iconclastic laws.

The success of Leo's and Constantine's religious reforms, their antimonastic stand, and the spread of iconoclasm were accompanied by a vigorous and successful Byzantine foreign policy as well. Along the Byzantine-Arab frontier in Syria, relations were stabilized and a rich and productive frontier culture began to make itself evident, perhaps suggested best by the later epic poem *Digenes Akritas,* which concerns the exploits of a half-Arab, half-Greek frontier hero in an idealized milieu that evokes an atmosphere of learning, love, heroism, and rough toleration of enemies. The struggle with the Slav and Bulgar population in Greece, the Balkans, and the Black Sea continued vigorously, and large numbers of Slavs were transplanted into various parts of the empire to repopulate depleted districts. The bubonic plague that ravaged the empire between 745 and 747 was yet another crisis to be overcome, and Lombard threats to the outlying Byzantine territories in Italy resumed once again. These difficulties called for decisive action, and Leo III and Constantine V proved to be remarkably although not completely successful rulers. Stringent economic and agricultural reforms, successful military organization, discipline, and strategic planning, and ecclesiastical reforms characterize the reigns of both. Not only the stabilizing and tough defense of the frontiers and their political activities, however, but the ecclesiastical administrative reforms of Leo III also deserve mention.

Part of the policy of Leo III was his determination to strengthen the authority of the patriarch of Constantinople, since 451 the preeminent ecclesiastical leader in the east, and second in dignity only to the bishop of Rome. During Leo's first moves against the icons, he encountered the firm resistance of Pope Gregory II (715–731), many Italian ecclesiastics, and Pope Gregory III (731–741). The intransigence of the Latin church may well have contributed to Leo's decision to reorganize drastically the ecclesiastical provinces subject to the patriarch of Constantinople. Leo first deprived the pope of the rich lands in South Italy and Sicily that had constituted such a substantial part of papal income. Leo then withdrew these two areas, as well as the whole province of Illyricum, from the pope's jurisdiction and placed them under that of the patriarch of Constantinople. At the same time, around 733, he also attached to the patriarchate several Anatolian ecclesiastical provinces hitherto under the jurisdiction of the patriarch of Antioch. At one stroke, Leo increased vastly both the jurisdiction and prestige of the patriarchate of Constantinople and lessened nearly to insignificance those of the bishop of Rome. The reigns of Leo III and Constantine V produced significant changes in the Byzantine world, and they brought to the fore the particularly pressing question of the rivalry between Greek and oriental cultural traditions, which focused upon, but did not restrict itself to, the question of images. We will consider the consequences of iconoclasm at the end of the eighth and beginning of the ninth centuries in a later section. Our immediate concern is the problem of the new impoverishment of the bishops of Rome and their status in the west. The loss of territory and subordinate jurisdictions seriously challenged the position of the bishop of Rome. However, other problems loomed even larger as the middle of the eighth century approached. A restored and ambitious Lombard monarchy, first under Liutprand (712–744), and then under his more ruthless successors Ratchis (744–749) and Aistulf (749–756), moved against the powerful and largely independent Lombard duchies to the east and south of Rome, those of Spoleto and Benevento. The tactical importance of the position of Rome and the weakness of the unsupported Byzantine garrisons in central Italy made the independence of Rome more precarious, and when Aistulf finally captured Ravenna, for two centuries the chief seat of Byzantine imperial power in Italy, he placed Rome under his own authority.

The Byzantine reduction of papal authority and jurisdiction, the military weakness that resulted in the collapse of imperial forces before the Lombard advance, and the uncertainty of Lombard intentions all forced the popes, who were unable and perhaps unwilling to treat with the Lombards, to seek allies beyond the Alps. As we have seen, the middle of the eighth century was a period of crisis and instability in many parts of Europe, and the papal approval of Pepin's revolution in 751 drew the bishop of Rome and the king of the Franks closely together. In 754, when the Synod of Heireia pronounced firmly against the cult of images, when only Byzantine emissaries, not troops, were forthcoming from Constantinople, and when Aistulf's forces were threatening Rome more ominously, Pope Stephen II (752–757) made his way to the kingdom of the Franks. There, he implored Pepin for aid, which he obtained in spite of considerable resistance among the Frankish magnates and Pepin's doubtful security so soon after his revolution. Stephen crowned Pepin and his sons Carloman and Charles kings in perpetuity, making Pepin *patricius Romanorum,* a title implying the status of special protector of Rome. The relationship between the pope and the king of the Franks, tentatively begun earlier in the century, established firmly by the approval of Pepin's revolution in 751, and cemented by the meeting between Pepin and Stephen II in 754 had enduring consequences, both for the future history of Italy and the papacy and for the concept of Frankish protection of the Latin church.

Thus, events in Constantinople and Lombard Italy, the plight of the bishop of Rome, and the determination of Pepin to aid the pope formed a concatenation of influences, none of which intended or foresaw, but all of which together compelled, the Frankish entrance into Italy. In 754 Pepin marched into Italy and forced Aistulf to promise to return to the pope Ravenna and other territories. In 756, however, Aistulf once again marched on Rome, and once again Pepin descended upon Italy, this time compelling the restoration of Ravenna and the duchy of Rome and laying the foundations for the papal state. The next few years consisted of tensions among Desiderius, the successor of Aistulf, the pope, Pepin, and the Byzantine emperor, whose diplomacy appears to have been effective in preventing a stabilizing of the agreements of 756. Byzantine overtures to Franks and Lombards, the death of Pepin in 768 and the succession of two kings over the Franks, and crisis-filled papal successions and continued rivalry among ecclesiastical factions in Rome precipitated further difficulties. In 771, Charles's brother Carloman died and Charles assumed the sole kingship of the Franks, Carloman's wife and children fleeing to Desiderius. In 774, Charles finally arrived in Italy, was formally received into the city of Rome by the pope, compelled the surrender of Desiderius, and was crowned king of the Lombards at Pavia. The Lombard kingdom of Italy was at an end.

During this same period, between 754 and 790, the popes ceased sending notification of their election to the emperors at Constantinople and sent such formal notification instead to the kings of the Franks. Imperial portraits disappeared from Roman coinage and were replaced with portraits of the issuing popes; popes ceased to date their official documents in terms of imperial reigns, doing so instead in terms of their own. In spite of continuing difficulties and Lombard resistance, the papacy in the second half of the eighth century reconstituted itself a distinctly Latin power and slowly removed the lingering traces of imperial authority from central Italy.

By 780, new negotiations appear to have restored temporary good relations among the pope, Charles, and Byzantium. The Papal State had begun, and the extension of Charlemagne's power had brought him not only the iron crown of the Lombards, but a newer and closer relationship with the pope and a renewed official status *vis-à-vis* Rome and the Roman church. This aspect of the expansion of the Frankish kingdom opened the way not only to a double royal title, "King of the Franks and the Lombards," and the appended Roman designation *patricius Romanorum,* but also to the idea of a new title appropriate for all of the lands Charles ruled, a renewed imperial title in the west.

THE CAROLINGIAN RENAISSANCE

The expansion of the Frankish kingdom under Charlemagne, particularly into Saxony and Italy, placed in Charles's hands resources greater than those of any of his predecessors. With the exceptions of Moslem Spain, Britain and Ireland, Scandinavia, and the lands of the pagan Slavs east of the Elbe and the Byzantine territories in South Italy, Charles was the master of Europe. King of the Franks and the Lombards and *patricius* of the Romans, his son Louis a subking in Aquitaine and his son Pepin subking of Italy, he was the greatest ruler in the west, a personage for the Byzantines and the Arabs both to deal with. In the third quarter of the eighth century Charlemagne exchanged embassies with Constantinople, Baghdad, Cordoba, and Rome, as well as establishing trading and diplomatic relations with the rulers of Mercia in

England, the king of the Danes, and the leaders of the pagan Slavic peoples to the north and east. His power reached farther than that of any western ruler since Theodosius I at the end of the fourth century, and his reputation, both as protector of the Church and as the "Iron Charles," pitiless, formidable, and victorious, reached even further. We have already seen the domestic arrangements according to which Charles governed this vast kingdom, and the consequences of his intervention in Italy. It is now necessary to turn to the transformation that his success and his patronage effected in eighth-century thought and learning.

Not the least striking aspect of the reign of Charlemagne is the sudden availability of new sources of contemporary information. The traditional records of the past, the monastic annals and such histories as Gregory of Tours's *History of the Franks* and Bede's *Ecclesiastical History of the English People,* gave way to new materials. Not only did the monastic annals continue, but new compilations were assembled, some probably at the royal court itself, and these offer us far more information than even the best-informed monastic chronicler. A number of other histories appeared, including several that take every opportunity to emphasize the role of the Carolingian house and sometimes to color unfavorably the last Merovingian kings. Some of them have the air of propaganda for the Carolingian cause, and others, probably originating close to the court, often gloss over or ignore completely some of the military difficulties and rebellions of the king. These annals and histories were sponsored by the king and the magnates and great ecclesiastical officers. More than his predecessors, Charlemagne instituted an active support of intellectual endeavor, and much royal money, as well as favor, stood behind this burst of literary activity. The king's material patronage extended to artistic as well as literary work, and we must keep in mind the role of the king as patron as we survey the results of this new activity.

Perhaps it is easiest to approach the intellectual activities of Charles's reign from the point of view of order. Above all, Charlemagne considered himself a corrector, a reformer of corrupt customs who sought to bring much human activity, particularly spiritual activity, back into line with an imagined ideal of propriety, which was the proper human conduct aligned most closely with God's plan for the operation of the universe. This concept of *ordo,* which has cosmological as well as practical implications, underlay many of Charles's reforms, explains his wide variety of interests, and perhaps explains his frequently expressed regrets, especially toward the end of his life, at having done so little to make the world, as he said, "truly Christian." Unlike his father and grandfather, Charlemagne appears to have possessed a broad vision of his place as king, a vision in which his personal responsibility for rectifying church and kingdom looms particularly large, in which his sense of mission was directed primarily at the eradication of abuses and disorder and at the restoration of an ideal pattern of life on many levels. Such a concept, which was probably formed slowly, underlay Charles's meticulous care to restore proper rules for ecclesiastical offices; the assiduity with which he ordered exact copies of the Benedictine rule, the Roman Sacramentary, canon law, and the writings of the church fathers; and his concern for the maintaining of records of his own activities—his correspondence with Byzantium and with the papacy, the ecclesiastical deliberations of his church councils, and his sponsorship of the court annals. It is from these efforts and from Charles's eagerness to provide a learned and well-trained clergy that the rest of the literary output of the royal circle derives, and it is the official literary undertakings that loomed with greater importance in the eyes of the king.

In order to promote these intellectual reforms, Charles developed the palace school, transforming an older institution for the training of young boys into an academy where literary learning and other forms of training were combined under the watchful care of the king himself and the scholars he brought to court. Out of the court school and the monastic schools, which now included external pupils along with the young novices, there developed not only the wider spread of learning and literary patronage that characterizes the ninth century, but the replacement of the cumbersome and difficult Merovingian style of handwriting by a new orthography that carefully separated individual letters and was much easier to read. The Carolingian minuscule, as this new hand is called, appeared first in the 780s and circulated widely thereafter. This script became the basis not only for the orthographic reforms of the eighth and ninth centuries, but for those of the fifteenth century, and it constitutes one of the sources for later typefaces and modern orthography. Education, handwriting reforms, and patronage reflect Charlemagne's care that his reforms should be thorough and fundamental. The *Admonitio generalis* of 789 publicly disseminated the king's views to his subjects, and subsequent royal pronouncements, whether in such letters as the *De litteris colendis* to the monks of Fulda or the more public capitularies (royal announcements of policy and law that were divided into chapters, *capitula*), reflect the king's persistent concern for the roots of the more ambitious reforms he had in mind.

Charlemagne's great search for the authentic versions of basic ecclesiastical texts had other consequences besides the reform of education and handwriting. First, the king's acceptance of a given text assured that text an enduring and prominent role in subsequent intellectual history. Thus, the *Dionysio-Hadriana,* the collection of ecclesiastical law that was sent to Charlemagne by Pope Hadrian in 774 and consists of the work of the great fifth-century ecclesiastic Dionysius Exiguus, became the foundation for all later collections of canon law and inspired the great canonists of the eleventh and twelfth centuries in their own compilations, traces of which exist in ecclesiastical law, both Protestant and Catholic, of the present day. The Sacramentary that the king received in 786, also from Rome, became the foundation for Continental ecclesiastical liturgical practice, just as the 787 copying of the rule of St. Benedict became the fundamental basis for monastic reforms during the next five centuries. The importance of Charles's concept of order is seen clearly enough here: the works he considered essential for his reforms remained particularly prominent and, as a result of their circulation, further influenced later intellectual development. Moreover, Charles's reliance upon Roman practice and Roman copies of these documents further strengthened the bond between the Franks and Rome and further spread the spiritual authority of the successors of St. Peter.

The king's interest in the fundamentals of education and the principles of reform and restoration of the right order of spiritual life had other consequences as well. The spread of educational institutions speeded the production of classical texts of poetry and prose, and the earliest manuscripts of many of the classical Roman and Greek authors that we now possess date from the late eighth and ninth centuries. This revival of interest in classical literature was, however, distinctly secondary to Charles's other interests. Charles had no remote idea of restoring the culture of pagan Rome, but rather of using that culture, or some of its traces, in restoring a proper kind of Christianity among his subjects, clerical and lay. Moreover, not only did classical literature circulate more widely and classical learning show its traces in other aspects of literary production, but the Germanic language of the Franks appears in the late eighth century chiefly in the ecclesiastical texts that required the use of the vernacular, but also in Charlemagne's noted fondness for collections of the old Germanic heroic poems, which one source tells us he had collected for his own enjoyment and which several scholars have attempted to reconstruct.

Between the troubled period 768–774 and the later triumphs of the king lies the story of Charlemagne's personal energies in organizing his kingdom and his assembling a body of loyal and able assistants and servants. It is to the latter that we now turn. The court of Charlemagne attracted, as might be expected, many of the most powerful figures in the kingdom, from royal relatives to ecclesiastical leaders to counts and marquesses on visits from their own districts. The palace school attracted the children of those in the palace and those close to the king. Yet, surprisingly, most of the figures whose names are associated most closely with the intellectual reform of Charlemagne's reign came to the king from great distances. Peter of Pisa and Paulinus of Aquileia, grammarians, and Paul the Deacon, historian of both the Lombards and the bishops of Metz, all came from Lombard Italy in the 770s and 780s. A new stream of exiles from Moslem Spain led Theodulf, a Visigoth and later, bishop of Orléans, to the palace, where his administrative, theological, and literary skills earned him the respect of Charlemagne and others. Dicuil the geographer and Dungal the astronomer came from Ireland. A number of other figures were native Franks, drawn to the intellectual life of the palace circle of scholars perhaps both by its novelty and by the obvious delight Charlemagne took in the company of these learned clerics.

The man associated most closely with the revival also came from a great distance. Alcuin was an Englishman, a monk at York, and the heir of the great tradition of English Christian learning that dated from the day of Theodore and Hadrian in the seventh century and had been crowned by Bede in the early eighth. Boniface, too, had emerged from that culture, and in a sense Alcuin may be considered the culmination of that tradition of eighth-century Anglo-Saxon influence upon Continental Christian culture. Alcuin was born around 730, and rose to become the head of the school at the church of York. He traveled to Rome in 780–781 in order to bring back the *pallium,* the stole of white wool that symbolized the papal approval of an archbishop, to his superior, Eanbald. Upon his return journey Alcuin met Charlemagne at Parma and was invited to come to the king's court after completing his mission. From 782 to 796 Alcuin was a fixture at the court of the Frankish king, exercising his influence particularly in the palace school, of which he became the master and which he reformed along the lines of the kind of learning developed in the English tradition. After a brief return to England between 790 and 793, Alcuin returned to Charlemagne's court, this time to become a spiritual adviser on a plane higher even than that which he had occupied as head of the palace school. In 796 Alcuin retired from court and became abbot of the great monastery of St. Martin at Tours, although he remained Charlemagne's most influential adviser, producing from the *scriptorium* of the monastery and through his own extensive correspondence the most important literary works of this first phase of the Carolingian-sponsored revival of learning. Alcuin's friends and students constituted the intellectual elite of the early ninth century, and his influence can be seen in the intellectual tradition of the great ninth-century monastic schools and their teachers. In the twenty-year association of Charlemagne and Alcuin it is possible to observe the extraordinarily close relationship between the most powerful ruler in the west and the individual who, probably more than anyone else, was his guide and consultant on the most important intellectual issues of his day.

In spite of the pervasive influence and wide learning of Alcuin, however, one other figure from these early years of the Carolingian revival should be noted. Among the court officials and scholars who met in these periodic study groups that gathered informally around the king and discussed matters of political and intellectual interest was Einhard, a layman from the Main valley who came to court in 793. He was born in 770 and spent his youth at the school of the monastery of Fulda, the most important of St. Boniface's monastic foundations and later perhaps the greatest center of learning in the kingdom. Einhard was one of its earliest products. Taught to read and write, and doubtless having acquired a considerable degree of competence in other aspects of institutional administration that could also be learned at a great monastery, Einhard joined Charlemagne's court, quickly became a well-known figure among the literary talents there—he is mentioned in several poems and letters from the period—and after 796 became supervisor of the royal building program, which focused his energies on the construction of Charlemagne's palace complex at Aachen. Many of the members of Charlemagne's intellectual and social circle acquired nicknames from classical or biblical literature: Charles himself was called "David," Alcuin

"Flaccus," after Horace, and Einhard "Bezaleel," after the Old Testament builder of the Temple.

Einhard remained a layman throughout his life, and his achievements, from his early days in the intellectual circles of the court, through his building career and his diplomatic missions, to his end as the lay abbot of the monastery of Seligenstadt, would themselves make him a figure of considerable importance for our understanding of the middle ranks of Charlemagne's courtiers and friends, even in the absence of a single work that may well be the most important literary production in Europe between Bede's *Ecclesiastical History* at the beginning of the eighth century and the Latin epic poem *Waltarius* from the middle of the tenth. Sometime after Charlemagne's death, Einhard wrote the king's biography, the first secular biography in modern literature. Hitherto reserved for the lives of saints or for the episodic achievements of ecclesiastical leaders, as was the case with Paul the Deacon's *History of the Bishops of Metz*, the genre of biography was renewed by Einhard as a fitting tribute to the importance of the life of his master, particularly, it may be suggested, in the light of the troubled days of the 820s and 830s. Whatever the occasion of its beginning, Einhard's *Life of Charles the Great* reintroduced the life of the secular hero into literature and exerted an enormous influence upon the genre of biography in later centuries. Through Einhard's prose, a mixture of classical and Carolingian styles (he borrowed several phrases and passages from Suetonius's *Lives of the Twelve Caesars*), which continually resists the tendency to describe a type and which shows us again and again what can only be considered fairly close to eyewitness reporting, the figure of Charlemagne emerges from chronicle and capitulary into something resembling immediacy and individuality. Charles was born in 743, eight years before his father's palace revolution, and when he was eleven, he and his brother Carloman were crowned with their father on the occasion of Pope Stephen II's visit to the Frankish king to ask his aid against the Lombards. But Einhard begins his biography, not with the birth of Charles, but with a description of the circumstances behind Pepin's ascent to the throne, including a strong denunciation of the incompetence of the last Merovingian kings that may well be considerably overdrawn. Einhard's *Life* continues through the troubled relations between Charles and his brother Carloman and Charles's single rule from 771 on. He then proceeds topically, from an account of Charles's battles and his relations with other rulers (which includes a description of the famous elephant, Abdoul Abaz, sent to Charlemagne by Harun al-Rashid, caliph of Baghdad), to Charles's building activities, particularly the construction of the palace at Aachen. In chapters 22–27 there is a remarkable description of Charlemagne's person.

> Charles was large and strong, and of lofty stature, though not disproportionately tall [modern estimates agree that Charlemagne was nearly six feet four inches tall, evidently an unusually great height for a Frank]; the upper part of his head was round, his eyes very large and animated, nose a little

long, hair fair and face laughing and merry . . . although his neck was thick and somewhat short, and his belly rather prominent; but the symmetry of the rest of his body concealed these defects. His gait was firm, his whole carriage manly, and his voice clear, but not as strong as his size led one to expect.

In accordance with the national custom, he took frequent exercise on horseback and in the chase. He enjoyed the exhalations from natural warm springs, and often practised swimming.

He used to wear the Frankish dress—next to his skin a linen shirt and linen breeches, and above these a tunic fringed with silk; while hose fastened by bands covered his lower limbs; and shoes his feet; and he protected his shoulders and chest in winter by a close-fitting cloak of otter or marten skins. Over all he flung a blue cloak, and he always had a sword girt around him, usually with a gold or silver hilt or belt.

He despised foreign costumes, however handsome, and never allowed himself to be robed in them, except twice in Rome. On great feast days he made use of embroidered clothes and shoes bedecked with precious stones, his cloak was fastened by a golden buckle, and he appeared crowned with a diadem of gold and gems, but on other days his dress varied little from the common dress of the people.

Einhard comments further on Charlemagne's moderate eating and drinking habits, his long working sessions punctuated by short periods of sleep, his readiness of speech, his interest in languages, and his religious enthusiasm. The personal affection of the writer for his subject is clear throughout the work, and in spite of occasional exaggerations, the biography allows us a remarkable glimpse of a late eighth-century ruler through the eyes of a man who knew him personally and had observed him closely.

In the end, Einhard rather than Alcuin offers us the easiest access to Charlemagne and the broadest background for understanding the king. A semiliterate barbarian ruler, a second-generation king who rose from a coup d'état and who had to struggle ruthlessly for his own throne, a Frank not much different visibly from those around him, he was nevertheless considerably more. His interest in learning, his extensive patronage of ecclesiastical and secular culture, and his continual involvement in the affairs of a growing kingdom mark him as something more than an exceptionally ambitious barbarian prince. The legacy of his intellectual patronage influenced the thought of Europe for centuries. Einhard's biography, as does no other document, shows us both the Frankish warrior and the king, whose new ideal of kingship influenced royal practices so pronouncedly at a critical moment in Europe's history.

FRANKISH KING AND *IMPERATOR ROMANORUM*

From many points of view in the third quarter of the eighth century, Charlemagne appeared to occupy a position considerably different from that of most Germanic kings. By the 770s, Charlemagne's military successes had been recognized even beyond the borders of his kingdom. In 776, the Anglo-Saxon Cathwulf had referred to Charles's kingdom as the *Regnum Europae,* the kingdom of Europe, thus reviving the obscure territorial designation, Europe, to indicate the breadth of Charles's new power. In the last decades of the century, Charlemagne's relations with the kings of Northumbria and Mercia indicated their inferiority to him, as did the tribute from the increasingly powerful King Alfonso II of Asturias in northern Spain. Shortly after 780, Empress Irene of Constantinople negotiated with Charles concerning a marriage between Charles's daughter Rotrud and Irene's son Constantine VI. This recognition, along with the embassies from Harun al-Rashid and the overtures from the Christian inhabitants of Jerusalem that reached Charles in 800, indicate one level of his position. The prestige of the king of the Franks was greater than that of any other Christian ruler. The magnitude of the impression made upon contemporaries by Charles's successes should not be underestimated in the rather more theoretical discussions that follow.

We have already seen how Charles's concern with ecclesiastical questions began early in his reign and, if anything, increased markedly toward the end of the century. The 780s witnessed extensive ecclesiastical reforms in the capitularies issued by Charlemagne. During the period 787–791, the first suppression of iconoclasm in Byzantium had resulted in the Council of Nicaea of 787, whose canons, agreed upon by Pope Hadrian II but badly translated into Latin, reached the Frankish kingdom and elicited a complex response written principally by Theodulf of Orléans but signed by Charles. This response, the *Libri Carolini,* strongly criticized the iconodule position, challenged the right of Irene, as a woman, to rule the empire, undercut the claims to ecumenicity of imperially sponsored church councils, and reiterated the traditional orthodoxy of the Franks, Charles's conversion of infidels, and the traditional ties between the Franks and the pope, the true authority for the determination of orthodox beliefs. At the Council of Frankfurt in 794, the Carolingian king and high churchmen dealt with the heresy of adoptionism, a dispute concerning the natures of Christ that reflected a rivalry between the Christian churchmen of Moslem Spain and those in the Christian kingdom to the north. Throughout the 790s the correspondence of Alcuin, Charles's closest adviser during these years, reflected a great concern for the survival of orthodoxy and the dangers to orthodox belief posed by various parts of Spain and Italy. In 797 Charlemagne issued the *Capitulare Saxonicum,* a broadly conceived and diplomatic approach to a program for the peaceable introduction of Christianity among the Saxons and Slavs, a program very different from the earlier, more brutal policies of Christianization that the king had insisted upon. From 795 on, another ecclesiastical crisis confronted the king. Pope Leo III, Hadrian's successor, had encountered formidable opposition in Rome, been accused of crimes, and kidnapped. The last years of the century saw both Alcuin and Charles particularly concerned for the situation of the pope and the consequent welfare of the Church. These ecclesiastical concerns, which show a steady sharpening of Charles's

Plate 9 courtesy Thames and Hudson Ltd., London.

MATERIAL CIVILIZATION, 800-1450. One of the great themes of European history between the eighth and the sixteenth centuries is the increasing control over the material world achieved by laborers, builders, peasants, and artisans and the exploitation of this control by patrons and landowners, clerical and lay. The plan for a proposed new monastery at St. Gall in Switzerland was never followed through to the construction stage, but the artist Alan Sorrell has reconstructed the appearance of the monastery as it would have looked had the plan been followed (Plate 9). The worlds of prayer, residence, and work are intelligently divided, and the plan is a marvel of engineering theory for the early ninth century.

Plate 10 courtesy Bild-Archiv der Osterreichische Nationalbibliothek, Vienna.

Depiction of the various labors that an agricultural world required in the different months of the year (Plate 10) often decorated astronomical manuscripts, as they did this tenth-century manuscript page.

Plate 11 reproduced by permission of the British Library Board. Additional Ms. 18850, f.17v.

One of the best sources of pictorial information concerning building is in illuminations of the construction of the Tower of Babel, *Genesis:* II (Plate 11), as shown here from a fifteenth-century manuscript. The construction techniques are those of the fifteenth century, and particularly interesting are the platforms supported by beams jutting out from the upper walls, from which workers construct the next course of walls.

Plate 12 courtesy L'Italia Magazine, ENIT, Rome.

Finally, perhaps the most characteristic feature of early European economic life is the market with its shops (Plate 12), here depicted in a fourteenth-century fresco from northwestern Italy.

ecclesiastical ideas and his concept of his own role, as well as the influence of articulate advisers, occurred at the same time as the first successes of Carolingian educational reforms and the building of the palace at Aachen, which had been under way since 794 and reflected a new conception of a palace-capital for the king.

The style of the buildings at Aachen appears to have been an imitation of the imperial palace at Constantinople as well as of earlier imperial monuments in Italy, particularly in Ravenna and Rome, and is quite distinct from earlier Frankish royal dwellings. In addition to this form of imperial imitation, several scholars have noted that from early in his reign, Charlemagne borrowed several devices that were the unique right of the Roman emperor at Constantinople, among them the use of the monogram and the lead *bulla*, or seal, on documents. These developments in palace building and design, court ceremonial, and diplomatic (the formal process of drawing up official documents), and the motifs of imperial themes in the court art of the 790s suggest a new status beginning to emerge in the mind of the king of the Franks and those around him. Some of this status may be gathered from a letter written by Alcuin to Ethelred, king of Northumbria, in 793. In this letter, Alcuin draws a sharp portrait of the ideal Christian king. After denouncing the evils he has heard of in England, Alcuin berates its kings for their irresponsibility, their neglect of their God-given powers, and their un-Christian way of life. He then goes on to praise the idea of a Christian ruler.

> Nothing defends a country better than the equity and godliness of its princes and the intercessions of the servants of God. Remember that Hezekiah, that just and pious king, procured from God by a single prayer [the destruction of] a hundred and eighty-five thousand of the enemy . . . by an angel in one night. Likewise with profuse tears he averted from him death when it threatened him, and [so] deserved of God that fifteen years were added to his life by this prayer. Have decent habits, pleasing to God and laudable to men. Be rulers of the people, not robbers; shepherds, not plunderers.

Alcuin's conception of a new kind of kingship, echoing as it does the writings of Bede and the coronations of 751 and 754, strongly colored his fears for the Church in the last years of the eighth century. Who else fit the description of a Christian Hezekiah better than Charles? To whom had God already given all the Christians in the west to rule and all the non-Christians to convert? And had not Charles done this well? By 794 Alcuin had referred to Charles as a *novus David,* a new David.

Between 795 and 797 two new crises of universal portent appeared: a revolution in Byzantium and the assault on Pope Leo III. The iconoclast movement under Emperors Leo III and Constantine V had placed the relations between the Latin and Greek parts of the Church under great strain and had stirred up sharp divisions in Byzantine intellectual, political, and spiritual life. The reign of Constantine V in particular, which was marked by the sharpest persecutions of the iconodules, was also a period of considerable military triumph and great strengthening of the Byzantine state. At Constantine's death in 775, he was succeeded by his far less competent son Leo IV, who died five years later, leaving his wife, the empress Irene, and an infant son, Constantine VI, to succeed him. Irene governed in her son's name and, an image worshiper herself, worked to undo the results of the iconoclast movement. In 787 the council of Nicaea reversed the earlier ruling against icons issued by the Synod of Hereia and reopened good relations with Rome. Irene, as we have seen, negotiated briefly with Charlemagne concerning a marriage between Charlemagne's daughter and Constantine VI. Irene, however, thereby alienated a considerable segment of the Byzantine ruling class, particularly the Asiatic soldiery, and her ambition led her to blind her son (thereby ritually making him unfit to rule) in 797 and to rule from that date as sole empress in her own name.

Irene's sex raised the question in the west, and perhaps in the east as well, as to whether or not a woman *could* hold the imperial office. Such a constitutional problem had never risen before, and the novelty of the idea may well have alienated further not only the Franks and the pope, but Irene's own subjects as well. Certainly, some Frankish sources after 800 observe that both Charlemagne and Pope Leo considered the imperial throne vacant in 800. Between 800 and 802 Charles and Irene even negotiated the project of their marriage. Irene, however, was overthrown in 802 and replaced by Nicephorus I (802–811), who renewed Byzantine resistance to Charles's imperial pretensions.

The question of the Byzantine view (or views) of Charlemagne's imperial status needs to be clarified by the observation that neither the title of *patricius* nor that of *Caesar* was given in the empire without the emperor's permission. In the eyes of the Byzantines, the empire and the Church were coterminous, and the Byzantine emperor was the head of both, and hence of the "family of rulers," those who ruled Christian peoples and had contact, however insubordinate, with Byzantium. The title *patricius* had been given to many allies of the empire before Pepin and Charlemagne received it, and in the early eighth century Tervel, khan of the Bulgars, had been made Caesar by Justinian II. A century after 800, another khan of the Bulgars was even named emperor, but in a style that indicated subordination to the emperor at Constantinople. Thus, it is not impossible that Charlemagne's claim could have been acceptable to Irene in this sense, and that it could have been accepted by Nicephorus I if not for the fact that it had been accepted by the hated Irene. In any case, Byzantine resistance to Charles's imperial title became strong after 802, and not until 812–813 was an agreement reached, one that, as we will see, recognized Charlemagne's imperial status, but on a level distinctly inferior to that of the emperor at Constantinople.

The crisis that struck Pope Leo III, however, was of more immediate consequence. The charges launched by Leo's enemies against him were such that they could only have been tried in an imperial court. The consternation of Alcuin and Charlemagne was quite real, and Charlemagne's letters to the pope reveal his concern for the moral crisis at hand. They reveal also Charles's conception of himself as a corrector of ecclesiastical abuses, even those at the highest level.

> It is incumbent upon us, with God's help, to defend Holy Church outwardly with weapons everywhere against attacks by pagans and devastation by infidels, and to consolidate her inwardly through the understanding of the true faith. It is your task, Holy Father, like Moses, to lift up your arms in prayer and so to aid our army that by your intercession the Christian people, under God's guidance and guarantee, may always be victorious over the enemies of His holy name.

By 799 both Alcuin and Charles shared an acute sense of an ecclesiastical crisis with Pope Leo at its center. Echoes of both the Byzantine and Roman difficulties resound in a remarkable letter written by Alcuin to Charles in 799:

> Until now, there have been three men of highest rank in the world. The first is the apostolic sublimity, governing from the throne of the blessed Peter, prince of the apostles, as his vicar. . . . The second is the imperial dignity and power of the other Rome [Constantinople]. . . . The third is the royal dignity which by the dispensation of our lord Jesus Christ is conferred upon you as the governor of the Christian people.

Alcuin then remarks upon the present weakness of the papacy and the crimes of the empress Irene, and he concludes:

> The royal dignity is more excellent than the other dignities in power, more shining in wisdom, more sublime in rank. Now on you alone rests the tottering safety of the churches of Christ. It is for you to avenge crimes, to guide the erring, to console the sorrowing, and to raise up the good.

In Alcuin's view, at least, Charles's royal dignity, originally the third of three supreme powers, is now the only one available to sustain the Christian Church and people. Charles, like Hezekiah and David, the just king, must now act alone and imperially.

In April of 799 Pope Leo was kidnapped by his enemies, but he escaped and made his way to Charles at Paderborn. In November, 800, Charles arrived outside Rome and was greeted by the pope with the ceremonial procedures appropriate for an imperial entrance into the city. Early in December, Leo cleared himself of all charges by an oath of purgation, and the ensuing synod probably decided to crown Charles emperor, possibly at the urging of Frankish clerics then present. On the evening of December 25, following the third mass of Christmas, Pope Leo placed a crown on Charles's head and declared him emperor of the Romans, the imperial *laudes* were chanted, and the pope prostrated himself in the formal *proskynesis* before the emperor.

Several sources remark Charles's displeasure with his coronation, but scholarship has suggested strongly that such displeasure could not have been caused by utter surprise. Undoubtedly, Charles knew of his forthcoming imperial coronation, and his anger may have been directed at the form it took, although that form was technically correct except for the pope's placing of the crown on the emperor's head. Technically, the Roman people created an emperor by acclamation; the pope (or the patriarch of Constantinople, for that matter) had no constitutive hand in the affair. What may have been Pope Leo's desire to associate himself with the coronation as further insurance against his enemies (he could not have suggested even remotely that the pope had the authority to crown an emperor), may account for the emperor's displeasure. The imperial title, when problems of diplomatic were worked out, was *Karolus Serenissimus Augustus, a Deo coronatus, magnus et pacificus imperator, Romanum gubernans imperium, qui et per misericordiam Dei rex Francorum et Langobardorum* (Charles, most serene Augustus, crowned by God, great and pacific emperor, governing the Roman Empire and through the mercy of God King of the Franks and of the Lombards). However many other reasons may be adduced beyond those suggested here—and there are many—Alcuin and Charlemagne regarded the new power and legitimacy of the king of the Franks and the Lombards as particularly favored by God and therefore suitable to be increased by the divinely ordained title of emperor of the Romans.

12

POLITICS, SOCIETY, AND ECONOMY IN NINTH-CENTURY EUROPE

FROM *RESPUBLICA CHRISTIANA* TO SEPARATE KINGDOMS, 814–888

Of Charlemagne's twelve children, only one survived to succeed to the emperor's vast legacy—Louis, called "the Pious," who reigned from Charlemagne's death in 814 until his own death in 840. During the last years of Charlemagne's rule, some of the controls over the old emperor's vast dominions slipped from his hands, and the thirty-six-year-old Louis faced the extraordinary difficulties not only of ruling the empire but of asserting his authority in the face of resistance from well-entrenched nobles, churchmen, and factions. The essentially personal rule still required of a ninth-century monarch, even one who was emperor of the Romans, king of the

Franks and Lombards, and lord of most of Europe, demanded that Louis reform the palace and establish his own counselors securely around himself, thereby necessarily creating personal and family resentment. After removing many of Charlemagne's old counselors and attempting to reform the process of governance, Louis paid great attention to the question of ecclesiastical reforms. Guided by his spiritual mentor, Benedict of Aniane, Louis undertook a reform of monasticism more effective and enduring than that of his father, and developed a much more complex concept of his own imperial duties. The circle of advisers with whom Louis surrounded himself contained men as remarkable as those who had served Charlemagne. Benedict of Aniane, Hilduin, and Helisachar, among others, continued the difficult task of establishing the order of governance across the empire, continued the literary and artistic patronage that produced in the ninth century a powerful and enduring intellectual movement, and attempted, with the emperor, to come to grips finally with a question that Charlemagne himself had repeatedly asked at the end of his life: *"Utrum vere Christiani sumus"*—"Whether we are truly Christians."

Yet the title of emperor provided Louis with no more actual resources for governance than it had his father. To a certain extent, the precocious development of some ideas and institutions during the reign of Charlemagne even tended to weaken the royal-imperial authority of the king. The growth of the church among the Franks and the impact of Charlemagne's reforms made the Carolingian higher clergy, particularly the bishops, especially vociferous in claiming to be independent of the emperor. These stress points became more important with the issuance of the *Ordinatio imperii* of 817. In this remarkable document, Louis violated traditional Frankish laws of equal inheritance among male children and relegated two of his sons, Pepin and Louis, to the position of border rulers subordinate to their imperial brother Lothair. Louis in Bavaria and the east and Pepin in Aquitaine and the west were viceroys for a superior ruler. The growing self-consciousness of the prelates, resentment against Louis's constitutional novelties, and the birth of a fourth son, Charles, in 825, led to considerable stresses and to another constitutional reform in 829.

The role of personal loyalty was critical in the ninth century. Royal capitularies, private correspondence, and ecclesiastical literature reiterated, with an intensity that only indicates widespread disaffection with the existing state of loyalty the demands of personal oaths of loyalty to superiors. The men around Louis, particularly the men he appointed to govern far away from him, had to be trusted. In 818, Bernard, King of Italy and Louis's nephew, was brought to the emperor and charged with treason. Blinded, Bernard died a short time later, thereby signaling the onset of insecurity that colors the last part of Louis's reign. In 829, Louis issued a new program for the legacy of the empire, one that took account of the existence of his new son, Charles.

The criticism of the Frankish bishops, the disaffection of many nobles and members of his own family, and his own pangs of conscience in the case of Bernard were not the only difficulties that Louis faced between 818 and 833. Economic decline, raids on the frontiers by the Scandinavians, the Bretons, the Arabs of Spain, and the Slavic peoples to the east all preoccupied the emperor, and the institutions of governance to which his father and he had devoted so much time and energy seemed not to work. Complaints mounted, and in 830 an abortive revolution by his sons was stopped by the emperor's firmness. The next two years, however, witnessed no change for the better. In 833 another revolt succeeded, Lothair, Pepin, and Louis forcing their father into retirement. An assembly of bishops hostile to Louis tried him for his alleged sins. Those sins were so great, they claimed, that Louis must be subjected to a perpetually disabling penance for the rest of his life, and must never again be canonically permitted to take up the sword and rule the empire. Louis was subsequently confined at Aachen in Lothair's custody. A year of Lothair's rule turned out to be enough for his brothers, however, and Louis was freed and then rehabilitated at another ecclesiastical assembly in 834. From 834 until his death in 840, Louis faced continued revolts, invasions from the north, and continued resistance to his governance.

At Louis's death in 840, a struggle for territory ensued among the surviving sons, Louis, Lothair, and Charles. At the Treaty of Verdun in 843, three kingdoms were cut from the old empire, *Francia Occidentalis* in the west going to Charles, *Francia Orientalis* in the east to Louis, and a middle kingdom extending from the North Sea through parts of modern Germany, France, and Switzerland and ending south of Rome, along with the weakened imperial title, to Lothair. These divisions, so counter to Louis the Pious's early visions of the intactness of the empire, recognized the old principles of divided inheritance and the new realities of regional interests.

In the years that followed the Treaty of Verdun in 843, a new regionalism, based in part upon the acquisitions of some of the Frankish nobility during the reigns of Charlemagne and Louis, slowly overcame the momentary central authority created by the remarkable personality of Charlemagne. Beginning in Burgundy and spreading to other borders, there emerged specialized frontier commands based upon the Carolingian concept of the frontier march. These internal frontiers conferred considerable powers on the nobles who administered them nominally in the kings' names, and the second half of the ninth century witnessed the shaping of blocs of territory under individuals with extraordinary powers, based partly upon the old Carolingian counties and marches and partly upon the ethnic divisions of old separatist territories such as Aquitaine and Bavaria. In the course of the late ninth and early tenth centuries these concentrations of command and power became detached from the kings, and in the late tenth and the eleventh centuries they slowly emerged as "counties" and "duchies," powerful territorial principalities whose lords formalized their status after two centuries of struggle and indifference to the claims of larger loyalties. The holding of royal lands by members of a single family throughout several generations, the institution of lay abbacies, by which laymen were appointed abbots of wealthy ecclesiastical properties, and the new forces of family and factional interest created new kinds of power in the kingdoms after 843 and gave to the surviving aristocracy both a new sense of solidarity and new powers.

The divisions of the imperial and royal lands after 843 resulted from the survival of older Frankish laws of inheritance. Those same laws became operative upon the deaths of Louis the Pious's three sons. When Lothair died in 855, his great Middle Kingdom, which contained the twin capitals of Rome and Aachen, was divided among his own three sons: Louis II (855–875) became emperor and ruled only Italy, Lothair II (855–869) obtained the northern parts of the Middle Kingdom and subsequently became memorialized in the territorial name for this area, Lotharingia, later Lorraine, and Charles (855–863) obtained Provence. When Charles died in 863, Provence was divided between Lothair II and Louis II, and when Lothair II died in 869, Charles of *Francia Occidentalis*, or Charles the Bald as he is known to history, and Louis of *Francia Orientalis*, or Louis the German, divided his kingdom. When Louis the German died in 875, his kingdom was divided among three sons. These family divisions of kingdoms that had themselves been reluctant divisions of the single kingdom of Charlemagne and Louis increased the kings' dependence upon the support of regional nobility and clergy. The idea of empire, which had its roots in Roman, Anglo-Saxon, and Carolingian ideas and events in the late eighth century and received under Louis the Pious the more complex imprint of spiritual mission, survived only in Rome, sustained by a series of popes whose own difficulties seem far more local and immediate than the transcendental issues of imperial theory and practice. The reigns of Lothair (843–855), Louis II (855–875), Charles the Bald (875–877), and Charles the Fat (881–887) as emperors are of far greater importance in regional history than in the history of the empire.

The struggles for political survival and the difficulties created by the complex questions of royal and imperial succession were only two of the problems that faced the Carolingian rulers of the late ninth century. Local revolts, invasions by Bretons, Northmen, Arabs, and later, Magyars, economic decline, and a diminishing level of communications all made it extremely difficult to rule. The presence of local centers of power meant, among other things, that young princes had fewer opportunities to learn their trade in great courts such as those of Charlemagne and Louis. Many rulers of the late ninth and early tenth centuries were backwoods princes ruling backwoods kingdoms, their imaginations as limited as their political horizons and their restricted powers. Immediate defense, family interests, and, whenever possible, expansion at the expense of others occupied them throughout their lives.

The nobles who witnessed the transformation of the Carolingian monarchies during the late ninth and early tenth centuries had acquired their power largely in the service of the early members of the Carolingian dynasty. To the lands that they gave out only for life and only in return for service and continued loyalty, the first Carolingians had attached a number of powers that would later be considered "public." The retention of some of these powers by ambitious and energetic nobles who also managed to retain the lands themselves increased the informal power of the aristocracy. Lands and powers both were conferred by the kings upon the receipt of an oath of personal loyalty. From the early ninth century, these oaths were surrounded by ecclesiastical sanctions as well, and the man who "commended" himself, who rendered homage to his superior, created not only a sanctified personal bond between them, but also, when in addition the superior conferred a *beneficium* on the vassal, lands or incomes to be held for life. Originally, the oath of homage and commendation had no connection with landholding or with the lifetime acquisition of royal rights to lands so held. Several generations passed, however, and those who held benefices tended to try to retain them in their own families. The slow gravitation of lands, powers, and incomes held for life toward lands, powers, and incomes joined slowly and subtly to personal or family property occurred throughout the ninth century. The very check upon disloyalty that the lifetime tenure of a lord's property was intended to constitute turned into a spur toward disloyalty and the growth of personal and family inerest. In 877, in a document known as the Capitulary of Quierzy, Charles the Bald issued stern injunctions against the inheritability of royal benefices, assertions of the king's right to appoint anyone he chose to vacant honors, and the identification of territorial gifts with the rules governing offices. These concerns of the king indicate that the hereditary principle was already making inroads, and that great noblemen had long been building private power with what had earlier been royal gifts. The new dependence of the rulers on the loyalty of a group of ambitious warlords prevented them from stopping this process, and by the early tenth century new bases of aristocratic power and new ties of dependency had spread throughout the old kingdom of the Franks, which were on the verge of disappearing into legend.

The fragmenting of the old kingdom of the Franks and the more recent empire witnessed other crises besides invasion, dynastic rivalry, and the growing power of a newly strengthened aristocracy. The Frankish clergy, particularly the bishops, had asserted their spiritual autonomy during the reign of Louis the Pious and had played key roles in Louis's disgrace and penitence in 833 and his rehabilitation in 834. Louis nevertheless extended the ecclesiastical reforms begun by his father in 802. He undertook to legislate matters concerning the support of clergy, particularly in churches and monasteries controlled by laymen, and the duties owed by the clergy to the king. And the royal support of the church extended to the continuation of missions to the Saxons and to the beginning of what turned out to be a vastly premature mission to christianize Scandinavia.

A remarkable series of documents surviving from the second and third quarters of the ninth century reveal many ecclesiastical concepts of public order and the respective rights of churchmen and kings. Written either as tracts on the ordering of the palace or as direct instructions to kings on how to rule well, these documents have been given the collective generic name of "Mirrors for Princes." In them, most of which were written by high ecclesiastics, one can by reading between the lines trace the changing attitudes of Frankish churchmen toward the temporal rulers.

Another series of documents that reflects the ecclesiastical crises of the ninth century had much more enduring consequences. This was the series of collections of ecclesiastical legal privileges that included a number of forged documents whose authenticity was unquestioned for several centuries. The period between 750 and 900 spawned a considerable number of forged documents, the most striking ones touching upon questions of ecclesiastical authority. At the end of the eighth century a Roman cleric, drawing upon earlier legends of Pope Sylvester I (314–335) and eager to justify papal claims to certain legal privileges in Rome, forged a remarkable document known as the Donation of Constantine, which purported to be a charter in which Emperor Constantine gave to the pope rule over imperial lands and palaces in the western part of the empire. The fictitiousness of this document, although long suspected, was not established formally until the fifteenth century, when the scholar Lorenzo Valla submitted the text to a minute linguistic and diplomatic analysis. The Donation of Constantine was but the first of a series of false documents whose purpose was to further what in many cases were relatively limited interests. The scope of these forgeries, however, and their astonishing breadth of legal overkill, gave them importance not only in the immediate circumstances of the ninth century, but in later centuries as well. The interests of the bishop of Le Mans in several lawsuits of the ninth century produced a remarkable collection of fraudulent documents known as the Le Mans Forgeries. Around 890, a Frankish cleric in Moravia presented forged documents to Pope Stephen V that were intended to impugn the orthodoxy of the great missionary to the Slavs, St. Methodios, and, incidentally, to further his own career in ecclesiastical politics. Unfortunately, the pope believed the documents and, among other things, prohibited the use of a liturgy in Slavic for churches of the Latin rite. The most influential collection of forgeries, however, were the False, or Pseudo-Isidorean, Decretals, produced in the mid ninth century to shore up the authority and unity of the Frankish bishops. This collection, which had a long and lively career in the politics and ecclesiology of Europe until the seventeenth century, purported to contain authentic letters of pre fourth-century popes and many letters of later popes, as well as canons of councils. Most of the alleged papal material in this collection consisted of forgeries that were very accomplished and, incidental to the primary purpose of the collection, particularly authoritative on the point of papal power. The Frankish bishops, challenging the authority of their archbishops, saw in their own rank and in the papacy the true unity of the Church. The skill with which many of these forgeries were produced is one slight piece of evidence for the considerable interest in learning and in Church history that the Frankish clergy of the ninth century possessed —another aspect of the lasting consequences of the Carolingian renaissance.

The Frankish higher clergy of the ninth century constituted a broad spectrum of intellectual talent and political energy. In their conflicts among themselves, with the kings, and with papal claims of authority, such prelates as Ebo of Reims, Hincmar of Reims, Agobard of Lyons, and Jonas of Orléans made the Frankish episcopate one of the most dynamic ecclesiastical and political forces in early European history.

The proposed, postponed, and effected divisions of Charlemagne's legacy in 806, 817, 829, and 843 illustrate the clash between old and new principles of public law in the ninth century, as do the clashes among the Frankish higher clergy. The kingdom of West Francia under Charles the Bald, the Middle Kingdom under Lothair, and the Kingdom of East Francia under Louis the German, all of which emerged in 843, survived, as we have seen, only until the death of Lothair in 855, at which point the Middle Kingdom was divided into three parts. In 869 both Charles the Bald and Louis the German claimed Lothar II's kingdom, and at the Treaty of Meersen in 870, Lotharingia disappeared, split between Charles and Louis. In 876 Louis the German died, and his kingdom of East Francia was divided among his three sons: Carloman was king in Bavaria; Louis the Younger was king in Saxony; Charles the Fat was king in Alemannia. In 877 Charles the Bald died, also leaving children, and his kingdom of the West Franks passed for a brief two years to his son Louis the Stammerer, who died in 879. Louis's two sons survived him only until 882 and 884, and by the latter date Charles the Fat, emperor since 881, was the only surviving Carolingian ruler. For three years, until his illness and deposition in 887, Charles the Fat ruled nearly the whole of Charlemagne's territories. But his rule was an empty one, and at his death in 888 the disintegration of the kingdoms proceeded quickly. Non-Carolingians assumed crowns in Provence and West Francia; the imperial title became the object of the princes of central and northern Italy; the new local powers in the Latin West turned to face new invasions from the north, south, and east; and local groups of nobles conferred hollow crowns upon the strongest of their number with little concern for legitimacy or Carolingian blood.

POPULATION AND FORMS OF SETTLEMENT

The great victories and high imperial claims of Charlemagne and his advisers must not overshadow the king's concerns for the less dramatic affairs of day-to-day life. Much of Charlemagne's energy and interest was devoted to the organization of the royal estates and the strengthening of population centers comprising subjects who were loyal to him. Many of the capitularies of the ninth century deal with agricultural life and practices, and it is in this century that we begin to find documentary evidence concerning the lives and work of many people who never found their way into the poems and chronicles that constitute the materials for political and military history during this period.

Until long after the ninth century, the vast majority of the population of Europe consisted of rural laborers whose work supported the ecclesiastical and temporal orders. Plague and the subsequent population decline of the sixth and seventh centuries was succeeded by modest population growth between 700 and 850. That growth slowed after 850 almost to a standstill, and not until a century later, after 950, did substantial population growth begin once again, this time to continue uninterrupted until the end of the thirteenth century. The small, stable population of the ninth century consisted mostly of farmers, free and unfree. The units of land on which they lived and worked were called by various names, depending upon the purposes of the sources that describe them. Certainly, many free villages and hamlets survived from Roman and early Germanic times, their population ranging from ten or twenty persons to two or three hundred, their structure and numbers varying in different parts of Europe. Surrounding these villages were house-gardens, and beyond them were the larger fields, woodlands, and wastes that covered Europe until well into the nineteenth century. In addition to these settlements, however, there existed much larger units, the great estates owned by nobles of ecclesiastical institutions or by kings, and of these much more is known. For instance, Charlemagne left precise instructions for the stewards of his estates. Early in the ninth century, Abbot Irminon of the abbey of St. Germain-des-Prés near Paris compiled a list of the territories owned by the monastery and the duties and rents owed by the tenants. The *Polyptic,* as this famous document is known, is not the only ninth-century source of this kind of information. Other monasteries kept similar records, and it is from these that much of our knowledge of ninth-century agriculture and settlement derives.

The patterns of settlement of this small population reinforces one historian's description of early Europe as a land of "vast, disorganized spaces." Villages, hamlets, and estates located on light soils that were easily drained and plowed contained the greatest population densities. Much of the rest of the land comprised forest and wilderness, far smaller human settlements, and vast areas of uninhabited land separating population centers. The working peasantry was poorly equipped with tools and animals, highly vulnerable to natural or man-made disasters, and lacked in all too many instances the necessary capital required to construct or acquire such labor-saving devices as water mills or durable iron agricultural implements. The inefficiency of much of this agriculture meant that large areas of land were needed to support relatively few people and that such fertilizing techniques as extensive manuring were impossible. The virtual absence of roads, the high cost even of water transportation, and the lack of manpower made communication difficult and extensive transportation of goods, particularly low-cost bulk goods, prohibitive. Even the lords of many great estates traveled from one to another to consume their share of the produce. They could not, except under very exceptional circumstances, have their supplies sent to them.

When a lord arrived at one of his estates, he stayed at his house, which was usually a primitive building by modern standards and was constructed generally of wood and plaster. It is important to note the physical discomfort of domestic architecture until the sixteenth century.

Houses were cold, damp, and utterly lacked privacy. The wealthy lived usually in a large single room and the peasants in tiny wood and daub huts. Surrounding the "manor" house were a number of outbuildings for processing the work of the estate. These were all grouped around a courtyard (a barnyard would be a more accurate description). When the lord was absent, as he usually was, the entire complex was managed on his behalf by a bailiff or steward, the *vilicus*. Each manor tried to be as self-sustaining as possible, although this was difficult unless some materials, particularly iron and wine, were imported. The remainder of the estate was divided into cultivated and uncultivated lands, the latter often available to all the tenants on the estate as a place to gather firewood or other forest products or for use as grazing land. The cultivated land was divided into units, each of which was called a *mansus*. In theory, a *mansus* was to support one family and consist of sufficient land to be plowed by one team in one year. In fact, *mansi* were of widely differing sizes, sometimes containing several families, and there was no correlation between the productivity of land and the number of persons settled on it.

The great estate was usually called a *villa* and was usually divided into two parts: the demesne, a piece of land worked directly on the lord's behalf, and tenancies. The lord's demesne was technically a *mansus*, like the other territories, although it was much larger than a single peasant *mansus*, the work done on it was more varied, and its labor force was larger. The aristocratic demand for abundant food and the relatively primitive agricultural methods of the period meant that a powerful aristocratic family would possess several villas, moving from one to another as the supplies of each were exhausted. The land that fed the lords was extensive and required considerable manpower, which was always at a premium. Thus, a large servile population, which was used for both domestic and field work, was needed to labor on these estates alongside free and half-free agricultural personnel. However, in a year governed primarily by the work rhythms of the agricultural calendar, the labor needs of the lord were partially fulfilled by the occasional service of free and half-free laborers, and, thus, the lord did not have to support a slave labor force throughout the year. The tenancies were sometimes let to peasants in return for cash rents, but more usually for clearly specified labor services on the lord's demesne. Often, the tenanted *mansi* of the ninth century contained more people than could work on the land of the *mansus*. In such cases, the labor of this surplus population produced for the lord those items that constituted part of the rent from each *mansus*.

The lord's demesne, itself a huge oversize *mansus*, and the satellite *mansi* of tenant farmers constituted an agricultural unit that could be put to varied uses. Some villas were owned by an ecclesiastical institution or by the king himself, rather than by the lord. In many cases, representatives of the king or the church lived on the demesne but sent the produce elsewhere. The records of royal and ecclesiastical institutions constitute the best evidence that exists for ninth-century rural society. This evidence, however, must not be spread too thinly. Royal instructions often describe an ideal, not an actual situation. The management techniques available to a monastery such as St. Germain-des-Prés did not exist everywhere during the ninth century, and it is not wise to assume that the villa system, with its divisions of demesne and *mansi*, was ubiquitous, or even widespread within a single region. Free peasant holdings, small villages, and the traces of other systems of land operation survive in sufficient numbers to warn the student to be cautious about attributing a uniformity and continuity to the villa system that it cannot be shown to have possessed.

In some areas, systems of landholding and land management that antedated Germanic inhabitants continued to operate as late as the ninth century and beyond. The divisions of fields, the plowing and harvesting cycles, the size and shape of villages, and the relatively free status of peasants varied from Ireland to Germany, from Frisia to Italy and Spain. Techniques of land use varied between the northern and southern parts of the kingdom of the Franks itself, and new systems were often introduced when Frankish immigrants moved into new territories east of the Rhine. The condition of agriculture constitutes one of those social and ecological rhythms that does not fit readily into other conventional divisions of history. Not only in terms of agricultural techniques, however, but in terms of institutions of social control as well, the ninth century witnessed both the continuity and transformation of older customs and the imposition of new ones. Old public duties and more recent ones—such as contributing a tax for the support of the army— continued in extended or attenuated forms; often, obligations attached to certain pieces of land did not coincide with the legal status of the tenants of that land; primitive techniques of labor management often led to overcrowded or deserted villas; a tendency to equalize the complex statuses of different degrees of free and unfree peasants existed side by side with an increasing economic differentiation among the peasantry; finally, the notorious reluctance of most of the lords even to consider capital investment in agriculture perpetuated the grim cycle of impoverished peasants supplying the needs of masters with limited wants and limited interests.

The ninth century witnessed opportunities for improvement and change in agriculture and the use of the land, but the narrow universe of Carolingian society responded little. Small villages and towns, tiny markets and fairs, areas of intensive proto-rational cultivation and areas of wasteful, relatively unproductive cultivation constituted most of the social and economic foundations of the Carolingian Empire. And among these areas of settlement, separating them and working against their communication, was the forest and waste that constituted most of the physical area of western Europe. The need for internal colonization in the ninth century was as great as that for territorial expansion and external colonization.

THE DISTRIBUTION OF WEALTH AND POWER

The peasant, whether free or unfree, looked to his lord for protection and the enforcement of his rights. The lord had a "house" in each villa and was the principal local contact with the greater powers in the kingdom. We have seen the role played by particularly powerful followers during the periods of the migrations and establishment of the earliest barbarian kingdoms inside the western Roman Empire, and we have also seen the unique relationships between the Merovingian kings and their followers, the reforms of Charles Martel, and the remarkable loyalty of the Frankish aristocracy to Charlemagne, at least in the early part of his reign. From the seventh to the nineteenth centuries, the world of the West was controlled largely by—and in the interests of—the members of a single social rank, the aristocracy. That rank was not always a "class" in the modern sense, nor did its members always and everywhere wield the same kind of power consistently. Its history was different in different parts of Europe, and its origins were diverse. The successful continuation and increase of family property and influence, faithful service to the king, military prowess, unchallenged gangsterism—all these account for the formation of aristocratic classes from the eighth century on. Since between the ninth and the thirteenth centuries wealth and power meant control over land and its inhabitants, the history of this aristocracy is in large part the history of the means of acquiring that control, of continuing to hold it, and of exercising the fiscal, judicial, and social rights attached to it. It is also the history of the social bond that that control implied and of the communities created by its exercise.

The remnants of Roman public offices, portions of land formerly belonging to the imperial fisc, the vast personal wealth of the barbarian kings, and the privileged status of conquering immigrants all contributed to the formation of the nobility between the fifth and eighth centuries. Service to the king, military leadership, and family territorial holdings installed or maintained many people in, or removed them from, the ranks of nobility. From the sixth to the eighth centuries, the massive emptying of the treasuries of gold and land of the Merovingian kings, the growing lay domination of ecclesiastical properties, and the noble acquisition of land from those too weak to defend their rights of possession continued to enrich the nobles. And the new opportunities offered by service to the Carolingian kings of the eighth and ninth centuries, the practice of intermarriage between wealthy families, the practice of passing the same names down through noble families, the consciousness of lineage (however fictitious such lineage tracing often was), the selection of marriage partners from among a group of noble families by kings and members of the royal family, and the sheer necessity of disposing of force and authority over vast, disconnected estates all contributed to the formation of a nobility with growing wealth and power by the ninth century.

The ninth-century Carolingian nobility was not only primarily

Frankish and lay, but ecclesiastical as well. From the eighth century on, noble families placed their relatives on episcopal thrones, at the heads of monasteries, and in the clerical household of the kings. Most ninth-century saints had noble blood, and, thus, ecclesiastical and lay powers shared a community of background and interest that strengthened and shaped the church and tied it more closely to the ruling groups in Frankish society.

When peasants, merchants, and the lower clergy regarded the nobility, they saw primarily arrogance, force, and the unrestricted consumption of agricultural goods. The economic universe of the Carolingian Empire was considerably limited, apart from the purchase of luxury goods, and the sign of noble life was primarily the unrestricted access to sufficient food and domestic comforts. When the lord arrived at his villa, a supply of food, drink, firewood, and clothing awaited him and his entourage, a supply painfully collected since his last visit. If supplies were not sufficient, the bailiff and the peasants felt the lord's anger, and when supplies were consumed, the company departed to the next villa. While in residence, the lord hunted (a privilege long conserved for the aristocracy), ate, gave gifts, and attended to estate business with his managing staff.

In the eyes of the nobility, however, life appeared somewhat different. Pride and the unrestricted expression of emotion were valued attributes, deriving in part at least from consciousness of family prestige, personal honor, and the sense of self—the ingrained fear of being shamed that is characteristic of what anthropologists have designated as "shame cultures." Personal status was further enhanced by *magnanimitas*, "great-heartedness," or, in practice, gift giving on a lavish scale as a means of enhancing personal reputation and creating bonds of social dependence that were nonexistent under any other conditions. Kings slowly gave away their entire wealth, and the nobles were constantly tempted to do likewise, for the more followers a lord could feed, house, and claim, the greater his status was. Rule over land and royal grants often gave legal privileges, "liberties," to nobles, who were thereby also set off from others in terms of what we are tempted to call public status. The *wergeld* for nobles was greater, the legal ritual at their trials was significantly different, and the punishments, when these were inflicted on them, were less than those meted out to other people. By the end of the ninth century, wealth and power in the Carolingian world were firmly in the hands of an increasingly self-conscious noble class.

TRADE AND COMMUNICATION

The needs of ninth-century Carolingian society that could not be met by local forces of production were generally narrow and specialized. Although the trade of the ancient Mediterranean world, as well as that of the Arab and Byzantine worlds, was carried on with a fine-quality gold coinage, the minting of gold coins began to decline in the west in the late seventh century, and by the ninth century silver coins constituted the primary currency throughout Europe. Although gold remained available in the form of bullion—treasure, Arab or Byzantine coinage, and works of ecclesiastical significance—from the eighth to the thirteenth centuries the coinage of Europe was silver. The rights of minting were usually in the hands of the king or those to whom he specifically entrusted them, and the large volume of financial exchange in gold that characterized the thriving trade of Byzantium and the Arab world circulated around the Carolingian west like a great river around an island. Only in early eighth-century Lombard Italy did trading connections with Byzantium sustain economic growth and the presence, however attenuated, of a native class of merchants in northern Italy. During the eclipse of town life and trade in transalpine Europe during the ninth and early tenth centuries, the towns and trade of Italy were never assimilated fully by the land-oriented economy of the Carolingians. The rise under Charlemagne and Pepin of the regional landed families of Austrasia to positions of great power throughout the empire is reflected in their regional patronage of jewelry and ecclesiastical decoration, areas in which considerable commercial activity was necessary. Lay control over church lands, which dated from the time of Charles Martel, and the formation of connected magnate families by marriage, concentrated much financial power in new configurations of society, and the extent of Charlemagne's rule brought the regularizing forces of Frankish protection and institutions to the very edge of the Arabic and Byzantine worlds, as well as to the worlds of the Scandinavians to the north and the Slavs to the east.

The frequent notice of merchants and traders taken in ninth-century documentary sources, the road taxes and fees that abound in the ninth century, the Carolingian efforts to rebuild roads and bridges, Charlemagne's work on the coastal areas of northwestern France, where he built lighthouses and maintained important trading encampments such as Quentovic and Duurstede, and even the enormously labor-intensive proposed canal linking the Rhine and Danube rivers, all point to a lively trade world of the ninth century, sometimes not on a small scale. Wine, grain, salt, weapons, and cloth moved on the rivers of the Carolingian Empire, and although this trade was narrow and specialized, its existence reflects a side of Carolingian culture that should not be overlooked in the great emphasis upon agriculture and the overall commercial spectrum, itself usually narrow.

Local markets connected the rural regions in economic relationships that were different from the internal structure of the *villa* and the free village, and occasionally, as in ninth-century Paris, larger fairs offered individuals the opportunity to acquire materials not on the local market and to encounter people from distant parts. Charlemagne's empire, however, was primarily land-based, and it was most secure on the land. Much of the king's income was spent on fortifications against the Danes and in Saxony against the pagan Slavs. But sea power was not a Frankish strong point, and neither in trade nor in security was the Carolingian Empire in any way a match for the superior sea forces of Byzantium, the Arab states, or the seafaring Northmen from Scandinavia. The growth of Arab sea power in the early ninth century made every Christian (and Arab) coast vulnerable to pirate raids, and reflected the institutional weakness of even the best naval forces in the ninth century. Even the great Byzantine navy proved remarkably fragile once imperial support was withdrawn from the sailors and townsmen of the empire. From 820 on, another sea power, that of Scandinavia, also exerted considerable pressure upon the Carolingians.

The ports of Quentovic and Duurstede connected the Carolingians not only with England—and there survive several letters from the ever busy Charlemagne to Anglo-Saxon English kings in which the emperor complains about trade matters—but with the traders of the north as well. Between 400 and 800, the Scandinavian Iron Age witnessed the growth of a relatively stable and prosperous society that by the ninth century had already begun to expand internally and southward, into what is now northern Germany and Holland. This culture had contacts with the southern and eastern worlds, and by the fifth century there even appeared a settlement—Helgö on Lake Mälar, near Stockholm—whose primary function appears to have been trading. Among the finds in recent excavations at Helgö was a sixth- or seventh-century bronze figure of Buddha, indicating the range of indirect contacts open to Scandinavia during this period. By the ninth century, this society had established trading contacts with the south—trading contacts that perhaps remind us of the picture of trade in the *Odyssey*, in which traders became pirates without warning and were uniformly described as "fierce, greedy, cunning men." The tough merchant-pirates of the early ninth century heralded, as we shall see in Chapter 13, a new wave of invasions. In their contacts with the Carolingian world before the invasions, however, they participated in the trade of the period, and their skills as shipbuilders and navigators and their commercial and social energies must be noted as well as their military ferocity: both aspects of these Northmen had enormous consequences in the history of the West.

Another aspect of long-distance trade was slaves. In the west, slavery had survived the decline of Roman authority and wealth, the rise of the barbarian Germanic kingdoms, and the views of the church. By the eighth century, however, the population of slaves in the west appears to have begun to drop, and by the tenth century slavery was virtually extinct as an institution and remained so for three hundred years. Besides the natural economic problems posed by a large slave population —the expense of sustaining slaves, particularly children, the old, the sick or the injured; the uncertainty of slave supplies; and the existence of an economy in which slave labor was either essential or extremely profitable—the ninth and tenth centuries witnessed a decline in the status of the lowest class of half-free peasants to near slave status which eliminated the need for large bodies of slave laborers. The slave supply, which in the ninth century came largely from the pagan Slavs east of the Carolingian Empire, also shrunk as Slavic states emerged in the ninth and tenth centuries and became converted to Christianity. Slave trade routes, however, survived in ninth- and tenth-century Europe. From the east, slave routes touched at Venice, Regensburg, Metz, and Verdun and continued usually into the Arab world—either through Venice or other Italian ports or across Frankland to Barcelona—and into Moorish Spain. The slave trade slowly became restricted to the selling of non-Christian (that is, pagan Slavic or Scandinavian) slaves to non-Christian owners (Moslems or Jews). Ecclesiastical legislation against slavery, particularly against the enslavement of Christians by non-Christians, remained more hopeful than effective, although with the decline of slavery in the west in the late ninth and tenth centuries, such ecclesiastical rules became stronger.

Extensive trade, of course, implies an extensive communication system. The limited trade of the Carolingian Empire reflects other aspects of that culture that we have already noted, particularly the difficulties of communication. The efforts of Charlemagne and Louis the Pious to build roads and bridges often required more money and labor than the kings had available, and the dangers of roads closing up, bridges falling, mountain passes blocking up, and rivers being too cold or seas too heavy for ship traffic loomed far larger in the ninth and tenth centuries than they have since. Although messengers and diplomatic missions traversed Europe regularly, and missionaries and pilgrims traveled back and forth from distant frontiers, communication in Europe remained primitive. Increasingly pronounced language differences threw up barriers to communication, as did the ambiguous status of immigrants, new artistic styles, and new ecclesiastical customs. To know what was going on, even relatively close by, was often difficult, and even the considerable increase of written documents under Charlemagne and his successors made at best a small impression on the vastness and disorganization of the empire. Louis the Pious tried to call general assemblies more frequently, but he appears not to have been successful. The sheer inertia of distance and immobility imposed iron limits on even the best communicational intentions of the ninth and tenth centuries.

13

BYZANTIUM AND THE CRISIS OF THE WEST, 802-950

CENTRAL AND EASTERN EUROPE TO 900

The westward migrations of peoples from western Asia did not cease with the arrival and settlement of the Avars in the Carpathian Basin in the sixth century. Between the sixth and the eleventh centuries, the westward movements of such later peoples as the Bulgars, Khazars, Magyars, and Pechenegs churned up the settled peoples between the River Don and eastern France, became new and powerful threats to Constantinople and the Latin West, and influenced the shape and the character of Central and Eastern Europe. In the ninth and tenth centuries their migrations drastically transformed both patterns of settlement and routes of communication between Greek East and Latin West, and their movements influenced the rise and fall of new societies among the Slavs. The arrival of the Avars had displaced many Slavic peoples, driving some with the Avars into Greece and the Balkans, and cutting off others, the northern Slavic peoples, from these southern Slavs. When the Avar hegemony was destroyed by the armies of Charlemagne in 796, parts of the southern and northern Slavic peoples entered the orbit of Carolingian power and Roman influence. "German" and "Slav" are imprecise labels of convenience far more than they are designations of specific ethnic or racial differences. The differences among Germanic peoples who entered western Europe after the second century A.D., some of whom mingled with peoples of Asiatic or Iranian stock, were so many, as we have seen, that the term "Germanic" is little more precise in meaning than "non-Roman." The complex relationships between Germans and Germans, Germans and Slavs, and Slavs and Slavs are characterized by the same hostility and friendliness, ferocity and interest, long-range plans and acts of expediency. The labels "German" and "Slav" imply no "natural" internal unity, other than linguistic, and no "natural" hostility to other peoples. Different groups of Slavs possessed widely differing cultures, patterns of settlement and social organization, and alliances both within and without the Slavic world. There is, in short, no more convincing a "racial" explanation of the history of central Europe than there is for that of western Europe. Local experience and change, political alliances, and the growth of a distinctive religious culture dominate the early history of both regions, and the alleged antagonism between Slavs and Germans vanishes as a force in history once the common experience of early Europeans is considered as a whole.

One of the most striking results of the weakening and destruction of the Avar kingdom was the emergence in the late eighth century of the first Slav state, the Great Moravian Empire. Centered in the valleys of the Danube and the March (Morava) rivers, the Moravian Empire was ruled by a single dynasty, descended from Mojmir, throughout the ninth century. The growth of a thriving agricultural economy was aided by the kingdom's encompassing of several different trade routes, and by the mid ninth century there are even signs of town development. As we have seen in the cases of other peoples, the Slavic transition from a tribal society to a post-tribal agricultural society involved particular stresses being placed upon traditional cultural institutions, one result of which was that Christianity made substantial headway among the Moravians during the ninth century. Mojmir was baptized around 825, and pressures from the bishops of Bavaria, particularly Passau and Salzburg, brought the influence of the Frankish church into Moravia. The Slavic inhabitants of Carinthia, to the southwest of Moravia, also began the process of conversion, although Carinthia was shortly absorbed into the frontier territories of Carolingian Bavaria. The prosperity of Moravia was equaled by its diplomatic importance in the second half of the ninth century, and to understand this importance we must consider the second great power in south central Europe during this period, that of the Bulgars.

Early in the seventh century the Bulgars lived around the sea of Azov, where they were for a time one of the Byzantine-allied Asiatic migrating peoples. The westward migrations of the Khazars from the Don Valley drove the Bulgars west, and around 670 they crossed the Danube against imperial orders and began to build up a strong state among the Slavic peoples along the southwestern coast of the Black Sea. During the late seventh and eighth centuries, the Bulgar power extended from the Black Sea across northern Greece and the Balkans to Albania. In 681 the Byzantine emperor was forced into a peace with the Bulgars. During the same period, the much greater Slavic population of the area came to predominate culturally and linguistically in the Bulgar kingdom as that kingdom grew in power and became a great threat to Constantinople.

Both Byzantium and Moravia felt the pressures of powerful neighbors in the second half of the ninth century. In 862 Louis the German, Charlemagne's grandson, entered into diplomatic relations with the Khan of Bulgaria, thus threatening Moravian independence, and in 863 Moravia made overtures to Byzantium. The diplomacy of Byzantium, as we have seen, consisted chiefly of setting one barbarian people against another, often with considerable success and sometimes with long-range consequences unforeseeable at the time. Early in the seventh century, for example, Byzantine diplomacy appears to have attempted to stop the Avar-Slav expansion to the south by urging other peoples to settle in their rear, to the north and west. One of the consequences of this diplomacy was to people south central Europe with a powerful pagan bloc whose existence and settlement hampered and finally destroyed overland communication between the Greek East and the Latin West between 600 and 800. Early Byzantine aid was behind some of the prosperity of the Slavs of Bohemia and Moravia in the rear of the Avars in the early seventh century. During the same period it is likely that the Croats and Serbs were induced by Byzantium to settle in the south, oppose the Avars, and occupy the lands along the eastern Adriatic, where they still live.

In 863 the Byzantines responded to the Moravian overtures by sending two brothers, the great apostles to the Slavs, SS. Constantine (Cyril) and Methodios, to organize the Moravian church. Cyril and Methodios were two of the most striking products of the great reforms of learning, religious devotion, and diplomacy that had grown up in early ninth-century Byzantium. Their lives had been spent in learning and diplomacy, and their activities had carried them as far as the eastern shores of the Black Sea and now took them west into Moravia. Both the Latin and the Greek Christian churches had long recognized the need for preaching and establishing the texts of prayers and creeds in the vernacular languages of the peoples among whom their missionaries proselytized, although both churches were reluctant to allow the high liturgy to be spoken in languages other than Latin or Greek. Another sign of the cultural differences developing between east and west was Byzantium's increasing willingness to permit the wider use of vernacular languages, and this openness laid the foundations for the emergence of literary languages among many Slavic peoples, particularly the Russians. The Latin church, however, retained its hostility to vernacular liturgies, and much of the friction between Latin and Greek ecclesiastical figures in central Europe hinged upon this issue. The greatest achievement of Cyril and Methodios was precisely the establishment of a script for the Slavic languages. The mission was successful, and in 867 Cyril left Moravia for Italy in order to see the ordination of his first prepared converts. In 867 Pope Hadrian II ordained Cyril's priests, established an ecclesiastical structure in Moravia, and sponsored the singing of the first Slavic liturgy in the Lateran. In 869 Cyril died in Rome, and Methodios was appointed to succeed him as bishop of Moravia. The Roman-Moravian ecclesiastical connection exacerbated the rivalry between Roman and Frankish churchmen, and between 870 and 873 Methodios was tried by a Frankish ecclesiastical court and confined in Germany. Freed, he returned to Moravia, journeyed to Constantinople in 881, and died in Moravia in 885. His greatest historian has called St. Methodios "the last great father of the universal Church," largely for his role in bridging the gulf between the Greek and Latin churches in the important lands between them. The two brothers have long been regarded as the patron saints of the Slavic peoples.

After growth and prosperity under the successors of Mojmir, Rastislav (846–869), and Svatopluk (870–894), the Moravian Empire grew weaker at the end of the ninth century. Under Mojmir II, regional moves toward independence, coupled with the devastating raids of the Magyars and the hostility of East Frankish leaders, destroyed the empire entirely. The first great Slavic kingdom came to an end at the end of the ninth and the beginning of the tenth centuries. But the place of the Slavs in Christendom had been firmly established, and the Moravian Empire was succeeded by stronger and more enduring Christian states: Bohemia, Poland, Croatia, Serbia, and, by the end of the tenth century, the Christianized Magyar kingdom of Hungary.

CRISIS AND RECOVERY IN BYZANTIUM, 802–904

The reign of Empress Irene (780–802) had weakened the Byzantine army, failed to come to full terms with the iconoclastic movement, and witnessed the crowning of an emperor, Charlemagne, from among the barbarian peoples. Irene was deposed in 802 by a revolution that placed Nicephoros I (802–811) on the throne. From the reign of Nicephoros on, Byzantium faced military threats along most of its frontiers and suffered severe internal dissension. Not until the end of the ninth century was the empire finally stabilized.

The troubled relations between the Franks and the Byzantines were, of course, exacerbated by the coronation of Charlemagne in 800. Not until 812 did the two sides reach agreement, the Byzantines recognizing Charlemagne's title of emperor and formally referring to him as the brother of the emperor at Constantinople, thus fitting Charlemagne's claims into the old Byzantine theory of a world "family" of rulers at whose head stood the Byzantine emperor. From 813 on, a new official formula reminded all other rulers of their place in this hierarchy; from that date, the formula *ton Rhomaion*, "of the Romans," appeared after the title *Basileus*, "Emperor." Charlemagne too was a *Basileus*, but not "of the Romans"; nor was Symeon of Bulgaria, who claimed the status of Emperor in the first quarter of the tenth century. No matter how driven to recognize such titles, the Byzantines reserved for their own emperor the title "Emperor of the Romans," a single head of a single empire to which other nations were necessarily subordinate.

Yet Byzantine diplomacy, even though it could hedge when necessary, faced considerable opposition throughout the ninth century. The armies of the caliph of Baghdad, Harun al-Rashid, the legendary ruler in the *Arabian Nights*, drove into Asia Minor, and the growing power of the Bulgarian Empire on the western shores of the Black Sea posed threats similar to those posed in the first quarter of the seventh century. From 805 to his death in 815, the Bulgar khan Krum devastated Byzantine territory in Thrace, and in 814 he brought the Bulgar armies to the walls of Constantinople. Under Leo IV (813–820) the threats from both Bulgars and Arabs subsided. Between 813 and 815, as part of the military and social reforms of the empire, Leo began the process of restoring the doctrines of iconoclasm, which enraged orthodox churchmen but represented a reversal of Irene's policies and the weakness of the administrations of her two successors. Economic pressures and political disaffection led to the most serious revolt since the Nika riots of 532. For two years (821–823) the armies led by Thomas "the Slav" ripped the empire apart, besieged the city of Constantinople once again (821), and exacerbated the economic difficulties of the rural provinces. In spite of the successful reign of Emperor Theophilus (829–842), the empire still faced outside enemies and internal problems of considerable magnitude. Under Theophilus's son and successor Michael III (842–867), iconoclasm was abolished for the last time and the efficiency of Michael's great minister Bardas succeeded in mobilizing the resources of the empire and introducing remarkable reforms in secular education, ecclesiastical life, the military, and the peasant economy. The university at Constantinople was reopened under the direction of Bardas himself, and under Bardas's great contemporary, Patriarch Photios, a new energy was given to religious studies as well. Such men as Bardas, Photios, Leo the Mathematician, and the linguist and missionary St. Constantine (Cyril) led an intellectual renaissance easily comparable in importance and influence to the military and social reforms of the imperial administration.

The Byzantine revival of the 860s was not, however, without its darker side. From the reign of Irene to that of Basil I (867–886) ecclesiastical problems became hopelessly intermingled with politics, and the ending of the iconoclast struggle in 843 did not end the difficulties of the church. The intellectual revival of the 860s reflects the energy and talent of the Byzantine clergy and secular administrators, but the pitch of religious feeling ran high in Byzantium, and Bardas and Photios were not without powerful enemies. Some of these charged Photios with having ousted the rightful patriarch, Ignatius, and in 859 took their case to Rome, to the court of the pope, at that time the capable and visionary Nicholas I (858–867). Thus, the relations between Byzantium and the West, long made fragile by problems of communication and language, and exacerbated by the western loss of the provinces of Illyricum and Sicily at the hands of Leo III in 751, the iconoclast struggle and the rise of the Frankish clergy, and the coronation of Charlemagne in 800 and the subsequent diplomatic problems of Byzantium's recognition of that title, were strained further by the clash between the able, ambitious, and dominating patriarch of Constantinople and the first pope in a century to develop a consistent theory of papal authority over the universal Church. The ensuing quarrel, one of the most important steps in the process of the alienation between the Greek and Latin churches, is complex. Aside from the troublesome question of Photios's canonical succession to the office of patriarch, there lay the deeper question of the rivalry between the monastic community of the empire, which regarded spiritual affairs as strictly the province of monastic churchmen, and the community of the court and the higher secular clergy, which regarded temporal and spiritual affairs as inextricably intertwined. In addition, the vexing questions of Moravia and the kingdom of the Bulgars came to the fore when, as we have seen, Moravia requested Byzantine missionaries and Bulgaria opened communications with Rome. In 863 the brothers Cyril and Methodios were in Moravia, and in 864 Khan Boris of the Bulgars converted to Christianity and requested an autocephalous church of the Bulgars. This the Byzantines were unwilling to grant, so Boris turned to Pope Nicholas I, sending a long list of questions regarding liturgical and theological problems. Nicholas's answer, the famous *Responsa ad consulta Bulgarorum,* is a remarkable condemnation of certain portions of Byzantine Christianity as well as a striking example of Nicholas's vision of the universal authority of the papacy.

The political and ecclesiological aspects of the quarrel led to rifts, charges, and countercharges. The next stage of the conflict, however, raised questions of theological import. Photios accused Pope Nicholas of heresy, charging that the Latin usage of the Creed erred in stating the doctrine of the Double Procession of the Holy Ghost, the famous *"Filioque"* dispute that still divides the Eastern Orthodox and Roman communions. In short, the Creed, as it had developed in the West, stated that the Holy Ghost proceeds from the Father *and the Son—Filioque—*instead of from the Father alone. On this question Photios accused Nicholas of heresy and declared him deposed.

The dispute, both within Constantinople and between Constantinople and Rome, dragged on, through Photios's own deposition in 867, his restoration in 877, the palace revolution of Emperor Basil I (867–886), and the rise of a new Bulgarian threat at the beginning of the tenth century. The schism that has been called the Photian Schism shows the strains in the relationship between the eastern and western branches of the Church, the growing dangers faced by two prelates—the pope and the patriarch of Constantinople—who formulated ideas very close to universal authority, and the role of the Frankish higher clergy in formulating Roman policy, both in dogma and in the mission field.

The ecclesiastical difficulties of the 860s were rivaled by new military crises. In 860 a fleet from Kiev attacked Constantinople, but was repulsed—the first hostile contact between Byzantium and the society out of which the first Russian principality grew. Under the powerful Khan Symeon (893–927) a new Bulgar attack on the empire was launched, and between 911 and 925 the Bulgar threat loomed very large on the Byzantine horizon. In addition to the Bulgars, the Arab domination of the eastern Mediterranean, their occupation of Sicily, their landholds in South Italy, and their control of the island of Crete posed a threat to Byzantium. In 895 Byzantine diplomacy introduced the Magyars to the west, inviting them to attack the Bulgars from the rear. Symeon of Bulgaria, however, induced the Pechenegs to attack the Magyars, and in their flight from the Pechenegs, the Magyars drove not south toward Bulgaria but west toward Moravia. Between 896 and 909, the Magyar hordes destroyed the Great Moravian Empire and settled on the plains of Transylvania, from which they proceeded to launch raids into Germany, Italy, and Poland. The Pechenegs moved west to take the place that the Magyars had vacated. In 904 Arab raiders sacked Thessalonica, the second city of the empire, and as the tenth century opened, Byzantium appeared to be threatened by overwhelming external enemies and severe internal religious and social dissent.

THE NEW INVASIONS OF EUROPE: ARABS, MAGYARS, AND VIKINGS

The ninth and tenth centuries witnessed the last invasions of Europe until the attacks of the Mongols in the thirteenth century. The new invaders—Arab raiding parties, Magyar hordes, and Viking pirates—struck the death blow to the precocious but troubled society of Carolingian Europe. These invasions transformed not only western Europe but the East as well, bringing the principality of Kiev within the orbit of Byzantine influence, transforming the map of central Europe, changing the balance of power between the Christian and Islamic worlds, and drawing the Scandinavian and Hungarian peoples into the civilization of the Latin West.

After the initial establishment of Arabic power in Spain and the brief early eighth-century thrusts by the Arabs into southern Gaul, Arabic expansion took place more slowly. The growing power of the Caliphate of Baghdad after the middle of the eighth century and the power of

Carolingian armies tended to stabilize the long and vague frontier between Latin Christendom and Islam. In the late eighth and early ninth centuries, however, Arabic sea power grew slowly, and independent bands of sea raiders began to strike at southern Europe and the eastern Mediterranean with greater and greater success. In 890, Islamic strongholds were established at St. Tropez and at La Garde Freinet on the southern coast of France. From these positions, Moslem raiders penetrated the towns of southern Gaul, northwestern Italy, and even the mountain passes of Switzerland. The rise of local centers of Moslem power in North Africa and the Near East followed the decline of the caliphate after the death of Harun al-Rashid (786–809). Independent Moslem states in eastern Persia grew up, and the separatist movements that had begun in the eighth century with the independence of Spain (756) increased. In 868 Egypt became independent under its own dynasty. From the mid ninth century on, the power of the caliph in Baghdad was reduced by the growing power of local governors and military leaders, and the Ummayad dynasty of Spain, the Aghlabid dynasty of Tunisia, and the Fatimid dynasty of Egypt operated virtually independently.

The ninth century witnessed both the growth of Moslem sea power and the ambitious expansion of local rulers. By 900 Sicily had fallen to the Moslems, and in the course of the ninth century Moslem raiders established bases at Bari and Garigliano and raided into the heart of Italy. The military and economic supremacy that the Moslems achieved during the ninth century inflicted terrible burdens on Europe, and not for another century was the Moslem dominance of the Mediterranean and the vulnerability of Europe checked.

The long duel between the Bulgars and Byzantines resulted, as we have seen, in the well-known Byzantine tactic of attempting to set one barbarian people against another. In this case, the Byzantines invited the Magyars to attack the Bulgars in 896. The tactic backfired, however, when the Bulgars convinced the Pechenegs to attack the Magyars, a move so successful that the Magyars fled west and destroyed the Moravian Empire, established themselves in the plains of Transylvania, and probed further west on raids into Germany, France, and Italy. The Magyars were a Finno-Ugrian people, related in language and origins to the Finns, who had occupied Finland much earlier. Their other name, Hungarians, derives from one branch of their people, the Onogurs. Penetrating into Moravia, the Magyars occupied the land in a manner similar to that of earlier barbarian invaders of Europe. Their royal dynasty, which descended from the migration-king Arpad, held little real power, and the war leaders who ruled the people and land began to launch raids further west. Between 898 and 920, Magyar war bands descended into Italy, Burgundy, eastern France, and particularly into Germany.

The western reaction to the Magyar invasions was one of virtually complete helplessness and terror. Document after document portrays the Magyars as terrifying, invincible hordes against whom no defenses could stand. For the first half of the tenth century, Europe had no defenses against the Magyars except for its vast spaces and the diminishing rewards gained by Magyar raids. The process of settling in the Pannonian Basin and of establishing a sedentary community with agricultural roots and some degree of political stability took the Magyars nearly a century. Not until the second half of the tenth century did the beginnings of the kingdom of Hungary take shape, the process of Christianization gain ground, and the social and economic basis of the raids in the west lose their strength. With the Moslem sea raiders, the Magyars constituted the second wave of ninth- and tenth-century invasions.

The third wave was that of the Scandinavian peoples. The establishment among the Carolingians of a powerful military power with expansionist aims eliminated many peoples that had served as buffers between them and other powers. The destruction of the Avars brought the Carolingians into contact with the southern Slavs, just as the destruction of Saxon resistance had brought them up against the formidable northern Slavic peoples, the Wends, Obodrites, and Liutizi. The subjugation of the Frisians may well have brought Carolingian arms against those of the Danes. During the last years of Charlemagne's life, Danish expansion south and east had precipitated several military clashes between Danes and Franks. Other parts of the west had encountered Scandinavian raiders even earlier. In 788 a raiding party landed at Wessex in southern England and killed the king's representative. In 793 the island monastic community of Lindisfarne was sacked and burnt. After the first quarter of the ninth century, the Viking raids increased in frequency and destruction. Informed of the unprotected wealth of the south, raiders from Norway and Denmark sailed south summer after summer, returning to Scandinavia for the winters. Their superbly built ships were not only the finest ocean-going ships of their time—and some of the best of any period—but their shallow draft allowed them to sail far up-river, attacking Rouen and Paris on the Seine, Trier, and the Frisian seaports of Quentovic and Duurstede. The Viking ships, carrying between 50 and 100 men and propelled by a single great sail and banks of oars, imposed a frightening presence on the European seaboard. They ravaged undefended ecclesiastical properties, continually defeated the small armies that the kings of West Francia fielded against them, and sacked the little towns that lay in their path. The weakness of organized resistance to these raids gave plenty of opportunities to local lords who could protect weaker people from the raiders and assume in their own hands many of the powers of governance that they once held directly from the kings. In many cases, what the Vikings left, or did not touch at all, also fell into the hands of powerful warlords. This was particularly true of ecclesiastical property. This double effect of the Viking raids should not be overlooked; Carolingian Europe was defenseless, but it was defenseless in particular ways, ways that did not exclude opportunities for strong and ruthless lords to increase their power at the expense of the victims of Viking raids and their own neighbors.

The paths of Scandinavian expansion were many. Norsemen moved chiefly into Ireland and western England; Swedes moved into the eastern Baltic and across northwestern Russia to Lake Ladoga, then down the great north-south river systems of Russia to Novgorod and Kiev, trading and raiding alike, until they came into contact not only with Byzantium across the Black Sea, but with Arab merchants on the Volga and the Sea of Azov. The Danes attacked eastern England, Frisia, and the Rhineland and then penetrated up-river into the heart of the old kingdom of Francia itself. By the middle of the ninth century, the patterns of raiding had changed. Groups of Scandinavians established winter quarters in Europe, and the raiding parties grew larger—they turned, in fact, into expeditionary armies seeking land to take and settle. By the 850s there were Norse settlements in Ireland, and in 865 the famous Great Army landed in England and stayed. By 878 a substantial part of northeastern England had fallen under Danish rule. In 911, the king of West Francia, Charles the Simple, sought to enlist some Vikings in his own service against others, and formally ceded to Rolf, a war leader, a small territory at the mouth of the Seine that became, under Rolf's successors, the kernel of the great eleventh-century duchy of Normandy. By mid-century, Viking raids show every sign of careful planning, coordinated operations, and the intentions of Viking leaders to establish settlements in western Europe.

The imposition of strong local rule in Scandinavia and the habit of exiling troublemakers probably accounted for the presence of many men in the Viking hosts of raiders. Certainly, later sources make the point that some people, unable to live under the new lordship forged by local rulers, removed themselves from home to wander across the sea. The expeditions, of course, increased the process of stabilizing political rule at home. With the most dangerous and resentful warriors off raiding, political rule could be consolidated even more quickly, and by the tenth century strong kingdoms appeared in Denmark, Norway, and Sweden. The Vikings may have been resentful, and they may even have been in the service of great lords; they were certainly tough and ruthless; but they were also extraordinarily talented. They were remarkable shipbuilders, perhaps the greatest the world had yet seen between the Bronze Age, and they equal the great Polynesian ships of a later period. They were particularly able to survive on the risky sustenance of raids, a little trading, threats and tribute, and long voyages over unknown seas. They could act with remarkable cohesion when necessary, and, hence, their small forces nearly always won in pitched battles. They were drawn, as historians have said, by the smell of gold, but they brought with them more than destruction. They gave, for example, an entire marine vocabulary to the French language, and in general they brought a new maritime world into the consciousness of Europeans. Although Irish monks had landed in Iceland in the eighth century, the Scandinavian expansion of the ninth witnessed the exploration of the island between 860 and 865 and its initial settlements in 874. Thirty or forty thousand Norwegians settled the island in the last quarter of the ninth century, many possibly fleeing from the strong personal rule of Harald Fairhair in Norway.

The settlers of Iceland traced their early history on the island in a remarkable document called the *Landnamabók*, which dates from the twelfth century. The privately owned farms and roughly egalitarian society of Iceland not only survived and grew, but tied itself to the Continent by its exports of fish and the constant travel of its people. By the twelfth and thirteenth centuries, the early stories of Norse Iceland began to be worked up into heroic tales called sagas, perhaps the last genuine European epics. In many cases, however, the quarrelsome character of the settlers did not change in the new land. In 984 Erik, another exile, this time from Iceland itself, discovered the island of Greenland, which was settled by the end of the tenth century. Erik's son Leif sailed even further west, and around the year 1000 appears to have made a landfall on a place he called Vinland, certainly none other than North America. The Norse settlements of Iceland and Greenland were not isolated episodes, totally distinct from the raids in the south. By the end of the tenth century, not only had western Europe received a new maritime vocabulary, it had been expanded enormously by the Atlantic voyages of the Norse.

The Vikings were the last and in some ways the most influential of the new invaders of Europe in the ninth and tenth centuries. We see their influence not only in the direct traces of their presence, however, but in the changes their presence made. Patterns of land settlement and landholding were transformed as regions were depopulated and later resettled, or as local lords assumed more and more powers of defense in the face of threatened or real invasions. Laymen stepped into the administrative shoes of the great abbots and bishops of Carolingian Europe, and the powers of the last Carolingian kings were shown to be empty. Now it is time to look for a moment at some of the immediate political consequences of the Viking presence.

As late as 825, it seemed possible that the foundations of the new Frankish Empire laid by Charlemagne might survive. Under Louis the Pious the educational reforms of the earlier generation produced a remarkable group of able and learned ecclesiastics, who in turn attempted to further the religious reformation begun by their predecessors. For the most part, the aristocracy still obeyed the king and the king's officials. The older, more archaic title of king of the Franks was dropped by Louis in favor of the new and, for the moment, more accurate one of emperor. Even the *Ordinatio Imperii* of 817 recognized the importance of the imperial title and violated the customary Frankish laws of inheritance in attempting to preserve the reality of the new realm. Between 840 and 888, however, as we have seen, all of Louis's attempts came to grief. The empire was partitioned and repartitioned, and by the tenth century the imperial title itself signified only the obligation to protect Rome. The kingdoms that had been created for Louis the German and Charles the Bald had themselves been partitioned, reunited, and partitioned again, drawing resources, men, loyalties, and wealth into ever smaller particularistic units, which themselves threw up frontiers against one another. In spite of the great ambition of such rulers as Louis the German and Charles the Bald, which extended in the case of the former to negotiating with the Bulgars and encroaching on the Moravian Empire and in that of the latter to imitating Byzantine court ceremonial, the reduction of royal wealth and territory on the one hand, and the growing strength of the aristocracy and the episcopacy on the other, reduced even able rulers such as these to intermittently effective warlords.

The Arab and Viking invasions reduced the power and and number of high churchmen. The real heirs of Carolingian Europe, or what was left of it, were the surviving new nobles, individuals who combined family lands with royal lands and church lands, spreading the official titles of old royal offices such as count, duke, or marquis over lands those offices had never included and ruling in a way that had never been justified by those titles. The aristocracy of tenth-century Europe were in many cases not so very different in their methods from the new ruler of the lands around the lower Seine, Rolf and his Viking companions.

Although Charlemagne's rule never extended to England, it is clear that English clerics played a distinctive role—perhaps the most distinctive role—in shaping the intellectual culture of the Carolingian period. In addition, Charlemagne corresponded with English rulers, sometimes in a not altogether cordial manner. During the late eighth century the kingdom of Mercia rose to eclipse that of Northumbria, but Mercian power was already on the wane before the rising strength of the southern kingdom of Wessex when the Viking invasions dealt it its death blow. In 851 the Vikings first wintered in England, and in 865 the appearance of the Great Army under its leader Guthrum opened the large-scale Danish settlement of northeastern England. In 867 Northumbria fell before the Danes, and the pressure of the Danish forces reduced considerably the remaining strength of Wessex. The 870s witnessed the consolidation by the Danes of the large territories they had won and the extension of continued pressure on Wessex. In 871, 875, and 878 the Danes attacked the Wessex forces, and on the third attempt they succeeded in driving the king of Wessex, Alfred, into a prolonged retreat in Somerset. However, Alfred emerged from Somerset the following year to defeat the Danes and witness the conversion of Guthrum to Christianity.

The small part of England that Alfred now controlled was not a sufficient basis for a large-scale assault on Danish forces. For the next twenty years, Alfred set about fortifying his lands south of the Thames. These fortifications were erected and maintained by local residents, and with their aid Alfred continued the defense of Wessex and began to expand his power to the east. By 886 he had taken London, and by his death in 899 he had laid the foundations for the expansion of the kingdom of Wessex into the kingdom of England. Alfred's descendants, combining their military strength with claims of royal legitimacy, began the long task of restoring Anglo-Saxon rule throughout the island. The Vikings in England, clearing away the many small kingdoms into which the island was divided, created the opportunity for the rulers of Wessex to create the foundations of the later English monarchy. Throughout much of the tenth century, Anglo-Saxon England was the most developed and unified kingdom in all of Europe.

The experience of England differed sharply from that of the small kingdoms on the Continent. The ephemeral rule of Charles the Fat over East Francia and West Francia between 885 and 887 was simply the culmination of two generations of royal and family rivalry. The real powers in these kingdoms were the great lords who fought, ruled, and guarded them on behalf of the king. The raids of the Arabs, Magyars, and especially the Vikings formed a continual threat to the Carolingian kings from the middle of the ninth century on. The Viking siege of Paris in 885 and 886 testified to the emperor's powerlessness, and when Charles was deposed in 887 and replaced by his nephew Arnulf of Carinthia, the strength of local centers of power became universally clear. Rule in France went not to the remaining Carolingian, but to Eudes, a descendant of Robert the Strong, count of Paris; separate kingdoms in Burgundy and Provence emerged; the imperial crown itself became the object of dispute among the great lords of northern and central Italy. Arnulf of Carinthia, the last able Carolingian ruler, held power until his death in 899, the same year that Alfred of Wessex died.

The different conditions of their respective monarchies at the deaths of Alfred and Arnulf offer further evidence of the collapse of authority on the Continent. The last years of the eighth century had witnessed the shaping of a formidable Frankish military force, which was expensive to muster and maintain but was undefeated because the plans for its offensive operations were carefully drawn up by Charlemagne before each campaign. The Frankish host was, even in its greatest days, too cumbersome an instrument for defense. By the end of the ninth and the beginning of the tenth centuries, it no longer existed. Local forces, commanded by local leaders owing (but sometimes not paying) allegiance to kings of smaller and smaller kingdoms or to remote and dubious emperors, bore the brunt of the Viking raids and the pressure of their neighbors. These temporary commands over loosely defined (and loosely conceived) territories constituted the basis for the subsequent growth both of later kingship and of the territorial principalities that constituted the political communities of the later tenth and the eleventh centuries. One consequence of the invasions was to clear away the wreckage of Carolingian institutions and older, restrictive patterns of landholding and settlement.

THE MACEDONIAN DYNASTY AND THE FLOWERING OF BYZANTINE CIVILIZATION

At the beginning of the tenth century, the outlook for Byzantium was nearly as bleak as that for the Latin West. A stronger and more hostile Bulgarian Empire to the north and west, successful demonstrations of Arab sea power in the eastern Mediterranean, and a new and dangerous enemy rising in Kiev all threatened the empire. Arabs, Magyars, and Vikings devastated the west, and the enemies of the east appeared, if anything, more dangerous. The Bulgars, settled since the eighth century, posed a more organized and continuing threat than the Magyar raiders; the Arabs of the eastern Mediterranean drew upon far more ready financial and military resources than the Arabs of the central and western Mediterranean; the warriors of Kiev, although fewer than their opposite numbers in England and France, were no less ferocious. Moreover, the Byzantine Empire possessed one weakness that the west did not: a center. Total capitulation of the west was impossible, because there was no crucial center of western economic or political life that, when captured, could bring down the rest of the continent with it. Even if Paris had fallen in the siege of 885–886, the loss of a town with no more than a thousand inhabitants would have made little difference in the quality of western resistance. The Byzantine Empire, however, possessed precisely such a center—the great city of Constantinople. There was a target, and there, if an attack was successful, was the life of the whole empire. For centuries, armies had marched and enemy fleets had sailed to its very walls; several times between the sixth and the tenth centuries, in fact, the empire had contracted to the walls of the city. But the walls had always held. And they also held in the tenth century. Rooted in the great city, the Byzantine Empire was more vulnerable to the late ninth- and tenth-century invasions than the West, but was wealthier and far better prepared to resist. The crisis of the early tenth century was followed by a triumphal recovery, and the tenth century ushered in not a Byzantine collapse, but the flowering of Byzantine power and civilization.

The Byzantine triumph of the tenth century had deep roots in the imperial history of the mid ninth century. During the reign of Michael III (842–867) the military success and institutional reforms of Bardas and the intellectual revival and ecclesiastical policies of Photios had done much to repair the disasters of the period between 780 and 811. The reign of Basil I (867–886) introduced the able Macedonian dynasty to the imperial throne, and Basil's dynastic successors Leo VI (886–912), Constantine VII Porphyrogennitus (913–959), and Basil II (976–1025) slowly built upon the attempts of the earlier Amorian dynasty to strengthen the empire. The foundation of new *themes,* the expansion of missionary activity and diplomacy, the collaboration of the patriarchs of Constantinople with the emperors, and the great patrician civil servants of the ninth and tenth centuries constituted the foundations of Byzantine survival and triumph. Palace revolutions, usurpations of the throne, and military blunders in the face of new enemies failed to undo the work begun in the mid ninth century. The administrative and legal genius of Leo VI and Constantine VII was augmented by skillful generals, several of whom even usurped imperial rank temporarily yet strengthened the defenses of the empire. Under the first of these, Romanus I Lecapenus (920–944), the threat of the Bulgarian ruler Symeon was finally turned back. In 911, and again in 945, trading treaties were signed with the rulers of Kiev. During the last years of Romanus's reign, Byzantine forces succeeded against the Bulgars, the Moslem forces of Syria, and the attacks of the Kievans, and participated in operations in South Italy and even in southern France against the Arab raiders there.

Romanus also resisted the growing powers of the landed aristocracy and legislated in favor of the farmer-soldiers, the settlers of the *themes,* on whom most of the Byzantine military success had long rested. Under Basil II, the final period of Byzantine triumph was ushered in with the conversion to Christianity of Vladimir, Prince of Kiev, in 989, and in the final war to suppress Bulgaria, which took place between 986 and 1019.

The successful defense of the empire and, after the first quarter of the tenth century, the rapid and virtually unopposed expansion of its power to the Euphrates, Crete, South Italy, Hungary, and Russia reveals both the great strength and the administrative wisdom of its ninth- and tenth-century rulers. The appearance not only of a series of successful, learned, and able emperors and successful generals, but also of great churchmen and scholars, an ecclesiastical administration that skillfully included missionary activity alongside diplomatic negotiations, and a talented civil service of urban aristocrats constituted the direction of imperial policy. The basis of that strength, however, consisted of the farmer-soldiers of the *themes,* the busy commercial activities in the cities, and the most successful mobilization of state resources since the fourth-century Roman Empire in the west.

Besides its military, political, and economic survival, however, Byzantium continued its renaissance of scholarship and literary activity, its remarkable innovations in the liturgy and in religious art and music, and its creation of a style of urban life that astonished ally and enemy alike. From Hagia Sophia and the imperial palace the influence of Constantinople extended throughout the empire and into the lands beyond it, and the city became as much a legend to the traders and warriors of northern Russia as to those of eastern Persia and North Africa. Between the seventh and eleventh centuries, only one other city, the Baghdad of Harun al-Rashid, gave rise to a similar image and a similar legend. In Rome, the language of imperial politics had survived to disguise the politics of central Italy. In Constantinople, the empire was an extension of the city. The imperial visage on imperial coins was carried to the far corners of the Byzantine world and beyond by missionaries, soldiers, diplomats, and traders. In what one historian has called "the Byzantine Commonwealth," the theory of the "family of rulers"— according to which the emperor was at the head of all the rulers of the world—came closer to reality around the year 1000 than it ever had before.

ROME, THE PAPACY, AND THE FRAGMENTS OF THE CAROLINGIAN IDEAL

Throughout the eighth century the Lombard threat and the calculated indifference of the iconoclast Byzantine emperors posed great difficulties for the papacy, difficulties that were compounded by the growing pressures constituted by aristocratic interest groups, particularly those with

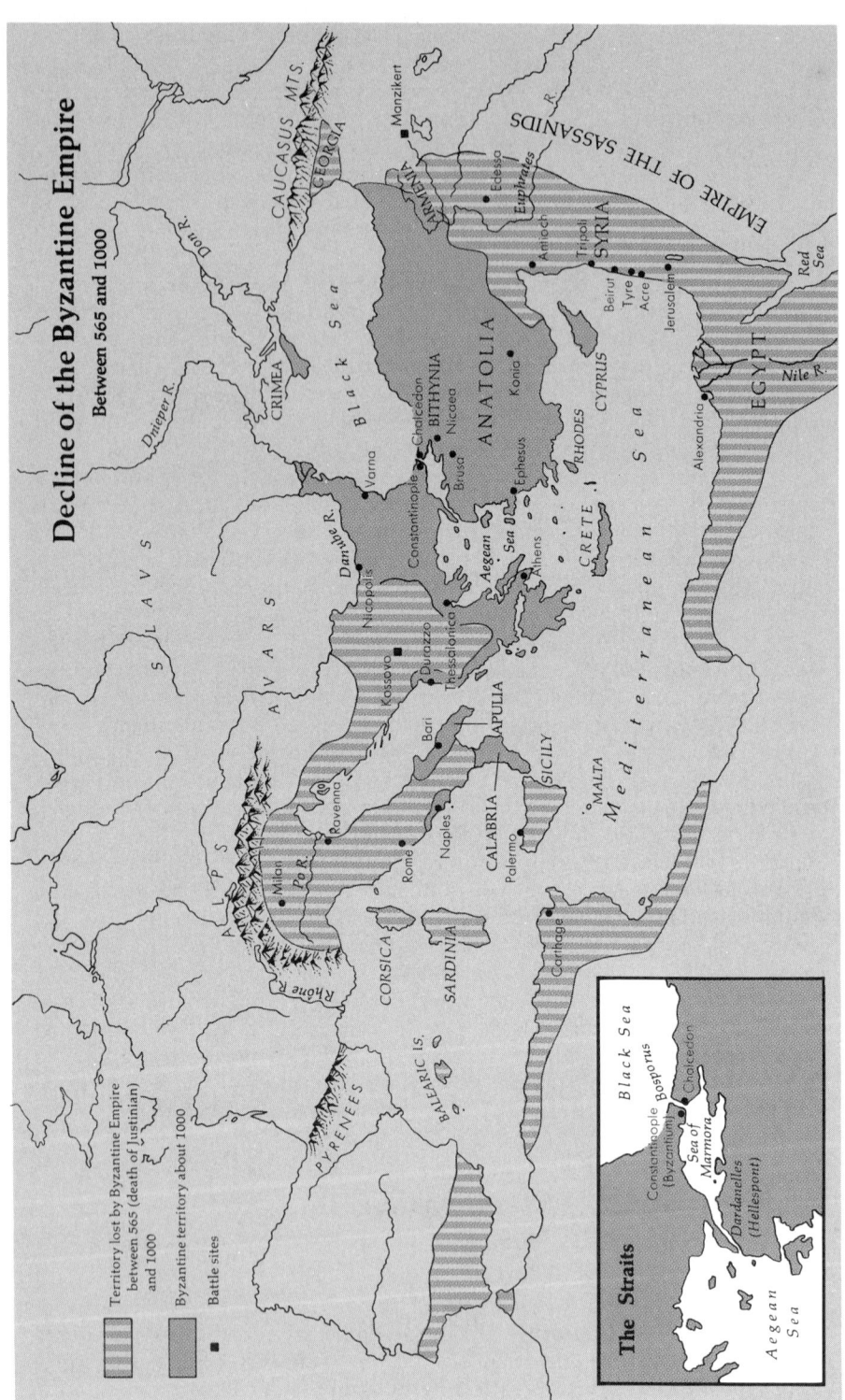

Byzantine titles and those whose roots were in the administrative affairs of the Lateran palace. During the pontificate of Hadrian I (772–795), a remarkably able governor, the Lombard threat was balanced by energetic and friendly relations between the pope and Charlemagne. Hadrian also made important attempts to reconstruct a distinctly Roman control over territories that had long been lost to the Lombards and others, and in his reforms of rural agriculture, his rebuilding of local churches, and his firm governance of the city of Rome, Hadrian contributed greatly to the subsequent formation of the Papal State. Hadrian's successor, the unfortunate Leo III (795–816), continued some of Hadrian's building projects in Rome, but his more vigorous enforcement of papal claims to other lands alienated the Roman aristocracy. Leo's difficulties were resolved only with his hearing before Charlemagne in 799 and in Charlemagne's coronation as emperor of the Romans (and protector of Leo) in 800. From that date on, however, the papal power in Rome had to contend with the power of the agents of the Frankish kings. The Papal State for which Hadrian and Leo had to settle was far smaller than the one they had hoped to build with Frankish help, and the establishment of Frankish subkings in Italy—first Charlemagne's son Pepin and then, in 813, Pepin's son Bernard—restricted the political authority of the popes even further.

South Italy had always posed diplomatic problems for the popes, problems arising from both Lombard and Byzantine forces. The absence of a coordinated system of defense to the south of Rome and the growth of Arab sea power in the first years of the ninth century opened the way to a striking series of Arab victories between 827 and 848, among which was the conquering of Sicily from its Byzantine authorities. These victories established Arab power throughout the western coast of southern Italy. The divisiveness of the rulers of South Italy posed one difficulty; another was the new interest in Italy taken by the descendants of Louis the Pious. Lothair, Louis's son and imperial successor, bequeathed his own kingdom of Italy to his son Louis II in 843, and Louis undertook to establish for himself an Italian kingdom based upon the whole of Italy. Roman resentment, sharpened by the rebuilding of the city and a revival of interest in Roman history, came to a focus when, during the pontificate of Sergius II (844–847), the pope's claims for the direct dependence of Rome upon the emperor were reluctantly recognized by Louis II, the power of the local Roman nobility in papal and city affairs grew to be decisive, and the city of Rome itself was sacked by an Arab raiding force (846). Under Sergius's successor, Leo IV (847–855), the defense and rebuilding of Rome were begun with great zeal. By 852 the Leonine City, which involved the ringing of the area around the Vatican with fortifications, had been completed, and the rebuilding of Rome had been undertaken by Emperor Lothair. The defense of the western coastal regions against further Arab attacks was increased by Leo's promise of spiritual benefits to all who participated in that enterprise.

The practice of the papal coronation of the emperor, devised by Leo III, was repeated by Pope Stephen IV in 816 for Louis the Pious and by Pope Paschal I for Lothair in 823, thus establishing, under three very different sets of circumstances, the papal role in imperial coronations. The long rule in Italy of Louis II (843–875), Lothair's son, witnessed the assaults upon papal primacy by Patriarch Photios and Emperor Michael III in Byzantium, and the continued assaults of Arab raiders throughout the ninth century. After mid-century, the popes were often embattled rulers who asserted the authority of the papacy in stronger and stronger terms against increasingly hopeless odds.

Nicholas I expounded more consistently than any pope in more than two centuries the theory of a Christian empire in the west constructed to protect and further the interests of the Church. In a series of letters to rulers of both east and west, Nicholas laid down systematically the principles of the relations between temporal power and spiritual authority, and his insistence on these principles, even in the face of adversity, contributed to the later development and extension of claims of papal authority throughout Christendom. Pope John VIII (872–882) faced even greater political crises than Nicholas. The death of Louis II in 875 led John in search of a ruler for Italy who was capable of establishing peace in Rome, defending Italy against the Arabs, and quelling the growing rivalry of the great duchies of Spoleto and Benevento in the center of Italy. At first crowning Charles the Bald as emperor in 875, John later supported Boso of Provence, and finally Charles the Fat, who was crowned emperor in 881 and was the last of the Carolingians to rule, however nominally, an empire nearly as extensive as that of Charlemagne. John's difficulties with the imperial succession were compounded by the internal strife among Roman noble and clerical factions and by the Arab threat. John himself led troops against the Arabs, and in his evocation of the need for all Christians to come to the defense of a threatened Rome, he coined the term *Christianitas,* Christendom, to designate the universal community of Christians with Rome as its center and the pope at its head. The decline of Carolingian authority, however, and the increasing power of the dukes of Spoleto and Benevento harassed John during his last years, and upon his assassination in 882 only the theory of a Latin Christian Empire had been forcefully enunciated. The institutions that might have given that theory substance were in total disarray, and the office of the papacy itself soon fell into the hands of local powers.

During the third quarter of the ninth century, the struggle among oligarchs to control ecclesiastical positions and ecclesiastical wealth in Italy overshadowed both imperial ideals and the enhanced papal claims of Nicholas I and John VIII. The houses of Friuli, Spoleto, and Benevento, and later that of Tuscany, claimed predominance on the basis of wealth, ecclesiastical connections, and relations with the families of the rulers of the Frankish kingdoms and with the houses of various popes. The assassination of John VIII in 882 and the deposition and death of Emperor Charles the Fat in 887–888 marked the end of the last traces of traditional Carolingian authority in Italy and the end of papal independence of the local aristocracy. In 891 and 892 members of the house of Spoleto, Guy and his son Lambert, were crowned emperors by Pope Stephen V and Pope Formosus. A brief Carolingian resurgence occurred in 895 when Arnulf was crowned emperor by Formosus, but both died the next year. In a scene of bitter recrimination and personal and factional vengeance, Formosus' successor, Stephen VI, had his predecessor's remains exhumed, clothed in pontifical vestments, and tried for various crimes. The corpse of Formosus was convicted, the dead pope's acts were annulled, and the body was dismembered and thrown into the Tiber. The trial of the corpse of Formosus echoed in Roman history for many decades, and political factionalism made the papal title simply an adjunct of aristocratic parties clamoring for power in the center of the peninsula.

The greatest of these families was that of Theophylact, a man who had risen in the papal administration to join the senatorial ranks of the most powerful aristocrats in Rome. Theophylact, his wife Theodora, and their daughter Marozia exerted considerable influence, and they used it to arrange the election of their ally John X (914–928) as pope. The forces of Theophylact and his family, Duke Alberic of Spoleto (who married Marozia), and John X combined with the revived Byzantine interests in Italy to defeat a major Arab force on the Garigliano in 915. The aristocratic rivalry in Italy continued, however, and in 932 Marozia's son Alberic emerged as the supreme lay ruler in central Italy, dominating even his brother, Pope John XI. Alberic began ecclesiastical and administrative reforms, encouraged a new literary consciousness of the imperial traditions of Rome, and instituted new contacts with the Byzantine Empire, particularly a restoration of Byzantine political forms in Italy. The last of the Italian "emperors" had died in 923, and Alberic's domination, which lasted until his death in 954, introduced a considerable degree of stability to Roman affairs. Alberic was survived by his young son Octavian, who inherited not only his father's power and wealth, but the papacy itself in 955. The pontificate of Octavian as John XII (955–964) was characterized by a falling away from both the high ideals of the ninth-century popes and the political stability of the reign of Alberic.

By 962 Rome had separated itself from the growing internationalism of the late Carolingian Empire and had reasserted its imperial heritage, chiefly to defend its local interests. The office of the papacy, closely associated with the idea of a universal Christian society, had been occupied by examples of both the best and the worst popes that any century ever produced. The growing power of noble families and their transalpine alliances posed constant threats to the pope's vision, and at times the universalist claims of Romans and popes alike sounded like empty boasting. Yet the tenth century also witnessed some striking achievements. The Arabs had been driven off, and the theory of papal primacy had, if anything, been enunciated more powerfully than ever before. The papacy remained the focus of Roman thought and society, and once the particularism of the mid-tenth century was overcome, the fragments of Carolingian universalist ideals rejoined in the image of a restored empire.

PART **FOUR**

CHRISTENDOM:

Material Civilization
and Culture, 950-1150

14

THE SOCIAL AND ECONOMIC TRANSFORMATION OF THE ELEVENTH AND TWELFTH CENTURIES, 950-1150

POPULATION GROWTH AND NEW PATTERNS OF SETTLEMENT

The differences that permit us to distinguish between cultures and civilizations consist not only of aesthetic, spiritual, and intellectual styles, but of other elements as well, ones that reflect substantially the fabric and structure of material life. The transformations of the Mediterranean world and Roman Europe had entailed large and distinctive shifts in population, patterns of settlement, and social structure. The Germanic and Slavic settlement of parts of Roman Europe and, in addition, vast areas of land that had never been a part of the Roman Empire continued these shifts, although without completely obliterating earlier forms of settlement. The cultural transformation from nomadic or settled pastoral societies to agricultural societies affected the settlers of Europe from the Iron Age Celts to the Magyars, and with the virtual end of the migrations and invasions by the middle of the tenth century, not only were many older forms of settlement swept away, but new patterns were established, patterns that, according to some historians, endured in many parts of Europe to the twentieth century and thus suggest, in this respect at least, the label "Traditional Europe" to describe European society between the tenth century and the Industrial Revolution. In the world of traditional Europe, the majority of the population lived and worked in rural areas, urbanization was linked closely to the population levels and activities of cities and the regions immediately surrounding them, and the social order was based on status differences rather than on clear-cut class differences. The roots of Traditional Europe are to be found in the settlements of the fifth through the tenth centuries and in the society and culture that emerged from these between the tenth and the fourteenth centuries.

One of the most striking shifts of the period between the tenth and the thirteenth centuries was the transformation of settlement patterns and the growth of the European population. A glance at some of the most striking features of the world around the year 1000 may serve to highlight the most important of these. In terms of urban settlements, for example, the greatest city of the Western world around the year 1000 was Constantinople, with a population somewhat larger, perhaps, than 300,000. Such cities as Antioch, Thessalonica, Córdoba, and Cairo, all in the Byzantine or Islamic worlds, ranged between 50,000 and 100,000 in population. No city in the Latin west remotely approached these urban concentrations. Paris had just begun to spill over onto the banks of the Seine from its original location on the Ile de la Cité, and the large areas enclosed by the walls of Rome and Milan were used mostly for farms and pasturing. By the mid fourteenth century, however, western Europe possessed at least four cities—Milan, Venice, Florence, and Genoa —that approached 100,000 in population and at least a dozen or more between 20,000 and 50,000. Considered against the background of Byzantine or Islamic—or modern—urban growth, these totals may well seem small, but they reflect a profound transformation of the social structure and an increase in population that are fundamental to the history of European development.

Between Scandinavia and Spain, Ireland and Russia, late tenth-century Europe probably numbered around 38 million people. Most of this population was distributed very unevenly in densely populated rural agricultural communities, which were irregularly spaced, isolated, and highly particularistic in their economy. Most of the population growth before and after the Carolingian period took place within these isolated centers; little effort was made to expand the areas of settlement and there were few successes in expanding the upper limits of potential growth. By the mid fourteenth century, in contrast, the population of Europe stood at around 75 million, before it was decimated by the wave of famine and plague from which it took two centuries to recover. This doubling of population in a space of three centuries was in part the result of the breaking of the Carolingian patterns of settlement, migrations into new lands, and the cultivation of many areas that had been vast and deserted since early Europe. Thus, not only did the European population grow at a startling rate, but between the tenth and the fourteenth centuries it transformed the older patterns of settlement, expanded into new lands, and rearranged the demographic and economic map of the West.

In the history of preindustrial societies, the fundamental mechanism of demographic and economic growth is the relationship between the number of people and the way in which they settle, on the one hand, and the level of agricultural productivity they achieve, on the other. The label "growth," of course, covers many complex processes, in which such elements as diet, life expectancy, marriage and reproductive patterns, the age profile of populations, and the strengthening or weakening of traditional social bonds all play important parts. And some of these must be considered with some attention if the complex character of European demographic and economic development is to be understood.

The sources of evidence for the demographic history of early Europe are varied and highly irregular. Some areas in some periods offer abundant information; most offer little or none. Such documents as the polyptics of the ninth-century Carolingian abbeys, later tax registers, manorial accounts, and occasional larger surveys, such as that carried out in England in 1086 for William the Conqueror and compiled into Domesday Book, all offer some help, but no documentary sources can remotely match the statistical resources and statistical consciousness of post-eighteenth-century Europe. Our information concerning medieval populations has increased considerably through the application of recent disciplines such as archaeology, statistics, and the formal discipline of demographic studies itself.

Most Europeans, before and after the population growth in the tenth century, had a short life expectancy; women died at a younger age than men, and, except in the towns, the ratio of men to women remained high. With the general tendency toward monogamy and the uncertainty of serial marriages, certain brakes were placed upon raw population growth. Other cultural patterns contributed to these brakes. Requirements of age and wealth in arranging marriages, the cultural and religious regulations surrounding intercourse, childbearing, and child rearing, and patterns of inheritance and age profiles in the population are examples.

The history of population is not merely the history of the increase or decrease in the raw numbers of humans inhabiting a given location during a given time. Such general terms as "population growth" are convenient labels for a complex process that must take into account available food, specific diet, the ratio of men to women and their ages at marriage, the age structure of a population (how great a percentage of the total belongs to each of several different age groups), mortality rates, life expectancy, and the percentage of a whole population available for reproduction. We have already considered some of the demographic limits upon earlier societies, particularly those of the barbarian neighbors of the Roman Empire, and we have seen that agricultural societies supported greater population densities than nomadic hunting or pastoral societies. One of the great clichés in western films shows the pastoralist cattlemen outraged at the "crowding in" of agricultural settlers, "homesteaders." Population differences, of course, entail cultural and social differences as well. Agricultural society, as European society was and remained until the nineteenth century, is also more susceptible to improved technological and material techniques than other forms of preindustrial society.

Between 900 and 1300, an agricultural revolution permitted the numbers of Europeans to increase and the structure of European society to change in such a way that large numbers of people were freed from the necessity of producing their own food and thereby permitted a degree of social diversification that led to the expansion of cultivated lands, new patterns of settlement, the development of urban and commercial centers, and the rise of a rich and varied culture. Although these changes did not occur everywhere or at the same rate and distribution, the effects of their most influential occurrences are clear. Different systems of plowing and planting led not only to an increase in the food supply, but to a broadening of its variety and to the introduction of new dietary elements, the most important of which were vegetable proteins. The devastation of the ninth and early tenth centuries opened new forms of land for cultivation. Around the tenth century, although fertility rates remained high, mortality rates dropped, and the increased production of food did not lead everywhere to a direct increase in food available per capita, a brake on population growth that often occurs when high fertility rates are not matched by corresponding improvements in food production. From 1100 to 1320, life expectancy increased significantly among Europeans, until a level was reached that, except during prolonged periods of plague and famine, remained characteristic of European populations until the late nineteenth century and remained higher than that of underdeveloped non-European peoples until the present day.

The social characteristics of this population change must be kept in mind. Children, when they survived, ceased to be dependents at an early age and joined the labor force. Persons who survived past fifty often had to contract with their families for their future support as part of the complicated process of turning over a farm from one generation to the next. The delicate requirements for an adequate labor force could be upset by too great a number of young people entering a force in which there was too little for them to do; this trend was particularly true of the aristocracy, which throughout the period 900–1300 tended to overpopulate and thus created a potential downward social mobility for its excess children. Fortunately, this potential downward mobility was in part compensated for by the increased opportunities available for a career. No excess, unlanded noble children became peasants, although their grandchildren might, and many of them entered religious life, populated the towns, entered trade and commerce, or undertook mercenary service in the periodic wars that required larger military forces than normal. Whenever mortality rates increased, the problem arose of minor children inheriting properties that required strong management, and so one example of population structural change suggests wider-reaching changes in social relationships. A burgeoning peasant population, on the other hand, might be induced to send its excess labor to open new areas for cultivation, as also occurred between 900 and 1300. Sometimes, as in regions of northern France, the Netherlands, and central Germany, the new areas matched or improved upon the productivity of the old, and the roots of lasting communities were set down. In other areas, the initial settlements were made by smaller numbers of people on very marginal land that required heavy, continual maintenance, and so a slight decrease in population—caused by disease, famine, or other natural disasters—would ultimately lead to the abandonment of this land and the migration of its population to other places. This second instance occurred increasingly from the late thirteenth to the fifteenth century.

Increasing population between the ninth and the late thirteenth centuries, however, led to new settlements in many places, and to the cultivation of previously uninhabitable lands (by draining swamps, reclaiming lands from the ocean, as in the Netherlands, and cutting down forests). Scholars have estimated that by the end of the thirteenth century, more land in Europe was under cultivation than at any time before or since. The new settlements took different forms. When a lord with uninhabited lands supervised their colonization, as lords did in northern Germany, Ireland, and northern France, the patterns of settlement in the new lands resembled those of the old and involved similar conditions of service and social status. When lands were let by inactive landholders, particularly remote lords and ecclesiastical establishments, individual entrepreneurs would be empowered to offer attractive terms to the colonists, acquire such concessions as milling and baking rights for themselves, and literally guide the new inhabitants to their new land, rather like the wagon masters in the nineteenth-century United States. Cities, too, required a steady increase of settlers from the countryside. Traditionally, cities do not replace their own populations, and steady immigration is required in order for urban populations to sustain their numbers or to grow. Migration to the cities—indeed, the entire urbanization of early Europe—took place in the period between 900 and 1300.

In order to provide the food supply that would ultimately sustain and increase population growth instead of operating to check it, as food supplies normally do in preindustrial society, smaller acreages of land needed to sustain larger numbers of people, and this in turn meant that not only did productivity have to be increased, but land exhaustion had to be prevented. Patterns of land use emerged in which crops were rotated in such a way as to restore the earth and at the same time produce needed food products. New sources of power had to be found, and an improved agricultural technology had to be encouraged and developed. These steps, almost beneath the conscious awareness of historians of industrial Europe, were the fundamental elements of the growth of population in Europe between the ninth and the fourteenth centuries. This growth, which helped to close up the vast spaces between centers of early European settlement and push the borders of that settlement beyond the Elbe and the Hispanic frontier, not only constituted another great agricultural revolution, but was also the key to the later development of Europe. Behind history are human beings, and behind particular humans and groups of people stand the complicated raw numbers of demographic study. These constitute the essential basis of the making of Europe after the ninth century.

SUSTENANCE AND SURPLUS: EUROPEAN AGRICULTURE

An increase in birth rate as a result of increased fertility entails a greater number of mouths to feed, and so for population growth to actually occur, mortality rates must be transformed and the amount of food available per capita must be maintained at earlier levels or, ideally, increased. The population of Europe grew between the ninth and the fourteenth centuries not only because of increased fertility, but because those who were alive and those being born had better chances to survive. The elements that have measurably affected the age structure and life expectancy of post-eighteenth-century populations—improved medical techniques, the industrialization of agriculture, the full weight of a vast program of scientific research, and the intensive development of natural and human resources—were wholly absent from this growth. As one historian has accurately stated, the Middle Ages witnessed an underdeveloped society pulling itself up by its own bootstraps. Between the ninth and the fourteenth centuries, people in Europe produced more and better food than they ever had before. The growth of population is a fundamental element in the development of medieval society, and the agricultural transformation of the period is the means by which population growth came to be sustained.

The fertility rate of the population of Carolingian Europe was high, but the mortality rate was high as well. The large amounts of land needed to sustain single families and to produce sufficient surplus for the clergy and for the nobles and service personnel of the courts required intensive cultivation and absorbed the energies of the population. That population cultivated grain, for the most part. As bread, porridge, and ale, grain provided the primary element of diet for many centuries. Two striking consequences of the population growth and agricultural changes after the tenth century were the improvement in the extent of cultivation and in

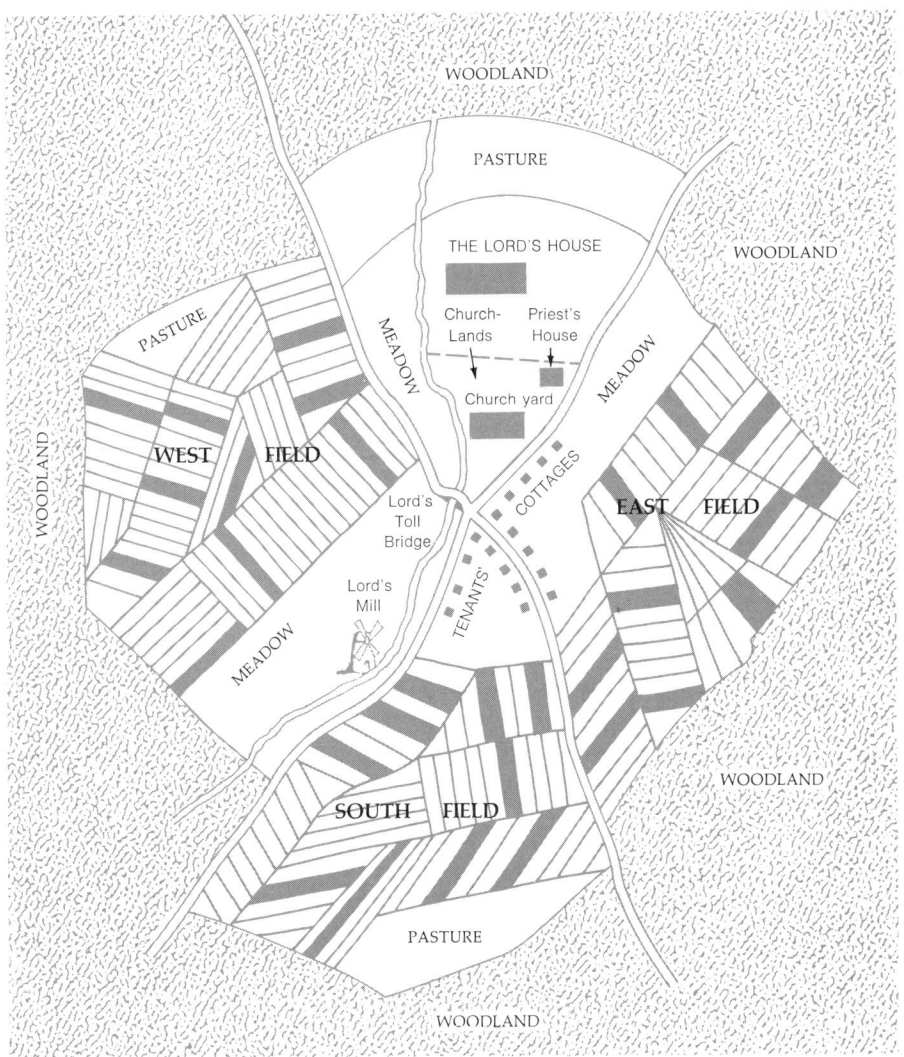

Plan of a medieval manor: the solid strips are the lord's demesne.

the quality of grain and the addition to the diet (first that of the nobles, later that of townsmen and peasants) of vegetable proteins, meat, and fish. These dietary additions, however, were never uniform or extensive. Nobles tended to consume more animal protein than vegetables, and peasants more vegetables than animal protein. Nobles and townsmen ate bread made from progressively finer-milled flour, whereas peasant bread remained coarse and was often baked from barley, rye, or oats. Bread, the staple of life, was one of the foundations of manorial wealth and economy. The planting and harvesting of grain brought the lord of the manor his large share; the lord's mills ground the grain to flour, and the lord's ovens baked the flour to bread. Slowly, the diet of Europeans widened. The signs of this include the introduction of vegetable protein and soil-renewing crops at a second spring planting; the expansion of the arable at the expense of the forest (and sometimes the lord's treasured hunting rights therein); the growth of markets that traded in food as well as in other material goods; the growth of dairy and stock herds; and the increasingly widespread use of viticulture, the turning over of vast fields in some regions into vineyards.

By the thirteenth century, commercial agriculture had expanded into industrial agriculture. Flax, hemp, and dye plants all constitute signs not only of agricultural sustenance, but of a sufficient surplus of basic foods to enable lords and peasants both to take such audacious and risky steps as committing precious farmland to crops and herds that, by themselves, could not sustain life in the locality and thus depended upon the regularity of a commercial market. The agricultural revolution of the eleventh and twelfth centuries greatly increased the market economy of Europe, and for two and a half centuries the security of the market permitted a vast agricultural expansion and a surplus that generated not only a transformation of older systems of landholding and service, but the clearing of new lands, the establishment of new settlements, and improved routes of communication and trade. Not since the appearance of commercial agriculture in Greece in the eighth and seventh centuries B.C. had a similar agricultural revolution taken place. Not until the agricultural reforms of the eighteenth and nineteenth centuries and the transformed economy of industrial Europe did a comparable revolution occur again. In this last revolution, agricultural society gave way to industrial society, which, in the Western world at least, broke the oldest cycle of life that humans have ever known.

Population growth, changes in demographic proportion of different age groups as percentages of the whole population, and the steady production of a food surplus over a larger and larger area of land are the most striking features of the agricultural history of the period between the ninth and the fourteenth centuries. Behind these, however, lie a mass of data that indicate vast regional variety and the presence of new techniques of farming and organizing labor. Older views of the agricultural history of this period often emphasized the uniform presence of the manor —the estate divided into demesne and *mansi,* with demesne labor performed both by resident peasants and by the occupants of the *mansi*—at the expense of other forms of agricultural organization. The survival of free farms (allods) and free villages, the new circumstances of farms cleared out of forest or wasteland, and the variety of farms that might be attached to a demesne but not grouped in its immediate vicinity at all have recently altered this older picture. The best and most attractive documentary sources, from the *Polyptic* of Irminon in the ninth century to Domesday Book in the late eleventh century, offer a picture of uniformity (sometimes a highly idealized picture of uniformity) that leads to oversimplification of the diversified kinds of units that characterized European agriculture.

One force for diversity lay in the character of the farming community itself. Although the rhythms of life and the essential occupations of farming communities were similar everywhere, each community had come into existence and acquired different rights on its own. It is, in fact, the sum total of the rights of both lord and peasant that gave each community its separate identity. Such rights were generally adjudicated in courts held on a manor, and the "law" of each manor was different from the laws of other manors. To be sure, the avaricious landlords of the ninth and tenth centuries attempted to assume control over the administration of law in a given territory, but the law they controlled by holding a manor court or a village court and compelling attendance was a customary law that had grown up with the community itself, that had been remembered, redefined, and reargued from generation to generation, and touched all communal aspects of manorial life, from the lord's rights to the number of pigs that farmers could turn loose to root in the forest. The exchange between lord and peasants in the manorial court, the hammering out of the customs of each manor and village, the community response to newly cleared land or new agricultural techniques all constitute an important part of the diversity and quality of rural life in early European history.

Agricultural communities of different kinds became the essential modules of European society. Irreducible to smaller units, trampled over by invaders and defenders, worked by serfs and free peasants, their success and failure altered the rhythm of county and kingdom alike. There was room for settlement everywhere, but little room for strangers. "And with regard to lordless men, from whom no justice is to be obtained," said a law of King Aethelstan in tenth-century England, "we have ordained that their kindred be commanded to settle them in homes, where they will be subject to folkright, and find them lords in the popular court." This text says much about tenth-century ideas of social status and social relations: every man had to have a lord, for the business of this tenth- and eleventh-century world was done by lords, nominally on behalf of others. In spite of the diversity of working and living conditions, however, population growth, new settlements, and an expanded and increased food supply all suggest a new productivity from labor. The ending of the invasions and the gradual establishment of territorial lordship imposed some degree of new security and regularity upon agricultural life, but the basis of the agricultural transformation of Europe was the increased productivity of population and land.

There was much work to be done, but from the tenth century on, there was also a new kind of help. From this century date the earliest references to new sources of power and labor-saving devices that constitute such a distinctive feature of western European history from the seventh to the nineteenth century. By the sixth century there is evidence of the increased use of water power, which was at first used chiefly to turn mills but by the twelfth century was employed in a remarkable variety of ways. The sixth-century volume of saints' lives by Gregory of Tours mentions one of the earliest examples of its use:

> The Abbot Ursus [d. c. 500] . . . had the idea of [diminishing] the labor [of his brethren] by establishing a mill in the bed of the river Indre. Fixing rows of stakes in the river, with heaps of great stones to make dams, he collected the water in a channel and used the current to make the wheel of the machine turn with great speed. By this means he diminished the monks' work and one brother could be delegated to this task.

Although the water mill had been known to, and used sparingly by, the Romans, it began in the tenth century to be used more regularly for a wider variety of tasks. As important as the wider use of the water mill was the revolution in the use of animal power for plowing. The development of the stirrup and the breeding of the great and expensive war horses that appeared in Europe early in the eighth century represent another new power source. Less spectacular but ultimately more important were two further ways in which the horse was employed in society. Widespread use of the faster and more versatile horse in agricultural life had been hampered under the Romans and in the early Middle Ages by the limitations on the weight a horse could pull, limitations imposed by the traditional system of harnessing. A tight collar around the horse's neck choked off the animal's air supply if too great a weight were placed against it. The great French historian Richard LeFebvre des Noëttes, in conducting research on agrarian history in the twentieth century, discovered that a new system of harnessing horses had appeared during the tenth century. The new horse collar allowed the pressure points of the load to be placed on the horse's shoulders instead of the throat, thereby exponentially increasing the pulling power of the animal. The horseshoe, too, appeared around this time. It complemented the increased pulling power of the horse by improving both footing and traction and by protecting the hooves against the damp, heavy clay soils of northern Europe. Thus, an animal of hitherto limited military and domestic use suddenly became the second great nonhuman power source available to Europeans. The third source was wind, and by the end of the twelfth century windmills had appeared. The power revolution of the tenth through the twelfth centuries was the first major development of nonhuman sources of power since the domestication of oxen and the invention of the ship, and the most important before the discovery of steam power in the eighteenth century.

These new sources of power were soon put to work. By the twelfth century, water mills and windmills were used in different phases of the process of cloth manufacture, and soon they were turning saws and triphammers. The horse, and the ox, were used in front of an equally important machine, the heavy plow. The plow of the Mediterranean and Near Eastern world had been developed for the soils of that world, light, sandy soils that were easily broken and pulverized. The agricultural engineering of the ancient world was not concerned with plowing techniques, but with water engineering—the complicated business of keeping the dry soils moist, either through irrigation or planned flooding—and with terracing and supporting fragile hillside fields. North of the Alps, the soil is different, and the Mediterranean scratch plow proved barely effective against the heavy, poorly draining clay soils of the north. Although literary references suggest that the sixth century witnessed the appearance of a new kind of heavy plow, archaelogical research indicates that it may have been invented even earlier. The new plow, called a *carruca* by the sources (as opposed to the Mediterranean *aratrum*), appears to have begun to circulate widely after the ninth century. Several features of the new plow bear closer examination, because they helped transform social as well as mechanical relationships. The new plow consisted of three parts: the coulter cut the sod, the plowshare lifted and turned the earth to a considerable depth, and the mouldboard shaped the turned earth into a furrow. Thus, the actions of these three parts cut earth, raised important soil elements to the surface, and provided for essential drainage. Yet in order to operate efficiently, the new plow required more than sources of horse or ox power. First, it required considerably greater power than the older plow: not one or two oxen or horses, but six or eight were needed to pull its load, and the thinness of early medieval population and the unlikelihood that a single peasant would possess eight oxen suggests that a pooling of plow teams was necessary. Second, the ideal way to plow a field was to move in a straight line as far as the pitch of the field would permit. The long narrow fields of the world of the heavy plow contrasted sharply with the square fields of the cross-plowing techniques familiar to the older scratch plow. Thus, the heavy plow introduced a degree of peasant cooperation, a redesigning of fields, and an increased labor productivity that made headway faster in lands hitherto unsettled or vacated rather than in lands crowded with peasants who had divided their fields in traditional ways. The new plow required a long field (measures of field lengths varied greatly), a headland at the end to permit the plow to make its great turn, and the laying out of fields in a way that saved time for peasants going to and from work.

The old and the new systems of plowing operated on land whose use had been developed over centuries. Because animals were few and were often turned out to graze when not working, much animal manure was lost. The necessity of fertilizing the heavy soils of Europe or letting them rest fallow in order to restore their fertility directed that early plow lands generally be divided into two parts. One field was planted in the spring and the other left fallow, the process being reversed every year. The fallow field was restored in part by animals grazing over its grass and stubble and leaving their manure to restore its soil. Around the eighth century, however, possibly earlier, another system appeared. Instead of two fields, one of which (and hence one half of all the arable land) lay fallow, the new system divided the field in three. In this system, one field was planted in the fall with grain, one was planted in the spring with spring grain and peas, beans, and vetches, and the third lay fallow. Both the winter and spring plantings were harvested in the late summer, at which point the cycle altered: the fallow field became the winter field, the winter field became the spring field, and the spring field turned to fallow. The advantages of the three-field system are obvious: the amount of land that was out of use was reduced from one half to one third; the varieties of vegetable protein from the spring planting improved and varied the diet; the same spring planting, by growing beans as well as grain, returned valuable nitrogen to the soil; and the rotation of crops meant that the exhaustion of the land by exclusive grain growing became less likely. The two- and three-field systems were not, of course, serial. That is, both systems survived, along with other kinds of agricultural practices: land might be cleared, sown for a few seasons, and then left fallow indefinitely; some land might be cultivated intensively and continuously while most of the rest of the arable was cultivated and left fallow in alternate years or planted one year and left fallow for two or three. To impose a uniformity upon medieval agricultural practices, whether in the form of an imaginary "ideal" manor or a uniform system of cultivation, is to distort seriously the variety reflected in, and the chronology of, agricultural history.

Besides fallowing, only two other methods of fertilizing fields artificially were in use: manuring and marling. Marl, a limestone clay, was rare and used only in certain regions. Manuring was always a problem because there was little of it, much of it was lost, and what there was was used most intensively in the kitchen gardens immediately around the farmhouses. The great revolution in fertilizing did not occur until the seventeenth and eighteenth centuries.

The organization of village life, the spiritual needs of the peasants, and the feasts and work schedules of the year were all linked to the rhythm of planting and harvesting. Family structure, local law, the clearing of new land, and festivals all imparted a distinctive character to medieval agricultural life, although the precise nature of that character varied from village to village and from region to region. Some things did not change. The seed-to-yield ratio remained terribly low, and people were subjected to floods and droughts, to plagues and animal sickness, and to degrees of heat and cold, darkness and light that would be extreme to a modern reader. Small plaster and thatch houses, the proximity of farm animals, long periods of inaction and bare subsistence, and the barely controlled fury of village and family society all colored the working year. And yet these roots, fragile in many ways as they seem, supported the transformation of European society between the ninth and the fourteenth centuries.

MARKET, TOWN, AND CITY IN AN AGRICULTURAL WORLD

The vast patterns of plowed fields, fallow land, forest, vineyard, and waste that constituted both the foundation and the background of early European social and economic history took different forms for different purposes. The manor and its divisions were both economic and legal units. Village and hamlet were economic units whose purpose was to cultivate the surrounding countryside effectively. Purely administrative units—the hundreds, wapentakes, boroughs, and castellanies—existed, not primarily for the purposes of their peasant and noble inhabitants, but for the administrative uses of higher powers. People paid suit at a particular court and tithe to a particular church according to custom and legal obligation. The overlapping of different kinds of communities on the same land has often given rise in the past to attempts to describe all units as if they had the same character and purpose—again, resulting in oversimplification of the complexities of rural life. Between the tenth and the twelfth centuries, as many historical studies have shown, peasant communities not only fought their lords in manor courts but could on occasion carry their fight to higher courts—to that of the king, for example, and even, in one famous case, to that of the pope. During the same period peasant families, especially in areas such as the Iberian Peninsula, Germany, and northwestern France and England, could accumulate relatively large tracts of land and grow comparatively wealthy. Also, the specialization of regional agriculture led to the development of trade and markets, which imparted a commercial character, at least in part, to even the most remote rural areas of Europe. Popes, high prelates, monasteries, kings, great lords, small lords, and communities themselves all regarded the divisions of territory from different points of view; all struggled to maintain their own legal rights, and some struggled to acquire new rights, often at the expense of custom and authority. It is in the play among these different communities that much of early European social and economic history is to be found. Reluctant to change, tied largely to the rhythm of the agricultural year, and largely impoverished, the communities of Europe between the tenth and the thirteenth centuries have often been regarded as static, anarchic, and heavily traditional. Yet out of these communities emerged in a remarkably short period many institutions that modern historians consider the essential characteristics of traditional Europe: complex trade, industry, and financial institutions; complexes of large towns and cities; movements toward centralized government and the rational exploitation of economic resources; a vigorous and extensive spiritual revival; and an intellectual community whose horizons knew no bounds.

Of all the different kinds of early European societies, that of the city has received the most attention, probably because urban development has always seemed less characteristic of preindustrial Europe, and hence, more "modern." Yet to understand the growth and character of medieval cities, we must first understand something of other communities —from the rural village to the monastery and to the household of a medieval bishop—because medieval cities, like these communities, were social organisms and were dependent upon their surrounding countrysides. We have already seen that the characteristics of the agricultural economy bound peasant groups into a community of enterprise and management and that the legal affairs of the manor and village bound them into juridical communities. The village church had a similar effect. The history of ecclesiastical administrative units is long and complicated. At the beginning of the period under consideration—that is, around the middle of the tenth century—churches were of several kinds. The bishop's own church was the chief church of the diocese. Attached to it were local churches, oratories, and baptistries, served by members of the bishop's ecclesiastical household and supported by the bishop. On the other hand, many churches were privately owned, for old Germanic law made clear distinctions between the function of a church and the rights of ownership over it, its furniture, the land on which it stood, and the collection of individual rights originally acquired by it or assigned to it. The lay proprietor assigned the priest to the church and could compel certain people to use his church rather than another. The only obligation upon the owner of the church was that he support a priest and maintain the services in it. Above these obligations, which had been the focus of much Carolingian legislation, the income of the ecclesiastical property was treated in much the same way as the income from a manor or a vineyard: it belonged to the lord. Without doubt, this system had many spiritual shortcomings, and throughout the eleventh century a movement built up to destroy, among other things, this system of proprietary churches. Not until much later in European history did anything resembling the closely organized diocesan and parochial structure of modern ecclesiastical administration spread widely through Europe. Between the ninth and the fourteenth centuries, certainly, local churches were much more obviously (and legally) an integral part of the village community, and lord, peasants, and priest (who himself had to farm, was occasionally married, and often was born in the neighborhood) constituted a community of interest. More than the region or kingdom, the village constituted the peasant's "native land"—in French, his *pays*. By the thirteenth century the village community was responsible not only for agricultural production, but for criminal apprehension in the district, the assistance of royal agents and investigators, and the maintenance of roadways and waterways. The village church usually compelled the community's attendance at religious feasts, offerings, baptisms, marriages, funerals, and burials. After the Fourth Lateran Council of 1215, the parish also compelled annual confession and communion. The patron saint of the church was also the patron of the village community, and the church and its burial ground functioned as a place of refuge, assembly, and festivity—often to the chagrin of higher ecclesiastical authorities. Within the parish were religious fraternities, another kind of community, whose members banded together to care for the sick, bury and pray for the dead, and celebrate together, distributing food and clothing to their members at least once a year. The church, its priest, and its yard offered protection from both natural and supernatural disaster.

New villages arising on hitherto vacant lands experienced a sense of community in their very isolation from traditional village organization and custom. Their inhabitants, often drawn from widely separated areas and possessed of lists of specific privileges, possessed even stronger senses of common interest than older villages. Just as it is inaccurate to consider rural society at this period as being static and uniform, so it is an oversimplification to consider it as being rigidly stratified. In the ninth century, King Alfred of Wessex had written that society was divided into three parts: "A king's raw material and instruments of rule are a well-peopled land, and he must have men of prayer, men of war, and men of work." In the eleventh century both Bishop Adalbero of Laon and Bishop Gerald of Cambrai echoed the conventional division: "From the beginning human kind has been divided into three parts, prayers, farmers, and fighters." At the end of the twelfth century, some lawyers added a fourth stratum, "town dwellers." A fourteenth-century English sermon notes that "God made the clergy, knights, and laborers, but the Devil made townsmen and usurers." Another disgruntled commentator in the fourteenth century added to the Devil's creations "students of universities." These are the general categories in terms of which people from the tenth to the sixteenth centuries envisaged the structure of society. We have already seen the slow shaping of the idea of an aristocracy (essentially, "those who fight") from the seventh century on. Yet strong-armed peasant farmers who served a lord or king might well wield authority equivalent to that of nobles, and the parish priest who was the serf of the landowner and proprietor of his church fitted socially into the class of "those who work" rather than the class of "those who pray." Villagers, priest, and lord, however stratified their lives appear, nevertheless constituted the village and manorial community. Lords retained power, but they also provided defense and patronage; peasants became more free from servile obligations, but most regarded the place of the lord as "natural" until the late eighteenth century; the ecclesiastical reforms after the late eleventh century broke the proprietary system and elevated the status of the clergy, but the local priest remained a secure part of the village community.

Large villages, particular ecclesiastical establishments, and many towns possessed other signs of community besides the continuously interdependent lives of lord, peasants, and priest. The economic opportunities offered by the gradual disappearance of servile status and its replacement with rents in money and produce, the rise in the number of markets and fairs, and the increased circulation of cloth, wine, and spices gave even the most local centers of economic exchange some contact with the world beyond. Although many, probably most, of the local markets and fairs dealt primarily with local products and local needs, some markets and fairs attracted royal attention. Merovingian and Carolingian rulers had sponsored fairs in Paris, and throughout the Carolingian sources we see the figures of traders, stewards, merchants, and slave traders. The supply of the great secular and ecclesiastical houses and courts depended upon some long-range trade, and some of the materials of this trade made their way into more remote centers of habitation. In ninth-century northern Italy and tenth-century Rhineland more and more fairs appeared, and they evidently prospered. The presence of a market or larger fair did not make a large village or town a city, but the existence of markets and fairs increased the circulation of goods, money, and people in the village or town and raised problems of communication and exchange that continued to help open the economic and cultural horizons of rural Europe.

The towns of ninth- and tenth-century Europe had sprung from a mixture of different origins. The ruins of old western Roman imperial cities and provincial administrative centers did not reach or surpass their old dimensions until after the twelfth century. Some towns and cities, occupied by the leaders of the early Germanic kingdoms, survived as royal residences. Charlemagne, as we have seen, built up Aachen as a royal residence at the beginning of the ninth century. But Charlemagne's successors did not reside in Aachen, and the once thriving town declined through the ninth century. Some towns, such as the ports of Quentovic and Duurstede, thrived through the eighth and ninth centuries only to be obliterated by invasion and never resettled. Towns, like fields and vineyards, are complex entities requiring continual maintenance of their fabric. Many of the older Roman cities simply decayed: roads were not repaired; walls, buildings, even churches were left abandoned. Animals and crops were raised within the boundaries of old urban centers. Further dilapidation took place when the building materials of the old cities were used for other purposes. The dismantling of the public architecture of the old Roman cities had significant consequences; one of which was that by the ninth century, few builders were capable of restoring anything resembling the physical features of older monumental architecture.

What was left of old cities, however, was often enough to permit them to be used as fortresses against invasion. The fortified towns drew people into them in time of invasion, and some undoubtedly stayed. Moreover, the slight trade of the eighth and ninth centuries made these fortified towns attractive to merchants, and the *portus*, the center of transportation and market facilities, often grew up at the edge of such fortified areas. Especially along the great rivers of France and Germany, trade, communications, and fortifications all contributed to the continuation of some forms, at least, of urban life. Outside of northern Europe, however, city life survived in more clearly marked ways. The Islamic cities of Spain and the cities, at least most of them, of the East Roman Empire thrived on the two ends of the Mediterranean. In South Italy, particularly after the Byzantine reconquest of the ninth century, such towns as Bari, Amalfi, Salerno, and Naples remained in contact with northern Italy and Byzantium. In northern Italy, Rome remained a shell of the old imperial city, although the papacy and the ecclesiastical affairs of the city sustained its concentration of population. Such port towns as Genoa and Pisa recovered slowly from the Lombard and Arab domination, but by the end of the tenth and the beginning of the eleventh centuries, the small fleets of both cities had begun to regain some maritime success. The conquest of Corsica, Elba, and Sardinia in the beginning of the eleventh century marked the new rise to prosperity of Pisa and Genoa.

One extraordinary example of urban growth took place in the west. At the head of the Adriatic Sea, a region of lagoons, islands, and marshes had long sheltered a population of fishermen and small marine towns. The invasion of the Lombards late in the sixth century had driven many wealthy Italians into these regions, and by the end of the eighth century the town of Venice had emerged. Under Byzantine control (except for its capture by Charlemagne's forces in 809), and always maintaining its close maritime and commercial ties with the Byzantine Empire, Venice developed a mercantile fleet and throughout the ninth century engaged in trade with Byzantium and the Islamic world and with the hinterland of the Po Valley. Salt and slaves constituted the earliest bases of Venetian prosperity, and by the tenth century Venice was the central western trading depot for Byzantine and Islamic commerce. The remarkable growth of Venice was quite unique, however, and few cities of the west could compare to Venice in wealth and power before the thirteenth century.

One hindrance to the growth of towns was the lack within the towns themselves of local authority sympathetic to the idea of growth and diversification. The old Roman *civitas* had been the administrative center of a region, and its governor and *curialis* class, often aided by imperial and private largesse, maintained both the physical city and its enterprising economic life. Roman cities, however, even in the best of times, had not been strong economic units, and with the decline of western imperial power the *curialis* class and the governors had gone, leaving only the bishop or the lord of a nearby region, whose interests were those of the rural landowner rather than those of an urban authority. Yet even in such cases as these, the necessary complexity of managing the affairs of an episcopal establishment required the continual presence of individuals designated in the sources as *negotiatores,* merchants who supplied the court, and a mixed population of artisans. Some of these towns grew because others nearby had been demolished by invasion; some were located on pilgrimage routes; some were fortified centers, markets for grain and the exchange of foodstuffs, or points of departure for routes of migration to the east or north. Many towns included properties of landowning nobles, as well as ecclesiastical establishments besides the bishop's church and palace. The role of the great and lesser nobility seems to have been particularly strong in the development of town life, particularly in northern Europe. The monasteries, originally on the edges of old Roman cities, became part of the nucleus of new cities that spread out and around the old Roman *forum* and the church or monastery. Fortified castles with hovels crowding around their base also became such urban nuclei. In these towns, markets sprang up, often, particularly in the case of woolen cloth, dealing in the materials of long-range and local trade. New habits developed among the leaders of town society. Local law, for instance, often failed to accommodate the needs of the temporary and diverse populations of market towns; local coinage might be insufficient; strangers, however attractive the goods they brought, were generally suspect. It is probably wise to consider the earliest urban settlements as having in common simply one or two functions—such as fortress or monastery on the one hand, and a *portus* or artisanal section on the other—that were originally separated but became part of a single urban unit when the defensive walls were expanded to encircle the several separate sections of activity and residence. The legal and monetary difficulties of urban life then were so apparent that reforms in the law and coinage became uniform throughout the town, and the town itself began to seek particular privileges from its overlord, most frequently the privilege of running its own affairs. The new walls, which, in most European towns, were continually rebuilt outward until the fourteenth century, enclosed not only ecclesiastics, lords, artisans, and merchants, but Jews as well, and within the walls appeared structures unique to the town's new needs: permanent market stalls, squares, and new churches. There also appeared larger houses, with stone on the ground floor and wood and plaster on the upper floors, in which work or business was conducted on the lower level and the workers resided on the upper. Towns developed official systems of weights and measures and built great cranes for lifting large weights, facilities for transients, animals as well as humans, and, by the end of the tenth century, town halls. All of these stand at the beginning of urban expansion in the tenth and eleventh centuries. The twelfth, thirteenth, and fourteenth centuries witnessed further additions to the physical city: paved streets, the expansion and rebuilding of tenth- and eleventh-century town halls, the great urban cathedrals, and, by the thirteenth century, a series of rigid ordinances regulating the physical appearance and kinds of activity in the town.

The stages of the physical city emerged slowly and differently in different regions. Older sections, when they were not torn down, consisted of haphazard buildings and tiny streets crowded against one another; fortified houses with great towers standing in winding, cobbled streets that a modern city dweller might charitably call alleys; old, tiny churches tucked in back of great new cathedrals, which themselves became "city" churches by the end of the thirteenth century. The vast, open naves of the new cathedrals were designed to make the preacher visible and audible to crowds of people inside, a repetition of the town square and its speakers out of doors. No western European city became the equal of Constantinople until the fourteenth and fifteenth centuries, and visions of that ultimate city are recorded in much of the travel literature of the twelfth, thirteenth, and fourteenth centuries. But some western cities seemed almost as mysterious and grand to contemporaries. Venice, covering her many islands and linked by canals, was the great western *entrepôt* of Mediterranean trade. Great fleets tied up at her docks, and their wealth, before it was conveyed to the hinterland, glorified the city. Huge palaces, vast squares, and new churches revealed a strong Byzantine influence, and the isolation and wealth of the city rendered it virtually independent of other powers by the eleventh century. Rome, in the eleventh century still a city of ruins and jerry-built fortified castles, had made some attempts at restoration in the ninth century, and the papal reforms of the eleventh and twelfth centuries restored some of the material grandeur to the spiritual center of Latin Christendom. The increase of business at the papal court during the twelfth century continued to help restore the physical fabric of the city, but not until the rebuilding program of the early sixteenth century and the vast urban redevelopment at the end of the sixteenth century did Rome again stand out in its old grandeur. Yet spiritual Rome was as impressive to western pilgrims as the material splendor of Byzantium and Venice—and safer. More orthodox than the Greek capital and less given to the mysterious ways of trade and moneymaking than the inscrutable Venetians, Rome attracted more affection from contemporaries. Other towns also stand out by the eleventh century, and the pattern of their distribution suggests strong economic functions. The coastal cities of northwestern Italy, southern France, and England; the riverine towns of the Rhine, Seine, Meuse, and Po; and the towns situated across, or better yet, at the intersection of trade and pilgrimage routes and mountain passes all show a precocious and generally steady development.

Towns were always a part of the economic and political life of their regions. They were never independent of their surrounding territories, particularly when population growth and the need for food supplies and room to expand brought their power into the countryside. By the twelfth century the life of the town was an intimate part of regional history, and urban history must allocate a chapter to this delicate and important aspect of urban life.

Political revolutions were rarely, if ever, the origin of town life, but they generally followed soon after a town grew in size and importance. The relatively crowded population of urban areas saw more readily the necessity of mutual support and action, particularly in clearing the way for the economic activities of the town to function properly. Not only merchants, of course, but urban nobles and some ecclesiastics shared the desire to acquire more power over their own affairs, and from the eleventh century on, coalitions of nobles, merchants, and leaders of wealthy artisans attempted to develop local authority that was outside the control of the traditional powers. Military leaders, heads of the urban courts, officials whose status in the town gave them a role in episcopal affairs (and, when a bishop's throne was vacant, virtually the entire administration of the diocese's property) formed groups, generally called communes. From the first quarter of the eleventh century, these groups often wrested from the count and bishop administrative and legal control of the cities in which they lived and had a shared interest. The new communes, which were often bitterly and savagely resisted, regulated town law and institutions, appointed their own town officials from among an urban patricate that usually consisted primarily of noble and wealthy individuals, and distributed their new authority across a system of offices and powers that aimed to increase the prosperity of at least that part of the population that counted as citizens. By the twelfth century, communes had begun to acquire charters from royal and episcopal authorities that specified their hardly won rights and powers. Within the cities, there was an increasing regulation of both economic and political affairs, as well as the beginnings of a new kind of social mobility.

The new village community, the market, and the town and city are remarkable social and economic aspects of the population growth and agricultural revolution that took place between the eighth and the thirteenth centuries. Complementing and influencing one another, each nevertheless also developed particular kinds of consciousness and different modes of perception—of the individual and the family, of the region, and of the world. Their political and spiritual needs differed also, and the great spiritual and temporal powers of the tenth through the thirteenth centuries had to consider these needs as their own character changed. To overvalue one of these institutions—the city, for example —at the expense of the originality and importance of the others is to fail to understand both the continuing agricultural and social base of early European society and the particular kinds of communications that existed among these institutions. The roads and tracks that sprang up to link town and village, city and city, and the rivers that also linked them grew crowded with ecclesiastics and merchants, agents and soldiers, pilgrims, students, and farmers. These avenues were also used by untouchable lepers, madmen, fugitives, and runaway serfs. The changing of the units of European society after the tenth century changed the way in which information and ideas, as well as money and power, were distributed.

COMMUNICATION AND TRADE, TECHNOLOGY AND INDUSTRY

Except for England, writing in the tenth and eleventh centuries meant writing in Latin—or, in the Slavic countries, in Old Church Slavonic— and in Greek in the rest of the Byzantine Empire. The institutions that had struggled to preserve literary Latin—the schools, a broader-based literary public, the cosmopolitanism of the imperial administrative classes —had all disappeared in the West, and late Christian Latin became the most widely used literary language, although its development was influenced by the appearance of other languages. Some of these, derived from different Latin dialects, became the prototypes of the modern Romance languages: Italian, French, Spanish, Portuguese, Provençal, Romansh, and Romanian. Others, derived from the old Germanic languages of the fourth through the sixth centuries, became the prototypes of recent Germanic languages: German, Dutch, the Scandinavian languages, and English. Old English was the first of these vernacular languages to develop its own complex literature, and literary Old English thrived in the tenth and early eleventh centuries. By the eighth century, ecclesiastics were insisting that preaching be conducted in the appropriate vernacular languages, although, as we have seen, Latin Christianity drew short of dealing with the question of conducting liturgies in the vernacular. In Byzantium, on the other hand, although the use of Greek for all liturgies was favored, Slavic-speaking peoples were able to continue to use Old Church Slavonic for the liturgy. The linguistic achievements of SS. Cyril and Methodios were as considerable and had as lasting an influence as their missionary activities.

The church fathers had explained the origin of diverse languages by commenting upon the episode of the Tower of Babel (Genesis 11) and suggesting that its corrective in New Testament history was Pentecost, when the Holy Ghost imparted to the assembled apostles the gift of speaking in tongues (Acts 2). This recognition of the place of vernacular languages bore fruit in the ninth and tenth centuries, during which glossaries appeared giving vernacular equivalents for Latin terms, and spiritual works were translated into Germanic and Romance languages. Latin, chiefly a possession of the clergy, also survived in some places, such as Italy, as a language of laymen as well. The growth of population and the increased communication systems opened up by new villages and roads, markets, and pilgrimages gave the new languages and their innumerable dialects the opportunity to rub against one another and to develop into zones of linguistic similarity. These were not yet contiguous with any political boundaries, nor did they function until much later as elements of "nationalistic" feeling. In many cases, it took centuries for vernacular languages to develop the powers of abstraction and the complex structures that enabled them to equal Latin. Yet the constant give and take of linguistic influences, of the borrowing of words, syntactical structures, and rhetorical techniques made the relationships between medieval Latin and the vernacular languages constantly fertile, exciting, and productive. The shaping of linguistic communities constitutes an important chapter in the history of the ninth, tenth, and eleventh centuries.

Spoken and written language constitutes one element of the transformation of communication during this period. Pilgrimages and the circles of devotion to particular saints and holy places constitute another. The increased movement of people in eleventh-century Europe increased the number of those who, either as an official penance or because of personal choice, went on pilgrimages to distant places. At the end of the fourteenth century, the English poet Geoffrey Chaucer used the device of a pilgrimage to introduce the reader to a number of different character types. Much earlier, the pilgrimage had also served a similar purpose: traveling through distant lands (sometimes to Jerusalem itself), the pilgrims heard strange languages and saw sights not found at home; at inns, monasteries, and hostelries they exchanged accounts with other pilgrims; when they returned, they brought back devotions to new saints and helped build churches in new ways. The circulation of pilgrims and the circulation of the cults of distant saints touched the farthest corners of Europe. Scandinavian, English, and French pilgrims went to the shrine of Santiago (St. James) at Compostela in northwestern Spain, or to Rome, or to Jerusalem. Alongside these great pilgrimages were many local ones as well, including pilgrimages to most of the episcopal centers. The first name contemporaries gave to the Crusades was that of pilgrimage, and the influence of pilgrimages and saints' cults represents another link in the communication of the tenth and eleventh centuries.

Just as monasteries and hostelries grew up along key points of pilgrimage routes, the *portus* and the enclosed market stalls grew up at key points along the routes of trade. For in trade, too, strangers came to new places to transact business. At first, merchants (who might also be part- or full-time pirates, thieves, or even pilgrims) were regarded with suspicion. *Homines duri*, "hard men," they were called, and their lives involved more risks than pleasures. In an age that regarded with suspicion even the standardization of weights and measures, merchants were few and hostile: they spoke a different language; they might be Jews; they came from God knows where and certainly didn't look like people from around here. These qualities alone made them highly suspicious, and it is not to be doubted that the merchants in turn regarded the locals with equal suspicion and hostility. The increased number of local markets increased the frequency of trade, and by the eleventh century the merchant was a more common sight, still suspicious but more easily accepted—if he stayed where he was told, sold only for the duration of the market and fair, dealt fairly and paid his bills, and left.

Yet even this slight improvement in market conditions generated great changes. The great merchants of the Byzantine and Islamic worlds traveled freely and widely across the Western world, and their journals, descriptions of trade and travel conditions, and correspondence illuminate whole areas that no western source discusses. From Scandinavia through Russia, western India, Persia, and North Africa and Spain, Islamic, Jewish, and Byzantine merchants had already created a commercial world far more complex than anything the West knew by the eleventh century. Yet the markets and fairs of eleventh-century Europe slowly laid down the conditions for the appearance of a similar kind of trade in the West. The needs of merchant groups, even though they stayed only a few days or weeks, were different from those of the local people. Methods of measure, calculation, and payment varied enormously across Europe. From the volume of baskets and barrels to the length of cloth, monetary equivalents, weights, and guarantees for good conduct, western Europe was a vast spectrum of local customs. Rights and privileges, accommodations, credit, coinage, uniform weights and measures—all these had to be worked out, and in doing so Europeans worked steadily toward establishing a process of standardization that not many people liked, but that many—more and more—were willing to tolerate in light of the advantages they brought. By the eleventh century, the climate for long-range and local trade was improving, and the *homines duri* were becoming a customary sight. The image of the merchants changed slowly from that of "hard" men, to that of "sly" men, and ecclesiastics worried more about the merchant's soul and avarice than about his sword and wrath. And that, in terms of the viability of a market economy, is a slight but unmistakable improvement.

Between the eighth and the twelfth centuries, Europeans developed new ways of dealing with one another. They also developed remarkable new ways of dealing with the physical world. The horseshoe and horse collar, the heavy plow and mouldboard, the windmill and water mill were steady agents of the transformation of agricultural life, and the upsurge in productivity that followed is all the more remarkable because it took place against the constants of a fixed seed-to-yield ratio, a general shortage of metal tools, the problem of insufficient fertilizer, and a reluctance on the part of managers to support anything resembling research or rational management practices. Agriculture was a spectacular example, but not the only one, of the new role of technology in western society. Various technological achievements in China and the Islamic and Byzantine Empires surpassed anything the late Roman and Germanic west was able to accomplish. Yet by the twelfth century, the West had begun to outstrip the technology of these eastern cultures, and by the fourteenth century it was clearly ahead of them. This aspect of the western experience is both crucial and difficult to explain. It became crucial because it led the way, first, to improved agricultural and industrial conditions, and, later, to a way of life and a culture that has been accurately labeled "industrial." It is difficult to explain because it produced not only individual inventions, but social and intellectual changes that made western society "technology-prone"; that is, it not only solved individual problems, it also contributed to a way of looking at the physical universe and a habit of extending the application of new discoveries that exponentially increased the ease with which westerners dealt with the material world. In time, its consequences made their way to the roots of social existence, but its own immediate consequences were startling enough: the productivity of the laborer was vastly increased, and a remarkably varied agricultural economy with a steady surplus was created. Against the history of the productivity of labor in the ancient world and the attitudes toward labor in early European and Mediterranean history, these changes seem even more remarkable. Not only did they transform work, they transformed the worker as well.

The early history of the water mill reflects many of these characteristics. By the eleventh century, not only had this method of grinding grain spread more widely than before, but new applications of the principle of water power appeared with great frequency. New forms of the distribution of rotary motion adapted the water mill to purposes as diverse as stamping cloth and powering forges for the smelting of iron ore. The scope of the use of these new devices suggests a propensity for the application of technological developments to industrial use very quickly, more so than in the relationships between technology and industry in earlier periods and in other civilizations. The organization of new monasteries and settlements in hitherto waste land, the increase in the demand for such products as cloth, iron, and salt, and the existence of a complex market all contributed to the spreading use of technological developments and their application across a broad band of the labor spectrum. Although the scale of such development was very small by modern standards, the fact that it existed at all is significant. Very large-scale agriculture and small local centers of industrial enterprise were the driving forces of medieval economy.

Medieval industry, also very small by modern standards, nevertheless was an effective force by the tenth century. The processing of fine wool in England, Frisia, and Scandinavia was often part of the work of the manor rather than a highly specialized occupation, but by the ninth century the fame of English and Frisian cloth had spread throughout the Continent, and by the eleventh century it was known as far as Russia and was sold in the markets of Italy and the Islamic world. By the twelfth century, centers for the finishing and sale of wool had arisen in the towns of Flanders, and the market for wool stretched from Flanders to Italy, where, by the thirteenth century, the wool industry had grown to major proportions. Like the early wool industry, the mining industry began small. The great Roman mines, some of which were five hundred feet deep, had ceased to be worked by the sixth century, and most medieval mining consisted of one form or another of surface workings. Iron, silver, and gold were the earliest products of these techniques. The great silver strikes of the tenth century in Goslar and in the twelfth century in Saxony helped increase Europe's output of precious metals. Iron was valuable during this period because of its wide use in techniques for hardening steel, some of which may have dated from the ninth century. Mining communities—which were especially numerous in the eastern Alps, at first, and then in Bohemia, northern Spain, and England—tended to be more independent than their agrarian counterparts, and some application of nonanimal power sources to the problems of lifting, forging, and draining in the mines appeared early. Although the stubborn problems of deep mining remained unsolved until the fifteenth century, auxiliary techniques already existed that later came to be applied widely. Techniques for casting molten soft metals, particularly bronze and tin, into objects as complicated as great bells were known by the twelfth century. Between the twelfth and the seventeenth centuries, the development of the blast furnace and the application of casting to the manufacture of iron produced cast iron and dramatically widened the horizon of metallurgy, as did the development of hard-steel chisels for sculpture.

The production of wool and metal is striking at first, not because of its volume or its role in the reorganization of social life, but because of its role in the market economy. Such activity required capital, time, a skilled labor force, and a market in which to sell the goods produced. In times of crisis, it also required credit and legal protection, and the opening of new mines often required the importation of skilled miners. These aspects of the primitive industry of early Europe helped not only to spur the material civilization of the period but to contribute to the circulation of capital, the diversification of the labor force, and the establishment of long-range market relationships in a society still largely agricultural. From the sheepfolds and the mines, wool and metal traveled a route of workmanship that reveals the early presence of skilled dyers and cloth finishers, ironworkers, goldsmiths, and minters. Although these activities constituted a small proportion of the economy of eleventh- and twelfth-century Europe, they were sufficiently important to attract the patronage of lords and kings, and they contributed to later territorial wealth and to the first theories of political economy in the fourteenth and fifteenth centuries.

The early wool and mining industries were small in scale and rudimentary in equipment. In the matter of large-scale building, however, the tenth through the thirteenth centuries witnessed remarkable achievements. The techniques of elaborate construction in stone were well known to the ancient Mediterranean world, but north of the Alps the majority of buildings were made of wood, or of plaster, daub, and thatch. After the tenth century, however, the development of stone building north of the Alps was rapid and widespread. The enormous expansion of building in wood and stone after the tenth century raised economic problems on a considerable scale. The need to acquire supplies of timber and stone, often from great distances, the problems of transportation and of the recruitment of a labor force (which had to be much more skilled on the average than the agricultural labor force), and the preparation and organization of labor on the building site raised difficulties that had to be solved. The presence of master masons, managers of accounts, quarry operators, and the myriad other types of workers necessary to construct castles, churches, or great halls is well attested by the late eleventh century. The building boom of the eleventh, twelfth, and thirteenth centuries developed in the building crafts a large number of skilled, mobile, and highly disciplined workmen.

Between the ninth and the thirteenth centuries, parts of Europe were drawn closer together by communication routes, new patterns of settlement, new economic relationships, and the consistent production of an agricultural surplus. The steady growth and spread of population not only pushed the frontiers of settled life out into waste places, but began the internal process of colonization—bringing people closer together. Travel became easier and more frequent, knowledge of different parts of the world circulated, and the vast stretches of open sea in the Atlantic and the vast steppes of South Russia were drawn within reach of a common market society. Not until the opening of the Mediterranean-Atlantic sea routes and the opening of land routes to Asia in the thirteenth century and the development of ocean routes and railroads between the sixteenth and the nineteenth centuries did comparable expansions take place. Language, the arts, the organization of labor, and the exploitation of material resources and technological processes were all part of this expansion, which was the beginning of the process by which the natural resources of Europe were systematically exploited to shape a new society.

15

POWER AND SOCIETY

LORDSHIP AND POLITICAL COMMUNITIES

Both late Roman imperial society and the early Germanic kingdoms had recognized the exceptional relationships between powerful and weaker men, and no forces between the third and the tenth centuries grew more rapidly than those that defined these relationships. The complex vocabulary in Latin and the Germanic languages that described relationships between lord and man also described relationships between the emperor and his subjects, God and mankind, a particular patron saint and "his" church and other possessions, and the rights of the head of kin or household. After the establishment of the barbarian kingdoms and the rapid and extensive spread of Carolingian royal power and authority, the men of the king—his vassals—carried out the king's orders, often far from the king's person and residence. Royal service had become progressively more attractive to the independent Germans, particularly when the rewards to be had in it included the wealth of the old imperial territories that had passed to the descendants of Clovis and the wealth of the church lands that had passed to the servants of Charles Martel. Great landowners did not disdain entering the service of a wealthy and famous (and generous) king, nor did lesser men disdain entering for the same hope of reward or adventure, or protection, the service of the great lords who served the king. The terminology of such service originated in the Latin, Celtic, and Germanic words designating humble slaves and servants, but the honorific character of this terminology increased in proportion to the rank and prestige of those willing to accept such positions.

As a nobility with varying degrees of personal wealth and ties to the king grew in number and power, the office of king itself, as we have seen above, also grew. To consider the political conditions of the late ninth through the late twelfth centuries as the result of some sort of decay of "central governmental authority" is misleading; the office of king and the powers and character of the nobility grew and developed together between the third and the ninth centuries. The power and spiritual authority claimed on behalf of Charlemagne and Louis the Pious was far more a novelty among the Franks than the growth of large private armies, territorial princes, and communities of dependence and lordship. Ninth-century glosses, lists of Latin words with vernacular (Old English or Old High German) equivalents, suggest that in this period Germanic words designating lordship were considered the synonyms of the Latin words that designated various forms of semipublic lordship in the late years of the Roman empire. The king was a particularly great lord, and the head of a large household was a small lord, but the idea of lordship was common to both. Later theories and institutions of kingship and aristocratic rank grew in different directions out of the common idea of lordship.

In spite of the work of the Carolingian clergy and of energetic rulers such as Charlemagne and Louis the Pious, kingship remained limited by the wealth and following a king could command. The partition of the empire in 843 and the subsequent repartitionings throughout the later ninth century meant that no matter how exalted a concept of kingship an individual king might have (and such kings as Charles the Bald and Louis II had exalted conceptions indeed), his authority was limited by his resources. The kings of the partitioned kingdoms declined in personal power, wealth, and authority. Non-Carolingians, such as Boso of Provence and, at the end of the tenth century, Hugh Capet of *Francia,* acceded to the office of king, and by the early tenth century the imperial title, now simply the designation of the most successful defender of Rome, passed out of the Carolingian family entirely. The Anglo-Saxon kingdoms of England were literally picked off one by one by Viking raiders until the dynasty of Wessex, in the person of King Alfred, was the last one left. The Anglo-Saxon kings that ruled all England at a later time descended from the last legitimate Wessex kings of the late ninth century. The office of king among the Slavic peoples in Poland and Moravia and among the Magyars in Hungary resembled early Frankish kingship in its limitations. Thus, the ninth and tenth centuries witnessed the weakening of the royal resources of individual rulers, not a decline from some earlier imaginary public kind of kingship that the ferocious and disloyal nobility simply chewed up.

The shrinkage of the Frankish and English kingdoms were related to the new military crises of the ninth and tenth centuries. It was hard to mobilize the vast armies of the Franks against the lightning-swift raids of the Arabs, Magyars, and Vikings. The perennial problem of royal control over ambitious and kin-conscious vassals grew worse as lands belonging to the king and awarded only for a period of service slowly became hereditary and, later, inextricably confused with land that a family already owned. In an age of sloppy or vague records, or no records at all, such a process was not particularly surprising. During this period the church was sometimes not able to keep accurate lists of bishops, and monasteries and episcopal sees tended to move from one place to another with great frequency. Often, partitions and repartitions of kingdoms further confused traditions of landholding, and the extinction of one family sometimes offered another family irresistible opportunities for territorial expansion, usually at the expense of a distant lord, church, or king. Finally, the most successful solution to the new raids of the ninth and tenth centuries also raised the power of lords. The vast Frankish armies were too slow and cumbersome against the raids of the invaders, but small local forces holding fortified places could sometimes hold the raiders up or make life very difficult for them, particularly when, slowed down by a load of booty, they passed by such a place. Sometimes the descendants of the old Carolingian counts successfully led such defense; sometimes new and obscure men took and held a fortified place, often in the face of local as well as invaders' interference. The titles taken by these local warlords echo those of the eighth and early ninth centuries— counts, dukes, marquesses, viscounts, earls—but they were often not held by the same individuals who originally received them, and sometimes the title changed at the whim of the current lord. What Rolf the Viking received from Charles the Simple of France was the title of count. As the dynasty's holdings slowly expanded to cover almost exactly the old Roman province of *Lugdunensis Secunda* and the archdiocese of Rouen, the counts briefly became marquesses, and later dukes. As duke of Normandy, William the Conqueror enjoyed a title that no one had ever given his ancestors; but then, no one was in any position to deny it to them when they casually decided to take it.

Thus, what might be considered as a service and administrative map of late Carolingian Europe came to be a map of the real local territorial commands, some of which dated from the days of Charlemagne and before, and some of which dated from very recent times. The rulers of these commands recognized the preeminence of the kings in some circumstances, but in most of their actions they were virtually independent.

Some of their territories, such as the duchy of Normandy, grew to substantial proportions; others, such as the tiny counties and castellanies of Gascony, the Rhineland, northern Italy, and Castile, remained small, and in such cases their lords enlisted the protection of larger landholders, who allowed them to keep their lands and titles. Some of the great lords extended forms of social control similar to those they employed on their own lands to other parts of the territories they claimed. By succeeding over a few generations in establishing their rights to rule and excluding the rights of others, including the direct rights of the king, these great lords built up principalities that were territorial as well as personal or dynastic; the conception of a territory became inseparable from the question of who ruled it and what law was administered on it. Thus, between the ninth and the thirteenth centuries, the character of lordship expanded from rule over individuals to rule over people and land. The process was not clear-cut, nor would the individuals and dynasties who constituted the new lordship have understood it in quite this way. These individuals considered powers, liberties, and rights in complex ways: an eleventh-century lord would understand a modern analysis of his power only if it dealt with such terms as his privileges, rights, dues, and possessions; he understood "power" not in the sense of private rights contrasted with "public" rights, but as individual possessions, which contrasted with nothing else known to him. Lord, king, and free peasant all enjoyed privileges that complemented one another: there were powers outside those of the king and other powers outside those of the lord. The political world of the tenth and eleventh centuries consisted of communities of power that dovetailed in different ways from those that modern conceptions of "public" and "private" rights and obligations can easily or accurately describe.

The county of Flanders, for example, was part of the old *pagus Flandrensis,* a particularly important defensive unit extending from the North Sea to the Rhine that was given by Charles the Bald to Baldwin I Iron-Arm in the mid ninth century. In the turbulent conditions of the West Frankish kingdom at the end of the century, the county was reorganized under Baldwin II (879-918), was ruled briefly by a "marquis," Arnold I (918-965), and under the remarkably able and energetic Baldwin V (1035-1067) expanded to the east and laid the basis of the prosperity and prominence that the county enjoyed in the late eleventh and early twelfth centuries. Baldwin V was the father-in-law of William the Conqueror, and his grandson Robert II "of Jerusalem" (1087-1111) was one of the leaders of the First Crusade. From Carolingian defensive command to prosperous and proto-urbanized territorial principality whose ruler could depart for Jerusalem—the story of Flanders is dramatic, but no more so than that of Normandy, whose ruler during the reign of Baldwin V was Duke William the Bastard (1028-1087). William became duke at the age of seven, witnessed the assassination of his guardians by the time he was twelve, spent his adolescent years putting down savage revolts, extended a legal claim to the throne of England in 1066, and vindicated his right by war during the same year. The early eleventh century witnessed the establishment of ruling comital dynasties in Flanders, Arras, Amiens, Chartres, Tours, Blois, Troyes-Champagne, and Anjou; ducal dynasties in Normandy, Rennes (for all of Brittany), and Aquitaine; numerous small localities were ruled by viscounts, vidames, and castellans; and large ecclesiastical properties remained under the protection and effective rule of lay lords.

The crown of West Francia had been given to the powerful dukes of Francia (the old Neustria) late in the ninth century, and in 987, one of their descendants, Hugh Capet, began a dynasty whose direct male line lasted until 1327. The old kingdom of the western Franks, West Francia, had dwindled to the area between Paris and Orléans known as the Ile de France, and its last ninth-century defenders had become its kings. Part of the later history of France stems from the fact that the rulers of Francia were called kings, instead of dukes or counts, and as kings and successors to the Carolingians they could later make claims that began the process by which the later kingdom of France was assembled. In the year 1000, however, the Capetian kings of Francia, ruling areas far smaller than those of other lords, bore little resemblance to their Carolingian predecessors or to their Capetian successors.

When the Carolingians had assimilated the eastern territories in the eighth and ninth centuries, they had installed Frankish officials as counts and some royal vassals to help them. They had also employed the Frankish clergy, in monasteries and episcopal sees, to aid in the process of conversion and acculturation, but the total numbers of a Frankish ruling group remained much smaller in Germany than in France or Italy. The old tribal units became the Frankish duchies of Saxony, Franconia, Lorraine, Swabia, and Bavaria, each with its own customs and general tribal associations, but each ruled by a Carolingian Frankish count and heavily populated with Frankish clergy. At the death of Louis the Child in 911, the dukes tried to make the best of things by electing Duke Conrad of Franconia as king over themselves, and in an attempt to associate this non-Carolingian with Carolingian legitimacy, they had him anointed by the clergy, the first instance of an East Frankish king being so enthroned.

The reign of Conrad I (911–918) reflects the difficulties of kingship and lordship in the tenth century. Relying upon the power of the bishops of the great dioceses of Constance, Mainz, Salzburg, and Passau, Conrad launched an attempt to make himself king in fact as well as in name over East Francia. His attempts to increase and spread his own power encountered energetic resistance from the other four dukes, who in turn began to articulate their territorial commands and lordship in order to turn their duchies into territorial principalities, and in this they were successful. Conrad's power weakened rapidly, and at his death in 918 the German duchies were stronger and better organized than ever before. Instead of the many territorial lordships that characterized the lands west of the Rhine, the lands east of the Rhine witnessed only the consolidation of ducal power in the five duchies of Saxony, Franconia, Lorraine, Swabia, and Bavaria. Joined to the dukes' earlier military power were the beginnings of territorial lordship and, in effect, the birth of new German principalities. The growth of the ninth- and tenth-century nobility and of territorial principalities is as much a chapter in the history of European communities as in the history of European invasion and post-Carolingian "anarchy." In imposing their own rule, the small and great lords, who controlled lands ranging from tiny single castles in Castile to the great Duchy of Saxony, also made themselves responsible for the keeping of the peace, the privileges of diverse communities, and the safety of the Church. In return, they received, sometimes grudgingly, loyalty and prestige. They ruled the most manageable territories that the tenth and early eleventh centuries could create. As we will see, they also patronized the beginnings of the agricultural revolution and the eleventh- and twelfth-century spiritual revolutions as well. Often enough, they were brutal, suspicious, abrupt, and ferocious. Yet they were also devout, after their own fashion, efficient, and ambitious for their dynasties and their territories. Often possessing no family history, they had histories made up; lacking traditional legitimacy, they cultivated the remnants of legitimacy in the monasteries and the holy men of the tenth century. Unlike the newly Christianized kings of Norway, Poland, and Hungary, they did not become saints, but they cultivated those saints they could find, and they did become pilgrims. The reason William the Bastard succeeded to the dukedom of Normandy in 1035 was because his father, Robert, had died on a pilgrimage to Jerusalem. Some lords went two or three times, and to Compostela and Rome as well as to Jerusalem. They ransacked land and labor alike for their fortresses, but they also gave away favorite hunting lodges to monks, allowed exceptional privileges to colonizing peasants, and sometimes entered the religious life themselves after a lifetime of looting and fighting. In practice, they became successful warlords; in theory, they retained spiritual horizons and ideas of loyalty to higher powers that held the germ of wider social bonds and larger political communities.

THE NEW GERMAN MONARCHY AND THE IMPERIAL REVIVAL

By the second quarter of the tenth century there were many kingdoms, or at least territorial principalities that their rulers called kingdoms, throughout Europe. The kingdoms of Asturias and Leon in northern Spain were soon joined by those of Castile, Portugal, and Aragón. The Wessex monarchs of late ninth-century England had driven back the Viking raiders and the Danish immigrants, and Alfred (871–899), Edward the Elder (899–925), Aethelstan (925–939), and Edgar (959–975) shaped a monarchy that was recognized throughout England. By the tenth century a kingdom of Scotland had also come into being, as had kingdoms in Norway, Denmark, Sweden, Poland, and Hungary. The old kingdom of the West Franks and the Middle Kingdom held, besides the fifty or sixty territorial principalities, the Kingdom of Francia and those of Burgundy and Provence. In England, Poland, Hungary, and Francia, strong ecclesiastical echoes of earlier liturgical monarchies gave additional legitimacy to ruling houses; in many other kingdoms, strong-handedness and well-supported legal and military claims vouched for the legitimacy of the new royal houses. Many of these kingdoms were no more stable, and possessed no more traditional legitimacy, than many of the territorial principalities, and by the twelfth century many of them had passed away. Those that survived—England, Scotland, France, the Scandinavian monarchies, Poland, Hungary, and Germany—grew slowly into territorial monarchies during the twelfth and thirteenth centuries. Those that disappeared became principalities or subkingdoms within greater powers.

The fate of the German monarchy of Conrad I was not quite like any of these kingdoms. Reconstituted under non-Carolingians in 911, the kingdom soon witnessed the strengthening of the duchies and long struggles between kings who had been dukes and dukes who resented royal interference in their own principalities. The ducal origin of the tenth-century German monarchy prevented the development of purely royal resources outside the personal resources of the ascending duke, and the royal struggle to make the crown hereditary in a royal dynasty was countered by the ducal struggle to make the crown elective. The great ecclesiastical powers of Germany, from the prince-bishops of Trier, Mainz, and Cologne to the monasteries of Fulda, Corvey, and Reichenau, alternately supported the monarchy and the princes. Briefly, between 918 and 1075, the new German monarchy seemed to carry all before it, and a series of strong kings from the Saxon and Salian dynasties, basing their powers in Saxony, Bavaria, and Franconia, rose not only to the effective rule of Germany, but, after 962, to the title of Holy Roman Emperor, thus appearing to reconstitute the old title, if not the territorial extent or character, of the empire of Charlemagne. Charlemagne was never far from these new rulers' thoughts, and from the end of the tenth century to the third quarter of the eleventh, they worked closely with the papacy and engaged in Italian as well as German affairs far more intensely and far longer than Charlemagne or his successors ever had. After the third quarter of the eleventh century, conflicts between individual emperors and popes, high churchmen, and German nobles weakened the power of the monarchy. The twelfth century witnessed the struggle of a new royal and imperial dynasty, that of the Hohenstaufen of Swabia, to create a territorial monarchy in Germany. The failure of the Hohenstaufen and the growing powers of the ecclesiastical and temporal princes circumscribed the authority of the kings of Germany from the fourteenth century to the abolition of the Holy Roman Empire by Napoleon Bonaparte in 1806.

The resistance of the four remaining Frankish dukes to the efforts of the fifth, Conrad I, to extend his recently acquired royal power led to outright military resistance and to the strengthening of the internal rule of the duchies. At his death in 918, Conrad I designated the duke of Saxony, Henry I the Fowler, as his successor, and Henry immediately took up the costume and the claims of the old East Frankish monarchy. Henry ruled like a Carolingian king, and his authority over the counts, control of the church, and direct royal rule of old Carolingian lands in other duchies besides Saxony reflect the tradition of East Frankish kingship that had begun with the empire of Charlemagne and Louis the Pious and had been hastened in its development from the rule of Louis the German on. Henry I was succeeded by his son, Otto I (936–973; emperor of the Romans, 962–973), who was made king at Aachen, where he was invested with the sword belt, sword, cloak, bracelets, scepter, and staff of the Carolingian kings, anointed and crowned by the bishops of Mainz and Cologne, and ritually served at table by the dukes of Lotharingia, Swabia, Franconia, and Bavaria, who took the roles of servants at the ceremonial meal. Otto acquired Franconia in 939, installed one brother, Henry, as Duke of Bavaria and another, Bruno, as Archbishop of Cologne, and proceeded to take directly into his hands not only the royal lands and comital offices of the old Carolingian East Frankish kings, but the administration of the affairs of churches and monasteries. By creating a base of power in western Saxony and Franconia, making members of his own family the most powerful subjects in the realm, and appointing advocates to draw the affairs of churches directly under royal control, Otto I moved at a remarkably rapid pace to establish a durable monarchy and cripple the growing powers of the duchies. In the great ecclesiastical rulers of Mainz, Cologne, Magdeburg, Würzburg, and Bamberg, the monarchy found able and effective servants. The prelates of Germany thus became a kind of special royal aristocracy, furnishing money, soldiers, administrators, and powerful allies to the kings, whom they recognized as possessing a particular liturgical character that set them off from other laymen and enabled them to rule the affairs of the German churches. Otto I's vigorous rule received further recognition when, in 955 on the River Lech, Otto led an army that annihilated a raiding force of Magyars. In the course of the tenth century, under Henry I and Otto I, German armies were successful against the Danes and against the western Slavic Wends and Sorbs. The development of powerful eastern Frankish commands, backed by the expanding German church, brought the German frontier up against those of the Danes and Poles. The success of such German military leaders as Hermann Billung in the north along the Baltic and Count Gero from Meissen to the Oder River pushed Saxon arms eastward toward the Slavs. A series of missionary bishoprics was founded or reformed. Hamburg, founded in 834 and merged with Bremen in 864, was originally the chief missionary bishopric for the Scandinavians and Slavs. By 948 Otto had established new bishoprics across the north and east, bringing German settlers and clergy into the Slavic heartlands. The military success of men such as Hermann Billung and Count Gero, and the ecclesiastical and social authority of the bishops of Hamburg-Bremen, Havelberg (948), Brandenburg (948), Magdeburg (962), Prague (973), Passau, and Regensburg represented a strong German power poised for indefinite expansion to the east. The pagan Slavic Wends stiffened their resistance to Saxon advance, but the thrust of Otto's kingdom to the Slavic east loomed as a large problem for the Slavs after Otto's victory on the Lechfeld in 955.

Across the south of Germany and to the southwest lay the duchies of Swabia and Bavaria, territories that traditionally had interests in Italy and the lands of the southern Slavs. To the southwest lay the kingdoms of Provence and Burgundy, also having Italian interests. Rudolf II of Burgundy (912–937) attempted to acquire Swabia and Provence; Hugh of Provence briefly acquired northern Italy and attempted to reconstitute the old Middle Kingdom by succeeding Rudolf II in Provence and Burgundy; from 949 the dukes of Bavaria and Swabia (the latter, Otto's son Liudolf), Marquess Berengar of Ivrea, and Otto maneuvered for power in northern Italy, attempting in various ways to link under individual control two or more territories on either side of the Alps. Provence, Burgundy, Swabia, Bavaria, and northern Italy constituted a real and dangerous sphere of action for ambitious nobles, and Rudolf II, Hugh, Liudolf, and Berengar were all able and ambitious men. Against the growing power of Berengar, Otto I descended into Italy in 955 and established his own authority. In 962 Pope John XII crowned Otto emperor of the Romans.

Thus, for the first time since 923 there was an emperor in Rome. For the first time since the death of Louis the Pious in 840 there was an emperor of the Romans who did not possess extensive lands in the Middle Kingdom. All the claimants to the imperial title in the ninth and tenth centuries came from Italy, Provence, or Burgundy, all important parts of the Middle Kingdom of 843. Thus, when Otto I moved into Italy after having exerted his power in Swabia, Burgundy, and northern Italy, he came as the descendant of the rulers of the Middle Kingdom and the heir to their imperial crown. His East Frankish kingdom in Germany strengthened that claim, and his marked and enduring successes against the Danes, the Slavs and the Magyars marked him in addition as a defender of the faith. Otto I inherited the political horizons of the late Carolingian world.

The imperial reign of Otto I remained colored by the Frankish traditions that he had inherited and his long career north of the Alps and the attitudes of his supporters on the Saxon and Slavic military and missionary fronts. Otto's continued presence in Italy, however, and the youth and the atmosphere of the upbringing his son and grandson received transformed the "northern" imperial idea into one that drew more heavily upon Roman history and papal experience.

Upon his death in 973, Otto was succeeded by his son Otto II (973–983), whose struggle with the new Arab raids in South Italy led to his defeat at Cortone in 982, the signal for a vast Slavic uprising in Germany and the weakening of his imperial position. Otto II died in 983, leaving a three-year old son, Otto III (emperor, 983–1002), and an empire badly in need of governmental reforms. In Italy minor nobles and powerful churchmen had managed to weaken the imperial control of ecclesiastical properties, and under Otto II and Otto III German administrators were brought to Italy to protect the imperial regalian rights. This reform began a process of "internationalizing" a German aristocracy, much in the same way that the rules of Charlemagne and Louis the Pious had "internationalized" the Austrasian nobility by spreading its members throughout the empire in the royal service.

Pope John XII had crowned Otto I, but he soon found that Otto's idea of his imperial role was not the same as his own. At a synod in Rome in 963, John XII was deposed, and a stream of German churchmen descended into Italy to advise the emperors, including one who became Pope Gregory V (996–999). The most remarkable of them, Sylvester II (999–1002), was the Aquitanian scholar Gerbert of Aurilliac. From the death of Otto II in 983 to that of Otto III in 1002, the energies and talents of transalpine Europeans were exercised in the establishment of a rapport between popes and emperors supported by able and loyal churchmen. Otto II had married the Byzantine princess Theophano, and the court of Otto III, their son, reflected the splendor of Byzantium and was supported by the new wealth and talent of German and Italian servants. The splendor of the court of Otto III drew Romans' attention from the claims of the Byzantine Empire, revived the old legends of Rome and Charlemagne, and encouraged the process of building effective large-scale governmental institutions in both Germany and Italy.

At his death in 1002, Otto III was twenty-one years old. He was succeeded by his cousin Henry II (1002–1024), during whose reign there began a process in which the recent Ottonian attempts to establish a system of governance directed from the imperial court gave way before a policy of balancing powerful factions one against the other. Under Conrad II (1024–1039) and Henry III (1039–1056), the imperial title was linked more firmly to the kingship of Germany, and means and personnel of government were sought that could conserve the resources of the monarchy and would not give too much allegiance to the aristocracy. The continuing association of the emperor with high churchmen during the reign of Henry III and the practice of raising unfree men to positions of great administrative authority were important parts of this development.

The great royal churchmen and the unfree *ministeriales* were the chief agents of the emperors, and as imperial power grew, so did the power of the aristocracy and the wealth of the empire. The social and economic changes of the early eleventh century increased the prosperity of all groups in German and Italian society. The silver strike at Goslar late in the tenth century gave the emperors a freer hand, and throughout the eleventh century they attempted to build, with Goslar as a base, a string of royal fortifications and a class of absolutely loyal servants. These attempts were the result of the imperial need to consolidate and regularize imperial authority and practical power over the free nobility and the ecclesiastical establishments founded by them. During the reign of Henry III (1039–1056), the Salian emperors achieved their greatest success. Dominant in Italy and Germany, they not only extended their power but ruled the German and the Roman churches, patronized ecclesiastical reform movements, and developed a loyal and dependent class of administrators. At the height of his power, from 1045 to 1056, Henry III was the strongest ruler in the Latin west and his power was consolidated and distributed the most effectively. King of Germany, he was also emperor of the Romans. His power reached from the Baltic Sea to south of Rome, from the Rhine to the Oder. His subjects, though restive, were powerless; his neighbors, Slav, Scandinavian, and Frankish, were vastly inferior in power, organization, and prestige.

CHRISTENDOM AND THE EAST: THE BYZANTINE SPHERE AND KIEVAN RUSSIA

By the first quarter of the tenth century, Croatia had become a Latin Christian kingdom, and by the eleventh century its old coastal cities, particularly Ragusa and Durazzo, had increased in prosperity, though they were overshadowed by Venice. Late in the eleventh century, the crown of Croatia was assumed by the rulers of Hungary, and the domination of Venice along the coast drew Croatia firmly into the affairs of the Latin west. Serbia too had become Christianized in the late ninth century, although the long struggle between Byzantium and Bulgaria in the late tenth and early eleventh centuries made church organization or concerted attempts at conversion difficult. The Adriatic coastal towns also sent influences inland, and beginning in the eleventh century the kernel of a Serbian kingdom that sought independence from both Byzantium and Rome developed. Although the great kingdoms of Hungary, Bulgaria, and Byzantium overshadowed such smaller principalities as Croatia, Bosnia, and Serbia, local traditions continued in these areas, and in the case of Serbia they presented the opportunity for a powerful independent monarchy to rise between the twelfth and the fifteenth centuries.

The Slavic principalities extending east from Germanic Europe thus reveal a mixture of Slavic, Latin, and Germanic influences tempered in the eastern regions by the influence of Bulgaria and Byzantium. The great trade routes generally bypassed Croatia and Serbia, either running north up the Danube valley to Hungary or along the sea and the coasts, touching Durazzo, Ragusa, and Venice. During the eleventh century, however, the power of Byzantium and the revival of a strong papacy with ambitious protectors in the form of the Norman rulers of South Italy gave to this area a considerable degree of importance in terms of the relations between Constantinople and Rome.

The slow triumph of Latin Christianity in central Europe is one of the many signs of the shifting balance of political and cultural influence that took place between the Greek and Latin churches during the period between the ninth and twelfth centuries. In spite of the glories of late tenth-century Byzantium and the destruction of the First Bulgarian Empire by Basil II in 1019, the energies and influence of Byzantium were pointed in directions other than the distant west and northwest. Constantinople, with its Greek as well as Roman heritage, had always looked to wider lands than the west alone. Often, Syria and Anatolia, the coasts and hinterlands of the Black Sea, and the eastern Mediterranean were more important spheres of action than the western parts of the Greek peninsula and the upper reaches of the Danube. The long duel with Bulgaria had emphasized this aspect of Byzantine policy, as did the long history of Byzantine diplomatic relations with the peoples to the east and north of the Black Sea. Constantinople had even developed an overland silk route from China that circumvented Islamic Persia. The shrinking ecclesiastical and political communities of the western Greek peninsula and the Slavic and Ugrian lands beyond Bulgaria did not play the important roles of the key Byzantine lands on the eastern and northern coasts of the Black Sea. There, at the termini of trade routes that went far back in time, lay crucial Byzantine economic and diplomatic interests. And there, from Bulgaria to Russia and beyond to the Caspian Sea, lay the future of Byzantine influence.

The northern coasts of the Black Sea had long constituted one of the most important routes for east-west migration. The establishment of settled Frankish and Slavic societies in Europe, the rise of Bulgaria, and the power of Byzantium did not so much check new migrations as exploit them for diplomatic purposes. Thus, the Byzantines had called in the Magyars against the Bulgars, the Bulgars had called in the Pechenegs against the Magyars, who fled to the west, and the Byzantines entered an alliance with Kiev to help finally crush Bulgaria. The old alliances between Byzantines and peoples farther to the east were maintained by the cementing of relations between the Byzantines and Khazars in the eighth century, a key element in Christian-Islamic relations in western Eurasia.

The Khazars, a Turkic people, had risen to prominence in the lands between the Black Sea and the Caspian Sea in the seventh century. They fought the expansion of Islam, and in 737 were defeated by an Arab army that had come up the Volga. The Arabs were unable to follow up their victory, however, and throughout the eighth and ninth centuries Khazaria increased in power and in wealth—the river trade of the north and the overland trade routes through central Asia passed through its lands. In the ninth century, possibly earlier, the ruling classes of the Khazars adopted Judaism, and their relations with Byzantium extended to the tenth century, when their power was broken first by the Pecheneg horde and later by the growing power of the princes of Kiev.

Byzantine policy concerning the Black Sea area had always been aimed at checking the expansion of Islam and establishing a balance of power that would prevent any single people from growing sufficiently powerful and hostile to threaten Byzantine economic interests in the area. Byzantine efforts were remarkably varied; they included formal diplomatic missions, ecclesiastical attempts at conversion, tribute, bribery, and dynastic marriages. The Byzantines were astonishingly skillful in impressing pagan peoples, and they developed the rules of diplomatic etiquette to a high degree. In addition to formal contacts, the Byzantines were also masters of exploiting the material and cultural differences that separated them from the nomadic peoples to the north. In the fourth century, Olympiodorus of Thebes went on missions with a parrot that spoke Greek. The accounts of pagans visiting the city of Constantinople echo the wonder and envy of all visitors to that city. In the ninth and tenth centuries, Byzantine court ceremonial was refined and perfected. Many of the aspects of this ceremonial that the sources describe were obviously designed to impress strangers. Thrones that were lifted by invisible hydraulic machinery propelled the emperor many feet into the air before astonished, prostrate visitors. Golden trees with animated singing birds, metal lions that were made to roar artificially, vast churches and mysterious ceremonies, and the vast, pulsing life of the city itself—all these were also part of Byzantine dealings with others. Dazzled, bewildered, bitterly resentful, envious, and impressed, the visitors to the city between the ninth and the thirteenth centuries all agree, in the records they left us, that Constantinople was considered a marvel, even by the urbanized Moslems of Persia and Egypt. To Pecheneg hostages, Kievan emissaries, or Khazarian traders, the city seemed a miracle, and it worked upon their memories long after they had departed.

The northern, eastern, and western coasts of the Black Sea posed problems of diplomacy as complex as any faced by Byzantium in its history. The establishment of a strong Bulgarian empire on the west coast engaged Byzantium in constant military and political struggles, and the threat of Islam between the Black and Caspian Seas in northern Persia dictated a strong Byzantine alliance with the Khazars. The strong Byzantine towns in the Crimea and along the eastern coast were close to many of the dangerous nomadic Eurasian peoples who roved South Russia from the Dniester to the Volga. Inland, to the north of the Black Sea, lived other peoples who were also drawn into communication with Byzantium. North of the Khazars, along the middle and upper Volga, lived the Volga Bulgars, who adopted Islam in 922. North of the Pechenegs and Magyars, occupying part of the South Russian steppe, forest-steppe, and northern forest, lived Slavic peoples who themselves had begun to form large political units by the seventh century and by the ninth century had witnessed the establishment of adventurous states in Scandinavia, central Europe, and Bulgaria. The movement of peoples, goods, and armies in the ninth and tenth centuries was not exclusively a problem of the western parts of Europe. For purposes of defense, and in order to participate in trade and to engage in profitable diplomatic negotiations with Byzantium, larger political units came into existence, and from the mid ninth century on, a series of Russian principalities began to play more and more important roles between the Gulf of Finland and the lower reaches of the Dnieper River. By the tenth century, a particularly strong principality that was centered in the town of Kiev had emerged, and the history of this principality is a key element in the history of eastern Europe.

From the Gulf of Finland and Lake Ladoga in the north to the

Black and Caspian Seas in the south, Russia consists of a series of horizontal climatic and soil belts that contrast sharply with each other. From the north down to Kiev on the Dnieper, a belt of heavy forest gives way to the area of forest-steppe, islands of forest among open grasslands. Kiev itself stands in the zone of so-called Black Earth, a rich, humus-retaining soil that needs little fertilizer to produce excellent harvests. To the south and east of Kiev stretch the western reaches of the great Eurasian Steppe, open grasslands that had for centuries constituted the track for migrations of nomadic peoples from Eurasia. To the west and north of the Caspian Sea stretch vast areas of arid land. The great river systems of Russia offered navigable waterways even more extensive and remarkable than those of western Europe. Of these systems, the Duna-Dnieper and the Volga-Oka offered waterways that sped communication and trade from the Baltic north to the farthest south. In spite of the vast spaces of steppe and forest, the river systems bound Russia together and oriented its outlook to the Baltic and Black Seas.

Moslem merchants, travelers, and artifacts left traces in Russia from the eighth century on; Byzantine gold and goods found their way there long before Byzantium and Kiev were in contact. The great forest riches—wood, wax, honey, and furs—permitted a healthy trade, and long-distance trade appears to have played a greater part in early Russian history than in that of many lands further west. The agricultural produce of Russia, although rich and important, was not tapped in full until centuries later, when the forests and forest-steppes were cleared, plowed, and harvested by large organized agricultural units with heavy equipment. The Jewish Khazars, the Islamic Volga Bulgars, the Greek Christian Byzantines and Bulgarians, and the Latin Christian Hungarians, Poles, and Scandinavians surrounded Russia with cultures that were developing rapidly and religious pressures that were obviously connected with the material prosperity of those who exerted them.

By the ninth century, the tribes of North and South Russia, the immigrant peoples who also lived in the region—from Goths in the Crimea to Finno-Ugrians and Scandinavians in the north and west—and the peoples living on the borders of the tribal lands had begun to witness the shaping of even larger principalities that soon overshadowed the tribal system itself. The attractions of trade and the eminence of the Khazar kingdom, the increasingly complex forms of social and economic activity among the Russian tribes and the importance of such towns as Kiev as trading centers, and the political pressures from neighboring peoples all contributed to the shaping of proto-principalities by the middle of the ninth century. One of the most hotly debated questions in Russian historiography concerns the next stage of early Russian history, the shaping of the principality of Kiev and the unification of the Baltic-Black Sea waterway system into a single political unit. Two disputed accounts exist. According to one, the name *Rus* was borne by Swedish traders and warriors who acquired control of northern Russia in the first half of the ninth century. Rurik, who allegedly founded Novgorod in 862, was succeeded by even more adventurous sons and relatives, two of whom,

Askold and Dir, captured Kiev from the Khazars; another son, Oleg, united Novgorod and Kiev in a single principality. The chief point of contention between this "Normanist" interpretation of the foundations of Novgorod, Kiev, and the single kingdom that united them both and its opponents lies in the character of Rurik, Oleg, and their successors. Clearly, by the end of the tenth century the princes of Kiev were Slavic, and another approach to the early political history of Russia argues that western Slavs, not Scandinavians, established the first political settlements. The argument is complex, and much of it has been clouded further by later nationalist and ethnic considerations that have little to do with historical accuracy. Throughout the early history of Europe, it is precisely the mingling of peoples, particularly in the shaping of kingdoms and principalities, that has been marked. From the war bands of the migration period to the settled kingdoms of the tenth century, the mixture of peoples was inevitable. Ethnic differences such as those argued about in the twentieth—or, worse, the nineteenth—century can hardly be said to have existed in early Europe. Similarities in customs and the common experience of a largely homogeneous economic world probably counted for more than Scandinavian or Slavic origin. As we have already seen, the early history of Bulgaria witnessed the imposition of a Turkic warrior group over a large Slavic population, which soon assimilated the new lords and even caused their language to disappear. There is no question of the Slavic character of tenth-century Kiev; the chief question is to what extent Scandinavians contributed to its development.

The rulers of Kiev were drawn farther south. In 860 a sea raid upon Constantinople was carried out by Kievans, in 907 Oleg launched a full-scale attack on the city, and in 911 a commercial treaty between Kiev and Constantinople was drawn up. Oleg's successor, Igor (913–962), attempted, not always successfully, to expand the southern reaches of Kievan power. Under Igor's son Sviatoslav I (962–972), the Kievan principality struck against the Khazars, destroying their empire in 967, and became the most powerful force north of the Black Sea. More frequent encounters with Byzantium and the attractions of neighboring Christian states led to the conversion of the Kievan principality to Greek Christianity during the remarkable reign of Vladimir (980–1015), the greatest of early Russian rulers. The conversion of Vladimir in 988, his close ties to Basil II of Constantinople, his role in helping Basil destroy the First Bulgarian Empire, and his marriage to the Byzantine princess Anna laid the foundations of the close ties between Kiev and Byzantium that remained for centuries.

The reign of Vladimir witnessed a far-sighted—and overambitious—attempt to consolidate Kievan power throughout the northern Black Sea region. However, the principality of Kiev was still a fragile political unit, and throughout the eleventh and twelfth centuries princely factions struggled for hegemony over it. Under such rulers as Yaroslav (1019–1054) and Vladimir II Monomakh (1113–1125) a single prince asserted his authority, but for much of the rest of the time princely territories vied with one another for supremacy. The foundations of ecclesiastical life laid by Vladimir, however—from the building of churches and the patronage of monasticism to the adoption of a Russian literary language from the liturgical Old Church Slavonic—went deeper than political lordship, and the spiritual development of Russia after the tenth century is a remarkable history in itself. Yaroslav (1019–1054) connected his house by dynastic marriages with the royal houses of France, Hungary, and Norway; England and Sweden later became connected with the house of Kiev. These dynastic practices increased not only political communications, but trade and cultural exchanges as well. As late as the early twelfth century, Kievan princes considered becoming vassals of the papacy. These instances of political and ecclesiastical diplomacy indicate the place of Kievan Russia in the world of early Europe. By the times of Vladimir I, Yaroslav, and Vladimir II, Kiev and all Russia, under the aegis of Byzantium but in contact with other European powers, had consolidated its early trade and military connections with the Islamic and Christian worlds and had closed the Baltic-Black Sea connection through its own power. The prosperity of Kiev and Novgorod led to that of other towns, and the rich spiritual and cultural influences of Byzantium traveled up the great rivers along with gold, silks, spices, and brides. To the northeast lay the uncleared forests, already opening to colonization in the eleventh century. To the south and the east lay the nomads of the steppe. The Pechenegs were neutralized in the eleventh century, but they were followed by the Polovtsi (Cumans) in the twelfth, against whom the Kievans waged a long struggle. By the end of the twelfth century, however, the nomad problem still had not been solved, and the Byzantine conflict with the Turks heralded the more terrible conflict between Russia and the Mongols in the thirteenth century.

ROYAL LORDSHIP IN THE ELEVENTH CENTURY

In spite of the elaboration of royal and imperial titles and the residual sacral qualities of the name of king, kingship between the ninth and the twelfth centuries is understood most clearly when it is considered as a kind of lordship, whose power was similar to the power that lords wielded on large and small scales throughout the particularistic society of late Carolingian Europe. Royal power grew up intertwined with, and sometimes barely distinguishable from, the power of other lords. In the tenth, eleventh, and early twelfth centuries the role of kings as lords determined the foundations of the political strength of later territorial monarchies, and the strength of the king as lord of his own lands, as well as lord of the kingdom, was established in the world of lordship and communities between the late ninth and the late twelfth centuries. The growth of distinctive monarchies in England, France, and Sicily illustrates different facets of this process, and the role of the dukes of Normandy suggests the similarity of the roles of lords and kings.

The Anglo-Saxon monarchy from Alfred (871–899) to Edmund

(939–946), established itself in the form of a strong dynasty, which had led English resistance to Danish invasion and imposed the legitimacy of the line of Wessex kings over all the English peoples. By 954 the last Danish ruler in the north of Britain had disappeared, and by the reign of Edgar (959–975, crowned 973) an elaborate coronation ceremony had developed, one that involved the high clergy and a royal anointing and coronation oath after the older Carolingian model.

During the tenth century the Old English vernacular experienced its greatest age as evidenced in lyric and epic poems, sermons and scriptural commentaries, and the *Anglo-Saxon Chronicle*—the earliest vernacular national history of Europe—compilations of law, and translations from Latin. During the same period several accomplished generations of English churchmen, particularly St. Dunstan of Canterbury (909–988) and Aethelwold of Winchester patronized the arts and learning and supported the monarchy enthusiastically.

Because of its small size, the presence of a defeated common enemy, the claim of the royal house of Wessex to the sole monarchy of England, and the ecclesiastical and linguistic elements of the tenth century, the monarchy in Anglo-Saxon England appears to have been the most developed in Europe during the tenth century. Under the monarchy, tenth-century English culture and material life developed extensively. But the early eleventh century witnessed another Scandinavian assault, and the antagonism between the leading English magnates and Ethelred II, "The Ill-Counseled" (987–1016), revealed the insecurity of the monarchy as an institution. Cnut of Denmark succeeded Ethelred as king of the English, and in many ways Cnut's rule was a continuation of the English-style monarchy of his predecessors. Cnut's dynasty died out in 1042, however, and the last surviving son of Ethelred, Edward the Confessor, became king of the English. Edward's reign (1042–1066) did little to check the increasingly local and family interests of the great houses, and although the cultural vigor of eleventh-century England was unimpaired, the leadership of the kings foundered upon their lack of lordship. Upon Edward's death in 1066, the leader of the greatest and most troublesome of these houses, Harold Godwinson, claimed the crown, drove off a Norse invasion led by Harald Sigurdsson, and marched south to meet the challenge of the Duke of Normandy.

The claim of William, Duke of Normandy, to the throne of England was based upon the alleged promise of Edward the Confessor, who had spent much of his exile in Normandy, to make William his heir, a claim that William maintained Harold had agreed to. By 1066 the duchy of Normandy had grown far greater than the lands between the River Epte and the North Sea at the mouth of the Seine that Charles the Simple had deeded to Rolf in 911. Under a series of able and energetic rulers, the duchy had weathered the last Scandinavian invasions, the violence and particularism of local lords, and the weakness of the church. William, after having survived both his illegitimate birth and a perilous minority, had ruthlessly established his own personal rule throughout the duchy and vigorously defended it against his own nobles and the kings of France. In September of 1066 William, leading a mercenary army, launched an attack upon England, where he defeated the army of Harold, which had shrunk in the march from the north, and had himself crowned king of England.

A remarkable source for the history of the Norman Conquest is the Bayeux Tapestry, a long narrow woven cloth depicting serially the history of the conquest of England, from the death of Edward the Confessor to the crowning of William I. It was probably made in England on commission from Bishop Odo of Bayeux, the brother of William the Conqueror. The scenes follow one another with clarity and spirit, and the spiritual dimension of William's legitimate claim is particularly emphasized.

The reign of William the Conqueror (1066–1087) began as a continuation of the reign of Edward the Confessor, but William's need for resources and his subordinates' actions forced him to impose a strong personal rule. The resources of the new king of England came in the form of land—the lands of earlier English kings and the family of Harold Godwinson, as well as the lands confiscated during the numerous rebellions of the third quarter of the eleventh century. To defend these lands, William, like his contemporary, Emperor Henry IV, built numerous castles and peopled them with men who were loyal to him. In the course of his reign, William placed more and more territory and power in the hands of his Norman supporters, lay and clerical. During this process much of the old Anglo-Saxon culture faded into oblivion: the genius of Old English literature slowly withered in the face of the conquerors' Anglo-Norman language; the unique calendar of Anglo-Saxon saints and liturgical observances paled before the reform ecclesiology of the Norman Churchmen; the tough and troublesome Old English aristocracy slowly disappeared before the numerous Normans. And always, under William and his successors, England played only a partial role in the family's interests; Normandy and the affairs of the Continent occupied them much more deeply. Not until the thirteenth century did England alone become the primary concern of its kings.

The insular and Continental interests, the family connections, and the linguistic character of the new Anglo-Norman monarchy and aristocracy both drew England securely into Continental affairs and relegated it to subordinate status among the possessions of its lords and its ruling class. Upon William's death in 1087, his holdings were divided among his sons, following the Norman law of inheritance. William II Rufus (1087–1100) inherited England, Robert inherited Normandy, and Henry received a little land and money. Robert's incompetence and his need for funds with which to join the First Crusade (see Chapter 17) heightened his brothers' interests in Normandy, and upon the death of Rufus in 1100 Henry inherited England and made a strong bid for the control of Normandy as well, which he achieved by 1106. The reign of Henry I (1100–1135), the last of the Conqueror's children, was a period of the strengthening of the royal lordship of England and the delineation of the particular structures of governance that later came to characterize

English monarchy and the role of kingship in English society. Faced with pressing financial needs for his defense of Normandy, Henry I raised a group of men from the lower nobility—or sometimes from no nobility at all—to serve his interests in England. These royal servants, dependent solely upon the king's favor and backed solely by the king's power, turned their attention and energies not to traditional structures of privilege and the acquisition of great landed fortunes, but to the institutions of uniquely royal governance—the courts, tax systems, wardship, and administrative privilege—in order to funnel as much money as possible to the king. As a result, they strengthened these institutions and made the royal court the focus of governance and administration as well as of power and prestige. By making the royal law courts centers of recognized process and recourse for injuries, the servants of Henry I both offered wider opportunities to those who resorted to law and created a structure that was easily supervised by the king and his chief servants.

The energy and skill of William the Conqueror and Henry I managed both to preserve Anglo-Saxon monarchy and to impose a Continental-style lordship upon England. By the middle of the twelfth century a native English culture had begun to revive, a culture that lacked the earlier brilliance of Anglo-Saxon culture but was distinctive in its own right and drew more heavily upon French and Mediterranean influences. Moreover, in the late eleventh and early twelfth centuries the Continental concerns of its kings drew England more and more into Continental affairs and created for it the role of treasury for Continental enterprises. Not until the thirteenth century did England's role among its king's possessions change significantly, and with few exceptions the strength of English monarchy was built up by royal servants working for hard taskmasters. Henry I, who lost his one legitimate son in a shipwreck in 1120, left the kingdom and its cares to his daughter, Matilda, who had been successively the wife of Emperor Henry V and Count Geoffrey Plantagenet of Anjou. However, Henry's nephew Stephen of Blois, the son of William the Conqueror's daughter Adela and Count Stephen of Blois, assumed royal power from 1135 to 1154, and his reign witnessed a strong challenge to the organization of the realms of Henry I. Rebellions plagued Stephen's reign, and the final compromise with the supporters of Matilda placed Matilda's son Henry Plantagenet in the direct line of succession. Upon Stephen's death in 1154, Henry II Plantagenet (1154–1188) became king of England. Far more than his grandfather Henry I, however, Henry II had extensive interests upon the Continent. He was count of Anjou, duke of Normandy, king of the English, lord of Ireland, and, through his marriage, duke of Aquitaine. The history of England in the later twelfth century is inextricably bound up with the Continental empire of the Plantagenet house.

The 5,000 men who followed William to the Battle of Hastings did not carve up the kingdom among them, as did other contemporary invaders. William gave out his English lands carefully, and one of the greatest tasks he and his successors faced was not only to reward their followers —and thus retain their loyalty—without impoverishing the royal dynasty, but to keep these followers faithful. This close watch that William I and Henry I in particular kept over their great lords is reflected in many aspects of their reigns. In 1086 William I undertook to discover the true wealth of his kingdom and sent out teams of recorders to analyze every holding in England. The results of their work—incomplete and sometimes obscure as it was—were compiled into great registers called, collectively, the *Domesday Book*. This analysis of the wealth and distribution of wealth in England was one that no other contemporary kingdom could have produced. The practical royal control established by the conquest and by William's subsequent savage reprisals against rebels had made England a remarkably "manageable" kingdom, and *Domesday Book* forms a fitting prologue to the activities of Henry I's servants in the first half of the twelfth century.

Between 1066 and 1154 the style of Anglo-Norman monarchy in England was developed as a response to the existence of certain Anglo-Saxon institutions and the particular needs of the Norman kings. In response to problems ranging from landholding and inheritance to local institutions and the needs of royal finance, the kings and their servants built a series of structures that gave a distinctive tone to English royal lordship. Yet English royal governance was subject to most of the same circumstances that plagued contemporary rulers: the court was largely itinerant and poorly staffed; problems of communication and undifferentiated administrative institutions made much of the court's work confused and intermittent; record keeping was irregular and unsystematic. Within these limitations, however, William I and Henry I established an effective and enduring royal lordship, one that provided resources for the extensive Continental empire of Henry II and his sons during the second half of the twelfth century.

The king of Francia, whose vassal William of Normandy conquered England in 1066, was Philip I, son of Henry I of *Francia* (1031–1060) and Anna of Kiev. Philip and his successors, down to his great-grandson Philip II Augustus (1180–1223), witnessed the empire building of many powerful vassals, although none as markedly successful as the kings of England, who added, one by one, many French titles to their original title of Normandy. Unlike the royal lordship of England, that of Francia offered little in the way of local traditions and continuity to shore up the strength of the successors of Hugh Capet. The history of royal lordship in eleventh- and twelfth-century Francia is that of a shrunken kingdom whose lords were able only with great effort and good fortune to lay the foundations of the kingdom of France.

From its first division among the children of Louis the Pious in 817 to the extinction of the Carolingian dynasty in 987, the empire of the Franks broke up slowly and painfully into a series of territorial principalities, some with the name of empire, some as kingdoms, many as illegitimate "counties," "duchies," and "marquisates." West Francia, the kingdom of Charles the Bald, suffered further subdivisions throughout the late ninth and tenth centuries until, with the replacement of the Carolingian dynasty by that of Hugh Capet in 987, it had shrunk to the area around Paris bounded by Compiègne, Reims, and Orléans, containing even within its diminished borders many areas in which the kings were powerless. The shrunken kingdom was bordered by new principalities whose lords remained nominal royal vassals while in practice they behaved totally independently of the king. Hugh Capet (987–996) came to the throne of Francia with great respect for royal dignity but with as little dynastic legitimacy as Conrad I of Germany (911–918) earlier in the century. Hugh, his son Robert II the Pious (996–1031), and his grandson Henry I (1031–1060) continued the attenuated monarchy of late Carolingian Francia. The degree of this attenuation is visible in the diminishing number of royal charters for the south that are noted after 987, and in the narrowing geographical origins of those lords known to be at the royal court during the reigns of Robert and Henry. Vassals of the kings became also vassals to other lords for new territories, and independent lords and bishops acted largely on their own during the first half of the eleventh century. During this period, the kings of Francia were effective kings only where they were effective lords, and those regions consisted strictly of the royal demesne lands around Paris. The counts of Champagne, Blois, Chartres, Anjou, Maine, Normandy, and Flanders were far more powerful than the kings of Francia. But they were also rivals among themselves for greater territories, and they never collaborated against the weaker kings, but, rather, used their royal connections, even their vassalage, whenever it could be turned to their own advantage. Even this nominal recognition of the distinctiveness of the royal title helped preserve the kingship of Francia, however. In particular, the dukes of Normandy acknowledged their relationship to the kings. In theory at least, some of the traits of late Carolingian theocratic kingship differentiated the kings from the other great lords. During the reign of Robert II, for example, the legends of the king's power to cure certain diseases by his touch began to circulate, and the ecclesiastical literary patronage of Robert managed to preserve some of these important traditional attributes even in the most difficult days of the kings, when they were hard put to establish their lordship even in the heart of their own territorial demesne.

Hugh and Robert spent their reigns in trying to enforce their lordship over their own territories and expand their dominion over neighboring lands without marked success. Elected to the kingship, the early Capetians strengthened their hands by associating their sons (and later their wives as well) in their rule from an early date. Thus, although the monarchy of France was not formally declared to be hereditary until 1223, the genetic good fortune of fourteen generations of Capetian monarchs in having sons old enough to share power from the beginning of a new reign constituted the important element of continuity in the process of strengthening the dynasty. Indeed, much of the legitimacy of the Capetians was acquired through sheer dynamic endurance. The reign of Philip I (1060–1108) marked the beginning of effective royal attempts to establish lordship securely in the region of Île de France, to establish royal justice against arbitrary local lords, and to establish effective royal authority within the royal demesne. This process of creating a strong lordship within the compact territories ruled by the king was the real beginning of French monarchy. Exploiting both ecclesiastical and temporal resources, Philip paid little attention to the wider movements for ecclesiastical reform that stirred up Europe within his lifetime. Unlike William the Conqueror, he had little to gain by supporting the reformers, and like his other contemporary, Emperor Henry IV, he had much to lose. Excommunicated from 1092 to 1108, Philip went on no crusade and kept his political horizons limited. He made himself lord in his small domain, and his descendants built upon that lordship in expanding the horizons of French kingship.

The struggles of popes and emperors in the last quarter of the eleventh century and the first half of the twelfth made the kingdom of France an attractive ally for the papacy. Philip's son Louis VI the Fat (1108-1137) and his grandson Louis VII (1137-1180) developed this relationship, thus strengthening the dignity of kingship in France more effectively than any other monarchs of the period. The connection between France and the papacy lasted until the end of the thirteenth century and increased greatly the strength of the royal dynasty while it afforded the popes sure allies in their imperial struggles. The Capetian dynasty during this period also profited from the dynastic crises among the neighboring nobility. England, Flanders, and Normandy were all affected by French royal interference in their dynastic affairs. Such accidental opportunites, the consolidation of power within the royal demesne, the connection with the papacy, and the stubborn retention of the trappings of monarchical authority—often without the power to make them effective—all these constitute in large part the first century and a half of Capetian lordship and the slow creation of the kingdom of France.

The kingdoms of Leon and Castile on the Spanish peninsula, England, France, and Germany all faced different problems during the eleventh and early twelfth centuries and possessed different resources for dealing with them. One of the most spectacular instances of the shaping of royal lordship during this period was the creation of the Norman kingdom of Sicily and South Italy, not out of older Visigothic, Anglo-Saxon, or Frankish traditions, but out of the fragments of Byzantine and Lombard institutions and the dynamism and ruthlessness of an able Norman dynasty. "The Other Norman Conquest," as historians sometimes call it, created a state where none had existed before, a state whose establishment, character, and power made it the most powerful kingdom in Europe by the end of the twelfth century and a major point of contact among Christian, Jewish, and Moslem cultures.

The development of Byzantine strength in the tenth century had restored Byzantine control over much of South Italy, including its restive Lombard principalities and its largely Greek population. The eleventh-century crisis in the Byzantine Empire (see Chapter 17), however, weakened Byzantine control and sparked a number of Lombard revolts. In the course of one of these revolts, a number of Norman pilgrims were hired by the Lombard rebels, and in 1017, after some initial successes, they were defeated by Byzantine forces at Cannae. The next few years were spent by the Normans in consolidating the small territories they still held, acting as mercenary forces for the Lombard princes of Salerno and Capua—as well as for the Byzantine ruler of South Italy—and helping the balance of power shift. The Norman role in the Lombard attack upon Pandulf, prince of Capua, led to the awarding of the county of Aversa to Rainulf, thus creating the first Norman principality in south Italy, in 1029. Between 1038 and 1042, the troubled political fortunes of Byzantium dominated South Italian politics. An initially successful military force led by George Maniakes launched an attack upon Sicily, held by the Moslems since 878, but Maniakes was recalled to Constantinople. The following four years witnessed further political crises in Constantinople and in South Italy. Between 1025 and 1046 the brothers William Iron-Arm, Humphrey, and Drogo of the Hauteville family of Normandy arrived in South Italy, and William soon carved out for himself the countship of Apulia.

The accession of Pope Leo IX in 1049 began the increase in papal concern for the affairs of the church in South Italy. The political rivalry of the preceding three decades had greatly reduced ecclesiastical discipline, and as a major proponent of ecclesiastical reform (see Chapter 16), Leo was particularly vexed at the conditions in the south, so close to Rome. While Leo was preparing to intervene in South Italy, Drogo of Apulia and Gaimar V of Salerno, the most powerful southern princes, were assassinated—in 1051 and 1052, respectively. The imperial-papal army encountered the Norman force led by Richard of Aversa, Humphrey of Apulia, and Robert Guiscard at Civitate in June of 1053. In a furious battle, the Normans destroyed the Italian and German army of Pope Leo and captured the pope himself. Negotiations with the pope resulted in papal and imperial recognition of Norman possessions in South Italy. In 1057 Robert Guiscard, the brother of William, Humphrey, and Drogo, succeeded as count of Apulia. In 1059 Robert took an oath of allegiance to Pope Nicholas II, becoming a vassal of the papacy and in turn receiving papal recognition of his title of duke of Apulia and Calabria and anticipating his conquest of Moslem Sicily. From 1059 until his death in 1085, the career of Robert Guiscard was one of continual territorial aggrandizement and consolidation of his control in South Italy. Sicily was wrested from its Moslem lords by Robert's younger brother Roger between 1061 and 1068; in 1071 Bari, the last Byzantine stronghold in Italy, fell into Robert's hands; serious revolts were put down throughout the 1070s; then, in 1081, Robert launched the supreme attack, journeying across the Adriatic to assault the territories of the Byzantine Empire in western Greece. However, after some initial success Robert was called back to aid Pope Gregory VII in his struggle with Emperor Henry IV (see Chapter 16). Robert's army relieved the imperial siege of Rome and carried the pope with it to Salerno. Renewing his attack on

Greece, Robert died in an epidemic on Corfu in 1085, leaving his great dukedom to his son Roger Borsa, and the ambitions of his family to his other son Bohemund and to his younger brother, Roger, "the Great Count" of Sicily.

At his death in 1101, Roger the Great Count left his widow Adelaide and a young son, Roger II (1095–1154). Adelaide, one of several remarkable eleventh-century noble women, provided a successful regency for her young son until his coming of age and knighting in Palermo cathedral in 1112. Under the first years of Roger's rule, the Sicilian ports participated in the expansion of Italian maritime commerce and the diverse peoples and institutions of Sicily were welded into a governmental administration. In 1127 Roger's cousin William, Duke of Apulia, died, and Roger claimed the inheritance. After a dispute and prolonged negotiations with Pope Honorius II, Roger was confirmed in the succession, and in 1129 he succeeded to the duchy of Capua, thus uniting the entire south of Italy and Sicily under his rule. In 1130 Roger was pronounced king of Sicily, Apulia, and Calabria by a bull of Pope Anacletus II, and on Christmas Day, 1130, he was crowned in a formal ceremony at Palermo. He had, better than any other ruler, turned lordship into kingship.

The Normans and Capetians, remarkable rulers in different ways, illustrate by contrast as well as by comparison the diverse fortunes of royal lordship in the eleventh and early twelfth centuries. The Norman conquerors of England inherited and preserved many of the institutions and traditions of Anglo-Saxon monarchy; the Capetians of France slowly attempted to secure their authority in a diminished kingdom; the Normans of Sicily began as mercenary soldiers, and then became territorial mercenary warlords, counts and dukes of the former Lombard and Byzantine provinces, protectors of the papacy, potential invaders of both Byzantium and Moslem North Africa, and, finally, the successful kings of a multiracial kingdom whose capital was at Palermo and whose farthest northern boundaries were just south of the Papal States. The variety of political adventurism in the late eleventh century reveals how personal and circumstantial royal lordship really was and how slowly and hesitantly anything resembling nationalism or territorial statehood came into existence. By 1130, a Norman king with an Anglo-Saxon wife wore the crown of the old kings of Wessex; a Capetian married to a Russian princess wore the old crown of the West Franks; and the grandson of a minor Norman warlord wore a crown he had created for himself in a kingdom that included Arabs, Jews, Lombards, Greeks, and Normans. Such were some of the varieties of royal lordship at the beginning of the twelfth century.

16

SPIRITUAL REFORM AND THE CONCEPT OF CHRISTENDOM

LORDSHIP: POWER AND CULTURE IN THE ELEVENTH CENTURY

The ecclesiastical reform movements launched by the Anglo–Saxon missionaries and the Frankish kings in the middle of the eighth century led to a sharpening of the distinctions between the spiritual and secular life and to a kind of lay protectorate over ecclesiastical institutions that became, by the early tenth century, virtually a lay domination of the Church. This new spirituality and consciousness of the role of the Church in the world did not gain great influence between the death of Louis the Pious in 840 and the imperial ecclesiastical reforms of the Emperor Henry III in the middle of the eleventh century. The lay protectorate, however, shaped a culture and created an interdependency between spiritual and temporal powers that flourished in the late tenth and eleventh centuries. Institutions of lordship acquired a degree of spiritual authority, and lordly prelates directed ecclesiastical affairs with an outlook not essentially different from those of their lay brothers.

The image of God that most accurately characterizes the devotional spirit between the ninth and the twelfth centuries is that of God the Father, a powerful, remote, and frightening divinity whose power is revealed in natural disasters, the destruction of pagans, and the imposition of order within society. Depictions of the Crucifixion focused upon the majesty of the figure of Christ and the triumph of divinity over humanity, the figure often being simply superimposed upon a cross, elaborately costumed and surrounded by angels. More attractive was the theme of Christ in majesty, showing the risen, triumphant Christ seated in a mandorla, a halo-like space that indicated eternity, and surrounded by symbols of the Church, the evangelists, or material creation. In the most primitive terms, Christ and God the Father were great lords ruling the manor-hall of Heaven; at its most sophisticated the Deity was the lord to whom kings and emperors owed their roles and their accounting. In a relief panel at the shrine of Charlemagne in Aachen, the emperor is shown presenting a small church to the Virgin Mary. Such depictions of donors and patron saints abound in early medieval art, and they remind us of the particular relationships men conceived between the donor and patron. The tiny church held by Charlemagne is not a "model," but the palace church at Aachen itself, symbolically shrunken to become the gift exchanged between the emperor and the Virgin. The Gospels of the ninth– and tenth–century Frankish kings and German emperors also illustrate the rulers themselves receiving homage, often touched by the hand of God. This art gives a striking impression of the cooperation between rulers and divinity, the extension of the relation of lord and man, patron and client, sometimes friend and friend, to encompass and conceptualize even the relationships between humans and God. Kings and lords stood in just such an "informal" relationship with saints, maintaining the order on earth that God and the saints maintained in heaven.

Never before and never since this period have there been so many royal and aristocratic saints: Charlemagne, Edward the Confessor of England (1042–1066), St. Olaf, St. Stephan, St. Wenceslaus, even St. Vladimir I of Kiev. Lords who retired to monasteries after long and exhausting careers often became saints, and having a saint in one's lineage became expected of European ruling houses. The degree of social and political cooperation among bishops, abbots, lords, and kings would appear unheard of to a modern society that is sharply conscious of the "separation of church and state," for that phrase itself would have had no meaning in the tenth century. The Carolingian concept of a true Christian society on earth, ruled by the Christian Emperor and directed by cooperative ecclesiastics, corresponds neither to modern notions of *church* nor of *state*. In such a religiously undifferentiated world, it is understandable that saints, and God himself, led Christian armies to victory, that the Virgin could be depicted as receiving churches from an emperor, and that, in a mosaic at the Lateran, Charlemagne and Pope Leo III, each wearing the square nimbus signifying mortality, should kneel before St. Peter, with his circular nimbus signifying immortality, as his protégés. Tenth century vernacular accounts of biblical stories describe tenth century social institutions, and the glosses of Latin texts act as an instructive commentary upon the shaping of vernacular European religious and philosophical vocabularies.

Nor were lords and kings the only partakers of spiritual as well as temporal authority. The grandmother of Vladimir I of Kiev, Olga, became a Christian thirty years before her grandson, and her power during the minority of her son Sviatoslav I, Vladimir's father, was as extensive as that of any other early Kievan ruler. Olga was sainted, as were many of the remarkable female rulers of the tenth and eleventh centuries. Even those powerful women who were not sainted present striking tenth century portraits. Theophano, the Byzantine princess who married Otto II and was left a widow at twenty-seven, ruled effectively as regent for her son, Otto III, during his minority, and at Theophano's own early death in 991, her own aged mother-in-law, the dowager empress Adelaide, took up the regency and the troubled politics of Germany from 991 until 996. During the early stages of Otto III's majority after 996, the governance of Germany was in the hands of his aunt Matilda.

The practice that daughters of Byzantine emperors and Kievan princes travelled halfway around the then known world to marry strangers at their family's bidding was different only in degree from the marriage patterns of the lesser nobility, but the remarkable force of personality required for young widows and aged matrons to exercise personal rule during the tenth and eleventh centuries must not be overlooked. A great modern historian has pointed out that "there was a moment in the eleventh century when the regent in Germany was the French Agnes (of Poitou, widow of the Emperor Henry III), and in France the Russian widow of King Henry I." The female relatives of King Aethelstan of England married all over Europe in the mid-tenth century, and marriages of the royal children of the Kingdoms of Leon and Castile not only linked the Iberian kingdoms to each other, but brought money, ecclesiastics, and fighting men over the Pyrenees to carry on the battle against the Caliphate of Córdoba. The role of women in religion, ecclesiastical patronage, the power of the imperial convents in Germany, and acts and institutions of charity is frequently discussed. It is less frequently pointed out that in the tenth and eleventh centuries women ruled, sometimes long, and usually well. From the legendary Guibourc, the wife of the hero William of Orange, who shared her husband's battles, to the eloquent playwright and poet Hrotswitha, the nun of Gandersheim in the tenth century, the participation of women in this aristocratic world of lordship was thorough and continuous. These were not the elegant ladies of the later romances, however; they possessed functional, activist characters, and, until the transformation of European culture in the twelfth century, their place in aristocratic society was more independent and their power more real than at any time before the twentieth century.

The images and realities of divine and human power existed against a background of insecurity, an undifferentiated attitude toward social and natural disasters that laid heavy emphasis upon penitence and liturgical practices, ideas of historical causation based upon a limited concept of the human personality and a reluctance to distinguish spiritual from material causality, and a limited system of exact spatial or temporal measurement. Pilgrimages, public penances, the increasingly anxious search for "pure" religious practices and authentic devotion, and a literal dependence upon the clergy for services requiring organization and literacy as well as spiritual efficacy characterize the spiritual and intellectual life of the late tenth and eleventh centuries. The outward forms of religious conduct, like the outward, easily memorable forms of legal and political agreements, expressed what later centuries would replace with new theories of individual spiritual development and conscience, and new theories of the human personality.

Sometimes a single literary work illuminates a complex of attitudes better than a long descriptive analysis. In 954, Adso, the abbot of Moutier-en-Der, wrote a short treatise for Queen Gerberga of *Francia* called *Libellus de Antichristo,* The Treatise on the Antichrist. Basing his hurriedly written work on earlier Carolingian biblical commentaries on the Apocalypse, Adso described the future coming of the Antichrist, who will be born in Babylon of the tribe of Dan, raised by wizards, prophets, and criminals, and establish himself as a great religious leader and king. The emperor of Rome will go to the Mount of Olives and lay down his crown and scepter, and the triumph of the Antichrist will be at hand. The prophets Enoch and Elijah will attempt to warn the people, but the Antichrist will kill them and increase his persecutions until Christ himself comes again, destroys the Antichrist, and institutes a period of repentance before the Last Judgment. This prophecy told by Adso had a long future. A twelfth century Latin play, many later prophetic treatises, and political propaganda down to the sixteenth century reveal the attractions of the story to the culture of early Europe. Yet there are elements in the treatise that tell us specifically of the religious culture of the tenth and early eleventh centuries. First, the treatise is dedicated to a Queen, a layperson, ostensibly as a result of her curiosity, and it combines scriptural commentaries with popular legends and contemporary values. It tells us something of the literary public for such works, and the career of the Antichrist and Christ's war against him are described in colorful, blunt terms. Not only will the Antichrist perform terrors and wonders, but he will convert many Christians and Jews to his cause. Adso points out that the Jews who are not convinced by the Antichrist will be converted to Christianity by

Enoch and Elijah before the last persecutions. The biblical phrases that recur throughout the short treatise are used as prophecies whose picturesque fulfillment is the thread of the story.

Legends of Charlemagne had already created, by the end of the tenth century, the image of the aged, heroic emperor defending God's kingdom against God's enemies, and the threats of invasion and disaster sharpened this image of an earlier, more heroic time. Asser's life of King Alfred of England was modelled upon Einhard's biography of Charlemagne, and a number of poems, saints' lives, and legends had begun to accumulate around the Frankish king and Roman emperor. The intellectual climate of the mid- to late-tenth century is thus accurately reflected in the *Libellus de Antichristo*. The work also reflects upon what have sometimes been called the excessively grandiose political visions of the ninth and tenth centuries. From Charlemagne to the Saxon emperors to Vladimir I of Kiev, the vision of large scale empires seems to contrast oddly with the rudimentary administrative institutions of the period. Yet such short lived empires were founded, and their survival, however brief, contributed to the idea of empire. Not even the extension of empire over non-Christians was excluded. The idea of the Antichrist was rooted in real political ideas as well as in the traditions of scriptural taste and the character of Carolingian biblical commentaries. It is precisely in the amalgam of such diverse visions that the character of the tenth and eleventh centuries is best seen.

Other elements in the *Libellus de Antichristo* also cast light on the character of tenth century European culture. The vision of the work is universal, but the specific knowledge of the author is not. Jerusalem, the Mount of Olives, Babylon, all possess symbolic rather than literal features, and the worlds of Judaism and Islam are subordinated to the great dramatic conflict between the Antichrist and Christ. Before the late eleventh century the place of Jews and Moslems in the European world was quite different from its later history. Pilgrimages were made to Jerusalem in the tenth and early eleventh centuries, although the route was often difficult and sometimes the traditional Islamic tolerance of Christian pilgrims was violated by individual rulers. The European Christians of the tenth and eleventh centuries, however, knew little of Islam or Judaism. Some knew of the Saracen raiders in northern Spain, southern France, the Alpine passes, and south Italy, but they knew very little of Moslem beliefs and practices; sufficiently little, it may be said, so that there existed little momentum for ideological warfare between Christianity and Islam. When the Crusade movement began in the eleventh century, it represented among other things a new Christian selfconsciousness and a new kind of hostility to Islam. Along the Moslem Christian borders, in Spain, southern France, Italy, and Anatolia, there grew up a rough border contact in which the fighters on either side came to resemble each other more than they resembled other representatives of their culture in the hinterlands. The tenth century Byzantine epic, *Digenes Akritas,* and the twelfth century Spanish epic *El Cantar del Mio Cid* describe such a frontier world; rough, heavy-handed, possessing a complex ethical code but little touched by considerations of religious doctrine and practice.

The knowledge of Judaism on the part of European Christians was similarly limited. Jewish communities had existed in the cities of the Roman world, and they had survived the fall of the empire in the West, with their inhabitants probably maintaining some degree of urban life as well as depending more and more upon the countryside and rural landholdings. Aside from the persecutions of Visigothic Spain in the seventh century, the customary Christian revulsion against Judaism remained more literary than active, and Jewish communities existed in large numbers in Toulouse, Cologne, Ravenna, Rome, Constantinople, and Trebizond on the Black Sea. Although there were several Byzantine laws restricting Jewish states and activity, the Jewish population of the Byzantine Empire lived in the Greek peninsula, western Asia Minor, and the region of Antioch. Throughout the Khazar kingdom, of course, Judaism was particularly favored. Two of the most remarkable documents of the ninth century consist of a letter from the court official and physician of the Caliphs of Cordoba, Hasdai Ibn Shaprut (915–970), a Jew, to the King of the Khazars inquiring about the Jewish kingdom, and King Joseph's answer, written about 960. Hasdai also wrote to the Byzantine court to protest Byzantine persecution of the Jews. Such communications (the letter of Ibn Shaprut appears to have been carried through Germany, Hungary, and Russia by a German Jew) were not new in the Mediterranean world, and even among the Moslems travelling Jews were not a surprising phenomenon. Ninth century Persian sources describe the Radanite Jewish merchants, who travelled from Europe to China, both overland and by a coastal sea route from Arabia to the South China Sea. Remnants of the last of these communities, the Jewish community at Kaifeng, survived into the twentieth century. Prosperous Jewish communities in Mesopotamia produced the great Babylonian Talmud by the sixth century, and, far to the north, Jewish traders, many of whom dealt in slaves, are represented on the reliefs of the bronze doors of the cathedral at Gniezno in Poland, being presented to the king by St. Adalbert of Prague. Although sporadic complaints about Jewish privileges, such as those of Bishop Agobard of Lyons in the ninth century, and an occasional Christian scandal, such as the conversion to Judaism of Bodo, an imperial court chaplain of Louis the Pious around 840, Jewish settlement in the Christian world was relatively untroubled. The social forms of pre-eleventh century Europe allowed such coexistence, and it is probable that Jews played social roles generally similar to those played by Christians until after the middle of the eleventh century. Christian selfconsciousness, in the case of Judaism as in that of Islam, had not yet begun to exert private and public hostility against religious differences.

Over the towns and farms, castles and roads, there loomed in the tenth and eleventh centuries the shadows of the monasteries. Perhaps the most successful and dynamic social institutions produced by the late ancient world, monasteries had sheltered religious and cultural change in Ireland, England, southern France, and Italy. The ecclesiastical reforms of the mid-eighth century depended upon the energies of Anglo-Saxon monks, and the first ecclesiastical administrations of Germany and, later, in the Slavic lands to the east, were based on monastic missionary activity. The Carolingian renaissance and empire would have been inconceivable had they not patronized monasteries and received aid in return. The monasteries had suffered in the late ninth and early tenth centuries, but they were generally equipped to survive and keep their communities intact, even though they had to move from place to place to avoid the invaders. Stories of such monastic wanderings in the late ninth and early tenth centuries are not uncommon, and, taking their relics and sacred books with them, monks trudged from place to place hoping to find sanctuary from the Northmen, the Magyars, or the Saracens. In other places, however, the monastic rule, never thoroughly reformed since the days of Louis the Pious and St. Benedict of Aniane, weakened, and the strictness of houses grew lax. Even the rough warlords of the early tenth century realized that the quality of monasticism was of particular importance to their own spiritual lives, and the monastic patronage on the part of these dynasties contributed heavily to the reform of monasticism that swept the tenth and eleventh centuries. By the end of the eleventh century, the great monastic establishments of Cluny and elsewhere had erected massive churches and cultural structures that complemented the aristocratic leadership of Europe. The role of monastic practices in shaping the culture of the tenth and eleventh century aristocracy is an important element in the study of early European social and cultural history.

The impulse toward monastic reforms had encountered stiff resistance even in the days of Boniface and, later, those of Charlemagne, Louis the Pious, and St. Benedict of Aniane. Not many monasteries accepted the rule of St. Benedict of Nursia; the inroads of the invaders and the secularization of ecclesiastical properties by lay abbots and "protectors" weakened the resources of even the oldest and strongest Carolingian monasteries. The first stirrings of monastic reform reveal the aristocracy and individual reformers working closely together. Such early movements, however, depended precariously upon the continuation of reform after the deaths of its main proponents, and in many places reform began, but it did not survive. In Lotharingia and Flanders, a young nobleman named Gerard of Brogne (ca. 890–959) founded a new monastic community on his own lands and appears to have attracted considerable renown for the effectiveness of his administration. Other lords gave him decaying ecclesiastical properties in Lotharingia and Flanders, but Gerard's movement flagged with his death and those of his patrons. At Gorze, also in Lotharingia, a reformed ascetic monastic center was established in 933 by Bishop Adalbero of Metz, and the ecclesiastical life and extensive patronage among the Lotharingian nobility and the Saxon and Salian emperors made Gorze a center of widespread monastic reform, with Gorze monks often being sent to older houses to reform them. The reforms at St. Maximin at Trier extended into Bavaria and from there to Montecassino itself. From Trier monks went out to the eastern frontier to become abbots of eastern imperial monasteries, and a monk of St. Maximin was the first archbishop of the important see of Magdeburg. A monk of Trier even was sent to Kievan Russia when it appeared that Russia might convert to Latin, instead of Greek Christianity. These monastic attempts at reform in the empire and Flanders were significant, but they proceeded slowly and depended for much of their vitality upon individual patrons and particularly able abbots.

Other movements for reform occurred in the Duchy of Burgundy and in Italy. Italian monasticism, for many years closer to the roots of the Benedictine rule and influenced by Byzantine institutions and monastic culture, particularly witnessed the development of eremitical forms of monastic life. Such impressive figures as St. Nilus (905–1004), who established a series of monastic foundations, particularly that of Serperi near Gaeta in southern Italy around 960, exerted an influence in far wider circles than Italy proper. Otto III patronized St. Nilus and brought his influence to Rome; St. Adalbert of Prague had stayed at Serperi several times. St. Romauld (952–1027) spent a lifetime of eremitical wandering throughout Italy and Catalonia, founded several reform houses, in particular Camaldoli around the year 1000, and left a legacy of strict monastic life, both communal and eremitical, that constituted a powerful training ground for the reformers of the later eleventh century.

The most influential and best known center of reform, however, was the monastery of Cluny. Established in 910 by Duke William the Good of Aquitaine, Cluny was remarkable from the beginning because the Duke gave the monastery, not to the abbot or a lay protector, but to St. Peter. The monastery was independent of all authority but that of Rome, resembling those new kingdoms and principalities such as Poland and Hungary whose rulers had made themselves vassals of St. Peter and thus entered into a particular relationship with the papacy. The power of the spiritual attraction of Rome, even in the dark days of the late tenth century, was considerable, and the image of Rome moved people far away in a manner that it is difficult to reconstruct today. The freedom of Cluny from all authority but that of Rome, its increasingly vast resources in land and monastic establishments, its growing attraction, through the distribution of relics and the institution of pilgrimages, and the remarkably high order of ability of its great abbots and their subordinates made Cluny a powerful influence for spiritual reform. A series of distinguished abbots, from the first abbot Berno (910–927) through Odo (927–942), Aymard (942–954), Mayeul (954–993), Odilo (993–1048), and Hugh (1048–1109), to the height of the monastery's influence under Peter the Venerable (1122–1156), saw the reform emphasis upon a new spirituality reflected in great emphasis upon and lengthening of the monastic liturgy, splendid large churches, and richly wrought vestments and vessels, and brought the shadow of Cluny to corners of Europe hitherto remote from major ecclesiastical influence. The abbot of Cluny could select his own successor (and the talents of the first abbots are eloquent testimony to the care with which this was done), and the affiliation of Cluny-reformed or -founded monasteries with the monastery of Cluny itself was strictly regularized. All Cluniac houses were priories, and the only abbot of these 1500 or so institutions was the abbot of Cluny. Such organizational supports enabled Cluniac houses to act together, afforded considerable opportunities for the work of such reformers as St. Odo, and extended Cluny's influence not only to northern France and the Rhineland, but to Rome and northern Italy. The great tenth and eleventh century abbots of Cluny were familiar sights in the Alpine passes and in Rome itself. The kidnapping of St. Mayeul by Arab raiders in the Alps has been alleged, in fact, to have been the rallying point for the final southern French assault that destroyed the powerful Arab stronghold of La Garde Freinet toward the end of the tenth century.

Cluny even influenced those centers of reform that were not directly affiliated with the Cluniac organization itself. Under Richard of St. Vanne at Verdun (1005–1046), Lotharingian and Cluniac reforms extended into Normandy, where the ambitious dukes, descendants of Rolf the Viking, undertook extensive monastic patronage, and under them the Norman foundations of Bec and Fécamp became particularly noted centers of piety and learning, and these in their turn influenced English monasticism after the Norman conquest in 1066. Under St. William of Volpiano (990–1031) the reformed monastery of St. Bénigne at Dijon acted as an independent center whose influences reached into Normandy and Italy as well. Under such influences nonmonastic groups made organizational responses. In the course of the late tenth and eleventh centuries, the clergy of cathedral churches, the canons, began to live increasingly regularized lives according to monastic organization.

The chains of monastic reform are long and often confusing. Yet the tenth and eleventh century monastic reforms, like the foundations of the frontier bishoprics and archbishoprics of central and eastern Europe, constituted social and cultural events of immeasurable importance. The new spirituality of the tenth century might have died, as other similar movements had in the past and would in the future, if it had not been sustained by the remarkable cooperation of the new nobility and found principles of organization that permitted it to thrive. In return, the monastic institutions of the eleventh century undertook to improve the spiritual life of nobles and peasants alike. The question of the contact between ecclesiastical institutions and the lay nobility and peasantry is a complicated one. The new monastic institutions, however wealthy and ascetic they might be, were driven by an intense spirituality that extended to laymen as well. From the eleventh century, lay patrons were enrolled in Cluny's prayers for the dead and commemorated in the impressive Cluniac liturgy. Cluny instituted the celebration of the feast of All Souls, commemorating both lay and clerical patrons. The elaborate and extended Cluniac liturgy influenced the laypeople who observed it, and the routine of monastic prayer became the foundation of the first lay prayerbooks, including the superb books of hours painted at the end of the fourteenth and fifteenth centuries. The churches of Cluny, particularly those designated Cluny II and III, were resplendent examples of a blend of worldliness and monastic retreat. Under the impetus of monastic reform, and not always under the auspices of Cluny, important architectural and sculptural developments took place. Out of northern Italy, southern France, and Catalonia came the remarkable Romanesque style, and from Germany there developed an imperial ecclesiastical architectural style and in northern Spain and southern France there emerged the pligrimage church, with long aisles circling the altar and the relic shrine behind it. The pilgrimage church, of course, could suit nonmonastic establishments as well.

There is perhaps no greater monument to the synthesis of aristocratic reform monasticism and the social codes of the eleventh century aristocracy than the great church, now destroyed, of Cluny III. Begun in 1088, the building was completed, after several disasters, in 1130. Until the rebuilding of St. Peter's in Rome in the sixteenth century, Cluny III was the largest church in Latin Christendom, and its ambitious architecture and glorious decorations represented the pinnacle of aristocratic monasticism. Later, in the twelfth century, monasticism underwent other reforms, designed particularly to separate monks from the world, and in the course of this new movement, Cluny and other eleventh century monasteries came under heavy attack for their worldliness, their love of material beauty, and their elaborate liturgy and ceremony. For the world of the eleventh century in which Christians from Norway, Novgorod, Gniezno, Kiev, and Ragusa mingled with Christians from the old Roman and Germanic lands to the west, Cluny III represented precisely the fulfillment of the old Carolingian ideal—lay patronage and protection creating the setting and the security for religious people to raise the value of human life and activity, to purge it by their prayers, and to accept the bodies and souls of their patrons at death. Such a religious culture was not particularly spiritual or concerned with the development of the mind and emotions, but it attracted the attention and energies of those it served, and it played a key role in circulating religious, social, and cultural values not only among the warlords of Europe, but also among the peasants and pilgrims who left their tedious routines to find, in a physical pilgrimage, some echo of the spiritual pilgrimage of which they had an inkling.

IMPERIAL REFORM AND THE ELEVENTH-CENTURY PAPACY

The emperor, by virtue of his anointing and coronation, was a particularly select defender of the Church; his status was that of a cleric as well as a layman, since he held *ex officio* several important ecclesiastical offices; until the end of the eleventh century, the imperial coronation was considered a sacrament, and the emperor therefore a uniquely sanctified person. In the Carolingian tradition revived by the Ottos, one of the emperor's first duties was the defense and ordering of the church, and in the course of his reign Henry III (1039–1056) showed himself one of the ablest and most dedicated ecclesiastical reformers since Louis the Pious. Not only did the emperors of the late tenth and eleventh centuries weld Germany into a single kingdom, but through their patronage and assistance they established links between duchies, cultural influences, and a new economic prosperity that shored up their sacral imperial claims and made the emperor the strongest monarch in the Latin west. The visionary spiritual internationalism that brought the Ottos into contact with Poland, Bohemia, Kiev, Italy, France, and Byzantium possessed a firm footing in Germany itself.

Unlike his father, Conrad II (1024–1039), Henry III relied heavily on clerics and ecclesiastical offices and resources for his governance. His reign witnessed the continued emergence of the *ministerialis* class, a group of unfree men promoted to high administrative office by the emperor and owing their loyalty only to him. This class constituted an effective governmental resource and a challenge to the free nobility. The imperial control over Germany and the presence of a service aristocracy in the *ministeriales,* contributed to the prestige and power of Henry III. The improved conditions of material life led to a revived interest in devotional forms and in the question of ecclesiastical reform on a wider scale. With these ideals, Henry was in sympathy. Filled with a conviction of his own divine mission, Henry sponsored monastic and administrative reforms, aimed at strengthening the monarchy's hand against such recalcitrant powers as the duchies of Lorraine and Saxony, and relied more and more upon high ecclesiastics. The archbishopric of Bremen, under the direction of the great Archbishop Adalbert (1043–1071), was turned into a focus of imperial power opposing the free nobility of Saxony. The combination of high ecclesiastics and imperial *ministeriales* appeared to be a successful instrument during the reigns of Henry III and his son and successor Henry IV (1056–1106).

The priestly and royal character of the emperor and the particular circumstances of imperial dependence upon high churchmen for the governance of Germany gave great impetus to ecclesiastical reform. Another source of reform was a new religious consciousness that was reflected in the growth of reformed monasticism, the popularity of relics and pilgrimages, and the appearance of anticlerical and antisacerdotal criticism, whether as injunctions for moral reform or as heresy.

The heresies of the early Middle Ages had tended to be the isolated beliefs of monastic thinkers, difficult to discover and easy to censor. By the late tenth and eleventh centuries, however, new heterodox ideas appealed to a wider, nonmonastic public. Injunctions to lead a life of evangelical piety, injunctions that sometimes led to a rejection of ecclesiastical institutions, joined the increasing frequency of severe criticism of ecclesiastical practices and personnel. Clerical marriage and concubinage, particularly among the lower clergy, drew more and more criticism, and the practice of purchasing or unlawfully dominating ecclesiastical offices—or, rather more complex, the old Germanic legal distinction between the altar, the province of grace, and the church and its property, the province of the patron or owner—became denounced as simony, after Simon Magus, the figure in apocryphal scriptures who attempted to purchase "magical" powers from St. Peter. Reform monasticism and, later, reformers from other movements, thus focused upon Nicolaitism—clerical incontinence—and simony as two particularly heinous offenses and made them the objects of intense reform movements.

Throughout much of the eleventh century, laymen and clerics cooperated in purifying the spiritual life and eradicating ecclesiastical abuses. By the second half of the century, however, two distinct attitudes toward reform became apparent. The first, in the traditional Carolingian style, left it to the emperor and his clergy to eradicate abuses and rectify them, even to the point of removing canonically consecrated ecclesiastical officials, from abbots to popes; this power was justified by the emperor's quasi-sacral status. The other view, which possessed political as well as spiritual dimensions, attacked the entire idea of lay authority, whether that of local lord or that of the emperor himself, in the name of *libertas*, the freedom from any kind of interference at all that was guaranteed by God to the Church and its institutions. By the middle of the eleventh century, both views—their proponents cooperating with each other—resulted in the spread of reform movements. By the second half of the century, however, their ways divided, with enduring consequences for Christian society.

The religious history of Europe between 750 and 1050 had consisted of a long, intermittent process by which the nobility and the ruling classes in general were slowly made aware of distinctly spiritual obligations; at the same time, the higher clergy were drawn more and more to share the sympathies and many of the attitudes of the aristocracy, and were eventually drawn more and more from the aristocracy. By the middle of the eleventh century, both higher laity and higher clergy had come to resemble each other closely. The particular qualities that distinguished clergy from laity became blurred as laymen shared ecclesiastical duties and ecclesiastics performed secular work. Lay piety, in both high and low social groups, had equaled, and often surpassed ecclesiastical piety. To many, it appeared that the long-hoped-for conversion of the world had finally come about, and in the liturgical practices at Cluny, on pligrimages, and in the symbiotic relationship between monasteries and their patron families, a high degree of cooperation was indeed visible. To many, however, such cooperation signaled a contamination of the Church. The clergy were subservient to laymen and often hardly distinguishable at all from them; many clergy were unworthy of clerical status because their conduct was less exemplary than that of laymen; the threat of the Church being swallowed by the world was a violation of a divinely decreed right order of the universe, and in the name of that right order more and more complaints were made against established ecclesiastical practices. To be sure, spectacular abuses abounded. In the eleventh century, the archbishopric of Narbonne was bought from two noble laymen by another noble layman on behalf of his son, then ten years old. In many churches, the incomes of canons went directly to laymen living outside the church. In addition to such abuses as these, laymen acted as legal representatives or advocates of ecclesiastical property, enriching themselves at the expense of the church; laymen served as abbots of monasteries; and laymen invested ecclesiastical personnel with the symbols of office over which they possessed control, thus appearing in the eyes of many to violate canon law. Even the otherwise praiseworthy actions of laymen in founding monasteries and reforming existing monasteries seemed to some to be a tampering with the divine order.

The late eleventh century witnessed an outburst of different opinions concerning the condition of the Church and the role of laypeople in it. England, France, Germany, and Italy all produced a large body of literature on the subject—pamphlets, exchanges of correspondence, treatises, imperial edicts, and decisions of church councils. From the middle of the eleventh century on, however, the papacy began to play a stronger role in these debates, and by the end of the century the questions of reform had precipitated a conflict of international proportions between the papacy and the empire. Let us consider first, though, the effects of the early reform movement on the papacy itself, the major issues under discussion and their proponents, and the complex political and social relationships that undercut the purely theoretical arguments offered by both sides.

The roots of the tenth- and eleventh-century reform movements obviously lay elsewhere than in the papacy. The Cluniac influence, Lotharingian reform movements, the imperial German church, and the precocious, idiosyncratic ecclesiastical culture of Anglo-Saxon England all contributed to a movement that was widespread long before it touched Rome. At the end of the tenth century, the dynastic and political burdens borne by the papacy had been reduced somewhat by the energy of the Ottonian emperors, but the problems of central Italy still loomed large in the history of the early eleventh-century papacy. The coronation of Otto I as emperor in 962 by Pope John XII introduced, in the form of the Saxon emperors, a new power in central Italy, but even the most energetic and successful of the Saxon emperors had to ally themselves with one or another of the factions that struggled for control of central Italy, and, with it, the office of the pope. Some of the efforts of the Saxon emperors deserve particular attention because of the contact they reveal with a wider world than that of Germany and Italy, and of these, none has received more attention than the relationship between Emperor Otto III and Gerbert of Aurilliac, Pope Sylvester II.

Gerbert was born in Aquitaine around 955. He entered the monastery of St. Gerard at Aurilliac in Burgundy, traveled to northern Spain in 967, and he made his first visit to Rome between 967 and 970.

Having learned something of mathematics in Spain, Gerbert left Rome in 971 for Reims as archdeacon and schoolmaster, and at Reims he was the tutor of Robert, later king of France. In 982–983 Gerbert was appointed abbot of Bobbio, St. Columbanus's old monastery in northern Italy, but a dispute with his monks forced him to return to Reims, where he continued as teacher and secretary to Archbishop Arnulf. In 991 Gerbert himself was made archbishop of Reims. In 997 he returned to Rome, in 998 he was made archbishop of Ravenna, and in 999, at the order of his former pupil Otto III, he became pope, taking the name of Sylvester II and thereby echoing the first Sylvester, the alleged curer and converter of Emperor Constantine. In 1000 Gerbert crowned Otto III in Rome. He died in 1002.

Gerbert's learning was remarkably wide, even in such an age of distinguished thinkers and grammarians as the late tenth century. His interest in the study of logic and mathematics, acquired in Spain and pursued later, was perhaps his most original contribution to an intellectual world in which the principal fields of study were grammatical and literary, but Gerbert also revived interest in classical authors. Throughout his life he appears to have been happiest as a cathedral schoolmaster; indeed, many of the best records concerning his work are the writings of his pupils. Such a man appealed to Otto III, and the three brief years of Gerbert's papacy and Otto's cooperation suggest the possibilities inherent in imperial direction of the papacy. But the alliance was premature, for the cooperation of the factions in central Italy was still necessary for a strong papacy, and after 1002 the papacy once again became a pawn in these factional struggles.

Within a decade of Otto's and Gerbert's deaths, the papacy fell into the hands of the dynasty of the counts of Tusculum, and three pontificates, those of Benedict VIII (1012–1024), John XIX (1024–1032), and Benedict IX (1032–1044), continued this dynasty's power for thirty years. A revolt drove Benedict IX from the papal throne, only to put in his place Sylvester III (1044–1045), a representative of yet another aristocratic faction. The insecurity of Sylvester, however, and the threats of Benedict led a proponent of reform, Gregory VI (1045–1046), to purchase Benedict's acquiescence in vacating the papacy. Gregory VI was a man dedicated to reform and possessed of high principles, but the circumstances of his elevation encouraged reformers from beyond the Alps to intervene and establish a canonically proper pope. At the Synod of Sutri in 1046, Emperor Henry III, in what must be regarded as the height of the Carolingian theocratic imperial style, deposed Gregory, and, for good measure, Benedict and Sylvester as well. In their place, after having himself made *patricius,* and therefore technically in charge of papal elections, Henry installed a series of German popes, all loyal to imperial policies and all genuinely committed to the principles of reform. Of these popes, the most remarkable and effective was Bruno of Toul, Pope Leo IX (1049–1054). Leo brought with him representatives of the reform movements in Lorraine and Burgundy, who in turn expressed their vision of a reformed Church and papacy in their daily administration of papal affairs. Leo traveled across the Alps frequently, holding reform councils and synods, and his aides, particularly Cardinal Humbert of Silva Candida, slowly brought the earlier reform enthusiasm to bear on the idea of papal authority. Thus, one of the first results of the diverse reform movements and their different aims was to train a cadre of reformers who came to Rome in the train of Leo IX and pressed the idea of widespread moral reform into the service of the idea of papal authority. Henceforth, reform movements might pull in several different directions, but the strand that concerned ecclesiology and the authority of the pope remained strongest. The new stature of the pope was felt not only in France and Germany, but in Byzantium as well when, in 1054, Cardinal Humbert excommunicated the patriarch of Constantinople, Michael Kerularios, and briefly launched one of the most important of the schisms that separated Greek and Latin Christianity throughout much of the next nine hundred years (see Chapter 17).

Among those associated with Leo IX were a number of remarkable men. Cardinal Humbert was one of the most intense, prolific, and stubborn reformers the Church had ever seen; Frederick, son of the duke of Lotharingia, was chancellor of the Roman church between 1051 and 1055 and later became pope as Stephen IX (1057–1058); Hildebrand, a native Roman and a former chaplain of Pope Gregory VI, returned to Rome with Leo and entered papal service as an administrator, establishing a center for local Roman reform movements. At the hands of these reformers, the viability of papal governance of the Church became a reality for the first time in more than two centuries. The practices of simony, clerical marriage, and papal authority produced a significant body of literature that drew upon authorities in the distant past and took the varied forms of treatises, particularly those of Humbert, and collections of ecclesiastical laws, of which the *Collection in 74 Titles,* compiled in Rome, possibly under Humbert's direction, first established papal authority over the universal Church in the form of a legal code.

Such reformers as Humbert were often intransigent in the positions they took, and they encountered strong opposition. Humbert, for example, argued that not only should simoniacal bishops (those who had purchased their offices) be deposed as uncanonical, but that ordinations to the priesthood performed by them should be declared invalid. Against such uncompromising positions, such reformers as St. Peter Damian (1007–1072) argued a less rigorous position, that such ordinations did not depend upon the state of grace of the bishop and were therefore valid. Throughout the 1040s and 1050s, Peter Damian had been a part of the movement of ascetic monastic reform that had swept central and northern Italy, numbering among its leaders St. Nilus and St. Romuald, and influencing the Ottonian emperors and such important figures in northern Europe as St. Adalbert of Prague. As part of the movement consequent to Leo IX's papacy, Peter Damian was made a cardinal in 1057. His literary works dealt directly with the problems of clerical incontinence and simony. Representing a different strand of the reform movement from that of Cardinal Humbert, his views reflect the different emphases that reform enthusiasts might have. It is important to remember that the movement generally labeled Eleventh-Century Ecclesiastical Reform had many different facets and focuses, and that the practices and influences of such different centers of reform as Cluny, Lotharingia, northern Italy, and Rome did not always coincide or agree. Indeed, the variety of reform emphases and the central role of the papacy contributed much to the complex history of the Church in the twelfth and thirteenth centuries.

Like most popes, Leo IX also faced problems of a more purely political character closer to Rome. Not only was the threat of local aristocratic domination not obliterated, it revived after Leo's death when an opponent of Henry III, Godfrey of Lotharingia, married the marchioness of Tuscany and established and antiimperial influence in northern Italy, an influence that extended to Rome itself when Godfrey's brother Frederick became Pope Stephen IX in 1057. A greater threat emerged to the south of Rome. Early in the eleventh century, possibly through papal efforts, a group of Norman warriors joined local Lombard resistance to Byzantine rule, which had recently been strengthened by the efforts of Basil II. For the next several decades, more and more Normans descended into South Italy, and one of them, William Iron-Arm, son of Tancred of Hauteville, established himself as count of Apulia in conquered Byzantine territory in 1042. By 1050, the Norman principality had extended into Benevento, and in 1053 Pope Leo IX led a papal army against the Normans. The pope's defeat and his embarrassing imprisonment contributed to his death in 1054, and the establishment of a Norman principality in South Italy had become a reality.

The successors of Leo IX continued some of his reform measures, but two events in the next two years drastically transformed the alignments of power upon which much of the stability of the papacy and the empire depended. At Leo's death in 1054, Henry III's chancellor, Gebehard of Eichstätt, became pope as Victor II. In 1056 Henry III died, leaving only his five-year-old son Henry IV under the regency of his widow, Agnes of Poitou. In 1057 Victor II died, leaving an important papal vacancy at precisely the moment when imperial authority was at its lowest ebb in a century. After a turbulent conflict, Bishop Gerard of Florence, a Burgundian, was elected pope as Nicholas II (1059–1061). The progress of reform since the accession of Leo IX in 1049 and the strong papal overtones of such thinkers as Humbert focused papal energies upon the question of lay domination much more strongly. In 1059 Nicholas issued a decree concerning papal elections in which he declared that only the clergy and people of Rome were to have the right of designating and electing the pope. The decree of 1059 also forbade, for the first time, the acceptance of a church by a cleric from the hands of a layman. Although this decree was not aimed directly at the imperial relationship with the Church, it could be, and later was, so applied.

Another disputed papal election placed Alexander II (1061–1073) on the papal throne. Under Alexander the signs of renewed papal authority grew stronger. The reform of France was well under way.

The claims of William, duke of Normandy, to the throne of England in 1066 were strengthened by papal approval. The Church of Aragón adopted the Roman liturgy in place of the Mozarabic. In 1059, Robert Guiscard, the Norman ruler of Apulia, swore an oath of allegiance to the pope, thus reconciling the papal-Norman hostility. And in 1071 and 1072 the Normans of South Italy attacked and captured two strongholds that represented as much as anything the turning of the tide in the Mediterranean in favor of Europe—in 1071 Bari, the last Byzantine stronghold, and in 1072, Palermo in Sicily, an Arab stronghold. At the death of Alexander II in 1073, the fruits of the reform movement had given shape to a universal church directed by a strong and respected papacy.

THE PONTIFICATE OF GREGORY VII AND THE IMPERIAL CONFLICT

Hildebrand, chaplain of Gregory VI and administrator of papal affairs under Alexander II, was born in Tuscany and spent most of his life in one capacity or another in papal circles in Rome. Possessing no aristocratic connections and harboring a fierce, perhaps mystical, reverence for St. Peter and the city of Rome, Hildebrand professed as a monk, probably at Rome before 1046, shared the exile of Gregory VI in Germany, may have resided at Cluny in 1047–1048, and returned to Rome, as we have seen, in the train of Leo IX. Under Leo and his successors, Hildebrand exercised considerable influence. He became archdeacon in 1059 and chancellor of the pope sometime after 1060. During the funeral ceremonies of the deceased Pope Alexander II, Hildebrand was acclaimed pope, most likely irregularly; only later was he elected formally by the cardinals and the clergy of Rome. He took the papal name of his first patron and became Pope Gregory VII; he was about fifty years old at his election.

Gregory VII's reform policies were not identical with those of Cluny, Lotharingia, the imperial church, or even the local Italian reformers. His youth had been spent in the current of reform movements, but his rejection of withdrawal from the world in favor of reform of the world and his fierce devotion to the papacy and its patrons, SS. Peter and Paul, mark him as a genuinely individual reformer, one about whom even the closest contemporaries differed sharply in their assessments. St. Peter Damian referred to him as a "holy Satan;" St. Hugh, abbot of Cluny, wondered at Gregory's miraculous rise to great office, and the great Countess Matilda of Tuscany, daughter of Beatrice and stepdaughter of Godfrey of Lotharingia, became an intimate correspondent, one of the few Gregory possessed. Others drew back. Cardinal Hugh the White parted company with Gregory after a career in the service of the papacy in France and Spain; many transalpine bishops bristled at

Gregory's claims of universal jurisdiction for the papacy; finally, Emperor Henry IV repudiated Gregory, calling him a "false monk" and demanding that he step down from the throne of St. Peter, which he had stolen. Not only did eminent contemporaries differ about Gregory VII, but the vast amount of literature that was produced during his pontificate debated questions of ecclesiastical governance, temporal power and authority, and the proper order of the world with a vehemence and passion that is as surprising as it is sudden. Gregory's pontificate touched remarkably sensitive issues, and his actions and statements gave a new focus and a new intensity not only to the question of papal authority, but to that of the right ordering of the world.

Reformers such as Pope Leo IX (b. ca. 1002) and Peter Damian (b. ca. 1007) belonged to an earlier generation than Gregory, and they had witnessed in their own lifetimes the developing movements for reform in Lotharingia and northern Italy. Both cooperated willingly with the imperial domination of the reform movement, and their world views, if these can be spoken of casually, were not essentially different from the old Carolingian traditions of ecclesiastical-imperial reform. Leo and Peter belonged to the generation of Henry III. Occasionally, a member of this generation, such as Cardinal Humbert, might be more outspoken than they, but even Humbert was checked by other voices. Gregory, on the other hand, grew to manhood during Leo's pontificate, and his consciousness of the need for reform extended to a truly universalist viewpoint, one that possessed none of the loyalties that conditioned the work of men such as Leo and Peter Damian. Gregory saw the cause of abuses not in specific incidents that might be corrected, but in the whole ordering of the world; Gregory engaged in a great debate on the meaning of *Christianitas,* Christendom, between the two powers most responsible for it, the pope and the emperor. For Gregory, the problem was not primarily lay investiture of clerics, clerical incontinence, or the various forms of simony, but the structure of authority that created conditions in which these abuses could happen. Against the Carolingian-theocratic emperor, the Carolingian-independent bishops and archbishops, the great independent monasteries, and hostile political powers, Gregory set an alternative vision of contending societies on earth—Christian society and the city of Satan. Only the pope, at the head of Christian society and strengthened by the merits of St. Peter, could fulfill God's plan for the world; any challenge to such an ordering constituted a threat from the forces of Satan and had to be countered by whatever powers were required. Thus, part of Gregory's pontificate was devoted to outlining systematically the nature and history of papal authority. To this end, Gregory had his subordinates search out old collections of laws and literature, and some of the materials they found, particularly those touching papal authority, came from the great collections of forgeries that were produced in the ninth century, particularly the collection called Pseudo-Isidore. The *Dictatus Papae,* a list of papal powers and privileges intended to serve as an index of the diverse aspects of papal authority, was written by Gregory VII and included in the official register of his correspondence. Gregory's colleague Anselm II of Lucca published a collection of ecclesiastical law that focused upon papal authority, as the earlier *Collection in 74 Titles* had done. Gregory certainly had no intention of continuously invoking the most novel and extreme of the claims made on the pope's behalf, but in the process of organizing the authority of the pope, describing it in collections of canon law, and building an administrative system through which it was distributed regularly and effectively, he contributed substantially to the foundations of papal power in the twelfth and thirteenth centuries. Papal legates moved throughout Europe, and in some places permanent legates were established. The clergy of Rome, hitherto important chiefly for its liturgical functions, grew into an administrative body of the papal court, and the cardinals, titled priests, deacons, and bishops of key Roman churches slowly grew into an administrative body surrounding the pope. In the realm of ideas and in the affairs of day-to-day church governance, the pontificate of Gregory VII transformed and increased the theory and practice of papal power.

The public to whom Gregory and his supporters appealed was, as we have seen, wide and varied. In Cluniac circles, reform depended both upon Cluny's unique subordination only to St. Peter and upon the cooperation of the system's aristocratic patrons; in imperial Germany, reform was supported by the imperial church, its leaders appointed by the emperor and guided by the influences of reform monasticism such as those emanating from Gorze or Einsiedeln or St. Maximin at Trier; in England after 1066 it depended upon the mutual respect and cooperation between the pope and the king. In addition to these alliances and diverse publics, there was another. The reform movements had touched lower levels of society than the aristocracy, and in some cases higher authorities, even the papacy itself, supported the lower orders at the expense of legitimate and traditional, but unreformed, higher clergy. In Milan, a town whose population was growing and whose church still drew upon the immense prestige of its early leader, St. Ambrose, a revolt broke out in 1057. Led by priests and noblemen, the revolt attacked unreformed clergy, particularly the institution of clerical marriage. The efforts of the papacy to reach a compromise—which included sending to Milan at different times personages no less than Hildebrand, Peter Damian, and Anselm I of Lucca (later Pope Alexander II)—lasted for only nine years. In 1066 the revolt broke out again, and in 1070 the old Archbishop Guido of Milan resigned. The revolt of the *Pataria,* as the Milanese movement is called, spread to other cities in northern Italy, and these reform movements linked papacy and people against traditional episcopal authority.

The events in Milan following the resignation of Guido precipitated even greater clashes. The archbishopric of Milan, one of the most important ecclesiastical offices in northern Italy, and hence particularly important in the structure of the imperial church, was resigned to Emperor Henry IV, who appointed a candidate of his choice to the post. The topic of proper canonical election to ecclesiastical office, however, had come to the fore in the struggles over simony throughout the last half of the eleventh century, and the Milanese rebels, supported by the papacy, rejected the imperial candidate and elected another. Because the emperor remained firm in his choice, the Roman Synod of 1073 excommunicated five royal advisers for their role in perpetuating a simoniacal appointment.

The ensuing conflict between pope and emperor occupied the rulers of the Christian world for the next fifty years and drastically transformed both the old Carolingian structure of papal-imperial relations and the rulership of Germany. Although the conflict was not the only focus of the reform movement in the last quarter of the eleventh century and the first quarter of the twelfth, its actors were so prominent and its literature so broad and vigorous that it often overshadows other aspects of the relations between clerical and temporal power. With these reservations in mind, let us consider first the relative positions of Gregory VII and Henry IV up to 1073, then the course of their conflict until Gregory's death in 1085, and, in the following section of this chapter, the course of the struggle up to the Concordat of Worms of 1122 and the First Lateran Council of 1123.

Upon the death of Henry III in 1056, Henry IV succeeded to the German crown; he was five years old. Under the regency of his mother, Empress Agnes, and her counselors, the great imperial state shaped by the Saxon and early Salian emperors was threatened. Henry II, Conrad II, and Henry III had painstakingly attempted to shape a structure of governance by relying, in turn, upon the court bishops, the counts and lesser nobility, and the imperial church and the *ministerialis* class. The emperors had, generally successfully, regained lands formerly alienated from the royal domain. They had exploited the tenth-century silver mines at Rammelsberg and tentatively established a central residence at Goslar. Throughout much of Germany, imperial castles garrisoned by *ministeriales* represented royal authority. These attempts to establish a firm royal governance in Germany were countered by other forces. The general lack of ties of vassalage among the nobility and the disproportionately large number of free nobility and peasants meant that the king was more the king of each of his subjects individually than the king of them as a group, and many evaded royal control while consolidating their own power by depriving others of their freedom and by establishing rival monastic foundations whose control remained in their own hands. Much of the emperors' efforts had been directed toward Saxony, the least organized of all the duchies, and in 1070, 1073, and 1075, revolts in Saxony called forth repressive measures on the part of Henry IV. Henry had to depend more than ever upon the *ministeriales* and the imperial ecclesiastical hierarchy, and the crisis over the archbishopric of Milan between 1070 and 1073 pitted a powerful and successful emperor against a determined and zealous pope.

Between 1073 and 1075, Gregory did not press his newly enunciated powers against Henry, but Roman synods pronounced very strong regulations against lay investiture during these years. In 1076, a diet of German bishops meeting at Worms withdrew their obedience from Gregory, and Henry IV, as *patricius*, addressed a stinging letter not to Gregory VII but to "Hildebrand, not pope but a false monk." In Lent of the same year, at the Roman Synod, Gregory formally declared the emperor excommunicated and deposed, or at least suspended, from his imperial authority. Dissident elements in Germany quickly supported the pope, and the old resentment at Salian governmental policies flared up again, this time with a new and greater cause to which to attach itself. Henry, in one of the most dramatic moves of the conflict, crossed the Alps and in January, 1077, presented himself as a formal penitent before the castle of Canossa, where the pope was staying before crossing into Germany, and asked for absolution from the cleric who had condemned him. Inside the castle were Matilda, countess of Tuscany and a vassal of Henry, and Abbot Hugh of Cluny, Henry's godfather. At their request, Gregory absolved Henry, thus undercutting the resistance of the German nobility to Henry and alienating their cause from Gregory's own. The German dissidents, frustrated at what they considered the pope's betrayal of their cause, elected an antiking, Rudolph of Rheinfelden, and for three years civil war tore Germany.

Relations between Henry and Gregory broke down again, though, and again Henry was excommunicated and deposed, Gregory in turn recognizing Rudolph. The second excommunication and deposition, however, had an effect far less than the first, and the terms according to which Gregory recognized Rudolph were unpalatable to both the new king and his adherents. When Henry restored his own power in Germany and defeated Rudolph in 1080, he turned his full energies against Gregory. The Synods of Bamberg and Mainz in 1080 renounced obedience to Gregory and elected the archbishop of Ravenna, Guibert, as pope. Guibert took the title Clement III, and as an anti-pope he played an important role in central Italy and Rome until 1100. Henry entered Rome in 1084. There, he witnessed the election of Clement III and his own coronation as emperor by Clement. Gregory, shut up in the impregnable Castel Sant' Angelo, called for his Norman allies in South Italy, and Robert Guiscard led a formidable army into Rome, driving out Henry and rescuing Gregory but sacking and burning the city as well. Gregory, forced to flee amid the curses of the Romans, went south with Guiscard's army to Salerno, where he died on May 25, 1085. The quarrel between Gregory and Henry, precipitated by the irreconcilable needs of the German monarch and the dogmatic inflexibility of the pope, plunged the papacy once again into a political crisis. But the papacy had grown immeasurably stronger since the days before Leo IX, and its resiliency is nowhere better expressed than in the sequence of popes between Victor III (1086–1087) and Calixtus II (1119–1124), under whom the conflict was continued and finally resolved.

CHRISTIANITAS: THE CONSEQUENCES OF REFORM AND CONFLICT

At the death of Gregory VII, Desiderius, the abbot of St. Benedict's monastery of Monte Cassino, was elected pope as Victor III. Victor's moderation and willingness to compromise were neglected, however, and at his death in 1087 the greatest of the reforming popes, Urban II, ascended the pontifical throne. Born Eudes of Châtillon around 1035 to a noble Burgundian family, Urban was educated at Reims. Around 1068 he entered the monastery of Cluny, where he rose to become prior, and in 1080 he left Cluny to enter the service of the papacy. He succeeded St. Peter Damian as Cardinal-Bishop of Ostia and served as Gregory VII's legate to Germany. He was elected pope in 1088 at the age of fifty-three. Urban shared the reform convictions of Gregory, but in addition he possessed wide experience, great tact and diplomatic expertise, and personal contacts with the most powerful figures in Europe. The new Latin church in South Italy, the church in Spain and England, and the great network of Cluniac affiliations throughout France all supported Urban vigorously and loyally. By compromise and generosity, he won the allegiance of former supporters of Henry and further undercut the antipope Clement III. Urban's patronage promoted a new flowering of monastic culture, and his administrative reforms, coupled with the work of a brilliant generation of canon lawyers, greatly strengthened the practical powers of the papacy.

In addition to his extraordinary ability as an organizer and diplomat, Urban, more than Gregory VII, was in sympathy with wider attitudes concerning the nature of religious reform. The Peace and Truce of God in particular received his blessing, and at the Council of Clermont in 1095, Urban proclaimed the Peace and Truce for the first time throughout all of Christendom. His monastic and aristocratic contacts kept Urban well informed, and his awareness of widespread attitudes and values helped shore up the strength of his papacy. Nowhere is Urban's appeal and knowledge of the spiritual climate of his age better illustrated than in his promulgation of the First Crusade (see Chapter 17). His success and energy reduced Emperor Henry IV to impotence, and at Urban's death in 1099, two weeks after Jerusalem was captured by the crusaders, the papacy was in a stronger position than at any time since the accession of Gregory VII.

Urban was succeeded by Paschal II (1099–1118), who had been a monk in Italy and later Cardinal-Priest of San Clemente. During Paschal's pontificate, a number of attempts to settle the problem of lay investiture were made. The tacit freedom of the kings of England to invest their own high clergy came to an end in the conflict between King Henry I (1100–1135) and his archbishop of Canterbury, St. Anselm (1033–1109), which was resolved by a formal agreement in 1107, according to which the king ceased to invest his high clergy with the ring and crozier as well as ceasing to receive an oath of homage. The year 1107 also witnessed the reconciliation of the papacy with the excommunicated king of France, Philip I, and his son and successor Louis VI. In Germany, however, the intransigence of Henry IV, who died in 1106, and of Henry V (1106–1125) prolonged the conflict between pope and emperor, which extended dramatically to the capture of Paschal by Henry V in 1111 and Paschal's suggestion that the higher clergy divest themselves of all secular property and obligations, a suggestion bitterly rejected by the reform clergy. Paschal died in 1118 and was succeeded by the short-lived Gelasius II (1118–1119). Not until the pontificate of Calixtus II (1119–1124), the Burgundian archbishop of Vienne, was the conflict between papacy and empire settled by the Concordat of Worms in 1122. According to its terms, the emperor retained the right to oversee the free election of prelates, to decide between disputed candidates, and to confer the temporal privileges by means of the scepter. However, the emperor gave up the right of investiture with ring and crozier.

Between 1050 and 1125, the diverse strands of the reform movement within the Church and society had focused upon the papacy, sometimes inadvertently but more often deliberately. The issues of reform, ranging from clerical incontinence to the high constitutional question of investiture in Germany and England, tend to be overshadowed in their variety and spheres of appeal by the great papal-imperial conflict that has long been labeled the Investiture Contest. The dispute over investitures, as we have seen, precipitated a clash between emperor and pope that may be considered, in one respect, as the result of a particular set of political circumstances and personalities that arose between 1070 and 1076, and in another, as the ultimate collision of two conflicting visions of the world. The old Carolingian tradition, on the one hand, and the new vision of Christian society viewed by Gregory VII, Urban II, and their supporters among the reform movement, on the other hand, were ultimately incompatible. Yet elsewhere than in Germany and Italy, traditional and reform views became reconciled and accommodated each other more readily, particularly in France, England, and Spain. The constitutional role of the German bishops, however, unlike that of high clergy elsewhere, precipitated the conflict, and at its end the papacy emerged stronger than ever, whereas the German constitution was transformed forever and the monarchy was forced to seek new resources elsewhere. The age of theocratic kingship in Germany, which stretched from Otto I to Henry III, was over. The reform movement had entered the service of the papacy.

What emerged in the later twelfth century was a new Church as well as a new empire, and the investiture conflict must not overshadow the wider transformation of that Church. We have seen the changing role of the papacy and the position of individual popes, and witnessed the growth of papal collections of ecclesiastical law, papal letters, and increased organization in the administration of papal affairs. The cardinals became political advisers; a secretariat was established to regularize papal correspondence, and the form of papal correspondence was regularized; papal finances were also regularized: under Urban II, they were modeled upon the financial structure of Cluny. By precipitating conflicts and challenging traditional ecclesiastical structures, the long reform movement helped produce a vocabulary of concepts concerning rights, property, obligations, and legal responsibilities that was much more specific than earlier ideas and could be handled in juridical fashion more effectively. Indeed, the new juridical atmosphere of the papal court, the collections of canon law that followed those of the late eleventh century, and the juridical definition of papal and imperial powers strongly characterized the Church of the twelfth and thirteenth centuries. Traditional sources of relatively independent power, such as the bishoprics, slowly became worked into a hierarchical system that was headed by the pope and Curia and limited by the growing canonical authority of archdeacons and cathedral chapters. Legal appeals from local ecclesiastical courts to Rome increased, as did the papal habit of appointing judges delegate with pontifical authority to hear appeals locally. In terms of organization and structure, one of the most striking results of the events between 1050 and 1125 was the better articulated structure of the Church itself.

Yet the process of institutional reform was slow, and there was no evident completed model toward which reforms tended to point. Areas outside of ecclesiastical organization were also touched by the reform movement. Stripped of their Carolingian sacral character, an example of which is the increasing denial by Gregorian reformers that royal anointing conferred any sacramental qualities at all, temporal rulers during the twelfth century began to develop what some historians have called "the birth of a political consciousness" in spheres that had been sharply defined by the literature of the conflict. Monasticism, very close at the outset of the reforming movement to the world of temporal activity, now withdrew from that world. New monastic orders shunned the pomp and civility of Cluny and established their monasteries in the wilderness and instituted harshly ascetic rules. Accompanying this last great flowering of monasticism (see Chapter 21) were new religious movements among the lower clergy and the laity. Public preaching, communal groups of laypeople living religious lives, the new sharper differentiation between clerical and lay status, with its particular emphasis upon the priestly state, and the growth of new forms of education and a new pastoralism all transformed the Church from what it had been in 1050, and the concept of *Christianitas* along with it.

The old Carolingian world view of the emperor ruling the temporal and spiritual orders was replaced by a new, Gregorian vision of a universal church comprising all of society, at whose head stood the pope, who could call upon secular rulers for aid but could never be subordinate to them. *Christianitas,* Christendom, could be regarded as a single society, one for which Pope Urban could proclaim the Peace and Truce of God at Clermont in 1095. It was also a society that Urban could urge, at the end of the Council of Clermont, to take up the sword in defense of itself against the heathen. For after the conflict between papacy and empire, the Crusade movement is the most immediately striking demonstration of the new concept of Christian society.

17

CHRISTENDOM EAST AND WEST, 1025-1150

CHRISTIANITAS: THE ACCULTURATION OF AN IDEA

Homo peregrinus—man the pilgrim—was long a motif in Christian literature, as evidenced by a range of references from the purely figurative to the literal. Gregory the Great (590–604) mingled both senses when he wrote, "This life is only a pilgrimage: and to him who yearns for his true homeland, the place of pilgrimage is a torment." From the eighth century on, pilgrimages came to be assigned as part of, and sometimes in place of, public penances, and the tenth and eleventh centuries witnessed the proliferation of pilgrimages and the building of pilgrimage churches, which allowed the pilgrim not only to pray, but to perambulate the relics he or she had come to venerate.

One's own diocesan church or a purely local shrine was the goal of most pilgrimages. Few Europeans in the tenth and eleventh centuries had business far from their homes, and those who did were often resented and suspect. The pilgrimage, however, was both an image of all people's lives and an institution in which Europeans might come to meet and know one another, for the long journeys contributed not only to the circulation of devotional forms and artistic motifs, but to the communication of ideas and images across Europe. Languages, local feelings, and the fearfully limited horizons of most people were all ameliorated on pilgrimage, and the great routes to Rome, Jerusalem, or Compostela drew together the elements of a religious culture at a period when few institutions existed to perform that function. Later, by the late twelfth century, the idea of pilgrimage had slowly changed into the ideal of the crusade, that of the wandering knight-errant and of the poor preacher living a life of wandering apostolic poverty. In the eleventh century, however, the literal attraction of a pilgrimage was powerful enough to draw ferocious Norman, Angevin, and Anglo-Saxon nobles away from their work at home and send them into unknown parts of the world. It drew the poor and the wealthy, and by constituting a common experience to all, it sharpened the self-consciousness of a particularly Christian society.

The pilgrimage routes were the home not only of much eleventh- and twelfth-century devotion, but of Romanesque art and architecture. The pilgrim churches, drawing upon gifts and talent, presented visually the great force of eleventh- and twelfth-century devotion. In such churches as that at the small monastery of St. Savin near Tours, images that before had decorated only manuscripts appeared in large frescoes; later, at Conques, Moissac, and Vézelay, they appeared in carved stone over the portals of the church and at the heads of columns. These images were drawn from the manuscript-illuminating traditions of the Apocalypse, the books of Genesis and Exodus, and early commentaries on the symbolic meaning of these texts. The most arresting images of all, however, are the scenes of the Last Judgment, set in brilliant relief on the tympanum (the space over the entrance) of such churches as that of St. Foy at Conques or Vézelay. These scenes, striking in their order and message, remind the Christian upon entering the church of the future judgment. The ecclesiastical decorations of Cluny, the energy of the southern French churches, and the pilgrim routes all suggest a new devotional vitality in the eleventh century.

In the society of Heaven, too, this devotion is reflected. Among the most popular saints of the eleventh century was St. Michael, as the angel who drove Satan from Heaven; he is depicted as a fighting warrior. The shrines to St. Michael, ranging from Mont St. Michel in Brittany to St. Michael of Monte Gargano in Italy, reflect the popularity of other warrior saints: St. James, St. George, St. Maurice, St. Demetrius, and St. Theodore. Divine judgment and aid, battle, pilgrimage, the liturgical blessing of weapons and prayers for victory in battle—all these must stand beside the other aspects of tenth- and eleventh-century devotion. They formed the cultural roots of late eleventh- and twelfth-century Christian society, engendered in many the response to monastic and papal reform movements, and underlay the process of changing social ranks and values.

In Spain, the reign of Alfonso VI of Castile (1065–1109) witnessed the growing wealth of the northern Spanish kingdoms, which was derived not from trade or manufacture, as in Italy or Flanders, but from the wealthy Moslem south, which paid tribute and booty to the northern princes. The wealth of these Christian kingdoms, particularly that of growing Castile, is reflected in Alfonso's contribution to Cluny, which financed the building of the great church known as Cluny III. Renewed communication with France and Italy brought influences from both areas into northern Spain. Considerable influence was exerted upon the newly wealthy and expanding Castile by, first, French warriors and pilgrims, and then, with the substitution of the Roman rite for the Mozarabic liturgy, by French churchmen and monastic foundations and by French and Italian merchants. In 1085 Alfonso captured Toledo, the ancient Visigothic capital, and by the end of the eleventh century he appears to have vindicated the idea of warfare against the infidel.

Alfonso's greatest servant, Rodrigo Diaz de Vivar, who was called El Cid (from the Arabic *Siddi,* chief), illustrates some of the varieties of military life in eleventh-century Christian Spain. Commander of Alfonso's armies, El Cid fell out with Alfonso in 1081, entered the service of Moslem princes, was briefly reconciled with the king, and then undertook to conquer Valencia for himself. The independence and occasional indifference of El Cid to Alfonso's political difficulties, his willingness to serve under Moslems, and his adventurousness in Valencia suggest that the ideal of a Christian warrior fighting God's war was not especially strong, although the epic poem produced in the late twelfth century, *El Cantar del Mio Cid,* turned the frontier adventurer and warlord into a model Christian warrior.

Other literary evidence from 1100 on also picked up the theme of heroic warriors performing God's work. The epic *Song of Roland,* written around 1100, depicts a heroic campaign of Charlemagne against the Moslems of Spain and the heroism and death of Charlemagne's nephew Roland in protecting the imperial army's retreat from Spain. The poem, a powerful vernacular epic, had as its origin a short entry in the Carolingian annals for the year 778. The historical events of these annals are transformed in the poem into a vision of world conflict between Christians and Moslems, the burdens of defending Christianity placed upon Charlemagne, and the heroic adventurousness of Christian knights. The new value found in knighthood, the blessing of the knight's weapons and the sacramentalizing of the order of knighthood itself, the association of warriors and clerics performing God's work, all gave a distinctive shape to the social and cultural values of a Europe that had but recently emerged from the military and social chaos of the late ninth and early tenth centuries. The legends of Moslem wealth in Spain, the reputation of Alfonso VI, the careers of El Cid and Roland, and the growth of the body of Charlemagne legends all contributed to such an image.

Besides the successful beginnings of the *reconquista* in Spain and the spread of the monastic and papal reform movements, there were other social forces at work to institutionalize some of the aspects of the idea of *Christianitas*. The new strength of Rome, supporting some traditional powers—kings and bishops—and challenging others, derived in part from the increased vigor of the papacy and in part from the traditional strength of the spiritual image of Rome—the image that had attracted the donation of the kingdoms of Poland and Hungary—and, later, Castile—to St. Peter, and had offered a new kind of freedom to monasteries such as Cluny and its dependencies. Other movements as well derived support from the practical implications of *Christianitas*. From the tenth century on, in a number of different centers, movements of clergy and laymen had sprung up with the intention of curbing the violence of private warfare. It was not for nothing that warlords gave lands and incomes to the church, undertook penitential pilgrimages, and sometimes became members of monastic communities at the end of their lives. The nobility that had saved Europe from the invasions of the late ninth and tenth centuries was hardly better than the invaders when it came to enforcing its own—whether real or imagined—rights and wants.

The idea of peace had been surrounded with spiritual legitimacy in the gospels and the writings of the church fathers and echoed in the canons of ecclesiastical councils down to the tenth century. At a council at Charroux, near Poitiers, in 989, an assembly of bishops pronounced a solemn condemnation, over relics, of anyone who should attack a cleric or rob the poor. From this date on, longer and longer lists of specific prohibitions against attacking certain classes of people were issued by ecclesiastical assemblies, frequently with local laymen joining in the pronouncements. By the mid eleventh century, the Peace of God had become formalized; it designated protected classes of persons and regulated the character of violence. The Peace of God protected certain persons; the Truce of God, which soon followed, protected certain times. At first the periods of Easter, Lent, and Advent, and later the period every week from sundown Wednesday to Monday, were declared to be free of violence.

These movements did not consist simply of pious pronouncements by ecclesiastics. Laymen joined in the acts of proclamation, and by the end of the eleventh century the peace associations had emerged as powerful local groups, joined by a common oath and secured by a willing armed force. In some areas, these groups grew powerful enough to be considered local governments in themselves, and in strong local principalities such as Normandy, the Peace of God became the Peace of the Duke. Emperor Henry III publicly preached a peace sermon in Cologne cathedral in 1043, and as the end of the century approached, peace movements, peace associations, and the concept of the Peace and Truce of God themselves acquired great emotional and institutional strength. The lords against whom many of these movements were directed often found themselves either facing strong resistance or being invited to participate in the movements themselves. In the latter instance, lords could further legitimate their military prowess by casting an air of sanctity over themselves as warriors and over their particular warlike functions.

The late eleventh and early twelfth centuries witnessed a new burst of anti-Moslem and anti-Jewish expression. Christian attitudes toward the Moslems were a mixture of curiosity and perverse misinformation. To Bede, the eighth-century English chronicler, the Moslems were the descendants of Hagar and Ishmael, the Old Testament outcasts. To others, they were one of the scourges sent by God as a punishment for the sinful Christian world. To others still, they were a schismatic Christian sect whose doctrines were a perversion of Christian doctrines (some even constructed an imaginary Moslem "Trinity" consisting of Mohammed, Apollo, and "Termagant"), a view that influenced Dante's placing of Mohammed in Hell as a schismatic. For those in Spain, Sicily, and Byzantium who dealt with Islam on a day-to-day basis, however, there was, to be sure, much mutual understanding and even cultural sympathy, and Carolingian attitudes toward Islam had been marked, one historian has observed, by "caution and sobriety." El Cid, as we have seen, could casually feud with Alfonso VI of Castile and enter the employment of Moslem leaders without apparent pangs of conscience. So too could—and did—many others. Away from the frontiers, however, the new Christian self-consciousness generated strong anti-Moslem attitudes.

Islamic views of Christendom were characterized largely by indifference and occasional scorn. Arabic geographers' interest in Europe grew slowly, and when it first appeared in the ninth century it was more a product of the Arabic study of Greek geographers, chiefly Ptolemy, than a reflection of intense curiosity.

The world beyond Europe was filled, for most thinking Europeans, with hostile peoples and, following the legendary anthropology of late antique encyclopedias, strange and mysterious creatures, part human and part beast. Such limited knowledge, fed by new hostility and a new conception of the warrior class within a new ideology of Christian society, heightened the potential militancy with which Latin Christians regarded Islam. Thus, a new consciousness of the place of Christendom in the world developed in the late tenth and eleventh centuries, one that was strengthened by institutional changes and by the operation of the ideals of religious reform. The relatively "open" ideological world of late Carolingian Europe had accommodated many different kinds of beliefs. In such a world as that of the late eleventh century, it would be an error to discount the place held by such ideas on the part of a knightly class and ecclesiastical reformers, the rest of whose lives seem to have been alarmingly short-sighted and intensely practical. It is precisely in these groups that intense outbursts of feeling occurred most frequently. The Apocalypse was heady reading, particularly when there was little else to read—in a world whose size and problems were only slowly entering into the European consciousness.

THE CRISIS OF THE BYZANTINE EMPIRE
IN THE ELEVENTH CENTURY

At the death of Emperor Basil II in 1025, the Byzantine frontiers and interior provinces were secure for the first time in two centuries. The Bulgarian Empire had become a Byzantine province; the frontier with Islam was firmly in Byzantine hands; Kievan Russia and Armenia had both come under strong Byzantine influence, and, for the first time since the seventh century, land communications had opened with the western parts of Europe—South Italy and western Greece constituting the westernmost reaches of imperial authority. Although religious tensions had existed periodically between Greek and Latin Christians, there was no conception of a permanent separation of the churches, and Byzantine diplomats had even contrived means of comprehending the "imperial" title of the Saxon emperors without compromising the position of the emperor of the Romans as head of the universal family of rulers. The stimulating intellectual and religious developments of ninth-century Byzantium constituted a firm cultural achievement, and Byzantine control of the seas and the internal economy assured the empire of prosperity. By the end of the eleventh century, however, Byzantium had experienced a crisis of monumental proportions. The Macedonian dynasty died out in 1056, and no stable succession was established until the accession of the military aristocrat Alexius I Comnenus (1081–1118). Internal political rivalry between military landowning aristocrats and the imperial bureaucracy, the decline of the free peasantry and the reintroduction of mercenary soldiery, the reduction of government finances through large-scale exemptions, and the growing competitiveness of Italian, particularly Venetian, traders in the eastern Mediterranean and the Black Sea all produced severe internal stresses. In turn, these were exacerbated by new attacks, from the Turks in the east, the Pechenegs in Bulgaria, and the Normans in South Italy and western Greece. From the reign of Alexius I until the capture of Constantinople by the Latins in 1204, Byzantine strength declined perceptibly, and Christendom was transformed.

The pressures that weakened Byzantium in the late eleventh century were not light; they included some of the most difficult internal and external crises that the empire ever experienced. With the annexation of Bulgaria, the frontier of the empire crossed the Danube once again and brought Byzantine forces face to face with the Turkic Pechenegs, who controlled the northern and northwestern Black Sea coasts and launched frequent raids into Byzantine-Bulgar territory throughout the century. To the east of the Pechenegs were the Cumans, and the pressures of these peoples on the great migration route through South Russia entailed considerable expenditures of men and money by Byzantium. The Pechenegs, Uzes, and Cumans, like other peoples before and after them, were among the Turkic peoples who occupied the western parts of central Asia. Between the eighth and the tenth centuries, many Turks had been converted to Islam, and Islam became a useful political and cultural tie between the Turkish ruling groups and the nomadic Turkish peoples. As various Turkish peoples were Islamicized, the political complexion of eastern Iran changed, and Iran itself became a Turkish principality. In 1055 a Turkish leader entered Baghdad as a "deliverer" of the caliph, and at the same time Turkish armies moved through northern Iran and Anatolia against Armenian and Byzantine positions. Tughrul (1055–1063) officially became the *sultan,* the military commander under the rule of the caliph. Under Tughrul and his successors, Alp Arslan (1063–1072) and Malik Shah (1072–1092), the power of the Seljuk Turks grew in the Middle East, threatening both Egypt and Byzantium. In 1071, the same year as the Norman capture of Bari, the armies of Alp Arslan encountered the forces of Romanus IV Diogenes (1062–1071) at Manzikert and destroyed the Byzantine army. The troubled political and military administration of eastern Anatolia collapsed, and on the fringes of the Byzantine Empire there emerged an expanding frontier population of Turkish Moslems and disaffected Armenians and Cappadocians that succeeded in withdrawing the Byzantine eastern frontier well into what is now western Turkey.

The pressures of Turkic nomads on the Danube, Black Sea, and Anatolian frontiers were not the only assaults on Byzantine territory during the late eleventh century. From the early part of the eleventh century, bands of Norman military adventurers had participated in the revolts of South Italy. By the third quarter of the century a great Norman principality had been established there and had launched an attempt to reconquer Sicily from the Arabs. The Normans played a powerful role in papal and Byzantine affairs during the late eleventh and twelfth centuries. In 1071, the same year as the Byzantine defeat at Manzikert, the Norman armies captured Bari, the last Byzantine stronghold in South Italy and launched attacks across the Adriatic Sea, temporarily capturing Durazzo and threatening the western provinces of Greece. These defeats along every frontier and, in the east, well into imperial provinces, drained the military force of the empire and exacerbated the political struggles that constituted the second dimension of the Byzantine crisis of the eleventh century.

Byzantine armies failed in the later eleventh century in part at least because they had been weakened in another contest, that between the powerful military landowning aristocracy and the imperial civil servants of the capital. The land and military reforms of the sixth and seventh centuries had stabilized both the Byzantine peasantry and the army. Peasant soldiers fought in the armies under their district leaders, and the thematic organization of the countryside from Italy, Carthage, and Anatolia to Greece became almost the surest sign of stable governmental administration. However, the troubles of the late eighth and ninth centuries, which included the danger posed by the armies to iconodule emperors and the drift of peasant land out of peasant possession and into that of wealthy landlords, both weakened the armies and hastened the transformation of the military aristocracy into a wealthy, privileged landholding class. Under Romanus Lecapenus and Basil II in the tenth century, this aristocracy had been checked—in part by laws and in part by imperial force. In the course of the eleventh century, however, a series of internal disputes precipitated another crisis between the military aristocracy and the civil servants.

Basil II, who died in 1025, was succeeded by his brother Constantine VIII (1025–1028) and then, for the next twenty-eight years, by Constantine's daughters, Zoe and Theodora, and Zoe's three successive husbands, Romanus III (1028–1034), Michael IV (1034–1041), and Constantine IX Monomachus (1042–1055). Theodora's death in 1056 was followed by the accession of a series of short-reigning emperors who were compelled to engage in intrigue and political alliances and factionalism in order to maintain their power. For nearly half a century, the direction of the empire drifted while civil servants and military aristocrats fought one another in the absence of that key element of earlier Byzantine success, a strong emperor. Not until the triumph of the military aristocracy and the establishment of the strong Comnenian dynasty in the person of Alexius I Comnenus (1081–1118), whose thirty-seven-year reign did much to stabilize the empire, did a strong imperial hand once again take up the government of the empire and recognize fully the extent of its difficulties.

The struggle between bureaucrats and aristocrats occurred on a formidable scale. Immense wealth and power on the one hand, and a highly cultured, efficient bureaucratic elite on the other, jockeyed for position against each other with disastrous consequences. Public finance was eroded by the increasing frequency of aristocratic exemption from taxes, the increasingly large budget of the imperial courts, and the inroads of Italian trade into the Byzantine sphere. By the middle of the eleventh century, the great Byzantine gold coin, the *nomisma* or bezant, had been devalued, and the other strong support of the empire, the army, had been weakened because of the rivalry among the great factions. The invasions of the late eleventh century, then, struck an empire that had, within the half-century from Basil II to Alexius I, drastically reduced its ability to resist them.

The new invasions and the internal political struggle, with their attendant consequences for finance and the army, reduced the ability of the empire to respond to a rapidly changing world. The Slavic kingdoms and principalities that surrounded the core of the empire were restive; Italian traders, fresh from their successes against Moslem sea power, encroached upon the maritime commerce of the empire; ambitious Norman lords looked hungrily at the throne of the empire itself; Turks, Pechenegs, Uzes, and Cumans ranged in the heartlands of the Black Sea littoral and Anatolia. The *Chronographia* of Michael Psellus, a Byzantine courtier and civil servant, depicts with verve and color, but with an ominous indifference to larger issues, the period from 976 to 1078, and offers a singularly partisan narrative of what was perhaps the most critical century in Byzantine history.

Nor was the crisis without a religious dimension. The religious crises of iconoclasm in the eighth century, the Balkan rivalry and the Photian Schism of the late ninth century and ecclesiastical rivalries in the early eleventh century had placed great stress upon Byzantine society and culture. The great flowering of Byzantium between the ninth and the late eleventh centuries had included the spread of the remarkable Byzantine religious culture within and outside the empire. The position of the patriarch of Constantinople was strengthened by the reception of new territories under his jurisdiction—lands in and beyond the Balkans and in eastern and southern Anatolia. And from the middle of the tenth century, Byzantine monasticism was reinvigorated by the growing settlement of monastic houses on Mt. Athos, the "holy mountain." The Byzantine liturgy and church decoration, which in themselves absorbed much of the creative vision and energy that in other societies was reflected in secular literature and art, reflected a highly developed and complex orthodoxy. Out of the early religious struggles and the great combats of the eighth and ninth centuries there had emerged a powerful and enduring ecclesiastical structure, one that has survived both the empire itself and all of the distractions of the modern world. The Church had survived its innumerable quarrels with the emperors. The patriarchate of Constantinople under Polyeuctus (956–970) was strengthened against imperial intervention in ecclesiastical affairs, and under the brilliant, headstrong Michael Kerularius (1043–1058), both the patriarchate and the relations between the Latin and Greek churches experienced a crisis.

The difficulties of the bishops of Rome in the late ninth and tenth centuries were many, and their association with the new German imperial line and with the Norman conquest of South Italy had strained relations with Byzantium, as had the growing independence of the patriarch of Constantinople. The citizens of Constantinople possessed a growing conviction that only in their churches was a proper liturgy performed, and only in their ecclesiastical institutions was the law of God followed properly. The estrangements between Greek East and Latin West were many, some of considerable importance and some relatively trivial. The cumulative effects of such hostility, however, were profound, and under Michael Kerularius events brought this broad hostility to a temporary head. In a letter of bitter complaint Kerularius denounced Roman rites and practices, and in turn Pope Leo IX assigned the equally fiery and zealous Cardinal Humbert (see Chapter 16) to answer him. Humbert responded in an insulting letter and then, in 1054, went to Constantinople on a legation whose purpose, at least, was to smooth differences over. Disputes concerning protocol immediately broke out, each side took offense, and the cardinal laid a bull of excommunication of the patriarch on the altar of Hagia Sophia on July 16, 1054. At a Byzantine synod a week later, the cardinal and his party were in turn excommunicated, and the Schism of 1054, whose roots reached into the past, had begun. Although these excommunications were not lifted until 1965, the Schism of 1054 must not be exaggerated. It was not the first such break, nor was it the last, and certainly no one in 1054 regarded it as permanent. The events in Italy and Germany, papal reform ideas, the personalities of Humbert and Kerularius, and the orthodox faith of the Byzantines all contributed to the momentary focus upon differences that had necessarily grown up in three hundred years of separation, different cultural developments, and frequent misunderstandings.

In the 1070s, relations between Pope Gregory VII and Emperor Michael VII improved, even to the point of Gregory's suggesting that he himself lead a large army against the Turks and thus preserve pilgrimage routes to the Holy Land and help restore the unity of Christian society. These plans came to nothing during Gregory's and Michael's lifetimes, but by 1089 Pope Urban II (1088–1099) and Emperor Alexius I had reached a new agreement concerning the rights of Latins in Constantinople. Alexius's need for soldiers by 1095 and his restored relations with Urban II led him to send legates to the Council of Piacenza in 1095 requesting military aid for the defense of the empire. The prospects of shoring up the empire's defenses, reuniting Christianity, and restoring universal orthodoxy inspired Urban's favorable response to the request, and as Urban set out for the Council of Clermont shortly thereafter, the prospects of western aid being granted to Byzantium looked particularly strong.

HOLY WAR AND SINFUL SOCIETY: POPE URBAN II AND THE "PILGRIMAGE" TO JERUSALEM

The period between the eighth and the twelfth centuries witnessed many changes in the culture of Christian Europe, none of them of greater consequence than the changing attitudes toward war and its legitimacy. Early in Christian history St. Augustine had worked out a theory of limited justification for war. The war had, first, to be defensive and lawfully declared by legitimate authority. Soldiers must fight only in obedience to the commands of their superiors, and they must fight not out of hate, but out of the love of justice. The only exceptions to these rules were that wars might be offensive against a state that refused to rectify the wrongs done by its citizens to the citizens of another state, or against a state that refused to return wrongfully seized property. Such a theory sufficed not to stop Christians from going to war, but to prevent the development of wider theories before the ninth and tenth centuries. In the histories of Gregory of Tours and Bede, Christian kings waged legitimate wars to defend their peoples against bad Christians and pagans. In the legendary histories of Charlemagne and Alfred the Great, warfare became a common attribute of the sanctified king. Although liturgy and moral theology ringed warfare with severe strictures, including heavy penances, the pressures from defenseless clergy and the new aristocracy seeking spiritual legitimacy grew strong. North of the Alps, liturgies developed for the blessing of weapons and banners. The growth of the Peace and Truce of God justified forceful repression of those who broke the peace, and a new veneration of military saints spread widely in the tenth and eleventh centuries.

During the ninth and tenth centuries, military conflicts in Italy and on the Christian frontiers were frequently described as having divine approval. When Alfonso VI of Castile conquered Toledo in 1085, his reputation as a Christian hero grew. When in 1086 he was badly defeated at Sagrajas, his defeat was regarded as a disaster for Christianity. Military success, however, fell with greater frequency to the Christian side of many conflicts. By 1000 Venice had driven the Moslems from Bari and controlled the Adriatic. By the early eleventh century Corsica and Sardinia were cleared of Moslems. In 1087 the combined fleets of Pisa, Genoa, Rome, and Amalfi successfully attacked the North African city of Mahdiya; earlier, the Pisans themselves had conducted a similar raid on Moslem Palermo in Sicily. These were not, of course, ecclesiastically sanctioned wars, and the merchant-warriors of the Italian cities probably did not regard themselves as God's warriors, but the victories in Mediterranean and Germanic lands gave considerable impetus to the idea of force used against pagans occupying formerly Christian lands.

The papal wars in the ninth, tenth, and eleventh centuries in central Italy also contributed to a new idea of legitimate warfare. In 1049 and 1053 Pope Leo IX waged particularly bitter wars against the Tuscans and the Normans, and in the following decades, papal recognition of the causes, if not the particular conduct, for which some rulers fought was formally acknowledged in the process of granting papal banners to rulers so favored. Papal banners were sent to the Paterines of Milan in their struggle with the imperial archbishop; to those besieging Barbastro in Spain in 1064; to Christian armies in Sicily; and, in 1065, to Duke William of Normandy in his contest for the throne of England. This new degree of papal participation should be considered in terms of the new policy of rectifying the conduct of the world, a policy that took various shapes during the reform papacies of Leo IX, Alexander II, and Gregory VII, who in 1074 suggested that he himself lead an army to the defense of eastern Christians and at other times spoke of recruiting a "Militia of St. Peter" to serve the purposes of God on earth. In 1089 Urban II granted the same remission of penance as would have been received for the pilgrimage to Jerusalem to those who helped rebuild the city of Tarragona in Spain.

By the end of the eleventh century, then, the idea of war had undergone several transformations, not the least of which occurred during the reform papacy after 1049. Yet none of the elements described above prepares us completely for the uniqueness of the events of 1095–1099; at best, they suggest some cultural background for them. Much more important were other institutions and ideas, particularly those of penitence and pilgrimage, some of which we have described above. The eleventh century witnessed a growing acuteness concerning penitence, particularly insofar as growing lay piety and devotional thought became dissatisfied with the degree of completeness that ordinary penance and reconciliation with the Church constituted. The popularity of specialized penitential devotions grew, and the most popular of these were penitential pilgrimages and the protection of the penitent in the service and life of a monastery.

From the Council of Piacenza in March of 1095, where he had promulgated reforms and met Byzantine ambassadors, Urban II made his way into southern France, where he visited Cluny and Le Puy, whose bishop, Adhémar, later became the papal legate for the Crusade. Urban then traveled to St. Gilles, near Toulouse, where he spoke with Raymond of St. Gilles, count of Toulouse and a strong supporter of Urban. On November 18 Urban opened the Council at Clermont. The late eleventh century witnessed a great increase in the number of church councils across the Alps presided over by the pope personally. These councils had helped strengthen the cause of the reform movement, and at Piacenza and Clermont as well, by far the bulk of the council's business dealt with matters of ecclesiastical reform. The events of the First Crusade have overshadowed the extremely influential reform measures taken at Clermont. For the Council of Clermont had many other affairs with which to deal. In 1092, King Philip I of France had abandoned his wife and taken another, an act that led to his excommunication at the Council of Autun in 1094. Because of the important role of France in the reform movement, the case of King Philip loomed very large. So did the vast problems of the internal reorganization of the Church, the fight against simony and clerical marriage, the abuses of ecclesiastical and clerical rights by laymen, and the movement of the Peace and the Truce of God. In the best edition of the canons of the Council, sixty-one items of discussion are recorded, only two of which pertain to the Crusade.

When the Council ended on November 27, 1095, Urban made a public address to a large group of assembled laymen and ecclesiastics. It is certain that several of those present and others, such as Raymond of St. Gilles who arrived later, knew of Urban's plan. In a speech that has survived only in very different secondhand versions, Urban painted a picture of the distress of eastern Christians, and he offered particular remission of sin to all who would go to Jerusalem "not from the desire for fame or money" but out of true penitence. It may very well be that Urban had envisioned, not the outright mercenaries that Alexius Comnenus had asked for, nor yet a holy army fighting a holy war, but rather an armed penitential pilgrimage whose mere size and presence would liberate Jerusalem and strengthen the eastern Church; ideally, God's recognition of such a purified and invigorated Christian world would lead to a reunion of Greek and Latin Churches and the Christian Congress of the Holy Land.

From Clermont Urban continued to travel through southern France, and preachers both great and small proclaimed the pope's request widely. A number of documents, called *Excitatoria,* were produced to further the cause, and in these, which include a forged encyclical of the early eleventh-century pope Sergius II, the appeal was spread through the ecclesiastical and aristocratic world. Some laymen, of course, were prohibited from going because they were excommunicated—for example,

King Philip I of France and Emperor Henry IV. Others, such as King William II Rufus of England, displayed no interest. Many, however—far more, in fact, than Urban had ever considered even remotely—did respond. It may be that Urban had in mind an armed penitential pilgrimage composed largely of men from southern France and led by Raymond of St. Gilles and Adhémar of Le Puy. The four great armies that eventually set out in 1096, however, came from all corners of the Christian west, and several early marches were composed of the poor and the alienated from even wider circles of society.

If Urban's initial plan did entail the sole leadership of Raymond of St. Gilles, it soon passed. Armies slowly assembled in northern France, led by Hugh of Vermandois, King Philip's brother, and Robert of Flanders. Raymond of St. Gilles led the contingent from Toulouse, and Godfrey of Bouillon led a force from Lorraine. In addition, Bohemund, the son of Robert Guiscard of Norman South Italy, also led an army. These armies remained under their separate commanders, and there was no unified command during the expedition. The person who came closest to representing and directing the whole movement was the papal legate, Adhémar, bishop of Le Puy. Although legates were appointed later for each army, the armies were composed of great lords and fighting men. Not only had the spark of a penitential pilgrimage that seemed particularly designed for armed warriors struck widely, but the economic pressures upon the growing aristocratic population suggested to many landless men that the great enterprise preached by Urban II might be a saving experience. The noble population of the eleventh and twelfth centuries tended steadily to outstrip the resources that sustained the social and economic superiority of the nobility, and noble children who could not inherit property or could not live under the strict regulation of family life that limited property and growing populations entailed were continually faced with the danger of declining social status. The Crusade of Urban II drew large numbers of such individuals. Great nobles went because they had been going on pilgrimages for a century—Robert of Flanders, in fact, had just returned from such a pilgrimage to Jerusalem. The preaching by the pope of a universal Peace and Truce of God must have appeared to laymen and clerics alike as a millennial event, one that signaled the new beginning of Christian society preached by Gregory VII and Urban II. All of these forces worked on the composition, spirit, and modes of perception within the Crusading armies.

Great princes and busy ecclesiastics were not the only ones who responded to Pope Urban's plea. Unofficial preachers and visionary clerics and laymen appealed to a far wider group than that mentioned above. Although prelates took care to restrict the participation of clerics on the great pilgrimage, lower clergy, monks, peasants, footloose warriors, women, and the sick all responded. One preacher, Peter the Hermit of Amiens, preached the pilgrimage in northern France and Germany and led a swelling army of the poor, headed by poor knights, among whom was Walter the Penniless, on a long land route to the Holy Land. By midsummer of 1096, the ragtag armies of Peter and Walter had reached Byzantium. Permitted through Constantinople and led into Anatolia, they were slaughtered by the Turks. The forces of Peter the Hermit and Walter the Penniless illustrate in particular the millenarian spirit that moved across all levels of European society at the end of the eleventh century. Ill-financed and unorganized, driven by penitential zeal, they survived the rigors of the journey to Constantinople, ultimately the rallying point for later Crusades.

Behind the forces of Peter and Walter followed other informal hordes, led by men of far less ability than even these two. Under the priest Gottschalk and Emicho of Leiningen, these groups terrorized the Rhineland and Hungary, instituting terrible massacres of Jews on their way, and ravaged and plundered through the latter area until they were wiped out along the Danube, far from even Constantinople. The actions of Gottschalk and Emicho reveal a less well-known aspect of the consciousness of Christendom. In the cultural and legal traditions of the period before the twelfth century, the status of Jewish communities was regulated through the legal remains of late Roman imperial law and its later modifications and through the doctrine of the "living witness;" that is, the idea that Jewish communities had to be preserved in Christian societies in order to "prove" the triumph of Christianity and to await the final judgment, before which the Jews would, legend had it, be converted to Christianity. Some aspects of this view influenced the development of the Antichrist legends after the tenth century. Yet Christian communities had not always hewn to the letter of the law in the case of Jews. Anti-Jewish legislation and literature had sprung up in the Byzantine Empire under Leo III, Basil I, and Romanus I Lecapenus and in the West in Visigothic Spain, the writings of Agobard of Lyons, and the legislation of the Carolingian kings in the ninth century. In 1063 a military expedition to Spain had massacred Jews in southern France, and throughout the eleventh century riots against Jews had occurred intermittently. The legislation against Christian converts to Judaism was savagely enforced. In 1071 Archbishop Andreas of Bari converted to Judaism, raising a scandal throughout the Latin and Greek Christian worlds. Indeed, the anticipation of a vast and unprecedented transformation of the world that marked Christian participants in the First Crusade appears also to have moved many Jewish communities as well. When the gangs led by Gottschalk and Emicho reached Mainz and other Rhineland cities their hysteria and savagery turned fully on the Jewish communities, and in spite of some attempts at protection by bishops and local authorities, the massacres spread. In the rabbinical literature and in the *responsa* (decisions of Jewish courts) as well, the effects of the new persecutions of the late eleventh and twelfth centuries were apparent in the discussions of legal problems arising from forced conversions and other circumstances of the European Jews after 1096.

The organization of the main armies, the official expedition, took longer than the spontaneous movements of Peter the Hermit and the rapacious march of Gottschalk and Emicho. The sheer logistical difficulties of moving even one army to Constantinople were immense. The feat of bringing in four armies within several months of one another was unimaginable. It was also dangerous, for the Byzantines had expected nothing resembling the forces that converged upon Constantinople in 1097. Alexius I Comnenus, a skillful diplomat, supplied the crusaders and worked out legal treaties with each, forcing some of the leaders to take oaths of allegiance to him personally. He then escorted the huge army across the Bosporus, where the city of Nicaea was the first to fall to the western armies. After marching south through Anatolia, the westerners encountered and defeated a Turkish army at Dorylaeum and marched to Antioch. The long siege of Antioch, the exhausted condition of the Crusaders, and the increasing dissension among their leaders constituted the greatest hardships of the entire expedition. From late October of 1097 to June of 1098 the western forces besieged Antioch. Immediately upon the taking of the city, news of the approach of a vast Turkish relief force further disheartened the armies. During the preparations for the defense of the exhausted city, a Provençal soldier named Peter Bartholomew claimed to have found, guided by visions from Heaven, the Holy Lance with which the Roman soldier Longinus had pierced the side of Christ on the cross. Although not universally believed, the episode aided morale immeasurably, and at the end of June the Turkish army was defeated and the conquest of Antioch complete. Not until January, 1099, did the final march to Jerusalem begin. Led by Raymond of Toulouse, who was clad as a penitent and a pilgrim, the armies first sighted Jerusalem on June 7, and after a fearful five-week siege they entered the city on July 15, 1099.

Two principalities had already fallen to Crusading armies by the time Jerusalem came under siege. Antioch had fallen under the control of Bohemund, and Edessa, an Armenian principality to the east of Antioch, had fallen to Baldwin. The arrival of a Christian Italian fleet at Jaffa in July had brought precious supplies to the armies, and the engineering skill of the Genoese William Embriaco helped construct the catapults and battle towers that finally wore down the resistance of Jerusalem. The skill and endurance that had brought the Christians to Palestine, however, was overshadowed by the massacre that they launched once they had captured the city. Arabs, Egyptians, Jews, and resident Christians fell before them. Although many people survived and preserved some of the human riches of the city, the devastation was extensive, as the pent-up emotions of three years of immense hardships were released upon the bodies of the city's inhabitants. The massacre would not have pleased Pope Urban II, who, to his credit, probably intended no such bloodletting. But Urban did not know of it; he died two weeks before Jerusalem fell. The problems surrounding Urban's successor, particularly the case of the emperor and the cause of ecclesiastical reform, complicated the solution of the problem of the Holy Land.

BYZANTIUM, ISLAM, AND THE LATIN KINGDOM OF JERUSALEM, 1099-1144

The capture of Jerusalem brought Christians in force to the Holy Land, but it also raised serious questions concerning the organization of the captured territories. Many of the members of the expedition left Palestine upon what they considered the completion of their vows, and the forces occupying Palestine and Syria shrunk drastically. Byzantium maintained several claims against territories now occupied by Crusaders, particularly Antioch. The Moslem powers that had witnessed the capture of Antioch and Jerusalem now began to develop ways of coming to terms with the new forceful Christian presence in their midst. Godfrey of Bouillon was elected, not king, but Protector of the Holy Sepulcher. He reigned briefly and was succeeded by his brother Baldwin of Edessa, who assumed the title of king and worked vigorously to establish royal governance as the principal force in the Near East. By 1111 most of the cities along the coast had fallen into Crusaders' hands, the last, Ascalon, succumbing in 1153. During Baldwin I's reign (1100-1118) four great Crusader territories took shape: the principality of Antioch, the county of Edessa, the county of Tripolis in the center of the conquered territories, and the kingdom of Jerusalem in the south. These were the principalities with whose presence and its consequences both Byzantium and the Islamic world had to deal.

Alexius I Comnenus (1081-1118) had gotten far more than he had asked in the Crusading armies. He had certainly not asked for a crusade, for the simple reason that no one, in the Greek or Islamic East or Latin West, knew what a crusade was: the retrospective interpretation of the events of 1095-1099 took shape only slowly in western sources in the first half of the twelfth century, and it never took shape in Byzantine or Islamic sources, because neither Byzantium nor the world of Islam ever fully understood the western crusading movement. Alexius's attempts to control the Crusaders and, when control failed, to come to some sort of understanding with their leaders, were generally successful. Friction, hostility, and mutual antagonism certainly existed between the Latins and the Byzantines, but Alexius's great intelligence and energies managed to salvage a semblance of good relations and some continuing aid to the western armies. Some of Alexius's difficulties are brilliantly illuminated by the account of his reign, *The Alexiad,* written by his learned, perceptive and Latin-hating daughter, Anna Comnena. Alexius's reign had, of course, witnessed other problems besides those of the Crusaders. The campaigns against the Turks in Anatolia, which were not helped at all by the Crusaders, occupied his attention, as did the political affairs of the empire and the growing economic problems of Byzantium. But Alexius's son and successor, John II Comnenus (1118-1143), acceded to an imperial throne under very different circumstances from those of his father. Alexius had helped stabilize the Byzantine coinage, weakened from the mid eleventh century on, and he had attempted to tie the large landholders more firmly to the imperial service by converting grants of land, *pronoia,* into conditional tenures depending on military service, thereby strengthening the imperial army. Alexius had not, however, managed to overcome wholly the hostility between landowning aristocrats and imperial civil servants, nor could he reduce either the increasing costs of government or the burden of taxation on the whole empire.

John II worked most successfully with the army. A good general leading a renewed force, he made Byzantine power felt once more in the Balkans and in Asia Minor—in Serbia, Hungary, and against the Pechenegs. His successes in Asia Minor, aided by the growing dependence of the northern Crusading principalities of Antioch and Edessa, were remarkable and helped salvage some of the territories of Anatolia for the empire. At his death in 1143, John was already planning further military expansion toward the Crusader states and east into Asia Minor.

Yet the Byzantine military successes during the reigns of Alexius I and John II must not overshadow the deepening internal difficulties of the empire. The loss of territories in Asia Minor and South Italy had injured Byzantine economic life considerably. Venice, a state only nominally dependent on Byzantium, had grown steadily greater in the Adriatic and Mediterranean Seas throughout the eleventh century. Venice's growth began with its subjugation of Dalmatia in the year 1000 and included an increasing number of trade privileges throughout the century in both Christian and Moslem lands. It culminated in the Golden Bull of 1082, in which Emperor Alexius I rewarded the Venetians for their help against the Normans of South Italy with vast trading concessions and a relaxing of tariffs and tolls. From 1082 on, Venice captured a greater role in the economic worlds of Byzantium and the entire Mediterranean. In 1099 and 1100, Venetian fleets policed the Aegean Sea against both Moslem shipping and overambitious crusading fleets from other Italian cities, particularly Pisa. Venetian assistance to the crusaders in the first year of the protectorate of Godfrey of Bouillion was rewarded with considerable trading and legal concessions in the port towns of Palestine and Syria. Byzantine reluctance to continue Venice's privileged status in the empire after the death of Alexius I in 1118 led to Venetian plundering of Byzantine ports, and the relations between Venice and the empire, strained since 1118, grew steadily worse throughout the twelfth century. Byzantium grew less and less able to control its own commerce, and Venice grew wealthy from her increasing trade. The loss of land and manpower, the continuing high expenses of government and the heavy taxes drawn from a diminishing tax base, the slow process of strengthening the great landholders with grants of *pronoia* and rights of administration over church properties, *charisticum,* the bitter antagonism with the Norman kingdom of Sicily and South Italy—all these engendered severe and ultimately irreversible economic and social weaknesses that were barely concealed by the energies, wisdom, and unremitting skill of Alexius I and John II.

The lands that Europeans began to call simply "Overseas"—*Outremer*—constituted rather a new problem for the Byzantines than a solution to the old problem of the Turks. To the Moslem world, the success of the expedition of 1097–1099 and the subsequent establishment of Latin principalities in Palestine and Syria also posed new problems. The arrival of the Turks in the Islamic world in the eleventh century posed great problems of assimilation, particularly to an Islamic Empire that had shifted its center away from the old sub-Byzantine world of Palestine and Syria to the old heart of the Persian Empire in Mesopotamia and had witnessed, in the eighth and ninth centuries, the establishment of independent Islamic kingdoms ranging from Egypt to Spain. The Abbasid Empire had slowly transformed the position of the caliph from that of the deputy of the Prophet to that of a military autocrat and had coordinated industry, banking, and trade on remarkably complex levels. The Abbasid court at Baghdad became one of the wealthiest and most brilliant in the world. The image of the court at the time of Charlemagne's contemporary, Harun al-Rashid (786–809) was caught in part in the later *Arabian Nights*. Throughout the ninth century, the western parts of the caliphate began to break away, from Egypt to Spain, and the provincial governors of the eastern provinces took more and more authority away from the caliph. From 945 on, the caliph was dominated by the military commander of Baghdad, and sectarian revolts and the rise of a powerful line of Turkish secular rulers, from Tughrul (1055–1063) to Malik Shah (1072–1092) further weakened the position and strength of the caliphate. In the course of the fragmenting Islamic political world, local revolts became dependent upon a number of heterodox Islamic sects that had sprung up locally. In the West, sectarian movements in North Africa and Spain were growing stronger in the tenth and eleventh century, and the invasions of the Almoravids and Almohads in the eleventh and twelfth centuries played a powerful role in Spanish and western Mediterranean history. In Egypt, the Fatimid dynasty that had come to power in 969 reached its height under Mustansir (1036–1094), the great contemporary of Malik Shah, extending east to Palestine and Syria.

Yet the new sectional kingdoms in the Islamic world also remained unstable. Attacks from the Berbers, Turks, and the Christians in Spain and Sicily threatened their existence in the eleventh century. By the end of that century, the old Mesopotamian unity of the caliphate of Baghdad was divided among a number of Seljuk Turkish princes whose rivalry with one another was too great to permit them to ally instantly against the expedition of 1097–1099, and with the death of Mustansir Egyptian power drew back west of the Nile. The crusaders, unknowingly, had marched into a world of fragmented, mutually hostile Moslem principalities, and this disunity afforded them their first foothold in the Holy Land.

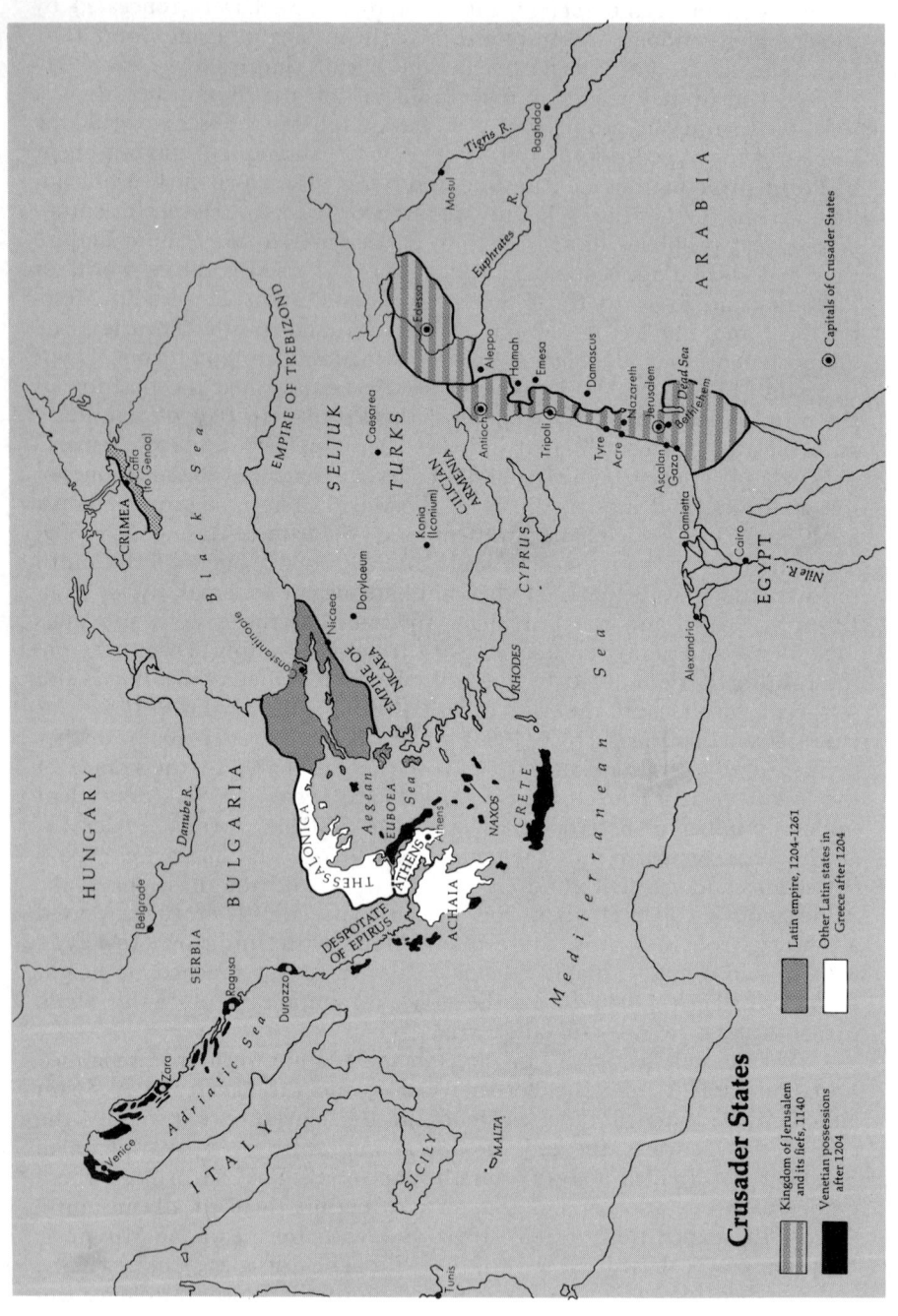

The first twenty-five years of the history of the Latin kingdom of Jerusalem and the other Christian principalities witnessed further Christian consolidation and the expansion of Byzantine strength in Anatolia and northern Syria. In 1127, however, a particularly able Seljuk prince named Zangi established a strong Moslem principality in the city of Mosul and expanded his territory at the expense of other Moslem leaders. By 1138 Zangi acquired power in Damascus, and in 1144 he successfully assaulted and captured Edessa, the first Christian principality to fall back into Moslem hands. Although Zangi was assassinated in 1146, his son and successor Nur-ad-Din (1146–1174) assisted in the defense of Damascus against the armies of the Second Crusade, and by 1154 Damascus itself had fallen into Nur-ad-Din's hands. By the middle of the twelfth century, a formidable new Moslem kingdom faced the Latin kingdom of Jerusalem.

The protectorate of the Holy Sepulcher ended with the death of its only ruler, Godfrey of Bouillon. Upon the accession of Godfrey's brother, Baldwin I of Edessa, the protectorate became a kingdom, the Latin kingdom of Jerusalem. The royal title gave Baldwin I (1100–1118) an advantage in prestige over the other great Christian princes of the Holy Land, the counts of Edessa and Tripolis and the prince of Antioch, but the establishment of a single Christian state uniformly dedicated to expansion in the face of Moslem hostility never took place. The army that had captured and sacked Nicaea, Dorylaeum, Antioch, and Jerusalem and had formed the core of the occupying Christian force bore little relation to a modern expeditionary force. Shrinking steadily in numbers as it approached Jerusalem, the Christian force consisted also of large numbers of the poor, women, children, lower clergy, and other noncombatants, whose often heroic conduct passed generally unnoticed and uniformly created a burden upon the military arm of the expedition. Two elements of these groups entered the growing body of Crusade legend in the first half of the twelfth century: Peter the Hermit, who later came to be credited with the entire plan of the First Crusade, and the Tafurs, a miscellaneous and savage body of the poorest members of the expedition that formed a kind of terrorist force at the edge of the main armies. In the twelfth century, both Peter and the Tafurs, along with Godfrey of Bouillon, became the subjects of later legends of the events of 1095–1099 and thus formed an important part of the growing European perception of the Crusade movement.

In addition to the problem of the pilgrim contingents, the Latin kingdom faced at its outset the problem created by the departure of the great princes, their work done, and the contingents that followed them. The small group of warriors that formed the core of the kingdom and the principalities engaged in continual warfare, and its ranks shrunk still more. They could be refilled only by fresh forces coming east from Europe, appeals for which were sent out steadily throughout the twelfth century. Moreover, conditions for establishing households and importing noncombatants also had to be established. The work of the first two kings, Baldwin I (1100–1118) and Baldwin II (1118–1131), was directed toward the securing of these conditions in the kingdom and, when they could, in the independent principalities as well. The strong kingship of Baldwin I in particular established the beginnings of a noble class, reestablished trade with the assistance of Italian merchants, and continued to pacify the Christian lands and hold off threats from Egypt and Damascus.

PART FIVE

CHRISTENDOM:
Authority and Enterprise,
1150-1300

18

THE MATERIALS OF A NEW LEARNING

SCHOOLS, CURRICULA, AND OBJECTS OF STUDY

Learning, usually the most fragile of social institutions, had occupied a prominent place in the reforms of Charlemagne, his advisers, and his successors. As we have seen, Charlemagne considered much of his work a restoration of a better, wiser age. His intellectual reforms consisted largely of restoring techniques of learning, authenticating fundamentally important texts of liturgy and law, and providing for a greater degree of thoroughness and continuity in the monastic and palace schools. These reforms, as admirable and surprising as they are, had two characteristics that must not be overlooked in any attempt to trace the character of thought and feeling in subsequent centuries: first, they occupied an extremely small number of persons, most of them religious, and hence depended for their preservation on the monastic centers where some trace of the reformers' influence lingered; second, they did not represent a divergence from the old pagan Roman curricular structure, but rather a new emphasis precisely upon the techniques of literary interpretation that had characterized late pagan and subsequent Christian learning since the fourth century. Throughout the ninth and tenth centuries, the study of logic and the mathematical complexities of the *quadrivium* remained the least emphasized subjects, and the study of literary exegesis and biblical commentary remained the predominant aim of educational activity. In the eleventh century, the purely exegetical orientation of education slowly changed, logic occupied a more and more prominent place in the scheme of study, and the increased number of translations into Latin of Arabic and Greek philosophy and natural science transformed the curriculum so that logic, mathematics, and science came to occupy the most prominent place in the curriculum and literary study was reduced to a preliminary level, rather equivalent to that of a modern grammar school or high school preparation. In conjunction with the transformation of the curriculum, there occurred a transformation of the schools themselves. From monastic academies whose primary purpose was to train monks, education moved, first, to the environs of the chapters of cathedrals, whose looser structure was more attractive to laymen and secular clerics, and, later, to schools that were separated even from the cathedrals—the early associations of teachers and students that became the medieval universities. These changes in both the substance and the social character of learning constitute a valid framework for a further exploration of more broadly based cultural changes: Latin and vernacular literatures and their public, and intellectual careers and patronage. The history of culture is not, of course, the history of education, yet the impact on literature and the arts of both the changing character of education and the new society that it served is so great that it is proper to begin our study with them.

The legacy of antique philosophy to later centuries was, as we have seen, extraordinarily diverse. Powerful traces of Neo-Platonism had shaped not only the high theology of Christianity, but its view of material creation as an inferior and illusory imitation of nonmaterial, mathematically perfect forms. The vast scientific and mathematical corpus of antique thought, from the Ionian philosophers and Aristotle to the mathematicians and astronomers of Alexandria, had never been translated into Latin at all, and the decline of knowledge of Greek in the West, itself under way long before the Christianization of the Roman Empire in the fourth century, had virtually deprived Latin-speaking westerners of access to that body of thought. Such strains of this body that had survived in the West had become part of that varied and diffuse Christian cosmology that had its roots in early commentaries on the book of Genesis and later Neo-Platonic Christian speculation on the character of the heavens. This cosmology was based in part upon Ptolemaic astronomy with its geocentric universe surrounded by a series of heavens, each made of a refined sort of material that was commonly thought to be crystalline and guided by celestial intelligences obeying the will of God. Because Aristotle had observed that terrestrial phenomena—including the weather—seemed subject to mutability and decay, he and his followers had distinguished between two kinds of creation: *physis*, the material world and its constituent parts, including the lower sky up to the orbit of the moon, and *uranos*, the "sky," that realm of regularly unchangeable creation that included the planets and what Aristotle thought to be the "fixed" stars. These two aspects of creation— a mutable sublunar world and a forever unchanging heaven (no nova was observed in the West until 1572)—were based upon the best science that the ancient world had produced, but they came down to later centuries detached from any consideration of methodology and from any conceptualization of further investigation; that is, they came as authorities, as classics that were not to be tampered with and certainly not to be refuted. There was, after all, very little to refute them with. Late classical antiquity had jettisoned much of the critical apparatus of early scientific thought, and the great encyclopedias of late antiquity, of which the last was the *Etymologies* of St. Isidore of Seville in the seventh century, had preserved both accurate and inaccurate scientific information, and they had preserved it as lore rather than as knowledge. As scientific lore it was assimilated into the cosmology of Christianity. Old, authoritative, accommodating itself to the level of enquiry that characterized the society of the seventh through the tenth centuries, the scientific legacy of late antiquity lived on in the Latin West in cosmology, theology, and in ancillary studies concerned with the interpretation of Christian literature.

Logic, too, was an ancillary study. Obviously far less essential to the needs of an illiterate society than literacy itself, the study of logic was hampered further by the nature of the materials available. To a society still struggling with the problems of literacy, those materials were, as R. W. Southern has pointed out, immensely repellent. They consisted of several tracts by Aristotle written as an introduction to the study of logic—translated and with commentaries by Boethius, the sixth-century Roman philosopher and public servant, and others—and the *Introduction to the Categories of Aristotle,* written by Porphyry, a third-century Neo-Platonist. The former had been the only results of Boethius's ambitious plan to translate all the works of Plato and Aristotle into Latin. The only work of Plato available was part of his dialogue *Timaeus,* translated by Chalcidius with commentaries by Chalcidius himself and Macrobius, fourth-century scholars whose familiarity with Plato leaves much to be desired. This slim body of introductory materials was hardly so inspiring as to make it very popular. Yet in it there were some extremely important ideas, for in translating Aristotle's introductory works to logic, Boethius had helped shape a Latin vocabulary capable of expressing and describing mental processes that had hitherto been available only in Greek.

The educational reforms of Charlemagne had resulted in the proliferation of texts of Scripture and of the writings of the church fathers, and they had created, or rather substantially enlarged, the literary public to whom these texts were available. To be sure, the monastic environment provided its own characteristics as well: the relative isolation of many thinkers, the limitations upon study posed by the number of books available at a given location, the accidental presence or absence of gifted teachers, and the energy with which abbots urged learning upon their monks (or with which monks accepted it from their abbots)—all these qualities determined both general and particular interests in learning. The remarkable intellectual productions of such ninth-century thinkers as John the Scot, Paschasius Radbertus, and Gottschalk of Orbais indicate some of that intellectual life at its liveliest and most depressing. The gradual accumulation of texts, however, and the increasing propensity of monks to move to where learning was known to be available contributed to a raising of learned awareness, not only of the vast extent of knowledge, but of the problems that only a familiarity with a great range of texts could make known. Scripture, men found, might appear to contradict other Scripture. One father might not only contradict another, but might contradict himself in another place. The study of logic, very gradually at first, seemed to offer a way out of these dilemmas, and by the late tenth century, logic appears to have begun to acquire a new prominence. The early studies of Gerbert, for example, took him to Reims specifically for the study of logic, and although Gerbert did not proclaim (as several thinkers would, two generations later) that logic was "the queen of the sciences," he and several of his contemporaries contributed to a new interest in the subject that is evident in the generations immediately following Gerbert.

Ecclesiastical controversies, which had followed so hard upon the Carolingian revival of learning, died down in the early tenth century, only to spring up more vigorously than ever in the eleventh. Questions of ecclesiastical reform, some problems of dogma, the increasing amount of propaganda literature, and the appearance of distinct points of view within a common system of communication all contributed to the increasing frequency of disputes that marks the eleventh century. One such dispute took place over the question of the real presence of Christ in the Eucharist; it involved two remarkable thinkers, Berengar of Tours and Lanfranc of Pavia/Bec. Berengar, a man of substantial learning and evident personal charm, was the first major thinker to apply techniques from Aristotelian logic to questions of theology. In a celebrated denial of the Real Presence, he argued that because "accidents" do not exist without their "substance," the "accidents" of the appearance of bread and wine in the consecrated bread and wine of the Mass "prove" that no change in "substance" has taken place; hence, these "accidents" are not the body and blood of Christ. The competence and the extent of Berengar's theories drew upon him the opposition of the more able Lanfranc, then abbot of the Norman monastery of Bec and later archbishop of Canterbury, and the exchanges between the two raised logic to the role of a major instrument in theological disputation. For Lanfranc defeated Berengar not by superior literary techniques but by being a better logician, and from the mid eleventh century on, the principles according to which Berengar had advanced his novel opinions and Lanfranc had refuted them were imbedded in all theological discussions of a serious nature.

The dispute between Lanfranc and Berengar on the Real Presence was only one of several intellectual issues of the eleventh century that indicate a new role for logical analysis. The scholar Roscellinus of Compiègne, also convinced that logical analysis was the best tool for considering truth, proposed the idea that only the data of experience and the name (*nomen*) we gave those data are real, and that the idea of universals that correspond to individual things and have a reality equal to them is false. Roscellinus's nominalism, as this approach came to be known, constituted one of two major theories of logic that were held during the following centuries. These two disputes and the complex arguments developed on both sides during the long controversy over simony and nicolaitism and the conflict between the papacy and the emperors at the end of the eleventh century inaugurated what might truly be called an age of disputation, and logical analysis came to play a more and more influential part in such arguments as the principles of these controversies were stated and restated in argumentative terms. The wide extent of the ecclesiological and political disputes and the new forms taken by disputes over questions of theology and dogma caused many to be suspicious of the new attraction that logic seemed to exert in the eleventh century, particularly when it was applied to questions of dogma or politics. In the ninth century, when John the Scot had been asked to refute the predestinarian heresy of Gottschalk, John's method and eagerness had pushed so far that "before the Irish philosopher could be checked, he had refuted sin and Hell" as well as Gottschalk. Such formidable energy as that of John the Scot, Berengar, and Roscellinus made many scholars reluctant in the eleventh and twelfth centuries to give logical disputation a free hand. Even though Lanfranc had proclaimed that logic, properly used, enhances faith, and even though Lanfranc's pupil, St. Anselm, represented the greatest triumph of logic in the service of orthodox belief that the West had yet known, logic was far from carrying all before it in the twelfth century, particularly in the realm of theology. It had become sufficiently popular to have achieved a firm place in the educational curriculum, and in doing so to have subtly transformed thinkers' approaches to the traditional problems of theology. But through the late eleventh and early twelfth centuries, the study of logic remained a subordinate part of the *trivium*, rather an intellectual exercise than a tool of theological criticism.

The slow rise of logic to renewed prominence during this period corresponded to another transformation, that of the schools. The monastic and palace schools of Carolingian Europe had constituted the intellectual arenas for the revival of learning of the ninth century. By the end of the tenth century, the cathedral schools had begun to acquire a larger share of the educational responsibilities of western society, and under an energetic and devoted bishop a cathedral school might grow and flourish spectacularly. Although the converse is also true—that under a lax bishop a flourishing school might soon expire—the cathedral schools of Reims and Chartres, Laon and Paris appealed to a broader range of students than the monastic schools, and it is in these cathedral schools that the new prominence of the study of logic made its greatest impression. The new direction of monastic reform in the late eleventh and early twelfth centuries moved away from that degree of involvement with the "world" that had in part characterized the flowering of monasticism in England, France, and Germany in the tenth and early eleventh centuries. This withdrawal of monasticism from its earlier involvement in the secular life around the monastery opened the way for the broad appeal of the cathedral schools. Moreover, the wide variety of activities that a cathedral had to look after, from administering law courts and estates to conducting liturgical services, generated a need for trained personnel, and cathedral service constituted an increasingly broader avenue into careers that led to high office and prestige. Finally, the growth of town life, a growth in which cathedrals played a prominent part, made the cathedral schools rather more accessible than monasteries, and the existence of resources, from housing and employment to books and teachers, drew ambitious students in greater and greater numbers. The late tenth and eleventh centuries witnessed not only a curriculum change of great significance, but a change in the character of educational institutions, at first on a humble level but later on a much more ambitious one.

READERS, BOOKS, AND LIBRARIES: THE MATERIALS OF LITERACY

Until the twentieth century, literacy was an attribute of only a small percentage of the population of the European and Atlantic community and of a much smaller percentage of the population of the rest of the world. Yet, in terms of religion and law, medicine and administration, early Europeans were, as Moslems called Jews and Christians, people of the book. Scripture, Sacramentaries, psalters, and sermon collections were but a few types of literary works that even low ranking clergy were expected to read. Lawbooks, medical treatises, and administrative handbooks grew more and more necessary after the eleventh century. Yet literacy remained the slowly acquired skill of only a few people, and communication between literate and nonliterate people remained that of the eye and ear: pictures, the spoken word, and didactic gesture sufficed for most forms of communication. Reading was the property of all literate people, writing that of fewer. The conditions of material civilization and social structure explain much of the illiteracy between the fifth and the thirteenth centuries. The collapse of the Roman urban educational system, the necessity of promulgating law after law urging that education be provided to candidates for the priesthood, and the general lack of a need for widespread literacy, oral communication sufficing instead, all contributed to this illiteracy.

The book itself underwent a transformation from the utilitarian Roman papyrus roll to, first, the *codex* bound at the edges and covered with wood or leather, dating from the second century A.D., and then to the sacred text carefully written on expensive skins and bound with gold and jewels, the text arranged dramatically on the page and accompanied by illustrations—a sacred thing in itself, almost an icon. The common papyrus of the ancient Mediterranean world slowly gave way in the West to parchment and vellum. Parchment was made from the skins of animals, usually calves; vellum, made from the skin of lambs, was rarer than parchment. Parchment was prepared for scribal use by a slow process that involved steeping the skin in a lye solution to dissolve organic materials, rubbing it with a pumice stone for smoothness (the flesh and skin sides of the parchment had different surfaces), softening it by means of crayon or chalk rubbing, evening it, cutting it to size, and then ruling it. Ruling consisted of punching tiny holes at line intervals and sometimes connecting them with barely visible lines made by a dry metal point. Generally, the scribe wrote the text, the rubricator inserted the red titles, and the illuminator added the illustrations required by whoever commissioned the book. This slow process of book production, the problem of obtaining enough skins, and the social and economic organization required to produce a book suggest some of the background of the place of literacy in early European history.

Before the eleventh century, older manuscripts, either those no longer needed or those containing pagan writing, were sometimes erased in order to provide new writing surfaces. Such manuscripts, called palimpsests, offer modern investigators the opportunity to recover texts that were overwritten by later scribes. Presentation books, the elaborately made manuscripts commissioned by rulers, magnates, or prelates as gifts or as service books for great churches, are triumphs of craftsmanship and art. They were characterized by gold-jeweled book covers, carefully smoothed and sometimes brilliantly dyed pages, and meticulously shaped scripts and illuminations.

The question of who could read these manuscripts is as complex as the techniques of manuscript production. In some general areas, literacy seems to have been more widespread than in others. Italy, southern France, and England before the tenth century seem to have had higher literacy levels than other parts of Europe. This state of affairs probably derives from the legacy of Roman society, for much of the literary production of the early Middle Ages was produced by and for the clergy, and hence had a limited appeal for the layman, particularly the warrior aristocrat and certainly the peasant and merchant. Charlemagne, for example, could read but not write; most tenth- and eleventh-century rulers were illiterate.

Beneath the character of reading materials and the occasions of literary production, however, there lies the more vexing question of the sociology of literacy. As V. H. Galbraith pointed out some years ago, many powerful figures of the early Middle Ages did not (or could not) read because they did not have to. Subordinate personnel, usually clerics, did the actual writing and reading aloud. In a world in which rulers were born and died surrounded by family and courtiers, oral communication was much more natural than writing. There was little privacy in this world, and a message spoken by a king or great lord carried more weight than a document written by someone else. Although the use of writing for administrative purposes increased during Charlemagne's reign and increased again after the tenth century, the need for a cultural system that trained large numbers of people to read and write and, equally important, generated the demand for written documents still did not exist.

The increasing complexity of social intercourse during and after the eleventh century began to alter the social conditions under which literacy had existed earlier. The spread of town life, the growing business of royal and princely courts, the movement of the schools out of exclusively monastic surroundings and into areas of cathedral and civic patronage, and the increase of both administrative and literary work in both spiritual and secular courts, all contributed to both the spread of literacy among more people and the function of literacy among new social groups. Not all people who needed to read documents had access to a cleric who would read to them. Lesser lords, merchants, and townsmen began more frequently to send their children to school, simply to enable them to perform basic record-keeping functions at home. And as court and civic records and legal and administrative handbooks became more necessary, civic and court officials had to be able to read them; however, literacy at this level was not accomplished until after the thirteenth century. Urban society felt these needs more quickly than rural society. In early fourteenth-century Florence there is evidence that the extraordinarily high figure of 40 percent of the children were educated at least to the level of literacy. If such a figure is correct, Florence far surpassed most of the rest of Europe, where the percentage of literate children was much, much smaller.

The spread of literacy from the monastic cloister and the clerical personnel of great churches and courts is reflected in the spread of the cathedral and informal schools of the late eleventh and twelfth centuries. Although most of the teaching in these schools was oral, literacy marched apace with it, and much of the literature of the twelfth century was produced by individuals who were the products of these schools. Probably not a significantly greater percentage of the population read for themselves the works of fiction and poetry, philosophy and theology that the twelfth and thirteenth centuries produced, but the very popularity of literature and the necessity of having administrative records made twelfth- and thirteenth-century European society more literacy-conscious.

The slowly produced illuminated manuscripts and the increasingly frequent utilitarian legal treatise or commercial record lead us to another consideration: What did one do with books if one had them and could read them (or have them read)? Outside of the monasteries and the cathedrals there were, before the twelfth century, no places where large collections of books were widely known to exist. Texts of particular works about which one may have heard were located unpredictably in whatever center of monastic culture they had happened to land. They were rarely recorded even in hand lists, never in anything resembling a catalogue, nor were they usually housed in anything resembling a modern (or an ancient) library. Those who owned books often could not read them, and they guarded them rather as valuable treasures than as media of communication. The "catalogues" of some early monastic libraries still survive, usually in the form of lists of titles scrawled on one or two folios of parchment. But even the term "library" in this sense is misleading. Books used for different functions were kept in different places. In the monastery, for example, the elaborately produced books for liturgical services were kept in the church itself; books that were read aloud at meals were kept in the dining hall, or refectory; those used for study were usually kept in the cloister, often along the south wall of the church, on shelves or in chests. As written instruments became more important in legal disputes, the habit of collecting one's "papers" grew, and family archives began. But alongside the literary and documentary purposes of written works loomed the phenomenon of forgeries, whether done for pious or criminal intent. With the emergence of forgeries, there also emerged a new interest in authentication and in the detection of forgeries. By the end of the twelfth century the widespread use of the written word, although this occurred within strict social and intellectual contexts, was becoming a part of European culture.

Not until the thirteenth century did anything resembling university or private libraries occur. These collections of books, pitifully small by modern or recent standards, represented, as we have seen, enormous outlays of resources and effort. The procurement and preparation of the writing surfaces, the sharpening of quills, the act of writing (seated in an upright chair, feet on a stool, the page on a tilted surface across the lap), and the circumstances of light, heat, cold, and fatigue all indicate both the physical difficulties of book production and the kinds and numbers of errors that inevitably crept into the texts and were multiplied as a text passed from copyist to copyist. Because binding was a complicated and often expensive process, it often happened that several different works were bound together, and when a knight or burger had only a few books, he sometimes placed them in a single binding.

By the thirteenth century, and probably earlier, the formalization of courses in instruction in the schools made identical copies of some works, those of textbook authors, highly desirable. In the course of the twelfth and thirteenth centuries, particularly as the schools incorporated themselves into corporations with enforceable legal rights, universities began to control the production of manuscripts of school authors by copyists and booksellers. Thus, some literary and technical works were produced in considerably greater numbers than others, particularly when they were included in the curricula of study at Paris, Bologna, or Oxford. These texts, usually put together hastily and far less attractive aesthetically than the splendid presentation codices, perished, of course, in far greater numbers, but with the lecture notes of students and the teaching notes of professors they contribute to our knowledge of the educational revolution of the twelfth and thirteenth centuries. That revolution also entailed a major increase in literacy and heralded the substantial increase in general literacy that marked the period after 1350 and in particular the period following the development of printing in the fifteenth century.

In 1387 Duke William of Guelders insulted the great Phillip the Bold, duke of Burgundy, by writing to him on paper instead of parchment. In the fifteenth century the duke of Urbino, the highly literate Federigo da Montefeltro, refused to include any printed book in his library. Besides the social, economic, material, and intellectual dimensions of the history of books and readers during this period, there is an honorific dimension as well. The splendid as well as the humble working manuscripts remind us of a world in which literary communications were as much events as utilitarian devices, and books possessed symbolic, gestural importance as well as functional significance. The meticulous art and craftsmanship of the best of early European book production remind us that the books themselves shared the aura of the sacred and the aesthetic theory of the period; serving, with relics, the function of guaranteeing oaths, they also shared the relics' status. Conveying, with the lecture, useful God-given knowledge, they also shared in the common attitude that they should not be prohibitively expensive, because, as moralists said, "Knowledge is a gift of God and ought not be sold." In the educational and devotional revolutions of the twelfth and thirteenth centuries, the written word played an incalculable role in the dissemination of thought and feeling, sensibility and forms of expression, information and speculation.

LANGUAGE AND CULTURE

The literary languages of Mediterranean antiquity, Greek and Latin, existed in a number of different forms. The divisions of written and oratorical language into different styles and vocabularies, the use of which depended upon the nature of the material being discussed, had been laid down by Roman rhetorical schools and handbooks of grammar. Literary language, with its divisions and stylistic rules, however, was certainly not the common speech of Greeks and Romans, and as we have seen, other regional languages, such as Syriac, Coptic, and Celtic, survived in the Roman world and even grew into wider use after the third century. The decline of classical Latin had already begun in pagan antiquity, and third- and fourth-century authors already reveal shifts in usage and vocabulary that distinguish their work from that of their predecessors. Particularly influential in this transition was the enormous influence of the kind of Latin used by ecclesiastical writers in the fourth and fifth centuries, especially the Latin of St. Jerome's Vulgate Bible and in it the strong influence of the Greek from which it was translated as well as the particular kinds of Latin Jerome chose to translate the original Greek. Finally, colloquial Latin seems to have made its way into texts more and more between the fourth and the seventh centuries, and in many literary records, from administrative documents to monastic chronicles, a Latin had emerged by the sixth and seventh centuries that was very different from the literary Latin of the Roman Republic and early Empire. When, after the eighth century, the teachers and scholars of the Carolingian period attempted to restore classical Latin, the language they produced contained the effects of the changes of the fourth through the seventh centuries. Throughout early European history, Latin remained the language of learning, ecclesiastical affairs, and serious discourse. It was commonly spoken by the learned, but it had to be taught to young children, and its role as a school language gave it marked social and cultural characteristics. Literacy in Latin sufficed for many centuries as proof of clerical status, and most of the literary and documentary materials before the fifteenth century were written in Latin.

Knowledge of Greek had begun to decline in the western parts of the Roman Empire by the third century and was virtually extinct by the fifth, although some areas, particularly South Italy, Ireland, and southern Gaul, preserved vestiges later than others. Latin also died out in the eastern part of the Roman Empire by the end of the sixth century. Not the least of the difficulties facing Greek and Latin Christians in their search for mutual understanding was this language problem and the uncertainties of the translations in which much of their communication with each other was necessarily carried out. There is little evidence of the knowledge of Greek in the West (outside of a few, mostly Irish, monasteries) before the ninth century, at which point the Irish philosopher John the Scot and the liturgical reformer Amalarius of Metz reveal a surprising acquaintance with the language. Not until the new interest in Greek and Arabic learning in the twelfth century, however, did the level of the knowledge of Greek rise even slightly. Even the early Italian Renaissance was much more distinctly a revival of interest in Latin antiquity, and not until the sixteenth and seventeenth centuries can there be said to have been anything resembling a widespread recovery of the knowledge of Greek in the West. The great contribution of Greek to Islamic civilization was the result of the translation of works particularly on astronomy and medicine from Greek into Syriac during the late empire and later, between the eighth and the eleventh centuries, from Syriac into Arabic. The Greek of Byzantium was a transformation of classical Greek; among other things, its pronunciation changed. Byzantine

Greek reached out to the Bulgars, Kievans, Serbs, and Croats, contributing theories of language, scripts for nonwritten languages, and the semantic values of an entire culture to these neighbors.

As long as it remained largely a school language, literary Latin tended to remain homogeneous and flexible throughout early European history. The regional variations of spoken Latin in late antiquity, however, changed at a much faster rate than literary Latin and laid the foundations for the vernacular languages of western Europe as they emerged, in their written forms at least, between the eighth and the twelfth centuries. Like the scripts of early European handwriting, which generally began as humble cursives and were then promoted to more respected uses, the forms of spoken Latin became so effective that they moved from a purely popular status to literary status. During the period of the formation of vernacular languages, influences from other languages shaped regional variations of popular Latin, and other forces, such as the social status of those using the language, the place where the shift from Latin language to Romance language occurred, and the surviving strength of non-Latin languages, all gave their distinctive shape to those vernacular languages that are derived from Latin and called Romance languages. Some of these languages survive today—Italian, French, Portuguese, Spanish, and Romanian—and some, such as literary Provençal, have recently declined.

Late Latin, especially late spoken Latin, contributed heavily to the Romance vernaculars of western Europe. Other languages, however, show little trace of Latin influence. Finnish and Hungarian belong to the Finno-Ugaritic family, a distinctly Asiatic family of languages. Basque remains from the pre-Indo-European phase of Europe's history, and many of the non-Latin languages of the Roman Empire survived until well into the modern era: Gallic, Coptic, Punic, Syriac, and many others lasted well past the transition from Latin to Romance vernaculars.

The second main group of European languages is the Germanic. The earliest written form of a Germanic language is Gothic, which is contained in the Bible translated by Ulfilas for the Visigoths in the fourth century. Not until the eighth century and after do extensive written examples of other Germanic languages appear, the first being Old English and Old High German. Even these languages, however, were influenced somewhat by Latin, particularly in the necessary expanding of their vocabularies as the material and spiritual circumstances of Germanic societies changed drastically between the migration period and the age of Charlemagne and after.

In the cultural world of early Christian Europe, language occupied a place of particular prominence. The divine inspiration of Scripture, the obligation to preach and spread the faith, and the supreme mandate to save souls all freed theories of language and literary expression from the limited context of late antique rhetorical theory by attributing to language a transcendental value in the divine plan of creation. To early European Christians, the episode of the Tower of Babel, described in Genesis, linked fallen human nature and pride to the linguistic diversification of the world. Against this confusion of tongues was set the episode of Pentecost, described in the Acts of the Apostles, in which the apostles were enabled to overcome the diversity of languages by divine inspiration. Having shown, people thought, that grace could overcome the most pronounced consequences of fallen nature, God had opened the plan of salvation to all peoples, Latins, Greeks, and barbarians. The early Church had advocated preaching in vernacular languages, and throughout the Carolingian period this responsibility was urged upon the clergy. Before the ninth century, both the Greek and Latin churches urged that preaching and praying be conducted in the vernacular, but both reserved the higher liturgical services to Latin and Greek. As we have seen, the missions to the Slavs of SS. Cyril and Methodios led to the shaping of a written Slavic language, and a native Slavic liturgy soon followed. Although the Latin church, after initial approval, did not continue to countenance Slavonic as a liturgical language, the Byzantine church did, thus contributing immensely to the cultural development of the eastern European world. In the West, Latin remained the only liturgical language, and ecclesiastical interest in the vernacular remained at a lower level.

The social transformation of the West during the tenth and eleventh centuries, however, gave great impetus to vernacular culture. The movement of people on a larger scale—on pilgrimages, Crusades, trade routes, and in search of learning—brought different vernacular speakers into more frequent contact. The slow process whereby Latin texts were provided with glosses, in which a vernacular word was written over or in a column next to a Latin text, expanded the vocabulary and the complexity of usage of the vernaculars. In some areas, particularly England, a precocious vernacular literature developed as early as the eighth century, whereas in areas that were particularly close to the old centers of Latin culture, particularly Italy, vernacular literatures did not appear until the thirteenth century. In the tenth century Aelfric, an English scholar, suggested that grammar, hitherto considered an attribute only of Latin and Greek, might be a property of English as well. However, it was not until the fifteenth century that the formal grammatical principles of western vernacular languages became generally known, described in reasoned texts, and introduced into the educational system. This late blooming of the idea of a vernacular grammar parallels the fourteenth-, fifteenth-, and sixteenth-century disputes as to whether or not vernacular languages were suitable for the highest forms of poetic expression, disputes that led to the sixteenth-century literary genre known as the "defense" of the vernacular.

Vernacular literature remained rare until the twelfth century, when German, French, Provençal, Spanish, and English works began to appear with greater frequency. By the late twelfth century there were attempts to translate Scripture into the vernacular in France, and from the twelfth century on, a sophisticated and elaborate court literature appeared in many European vernaculars. In the universities after the twelfth century, the need to improve the students' Latin was so great that the students were strictly forbidden to speak the vernacular; employees known as "wolves" prowled the student quarters trying to detect inadvertent lapses into a vernacular.

The vernacular languages of Europe did not emerge as tidily as modern political maps might lead one to expect. Regional differences remained pronounced in many areas until the nineteenth century, and in some areas until the twentieth. By Charlemagne's day the language of the Franks was already breaking up into Romance Old French and Old High German. Charlemagne himself probably spoke a language close to Flemish or German, and Einhard, his biographer, tells us that he loved to hear the old heroic songs of his people performed and that he even collected them and had them written down in a "songbook," which no longer exists. The biographer of Charlemagne's son Louis the Pious tells us that Louis in his youth was raised on similar oral literature.

One of the earliest monuments to this division of northern vernaculars is the document known as the Strasbourg Oaths of 842. Included in the ninth-century chronicle of Nithard, the oaths were taken by Louis the German and Charles the Bald, sons of Louis the Pious, in the process of the drawn-out disputes between them over their respective shares of the inheritance they received from their father. Charles, king of the West Franks, spoke to the assembled crowd in German, and Louis, king of the East Franks, spoke in Old French, each thereby addressing primarily the other's followers.

By the twelfth century, numerous regional variations of Romance and Germanic speech existed all over Europe, a situation that often made it impossible for neighbors to understand each other and that greatly hampered verbal communications over a wide area. In the vast area that later became the kingdom of France, for example, the north and south were divided by a line separating the Romance form in the north known as the *langue d'oïl* from the *langue d'oc* in the south and southwest. These designations derived from the manner in which the word "yes" was spoken in these regions, and they applied to very different Romance language forms. The language of the south produced a flourishing literature in the twelfth century, but that of the north lagged somewhat behind. However, there were many regional variations in each of these two conveniently large divisions, and in the north the problem was complicated by the presence of many Germanic dialects to the north and east and by the persistence of Breton and Anglo-Norman to the west.

The *langue d'oïl* exerted its influence farther away than France proper. Influencing the language of the inhabitants of the duchy of Normandy, it traveled with the Normans to England during the conquest of 1066. Before 1066, the rich old English vernacular had risen to considerable literary prominence, and a substantial number of translations from Latin were completed during the reign of Alfred of Wessex (876–899). This tradition continued through the tenth century, and the brief Danish conquest of 1016 brought more Germanic influences to England. Then, with the Norman Conquest of 1066, the linguistic character of English society changed drastically. Norman French became the language

The Materials of a New Learning   367

of the ruling aristocracy and churchmen, and a period of social opprobrium for Old English set in. By the twelfth century, Norman French was still the language of the rulers and nobilty of England, although a new Romance-influenced English language, known as Middle English, had appeared. Not until the reign of King John in the early thirteenth century, though, was there a king of England who could speak English.

By the twelfth century, the vernacular languages of much of Europe had become sufficiently capacious and complex to invite translations from many ecclesiastical literary sources. With the development of native French prose in the thirteenth century and German and English prose in the fourteenth, the vernaculars, Romance and Germanic, had achieved the foundations, at least, of their later development.

The intellectual energies of the twelfth century were also much taken up by translations from Greek and Arabic. By the early twelfth century, knowledge of the achievements of Arabic thought and the Islamic legacy of much of Greek learning had begun to make inroads in the West. In the late eleventh and early twelfth centuries, Adelard of Bath, an Englishman, traveled as far and wide as South Italy, Sicily, Greece, Cilicia, Syria, Palestine, and possibly Spain seeking out the knowledge he had heard of. Adelard returned to England for good around 1140 and spent the last ten years of his life probably in the royal service at the Exchequer, the accounting office. Adelard's literary works are not as immediately revealing of the wealth of Arabic thought as Adelard professed, but they do represent one of the early stages of what, by the late twelfth century, had amounted to a torrent of translations from Arabic works and, by the thirteenth century, from Greek works directly as well. The ninth and tenth centuries had witnessed the translation into Arabic of much of the corpus of earlier Greek learning, and westerners began to acquire some of this legacy through translations from Arabic. Both the Greek and the Islamic legacies acquired great popularity in the West. The work of Ibn Sina (d. 1037, Avicenna to the Latins) in medicine and philosophy remained fundamental to western thinkers between the twelfth and the eighteenth centuries. Ibn Rushd (d. 1199, Averroes to the Latins) was probably the greatest of all commentators upon Aristotle's scientific works. Jabir (d. 721) had written extensively on chemistry, Al-Khwarizmi (d. 850) on mathematics, including concepts of place holding and the introduction of the zero, al-Battani (d. 930) on trigonometry and astronomy, and Alhazen (d. 1039) on optics.

Spain appears to have been the first center from which the Islamic materials were passed on to the Latin West. Even apart from the great intellectual problems involved in translating Arabic and, later, Greek into Medieval Latin, particularly problems of equivalent terminology, the process of translation was extraordinarily complicated. First, the Arabic text was read aloud, then translated into one translator's own language, usually Hebrew or Old Spanish, and then retranslated into Latin, a process certainly not free from boundless opportunities for error and confusion. What is remarkable about the great age of the translators, however, is the very high level of skill and the vast energies they displayed. The city of Toledo provides a case in point. This city, long a center of Islamic learning, was captured by Christians in 1085. In 1126, the year of Adelard of Bath's first return to England, Toledo received a new archbishop, Raimund, who within four years began to develop a local team of Arabic translators. The greatest of these, Domenicus Gundesalvi, produced a vast number of translations. Once Sicily had fallen into Christian hands, it constituted another point of contact for the two cultures, and the remarkable Norman Sicilian court of the twelfth century produced much work as well, its eclectic population of Arabs, Jews, Greeks, and Latins rubbing elbows in the most cosmopolitan center of European culture before the seventeenth century. Under Raimund of Toledo the corpus of Ibn Sina's works was translated into Latin. At the twelfth-century court of Roger II of Sicily the great Islamic geographer Al-Idrisi dedicated his most important work to the Christian king personally. At Salerno, long the center of the most extensive medical learning in the Christian west, the translations begun in the eleventh century by Constantine the African and John the Saracen continued into the twelfth. In 1127, Stephen of Antioch, an Italian, translated the Al MaTaki, the greatest Islamic medical encyclopedia. Adelard of Bath translated Euclid's *Elements* into Latin from Arabic, and the greatest of the early translators, Gerard of Cremona (1114–1187), translated over ninety works, including Ptolemy's *Almagest,* the standard work on astronomy in Europe until the seventeenth century. In 1142, under the sponsorship of Peter the Venerable, Abbot of Cluny, the *Qu'ran* was translated into Latin for the first time.

In Sicily, Italy, and Hungary, the twelfth century also witnessed the first new translations from Greek. Such men as Burgundio of Pisa and Moses of Bergamo made the first new Latin translations of Plato and Aristotle since the days of Boethius in the early sixth century, and by the late thirteenth century most of the Aristotelian corpus and much of Plato had been successfully translated into Latin. Greek Christian theology, particularly the extremely influential writings of St. John of Damascus of the eighth century, was also translated into Latin.

The new learning that the translators made available to the Latin West was certainly not the only contribution of the great age of translators. Islamic medical, agricultural, and architectural discoveries also passed into western hands during this period, and the prominent role of Jewish translators marks the beginning of a new Christian interest in Jewish literature as well, although the anti-Semitism of much of Christian Europe after the eleventh century made translations from Hebrew a risky business, a problem that lingered into the seventeenth century. After the new reception of Arabic and Greek works, however, the influence of Jewish scholarly traditions of scriptural interpretation became particularly extensive during the thirteenth century.

The increasing sophistication and ease with which scholars handled Latin during the twelfth century, the strength of vernacular languages and literatures, and the input from Arabic, Greek, and Hebrew learning touched all of European society and marks one of the first of the great ages of intellectual cosmopolitanism in modern history.

THE MARKET FOR LEARNING AND LETTERS: EDUCATION AND CAREERS IN THE TWELFTH CENTURY

The internal transformation of curricula and the appearance of new schools, a wider use of the written word and a wider function for literacy, the appearance of efficient scripts, and the opening of linguistic horizons all played substantial roles in the intellectual revolution of the twelfth century, but they do not, by themselves, fully explain its character. The social consequences of the new learning extended more widely into twelfth-century European society than the limited literacy and firm social divisions of the period might at first suggest. Such revolutions do not occur suddenly, with the appearance of a few great thinkers whose ideas are so compelling that they carry all before them. The character of learning before the late eleventh century reflects the character of late Carolingian society. Occasional monasteries flourished briefly as isolated intellectual centers, and a few towns maintained schools. The courts of the Carolingian kings supported some scholars, but learning was almost exclusively monastic in character and necessarily subordinated to the practical needs of monastic institutions. Few people thought it worthwhile to set out on intellectual adventures in the world outside of their local region, and when, like Gerbert in the tenth century and St. Anselm in the eleventh, they did go off seeking wider knowledge, it was to other monasteries, cathedral schools, or courts. There was little sign that their search, even if it was successful, was appreciated or used by others, and the careers such men followed later generally depended little upon the state of their learning. Behind the revolution of the late eleventh and twelfth centuries, however, lay new social structures and new social values. There was a new demand for learning and letters, and those who acquired them could and did find careers open to them. There were new uses for ideas and learning in the twelfth and thirteenth centuries, and as we shall see in Chapter 19, the social conditions out of which the intellectual revolution grew helped generate new directions in the world of ideas.

The careers of Gerbert and St. Anselm reflect intellectual achievement in a society that exerted no particularly great demands for such achievement. The practical learning required in a monastery or a court was considerably different from that that later emerged in the twelfth century. There was little demand for the achievements of a Gerbert, and Gerbert became pope as much through his friendship and loyalty to Otto III and his experience as through his vast and increasingly suspect learning. In the course of the late eleventh and twelfth centuries, however, careers did come into existence that required learning, and people could use their learning as a stepping stone into ranks and functions that had been virtually closed to them a century earlier. The new energies of royal and ecclesiastical rulers—for example, Henry I of England—led these powerful figures to depend less upon the traditionally established lords and prelates of an earlier age than upon the services of men whom they had raised to power themselves, men who depended upon them alone for patronage and support and who, although they could be better controlled by their patrons, brought to royal and ecclesiastical service sharpened wits, the need to function efficiently, and a taste for the learning they had so painfully acquired. Such men and their taste and their patrons helped create some of the conditions that increased the demand for learning and letters in the twelfth century. The Church, faced with increasing business at Rome and in the great dioceses after the Investiture Contest, felt an increasing need for capable, loyal, trained assistants, and it had the great power to attract the men whom it needed. The twelfth century was probably no more noticeably litigious than the eleventh, but the new law courts of the towns and the courts of kings and princes and prelates had to be staffed. Moreover, lesser princes and prelates began to find that when their clerical business was not kept up, their revenues and status declined perceptibly. All of these potential patrons helped generate a new demand for learning and letters.

Traditional centers of learning, however, were not equipped to meet this demand. Monastic schools, irregularly and unpredictably staffed, had never intended to educate an entire society. When they had done so, between the sixth and the tenth centuries, they succeeded largely because the demands made upon them had been slight. By the twelfth century, education had to be found elsewhere. The cathedral schools, however, were scarcely any better. Not until late in the twelfth century could general steps be taken to insist that all cathedrals have a school and that certain subjects be taught in it. The quality of these schools depended upon the bishops and their chancellors, who had much else on their minds, and the few teachers able to excite a class. The schools for laymen that doubtless survived in Italy and southern France had always been small, and except for certain parts of northern Italy, they were not located in centers where the demand for them was strongest. Independent courses of instruction given by individual scholars existed, but these turned out few students at first. By the late twelfth century, the merging of several of these instructors at the cathedral schools at Paris and Bologna had paved the way for the universities of the thirteenth and fourteenth centuries. But between the decline of the monastic schools in the eleventh century and the rise of universities in the thirteenth, the centers of learning remained as limited, and flexible, as they had always been.

Sometimes, the study of individual careers illuminates cultural history better than generalizing. Peter Abelard was born to a minor noble family in Brittany in 1079. His father, Berengar, was in the service of the count of Brittany, and Abelard, as the eldest son, might have been expected to follow in his father's role. Berengar, however, already revealed something of a new world: he appears to have been solicitous for his children's education, and when Peter renounced a military career and started out upon a journey to school after school to acquire the training in dialectic that he wanted, Berengar appears to have raised no objections. Abelard studied briefly at Loches with the philosopher Roscellinus, and probably stopped off at other places before he arrived at Paris around 1100. Abelard began his studies there under William of Champeaux, archdeacon of Paris and a well-known logician. Relations between the two cooled noticeably after Abelard's aggressive personality began to reflect his independence of his teacher. Abelard then left Paris and established himself as an independent teacher at Melun and Corbeil; he did not return to Paris until 1108. In 1113, after five years of success in Paris, Abelard turned to the study of theology and shortly became a member of the cathedral chapter of Notre Dame and master of scholars at the cathedral. Youthful brilliance and success in Paris was, in the twelfth century as in the twentieth, a heady experience, and Abelard's natural independence made him, by all accounts, a difficult man to live with. He had begun an affair with Heloise, the niece of a fellow canon, after having become her tutor, and the story of their child, their secret marriage, and Heloise's uncle's bitter objections, culminating in the castration of Abelard and the claustration of Heloise, is well known. In 1116 Abelard entered the monastery of St. Denis, and Heloise took the veil at Argenteuil.

Until the time of his marriage, Abelard's career had progressed swiftly and with remarkable success. Although he had only taken minor orders, his marriage barred him from further ecclesiastical advancement. His old teacher, William of Champeaux, was archdeacon of Paris, then head of the monastic school of St. Victor in Paris, and then bishop of Chalons. Such a career would have been possible for Abelard as well, and Heloise, realizing this, appears to have bitterly advised against their marriage. From 1126 until 1136 Abelard remained in monastic life, first at St. Denis in Paris, later at the monastery of St. Gildas in Brittany, which he left in 1132 to resume his teaching. He returned to Paris, now fully grown into an intellectual center, and flourished until his theological writings were condemned at the Council of Soissons in 1140. Abelard then retired to the monastery of Cluny, under Peter the Venerable, where he died in 1142. Heloise, who had become the abbess of a monastery Abelard had founded for her, survived him by several decades.

The lives of Heloise and Abelard reflect the liveliness and informality of Paris in the early twelfth century. Heloise was brought up in ecclesiastical households, and although such households declined later on, the sociological background of such "church children" contributed a number of important individuals to the movement of learning. We will consider Abelard's role in the history of thought in Chapter 19. His career, however, from the child of a minor Breton knight to the master of scholars at Notre Dame in Paris, sheds considerable light upon the new circumstances of learning in the first half of the twelfth century.

When Abelard returned to Paris in 1136, one of his students was John of Salisbury, who had been born about 1115, raised in the old episcopal town of Salisbury, and then sent to Paris to study. After his studies were completed, in 1147, John joined the papal court and remained there until 1153, when he became the secretary of Theobald, archbishop of Canterbury. Europe in the 1140s and 1150s was full of opportunities even for men from places as remote as England. The chancellor of the papacy in 1146 was Robert Pullen, the English theologian, and from 1154 to 1159 the pope himself was the Englishman Nicholas Breakspear (Hadrian IV), who had previously spent many years in papal service. Under Theobald and his successor, Thomas Becket, John worked closely with the archbishops of Canterbury. Exiled in the 1160s, John was present at the murder of Becket in 1170. In 1176 John was elected bishop of Chartres, a post that he held until his death in 1180. John's friend and patron, Thomas Becket, descended from a prosperous Norman citizen of London, was sent abroad to Paris to study, moved in circles familiar to John, and became chancellor of England and then archbishop of Canterbury under Henry II.

Such careers as these, and there were many more as striking, illuminate the changing conditions in the world of governance and power. Learning now meant success, although many students failed to achieve the careers they sought and left bitter invective against those they thought prevented it. Even successful men such as John of Salisbury condemned the intellectual extravagance and bombast that sometimes passed itself off for learning, and they and others complained that true learning was bypassed as flashy superficial talents seemed to make all the headway. These criticisms have much substance, but they also remind us of the extent of the new learning and the offers it might have in store for ambitious, brilliant, or merely glib, aspiring officials.

Nor were the rising scholars only those whose social origins made them more mobile and adventurous than the rest. John of Salisbury and Heloise had come from ecclesiastical surroundings, Abelard from the backwoods of Brittany, Becket from the streets of London. One of Becket's contemporary students at Paris may have been Reginald von Dassel, not one of the greatest students at Paris, but a person of noble birth, who later became provost of the cathedrals at Hildesheim and Münster and, after 1156, the chancellor of the Holy Roman Emperor Frederick Barbarossa, whose uncle and biographer, Otto of Freising, had also studied at Paris. Such opportunities afforded ambitious students considerable incentive to seek out the best (or the most popular) schools and teachers and to cultivate among their contemporaries those who gave promise of one day being able to dispense patronage. Such a network of schools, scholars, career aspirants, and patrons contributed much both to the patronage of learning and the spread of the schools, and also to the institutions of administration and governance. They imparted a new style to the centers of power, and they patronized others like themselves. In short, in a world of established ranks and orders, they created that useful invention, the career, and its humble relatives, the occupation and the opportunity for administrative advancement. In shaping such a world, they also shaped the intellectual circumstances in which administration, communication, and educational institutions dealt with real day-to-day problems, shaped theories of law and governance, and contributed a new intellectual dimension to the old problems of society and its organization.

19

THE CONTENT OF THE NEW LEARNING

ANSELM AND ABELARD: FROM DIALECTIC TO PHILOSOPHY

Among those who wandered in search of learning in the eleventh and twelfth centuries, two men stand out as representatives of the early and later stages of the intellectual revolution of the period. St. Anselm was born at Aosta in northwestern Italy in 1033, received his earliest education there, and set out to find a more effective center of learning. In 1060 he entered the monastery of Bec in Normandy, where he studied with Lanfranc, also a native of northern Italy and then the monastery's abbot. In 1063 Anselm became the prior of Bec, and in 1078 abbot. In 1093 he succeeded Lanfranc as archbishop of Canterbury, and he died in 1109.

The generation that separated Anselm from Abelard witnessed significant changes in the location of centers of learning and the circumstances in which learning might be acquired. For Anselm, learning was necessarily monastic, and monastic schools flourished wherever patronage of monasteries happened to take root. The dukes of Normandy had lately taken to patronizing Bec, and pure chance drew first Lanfranc, then Anselm to that remote corner of their world. Anselm moved from the position of monk to those of abbot and archbishop, a progression not surprising in the monastic-influenced church of the late eleventh century. For Abelard, monasticism came only at the end of a career that had been surprisingly and dramatically cut short. Cathedral schools, independent teaching, the teaching position at the Cathedral of Notre Dame—these were the circumstances of the new learning a generation after Anselm. But there was more to the difference between the generations of Anselm and Abelard than cultural climates and social opportunities. Anselm was not wholly representative of eleventh-century monastic culture: he was a great logician, and would have been in any age the rival of Plato and Descartes. In his devotional writings he laid the ground for a system of dialectical analysis that developed further in the work of Abelard and those around him and led to the systematization of the study of law and theology and the development of a philosophical approach to many broader fields of knowledge and speculation. Upon the superstructure of the circumstances of the new demand for learning and letters, there arose a distinctive kind of thought and a fundamentally new approach to the problem of existence.

The slow rise to prominence of logic in the course of the eleventh century took place, as we have seen, within the format of the *trivium,* the initial study of grammar, rhetoric, and dialectic that constituted the core of education before the twelfth century, and sometimes constituted the only education available. The prominence of grammar and rhetoric derived from their essential role in interpreting and explaining Scripture and accorded with the limited extent of educational facilities. Logic, however, served as R. W. Southern remarked, as "an instrument of order in a chaotic world," and its rise was in part the rise of a new sense of just how chaotic the world really was. With the increased ease of communication and the growth of schools, increased study of Scripture and the writings of the church fathers revealed inconsistencies, contradictions, and paradoxes that even the most elevated rhetorical training balked at solving. Logic seemed to offer a systematic, disciplined approach to these fundamental problems, and it also shaped a mind in such a way as to help it consider other aspects of the human condition, for which it also had to find solutions.

The great power of an almost mystical faith and a lyric urge to render intelligible the doctrines held by faith informs and illuminates Anselm's dialectical method. Like Plato and St. Augustine, the personality of the thinker imbues his formal works of philosophical speculation, and this aspect of Anselm's character contributes to his personal reputation above and beyond the contents of his works themselves A second aspect of Anselm's thought may be considered his break with traditional concepts of the functional use of scriptural authority. From late antiquity to the eleventh century the authoritative character of received texts—from scientific encyclopedias to Scripture—had colored explanations of faith. The texts, authoritative in themselves, had only to be explained, their authority had only to be appealed to, in order to shape a convincing argument. In Anselm's writings, faith, which is posited as already existing, seeks not authority but understanding. *Fides quaerens intellectum,* "faith seeking understanding," became Anselm's own motto:

> "Neither indeed do I seek to know in order to believe, but I believe so that I may know."

"Knowing," in Anselm's sense, was not contrasted specifically with scriptural authority; rather, it opened avenues in the exercise of human faculties to areas that had hitherto been closed by the authoritative character of the received tradition. "Understanding" became a legitimate goal of the mind imbued with faith, and logic became its principal tool; the joy of human understanding according to the capacities that humans possess is legitimate and does not necessarily bolster a faltering faith but expands and illuminates an already grounded faith. Anselm's famous argument concerning the ontological proof of the existence of God may serve as an example. In his *Proslogion,* Anselm offered the definition of the deity as a being than which no greater can be thought to exist. Anselm, who possessed the Augustinian notion of the *vestigia Dei,* the "traces of God" possessed by fallen human nature, conceived human reason as one of the legitimate means of discovering God, particularly when reason's conclusions did not contradict Scripture. Reason, when published to its limits of conceptualizing, steps over the border to discover by its own efforts things that are necessarily existent, of which God is the only such being. Anselm's argument, which has attracted much commentary, praise, and criticism, is essentially an extension of his concept of the legitimacy of reasoning in the life of the Christian believer. For Anselm, if *fides* seeks *intellectum,* and if *fides* is proper, then the *intellectum* it discovers must necessarily point to a real truth. This legitimizing of reason in matters essential to the human condition is Anselm's great contribution to the history of thought.

The directions in which the development of logic traveled were, not surprisingly, the directions defined by the culture of Christian Europe. Thus, the proof of the existence of God, the doctrines of redemption and salvation, and the problem of universals all focused upon the concerns of Christians in the eleventh century. Anselm's Europe had inherited a view of the redemption of fallen humanity from St. Augustine, a view that stated that fallen humanity was legitimately in bondage to Satan because of Adam's succumbing to Satan's temptation. Satan had the right to exact death from his servant, humanity, and only Satan's mistaken claiming of Jesus for death broke his power over all of humankind. In the world of thought of the ninth and tenth centuries, this argument had acquired a rather narrowly regalistic accent, depicting man rather as a serf and Satan as a legitimate but wicked feudal overlord. In his treatise *Cur Deus Homo,* "Why God Became Man," Anselm rejects the arguments that God "had" to deal "legally" with Satan because of Satan's legitimate claim over man. Instead, Anselm argues, God became incarnate so that a being who was both God and man could render satisfaction to God for the loss He had suffered through man's succumbing to Satan. Here the focus is firmly upon the original offense to God and definitely away from the perplexing questions about Satan's legitimate rights over humans.

In his ontological proofs of God's existence, the discovery of which he claimed to be intelligible to human reason, and in his new approach to a theory of human redemption, Anselm used the techniques of logical analysis and the vocabulary of Aristotelian logical discourse. In developing these concepts and applying them to the crucial questions of the Christian idea of human existence, Anselm opened a road for reason that paralleled, but did not contradict, that of Scripture and accepted dogma. He began a fascination with reason that lasted until the late thirteenth century, when a new group of philosophers once again severely restricted reason's capacity to achieve the kind of knowledge about transcendental existence that Anselm had posited so hopefully. Between the late eleventh and the late thirteenth centuries, however, Anselm's approach opened up a new career for the study of logic and laid the foundations for a new philosophy.

Dialectic, or logic, applied at first to a broad spectrum of mental activities. The dispute between Lanfranc and Berengar of Tours, Roscellinus's theory of universals, the development of logical means to remove the apparent contradictions or inconsistencies of Scripture, and the systematization of legal texts all derived from the new role of logical analysis and definition. Theology itself took its initial shape from the logical techniques of the eleventh and twelfth centuries, and since theology alone dealt with the most important questions concerning human existence, it was through theology that logic developed into philosophy between the lifetimes of Abelard and St. Thomas Aquinas in the thirteenth century.

Anselm's thought and influence were not limited to the surroundings of Bec and Canterbury. His biographer, Eadmer, told the story of his life, and his writings were collected shortly after his death. Of those who learned from him, Anselm of Laon became a particularly well-known teacher; among others, he taught Abelard's first teacher, William of Champeaux. However, Abelard, who heard Anselm of Laon late in life, did not think much of the experience. St. Anselm's writings also influenced later twelfth-century thinkers, and the rise of dialectic, of which St. Anselm's work was the greatest example, went on to affect others, Abelard included. Anselm had, following Lanfranc, elevated human reason to a legitimate rank in the hierarchy of ways of knowing God, and those who followed him were now free to explore the myriad other uses of reason.

St. Anselm was a monastic teacher, a theologian, who used logic in traditional, unexceptional pedagogic activities in the monastery. His successors as logicians, however, were not always monks, and their work extended not only to the application of logical analysis to many other fields, but to the continuing application of logic to theology as well. William of Champeaux, like Abelard, ended his life in a monastery, but before that he had lived in a wider educational world. The upsurge of logic in the twelfth century resulted in its application to everything. At first, it was applied in the cathedral schools, such as those at Chartres, but cathedral schools were notoriously dependent upon the abilities and energies of their personnel; often, a single teacher illuminated one school briefly and then died or left, leaving the school with no continuing body of faculty or students. In Paris and Bologna, however, groups of masters appear to have established schools that were independent of cathedral authorities at first, and these two centers appear to have been sufficient for the slowly growing number of students who sought learning at them. After the twelfth century, of course, other centers were started, and some, along with Paris, Bologna, and Oxford, survived as universities. In the course of the twelfth century, however, these schools were still highly informal, barely structured, and still faced with tasks ranging from teaching Latin to explaining Scripture. That Abelard wandered from Paris to Melun to Corbeil to Paris and, after 1136, to Paris again, means that Abelard's "school" was wherever he was with his students, and his and other masters' students came and went as the spirit moved them. The curriculum was still that of the *trivium* and *quadrivium,* and Abelard's teaching involved largely the third part of the *trivium,* dialectic. Individuals might leave their study with Abelard to study dialectic with William of Conches and later theology with Gilbert de la Porée, counting their studies complete when they equaled or surpassed the available masters, stopped making progress, or simply found a patron and obtained employment. John of Salisbury was such a person.

The first application of logical studies was to that body of literary tradition that had long formed the materials for study in the West: a few works of Aristotle, Plato's *Timaeus* and commentaries on it, classical literature, and the works of the strange encyclopedists of late antiquity. For several generations learning meant no more than this, and without the influx of new materials it remained, with surprising and often original applications, essentially the study of a body of received literature. The translations from Arabic and the recovery of the works of Aristotle gave a terrific new impetus to this technique and challenged not traditional methods of teaching, but the tradition of received, authoritative literature. Once more the concept of "science" reached out to embrace new studies of nature and the natural world. The original, often brilliant, highly literary explorations of such men as William of Conches and Bernard Sylvester were still tied to the old body of knowledge and literary tradition, yet the organization of traditional materials by the application of logical principles prepared the way for the impact of Aristotle and the Arabs and for the expansion of reason's role from that of a support of scriptural revelation to that of a questioner of the problems of nature as well. In their new task, reason and logical method had been toughened by their application to other fields besides philosophy: theology and law.

THE INVENTION OF THEOLOGY

Assimiliating the new materials of Islamic and Greek thought, formal philosophy found its own track out of the lively but confusing intellectual world of the mid twelfth century. In the thirteenth, it became formally separated from theology. The twelfth-century headlong rush to apply logical analysis to all fields of knowledge had not always produced scholars as sensitive as St. Anselm. Many representatives of a still lively tradition of theological study savagely condemned the presumption of the logicians in extending their interests into the field of theology; Abelard himself fell afoul of the most distinguished theologian of his day, St. Bernard of Clairvaux, which led to his condemnation at the Council of Soissons of 1140. For although the freedom with which philosophical speculation was permitted to roam during the twelfth century was considerable—as in the great, speculative, poetic myths of creation that combined all twelfth-century learning, such as the *Cosmographia (De mundi universitate)* of Bernard Sylvester (d. 1167)—that freedom did not include immunity from the bonds of religious dogma, and that dogma was very much a general concern by the middle of the twelfth century. The formalization of theology was the result of both the new learning and the energetic activities of popes and councils from the First Lateran Council of 1123 to the Fourth Lateran Council of 1215. Within this century, a full-fledged theological system was erected, as were the mechanisms of dealing with those who attacked its principles or denied its content.

The theological interests of the logicians were determined by the rich intellectual problems inherent in an analysis of Scripture and doctrine and in the necessary reconciling of differences in interpretation; logicians used the helpful vocabulary of logical discourse in both of these areas of concern. To those theologians who remained firmly devoted to traditional methods of interpretation, such a course seemed both presumptuous because it raised a purely human science nearly to the level of probing divine mysteries with more confidence than modesty, and dangerous because it greatly increased the possibility of generating heretical beliefs, especially in those whose intellects were not as sophisticated as those of the logicians. Much of the attack on the new logical approach to theological problems came from men trained in recent methods of scriptural interpretation who were products of a new and intense wave of devotion that had appeared in twelfth-century monasticism. These men, such as St. Bernard's friend Rupert of Deutz, revived the old Augustinian scorn for *curiositas,* an unseemly and intemperate, and perhaps superficial and improper quest for knowledge, particularly when they witnessed the new teachers receiving the title *magister* ("master"), being equated in terms of authority with Scripture and the church fathers, and rising to positions of power in the Church and the world. Of Abelard's pupils, twenty later became cardinals, fifty became bishops, and innumerable others made their master's ideas felt throughout the

Christian world. These teachers, particularly Abelard, were now noted not for their sanctity (sometimes quite the opposite), as such men had been before, but for their learning, and this, to Bernard, Rupert, and others, seemed to turn the universe upside-down and to threaten the whole Church. Such were some of the results of the initial rush to logic and the equally vehement reaction against it.

The logicians and their followers were not the only new influences upon traditional theology in the twelfth century. The vast maze of Scripture, patristic literature, and pre-twelfth-century glosses and commentaries upon them were not organized or systematized in any form. The reform movement in tenth- and eleventh-century monasticism, the subsequent reform of the papacy beginning with the pontificate of Leo IX (1049–1054), and the battles and disputes attending the Investiture Contest and the papal launching of the First Crusade had all contributed to the restructuring of the Church. By the Concordat of Worms in 1122, many of the most hotly disputed issues had been temporarily settled, and the assembling of the First Lateran Council in 1123 published that settlement to the Christian world. Yet the task of the papacy and the Church seemed barely begun. New forms of secular society, new threats of heresy, the burgeoning business of the ecclesiastical law courts, and a new and articulate perception of the disorganized character of dogma and law all contributed to a movement to systematize the structure of the Church, to organize its law, and to define its dogmas.

Such work was carried out not only in the schools but in the papal court, in the great ecclesiastical councils, and in the work of papal legates sent throughout the Christian world. The papal court, reorganized under Pope Urban II (1188–1199), came during the twelfth century to consist chiefly of a group of higher clergy called cardinals. The cardinals, who originally were clergy of all degrees serving in the older Roman and suburbicarian churches, originally functioned chiefly as liturgical substitutes for the pope himself. In the electoral reforms of 1059, however, the cardinals were given a majority voice in the election of popes, and during the twelfth century they came to direct the administration of the church and advise the pope. On great occasions, the popes had held synods in Rome, particularly during Lent, and during the twelfth century these grew into the great church councils that drew prelates from all over Europe and issued collectively the decrees that slowly shaped law and dogma. Beginning with the pontificate of Gregory VII (1073–1085), particular ecclesiastical officials, either resident bishops or clerics sent from Rome, served as legates and carried powers similar to those of the pope himself, thus increasing the efficiency of church government.

The work of the papal court, cardinals, councils, and legates increased during the twelfth and early thirteenth centuries, and service in this government became an attractive career for an ambitious cleric. Others, not surprisingly, viewed this growth of administrative apparatus with considerable misgiving; St. Bernard complained to his protégé, Pope Eugenius III (1145–1153), about the increasing "worldliness" of the governance of the Church, just as John of Salisbury did to his friend, Pope Hadrian IV (1154–1159). By 1159, no longer were the duties of the clergy surrounding the pope limited to ceremonial functions, and no longer was widely recognized personal holiness sufficient for promotion to the rank of cardinal or legate. These duties had become careers, and one trained for them in the schools, not in the monasteries. A cleric might serve at the papal court for a time, as John of Salisbury did, and then serve elsewhere, maintaining his contacts with old colleagues and sometimes returning on diplomatic missions from his new master, as John did for Henry II of England.

This was the administrative structure of the Church that, during the twelfth century, defined law and dogma in councils, regularized the system of ecclesiastical courts, and precisely defined the boundaries not only of bishoprics and parishes but also of jurisdiction over monasteries. In the course of this work this administrative staff came more and more under the influence of ways of thought propounded in the schools and less and less under that of traditional monasticism. Such influence responded more readily to principles of systematization and regularization, and it tended to produce an attitude toward the organization of the Church and its beliefs more akin to law than to the traditions of the early Church. Law itself had undergone a significant transformation in the twelfth century. The vast disorganized mass of earlier ecclesiastical law, ranging from Scripture and patristic literature to miscellaneous papal decrees, conciliar canons, and royal charters composed over a period of seven centuries, was not handled easily in the twelfth-century Church. Several great thinkers early in the century, such as Burchard of Worms and Ivo of Chartres, had successfully put some order into some of these materials, much as had more particularly purposeful compilers such as Anselm of Lucca during the Investiture Contest. One of the most important influences upon the shaping of canon law, however, was precisely the development of principles of systematic organization of related ideas and topics in the schools of the twelfth century.

As we have seen, the confusion of ecclesiastical law and the purely literary and meditative character of theology before 1150 made these areas of concern attractive to the logicians, and many of them, from Anselm to Laon to Abelard, applied their new methods to these fields. Their methods are best seen in Abelard's famous work, the *Sic et Non*, "Yes and No." The *Sic et Non* was compiled by Abelard sometime after 1120, probably for the use of himself and his students. It consisted of a preface laying down a methodology of interpreting the texts and then a body of texts culled from the writings of the early church fathers, the texts being laid out in contradictory groups dealing with different topics. The aim of the technique was to apply reasoning to these apparent contradictions and so to resolve them. In his preface, Abelard reminded the student that interpreting the words of the fathers required some knowledge of linguistic change, corruption of translation or copying, the circumstances and contexts of the statements, their definitive or nondefinitive intention, and an establishment of a hierarchy of authorities. Other collections of patristic opinions and scriptural texts also appeared. In 1140 Gratian, a monk at Bologna, compiled a collection of such statements; it consisted of numerous texts by different authorities, and these texts were used to solve a systematic set of problems dealing with ecclesiastical law. Far more than Abelard's work, however, Gratian's collection was informed by a mind both legally acute and devout. From the beginning to the end of his work, Gratian imposed order, principle, and coherence upon the previously undigestible materials of ecclesiastical law. He marshaled over four thousand different texts from dozens of authors, sometimes using as many as seventy to clarify and illuminate the diverse sides of a single topic. Between the texts, introducing them and bringing each topic to a conclusion, is Gratian's own commentary, a model of lucidity and economy. Gratian's collection, although it always remained unofficial, became the model for later official collections of canon law (see the next section) and for the system used in theological works of grouping thematically related texts together for analysis. Around 1150, probably under Gratian's influence, Peter the Lombard, a master in the Paris schools and later bishop of Paris, produced his *Book of Sentences,* a systematic collection of scriptural texts and the writings of church fathers and masters dealing topically with theological wisdom. The works of Gratian and Peter Lombard became the schoolbooks for the later study of law and theology, in some cases being used until the beginning of the twentieth century. Arising in the schools and from masters such as Abelard, Gratian, and Peter Lombard, the principles of selecting, ordering, and typologizing diversified texts were now applied to the disciplines of law and theology.

Thus, the masters of theology in the schools moved further and further away from traditional methods of interpreting and explaining Scripture and later theology. The language of theological definition and explanation became more and more that of the schools of logic and the philosophers and less that of the meditative and literary traditions of the past. Not only did the new language and the new systematizing of thought and exposition explore further dimensions of the relationship between God and creation, it opened vistas in the definition of the human personality. As the tools of logic and philosophy became the tools of theology, specialization, training, and formal expression became necessary for theological study. In the course of this process, the nature and number of the sacraments was finally set at seven and their character was defined; the complex questions touching definitions of nature, grace, sin, and salvation and their attendant problems now received firm answers. In the teaching of theology, the master now proceeded to treat texts, no matter how traditionally authoritative, in terms of the questions they illuminated, and the choice of these questions and their complexity directed the thrust of study. In time, the questions, *quaestiones,* became the principal form of theological exposition. The master would pose the question, give a series of texts or arguments for the negative, hinge his discussion on a short statement generally beginning, "On the contrary. . . ," give his own analysis, and systematically reply to the objections raised in the first part of the discussion. Each question, therefore, possessed a symmetrical structure consisting of a kind of dialectical reasoning that was closely guided by the master. By the thirteenth century, the replies to the objections became not the marshaling of texts from the authorities, but expressions of the master's own reasoning. At the same time there appeared collections of questions on particular individual topics, such as marriage and penance. These were called summas, *summae,* and they became the standard forms for the pedagogic and literary exposition of theological thought.

The older scriptural commentators were not the only theologians who were bypassed by the new methods. The bishops, traditionally the custodians of doctrine, were also bypassed. The theologians of the schools, specially trained and possessing a methodology and a vocabulary —one might say a craft—of their own, became the leaders of theological speculation. Thus, the development of new forms of theological organization and exposition reflected the transformation of the older monastic-episcopal church in ways that paralleled the new organization of the papacy and its government, and these new forms participated in the character of the new learning. It is no accident that the name for this organization of knowledge and belief, theology, appears to have been coined by Peter Abelard.

THE PROFESSIONS: LAW

The principles of mental organization according to the precepts of logic infused both the schools and the more narrow confines of theology. But they did not stop there. Logic's virtue, so it seemed to those who professed it, could be applied to any field, and no area of twelfth-century life seemed better suited to its application than that of the law. The vast aggregate of different customs, procedures, exceptions, and authorities that constituted the panorama of twelfth-century law would have tempted any logician, and the importance of logical training in the schools strongly influenced men who later became legal functionaries in ecclesiastical and secular courts during the twelfth and thirteenth centuries. But the revival of logic was not the sole impetus to the new legal studies. A practical need for the organization of law was recognized by ambitious and energetic rulers such as Henry I of England and Roger II of Sicily, and both of these rulers and others as well, strongly influenced the systematization of law, first in their own royal courts and later throughout their realms. In addition to such a practical impetus, however, the late eleventh and early twelfth centuries witnessed a revival of the study of Roman law in northern Italy. This revival, providing teachers, students, and legal authorities alike with a model of a rational legal code, a method for its exposition, and the need to fit Justinian's laws to twelfth-century circumstances exerted great influence throughout the twelfth and thirteenth centuries and touched, however lightly, all the legal systems of Europe.

The *Corpus Iuris Civilis* of Justinian, published in 534 was a coherent, systematic body of law and one of the greatest intellectual triumphs of late antiquity. The *Corpus* was never effective in the western parts of the empire because of the political and social strife of the sixth and seventh centuries, but by the end of the eleventh century it had begun to attract the attention of a number of practicing lawyers and teachers in regions as separate as southern France, Lombardy, and Ravenna. Many of the first works to reveal the influence of Roman law were procedural handbooks, explanatory glosses, and the records of decisions circulated in literary or polemical works. In Bologna, the most influential of all law schools originated. Although the origins of this school are obscure, it appears that the first teachers of Roman law were scholars trained in the *trivium* and perhaps the *quadrivium* and who came to the teaching of law from the teaching of the liberal arts. The first of these, Irnerius (fl. 1088–1125), gave up the idea of compiling guides to legal procedure and summarizing the principles of the law and instead lectured directly on the texts of Justinian's work. In their method, and in the glosses (explanatory comments on individual words and passages), establishment of authentic texts of Justinian's work, and concepts of teaching, Irnerius and his successors used the same techniques that Abelard and the other school masters used in the development of dialectic. The new learning also made its influence felt in the teaching methods and expositions of these teachers of law. Their use of the process of explanation known as the *distinctio,* the distinction, reflected the logicians' desire to organize and to explain problems in a rationally comprehensible way. The *distinctio,* which also operated in expositions of ecclesiastical law, consisted of a general category that was methodically subdivided into its subordinate parts—the relations among these kept rigidly distinct—until the basic elements of the category had been reached. Working from these, the teacher then laid out an interpretation that was concise, orderly, and clearly comprehensible to the student. The *distinctio* and the *quaestio* became the two characteristic features of thought and expression in the learned literature of the twelfth and thirteenth centuries.

The *Corpus Iuris Civilis,* of course, had one immense advantage over the bodies of learning that constituted theology and canon law. It was already a systematic body of law, and it had only to be explained once the texts were established, not formed from diffuse materials. Hence, its teaching appealed to a wide group of problems much earlier than canon law and theology did, and its techniques influenced the shaping of both of these areas of concern. From the isolated definitions of words, brief lists of principal subjects, and collections of rules, the glosses lengthened into detailed examinations of the nature of each law, until by the end of the twelfth century individual sets of glosses by individual teachers came to be written separately from the texts of the law and were themselves compiled into *summae* for further study and disputation. By the middle of the thirteenth century the tradition of brilliant teachers at Bologna and the diversity of glosses and *summae* led to the production of a long summa by the great jurist Francis Accursius (d. 1260). This work summarized previous teaching and was so influential that it became the ordinary gloss, the *glossa ordinaria*, the standard exposition of the law that became required reading on the part of all students after its appearance in 1250. The gloss technique reminds us of the links among the different fields of learning. The Bible, too, acquired a *glossa ordinaria* during the twelfth century, as did Gratian's *Decretum* early in the thirteenth and the later collections of papal decrees that became official lawbooks.

The teaching, studying, and explaining of Roman law was not a formal school exercise, however. Students came to study the law of Rome because in many parts of Italy, southern France, and the alpine territories it was still held valid. These were the countries known in French as the *pays du droit écrit*, "the lands of written [that is, Roman] law," and there, as well as in Byzantium, Roman law still operated. Roman law was also recognized by the Church as the foundation of canon law: *non canonista nisi romanista*, "if you are not a Romanist you aren't a canonist," ran a student jingle of the thirteenth century. *Ecclesia vivit lege romana*, "the Church lives by Roman law," ran the more sonorous—and influential—pronouncement of the Church.

Yet even outside the Church and the lands of written law, the study of Roman law proved valuable. The rest of the Christian world, the *pays du droit coutumier*, "the lands of customary law," also found great attraction in the order and logic of Roman law. Techniques of judicial procedure and theories of evidence, including the infamous reappearance of judicial torture, all made their way into customary courts under Roman legal influence. The earlier legal universe of the oath, compurgation, and the ordeal slowly gave way before judicial reorganization springing from Roman legal procedures.

Indirectly, Roman law constituted a model for legal systems that remained formally independent of it. In England around 1188, a writer produced a work called *A Treatise on the Laws and Customs of England*. The author, allegedly Ranulf de Glanvil, revealed the influence of Roman law in many details, most importantly in his idea that the customs of England were susceptible of study by a treatise in the first place. In the thirteenth century, a royal justice named Henry Bracton wrote an extensive treatise, *On the Laws and Customs of England*, which carried ideas of organization and systematization even further. Between 1279 and 1283 Philippe de Beaumanoir wrote his treatise, *On the Cus-*

toms of the Beauvaisis (the region around the town of Beauvais in northern France), a work that showed great mastery of the principles of Roman law while applying them to a body of customary totally different.

In many respects, the creation of canon law was as significant as any of the developments discussed so far. From Gratian's *Decretum* through the unofficial and later official collections of papal legal decisions that appeared in 1234, 1298, and 1314, scholars and popes shaped a body of law that laid down a new, juridical view of the relationship between the individual Christian and the Church. This body of law remained valid and in use throughout Christian Europe until the Reformation of the sixteenth century and in the Roman Catholic Church until 1918. Part of its influence lay doubtless in the fact that Gratian's organizing principles displayed clearly where the greatest legal problems lay, and that the lack of a fundamental organization comparable to that of the *Corpus Iuris Civilis* left teachers and students much room to add their own thought to the body of scholarship on the law or to criticize Gratian's. From a course in the liberal arts, including dialectic, students moved on to read Roman law, and they might then go on to canon law, their minds sharpened by logicians, Romanists, and their own teachers of canon law. The first commentaries upon Gratian's collection are hesitant and elementary. Longer commentaries quickly appeared, however, modeled upon those produced by teachers of Roman law—summas, questions, and rules. Among the early canonists, or decretists, a number of scholars produced genuine contributions that greatly influenced later approaches to the teaching and the creation of church law. Such twelfth-century figures as Rufinus, Stephen of Tournai, and, the greatest of all, Huguccio of Pisa, were followed in the early thirteenth century by Richard of England, Alan of England, Tancred, and Johannes Teutonicus, who composed the *glossa ordinaria* to the *Decretum* around 1215.

As had been the case with those who studied logic, theology, and Roman law, the teachers and students at Bologna and, later, other centers of study, moved into the world of affairs and in their own careers approached the traditional duties of bishop, legate, and pope more and more from the point of view bred in them during their legal studies. Most accomplished canonists became ecclesiastical officials, from archdeacon to cardinal, and in 1159 Rolandus Bandinelli became pope as Alexander III (1159-1181). Under Alexander and the great many of his successors who also were trained in the law, the papacy reached the height of its authority and achieved a terrible clarity in its definitions of ecclesiastical law, especially in those areas that touched upon "constitutional questions" defining the relation of papal authority to that of kings, emperors, and prelates. Before the political theorists of the thirteenth and fourteenth centuries, the canon lawyers of the twelfth and early thirteenth centuries explored questions of papal authority and other topics with an originality and profundity that raised some of them to the highest levels of political theorizing the modern world has known.

Moreover, much of canon law touched areas that in the twentieth century are universally regarded as civil rather than ecclesiastical responsibilities. Questions of marriage, dowry, legitimacy of children, vows, wills, penance, and public authority all fell within the canonists' spheres of legitimate interest and so influenced these areas of life for centuries and in some respects still do. The rise of the "new theologians" in the traditional world of monks and bishops was accompanied by the rise of the "new lawyers." The Church was transformed by this specialization of theology and law. Older institutions persisted, and they still exist. But advocates of monasteries, bishops, archdeacons, legates, judges, and popes all came now from the ranks of the theologians and the lawyers, out of the schools, and they brought with them to their traditional positions new attitudes toward law and theology and new concerns for their role in Christian society—concerns, it should be noted, that were often disparaged, not only by representatives of older attitudes but by many individuals who charged that the new direction of ecclesiastical organization was away from the needs of simple Christians and more and more toward the temptations of the world.

The role played by the revival of legal studies in the general new learning of the twelfth century is large. Besides the specific revival, application, and inspiration of Roman law and the marked role of canon law, however, we have also seen the less tangible and direct, but equally powerful influences it exerted upon the legal thinking in areas where Roman law was not recognized. In short, law everywhere began to be subjected to the criteria of systematization, consistency, and rational analysis, whether it was Roman law, the customary law of England, or the customs of a region in France. These indirect influences contributed greatly to the role of law in the monarchies of the late twelfth and thirteenth centuries. Among their many other roles, medieval kings were law protectors, law administrators and sometimes lawgivers. The reign of Henry II in England (1154–1188) witnessed a vigorous royal effort to regularize the law followed in English courts, first in those on the royal domain and later throughout the kingdom. The legal enactments of King Louis IX of France (1226–1270) constituted an attempt to organize the law of the royal domain proper, with additions from Roman law; outside the area where royal law was recognized, in such provinces as Beauvais, regional customary laws were often written down, commented upon, and administered by men with training in Roman law, canon law, or both. One of the most remarkable examples of such a synthesis of traditional law, royal enactments, canon law, and Roman law is the book of laws for the kingdom of Sicily, the *Liber Augustalis,* promulgated by Frederick II in 1231. Drawn up by men who had studied at Bologna but were responding to the traditions of authority within the Sicilian kingdom, the *Liber Augustalis* was widely praised for its organization and succinctness. Not slaves to Roman law, but farsighted students of its potential helpfulness in structuring the law of Sicily, the authors of the *Liber,* like Beaumanoir a generation later, revealed how pervasive and influential the legal revolution could be.

THE MEDIEVAL UNIVERSITY

The schools of Paris in the days of Peter Abelard and for decades afterward consisted of the assemblies of students grouped around individual masters, the students paying the masters individually. These assemblies gradually came under the ecclesiastical jurisdiction of the bishop of Paris. In Paris and Bologna, the phenomenon of individuals coming together in a strange city far from their homes to study was a social and juridical novelty, and the very presence of the schools and the lack of a legal status for them rendered the students vulnerable to much of the inadvertent hostility generated by the inveterate localism of the twelfth century. Unprotected by citizenship, status, or privilege, students were subject to price and rent gouging, a lack of legal protection, and the perennial distresses of underfinanced strangers.

Long before the formal beginnings of universities, two institutions illustrate the precarious status of the new schools. In 1158 Emperor Frederick Barbarossa issued a privilege to those students on imperial lands—and Bologna was within the empire—that protected their status as students against the powers of a world that was reluctant to recognize the category. In his privilege, which is known as the *Authentic Habita* (from its opening word, *Habita,* the incipit, or beginning, by which many medieval legal documents were commonly called), Frederick laid down several clearly defined areas of protection for students. First, students might safely come to places where learning was to be had and might safely live there; second, no one was to injure the students or bring them into court to settle an obligation incurred by someone else from their place of origin. The document is humble, but it is the foundation charter for the modern concept of academic freedom. It is purely practical in intention, yet in the decorative phrases surrounding the injunctions Frederick wove the traces of a new attitude on the part of public authorities toward study in general. The scholars do good, said the emperor, and since all who do good ought to be under imperial protection, so will they be. Study is functional: those who learn teach the world, and they teach obedience to the subjects of God's servants (that is, the emperors), and in doing so they often expose themselves to danger, poverty, and insult. Then, in a remarkable parallel to the old Irish idea of "exile for the love of God," Frederick went on to note that scholars "make themselves exiles for the love of knowledge," and thereby excite "compassion." The mingling of traditional liturgical phraseology and expeditiousness is audacious and revealing. A second event that illuminates the circumstances of the earliest schools is the inception, a public defense of one's learning that began to be used in the late twelfth century. The inception has parallels, as the German historian Peter Classen has shown, with the formal rites of initiation into the order of knighthood, the oath of citizenship in the corporation of citizens of a town, and the ritual recognition of the status of master in a craft guild.

Thus, scholars, both students and teachers, slowly created a collective place for themselves in a society that jealously guarded its status ranks and savagely left unprotected the stranger without status. Indeed, the defensive measures taken by the late twelfth-century schools, measures that tried to achieve some degree of protection in an institutionally hostile world, consisted wholly of creating for scholars a corporate status that would be recognized. *Universitas*, the Latin term used to designate the schools, was a common word indicating any collectivity, from craft guild to confraternity to body of citizens, and the formal designation of the universities was *Universitas societas magistrorum discipulorumque,* "the university, or society, of masters and students." Other terms that were related to associations generally applied also to scholars. *Schola*, from late Roman imperial and Byzantine tradition, meant many different groups regarded simply from the point of view of them as a group. *Schola* in academic terms remained the designation of a master and his students together. Groups of *scholae* working in close proximity and having a similar character were called a *studium*. These terms possessed no collective juridical character, however, and privileges such as the *Authentic Habita* applied to scholars individually, giving them no collective rights and recognizing no collective juridical existence. The key event in the history of the universities occurred between 1200 and 1220 when the issuance of papal, imperial, and royal privileges entitled the scholars to act as a legal collective, an *universitas*, possessing the right to be represented legally as a corporation, to possess a seal, to collect and administer common funds, and to sue and be sued collectively in courts of law. Sometimes, as at Paris, the legal collective *universitas* was one of the masters alone; sometimes, as at Bologna, the students constituted an *universitas*. Through such societal and juridical changes, the universities came into legal as well as social existence by the middle of the thirteenth century.

In 1200 King Phillip II Augustus of France provided an extensive charter of privileges to the *universitas* at Paris, a document generally regarded as the foundation of the charter of the present university, and in 1231 Pope Gregory IX issued the decree known as *Parens scientiarum,* "the mother of knowledge," which afforded ecclesiastical privileges to the university of Paris and conferring on it by accident a title that it has borne honorifically since then. The universities of the thirteenth century, possessing by then legal existence, often suffered from the organizational problems that other "universities" suffered from: disputes between masters and students, between masters, students, and the officials of the diocese, and between scholars and townsmen. Possessing legal identity, universities could leave a city, negotiate with another city for accommodations, and move there, supervise lower schools in the vicinity, issue collective pronouncements on public questions, and regulate areas as diverse as the book trade and the rate of rents charged to students and teachers. For the universities were only legally, not physically—except for their members —existent. There were no university campuses, no libraries, no distinctly and exclusively university buildings. Lecture rooms were rented in private buildings; masters took students into their homes for residence and instruction, and students who did not live in a master's house had to find private lodging. Only slowly, through gifts, did individual buildings become university property. Even the earliest colleges consisted simply of endowed funds that paid for the housing, feeding, and instruction of poor students under masters' supervision; they were more charitable trusts than physical places. For example, the Sorbonne, the popular designation of the University of Paris, derives from the gift by Robert de Sorbonne in the thirteenth century of a charitable endowment for the support of poor scholars. The first buildings belonging to Oxford, Merton College, were left by Robert Merton, who had acquired them from Oxford Jews, who had refurbished them, renovated them, and thus helped originate the style of college buildings that is commonly called "Gothic."

Within these legal and physical circumstances, the schools developed their curricula and played out their role in terms of the new and the old learning. The triumph of logic, the subordination of the subjects of the *trivium* to the increasingly professional disciplines of theology and law, and the creation of the degree, the *licentia ubique docendi*—"the license to teach anywhere"—shaped their internal intellectual processes, just as their privileges, legal status, and endowments shaped their physical and social character.

The organization of the legal, economic, and social aspects of the universities influenced the development of the curriculums. The first course, a remnant of the old *trivium* and *quadrivium,* was called the Arts course, and its completion became a condition necessary for progress to the gradually evolving higher faculties. By the thirteenth century, the Arts course focused upon Aristotle's logical works and included some study in grammar through the works of Priscian and in rhetoric through the works of Donatus (Latin writers of the fifth and fourth century, respectively, whose books had constituted the core of the study of grammar and rhetoric ever since). During the thirteenth century the Aristotelian content of the Arts course expanded to cover much of Aristotle's work on natural science and, after the middle of the century, works on grammar and rhetoric written by contemporary masters, another sign of the powerful influence of twelfth- and thirteenth-century thinkers and another example of what its critics thought was the perfectly awful custom of equating the new "masters" with the older authorities. By the early thirteenth century, those interested primarily in letters were complaining that the sciences were sweeping the Arts field.

The student who arrived at the university at the age of fourteen or fifteen already knew how to read and write—Latin. His course of study, which usually lasted for five or six years, began with a two-hour lecture at six A.M. and was followed by more lectures, debates in logic, and supervised quizzes. He also attended extra lectures given on holidays. After five years, the student spent the period between December and March undergoing a series of formal disputations with delegated examiners (the determination), at the satisfactory completion of which he acquired the degree of bachelor of arts. If the student continued his studies (for bachelors were not official members of the nations), he faced several more years of study and disputation, examinations for the license to teach, and different lectures on prescribed books. After a formal initiation into the nation, he was awarded the master's degree in arts (the equivalent of the modern Ph.D.), after which he was expected to hold a banquet for his professors and friends.

The master's degree, which included the license to teach, was the customary place to break off studies if a career was the object. For different kinds of academic advancement, however, further work was required. The candidate for a doctorate in law had to spend five to seven years hearing and giving lectures on Roman and canon law, then submit to an examination in public, and then, during a long and expensive period of ceremonies, give his first public lecture and public debate and receive his doctoral privileges. The candidate for a degree in theology faced an even more difficult course. He spent as many as fifteen years hearing lectures, disputing, and reviewing the Bible and the *Book of Sentences* of Peter Lombard. He might copy down his master's lectures, write his notes, and submit them to the master, who would then revise them and allow them to circulate under his name—in short, "publish" them.

Upon the reception of the master's degree, the student could begin to lecture in the faculty of Arts (rather as graduate-student teaching assistants do today, but with more autonomy) while he worked toward his higher degree. The life of the masters was as full as that of the students. Official business, outside consultations, writing, engaging in disputes with rivals, preaching (for the master was a moral as well as an educational official, or, rather, the differences between the two were not as sharply marked then as now), and participating in the rich life of ceremony, labor, busywork, and responsibility that characterized life at the medieval university.

From the university the students went out into the world, and they took the world by storm. Any time spent at the schools, from a few years' residence to the full doctorate of theology, helped start a career. The methods learned and the subjects mastered then determined how the graduate viewed his work which in turn influenced profoundly, as we have seen, both the personnel of high ecclesiastical and secular offices and the style of the offices themselves. The bishops, archdeacons, cardinals, and popes of the thirteenth century came from the world of the university, and through their experience they transformed both the offices they filled and the world they managed.

20

THE CHURCH AND THE WORLD, 1098-1250

MONASTICISM AND CIVILIZATION

From the time of the earliest monastic settlements—those off the coast of southern Gaul and in Italy and Ireland between the fourth and the sixth centuries—the institutions and culture of the monasteries played an important—perhaps the most important role—in shaping the religious culture of the Christian west. Monasteries supplied bishops and popes to the church and the world; they offered examples of economic and managerial enterprise; when they sheltered scholars, the scholarship they produced not only advanced the literary efforts of Europe, but rescued many of the Latin classics and offered the only education available. When, in the eighth century, the movement for ecclesiastical reform began, it originated with wandering English monks who designed the pastoral and administrative churches of France and Germany. When ecclesiastical reform became a major program of Charlemagne's concept of the ruler's responsibilities, Charlemagne turned to the monasteries and their scribes and scholars; when they had established basic educational reforms, Charlemagne's successor, Louis the Pious, turned to the great reformer Benedict of Aniane, who vastly increased the influence of the Benedictine rule. The reforms of the tenth and eleventh centuries, from Cluny to Einsiedeln, raised the monasteries to a position of wealth and influence unrivaled by most of the remaining parts of the Church, and in the eleventh century, when Gregorian reform turned in the direction of ecclesiology, monasticism was again transformed. To a great extent, the history of monasticism is the key to the cultural history of Europe between the fifth and the twelfth centuries, and the monastic revolution in the twelfth century is an integral part of the complex transformation of European culture in other areas during that period.

One of the most important elements in the history of the eleventh century was the increasingly close associations between monasteries and their lay patrons and protégés. A new spirit of penitence inspired laymen to seek the intercession of the monks in their prayers and liturgies and to inscribe their names on the books of the dead for whom the monastery prayed, and in return they patronized the monasteries. Solemn public prayers, charitable or virtuous acts, penitential pilgrimages—all contributed to these close relations. People entered monasteries to share even more intensely in the spiritual perfection of the monks, often rejecting the world in doing so.

As we have seen, one of the objectives of the papacy, especially the papacy after Gregory VII (1073-1085), was to work intense reform in the world itself rather than to preserve the monasteries as asylums from the world. As H. E. J. Cowdrey has shown, this was one of the key points in the slow parting of the ways between Cluny and Gregory VII. In a broader sense, the twelfth century witnessed the growth in the world of other reform movements that rejected, implicitly or explicitly, the uniqueness of monastic retreat. On the other hand, twelfth-century monastic reformers saw with increasing clearness that the monasteries and the world had drawn too close. They regarded the monastic vocation not as a shelter for aristocrats with increasingly acute consciences, which role drew with it the virtues and vices of increased lay patronage, but as an occasion for the renewal of apostolic simplicity, utter withdrawal from the world, and a return to the simple letter of the Benedictine rule. As we shall see in the next section, this movement was but a single part of a much heightened interest in evangelical Christianity shared by monks, secular clergy, and laymen from all walks of life during the twelfth and thirteenth centuries. Such monastic institutions as Cluny, with its elaboration of the rule, its contacts with the world, its enormously intricate liturgy, and its great wealth, came under heavy criticism from reformers, and a new monastic movement gained greater and greater headway during the second half of the eleventh century; it burst into full flower in the twelfth.

In the eleventh century there appeared new monastic groups of Vallombrosa and Camaldoli in Italy, the monasteries of the Carthusians of eastern France, who developed their reformed order between 1080 and 1176, and the foundations of individual reformers, such as the remarkable convent at Fontevrault that was founded around 1115 by Robert of Arbrissel and consisted of four religious houses, all ruled by a woman. The most influential, and the most significant of the groups of reformed monasteries was the complex of monasteries that grew out of the reforms at Citeaux from the late eleventh to the late twelfth century. Founded in 1098 by a group of monks who sought a stricter rule than that at their old monastery at Molesmes, Citeaux (*Cistercium* in Latin, whence the name of the order, the Cistercians) was located in a remote and desolate corner of Burgundy. Under the abbot Stephen Harding (1070[?]–1134), the congregation lived according to a very strict rule—hewing, as they said, to the absolute letter of St. Benedict's instructions—simplified the complex liturgies of other monasteries, and introduced a program of hard manual labor. The first fourteen years of the monastery were difficult, but with the arrival of St. Bernard in 1112–1113, the order slowly began to expand. Between 1113 and 1115 daughter houses were founded at La Ferté, Pontigny, Clairvaux, and Morimond, and by the late twelfth century there were over three hundred Cistercian houses, as well as several hundred more following one variation or another of the Cistercian rule. For the simple letter of the Benedictine rule proved incomplete at Citeaux, and in 1114 Stephen Harding drew up the first version of a rule for Cistercians, the *Carta Caritatis*, "The Charter of Love," which supplemented the Benedictine rule by organizing and homogenizing the liturgies of the Cistercian houses, their relations with one another, and the relations of the order with the world. With the rule and the charter, the Cistercians revolutionized the nature of a monastic order.

One of the most striking features of the Charter of Love was the principle of the organization of the order. The abbot of Citeaux was, as at Cluny, the head of the order, but his leadership was modified in several striking ways. Reciprocal inspections of daughter-houses by abbots of founding houses and of founding houses by abbots of their daughter-houses, and the annual convening of all abbots at Citeaux to make collective decisions regarding the affairs of the order reflect the corporate character of the order as a whole. Cistercian recruitment was also versatile. Those who seemed less than suitable for participation in the full austerity of the monastic program were enrolled as *conversi*, lay brothers, and they came to operate the farms of the order and to live in granges out in their fields. For the monks themselves, life was strict. Only the most severe decorations were permitted in Cistercian churches—no bright colors, elaborate sculpture, bell towers, or metal crucifixes—and the cloisters were stripped of their elaborate ornament. A standard general model for all Cistercian churches emanated from Citeaux and Clairvaux and carried the architectural principles of the order into the farthest corners of Europe as the order itself spread south to Italy and Spain, northwest to England, and northeast to Germany and Poland.

The Order's use of its growing material wealth placed the Cistercians at the forefront of ecclesiastical influences upon European economic history. The wild, remote locations of the monasteries afforded a clean slate for the development of agricultural, pastoral, and industrial techniques, and the form of organization of the order improved the management of material resources considerably. In their new agricultural improvements, their sheep raising, and their development of non-human sources of power, particularly water mills, the Cistercians occupy a prominent place in the economic history of the twelfth and thirteenth centuries.

The spiritual and material success of the order, however, brought dangers as well. The immense popularity of the Cistercians, or White Monks, as they were also known, threatened to weaken the austerity and withdrawn character of the order. Again and again, Cistercians from St. Bernard and Rupert of Deutz on, became involved in the world's problems and controversies; again and again, gifts and privileges threatened to enrich the order beyond the visions of its founders. In a world whose troubled conscience had become more troubled, the Cistercian appeal found welcome ears, and Cistercian criticism doubtless weakened the position of other monastic orders, who were already under heavy attack from the growing towns, the schools, and the new administrators of the Church. But the Cistercians themselves could not remain invulnerable to these same forces. Cistercians too began to drift off to the schools and universities; Cistercian monasteries acquired decorations and wealth that generated further participation in a money economy and diverted many monks into the roles of financial managers; the appearance of the new ministry in the towns in the twelfth century and of the new orders of friars in the thirteenth weakened the exclusivity of the Cistercian appeal. Eugenius III (1145–1153) was the first Cistercian pope, a pope for whose spiritual welfare St. Bernard was so concerned that he wrote for him a handbook on the papacy, the *De Consideratione*. One of the greatest Cistercian popes was Benedict XII (1334–1342), who, like Eugenius, ascended the papal throne in troubled times for the Church. Benedict urged vigorous reforms upon the order in an attempt to recapture the twelfth-century spirit, but influential as those reforms were, Benedict could not stop the gradual decline of monasticism in the fourteenth-century Church.

The vigorous appeal of the Cistercian reform and the reforms of other less influential and less well-known orders constitute an important element in the intellectual and spiritual ferment of the twelfth and early thirteenth centuries. From monastic liturgies and techniques of scriptural interpretation there emerged influences that challenged both reforms and new methods of interpretation that emerged elsewhere, particularly those that developed outside the cloister. The Cistercians were vociferous in their criticism not only of other monastic orders and the secular churches, but of the new techniques of the schools, of the new directions in learning, particularly theology, and of the condition of pastoralism. To counter these influences, the Cistercians did not simply offer a rigid austerity and a puritanical view of the dangers of worldly temptation; in their liturgical and scriptural innovations, and particularly in their spiritual devotions, they opened new methods of spirituality that exerted powerful and enduring influences upon the world around them.

The view of the universe that regarded man as essentially powerless and considered the strength of the monastic community, and, by extension, the proper behavior of a whole society, to be one of the surest of the few roads to salvation slowly gave way between the tenth and the twelfth centuries to a new, more intimate concept of the relations between God and man. Most of the devotional and psychological vocabulary before the mid twelfth century offered humans little more than the way of penitence for an inevitably sinful life, and once penitence was achieved, it was to be preserved statically by acts of self-discipline, prayer, and spiritual caution. In the course of the tenth century, however, the monastic revival, the sanctification of many kinds of penitential acts, and the concept of a God who helps instead of simply judging man—in ordeals, battles, conversion miracles, and almsgiving—generated, or at least helped generate, feelings of a different kind about God. Instead of dread and penitence alone, we find a kind of human sympathy toward God, a new devotion to the human figure suffering on the cross, a new interest in depicting the Virgin and Infant in the naturalistic, domestic manner of a human mother and child. The monumental traditions of earlier artistic depictions continued, of course, but the fire of the new devotion made greater headway. From the limited human states of penitence and humility there evolved, first in monastic writings, the idea of spiritual development by the individual. And by the mid twelfth century a whole psychology of spiritual states, some of them described in a literature of intense lyricism, existed to explore the newly perceived variety of ways to reach God. In spite of the austerity of their rule, or rather because of it, the monks of the twelfth century, particularly the Cistercians, stood in the forefront of this movement. When they attacked the scholars, it was not from crabbed petulance but from a deep-seated fear that excessive analysis of essentially unfathomable mysteries weakened devotion. To understand their position, the modern student should remember just what a very inept or pedantic literary critic can do to his or her enjoyment of a great poem.

The greatest contribution of twelfth-century monasticism was precisely in this area of widened thought and the expansion of human feeling. The rigid discipline, the hard rules, and the frontier monasteries and farms all suggest the toughness and sternness of the reform movement. The aristocratic origins of many of its members, the remarkable corporatism of the order's administration, and its widespread success remind us of the strong links between even the new, withdrawn monastic movements and the world out of which they fled. For the historian of culture, however, it is equally important to note that the new devotion introduced and nurtured new forms of sensibility and opened new areas of a genuinely religious life to other clerics and laymen as well.

NEW FORMS OF DEVOTION, ORDER, AND DISSENT

The most prominent individual in the Cistercian movement of the twelfth century was St. Bernard, who also extended a great influence in the world outside of the Cistercian Order. In doing so, paradoxically, he adhered less to the Cistercian ideal and responded more to the spiritual needs of a world whose affairs he had ostensibly rejected. Bernard was born to a noble family near Dijon, and in 1112, with his brothers and a large group of other young noblemen, suddenly joined the new community of Cîteaux. Bernard's arrival traditionally marks the new surge of the order, and in 1115 Bernard founded the third daughter house of Cîteaux, Clairvaux. Throughout his life he remained devoted to the ascetic ideals of the Cistercians, and in spite of almost continual debilitating illnesses, his physical austerity became well known throughout Europe. His ascetic character, the burning lyricism of his devotional works, his concept of human dignity and virtue and the psychology of the ways in which man ought to love God, and his career as a model monk and abbot establish him securely in the greatest traditions of monasticism. Yet Bernard was also more than a monk. In spite of the ascetic character of his orders, he was also the most widely respected holy man of the twelfth century, and it is perhaps as one of the last and most outstanding examples of the type of the holy man, which developed in late antiquity, that his influence is best understood.

For Bernard played a role in the world outside of the cloister as extensive as that of any monk described in these pages so far. In 1128 he was the secretary of the Synod of Troyes; in 1130 his prestige alone swayed the outcome of the disputed papal election involving Innocent II and Anacletus II; in 1140 he attacked Abelard and secured the condemnation of some of his teachings at the Council of Sens; in 1144 he preached the Second Crusade and even traveled to Germany, first to put a stop to the resumption of the persecutions of the Jews and second to persuade Emperor Conrad III to join the expedition; in the last decade of his life he wrote a handbook on the papacy for the Cistercian pope Eugenius III, preached unremittingly against the spread of heretical doctrines, and all the time poured forth a large body of correspondence, treatises, prayers, meditations, and instructions to diverse groups and individuals in society. Such a life indicates the power of monasticism as an institution during its greatest age as well as the potential influence of a single holy man in a world that responded still more readily to ascetic devotions and personal sanctity than to the institutionalized routine of the organized Church.

The world of St. Bernard, the world inside and outside the cloister, is reflected in its interests and concerns precisely in those affairs in which Bernard participated. The life of synod and council, the role of the papacy, the formation of the Crusade movement, the relations among Christians, Jews, and heretics, and the new military orders and the rest of lay society that looked for some guidance for the new intensity of its

Plate 13 courtesy A. F. Kersting, London.

THE FACES OF GOD. One way to trace the changing forms of devotional psychology in early European history is to study the representations of the deity and the images they invoke. The figure of Christ Pantocrator (the Mighty Judge; Plate 13) is a popular Byzantine theme, here depicted from the twelfth-century apse of the cathedral of Monreale in Sicily. Remote and fearsome, Christ imposes a solemnity and an unreachable majesty upon the entire church.

Plate 14 courtesy Thames and Hudson Ltd., London.

The image of Christ in Majesty, triumphant and supreme, is another common early theme of pictorial representation (Plate 14), shown here from the ninth-century Frankish Lorsch Gospels.

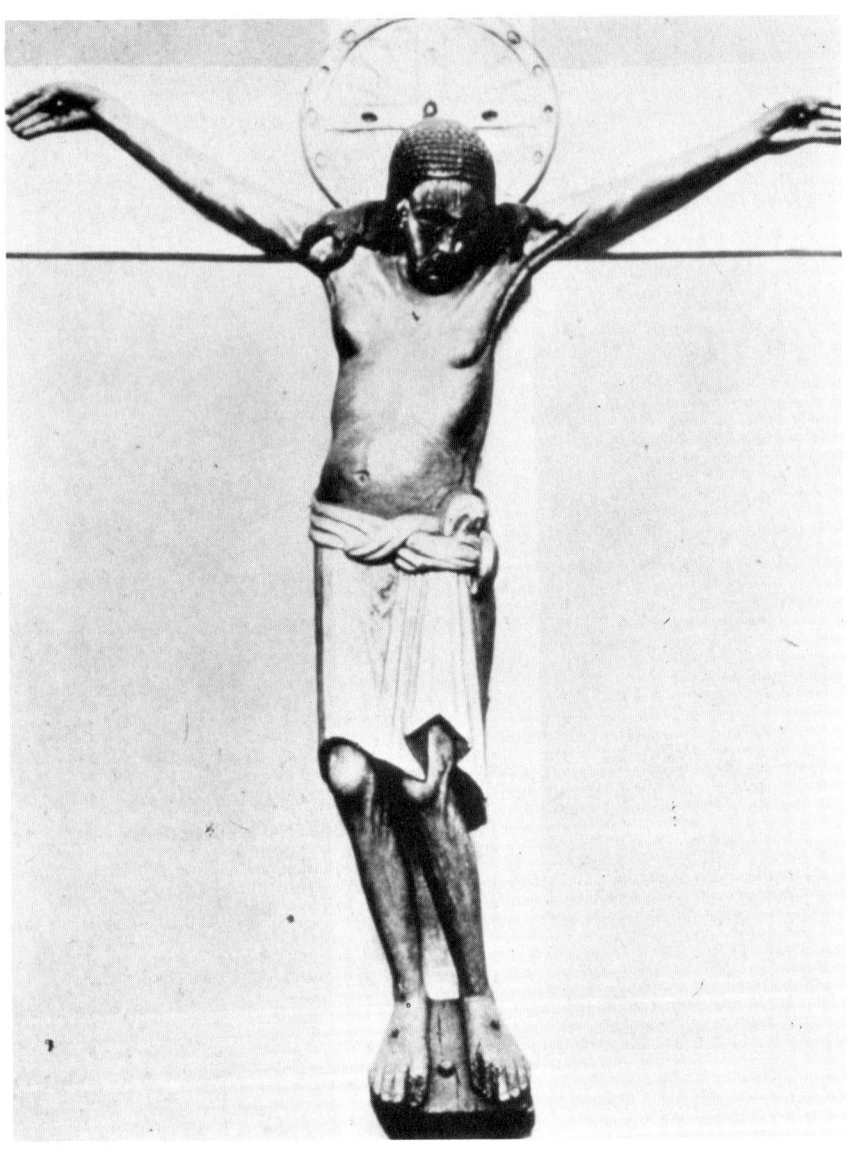

Plate 15 courtesy University of Pennsylvania.

By the tenth century, however, new images of the deity increased in popularity, particularly the dimension of the suffering human figure on the cross shown here in the crucifix made for Archbishop Gero of Cologne around 975 (Plate 15).

Plate 16 courtesy Archives Photographiques, Paris.

By the twelfth century, the theme of the love of the divine Creator for His creatures attracted artists and thinkers' attention, and the example here, from the north porch of Chartres Cathedral (Plate 16), shows the creation of Adam, with the look of tenderness upon the face of God in sharp contrast to that of the Pantocrator on the nearly contemporary apse at Monreale.

devotion—all these were the most intimate concerns of twelfth-century society.

We have already seen the role of synods and councils in defining dogma and ecclesiastical law, from the First Lateran Council of 1123 to the Fourth Lateran Council of 1215. These were the occasions when the pope and higher prelates met and set down the clear and unambiguous decisions of an increasingly articulate ecclesiastical structure and turned the intense reform programs of Gregory VII and Urban II into firm action. Although abuses, such as clerical marriage, took a long time—most of the century, in fact—to be completely eradicated, the work of these councils, shared by papal direction and taken up in individual dioceses by episcopal constitutions and instructions, was literally the shaping of the medieval Church. The problem of papal authority was part and parcel of the work of the councils. The high claims of Gregory VII and the prestige of Urban II could not be sustained in a program of papal power without the firm organization of the papal court and the Church as a whole. The varieties of papal action, from the pontificate of Paschal II (1099–1118) to that of Calixtus II (1119–1124), revealed the extremes of potential papal policies. The crucial papal election of Innocent II (1130–1143), whose outcome was influenced by St. Bernard, instituted a line of popes prepared to work out the details of achieved reform agreements and the foundations of ecclesiastical and dogmatic organization. The popes acquired new rights within traditional dioceses and witnessed the shoring up of papal authority in such works as Gratian's *Decretum* and St. Bernard's *De Consideratione*, in the flood of juridical appeals to the papal courts, and in the increasing appointment of papal legates and judges delegate to hear complex cases. Several popes early in the century, and more later, achieved the papacy after careers in the papal service. Hadrian IV (1154–1159), the only English pope, was the abbot of a chapter of canons near Avignon when he was invited into papal service, in which he spent most of his time in Scandinavia as papal legate and organized the church in Scandinavia. Alexander III (1159–1181), Rolandus Bandinelli, was the first graduate of the law school at Bologna to ascend the papal throne, and his acts, from his decree requiring a two-thirds majority in papal elections to his analysis of the authority of the office of judge delegate, put the stamp of legal training on the letters emanating from the papel chancery, which, in the course of the century, developed an organization and literary style that was unique among the courts of Christendom. Alexander's long conflict with Emperor Frederick Barbarossa created a new arsenal of legal arguments advanced by the papacy, and under Alexander III and his successors, particularly Innocent III (1198–1216), Gregory IX (1227–1241), and Innocent IV (1243–1254), the letters, or decretals, issued from the papal chancery became formative instruments of law within the Church. Unofficial collections of these papal letters began to appear in the late twelfth century, and the teachers at Bologna and elsewhere commented upon them, just as they commented upon the *Decretum* of Gratian. In 1234 Pope Gregory IX issued the *Liber Extra* (so called because its contents went beyond, *extra,* the earlier collection of Gratian), a collection of systematically arranged parts of papal letters since the mid twelfth century published with full papal authority and headed by a letter to the law school at Bologna instructing that the collection be taught as official Church law. The *Liber Extra* was divided into five books, which treated, respectively, the judge, the judgment, the clerical state, marriage, and crime. Each book was divided into titles, and each title was divided into chapters; each chapter consisted of a relevant extract from a papal decretal. The same letter might appear in several different places in the law code, depending upon the applicability of its parts. The *Liber Extra* was put together by Raymond of Peñafort, the great Spanish canonist and moral theologian, and like Gratian's *Decretum,* it acquired a number of commentaries, one of which, that of Bartholomew of Brescia, became the *glossa ordinaria.* The commentators upon the *Liber Extra* and subsequent collections became known as the decretalists, because they commented upon collections of papal decretals, and the commentators upon Gratian were called decretists, after the object of their study, the *Decretum.* In 1298 the lawyer-pope Boniface VIII issued another collection, the *Liber Sextus ("The Sixth Book,"* after the five of the *Liber Extra*), and several more small collections appeared in the fourteenth and fifteenth centuries. But the great age of canon law occurred between Gratian's *Decretum* in 1140 and the period 1298–1348. The law that was established then remained the law of the Church until the Reformation, and the law of the Roman Catholic Church until 1918. The greatest commentators, men such as Huguccio, Rufinus, and Stephen of Tournai in the twelfth century, Innocent IV, Hostiensis, and Guillelmus Durandus in the thirteenth, and Johannes Andreae and Guido de Baysio in the fourteenth, brought to their explication of the law an immense knowledge of the legal and social conditions of their age, and their extensive commentaries, later unjustly scorned by humanist intellectuals, constitute one of the richest sources for the history of legal, social, and political ideas that any society ever produced.

Although such critics as St. Bernard bitterly denounced the volume of legal business handled by the chancery, the legates, and the popes, the legal dimension of papal activity increased throughout the late twelfth and early thirteenth centuries and imprinted its stamp and style upon the activities of the papacy and the concept of the community of the Church. Popes of the late twelfth century, in fact, may be seen to alternate between men who desired to maintain papal authority to the letter of the law (and sometimes beyond it) and other men who were willing to compromise with opponents, to check some of the consequences of an excessively juridical conception of papal authority, and to cultivate devotion and piety rather than administration. This dichotomy may be more complex than it at first appears. The career of perhaps the greatest of the popes, Innocent III (1198–1216), reflects important dimensions of both aspects of the papacy. A man with some legal training and at thirty-seven the youngest of the popes, Innocent gave great impetus to the juridical side of the papacy. In decretal after decretal he laid down with astonishing precision and impeccable juridical reasoning the principles of papal authority, assembling throughout his pontificate a formidable body of legislation that gave concrete juridical shape to papal authority. Yet Innocent possessed a second side. His biographer devotes considerable attention to Innocent's care for the well-being of the Church—and of individual churches, on the restoration and decoration of which Innocent spent much money and time. He responded with a surprising swiftness to the new devotional movements of the early thirteenth century, particularly to the figures of St. Dominic and, above all, St. Francis of Assisi. The famous fresco of Innocent's dream of St. Francis holding up on his shoulder the falling church represents both Franciscan and Innocentian tradition, and warns the reader not to view Innocent solely as a lawyer and administrator acting within a narrow, legalistic tradition. Such mixtures are subtle, and they have often been lost in the wars of confessional historiography, but they were certainly present in Innocent and in many of his successors.

The Crusade idea and the rise of the military orders also received their fullest development in the world of St. Bernard. The complex sources of the First Crusade (see Chapter 17) took time to acquire a presence in the people's minds in the early twelfth century. Then, as accounts of divine inspiration, legends, miracle stories, and travelers' tales acquired wider circulation, the idea evolved of a divine plan protected by God and a responsibility for continued action. Thus, when Edessa fell to the Turks in 1144, St. Bernard was the most active preacher of the necessity of a second Crusade. At Vézelay, the crowds were so great that Bernard cut up his own habit to provide crosses for those who wished to take up the mission. Privileged status for Crusaders and their families and property was formulated in the chancery of Eugenius III. The fire of Bernard's eloquence moved the Second Crusade from Europe to its series of unmitigated disasters in Asia Minor and Syria, its ill-considered and hopeless siege of Damascus, and its retreat to Europe. To St. Bernard also fell the less enticing role of explaining the Crusade's failure.

The role of the twelfth-century holy man in the world did not cease with conciliar and papal counseling and preaching the Crusade. The intense growth of reformed monasticism in the late eleventh and early twelfth centuries was, after all, a reflection of a widespread devotional reform movement that touched people in all walks of life, women and men, religious and secular clergy. Bernard was a nobleman, as were many of his companions in the Cistercian Order, and he influenced movements that grew outside the cloister as well. Beginning in the middle of the twelfth century, the military orders, groups of fighting men who led the austere lives of monks when not in battle, were founded as service organizations in the kingdom of Jerusalem. Indeed, knighthood came to be in a sense sacralized at about the same time as kingship came to be desacralized. Gregory VII's idea of a *militia Sancti Petri*, "a militia of St. Peter," the papal recognition of legitimate combat for a proper cause, the success of the First Crusade and the legends of its heroes, particularly Godfrey of Bouillon, that began to circulate early in the twelfth century, and the growing legends of Charlemagne and his knights, of which the early twelfth-century *Song of Roland* is one example—all these contributed to the idea that knighthood was an order, and that it possessed a spiritual as well as a temporal condition.

In the Holy Land, a small group of knights took common vows of poverty, chastity, and obedience, as did monks, and then added the stipulation that they would protect pilgrims as well. Such a novelty, a religious order existing to wage war by force of arms, is one of the many varieties of religious experience that the twelfth century produced. This group, given rooms in what was then called the Temple of Solomon, took their name, the Templars, from their first residence. At the Council of Troyes in 1128 St. Bernard helped draw up a rule for their order, and the Cistercian influence on later military orders remained strong. St. Bernard went on to write a treatise, *In Praise of the New Knighthood*, which increased the popularity of the Templars, aided in recruitment, and spurred the formation of still other orders. In the course of the twelfth century, the Templars came directly under the authority of the pope, and, like independent monastic orders and privileged houses of the same character, they sometimes posed a problem to local structures of ecclesiastical and temporal authority in the Latin kingdom of Jersualem. In 1070, a hostel had been founded under the protection of St. John, and in the course of the twelfth century a new order of knights, the Order of the Knights of St. John of the Hospital, or the Hospitalers, took shape analogously to the Templars. They too became independent of all powers but the papacy. In the course of the late twelfth and thirteenth centuries other orders were formed as well, and in terms of their rules of varying strictness and intensity they constituted a bridge between the clerical and lay worlds. Both Templars and Hospitalers became privileged and wealthy, as did the Cistercians, and their history in the Holy Land and in Europe is checkered. The Templars developed into one of the most important and wealthiest financial institutions in the thirteenth century, serving as bankers to pilgrims and Crusaders alike. The military orders, the history of some of which extends in European affairs to the sixteenth and seventeenth centuries, represent one of many possible combinations of the new spirit of militant Christianity and the new self-consciousness of the order of knighthood. It is no accident that such a combination should appeal to the aristocratic holy man St. Bernard, or that the orders should have exerted a particularly wide appeal.

The Cistercian spirit and the new military orders did not, however, carry all before them. Among the tasks that took St. Bernard out of the monastery and into the world was that of preaching against heretics, and the rise of heresy in the twelfth century is a striking accompaniment to the vigor of the wide devotional movement of which the new administration of the Church, reform monasticism, the military orders, and the idea of Crusade and pilgrimage are other manifestations. Before the eleventh century, the sources for the history of heresy generally depict unorthodox belief as a phase of monastic controversy, rarely touching the general devotional character of the world outside the monastery and the episcopal and royal courts. Then, early in the eleventh century, sources indicate a wave of popular heresies that were championed by independent preachers, some of whom were priests, and that focused upon moral reform, the life of the clergy, and the doctrine of apostolic poverty. As we have seen, such movements, the *Pataria* of Milan being one striking example, provided some of the support for the reform papacy, particularly that of Gregory VII, late in the eleventh century.

In the course of the twelfth century a broader and deeper movement of heretical beliefs swept through Christian Europe. Not surprisingly, its roots have been the subject of much scholarly and confessional controversy. The term *haeresis* came into Latin from Greek, where it had originally designated generally the concept of "choice," and later referred specifically to the different beliefs of the philosophical schools. In Christian Latin usage it gradually acquired the meaning of doctrines held contrary to the teaching of the Church. The thirteenth-century definition of Robert Grosseteste conveys both the contemporary and the etymological meanings of the term:

> Heresy is an opinion *chosen* by human faculties . . . *contrary* to sacred scripture . . . *openly* taught . . . *pertinaciously* defended. Heresy in Greek, *choice* in Latin.

These meanings are important to remember in considering the development, spread, and content of heretical beliefs and the Church's response to them. The individual whose opinions ran counter to those officially proclaimed by the Church was not immediately guilty of heresy. He might be instructed, cautioned, asked to change his mind, or, in the manner used by St. Bernard, publicly denounced. For heresy to exist, it had to be openly maintained and taught; the concealed heretic did not emerge as a problem until later. Finally, the true heretic was one who, admonished and corrected, openly maintained and "pertinaciously" defended his opinion against all opposition. It must also be kept in mind that the usage of the word "heresy" was extremely loose in the early twelfth century. Abelard applied it to persons who held incorrect theories of grammar, and much of the conflict between Abelard and St. Bernard leading to the condemnation of some of Abelard's doctrines at the Council of Sens in 1140 used the term "heresy" in a way more reminiscent of the correction of an erring monk than of its later twelfth-century meaning. But the worlds of the cloister and the Paris schools were slowly drawing apart, and such conflicts grew sharper as later participants took up the two causes in the late twelfth and early thirteenth centuries. As far apart as they were drawing, however, the worlds of Abelard and Bernard were still closer to each other than either of them was to the popular world of devotion that was becoming more intense day by day. Indeed, "learned heresies" were rarely attacked as bitterly as the spreading popular heresies, and scholars retained a considerably greater latitude in their teachings than did popular preachers or heretical societies. One of the strongest condemnations made by the early Church, for example, was that against astrologers. This hostility, echoed in the influential twelfth-century thinker Hugh of St. Victor, did not prevent astrology from becoming a popular learned pastime, receiving, as it did so, the imprint of the Islamic thinkers whose popularity grew as the twelfth century wore on, slipping in the door of orthodoxy, as it were, just before that door slammed shut against heresy and other forms of the occult.

The roots of popular heresies, however, were more complex than scholars' disputes or monastic unorthodoxies. Just as the tenth century had witnessed a turn to the more human aspects of the crucified Christ and the depictions of the Mother and Child, so the tenth, eleventh, and twelfth centuries saw the increase in the veneration of the Virgin. Yet, side by side with this new sensibility and the new devotion it inspired, it appears that another set of attitudes evolved, attitudes that savagely attacked what was considered to be the confining of divine power in earthly material symbols. In the eleventh and twelfth centuries, groups led by preachers attacked churches, overturned altars, burned crosses, and bitterly denounced the clergy. Moreover, the reform movement of the eleventh century attacked simoniacal and Nicolaitan clerics, and some of its more extreme literature swerved very closely toward a general anticlericalism. The general crisis concerning the extent of the reform movement that worked itself out in the conciliar and papal decrees of the twelfth century also engendered uncertainty in the believing public, and both progressive reformers and hostile, traditionalist critics heaped scorn on the new burgeoning legal business of the papal chancery and the administration of the Church. St. Bernard's attacks upon the extravagance and materialistic Christianity of Cluny and the diversion of the papacy into the law courts found many ears and was echoed and distorted by many minds. Some scholars have drawn the distinction between movements of reform and movements of heretical unorthodoxy. Reform and dissent that became heretical were in part as sharply defined by the steps that churchmen took in defining orthodoxy with their challenges in mind, as they were by their own internal development.

Two further problems remain to be considered. First, there was on all levels of society in the eleventh and twelfth centuries a new urge toward the evangelical life as laid out in the Gospels, a search, as one great historian put it, "for the apostolic life." The Cistercian idea that the rule of St. Benedict embodied a program for translating the true gospel into action, the ideas of voluntary poverty and austerity and a common life that ran through monastic reforms and the congregations of regular canons in the twelfth century, the sacralization of such orders of lay society as those of knighthood, marriage, and religious confraternities—all these reflect a consciousness of the new evangelical spirit that touched nearly all people. This new movement touched both orthodox and heterodox individuals, as did the second problem the historian of heresy has to contend with: the changing material circumstances of society. We have seen the substantial transformation of the social and economic configuration of the earlier history of Europe in the tenth through the twelfth centuries. The simplistic approach that suggests a purely materialistic causation of spiritual change has generally been discarded, although the relations between heresy and social structures were clearly present and the growth of heresy as it took place in the twelfth century must certainly be explicable in terms of the new society among which it spread.

One common attack upon those whom the representatives of orthodoxy accused of heresy was based on charges of "novelty." "Novelty," "new ways," "excessive curiosity," were, of course, terms applied also to the new schools, but they suggest that representatives of orthodox beliefs did not think that the heretics they encountered were reviving the past heresies of the early Church. However, some of these representatives, and some modern historians as well, have studied the influence of one new movement, that of Bogomilism, upon the Latin heretics after the middle of the twelfth century. Bogomilism appears to have emerged as a heresy in the Byzantine Empire, found a home in Bulgaria, and moved west on trade routes and crusade routes in the early twelfth century. The Bogomils attacked much of the fabric of Christian orthodox belief. They echoed Manicheanism by denouncing material creation and the creator as evil gods and in emphasizing the exclusive goodness of spiritual beings. The exclusivity of the Bogomil influence has generally been rejected by recent scholars, and the roots of all Latin heretical movements have been located in the religious excitement of the twelfth-century conscience.

It is important to remark the regional varieties of Latin heresies, even those that pass under the generic labels of Catharism and Waldensianism. Different kinds of heretical beliefs came to the fore in different parts of Europe, and the ecclesiastical instruments of repression were applied with different intensities and different degrees of success in different regions. Generally speaking, those regions possessing a strong, relatively exclusive central governing authority, a vigorous but not necessarily learned community of higher clergy on the episcopal level, and means of social support or coercion tended to have a lower incidence of heresy than those that did not exhibit these characteristics. The roots of heresy, at least the social roots, can account for willingness to become heretical in beliefs and the response of the rest of society to the change in individuals or groups. In a society that is generally indifferent, heresy may spread unchecked, and when ecclesiastical institutions fail to channel popular devotion or even attract serious defenders, heresy attracts adherents.

The two best-known types of heresy in the twelfth and thirteenth-century world—Waldensianism and Catharism—flourished primarily in Provence and Languedoc in the south of France. Waldensianism, named for the merchant Valdes of Lyons, held the doctrine of the corruption of the Church, the priesthood of all believers, the necessity of preaching and reading Scripture in the vernacular, and apostolic poverty. This group, which resembled in many aspects other voluntary groups later accepted by the Church, differed from similar sects in its intransigence rather than in doctrinal content. Admonished, they would not accept ecclesiastical conditions; they were, in short, pertinacious. Catharism, whose name derives from the Greek word meaning "pure," was rather more complex. Sharing the Bogomil concept of a material universe created by an evil spirit, Cathar doctrine may also have shared the antimaterialistic revulsion that we have noted accompanying the growth of a "humanized" relationship between God and man. The Cathars held that human spirits were imprisoned in flesh, and for them the greatest sin was procreation, imprisoning another spirit in the material world. God sent Jesus, who only appeared to take on the characteristics of a human being, to show man the way out of the trap of material creation. None of the "human" aspects of Jesus—not the cross, not the passion, not the church that was built on these symbols had anything to do with God. The Church was a creation of Satan, and hell was Earth, imprisonment in the material world. The Cathar stages of initiation were two. One first became a believer, and then, after preparation, received the *Consolamentum,* the laying on of hands that turned a believer into one of the perfect. Once becoming a *perfectus* (or a *perfecta,* for one of the strongest attractions of many heretical doctrines was their recognition of the parity of men and women), one renounced excessive food and drink, sexual intercourse, and care for the body. One of the possible forms of death for the Cathar *perfecti* was the *Endura,* starvation, the ultimate rejection of material creation.

Catharism (sometimes called Albigensianism, because there were many Cathars at the town of Albi in southwestern France) flourished particularly in that southern part of France that historians have lately taken to calling "Occitania," the region where the *langue d'oc* was spoken and where customs different from those in the north prevailed. In these territories, which were ruled by hundreds of counts and viscounts, spiritually guided by a generally inept and impotent clerical hierarchy, and open to influences from Moslem and Christian Spain, Italy, and the whole Mediterranean world, Catharism grew to proportions that alarmed even the pope.

Cathars and Waldensians were, in one sense at least, part of a wide devotional movement that was rooted in the change of religious consciousness of the tenth through the twelfth centuries and is reflected by so many facets of the twelfth-century world. In the major encounters of St. Bernard with several aspects of this world, we have seen both the religious ferment and the new solutions to it that people discovered. At the time of Bernard's death in 1153, some of the problems that he encountered had grown; some had disappeared or been transformed. All of them, and his own life as well, reflect a vigor and a sense of discovery that were not yet wholly severed from older forms of piety. Bernard was a monk and remained one all his life. Abelard became a monk and died at Cluny. William of Champeaux, became a monk and then a bishop. Bernard's lifetime witnessed a monk who became pope. The holy man could still exert a moral force as prestigious as that of Rome, Rheims, or Cologne, but he worked in a more complex world, one in which personal holiness became a goal for larger numbers of people.

THE NEW PASTORALISM, HERETICS, AND JEWS

One of the bitterest charges leveled alike by reformers, dissenters, heretics, and even high churchmen was at the ineptitude and immorality of the clergy. Such charges had lain behind the success of the reform movement of the late eleventh century and directed the conciliar legislation of the twelfth. To a large extent, many of these charges were true. Yet it is difficult to know where to lay blame for what is, after all, an anachronistic charge. There were no training schools for clergy, bishoprics often were awarded for petty temporal reasons and with ecclesiastical connivance or the clergy's submission to temporal power, and the lowest clergy came untrained from the same class of people whom they served. When Peter Abelard became, briefly, the abbot of the monastery of St. Gildas in Brittany, he was appalled to find that his monks lived as if the reform movement had never taken place, and when he set out to reform them, a task in which he asked the assistance of St. Bernard, he was almost poisoned for his efforts. In spite of the powerful sacramental character of the clergy in the new theology, its conceived role as a separate sacred order in society, the prohibitions against clerical marriage took a long time—most of the twelfth century, in fact—to make substantial headway. Moreover, the Concordat of Worms of 1122 had not entirely deprived temporal powers of their right to appoint individuals to high ecclesiastical positions.

Yet one of the most pressing needs the twelfth century faced was precisely that of a clergy capable of putting the new theology and the new law into practice. "They are like dumb dogs . . . ," Innocent III remarked about some of the bishops of southern France, who would not or could not preach the gospel. The attractions of the Cistercian and other ascetic movements pulled candidates away from the secular church, and the schools and courts attracted others. Councils issued canons, and these canons were redrawn into episcopal constitutions, which were then disseminated in appropriate forms throughout each diocese, their efficacy checked by regular episcopal visitations. In such a system, the faulty link lay with the episcopal and its subordinate levels. The Italian and southern French town movements had taken considerable power away from the bishops, and the bishops, who still belonged to an earlier society of formalized status and were often of the noble class, felt ill at ease with the rootless and status-ambivalent townspeople. One of the great bases of the appeal that religious guilds, confraternities, and societies of all kinds possessed in the towns was their offer of a kind of community that the diocese or the parish was not able to provide. The evangelical movement attracted townspeople to wandering preachers who exhibited a rootless life of poverty and a faith of whose orthodoxy they were uninformed.

Although the great thrust of theological and ecclesiological reform in the twelfth century that culminated in the Fourth Lateran Council of 1215 recognized the pastoral needs of the Church, such needs can hardly be said to have begun to be met until the end of the thirteenth century. Even the remarkable movement in the field of moral theology that resulted in the work of Peter the Chanter and others between 1180 and 1230, in a sophisticated adaptation of theological dogma to specific cases and social needs, was felt only intermittently. Although by 1200 handbooks for confessors already reflected a new sophistication and a new and broader conception of the guiding of consciences, their influence was not uniformly felt. By 1200 the Church faced two pressing needs: it had to repress heresy by some means, and it had to address the problem of a more vigorous pastoral contact with the body of believers. The thirteenth century witnessed important and influential solutions in both areas.

In the case of heresy, the first efforts of the papacy had been to turn to those who seemed best to embody the spirit of twelfth-century religion, the Cistercians. But in spite of the occasional successes of a St. Bernard, the Cistercians found little sympathetic hearing, and like the bishops and lower clergy, they soon gave up their attempt to combat heresy. Some clergy and laymen, however, had seen the success of the wandering preachers who professed voluntary poverty, particularly in the towns, and they were anguished by the failure of the clergy to stem the spread of heresy. They were also appalled at the general ignorance of both higher and lower clergy, particularly when it encountered the always informed, scripturally based, eloquent arguments of heretical apologists. For the heretics had adopted the vernacular languages and the translation of Scripture into them. They appear to have maintained a higher level of literacy, and their schools accepted women as well as men. More than one southern prelate was embarrassed in debate by a well-trained heretical opponent.

One of the most significant organizational reforms of the twelfth century had been the movement to impose order in the chapters of canons, the clergy that served cathedral churches. Before the twelfth century, the jumble of traditions, privileges, and liberties that had gone virtually unchecked for centuries had left the cathedral clergy in a particularly sorry state. Other groups of clergy had felt the need for communal life that was based more on service to the community than monasticism was, and both of these groups found a solution in the course of the twelfth century. A loose directive written early in the fifth century by St. Augustine for a house of religious women became the foundation for the order known as the Augustinian canons. These were groups of cathedral priests and collegiate priests (that is, priests who lived together) who performed pastoral and service functions while living under an organized rule. The first group of Augustinian canons dates from 1060, the Premonstratensian Order from 1120, and the uniquely English Gilbertine Order from 1148. Although they could not perform wonders, the orders of canons regular substantially maintained much of the spiritual life of the areas they served. In 1206 one of the canons regular of the Spanish diocese of Osma, Dominic de Guzman, witnessed with his bishop the inefficacy of Cistercians attempting to refute heretics in Montpellier, and decided to organize a group of clerics trained to preach and to live in strict poverty, bringing to their mission none of the trappings of ecclesiastical authority that even the Cistercians refused, by 1206, to dispense with. For ten years Dominic worked with a small group of trained preachers, and between 1215 and 1217 the group dispersed to carry out its mission in different parts of Europe. Dominic himself went to Rome, where he encountered two remarkable individuals: Pope Innocent III and St. Francis of Assisi. Francis, born around 1182 to a wealthy merchant family of Assisi in Umbria, central Italy, had spent his youth and young manhood in the military and literary secular pastimes of his society. Suddenly, at the age of about twenty, he began to reject his own background and to circulate more and more freely with poor priests, lepers, and beggars. In 1206 he received his mission in a vision and began to preach. Francis and his first companions preached as laymen, rejected the ownership of property for themselves, and drew up a simple rule that attempted to translate the gospel into a program of action. Pope Innocent III, who was, as we have seen, both a capable and ambitious administrator and a man of great vision, accepted Francis's rule, and became a particular patron of the new group. In 1215 Francis met Dominic in Rome and the two men formed a deep friendship.

Both St. Dominic (1170–1221) and St. Francis (1182–1226) discovered in preaching and poverty two of the most effective keys to the pastoral needs of their age. Because of their poverty, the orders each man began acquired access to those who criticized the wealth of the established Church. By bringing the license to preach, hitherto a prerogative of bishops alone, to priests who were specially trained for the task, they finally began to approach heretical preachers on a level where both sides were equally able. In addition to the rights of St. Dominic's Order of Preachers (popularly, the Dominicans) and St. Francis's Order of Friars Minor (popularly, the Franciscans) to preach, other individuals were enabled to preach, although they were limited in their preaching to exhortation rather than the exposition of dogma. The wave of preachers over the thirteenth and fourteenth centuries had incalculable impact, and the literature of preaching influenced thought and literature in general for several centuries.

Both orders established their own rules, both acquired protection from Popes Innocent III and Gregory IX, and both made an enormous impact upon heretics and orthodox believers alike in their communal missions, stressing voluntary poverty, conversion, simplicity, and obedience to the Church. Yet both orders also bore the stamp of their origins. Francis directed his disciples by the magnificent example of his own personal humility and joy. He made a great vision out of his own abjection, and spoke of his marriage with "Lady Poverty." His personality appears to have touched profoundly nearly everyone he met, and the imprint he left upon the Christian culture of earlier and later Europe endures in the literature that sprang up after him, making him perhaps the most attractive of all Christians. Dominic, however, was a different kind of man. Familiar with the regularity and the order of the Augustinian canons, Dominic's organizational genius greatly strengthened his order, and his early and important decision to utilize the new universities as training grounds for the members of the order was a crucial step. The learning of the Dominicans (the Franciscans followed to the universities somewhat later and more reluctantly) proved a powerful tool in their mission, whereas the attractiveness of the Franciscans lay in their way of life and in the enormous personal prestige of their founder.

Yet the new orders of Francisans and Dominicans tapped only one side of the Church's new character, that of channeling the new spirituality by means of organizations that captured its essence and employed it in a pastoral context. There was another side to the thirteenth-century church, a juristic one, and that new feature was also called into play, particularly when the orders seemed less than successful. The existence of episcopal and papal courts had grown in the twelfth century, as we have seen, and the procedure used in them borrowed more from earlier ecclesiastical procedure and Roman law than from the kinds of law used in the lay courts of the twelfth century. Early European law, both temporal and ecclesiastical, was based upon the accusatorial process, in which a private accuser made charges before a judge and the accused party responded. This was the format of all trials, criminal and civil, including trials by ordeal, by judicial duel, or by compurgation. Another process was sometimes used, however, one that allowed the judge to act independently of an accuser when the accused was guilty of ill fame—that is, public notoriety. Episcopal visitations through a diocese used this procedure. In the course of the twelfth century the new familiarity with Roman law revealed the complexity of the inquisitorial procedure, in which, unlike the accusatorial procedure, the judicial authority itself might begin a case and inquire into its facts. The decretal *Ad abolendam,* issued by Pope Lucius III (1181–1185) in 1184, ordered all bishops to inquire after heretics within their jurisdictons—to conduct, in effect, an inquest. Early legislation against heresy aided the spread of the inquisitorial process, but the process was still used loosely and the chief punishment was anathema or excommunication.

In 1199, however, Innocent III published the decretal *Vergentis,* in which he increased the punishment of heretics to include the confiscation of goods and property. However, the chief importance of this text lies in its specific application of the old Roman-law idea of treason to heresy. Heresy became, in this decretal, treason to God, and the forfeiture of worldly possessions and excommunication were consistent with the penalties prescribed in Roman law, but they did not yet lead to the death penalty. In 1208, however, the papal legate Pierre de

Castelnau was murdered in Toulouse, and Innocent decided to launch an all-out attack upon the Occitanian center of Catharism. Innocent III launched the Albigensian Crusade against the heretics and their indifferent rulers, the counts of Toulouse; later, his succesors launched the Inquisition.

The Albigensian Crusade lasted from 1209 to 1229, and it both destroyed the heretical culture of Occitania and marked the terrible turning of the crusade against Christians. Innocent recruited an army from the north of France, and for two decades of intense military conflict, acts of brutality on both sides, and the slaughter of heretics and orthodox Christians alike, the knights of the north battered and destroyed the rich and varied civilization of the south. But the military campaigns did not entirely wipe out centers of heresy, and Innocent's successors, particularly Gregory IX (1227–1241), redoubled their efforts to urge bishops and councils to use inquisitorial techniques to discover hidden heretics. By 1233 Gregory IX had begun using the Dominicans and Franciscans as inquisitors, granting them powers that traditionally belonged to the bishops, particularly in those districts in which the bishops seemed ineffective. By entrusting inquisitorial powers to the orders, Gregory IX moved a long way toward establishing a permanent tribunal that discovered heresy by means of the inquisitorial process.

The continuous role of the Dominicans and Franciscans in the office of inquisitors developed the inquisitorial process quickly. Although most of their earlier coercive power had been psychological, financial, and sacramental, the inquisitors discovered the technique of "relaxing" recalcitrant defendants to "the secular arm," the lay magistrates who could use physical force without violating their canonical status. In the hands of the members of the Holy Office, the official title of the Inquisition, the inquisitorial procedure developed its first oppressive features: the concealment of the identity of witnesses and the specifics of evidence, the refusal of counsel, the demands to identify accomplices as a sign of repentance, the admission of evidence from hitherto unreliable witnesses, and, in Innocent IV's decretal *Ad extirpanda* of 1252, the admission of torture. Torture itself, judicial torture, had made its first reappearance in Europe since the Roman Empire early in the thirteenth century in the city-states of northern Italy, where it probably derived from both new kinds of crime and law enforcement and the revival of Roman law. By 1252 it had become an instrument of the Inquisition, and from that date until the eighteenth and nineteenth centuries, judicial torture spread from the town courts of Italy and the Inquisition's chambers into most of the criminal courts of the Christian world. Within a century, armed with its new powers, the Inquisition had crippled heresy in Occitania and the Church had acquired a formidable and terrifying instrument for detecting and extirpating heresy.

Preaching, example, and inquisition were the chief instruments with which the thirteenth-century church defended itself against heresy. As we have seen, the first two of these also launched a new kind of missionary activity, one that involved large-scale conversions of a peaceful nature and genuinely satisfied the devotional needs of many. Until the fifteenth century, the organization of episcopal rule became more effective, and heresy ceased after 1325 to be a substantial threat.

Heretics, as they came to be viewed by themselves and by the Inquisition and the Church in general between 1180 and 1250, were public dissenters, enemies of the Church, and, in the Church's eyes, traitors to God who deserved the harshest punishment. There were other groups in medieval society, however, and just beyond its fringes, who were not Christians, were hostile or indifferent to Christianity, and who also had a place in the Christian world view. These include the Jews, the Moslems, the "nations"—heathen tribes of Asia—the insane, lepers, and witches. Among these, the Jews require further consideration.

In the course of the twelfth century, the status of Jews in Christian Europe began to decline precipitously. The status of Jews before the twelfth century, as we have seen, was one of partial acceptance in parts of Christian society; in other parts, Jews were subject to outbursts of murderous hostility. The "crime" of the Jews, the allegation in many Christian writers' works that the Jews remained collectively responsible for the death of Christ, became a commonplace metaphor against which other, wholly unrelated crimes were rhetorically measured. Then, in the course of the eleventh and twelfth centuries, the irregular hostility of the Christian west became transformed in a programmed hostility that included formal treatises denouncing Jewish beliefs, literary "Conversations" among Christians, Jews, and Moslems, popular legends depicting alleged Jewish atrocities against Christians, particularly Christian women and children, and increased disabling legislation against the role of Jews in civil life. From the end of the twelfth century on, confiscations of Jewish property, mandatory wearing of distinctive signs and costumes, and juridical expulsion of Jews from communities and kingdoms, beginning in France in 1182, reflected the new widespread formalized hostility toward Jews in Europe.

There is considerable scholarly disagreement on the subject of the relative status of Jews before and after 1100. Certainly, taxes imposed upon Jews date as early as 1051 at Macon in southeastern France. The earlier Gallo-Roman status of the Jews, as well as Carolingian protective legislation, appears to have survived into the twelfth century. Some scholars, in fact, have gone so far as to regard many Jewish communities and individuals as wholly indistinguishable from their Christian contemporaries in the eleventh and early twelfth centuries. In a relatively economically undifferentiated society in which such overemphasized Jewish activities as slave trading, moneylending, and commerce can have occupied only a small part of the Jewish population, this view has much to recommend it and certainly serves as a salutary corrective to the fallacious image of the very wealthy Jews who bought their privileges and lived in great pomp, an image that runs from twelfth-century monastic writers to the pages of Sir Walter Scott's *Ivanhoe*. In fact, two clear ideas appear to date from the early twelfth century: the principle that the Jews have no legal rights except those granted them by the king, first adumbrated in England after 1135, and the necessity for firm pronouncements guaranteeing the safety of Jews from high ecclesiastical authorities. In 1120 Pope Calixtus II issued a decretal, *Sicut Judaeis,* reminding all Christians of this responsibility, and St. Bernard had to hurry to Germany in 1144 to stop the new persecutions of Jews that attended the preaching of the Second Crusade. By the second quarter of the twelfth century, the danger to the Jews appears to have distinctly increased. The new self-consciousness of Christendom, described in earlier chapters, may well have played a role in this new hostility. Certainly the anti-Moslem attitudes developed in the eleventh century came in part from the new Christian self-confidence, and the new humanizing of the figures of Christ and the Virgin may well have contributed to the hostility to Jews, whose imaginary atrocities in twelfth-century literature surely derive from this new devotional sentimentality. Finally, the attitudes toward and the treatment of Jews in the twelfth and thirteenth centuries must be considered in terms of the broader religious and social turbulence of the period. Ruling and governed elements in a society and culture develop their own distinctive insecurities which produce fear and hatred, and these fears are projected onto whatever groups are the aliens of the moment. The Jews, however deeply rooted and indistinguishable from Christians, were, in law, religion, and culture, the most visibly alien group, more alien even than the heretics.

The offices that had long been acknowledged to have an obligation to protect Jews—the emperors, kings, and popes—began in the late twelfth century to issue formal statements of protection, but also to exact from the Jews what the letter of the law (most of which dated from the fifth and sixth centuries) permitted. The financial scrambling of thirteenth-century monarchies, the popes' furious attack on heretics and dissenters, and such legislation as the requirement that Jews wear identifying marks on their clothing, which dates from the Fourth Lateran Council of 1215, made these "protectors" less useful than a reading of the law and the theory about the protection of the Jews might lead one to expect. Kings and popes, as it turned out, were very dubious protectors at best. What Gavin Langmuir has called "the balance of contempt and toleration laid down in the Church's doctrines" was impossible to maintain. And when it was overthrown, it was always on the side of contempt, brutality, and sacrilege. The twelfth and thirteenth centuries marked not only a new hostility toward individual Jews and Jewish communities, but the development of anti-Semitism in its most manifold and wide-ranging aspects. Prejudice, in any form or time, influences its victims as well as its possessors. Jewish communities acquired, both voluntarily and as a result of force, a new, diminished role in medieval society, and by the fourteenth century the beginnings of what later became ghetto life had evolved.

The liveliness of the tradition of rabbinic *responsa,* which revealed much of the social life in Jewish communities; the great traditions of Talmudic and biblical scholarship that culminated in the work of Rashi of Troyes (1040–1105) and that—through a successor, Joseph Bekhor Shor—influenced the Christian biblical studies of Andrew of St. Victor in the twelfth century, Hugh of St. Cher in the thirteenth, and Nicholas of Lyra in the fourteenth; and the role of Talmudic scholarship and such philosophers as Moses Maimonides (1135–1204) in shaping thirteenth-century scholastic philosophy—such debts were not recognized by a large public. By the mid thirteenth century, the image of the hated Jew had become a commonplace of general Christian culture, a commonplace that can, unhappily, still be invoked and is still invoked by many non-Jews in the twentieth century.

A higher degree of literacy, contacts wih Jewish societies in non-Christian lands, the rich Jewish philosophical and medical culture in the Mediterranean, even the translations of Christian Latin works into Hebrew and the flourishing of amatory poetry in Hebrew (and the existence of a Jewish minnesinger, Süsskind of Trimberg) characterized medieval European Jewish society. Yet, lacking rights, exploited by ambitious and greedy rulers in much the same way that those rulers exploited other classes of servants, from the *ministeriales* to the courtiers of the thirteenth century and the favorites of the fourteenth, facing the formal protection and the pragmatic powerlessness of the higher reaches of the Church and the unremitting and savage hostility of the lower classes, threatened with the destruction of the Talmud, and exiled from England in 1290 and from France in 1322, the Jews of Europe were driven, herded, attacked, and forced into the role of despised minority in which they remained, in general at least, until the end of the seventeenth century.

As more Christians discovered the full range of their own religious beliefs between the eleventh and the thirteenth centuries, they also perceived the differences between their own creeds and those of the Jews. These discoveries, the exploitation of the Jews by their rulers, and the rising sentimentalism that had as its ominous reverse side the legends of Jewish atrocities—all contributed first to the segregation of the Jews, then to their expulsion from kingdom after kingdom between 1290 and 1492, and, last, to the brutal caricature of their beliefs and humanity in the earliest anti-Semitic literature and propaganda.

The new orders and the Inquisition, the great variety of heretical beliefs, sects, and literature, and the transformation of the place of the Jews are among the most important indicators of the beliefs held in the Christian community during the twelfth and thirteenth centuries. Inquisition, defamation, and persecution are easy to condemn at any point in history, and the spirit of the early Franciscans remains as attractive to the modern reader as the spirit of the early Dominicans seems austere and forbidding. This variety of religious ideas, institutions, and attitudes characterizes the temperament of Europe during two centuries of its history.

CHRISTENDOM AS POLITY:
PAPACY AND EMPIRE, 1123-1250

The public, formal settlement of the main issues of the conflict between the papacy and the empire by the Concordat of Worms in 1122 did not resolve the vexing and tangled questions of the extent of and the limitations on ecclesiastical and temporal power. There was still no constitutional law for Christendom. Questions of investiture, and of all the relationships that it symbolized, were settled, as was the universal antipathy toward clerical marriage, and even temporal rulers appreciated the effectiveness of an able, trained, dedicated clergy. These issues, however, were not the ones that arose in the twelfth and thirteenth centuries to open the whole question of Christendom as polity on a new and more complicated level. In this section we will consider first the theory and practice of empire and the history of the emperors in Germany and Italy to the middle of the thirteenth century. Then, reviewing our earlier discussion of the growth of papal government, we will consider papal theories of the constitutional structure of Christendom. Finally, we will focus on the particular crises in the relationship between empire and papacy that occurred during the reigns of Frederick Barbarossa, Henry VI, and Frederick II and culminated in the deposition of Frederick II by Pope Innocent IV, an act traditionally regarded as the triumph, however momentary, of the papacy as the ruling authority in Christendom.

Between the accession of Otto I to the imperial title in 962 and the death of Henry IV in 1105, the empire, Roman Empire (tenth century), or Holy Roman Empire (twelfth century) was the most powerful monarchy in Europe. An incipient dynasticism, the prestige of the office of emperor, and the individual prestige and panoply of the Ottos made the German monarchy far stronger than the Capetian dynasty of France or the troubled kinship of Anglo-Saxon England between the death of Edgar in 975 and the death of Edward the Confessor in 1066. Against the territorial power of the dukes of Saxony, Bavaria, Swabia, Franconia, and Lotharingia, the Ottonian and Salian emperors set up their *ministeriales* and their imperial bishops. Silver strikes in the Rammelsberg Mountains near Goslar in the tenth century gave them capital in plenty, and Goslar slowly became something of a capital city for the emperors. The power of Henry III was felt in the world of ecclesiastical reform long before that of the papacy. The power of Henry IV was felt in Rome after the briefly triumphant Gregory VII had to flee the city and take refuge in the Norman south. But Gregory's attacks and internal revolts against the growing authority of Henry IV had taken their toll. Henry V revolted against his father, and the one clear consequence of the reformers' propaganda, the idea that the emperor was no longer a sacral person, aided in diminishing further the prestige of the imperial figure. When Henry V died in 1125, the princes of Germany reasserted the electoral principle and chose Lothar of Supplinburg, duke of Saxony. The period 1122-1125 was particularly important, in that Lothar had

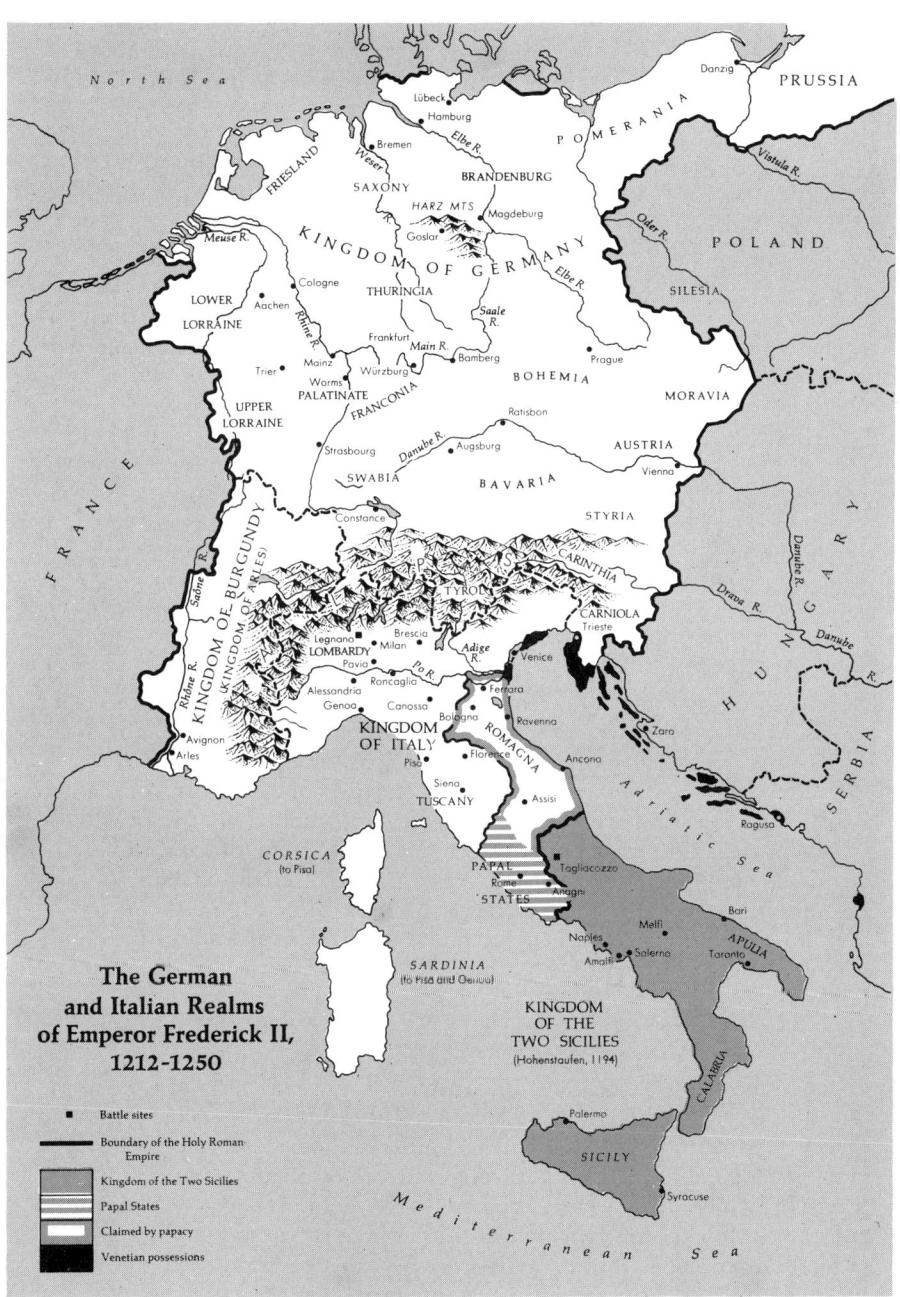

The German and Italian Realms of Emperor Frederick II, 1212-1250

to find a political and financial base of power, there being few imperial resources that were distinguishable from the Salian family properties. He employed the resources of his own duchy of Saxony and those of his allies Bavaria and Franconia and his acquisitions in northern Italy. And on the whole he employed them successfully. At his death in 1137, Lothar had developed the kernel of a powerful state, and his heirs, the Welf dynasty of Bavaria and Saxony, loomed as powerfully as had the last Salians. The fear of the major electors, particularly the archbishop of Trier, of another dynasty like that of the Salians rising to power led to the election of Conrad III as king of Germany in 1137. Conrad, the son of Frederick of Hohenstaufen, duke of Swabia, himself the son of one of Henry IV's strongest supporters, controlled the resources only of Swabia and the retrieved Franconia, and waged a battle to build sufficient resources to enforce his power throughout Germany, especially against Welf resistance.

Between 1050 and 1150 the German aristocracy also faced difficulties. The old traditions of requiring that inheritances be divided among children threatened to reduce individual family solidarity and real power. Yet the preservation of a major part of the inheritance, or the addition to it of imperial titles, offices, privileges, and monastic advocacies, threatened to alienate brothers and other relatives who received fewer or no shares. Vast amounts of wealth might suddenly shift within a single family if fathers died prematurely and left young children who could not protect their rights. Once a small section of one of the earlier great, loosely connected families acquired through its own or an ancestor's efforts wealth and offices that could be kept in one package, the focus of its energies became more narrowly dynastic. Rivaled by the *ministerialis* class of royal servants, the aristocracy of Germany constituted a turbulent, conservative body of rank-conscious nobles who were willing, as long as they did not lose their individual rank in the process, to become vassals of monasteries, bishops, or other nobles. Individual landholdings gave their names—and the privileges of rank attached to them—to the families who held them, all in the midst of royal rivalries and the building of such great dynastic holdings as the Welf control of Saxony and Bavaria.

When Conrad III became king of Germany in 1137 he began to collect under his own control properties that sometimes made him a vassal of monasteries and bishops. Instead of creating a royal domain, as did the kings of England and France, the kings of Germany first acquired territories by a variety of techniques, then attempted to install a homogeneous administration throughout all of them, regardless of the terms by which they were supposed to be held. Indeed, the means to enforce authority was always the aim of German monarchs, and the Hohenstaufen state, insofar as it may be called a state, had the search for effective authority as its constant rationale. The great houses of Hohenstaufen and Welf contended in a turbulent social and political world. It was not a world in which turbulent petty nobles prevented the formation of a true monarchy, but one in which noble families, great and small, attempted to acquire power and continuity, just as the kings attempted to acquire power and dynastic continuity. In many respects, this absence of a hierarchy of lordships, or rather the artificial hierarchy that took shape in the twelfth century, prevented the foundation in Germany of a monarchy similar to that of France. France possessed a hierarchy of lordships, and when the king of France extended his control in the late twelfth and thirteenth centuries, he controlled whole territories and their subordinate nobility once he controlled the major centers or acquired the major titles. In Germany, the king could not control the major centers, the duchies; rather he had to insert himself into whatever positions of lordship he could acquire by any means whatsoever. He was prohibited after the twelfth century, in fact, from keeping individual fiefs that fell into his hands for longer than a year. These could be administered homogeneously, but they could never give the king the power in the kingdom that anything resembling state building required.

Conrad III attempted to weaken the Welf family. The emergence in that family of Henry the Lion (1130–1195), the leader of the Welf faction throughout much of the century, not only preserved Welf interests, but maintained the family's strength. In addition to the Welf family, with its holdings in Saxony and Bavaria, Conrad faced other, only slightly less powerful families. In southwestern Germany the dukes of Zähringen were building a compact state, and the Babenberg and Wittelsbach families were alternately powerful allies and enemies. The great ecclesiastical princes, the bishops of Mainz, Trier, Cologne, Passau, and Freising, also constituted part of the aristocracy. Indeed, it was largely the fact of his mother's Welf blood and his father's Hohenstaufen blood that made Frederick I Barbarossa (b. 1125) the successful candidate for the crown of Germany after his uncle Conrad III's death in 1152. As a compromise candidate, Frederick ruled until his death in 1190. As king of Germany, Burgundy, and Italy and emperor-elect, he possessed great titular power, but his backing in Germany was crucial, and his first efforts were directed toward strengthening that support. In 1155 he invested Henry the Lion, who already held Saxony, with Bavaria, and consoled Henry Jasomirgott, his cousin and lately duke of Bavaria, with the newly created duchy of Austria in 1156 by means of the *privilegium minus,* a charter conferring particular privileges upon Austria. Barbarossa was an able diplomat, and he cemented bonds with the ruler of Hungary, Bohemia, Poland, and Denmark. In 1158 Frederick moved into Italy. Among his first actions there was the issuing of the *Authentic Habita,* the privilege for scholars. The decisions of the Diet of Roncaglia in the same year outlined Frederick's plans for consolidating imperial rule over Italy. However, Frederick quarreled with Pope Hadrian IV, and when Hadrian died in 1159 a double papal election placed two conflicting candidates on the throne of St. Peter. Cardinal Octavian, Barbarossa's ally, took the title of Victor IV, and his opponent, Rolandus Bandinelli, took that of Alexander III.

The disputed papal election was the first of Barbarossa's Italian problems. The second was that of the Italian cities of the north. Although the provisions of the Diet of Roncaglia were recognized by some cities, others, led by Milan, opposed them and closed their gates before the emperor. Frederick conquered Milan in 1162, but the disputed papacy dragged on, Alexander finally gaining the upper hand, largely because of French and English support. Frederick returned to Germany, and in 1165 he had Charlemagne canonized by the successor of Victor IV, the antipope Paschal III.

In 1167 the cities of northern Italy that opposed Frederick formed the Lombard League, and from 1168 to 1174 Frederick remained in Germany strengthening his resources and attempting to establish his dynasty in the person of his son Henry (later the Emperor Henry VI) as king of the Romans. Then, in 1174, he returned to Italy with an army, but he failed to capture Alessandria, a new city founded by the Lombard League and named after Alexander III, and he broke with Henry the Lion over the latter's refusal to supply Frederick with reinforcements. Finally, in 1176 Frederick's army was routed by the forces of the Lombard League at Legnano, and Frederick was forced to negotiate. In 1177 he and Alexander and the cities came to terms in the Peace of Venice.

Returning to Germany, Frederick resumed his conflict with Henry the Lion, who, in a series of trials, was deprived of his duchies and saw them transformed into new territorial commands. Along with Carinthia and Bohemia, which were made duchies before Frederick came to power, the raising of Austria, Styria, Westphalia, and Brabant to the status of duchies made ten duchies in all in the empire. Bohemia was raised during Frederick's reign to the status of a kingdom, and the king of Bohemia became one of the most powerful princes of the empire. After 1180 Frederick and his officials slowly established some order among the welter of nobles in Germany. They restricted the title of prince to a small number of nobles, they created the ten duchies, and they reinforced the developing hierarchy of lordships. In 1186 Frederick married his son Henry to Constance, daughter of Roger II of Sicily and later heiress to the kingdom of Sicily.

In 1187, when news of the fall of Jerusalem to the Turks reached Europe, Frederick took the Crusader's vow, but he drowned in June, 1190 in Asia Minor during the march to Jerusalem. His son and successor Henry VI (1190–1197) spent time and effort consolidating his reign in both Germany and Sicily before his untimely death in 1197. Henry left a son, Frederick II, but the child was only three years old, and the electors faced an imperial election in which the two main candidates were representatives of the traditional Hohenstaufen and Welf families: Philip of Swabia, Barbarossa's son and Henry VI's brother, and Otto of Brunswick, son of Henry the Lion. The disputed election was settled by the intervention of Pope Innocent III (1198–1216), who crowned Otto IV emperor in 1198. Otto's ambitions made him an unwilling tool of Innocent, however, and the relations between the Welf emperor and the pope deteriorated rapidly until Otto's death in 1215. With Philip and

Otto dead, Innocent then turned to the nineteen-year-old son of Henry VI, the half-Sicilian Frederick, who was crowned emperor in 1220. The uniting of the crowns of Germany and Sicily had never been acceptable to the papacy, or to the northern Italian towns. Frederick had spent most of his youth attempting to stay alive and exert some sort of a claim over his vast inheritance, and in his concessions to the nobles of Germany he revealed his preference for Sicily as the base of his power. His rule in Sicily and South Italy was ruthless and effective, a continuation of the able governmental traditions of the Norman monarchs whom he had succeeded. His court, like those of Roger II and Frederick Barbarossa, was filled with scholars and administrators, and his supervision of governance was thorough. In 1231 he issue the law code of the Sicilian kingdom, the *Liber Augustalis,* and in 1229, in spite of being excommunicated, went on crusade and through diplomacy won a treaty with the sultan of Egypt that permitted Christians access to Jerusalem. His intelligence and energy served him well, and when he encountered the power of Pope Innocent IV, his own resources, intelligence, theory of imperial majesty, and propaganda all swelled his claims. Frederick II's idea of a universal empire had become similar to that of his grandfather, Frederick Barbarossa, as supported by Roman law and a compact, well-governed kingdom, with the reserves of Germany in waiting. For the papacy the final question of imperial power was about to be answered.

The problems of the "constitutional" authority of the emperor within Christendom were thus an inextricable part of his authority as king of Germany, and the working out of any effective imperial ideology always confronted the specific political, economic, and diplomatic problems that the king of Germany (and, later, the king of Sicily), had to face. The popes too worked toward a theory of universal authority in Christendom, and they too were faced with specific political difficulties in central and northern Italy that sometimes impeded their design. They certainly lacked effective military power, and, hence, papal diplomacy played rather a different role in the history of the twelfth- and thirteenth-century papacy than diplomacy played in the Holy Roman Empire. We have already seen something of the complex process whereby a juristic conception of papal authority, based upon actual juridical activity and the theories of the canon lawyers, took shape between the pontificates of Gregory VII and Alexander III. The new system of church governance, new and differently trained personnel, and, in a sense, the new training of the popes themselves all contributed to this transformation. We must now consider some specific episodes in the history of the twelfth- and thirteenth-century papacy that exercised the new theories and the new institutions of papal governance, while changing the papacy's conception of the imperial power.

Among the ideas of papal authority that developed in the controversies of the late eleventh century, several acquired particular importance. St. Peter Damian had drawn the analogy between the papal court and the ancient senate of Rome; papal costume between the ninth and the thirteenth century, particularly the process by which the tiara and the papal mantle came to acquire significance, acquired a strong temporal symbolic meaning; several of the metaphors commonly used in papal correspondence also underwent a transformation that made them apply clearly to the temporal authority of the popes. In this process of shaping a theory that was ultimately expressed in rhetoric, liturgy, costume, and historical symbolism, the popes of the twelfth and thirteenth centuries found themselves dealing with very different sorts of temporal authorities. On the one hand, the claims of the papacy and its supporters that spiritual Rome had succeeded to the temporal authority of the Roman Empire and that therefore the emperor himself was in a sense a *vicarius*, or subofficial of the pope, could only be safely expressed of the emperor and of the temporal powers within the city of Rome itself. Such a universal argument, couched in juristic terms, had little applicability to kings and other temporal rulers outside the empire, and in dealing with these powers the popes made more of their moral teaching authority and of their specific legal powers on a smaller scale. On the other hand, the nobility of Rome also claimed, particularly after the mid twelfth century, that they were also the heirs of the Roman senate and that their authority could not be abrogated by the power of the pope. Thus, the highest kind of papal claim to universal authority could be applied most clearly and directly to the imperial office, whereas papal supremacy over kings and papal authority within kingdoms, counties, and duchies had to be couched in somewhat different terms. In the following pages, it seems advisable to distinguish between the audiences of papal theories. The Donation of Constantine, the theory of the *translatio imperii* (the concept that God had transferred, sometimes through papal agency, the *imperium*, imperial authority, from the Greeks to the Franks and from the Franks to the Germans), and other literature supporting the theory of universal imperial papal authority all set the pope over all men, but particularly over the emperor.

Translated into terms meaningful to twelfth-century people, this papal lordship was expressed in letters and symbols. In the twelfth century, a fresco was painted on the walls of the Lateran palace depicting the emperor Lothar of Supplinburg becoming a vassal of Pope Innocent II. At the imperial diet at Besançon in 1157, a papal letter was read to Frederick Barbarossa in which the imperial authority was referred to as a *beneficium* (the technical term for a gift conferred by a superior on an inferior) from the pope, and when the imperial court protested, one of the papal legates, traditionally Cardinal Rolandus Bandinelli, pointedly asked what the imperial authority was, if not a *beneficium*. The ritual for the investiture of an emperor in the twelfth century required the emperor to perform symbolic services for the pope that were highly reminiscent and suggestive of a subordinate relationship in the world of temporal lordship. These were some of the symbolic means by which papal ideas of universal monarchy were conveyed to laymen, even emperors. As we will see below, the papacy devised slightly different approaches to other temporal powers. In 1208 the *ordo* (ritual) for the investing of an emperor was also changed to express papal authority more effectively. The *ordines,* or directions for public or liturgical rituals, are extremely important sources for changes in the history of ideas, because they represent the gestural expression of theoretical abstractions, the most effective means of communicating to an audience the meanings of the rituals and the offices they transferred. At the investing of Otto IV in 1208, the emperor was no longer addressed as having been "crowned by God"; the imperial *laudes,* the public acclamation of and prayer for the new emperor, was drastically shortened and stripped of all implications of the sacramental character of the investiture. In his decisions concerning the disputed imperial election between Philip of Swabia and Otto IV in 1198, Innocent III had been accused by the German princes of intervening in an affair that was no business of his, but his letters to them on this subject between 1199 and 1202 established very clearly his conception of his own power. He did not, Innocent wrote, have any intention of interfering with the princes' right to elect the king of Germany, but, he pointed out, the king of Germany was only an emperor-elect, and he had to be examined for his suitability as a defender of the Church by the pope, and rejected if he was found wanting. This literature represents a careful distinction among princely rights, explicit papal rights, and universal papal responsibility for the whole Church, and the balance among them is very carefully maintained. These were some of the different methods by means of which the changing papal concept of universal authority developed in the late twelfth and thirteenth centuries.

There are, of course, other elements to consider. Each pope was an individual, having a unique life history and unique interests. As we have attempted to show above, popes did not automatically come to resemble one another or to hold the same ideas or to express them in the same ways simply because they became popes. Some emphasized compromise, peaceful negotiation, personal holiness, and moral admonition; others approached similar problems with a legalistic and meticulously considered position from which they would not depart; some were young, others old when they became pope; some had been monks, some legates, some lawyers, some were secure in Rome, some were driven from the city by opposing forces or antipopes and forced to wander throughout Christendom, or at least throughout central Italy. These and other sets of individual circumstances influenced each pope's concept of papal authority and each pope's shaping of papal policy. There was, to be sure, something of a cumulative building up of theories of papal authority throughout the twelfth and thirteenth centuries, but theory could be, and usually was, modified by events and personalities. Some of those events and personalities acquired great significance during this period.

The citizens of medieval Rome, unlike those of the city-republics to the north, held little political power. The presence of the papacy and the propapal emperors of the eleventh century, the lack of Roman connections on the part of foreign-born popes, and the existence of the Papal State in central Italy all contributed to the disabling of the turbulent Roman nobility. The great dynasties of the tenth and eleventh centuries had become only a few of many ambitious families who lived in fortified castles, often made from Roman ruins, and who retained the ancient titles of *consul* and *senatus* to describe what powers of office they held. The nobles and wealthy families of Rome constituted an intermittent problem for the popes of the late eleventh and early twelfth centuries, because in their struggles for power within Rome they often sided with one or another of contending papal candidates or massed in common hostility toward a single reigning pope.

The power of the nobles and the temporal resources of the papal court, however, were challenged by a new movement in the 1140s, one led by wealthy but nonnoble families who attempted to establish a commune—that is, a government of the city of Rome in which power was shared among a wide citizen body. Other towns in northern Italy had formed communes in the early twelfth century, as had towns in Flanders and as towns were doing in the kingdom of France. Some of these had been remarkably successful, driving out counts and bishops, bringing the nobility to heel, and establishing communal governments with some degree of continuity. In Brescia in the 1130s such a movement threatened the power of the bishop, and in 1138, partly under the leadership of Arnold of Brescia, a former student of Abelard, the bishop was expelled from the city. Arnold had focused his criticisms of the Church upon the question of temporal power, and in 1140 he reprimanded and was in turn condemned by St. Bernard at the Council of Sens. Arnold then traveled to Zurich in Swabia, and in 1145, when the commune in Rome rose against the pope and the nobles, Arnold went to Rome.

The Roman revolution centered in the Roman populace's anger at Pope Innocent II (1130–1143) for his mercy to the rebellious town of Tivoli, and between 1143 and 1145 the commune held its ground. In 1145 it defeated a papal army, and during the first two years of the pontificate of Eugenius III (1145–1153) it drove the pope from the city several times, consequently calling upon itself the eloquent wrath of St. Bernard. The year 1144 held other bad news for the pope: the city of Edessa in northern Syria fell to the Moslems, and the preparations for the Second Crusade had to take precedence over all else. Between 1144 and his death in 1153, Eugenius III was in the city of Rome only twice, briefly in 1149–1150 and again in 1152–1153. Arnold, who arrived sometime between 1145 and 1147, slowly assumed a greater and greater role, first as a moral reformer and preacher, later as a demagogue.

In 1154, after the short pontificate of Anastasius IV, a ninety-year-old career papal official, a canon regular and papal diplomat, the English Hadrian IV, succeeded to the papacy. Hadrian promptly placed Rome under an interdict, forbidding any ecclesiastical services to take place in the city. The population finally gave in and turned Arnold over to the pope. Arnold escaped, however, and the pope faced the problems of the arrival in Italy of Frederick Barbarossa. By a quick agreement, Barbarossa recaptured Arnold, entered Rome for his coronation as emperor, and destroyed the republic of the commune. In 1155

Arnold was judged guilty of heresy, turned over to temporal authorities, and hanged, after which his corpse was burned.

The disputed papal election of 1130, the Roman revolt, the fall of Edessa, the exile of Eugenius in 1144, the rise of Arnold in Rome, and the troubled negotiations between Hadrian IV and Frederick Barbarossa give us some idea of the problems of papal governance and the drains on papal energies from many different sources during a single twenty-five-year period. During the long pontificate of Alexander III (1159–1181), the pope spent only three years in Rome, the commune having revived again, and in the thirteenth century, after a truce with Pope Innocent III (1198–1216), the commune once again became a papal problem during the struggles between Pope Gregory IX and Emperor Frederick II. In the fourteenth century, when the papacy was headquartered in Avignon, the republic rose again with great initial success. Thus, although the theories of papal universal authority were often directed most successfully against imperialist claims, the day-to-day life of the popes often encountered such substantial political difficulties as the question of papal relations with the citizens of Rome.

Barbarossa's reign, shored up by the influence of the professors of Roman law at Bologna and his own court, witnessed a continual claim to imperial authority that ran counter to the papal thesis. However, such imperial claims encountered the substantial development of twelfth-century ecclesiological thought. In the first place, a new concept of the Church had emerged, one in which spiritual authority acquired greater power than temporal authority, even that of the emperor. Second, the new theology of penance extended both the moral and juridical authority of the Church into the daily lives of many more Christians. When the Fourth Lateran Council in 1215 decreed the necessity of annual compulsory confession to parish priests, it drove home this new moral-juridical priestly character. Third, the position of the pope within the Church had been greatly strengthened in the writings of the canon lawyers, men such as Gratian, Rolandus Bandinelli, and Huguccio of Pisa. Although there were not many texts in the *Decretum* concerning specifically temporal power, the few that existed often constituted starting points for extended discussions of imperial authority, particularly in terms of papal authority. And in the thousands of texts in the *Decretum*, papal authority is explored in every conceivable manner. In spite of St. Bernard's criticisms of the new juridical character of much of the papacy's business (criticisms that echo those of Arnold of Brescia and others holding divergent points of view concerning the role of the Church)—"Your power lies in sins, not in the problem of possessions"— the juridical character of papal authority has developed and extended in the work of three generations of some of the ablest lawyers the world has ever known.

When Frederick Barbarossa temporarily rebelled at holding the stirrup of the pope's horse at Sutri in 1154, he was criticizing a practice whose purely honorific character had come to be regarded as a sign of quasi-juridical subordination. Yet the changes in twelfth-century thought had greatly strengthened papal authority, and the pontificates of Innocent II, Eugenius III, Hadrian IV, and Alexander III reveal this practical strength.

The pontificates of Innocent III (1198–1216), Gregory IX (1227–1241), and Innocent IV (1243–1254) witnessed the most extensive application of the theories developed in the twelfth century. In a series of councils, exchanges of letters, and diplomatic agreements, these three popes gave practical shape to the juristic authority of the pope in a dramatic series of encounters with a wide spectrum of temporal powers. We have already seen Innocent III laying down a claim for papal authority in his correspondence with the electors of Germany in the dispute between Philip of Swabia and Otto IV in 1198. We have also seen the consequences of the decretal *Vergentis* of 1199, which identified heresy with treason to God and permitted the confiscation of a heretic's property. Between 1198 and 1209 there was no emperor in Italy, and Innocent's control of the Papal States and his guardianship of Frederick II in Sicily gave him more practical authority than many of his predecessors had had. In 1201 Otto IV acknowledged remarkably sweeping claims made on behalf of papal authority, and Walter of Brienne, a candidate for the crown of Sicily, gave equally broad recognition to papal authority. In 1201 Innocent wrote in the decretal *Sollitae* to the Byzantine emperor, making vague but serious claims to universal authority. In two decretals of 1202, *Venerabilem* and *Per venerabilem,* Innocent further defined his authority in cases of temporal jurisdiction. At the same time and for a while after, Innocent negotiated with the excommunicated king of France, Philip II Augustus, and with the excommunicated king of England, John. The pontificate of Innocent III, the busiest if not the greatest of the medieval popes, revealed the broad spectrum of jurisdictional areas across which the theories of papal authority could be spread and witnessed the extraordinary ability of the pope and his curia to turn such theories into the basis for practical decisions in hundreds of particular cases.

Innocent's pontificate also witnessed the removal of Otto IV and the final substitution of the young Frederick II for Otto. But Innocent did not live to see the final imperial-papal clash between Frederick and his successors. Although Frederick had promised to give up the kingdom of Sicily when he became emperor and to go on crusade, he lived up to the letter of neither of these promises, and Gregory IX (1227–1241) was forced to deal with Frederick at the height of his power.

When Frederick II came of age in 1208, his Sicilian inheritance was virtually in ruins. By intelligence and ruthless application, he managed to restore royal authority by 1223, and the *Liber Augustalis* of 1231 signaled the strengthening of that authority and the heavy-handed but effective governance of the kingdom. Nothing escaped the king's eye: coinage, taxes, commerce, practical justice—all these were administered by a trained, competent, and loyal body of servants. Yet the technical lordship of the pope over Sicily led to other difficulties. Frederick never attained the office of papal legate for Sicily, an office held by the kings of Sicily since Roger II. His power in Germany and northern Italy was far less than that of his grandfather Barbarossa, and in order to wring concessions from the towns and princes there, Frederick was forced to offer further privileges and exemptions. The powers of the imperial office were diminished, but Frederick's own native intelligence, his unremitting passion to an Augustan revival in his own age, and his grouping of able servants around him worked to restore the idea of empire in its full brilliance. But Frederick aroused suspicions too. His penetrating intelligence and his notorious scepticism deprived him of the sympathy outside Italy that he needed and raised questions about the orthodoxy of his beliefs; his open scorn for the papacy and other clergy deprived him of potential allies; his ceremonial and publicistic expressions of his concept of imperial authority did not sit well with parts of a world acquiring a first substantial taste of relative independence from overlords, no matter how glamorous they might at first appear.

Again and again Gregory IX hammered at Frederick's claims. Frederick's reluctance to hand over Sicily to his son, his refusal to go on crusade, his decision to go on crusade after being excommunicated, his oppression of ecclesiastical liberties—all these the pope contrasted with Frederick's imperial duties. When Gregory died in 1241, Frederick meted out harsh treatment to the conclave of cardinals electing a successor, and at one point Frederick exerted the old imperial claim to decide a disputed papal election. The brief pontificate of Celestine IV accomplished nothing, however, and not until 1243 did another pope ascend the throne of St. Peter—Innocent IV, Cardinal Sinibaldo Fiesco of Genoa, a member of a proimperial family, a superb jurist, and a man wholly lacking in what Frederick considered the irritable majesty and mystical intractability of Gregory IX.

Yet Innocent proved to be the ultimate opponent of Frederick. He refused to make concessions to the emperor's demands. He called a council for Rome, and when Frederick's forces scattered the fleet and captured some of the members arriving for the council, Innocent fled first to Genoa, and then to Lyons, where he called a general council for 1245. Although Frederick invoked the imperial right to call a general council himself if the pope did not act in the interests of the Church as a whole, the threat remained only a threat. In 1245 at the First Council of Lyons, Innocent tried Frederick, who was defended in proxy by Theodore of Suessa, condemned the emperor, and declared him deposed. Innocent's decretal deposing Frederick, *Ad apostolice,* summed up eloquently the whole canonistic tradition of papal authority, and declared that the emperor was the most suitable target against which that authority could be directed. In spite of Frederick's continued battles, his death in 1250 marked the disappearance of the last emperor capable of challenging papal authority in the tradition of the emperors of the eleventh and twelfth centuries, who were buttressed by new ideas of public law and new institutions of temporal majesty. By 1250 the papacy had triumphed.

Yet that triumph was over the one enemy against whom the powers of the papacy as spiritual head of Christendom could most readily be invoked. Other powers proved less tractable. Moreover, the papal success against Frederick II must be regarded as the success of temporary alliances, diplomatic skill, and the overextension of imperial resources at least as much as the triumph of a theory. For the forces under the pope's control were small, and papal uncertainty as to the conduct of allies was at least as great as papal confidence in the theory of authority. Papal finances, in spite of the efforts of Innocent III and Honorius III (1216–1227), remained small, and income remained difficult to collect. The personnel of the papal Curia were difficult to recruit and manage; during the first half of the thirteenth century, for example, the number of cardinals averaged about eight. Rulers everywhere could find seemingly legitimate excuses to decline papal requests for money, men, or crusade movements. Moreover, papal justice appears to have become less attractive after 1220, and popular dissatisfaction with the papacy—whether in the continuation of antipapal satire, the hostility of heretics and their sympathizers, or the lack of papal contact with popular devotion—spread widely during the thirteenth century. The conflicts between Gregory IX and Innocent IV and Frederick II were not the only papal encounters with temporal powers during this period. The papal interventions in England in the murder of Thomas Becket in 1170 and the interdict during the reign of John in 1208–1213, the excommunication of Philip Augustus, the Albigensian Crusade and the deposition of Pedro II of Aragón in 1208, and the suspension from governance of Sancho II of Portugal in 1245—all generated as much hostility toward the papacy as they served to display papal power. Finally, it is important to note that some widely respected moral figures of the twelfth and thirteenth centuries withheld their full approval from the papacy as an institution. St. Bernard, St. Louis of France, and others, men who possessed enormous personal prestige, never consistently approved the character of papal activity. These shortcomings were not eliminated with the papal triumph over the empire, and they became more pronounced at the end of the thirteenth century. The growth of papal monarchy was indeed based upon a concept of Christendom and a juristic theory of papal authority that were impressive and temporarily successful, but their chief victim was the emperor, not temporal authority in itself.

21

THE ROAD TO THE WORLD

COURTLY SOCIETY AND SECULARIZATION

The consolidation of public power in the hands of kings, the weakening of unrestricted ecclesiastical liberties within these kingdoms and in the city-republics of northern Italy and Germany, the increasingly articulated economic and social institutions of thirteenth-century Europeans, and the religious unrest of the period all signal, not any kind of homogeneous experience, but a diversity of changes that took different characters and took place at different rates in different parts of Europe. The vast and complex process that historians call "secularization" or "laicization" was certainly rooted in these changes. Several aspects of secular values were expressed in terms of older institutions—criticism of the clergy and the

Church, the new emphasis upon the chivalric life of the nobility, and attacks upon privilege—and some in new institutions—the character of life in the courts and towns of thirteenth-century Europe, the works of vernacular literature, new styles of devotion, and town design and building. Secular values expressed themselves also in current topics of philosophical debate, such as the question of the natural virtues of heathen and that of the limits of reason in probing the divine mysteries. The new styles of devotion, from private solicitude for one's own salvation to a new wave of lay patronage of shrines and churches, also reflected secular values. In the society of the new courts, however, those values stood out most sharply.

The story of noble residences, from farm and humble defense work to castle and country house, would tell as much about the history of the ruling classes of Europe as the history of costume, marriage habits, and legal privileges. The development of the court from the household of kings and nobles between the eleventh and the fourteenth centuries is far more, however, than the story of houses. For courts were ceremonial and functional centers of power and culture as well as residences. The lord and lady and their immediate relations, servants, ministers, retainers, and guests constituted a unique kind of community in which private and public affairs were inextricably mingled and in which the most prosaic details of everyday life were juxtaposed against the highest and most formal kinds of ceremony. Few castles, as we have seen, could be considered comfortable by modern standards, and the domestic design of these buildings reflects a culture far different from modern culture. Privacy, the separation of functions, and the perennially traveling society of country houses came later. Labor and materials cost a good deal in the twelfth and thirteenth centuries, as in the twentieth century, and the great castles of stone, which were built by skilled masons and employed materials that had to be transported a long way, prerogatives of the higher nobility. Wood and earth often remained the lot of the lower nobility. The society of the court, the society that dwelt in the great stone castles, was a common society in which individuals of all ranks mingled, privacy was unobtainable, and learning was acquired by watching and listening. Hunting and the extensive trappings of the hunt—from packs of dogs and huntsmen to equipment—tournaments, court duties, estate management, and, above all, regulating the domestic conduct of his inferiors, filled the noble's days.

During the course of the twelfth century, the life of the great courts acquired a style of its own—*courtois, höflich,* "courtly"—which spread from France throughout most of Europe. "Courtly" conduct was that accepted by the great courts, and it included manners, ethics, dress, skills, and speech. Next to the virtues of the warrior, the man who was *preux,* there emerged the virtues of the courtier, the *prudhomme,* the man who was well behaved. Books of manners are not common reading in the twentieth century, but in the twelfth and thirteenth centuries conduct revealed much about a person, and the ideal of a perfect type of conduct, courtly conduct, reveals much about the relative peacefulness and leisure of the thirteenth-century courts. For manners, in the sense in which the term was used in the thirteenth century, had much to do with what we would call ethics and breeding. The way of life of the good courtier was considered—sometimes explicitly, by such different figures as St. Louis IX of France and the German court poet Wolfram von Eschenbach—the layman's counterpart to the daily prayer of the monk. Yet courtly conduct was something more than part of the justification of a particular lay status against the traditionally recognized and more honorific status of the clergy. The configuration of noble households was changing during the twelfth and thirteenth centuries, and to some extent the new rules of courtly behavior accommodated this transition and perpetuated the new social and emotional relationships of the twelfth- and thirteenth-century European world. The figure of the woman as the object of amatory and erotic emotions, the fierce restriction of courtly status to the class of nobles below that of the king and his ministers, and the elaboration of a code of arms and military conduct may all be regarded as manifestations of this new spirit of a lower service nobility seeking a foothold in society that would explain both their inferior status and account for their high claims to parity with those who held greater wealth and power. Much has been made, too much, probably, of "courtly love," a phenomenon in the literature of the twelfth and thirteenth centuries in which a noble woman was loved by a humble knight who sang her praises and expected usually small—but sometimes substantial—favors in return. Not enough has been made of the other elements of courtly psychology. When, in a thirteenth-century romance about King Arthur, a knight refuses a kingdom because he would no longer be a knight and be able to follow the life of chivalry, or when, in the fourteenth century, the rigid rules of chivalric conduct impaired the tactical functions of whole armies, the influence of courtly culture becomes recognizable beyond the rather narrow amatory terms in which it is usually described. The life of the court expressed its demands and cohesiveness in terms of codes of conduct and psychological expressiveness, but it was rarely insulated from the concerns of the rest of the world. Dominicans and Franciscans found access to the court of Louis IX and to those of others; heretics too found shelter—in the courts of Occitania. The intimate contact between devotional movements and court life is often overlooked by historians whose attention is riveted on cities; yet court life is no older than the urban revival and no less representative of the attitudes and values of the twelfth and thirteenth centuries. In the courts, a secularized kind of life, an ideal of life possessing a dignity equal to that of the clergy, was first expressly enunciated. The heavy-handed fighting man of the tenth and eleventh centuries, who had to do penance for killing and whose hopes of salvation were few, slowly turned into the knight, whose ordination paralleled that of the clergy, whose brotherhood with all other knights discreetly concealed widening social differences, whose character as a *prudhomme,* as St. Louis once observed, was so dignified and meritorious that to say the word "filled the mouth."

The knight in turn became the object, or rather the vehicle, of a number of ethical ideals that influenced the image of the virtuous layman in all walks of life. That transition was not at all appealing to the knightly class, but its virtues were borrowed by the world of university students and teachers and the world of townsmen. Professors of law claimed parity with knights as "knights" and "priests" of the law. And the concept of "gentleness," with its complex earlier associations in the literature of love and knightly conduct, became in the late thirteenth and early fourteenth centuries imbued also with an ethical dignity that was close to virtue and constituted a major landmark in the history of social ideas and relationships. The slow process of transformation of the human concept of self that had some of its roots in the changing conceptions of the relations between man and God in the devotional revolution of the eleventh and twelfth centuries had other roots in the formulation of a secularized ideal of gentlemanly conduct. In this process of formation, which later extended from the courts to the towns and contributed much to the changing ideas of human dignity, courtly culture played a considerable role. The knight, like other social types, made a contribution far greater than his picturesqueness, quaintness, and archaic dignity; he helped in his own way to seek a measure of lay life that satisfied both material circumstances and the high demands of earlier moral theology. The knight and the court, just as much as the townsman, merchant, free peasant, and ecclesiastical critic, constitute part of the variety of secular experience that established the legitimacy of the lay status in early Europe. Far from being remote, idealized, picturesque institutions, the courts of the thirteenth century legitimated with a new ideal of the self a life of hard activity. Lords, courtiers, retainers, clergy, and poets in these courts absorbed influences from the world outside and created a sense of order and ethical conduct that accommodated their own status and evolved a set of values for an increasingly secularized world.

THE FLOWERING OF VERNACULAR LITERATURE

Literature presupposes a literary public, and the literary public of Europe before the twelfth century accepted largely the Latin literature produced by monks and a few literate laymen. Aside from the formal documents that constituted much of the influence of the written word during the age of Charlemagne, there was little reading for the literate laymen that did not have a touch of the monastery or the hand of the clergy in it. *Beowulf,* the greatest and earliest example of vernacular literature, was probably written by a monk, though for a lay audience, and the songbooks of Charlemagne's leisure hours were destroyed by his son, Louis the Pious, as a reaction against his own song-filled adolescence. In the late ninth and tenth centuries, European literature was Latin literature, and although the roots of Germanic and Romance vernaculars extend back to the eighth and ninth centuries, the literary remains of the vernacular languages are strikingly scanty. Sometimes, as we have seen, a precocious development of a vernacular literature might flower, as in ninth- and tenth-century England, Moravia, and Germany, but its roots were slight and events could wither it. The richness of Anglo-Saxon English disappeared during the eleventh and twelfth centuries, to be replaced, first, by the courtly Anglo-Norman language of the conquerors, and, by the end of the twelfth century, by Middle English—the language, first, of a few lyrics, homilies, and moralizing poems, and, later, of the remarkable profusion of literary works between 1250 and 1400 that culminated in the literary genius of Chaucer and the brooding, rough-hewn lyricism of the author of *Piers Plowman*. Old Church Slavonic died out as a liturgical language during the tenth and eleventh centuries, and even Old High German, whose literature in the tenth and eleventh centuries rivaled that of England, slowly gave way in the twelfth century to the more flexible and sophisticated Middle High German, the language of the great romances of early thirteenth-century German courts and the lyric poetry of German courtly amatory verse.

The adventures of literature are tied inextricably to the adventures of language. The long and distinct antagonism between the north and the south of what later became France are reflected not only in the differences between the *langue d'oïl* and the *langue d'oc,* but in the differences between the literatures produced in those languages. By the eleventh century, Languedocian had produced a rich tradition of verse, prose biographies of the troubadors, and a complex literary and emotional psychology that is still virtually untranslatable. Languedocian, even after the thirteenth-century decline of the courtly centers that supported and appreciated the work of the troubador poets, retained a lyricism and emotional impact that may be traced in such unlikely places as the vernacular prose reports of trials and the formal accounts of ecclesiastical assemblies. In the north, however, the lyricism and emotional exploration of the south is absent, and instead we find hard, grim saints' lives and tales of military valor such as the *Song of Roland,* an account of the adventures of Charlemagne's Spanish expedition of 778, expanded through transmission into a full-fledged exploration of the varieties of military virtue and sentiment, an account imbued with the already legendary figure of Charlemagne, whose struggle on God's behalf against the enemies of God constitutes a kind of "public" framework for the adventures of Roland and Olivier. Charlemagne and his successors also figure in the twelfth-century *chansons de geste*, "songs of deeds," which explored the idea of valor and loyalty in settings that reflect the decay of personal relationships and often use legal disputes as a stepping stone for the probing of the failures of traditional relationships. The great history of R. R. Bezzola, *Les origines de la littérature courtoise,* analyzes many of these works, and it is at its best in suggesting the increasing anxiety the authors show in attempting to display in literature the corrosive forces at work in the traditional world of lord and vassal.

Both northern and southern French literature have been studied in terms of their relative emphasis upon the role of women. Conventionally, the south has received high marks for its exploration of the amatory emotions and its role in making the relationships between men and women the object of intense exploration. In the literature of the north, women are fewer and their roles are conventionally subordinate, but to a reader of many years, they live with a freedom—an absence of what modern scholars might call role definition—that is wholly alien to the world of the south. It must be remembered that the role of women in early European society was generally open before the mid twelfth century. When women lost sacramental priestly status, when they became the objects of love, they achieved a new place in society. With the addition of marriage to the sacraments early in the thirteenth century, the marital *ordo* received new recognition. At the same time, however, the place of women was more closely specified and hence circumscribed. In the rough literature of the north, women guarded castles, fought battles, liturgically wept their heroes into heaven, owned property, acquired and dismissed husbands and lovers with a casualness possible only in a world in which their status was informal. Once it became formal, once poets (and poets' audiences) defined the role of the ideal women in terms of their morally elevating effect upon men, the role of women became circumscribed and limited. Such sex-role definition extends from the twelfth to the twentieth centuries.

The difference between northern and southern French literature, of course, covers more ground than I have illustrated here. The poetry of war, of saints' lives, of comedy and satire, and of public affairs also differs in each culture. The relationship between literature and social conditions is a complex one on which few literary and social historians agree. It can be said, though, that to cross from northern France into Poitou is to enter a new social and literary world. The divisions between northern and southern French literary interests, language, and styles reflect the enormous regionalism that pervaded European life in the twelfth century.

That regionalism could only be overcome by two forces: the spread of a new Latin culture and the growth of common feelings and attitudes among the literary publics. In the course of the twelfth century, both came about. In a brilliant study called *European Literature and the Latin Middle Ages,* the German scholar Ernst Robert Curtius displayed the rich intellectual and rhetorical culture of medieval Latin literature and suggested that its influence was felt throughout Europe after the twelfth century. When, in the late twelfth century, the fashion of the troubador lyrics of the south and the *chansons de geste* of the north both gave way before the increasing popularity of the courtly romance, tales describing the fictional world of King Arthur and his knights, romance literature swept Europe, from England and Portugal to Germany and Bohemia.

The legends of King Arthur, scattered obscurely through saints' lives and piecemeal histories, suddenly began to attract a great interest after the mid twelfth century. The Champagne poet, Chrétien de Troyes, wrote a number of works in which the court of Arthur served as a focus for the adventures of a different kind of knight, one whose adventures had far more to do with what a modern critic would call the search for an identity than with battles with Saracens or endless feuds over property and privilege. In several remarkable works, Chrétien established the world of Arthur's court as one in which personal identity was discovered through the solution of problems posed by adventure. The court represented order, stability, established identity, and public recognition. Outside the court, in the forests, lakes, and deserts of the literary landscape, lurked the elements of disorder, uncertainty, paradox, and unintelligibility. There, outside the court, the knight discovered who he was, and his trials legitimized him when he returned to the court to tell his story. In the course of the thirteenth century, the stories of Arthur's court expanded, and a Cistercian influence introduced the theme of the Holy Grail, reflecting the elevation of knighthood to sacral status. By the early thirteenth century, the great *Prose Vulgate* began to piece together all the stories linked to Arthur, and versions of the *Vulgate* are found in most European languages. By the time of Thomas Malory in the mid fifteenth century, the Arthurian corpus had become a great mine of secular themes, one whose political as well as emotional dimensions contributed elements to Malory's great epic the *Morte d'Arthur*.

The romances based on Arthurian materials expressed a varied spectrum of courtly concerns. Gottfried von Strassburg (fl. 1210) produced the brooding *Tristan and Isolde*. Among his contemporaries were the great German poets Wolfram von Eschenbach, whose *Parzival* and *Willehalm* contained new speculations on secular values and personal doubts, and Hartmann von Aue, whose *Der Arme Heinrich* and *Gregorius* included analyses of the layman's devotion and the conflict between role and conscience. The love lyrics of Languedoc were echoed in Germany, Italy, Sicily, and England.

In Scandinavia, the history of the tenth-century explorations and settlements in Iceland and Greenland fed a literature of adventure and social concerns—the sagas—and Scandinavian mythology, from pagan antiquity to the thirteenth century, contributed to the literature of the *Eddas*, long, complex poems exploring the remote past in the light of thirteenth-century concerns. In Kievan Russia, the *Song of Igor's Campaign* was the twelfth-century counterpart to the heroic literature of Scandinavia, early Germany, northern France, and the Spain of the *Song of the Cid*. Throughout the European world, folk literature, traditional themes, and common tales circulated widely, not excluding stories from Islamic, Byzantine, and Buddhist sources. These tales made their way into Latin as well as the vernacular literatures, and they became the common property of poets, storytellers, and moralists. Saints' lives also entered the stream of vernacular literature, and they contributed to the language of emotional discourse. In the thirteenth century the Franciscan influence, reflected in the *Little Flowers of St. Francis,* a collection of unique stories about the personality of St. Francis, influenced other forms of narrative, and the new devotional revolution of the twelfth and thirteenth centuries produced different types of saints and holy men, clerical and lay, whose biographies expanded the genre of biography itself. The lives of women saints contributed to the continued exploration of the self in an otherwise traditional genre. The comic stories of the *fabliaux* satirized both townsmen and knights and laid the foundations for the wide range of humorous tales of the fourteenth century, particularly those of Boccaccio, Sachetti, and Chaucer.

There existed also a vast body of literature of which much less is known. Popular songs, tales, verses, and moralizing stories are often neglected by scholars because of their dubious value as "great literature." Yet to the historian of culture, they reflect life and interests no less than do the more formally recognized works. The collections of miracle stories of Caesarius of Heisterbach at the beginning of the thirteenth century and Jacobus of Varagine at the end of that century were read by Europeans for centuries, and in some cases still are. The *exempla,* moral tales used to illustrate and enliven sermons, offer frequent insights into popular life and interests. The stories, jokes, and scurrilous verses quoted in chronicles and memoirs of such thirteenth-century writers as Salimbene offer glimpses of general life that are found nowhere else. From moralizing tales to outright scatology, medieval vernacular literature represents a widely varied, rich, and wonderful world of literary expressiveness. For the interested reader, these materials heighten and illuminate a culture on a level that is attained only incompletely in more formal documents and works of philosophy.

Perhaps a final example will serve to illustrate these remarks: the *Nibelungenlied*. The *Song of the Nibelungs* is a thirteenth-century epic poem written in Bavaria and based upon materials that date, in their Latin form, from the sixth and seventh centuries. It is the tale of the warrior Siegfried and his people and his wife, Kriemhild, the sister of Gunther, Siegfried's enemy. Following Siegfried's murder, Kriemhild plots revenge upon Gunther, and the ensuing action involves the whole world; Attila the Hun, Theoderic the Ostrogoth, and the heroes of the old Latin and German sagas are all drawn together. Yet the *Niebelung* poet does not revel in the wealth of legend, literary tradition, folklore, and violence he presents, but focuses the action and diversity in a masterly way upon the theme of Kriemhild's revenge. The place of this marvelous work, somewhere among the sagas, *chansons de geste,* and romances, reflects both the high command of literary skill that had been reached throughout Europe by the thirteenth century, and the complex relationships between medieval vernacular literature and the life of early European society. The historian can no more neglect this literature, nor forego learning the techniques required to read it with sympathy and understanding, than neglect the official documents and charters that constitute more customary reading. The complex associations between Latin and the vernacular literatures of Europe during the twelfth and thirteenth centuries remind us of the comparative character of all great literary study and the obligation of the historian to look at all available sources, not merely the least readable.

ARISTOTLE, AQUINAS, AND THE PLACE OF NATURE

For most thinkers between the sixth and the thirteenth centuries, nature was part of fallen creation, hostile and rugged in terms of people's experience in the physical world, and generally unintelligible. The character of education and learning during this period did little to dispel such attitudes. The division of subjects into the literary *trivium* and the mathematical *quadrivium* offered little scope for natural science, and no corpus of knowledge handed down from the past suggested a different way of considering material creation. Thus, a strong bias against the material world was reflected in the christological controversies, the Frankish criticism of Byzantine iconodulia in the late eighth century, the hostile attacks upon materialism in the eleventh-century church, and the outright attacks upon material creation by the Cathars and other heretical sects of the twelfth century. Material creation held a place in the hieratic scheme of understanding God's will for the world, but neither a love of nature nor indeed any concept remotely resembling the modern concept of nature occupied people's thoughts before the end of the eleventh century.

Between the early twelfth and late thirteenth centuries, however, attitudes toward material creation changed on many levels. Twelfth-century scientists began to acquire access to scientific works in Greek and Arabic that contained methods for rendering the physical world highly intelligible, methods that ranged from the study of geometry to the beginnings of biology and botany. By the thirteenth century, the works of Aristotle in natural science added to this corpus. New building and sculpting techniques created more tractable structures and enabled sculptors to reproduce naturalistically much of the objective world. Twelfth-century philosophers, poets, and cosmologists concerned themselves with material creation as a whole, and the new interest in Platonism in the early twelfth century, on the one hand, and the increasing desire to organize knowledge and dogma into a coherent system, on the other, led to new attempts to regard material creation as a single system, the application of such terms as *universe* and *nature* to manageable sections of it, and, in the writing of Bernard Silvester's *Cosmographia* around 1145, to the personification of nature as a goddess in an allegorical explanation of the universe. In the same period, of course, others besides sculptors, builders, logicians, Platonists, and poets developed a new interest in nature. The rediscovery of Roman law and the elaboration of canon law led to discussions of the problem of the law of nature, and political theorists of the twelfth century argued that political communities, being legitimate parts of God's plan for man, were also natural. These various ways of conceptualizing material conditions did not always interact and mutually influence each other, but it is clear that by 1150 an idea of nature and the natural had begun to appear as part of the common intellectual and emotional vocabulary of many people.

Against the increasing hostility of Manichean heresies that denied the goodness of matter, philosophers, poets, and cosmologists, as well as painters and sculptors, expressed natural phenomena in all their dignity. The intelligibility of the universe had become a widespread conviction by the thirteenth century, and the wonderful manuscript illuminations of God setting out to create the world with a carpenter's square in one hand and a geometer's compass in the other convey this certainty of the excellence of material creation. The remarkable statue on the north portal of Chartres cathedral shows a seated, infinitely compassionate God shaping Adam out of amorphous clay, the figure taking shape in God's very hands. In the late twelfth and thirteenth centuries, the arguments over the real presence of Christ in the Eucharist and the savage attacks of the Cathars were met with the new feast of *Corpus Christi,* and processions and paintings depicted the physical, human character of Christ more and more surely. These diverse examples from poetry, manuscript illumination, sculpture, and antiheretical liturgical reforms reflect the new respect and dignity accorded material creation during the twelfth and thirteenth centuries, and the new sense of participation in nature on the part of human beings.

It is in the world of formal thought and study, however, that the most striking examples of the new place of nature are to be found. The discovery and translation of Aristotle's works on natural science in the late twelfth and thirteenth centuries, together with the commentaries of the great Islamic thinkers, brought a vast mass of learning to the common thought of thirteenth-century Christians. These works were first read widely in the lower arts faculties at the universities, but early in the thirteenth century they were banned because of doctrinal opposition to certain Aristotelian propositions. The history of these new studies was radically altered, however, in 1240, when a German professor from the *studium* at Cologne, Albertus Magnus (Albert the Great), arrived at the University at Paris; in 1242 he assumed the Dominican chair of theology. From 1242 to his death in 1280, at the age of about eighty-three, Albert became almost the model of the ideal churchman. From Paris he returned to Cologne to establish a Dominican school; he traveled up and down from Rome to the Baltic as head of the German province of the Dominicans; he became bishop of Regensburg, served in administrative capacities throughout Europe, attended the Second Council of Lyons in 1274, and defended some of the work of his great pupil, St. Thomas Aquinas, at Paris in 1277. In the course of that enormously busy and varied life, Albert managed to begin successfully the process of accommodating the corpus of Aristotle's work with orthodox Christian belief.

The work of Albert was carried on and brought to towering completion by his pupil, Thomas Aquinas. Thomas was born around 1225 into the family of the lords of Aquino in southern Italy. From 1230 to 1239 Thomas studied at Monte Cassino, and in 1244, against the opposition of his family, he joined the Dominican Order. In 1245 Thomas was sent to study at Paris, where he commenced his work with Albert, and in 1248 he returned with Albert to Cologne. In 1254 Thomas returned to Paris, where he taught until 1259, when he was assigned to the papal court in various teaching capacities. Thomas returned to Paris and remained there between 1268 and 1272, at which point he went to Naples as head of the Faculty of Theology. In 1274, on his way to the Second Council of Lyons, Thomas died.

The work of Albert the Great and Thomas Aquinas represents other aspects of thirteenth-century culture besides the assimilation of Aristotle. Both members of one of the two most dynamic religious orders, both members of the new university community, both active advisers to the order and the papacy, both tireless scholars and workers, Albert and Thomas reflect the intellectual currents of their time, but they also stand out as exceptionally gifted and generous men, whose lives were filled with time-consuming and often tedious administrative work. It is important to keep in mind the careers actually followed by many thinkers of the twelfth through the fifteenth centuries. The role of professional intellectual was rare among them. The life of study and writing occupied only a small part of many careers, philosophers, theologians, law professors, and scientists often spending most of their time in administrative, preaching, or service jobs, often becoming bishops and archbishops, working their intellectual activities into lives crammed with other preoccupations.

The earliest Christian philosophy, from St. Augustine to the thirteenth century, had borrowed much from the Neo-Platonic metaphysics. The general indifference of Platonism to the material world coincided conveniently with the place of nature in western thought before the twelfth century. The great attraction of Aristotle was precisely the Aristotelian contribution to natural science, the emphasis upon describing and understanding the material world and its place in the divine order of the universe. Such an ambition, of course, presupposed new attitudes toward nature. That nature is consistent, intelligible, and capable of systematic analysis and description are three such attitudes. So is the idea that in studying nature the mind is led to a better understanding of metaphysics and theology. *Ratio,* reason, the uniquely human capacity to learn by using uniquely human faculties, in Aquinas' writings pointed the way toward the incorporation of physics and other natural sciences in the human scheme of knowledge, strengthened the thirteenth-century manifestations of interest in the material world and in the human agency.

It is thus possible for the nonspecialist in philosophy, literature, or art history to acquire a strong sense of the general significance of the work of the thinkers and artists of the twelfth and thirteenth centuries. At the beginning of the twelfth century, a manual written by Theophilus, *Concerning the Different Arts,* laid down the principle that the craftsman must understand the materials he works with, and this emphasis upon the necessity of human understanding, together with the idea that the material—and even the immaterial—universe is intelligible, links Theophilus with Aquinas, the great cathedral and castle builders—masons, glassmakers, and metalworkers—with the scientists of the thirteenth century, and the twelfth-century poets who personified nature and devised elaborate, learned creation myths with the poets who sent the individual knight away from the ordered world of the court into the chaos and mystery of the forest so that he could find both his own identity and the legitimacy of the rational world to which he returned. Thus, Aquinas, Albert, Aristotle, the artists, and the poets may all be seen as participating in the revolution in the concept of nature in the twelfth and thirteenth centuries that resulted in the rejoining of the dignity of the material world and mankind to that of the spiritual universe and its creator.

SECULARIZATION AND THE ACTIVE LIFE

The court, the vernacular literature of the layman, and the new place of nature and natural speculation are all aspects of the layperson's coming to terms with individual and social experience in space and time. Much of the evidence of this transformation of European culture is obscure: some of it is buried in semantic transformations, some in art, and some in the painstaking handiwork of manuscript illuminators and stonecutters. In many of the works of political theory and ecclesiology of the fourteenth century, several of the indirect consequences of this movement become clearer: the Christian layperson could lay a charge of heresy against the pope; the congregation of the faithful could exert pressure upon the clergy; and—hesitatingly in the work of thirteenth-century writers, more determinedly in the work of fourteenth-century writers—the council may challenge the authority of the pope. The inner subtleties of ecclesiological theory are not the places that historians of secularization often look for their evidence, but one of the surest measures of changing cultural values is the transformation of the relationships that any society considers essential at any particular point in its history. The individual's status as a Christian remained a primary concern, and subtle changes in the ways of conceiving, describing, and modifying that status often offer substantial evidence for changes in basic attitudes. Let us consider two general areas of human activity apart from ecclesiology and formal political philosophy in which some of the consequences of the changes discussed so far in this chapter may be seen: economic relationships and the creation of a political public. These broad questions may illustrate the complex and often subtle process by which the vague term "secularization" may be understood.

To a great extent, ideas and laws concerning economic relationships were a creation of churchmen, but they were a creation in much the same way that ecclesiastical political theory was: both economic and political practices were influenced by the Church's concept of its own *magisterium*, teaching authority, in the areas of faith and morals. The churchmen did not speak as economists or political theorists, but as guardians of the law of faith and morals, and when in that capacity they made pronouncements that touched wide-ranging social institutions, they exerted influences and encountered opposition that influenced the structures they dealt with. Nor was the relationship between the church and political and economic problems entirely one of outside observation and scrutiny. The Church itself was a complex economic institution with deep roots in the economic life of all Europe. Its institutions had to be regulated, protected, and exploited, often against the ambitions of laymen. The individual church constituted a particular center of local society, the physical building serving as a center of much social, including economic, life between the eighth and the seventeenth centuries. These complex relationships, from *magisterium* to economic interests to social role, all conditioned ecclesiastical attitudes toward economics. Ecclesiastical attitudes in turn influenced the social role of economic phenomena.

Before 1150, such complex relationships meant relatively little. The undifferentiated economic life of European society, the particularistic existence of most churches, including the church of Rome, the slight impact of the market and other complex forms of exchange—all these existed within the theoretical framework of ecclesiastical attitudes toward economics that had been shaped in the early Church and made into law by the fathers. The economic revolution between 950 and 1250, however, created problems and practices that increasingly came into conflict with traditional ecclesiastical attitudes, and both the laypeople engaged in the new economic activities and the ecclesiastics who faced the gap between theory and practice were compelled to think about these problems in new ways.

The long and painful process of redefining the spheres of ecclesiastical liberties that culminated first in the Investiture Conflict raised necessarily economic questions concerning church property and churchmen's economic relationships with lay patrons. The growth of the cost as well as the scope of ecclesiastical activity in the twelfth century, from the cost of pursuing cases in the papal court to the collections of tithe and the taxes for the Crusades of the twelfth and thirteenth centuries, raised many people's consciousness concerning economic relationships and the priority of ecclesiastical financial practices. One of the deepest roots of anticurial and antipapal satire of the twelfth and thirteenth centuries was the traditionalist refusal to countenance the new administrative and financial practices of the Church, even when these were necessary for the Church to perform its functions. The increasing discrepancy between incomes, social ranks, and methods of acquiring and spending money became particularly acute in the twelfth century, as the circulation of money increased and became a prominent aspect of social relationships in which it had not played a major role before. There remained many traditional ideas that could not easily be accommodated with these changes, particularly the rigid scheme of labeling human action in terms of the names of the vices and the virtues, and the essentially spiritual concept of the Church organization. The idea of a spiritual Church enmeshed in the affairs of the world was, as we have seen, part of the program of criticism of many people in the twelfth century, from such respected orthodox figures as St. Bernard and Pope Paschal II to such heterodox groups as the Waldensians and the *Humiliati*. Indeed, the ideal of apostolic poverty remained through the thirteenth century one of the most effective instruments for the mission of the Church to the cities, as may be witnessed by the Franciscan success.

The traditional vocabulary for describing the vices and virtues came from monastic spirituality and scriptural interpretation, and it derived heavily from the New Testament and the writings of the early church fathers. Thus, immorality was conceived less in terms of the individual's own personality and spiritual experience and more in terms of his fitting previously defined categories. All sinners of one habit resembled one another, as did people guilty of sins from related groups.

Before the twelfth century even the individual conscience was subordinated to a series of idealized types of sin or virtue. Such vices as pride, avarice, lust, and sloth, each possessing different characteristics, were represented differently in art, but all proud people tended to resemble all other proud people, all lustful people tended to resemble all other lustful people. Such a system did not survive unchanged in the twelfth century. Elements of character analysis from other sources, including the works of Aristotle, expanded and differentiated among the vices and virtues, just as, in other areas, individual traits were handled with more confidence and perception. Thus, in the course of the twelfth century the relatively inflexible concepts of vice began to change, just as did the variety of economic and political experience. Both traditionalism and change influenced new attitudes toward economic activity and morality between the twelfth and the sixteenth centuries.

Avarice, as a number of historians have shown, became regarded by many as the greatest of sins, displacing the traditional leader, pride, during the twelfth century. Traditional Roman scorn for commerce, early ecclesiastical criticism of the accumulation of wealth, and the rigid adherence to these traditions until the twelfth century left the early twelfth-century Church ill prepared to deal in a sophisticated way with the new economic climate.

Such topics as excessive wealth or profit, the morality of certain kinds of contracts, usury and interest, prices, life styles, penance, charity, and the question of restitutions preoccupied both lawyers and theologians in the Church, and both canon law and moral theology dealt with them, although with different aspects. Thus, different sorts of churchmen commented upon economic activity from different points of view with different purposes; theologians were concerned with the interior state of the soul, canonists with the outward adherence to ecclesiastical law. The former dealt with sin, the latter with criminal offenses. The theologians had a much wider scope of theory and practice, but the lawyers were subjected to jurisprudential restraints. These complex roles and purposes influenced the ways in which theologians and canonists approached questions of an economic character. "History," Frederick William Maitland once remarked, "does not move from the simple to the complex, but from the vague to the definite." It was precisely the vagueness, the blanket condemnation of most forms of economic activity, that made traditional ecclesiastical law and theology so hostile to the varieties of economic activity that proliferated after the tenth century. And, after the mid twelfth century, it was precisely the capacity of abstraction and definition that permitted lawyers to dissociate aspects of economic activity one from another that rendered Church law more favorable to many of these. A similar process has already been observed in other contemporary changes, from the legitimation of many aspects of knighthood growing from an earlier general condemnation of warfare and killing to the recognition of the virtuous place of marriage growing from an earlier general hostility to most manifestations of sexual relationships.

In the course of the twelfth and thirteenth centuries, the different concerns of canonists and theologians, the former for law and society, the latter for morality and salvation, afforded considerably greater dignity and freedom of economic exchange. Property, profits, and price were recognized by both groups, although the theologians also introduced the idea of the merchant's moral responsibility to make restitution when required and tended to formalize mercantile charity as a moral requirement and a guard against avarice. Thus, many merchants and financiers left large sums to charity on their deathbeds, not because the law required it, but because of their concern for their personal salvation. The history of the idea of usury may illustrate this relationship between legal freedom and moral restraint. Canon lawyers, dealing with what was called the external forum, the forum of law and social relationships, condemned notorious usurers but said relatively little about other forms of usury, especially those that were an inextricable part of raising capital in an increasingly complex economy. Those who might be guilty of occult usury were liable in the internal forum, that of conscience, but not in that of law. Further, a number of exceptional circumstances when even the new distinction might be broadened were recognized by both theologians and canonists. Such elements as risk, the usufruct on land held as a security for loans, financial penalties, gifts, and other factors mitigated the moral character of usury. To be sure, many loans and interest payments in medieval commerce resorted to these exceptions in order to avoid ecclesiastical censure, and to a certain extent such practices hampered the operation of a free economy. Generally speaking, however, theology and canon law both recognized the complexity of commercial and financial life in the twelfth and thirteenth centuries, and their solicitude for both law and morality is far more characteristic of their response to changing conditions than their long-reputed crabbed hostility toward economic activities. The process of juridical and theological reasoning, which lead to sharper distinctions and definitions of legal and moral practices, both increased the complexity of legal and theological thought and recognized the complexity of twelfth- and thirteenth-century economic activity and life.

The history of early European political theory and political life is often written in the vocabulary of nineteenth-century constitutional theory. Hence, historians are often all too prone to discuss parliaments, states, constitutions, and sovereignty as if these modern institutions had existed, with only slight historical disguises, from the twelfth century (sometimes earlier) onwards. In our study of lordship, kingship, ideas of authority, and the practical exercise of power, however, we have also seen the essentially expediential, associative, and traditional character of public power. We have seen ideas closely resembling that of the modern state influence the direction of the early European church. We have seen ideas and ceremonies that in the centuries after the fifteenth have always signaled monarchical absolutism signify a much less thorough and absolutist authority. We have seen legal and practical privilege, which essentially denotes nonmembership in a political structure, exploited in such a way that it is hard to distinguish from the elements that seem to predict modern political societies. Much of the problem of the study of the early European polity lies in conceptualization and terminology. Once we discard the categories of thought invented by constitutional theorists in the eighteenth and nineteenth centuries, once we stop seeking for the "seeds," "origins," or "beginnings" of modern institutions, if only for an edifying moment, we may reach a better understanding of how political society actually *was* organized, what people thought about it, and why they accepted it. Seeking the origins of modern institutions is, of course, a major job of historians, but it is also the historians' job to identify the institutions they are seeking the origins of, not to take those institutions at their scholarly face value, label them and conduct the search with an image of the object already in mind.

There are several "political" changes that the student of thirteenth-century history may note. We have discussed several of these above. For the purposes of the topic of this chapter, however, let us concentrate upon the idea of a political public—that is, that segment of society that, either by legal privilege from below or invitation from above, participated in the affairs that, as the lawyers said, "touched all." We have already seen the cooperative character of twelfth- and thirteenth-century kingship; coronation ceremonies, *Festkronungen,* crown wearings, the holding of formal courts—all these involved not only the display of the king but also the audience of his subjects. In the thirteenth century, other elements of kingly action involved other subjects, from wider areas than simply those entitled to be present at court.

First, the thirteenth century witnessed the slow process in which common language, common wide allegiances, common sets of rights, and the idea of a common history began to link subjects to the king in ways that were new. Such notions as the community of the realm, however restrictive in fact, offered in theory a common membership to lower ranks of society. It was not the lowest ranks of society, after all, who revolted against state authority between the fourteenth and nineteenth centuries, but those above. The revolutionaries of early modern Europe were the descendants of the political public of the twelfth through the fourteenth centuries. We have already seen how demands for taxation, first from the church for the Crusades, later from the monarchy for

Crusades, "emergencies," and "necessities of state," created a common community of taxpayers. Traditional rights to assembly and counsel giving, many of which dated in different parts of Europe from the late twelfth century and included both clergy and laymen, survived into the thirteenth and fourteenth centuries. The very process of the formalization of status, whether that of noble or burgher, attached the noble or burgher to the wider community that recognized that status. Finally, the double aspect of tradition and current necessity expanded the rulers' habit of holding assemblies that constituted, including king and subjects, a kind of voice of the realm. Regardless of how the representative process developed in different regions, regardless of how "legislative," "ceremonial," or "propagandistic" the assemblies of each kingdom were, the point to be made concerning all of them is that they consisted of a wider and wider group of subjects who, through privileged status, elective representation, invitation from the monarch, or voluntary participation, discussed in common the needs of the kingdom. In England, from 1258 and 1295 on, such assemblies became not a constitutional but a convenient means of conveying the king's and kingdom's needs to wide social ranks of subjects; in France, the Estates-General first served as propaganda vehicles in Philip IV's quarrel with Boniface VIII; in Castile, the Cortes remained powerful, but ultimately participated little in the expansion of Spanish monarchy after the fourteenth century.

Representative assemblies, common taxation, common recognition of privileged or corporate status, the very processes by which the king felt it necessary or useful to deliberate with his subjects concerning matters that ultimately touched all of them—these are far more important for the political experience of thirteenth- and fourteenth-century people than whether or not they were participating in a constitutionalist parliament, a locally powerful Cortes, or an ultimately powerless Estates-General. The creation of a political public, a group of people from different social and legal ranks who participated in various ways with kings and local rulers in matters that touched both the king and his subjects, is one of the most striking phenomena of the late twelfth and thirteenth centuries. The political public, regardless of the particular functions it or its elements may have assumed, was, like the economic public, another consequence of the experience of the twelfth and thirteenth centuries. Its chief characteristic is not absolute or limited monarchy, but the new meaning of the terms *public, common,* and *kingdom*. A new sphere of activity had emerged, and like the economic sphere, it received ultimately the cooperation of the church. The French bishops between 1294 and 1303 had to make hard decisions, but their successors had to make even harder ones. The polity had created its own public by 1300.

22

TEMPORAL AUTHORITY:
From Territorial Principality to Territorial Monarchy

THE KING AND THE KINGDOM

The temporal rulers of twelfth- and thirteenth-century Europe possessed both new resources and new ideas of governance. Population growth and new patterns of land use and settlement, agricultural prosperity and increased productivity, the growth of towns and the spread of trade all constituted new material resources. The ferment in political theory that resulted both from the conflict between spiritual and temporal authority in the twelfth and thirteenth centuries and from new views of the legitimacy of temporal authority, the personnel of the new princely courts and their learning, and the use of patronage and propaganda all shaped new ideas of governance and a new political theory. The essen-

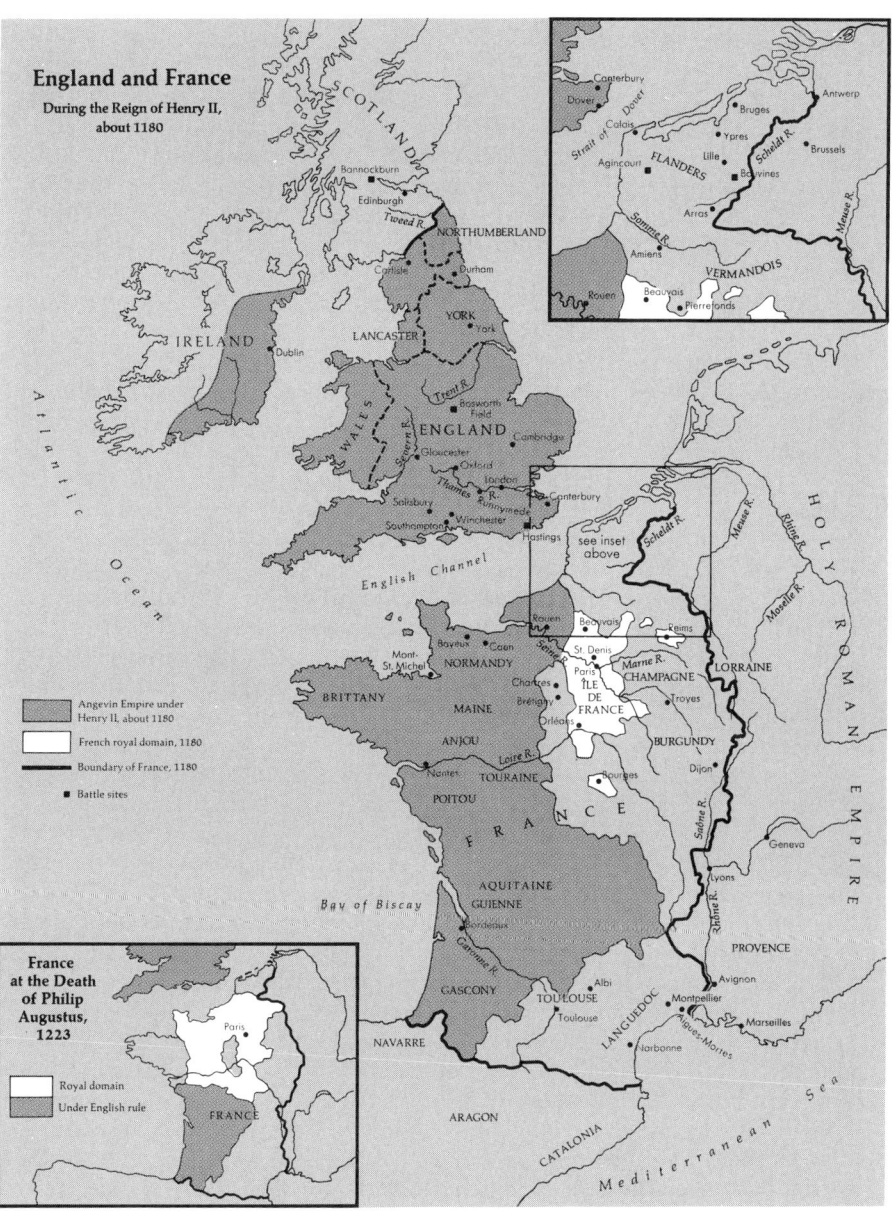

tially private person of the king slowly became a public person, and the king's rights, from being those of a somewhat exaggerated private individual, became identified with the rights and rituals of the abstract crown, throne, or kingdom. Deprived of his sacramental status in the battles of the Investiture Contest, the king in the twelfth century developed new grounds on which to base his claims to authority over the Church, to expand the area of life that his own governance touched, and to develop the idea of secular majesty. At bottom, however, princely power became transformed into monarchical power through the unremitting efforts of dynasties of rulers paying attention to the minutiae of daily business and the work of their servants. In and around these efforts emerged the theory and law that justified them and made them legitimate. In the course of these two centuries territorial monarchies began to acquire shape and depth, and they touched other ideas of community—language, xenophobia, and a common history—that they later took over and made their own. The twelfth and thirteenth centuries are the centuries of kings.

The kings of the eleventh and early twelfth centuries were kings of peoples: *Rex Anglorum* and *Rex Francorum* were the titles of the kings of *the English* and of *the French*. Not until the late twelfth and early thirteenth centuries did these titles change to *Rex Angliae* and *Rex Franciae*, "King of England," and "King of France." The process in which kingship was, in this sense, territorialized, is part of the process in which royal lordship and public law became imposed, with more and more acceptance, throughout individual kingdoms. The proper means of studying such "constitutional" changes is comparative. Kingship and the idea of public monarchy did not develop in all areas in quite the same direction or at the same pace. The histories of England, France, and Castile *as kingdoms* offers several diverse examples of the formation of early European states. We have already considered Germany and Sicily and Jerusalem in this light.

The "history" of modern states is often extended backwards in time and based upon an idea of the state that was developed only in the nineteenth and twentieth centuries. The ingredients of the modern state —continuity of a society in space and time, community of language, the appearance of impersonal institutions of governance and the impersonal loyalty of subjects and citizens, the idea of sovereignty, and the various aspects of a "national" consciousness—did not all coalesce in the twelfth- and thirteenth-century kingdoms of western and central Europe. "Nationalism" in its broad variety of forms, from the awareness of a common history and language to uncritical loyalty to the person or institution that temporarily embodies general values, became attached only slowly to the person of the ruler and, much later, to the idea of a state conceived apart from the ruler. The mobilization of state resources, a general test of modern states, occurred on a far smaller scale and for far shorter periods of time in thirteenth-century kingdoms. The concept of patriotism, or, conversely, that of a state with resources so great that universal coercion is possible, became attached only slowly to the idea of the kingdom. The words "politics," "polity," and "policy" appeared in most western languages only after the thirteenth century, and appeared in general use only after the seventeenth. When Henry VIII set in motion the proceedings that resulted in the divorce of Anne Boleyn in the early sixteenth century, jurists habitually referred to this constitutional question as "the *king's* great matter." For four centuries, king and kingdom were inseparable and interchangeable terms. It is in this light that we may consider early comparative "constitutional" histories of England, France, and Castile in the twelfth and thirteenth centuries.

One way in which kings transformed their roles was by taking on more business. Kings and sometimes emperors of the ninth and tenth centuries swore only to maintain the peace and to protect the church by doing justice, as their centuries recognized justice. Increasingly during the twelfth and thirteenth centuries, royal coronation oaths became longer, and the business that the kings swore to protect grew larger and larger. The ceremonies of kingship, from coronation to royal funeral, came to suggest transcendent ultra-personal obligations on the part of the kings. And in the twelfth and thirteenth centuries, taking upon oneself more obligations brought with it more privileges, more legitimacy, and more power.

At the death of Henry I of England in 1135, the barons became divided in their allegiance between Henry's daughter Matilda, the widow of Emperor Henry V and currently wife of Geoffrey Plantagenet, count of Anjou, and Stephen, Henry's nephew, son of William the Conqueror's daughter Adele and Count Stephen of Blois. The struggle between Matilda and Stephen gave opportunism and overreaching lordship their greatest opportunities since the Conquest. The Church, eager for widespread reform, sided with first one, then another, of the contestants. The nobles, eager to increase their own fortunes, also changed sides. The solution to the question of legitimate lordship, the designation by Stephen of Matilda's son Henry as his successor, brought Henry II (1154–1188) to the throne of England. Henry II's precipitate steps to strengthen the diminished crown of England included claims for alienated royal lands and rights, the extension of royal courts' jurisdiction into lesser courts, banishment of turbulent nobles, widespread investigations of royal officials, and a revival of Henry I's legal system. Yet Henry II was not primarily concerned with England, except as a base for his operations on the Continent. For Henry II of England was also duke of Normandy, count of Anjou, Maine, and Touraine, and duke of Aquitaine, through his marriage with the divorced wife of Louis VII of France, the remarkable Eleanor of Aquitaine. Indeed, the extent of Henry II's holdings on the Continent was as great as the whole of England, and Henry, a Continental by birth and speech, spent far more time in his Continental possessions than in England. England gave Henry a royal title to match that of his Continental overlord, Philip Augustus of France, and it gave him, when his servants managed it properly, sufficient income to pursue his Continental adventures. But for Henry II and his son and successor Richard I Lionheart (1188–1198), England was one of several territories

Plate 17 courtesy Bildarchiv Foto-Marburg.

POWER AND STATUS. The aristocracy, as it took shape in European society between the seventh and the thirteenth centuries, based its claims to status on its wealth, birth, the divine purpose of its role in society, and its place as patrons and protectors of the Church and the weak. Such figures as that of Eckhardt and his wife Uta, from Naumburg Cathedral in Germany (Plate 17) suggest both status and role, in the woman's crown and the man's sword and shield, as well as the remarkable sense of self that made the aristocracy a powerful force in European society down to the nineteenth century. Even in the memory of the past, contemporary ideas colored the depiction of past events. In this fourteenth-century manuscript (Plate 18) depicting the coronation of Charlemagne in the year 800, the costume and regalia of both the ruler and the ecclesiastics surrounding him are fourteenth-century in character. This capacity to translate even the remote past into contemporary images was both a strength and a weakness of the European royalty and aristocracy.

filz, le roi d'aquitaine & oment il donna
a bernart son neueu le roiaume de lombar
die. Et puis oment il fist assembler .v.
concilles el roiaume de france en diuers li
eus. pour amend lestat de sainte eglise.
Et de la desconfiture muchiel temp de grice
Et puis oment trumas le roi de bulgrie
fu desfis deuant costentinoble.
Ci comence li secons liures de lestoire le grant
Roy chailemaine.

Plate 18 courtesy Musée Goya/CASTRES, Photographie Giraudon.

—and the others were much more fashionable and interesting—that he ruled. Of Richard's ten-year reign, only brief periods in 1189 and 1194 saw the king in England. Neither Henry II nor Richard the Lionheart spoke English, nor did they wish to learn. They were lords first, then kings, and the resources of their kingship seemed less important than the exercise of their lordship on the Continent.

Henry II and Richard I were succeeded by Henry's son, Richard's brother John (1198–1216), the first king of England since the Conquest who spoke English and spent most of his adult life traveling up and down the roads of his kingdom. Under Richard and John, most of the overseas Continental empire of Henry II was temporarily lost, Normandy reverting to Philip Augustus in 1204. John was not an English king of England because he wanted to be one, but because he had no other place in which to be a lord.

The reigns of Henry II, Richard I, and John witnessed the laying of the foundations of the English monarchy, in spite of the focus of the kings' interests elsewhere. Under Henry II, the lordship of the king became a weighty and carefully supervised force. Henry extended the rights of lordship pertaining to the king far beyond those pertaining to other lords. He controlled the descent of fiefs held of the king and claimed the right to approve the heirs; he increased the king's share of income from fiefs that had been subenfoeffed to others; he expanded the role of the king's justices so that men in a given district were compelled to testify as a sort of grand jury as to crimes committed in that district; and he collected the fines, properties, and other wealth of convicted or escaped felons. Henry II also devised a number of efficient ways in which cases hitherto adjudicated on a local level might be brought to the king's court. In this process, Henry II and his justices developed a series of *writs,* simplified claims to royal court action that could be acquired, usually by purchase, by individuals whose possessions had been abruptly seized by others. The operation of a writ brought the king's justices into an affair, and the decisions of the king's justices became more and more generally recognized as the law of the land. Henry II's courts served two functions: they brought before judicial authorities cases that earlier might have escaped adjudication, and they increased the area of social life into which the authority of the king's courts might intrude. They brought the king home to many of his subjects who had never felt the presence of his hand. And they brought both authority and increased revenue to the king.

In his itinerant life, from Normandy to England, back to Normandy, and then to Anjou, Poitou, or the frontiers of Gascony, Henry II was far more interested in making himself a powerful count, duke, or king in those dominions in which he was count, duke, or king, than in creating a modern style of monarchy for England. Yet his vigorous pursuit of lost royal lands and powers, his clever and well-enforced intrusion of his own legal interests into fields that had hitherto belonged to others, and his insatiable thirst for regular revenue led to the foundation of a regular system of royal governance in England that survived long after the Angevin novelties in Normandy, Anjou, and Aquitaine had been forgotten. In one of his characteristic outbursts of legislation, the Constitutions of Clarendon of 1164, Henry II attempted, with great sense, to regulate the practical effects of some of the consequences of the Investiture Contest in England. In defining the king's rights in the area of church property and criminal acts by clergy, Henry stated the royal side strongly. But Henry II was not working in a sociological vacuum. He needed servants to enforce his decisions, and in one case his selection of a servant backfired. Thomas Becket was the son of a Norman merchant of London, attended the schools of Paris, and undoubtedly, like many others, came home to England full of the sense of intellectual accomplishment and style that he had admired in France. Catching the king's eye, Becket was made chancellor of England, and, successful at this, he was made archbishop of Canterbury by a grateful and hopeful lord. But there had become by the end of the twelfth century a great difference between the royal servants who had held great ecclesiastical titles in Henry II's time and those who, like Roger of Salisbury, had held them in Henry I's time. The difference was in large part the new devotional aspect of high ecclesiastical office. Becket proved as intransigent an archbishop as he had been a pliable lord chancellor. He bitterly opposed Henry's Constitutions of Clarendon, denouncing them in the new language of ecclesiastical liberties and churchly immunities that had recently acquired a sharper juridical sense among the lawyers of Bologna and Rome. Thomas fled England before the king's wrath, and his exile created embarrassments for the king and Pope Alexander III alike. Upon his return to England under a shakily concocted agreement, Becket again criticized the king, and several royal knights, taking a momentary outburst of Henry II at face value, traveled to Canterbury and slaughtered Becket as he conducted services in Canterbury Cathedral. Henry punished the murderers and underwent a severe personal penance for the crime, but his Constitutions of Clarendon survived, for the most part, and in this ecclesiastical matter, as in the case of his legal reforms, Henry II marked one major stage in the development of the monarchy of England.

His sons and successors nearly ruined most of Henry's work. Richard, far more than his father, devoted himself to the Continental possessions, to the Crusade, and to his rivalry with King Philip Augustus of France. Richard's virtue was in one sense to appoint useful, productive, loyal agents to administer England in his customary absence, and under these men the institutions first developed by the Conqueror and Henry I and brought to efficiency under Henry II continued to operate successfully. Upon Richard's death, however, the accession of John changed affairs considerably.

John was an energetic and intelligent king. But he lacked the command that his brother Richard had possessed, he was a bad general, and he lacked the ability to foresee the consequences of some of his acts. Some of these consequences had great impact upon the nature of the kingdom of England. In his quarrel with Pope Innocent III over

Innocent's appointment of Stephen Langton to the see of Canterbury without John's approval, John first withstood a five-year interdict between 1208 and 1213 and a personal excommunication. He then capitulated to Innocent, even recognizing him as the legal overlord of England. Such a title, consistent with the actions of several other kingdoms seeking papal protection, made John an ally of Innocent, and when the barons of England revolted against John's exactions, Innocent intervened with considerable success.

John exploited the devices used by his father and brother and their agents, but he exploited them without sharing other characteristics of his two predecessors: the fear inspired by Henry II and the respect and affection generated by Richard I. John's hand was heavy without being feared or respected, and his loss of Normandy to Philip Augustus in 1204, the consequent focusing of the barons' interests on their English affairs, his capitulation to Innocent III, and his share in the defeat of Otto IV by Philip Augustus at Bouvines in 1214 all contributed to the barons' resentment. In 1215, a coalition of nobles forced John to issue a charter (later nicknamed Magna Carta, Latin for Great Charter) specifically defining the limits of royal authority in areas that touched the barons' interests. Magna Carta, far from being a "democratic" or "constitutional limitation" on the king, was the extortion of privileges by an injured and outraged aristocracy. Innocent III, appealed to by John, promptly denounced the document as injurious to the dignity of the king. Magna Carta did, however, extract from the king the admission that the king ruled under law, and the later history of the Great Charter and the role of royal governance in England was influenced by this admission and the principles of governance it laid down.

John was succeeded by his infant son Henry III, whose extraordinarily long reign (1216–1272) consisted of a minority in which control of the government was in the hands of regents and papal legates, and a majority in which the king and the barons did battle once again. The thirteenth century in England thus witnessed a baronial attempt to weaken the position attained by the late twelfth-century monarchy in England by securing control of the king and his administrators. Although these efforts produced a much more serious baronial revolt in 1258–1265, they were not ultimately the guiding events in thirteenth-century England. The reign of Henry III also witnessed increased efficiency among the public servants of the crown; indeed, men began to speak more and more of the crown, and the concept of the crown as the abstract repository of public authority took shape and flourished during this period, and in spite of attempts to invoke the crown's authority against the king, the king and the crown were identified too closely to make such a separation possible. Moreover, the king had begun to attract lower-ranking nobles into his service and to extend the reach of his courts deep into the countryside. The ecclesiastical rulers of thirteenth-century England were on the whole loyal to the king and contributed what they could, personally and officially, to royal governance. The models of ecclesiastical administration and the penetration of royal service into further reaches of the countryside constituted two of the firmest achievements of royal governance during this otherwise troubled period. In the course of the thirteenth century the phrase "community of the realm" appeared, and in its many and diverse implications we may see the consequences of the work of Henry II, Richard I, John, and their agents, as well as the great lay and ecclesiastical protectors of Henry III's minority and the servants of his manhood. The cumulative effects of royal governance after 1154 took deep root, deeper than many of the barons realized. The tradition of royal law courts, with their reasonings and records, the royal exploitation of the unity of local communities outside of the traditional powers of great nobles, the royal use of local residents in royal juridical inquests, and the royal identification with "English" language, history, and society all contributed to the strength of the king. The reign of Henry III's son and successor Edward I (1272–1307) witnessed the bringing to a head of the baronial and communal conflict and the triumph of the king.

The idea of the "community of the realm" covers a wide area, some aspects of which are susceptible of constitutional historians' investigation and some of which remain elusive and undefinable. There is always more to a state, when it is a state, than a simple and articulated "constitutional" structure. In the reigns of Henry III and Edward I, England became more than the king's field of research in ways of extracting more and more resources, more than the personal royal lordship that John tried to make it. The identification of the king with the very institutions that gave security, order, and regularity to more and more people on diverse social levels, the respect and deference of the able thirteenth-century English higher clergy, the support of the papacy and, briefly, the king of France, and the character of Henry III and Edward I marked the success of a certain kind, a style, of monarchy in England that survived until the seventeenth century and, it can be argued, even later.

The kings of France faced a very different kind of kingdom from that of post-Conquest England. Until the early years of the twelfth century, the kings of "France" ruled, as we have seen, a small kingdom that extended from Paris to Orleans, a kingdom peppered with independent lords and castles that prevented the thorough subjugation of even the royal domain until the twelfth century. Far less powerful than the dukes of Normandy or the counts of Anjou or Champagne, the Capetian kings barely retained their royal holdings against the interests and indifference of the great lords whose territories surrounded and often seemed to threaten to engulf their own. The reign of Louis VI the Fat (1108–1137) commenced much of the development of the French royal house. Louis vigorously pursued the establishment of royal power in the royal domain, and in doing so he sided with the communal movements in the towns and the movements of new settlements in the wastelands on the royal domain. He patronized the church, particularly the abbey of St. Denis, and under his friend and biographer, Abbot Suger, St. Denis replied in kind by becoming the proclaimer of Capetian legitimacy and authority, in chronicles, biographies, and liturgies. At his death in 1137 Louis had begun to acquire for his dynasty the initially grudging respect that was the first requisite for great lordship.

The emergence of the king of France as a successful lord in his own domain of Île de France was the first condition necessary to establish his kingship in other areas, and in this work the reign of Louis VII (1137–1180) made permanent the achievements of Louis VI. It was Louis VII whom Frederick Barbarossa thought he could overawe into supporting the antipope Victor IV against Alexander III, Louis VII who offered shelter and support to Alexander, Louis VII who benefited in return from the increased respect of the papacy. Of all the participants in the ill-fated Second Crusade of 1147–1149, only Louis VII had his adventures recounted in an admiring light, in Odo of Deuil's *Journey of Louis VII to the Orient*, and throughout his reign Louis enjoyed a general respect for his piety, which is reflected in the memorials of St. Denis, Suger, and Odo. The Capetians were sufficiently highly considered outside the royal domain that William X of Aquitaine promised his daughter Eleanor to Louis VII. They were married in 1137, and the marriage, with numerous ruptures, lasted until 1152, when it was annulled and Eleanor received Aquitaine back. In 1153 Eleanor married Henry Plantagenet, duke of Normandy and count of Anjou, who became Henry II of England in 1154. She brought to Henry the great Aquitanian lands whose rule so consumed the rest of Henry's life and nearly all the interests of his son and successor, Richard I. The gain and loss of Aquitaine did not significantly diminish the prestige of Louis VII, however, and in other respects his reign continued the work of his father and began several new directions.

The reign of Philip Augustus (1180–1223) bracketed those of Henry II, Richard I, and John of England. Louis VII had watched Henry II attempt to exert his lordship over his diverse Continental possessions, the Angevin Empire, as historians have called it, without being able to do much about it. It fell to Philip Augustus to perform a double function. On the one hand, he had to attempt to expand the lordship of the king of France beyond the borders of Île de France, and on the other, he had to control the great lordship of Henry II and his sons on the Continent. Philip II Augustus's achievements have commonly cast those of his father and grandfather into the shade. Yet the lordship of Île de France, as opposed to the kingship of France, was an essential first step in establishing the Capetians as lords. The finances of Louis VII were raised to a respectable level, certainly equivalent to or greater than the income of the great princes whose territories surrounded his, with the exception of the whole domain of Henry II, in England and on the Continent. Philip Augustus was lord and exploiter both, for at the end of his reign he had vastly increased the territory in which the king of France was the direct lord, and he had vastly increased the size and royal control over income of the French crown. Philip Augustus came to the throne after the great lords, whose territories surrounded Ile de France, had turned these lands into territorial principalities.

As Philip acquired by inheritance new claims of lordship, voluntary homage, and various small and large territories around Île de France, he sent his own agents to his new lands, although he ordered that local customs and laws be observed. This combination of central supervision and local tradition characterized French law until the nineteenth century, and French political administration until the seventeenth. As Philip acquired new territories, he sent in his agents, *castellans* and *baillis*, much as Emperor Henry IV had done in Saxony in 1071–1075. In the process of expanding the royal domain, Philip sometimes found himself in the position of being technically a vassal of another lord. His solution, and one of the foundations of the French monarchy afterward, was that he could be a normal holder of the territory except that he could do no homage, because the king of France, as his chroniclers and advisers said, "is no man's vassal." Again, the special kind of lordship that the king claimed to possess represents an exaggeration of parts of the idea of lordship and an exemption of the king from other parts that normal lords might be subject to.

Philip's greatest achievement, however, was the beginning of the breaking up of the vast empire held on the Continent by the kings of England. The Angevin Empire consisted of England, the lordship of Ireland, the duchies of Normandy and Aquitaine, and the counties of Anjou, Touraine, and Maine. The king of England ruled more land in France than the king of France, and the rivalry between the Angevin kings of England and Philip Augustus was, as we have seen, sharp and unremitting. Philip Augustus and Richard hated each other without either being able to break the bonds of lordship that linked Richard, as vassal, to Philip, as overlord of Normandy and the other Continental territories. During the reign of John, however, Philip found his opportunities. John's violation of the marriage agreement between Hugh of Lusignan and Isabel of Angoulême brought Hugh's complaint to the court of Philip, who was overlord of both men, and Philip's insistence that John appear in court as a good vassal should was met by John's refusal. In consequence, Philip announced the confiscation of Normandy in 1204, and for the first time since the Conquest of England, the lordship of a king of France over his powerful English vassal was enforced successfully. The loss of Normandy precipitated the loss of other English possessions, and the acquisition of the wealthy duchy of Normandy and other lands vastly strengthened the financial resources and the lordship of the French king.

The chief tasks of Philip Augustus's successor, Louis VIII (1223–1226), consisted of extending royal lordship into the newly acquired lands of Poitou and Languedoc, the latter acquisition resulting from Louis VIII's invasion of Languedoc at papal request in 1226. Between 1226 and 1229, the forces of the king of France finally defeated the forces of the count of Toulouse and the resistance to the Albigensian Crusade, and the vast, rich, culturally diverse lands of the south came under the rule of the Capetian family for the first time. The consolidation of such territories took several generations, but the expansion of the realm and the direct rule of the king progressed throughout the thirteenth century. During the minority of Louis IX (1226–1270), which lasted until 1234, the regent of the kingdom was Louis VIII's widow, Blanche of Castile. In 1226, during Blanche's regency, a coalition of opposition to the recently acquired powers of the Capetians arose, led by the recently defeated enemies, the king of England and the counts of Brittany and Toulouse. Blanche overcame this revolt, firmly consolidated the power of the crown, and handed over to her son the full achievement of the Capetian monarchs of the preceding four generations. The reign of Louis IX was reckoned for centuries as the golden age of France. The king, personally devout, influenced by most of the devotional movements of his age, imbued with an active sense of justice, was the perfect type of the ideal thirteenth-century king—full administrative ruler and saint. The enormous personal prestige of St. Louis added another dimension to the status of the king of France, one that his descendants invoked, even in their most unsaintly moments. Upon his departure for the crusade of 1248–1252, St. Louis again made his mother regent, and under her rule and the firm establishment of royal agents throughout the realm, the governance of France, complex and many-layered as it was, survived and continued to operate. At Louis's death in Tunis in 1270, the domain of the king of France far surpassed that of the king of England, and the king of France could tap the wealth of far more people than could any other monarch in Europe. For with the expansion of royal lordship went the ability to mobilize the resources of far greater numbers of people, and the kings of France in the late thirteenth century were not only far wealthier, in subjects and money, than their rivals, but their administration, making centralization out of regional diversity, was more highly trained and closely supervised. Moreover, the power of the king had begun to attract to itself, through the legends of Louis VI, Louis VII, and St. Louis, the spread of the French language and the spreading French reputation for sense, scholarship, and holiness—the growing "cult" of France itself.

In 1270 and 1272, England and France saw new kings succeeding rulers whose long reigns, personal reputations for holiness, and success had contributed considerably to establishing their respective monarchies securely in each kingdom. By the third quarter of the thirteenth century, the monarchy in each kingdom had acquired a new prestige of its own and begun to link itself to the idea of a common history, a common language, and a common culture. These secondary traits that help constitute that vague aspect of statehood known as nationalism aided the monarchies, but they did not create them, nor could their importance be measured continuously. In many respects, England and France evolved quite different monarchial governments. The territorial compactness of England, the absence of strong local resistance to monarchical authority, the use of local aristocracies in royal service, and the precocious systems of financial accounting, taxation, and the administration of justice all characterize the development of the territorial monarchy of England between 1100 and 1270. France, on the other hand, faced a highly developed system of local powers, the necessity of a large and complex royal bureaucracy, and the development of a bureaucratic class loyal to the king rather than to a locality, and it took much longer to develop accounting and justice systems. By the end of the thirteenth century, however, the king of France held the edge in population, income, and extent of territory. During the long conflict between England and France that grew out of the rivalry between Philip Augustus and the Angevin kings and came to a head in the long war between England and France known as the Hundred Years War in the fourteenth and fifteenth centuries, these resources and the character of monarchical authority were tested in both kingdoms.

The expansion of royal power and authority in England and France took place in an atmosphere not free of lordly hostility and the use of force, but generally free of major invasions. The societies in the Iberian peninsula, on the contrary, shaped kingdoms during the very process of the *reconquista,* the expanding of Christian territory at the expense of the Moslem rulers of *Al-Andalus.* Thus, the "constitutional" structure of the kingdoms of Aragon, Castile, and Portugal, although it had several aspects in common with those of England and France, stands in sharp contrast to the expansion of royal lordship in the north. The history of the kingdoms of the Iberian Peninsula during the period between the eleventh and the fifteenth centuries is inextricably part of the history of the *reconquista.* The *reconquista* itself, of course, is a long and complex history, one in which the rough primitive culture of northern Christian Spain slowly and terribly came to terms with the rich, complex Arab and Jewish culture of *Al-Andalus.*

At the outset of the eleventh century, the Christian kingdoms in northern Spain, Leon and Navarre, were extended on the east by the small counties of Aragon, Sobrarbe, Ribagorza, Pallars, and Urgel, and the old Carolingian Spanish March in the northeast was broken up into the counties of Roussilon, Asturias, and Barcelona. The main thrust of the offensive lay with the kingdom of Navarre, whose ruler Sancho III the Great (1000–1035), drew the county of Castile from the old kingdom of Leon in the west and established his own prestige as far east as Catalonia and beyond the Pyrenees into southwestern France. At his death in 1035, Sancho divided his kingdom among three sons, leaving Navarre to Garcia IV (1035–1054) and creating kingdoms out of Castile for his son Ferdinand I (1035–1065) and out of Aragon for his son Ramiro (1035–1063). During the reign of Sancho III and Ferdinand I, Navarre became the channel through which aid in men, money, and monks came over the Pyrenees into the peninsula, links were forged with the reform movement in Rome under Gregory VII, and the loose warrior society of Castile began to bear the brunt of the offensive into the central plateau of the peninsula. Under Ferdinand's son and successor, Alfonso VI (1035–1109), the patron of Cluny, Toledo was taken in 1085, a large-scale program of repopulation was undertaken in the conquered territories, and the unique form of Castilian society emerged, led by a powerful and warlike warrior nobility and the councils of the privileged towns.

The initial successes of Castile, however, encountered a temporary setback when a Moslem puritan sect, the Almoravids, who had built up a large empire in western North Africa (1055–1080), came to the aid of the weak Moslem kings of Islamic Spain and constituted a severe threat to the kings of Christian Spain until the early twelfth century. They were followed by an even more fierce sect, the Almohads, who had destroyed their holdings in Africa and conquered their Spanish possessions by the middle of the twelfth century. Almohad domination of Moslem Spain lasted until the Christian victory at Las Navas de Tolosa in 1214.

During the twelfth century, the settlements in central Spain had taken the shape of the interests of the warrior aristocracy and the privileged towns. Herding, light agriculture, and war parties occupied the knights and townspeople, and the growth of the military orders after 1150 continued the military cast of the frontier. Dynastic disputes during the century led to the founding of a separate Portuguese monarchy under Afonso Henriques (1139–1185), to revolts on behalf of claimants to the throne that resulted in making the grip of the knights and herdsmen stronger, in opposition to the agricultural and commercial interests of a small part of the population, and to the separation of Leon and Castile once again between 1157 and 1230. The extensive commitment of newly conquered lands exclusively to herding had severe consequences in the later Castilian economy, when large-scale agriculture and trade, two of the most important institutions to shape England and France, were dramatically reduced in favor of the herdsmen. Shipping, agriculture, trade, and finance thus played a very minor role from the outset of the kingdom of Castile, and these functions were generally carried on by outsiders, often Moslems, Jews, and Italians. This economic "incompleteness" of Castile lasted through the last stages of the *reconquista* in 1492 and shaped the attitudes of Castile during the period of Spanish power throughout Europe in the sixteenth and seventeenth centuries.

The destruction of the Almohad forces at Las Navas de Tolosa in 1212 opened the way for a massive Christian assault toward the south, and under Ferdinand III of Castile (1217–1252) and James I of Aragon (1213–1276), the center and eastern parts of the peninsula were penetrated and resettled by Christian forces. In the process, the wealthy, varied, and prosperous economy of Islamic Spain was virtually destroyed, and the patterns of sheep and cattle raising at the expense of agriculture and trade were repeated in the south. In the kingdom of Castile itself, the authority of the clergy and the independence of the greater and lesser nobles checked the power of the king, and the traditional independence and privileges of the towns led to a kind of precocious parliamentary institution, the Cortes, in which representatives of the nobility, the clergy, and the towns defended their rights and voted taxes for the king. The first Cortes dates from 1188, but throughout the thirteenth century they became more numerous and vociferous.

Beginning in the mid twelfth century, the diplomatic problems between Castile and the emerging kingdom of Portugal, the royal defeats of the king of Castile by the Almohades, the growing pressures of Crusade psychology in Castile, underpopulation, and the granting of privileges to the nobility and the military orders all contributed to the instability of the Castilian monarchy. Perennial political troubles, such as dynastic conflicts, disagreements between spiritual and temporal authority, the lack of a continuous administrative class loyal to the crown, and the problem of finances troubled the kingdom of Castile as they did other kingdoms, but the Castilian monarchs had fewer resources with which to balance their own power against these problems. The king of Castile claimed the same royal status as his peers in England and France, but the unstable military and political conditions of Castile prevented him from becoming as practically effective as other rulers. The Crusade mentality of the Church and the military orders and the privileges of the nobility continually threatened the stability of the crown, particularly during crises of succession and crises following royal defeats. On several isolated occasions, however, a considerable courtly brilliance played over the crown of Castile. During the reign of Alfonso X *El Sabio* (1252–1284), royal patronage of Christian, Moslem, and Jewish writers and artists produced a remarkable flowering of culture, and Alfonso and his publicists even raised his name as a candidate for the throne of the Holy Roman Empire. But the last years of Alfonso's reign were darkened by political quarrels over succession, and Alfonso's overtures on the Continent were rebuffed. Not even the occasional brilliance of a single reign could establish the crown of Castile solidly over the heterogeneous, extraordinarily privileged, and economically incomplete society that its holder had to rule. The examples of the English, French, and Castilian monarchies thus offer highly distinctive examples of the varieties of royal governance in the twelfth and thirteenth centuries and of the different ways in which royal lordship grew into territorial monarchies.

TRADITIONAL STATUS IN A CHANGING POLITICAL WORLD

In the tenth and eleventh centuries, clergy and laymen alike agreed that Christian society consisted of three parts: those who fight, those who pray, and those who work: *bellatores, oratores,* and *laboratores.* "These three orders," wrote an eleventh-century bishop, "co-exist and may not suffer themselves to be separated. The services rendered by each one of them permits the work of the other two. Each in its turn is responsible for assisting the others." Society was divided into orders, a term at first exclusively secular but by the twelfth century already acquiring a sacral context. Knighthood was considered an *ordo,* and the knightly investiture was considered an ordination. Marriage constituted an *ordo,* as did, of course, the clergy. These orders entailed particular liberties appropriate to each. Out of the fighters there emerged by the twelfth century both the high and the low nobility, as well as the mercenary fighting man.

Out of those who pray there emerged during the twelfth century a reorganization of the clergy and the attendant problems of clerical status in a world of competing spiritual and temporal authorities. Out of those who work there emerged the serfs, free peasants, merchants, financiers, and artisans. By the twelfth century, in fact, the threefold division of early medieval society could be applied only in idealistic circumstances. It no longer accurately described the variety of status, power, wealth, freedom, and servitude that the twelfth-century world knew. By the thirteenth century, it was wholly inapplicable except in underdeveloped societies. No universally accepted substitute emerged in place of this threefold division. Slowly, the divisions between freedom and servitude, noble and nonnoble, clerical and lay, displaced the older simplistic model of society, and although some of the aspects of the older model survived as signs of class distinction, the world of the thirteenth and fourteenth centuries was more varied than that of the tenth and eleventh.

We have already seen the working of some of the forces that rendered the earlier model of social orders obsolete: the de-sacralization of rulership and the consequent search on the part of temporal rulers for a substitute "political theology"; the ability of serfs to purchase their freedom and the transformation into money payments of the obligations of those who did not; the separation of the clergy from the laity as a consequence of the Investiture Conflict; the impact of such diverse problems as family longevity, the new money economy, and the growth of royal power upon the early nobility. In the Church, the growth of explicit, institutionally articulated papal authority intruded on the earlier independence of the bishops, as did the spread of privileged monastic institutions such as Cluny and Citeaux. With the rise of the universities, the twelfth-century lay devotional revolution, and the growth of the pastoral consciousness, ranks of lower clergy became more numerous, and preaching, a traditionally episcopal prerogative, was opened to the lower clergy. The rise of a class of merchants, financiers, and entrepreneurs and the growth of independent or privileged urban structures introduced even greater dissonance between the possession of political power and the possession of wealth. In the course of the twelfth and thirteenth centuries, in one sense, each of the three older divisions of society became more varied. The "fighters" became graduated into a high nobility that defended and defined its privileged status as it hoarded its wealth and sought a function appropriate to its status, a middle and lower nobility increasingly dependent upon great lords and kings, and a large and motley collection of poorer fighting men, youths, and other kinds of retainers. Although the high nobility prided itself upon its prowess in arms and developed the idea of chivalry to glorify its status, the lower ranks as well claimed certain privileges of knighthood, thus constructing a kind of ceremonial unity among a group already breaking up into ranks of different wealth and power. The clergy also drew sharp distinctions among major and minor orders, prelacy, and the papacy. Yet the swarms of students, administrators, and wandering holy men of dubious clerical status, and the growing population of private chaplains, mendicants, lay people living under orders, and service clergy kept the border between clerical and lay status fluid and helped bring part of the clergy, at least, under temporal authority.

In peasant society, as well, the changing economic and political conditions of the twelfth and thirteenth centuries created a broad spectrum of people with different status, from the domestic slave and the serf, who were bound to the soil and forced to provide compulsory services to a lord, to the landless free laborer, the established peasant family, and the wealthy capitalist peasant farmers. "Family labor on family land" characterizes a peasant economy, and within the broad group designated as peasants, the experience of the growth of a money economy, the increased privileges offered to migrants and settlers, the changing system of courts and incomes from courts, and the sense of community in peasant villages all contributed to increased prosperity and freedom and at the same time broadened the economic spectrum of peasant life. In western Europe, at least, peasants generally became freer during the twelfth and thirteenth centuries, as the society in which they lived was in a slow process of reorganization.

By the end of the thirteenth century, in the west particularly, the growth of royal power touched the lives of more and more people on all social levels, became institutionally articulated through divisions of function within the royal courts, and exerted considerable control over the nobility by its dispensation of patronage and privilege. Status, determined by income, degree of freedom, legal privilege, and importance to the crown, began to displace the idea of *ordo*. Status remained a secular term, meaning condition, standing, or estate in life, and the circulation of such a term indicates the shift from the concept of a divinely ordained threefold society to a society of estates, reflecting both the recognition of the changing circumstances of human fortunes and the power of human agency to alter one's circumstances in life. As noble status became defined more self-consciously, other forces besides heredity were at work to allow acquisition of noble status. As peasants moved to towns, prospered in two or three generations, and moved back to the countryside richer than they had been when they left, or stayed, bought up more land, and hired more laborers, even the token ceremonies and payments indicating servitude became more and more onerous. The emergence of a free peasantry, a privileged nobility, both high and low, and a clerical status whose loyalties were increasingly divided between the hierarchy of ecclesiastical authority and the growing appeal of temporal powers all suggest the slow transformation of an early society of orders into a later society of estates.

In this changing social world, traditional claims were modified, confirmed in privileged status, or abolished. Sometimes they were sublimated, as in the romances of the twelfth- and thirteenth-century vernacular literatures. Sometimes they were savagely parodied, as in the fourteenth-century German poem *Meyer Helmbrecht,* in which the excessively ambitious son of prosperous peasants undertakes to dress as a lord and acquire a new identity. Sometimes they imposed a heavy burden on the falling and rising members of the aristocracy, bourgeoisie, and peasantry, as declining fortunes made some people cling desperately to former privileges and roles and rising fortunes made others divest themselves of their previous life styles and imitate those of superior ranks. Society did not fail to make savage fun of both, but even satire, especially social satire, is often liveliest when society itself is in a process of transformation. Drawing upon traditional values as well as new circumstances, satire reveals some aspects of a society in transition. In the courts and towns of the thirteenth century, the search for the clarification of status occupied all levels of society.

THE CONFLICT BETWEEN SPIRITUAL AND TEMPORAL AUTHORITY

The initial success of the Investiture Conflict, the growth of papal authority and a defined ecclesiastical hierarchy, the de-sacralization of temporal rulers, and the successful papal struggle with the last Hohenstaufen emperors all contributed to the political experience of the papacy and the assertion of the superiority of spiritual to temporal authority. Such superiority was spelled out in the writings and teachings of canon lawyers, popes, and the papal chancery, in the careers and ideas of individual holy men from St. Bernard to St. Francis of Assisi, and in the philosophical treatises of the thirteenth century. Debates upon papal power occupied the universities, and in the fourteenth century even longer tracts bearing such titles as *Concerning the Power of the Pope* appeared in appreciable numbers. Yet at the height of the theory of papal supremacy, there were other ideas that challenged its universal applicability. These ideas came from the stabilization not only of temporal political institutions, but of a temporal political theory that had grown up in the course of the thirteenth century. The famous conflict between King Philip IV of France and Pope Boniface VIII during the last years of the thirteenth and the first years of the fourteenth century is commonly regarded as the turning point in favor of temporal powers. But several characteristics of papal government, even at its height, contributed to this weakness in the papal position.

First, as we have seen, the material powers of the papacy were extraordinarily limited. More than any other force, the papacy depended upon loyal cooperation from other powers for the execution of its decisions. Second, the information received by the papacy, upon which many papal decisions were based, was often erroneous, and papal letters are sprinkled with such phrases as "if things are as stated" and "if this is really so." Third, the papacy's administrative weakness—a weakness that, in terms of personnel, was shared by all ambitious political structures before the eighteenth century—created delays in responding, confusion in the minds of litigants and jurists, and a constant state of disorganization in the papal curia. R. W. Southern's designation of "the ramshackle machinery of government of which Innocent [III] was both the slave and the master" is largely accurate. Fourth, the pope was both a local and a universal ruler. Locally, the affairs of the city of Rome and the wider circle of the Papal States occupied far more of the popes' attention than the grander questions of Christian society at large. The relations between the papacy and the city and Papal States had been, as we have seen, a problem in the eleventh and twelfth centuries, and only during part of the thirteenth century was papal security established, although it did not last much later than 1240. The local concerns of the papacy were far less easily solvable than some of the other Europe-wide crises of which the pope was the welcomed arbiter. Fifth, and less clearly demonstrable, were the consequences of a century and a half of papal activity in ruling Christendom in the minds of Christians themselves. Bitter antipapal and anticurial satire and invective commenced during the inital stages of the growth of papal administrative rule during the twelfth century. St. Bernard and John of Salisbury had sharply criticized the new legal and diplomatic activities of the papacy. Heretics and orthodox lay critics hammered away at the bureaucratization of the Church, and the successes of Arnold of Brescia in the twelfth century and the Spiritual Franciscans in the thirteenth revealed the widespread sympathy such views might obtain. The diversion of the Fourth Crusade to Constantinople and the launching of the Crusade against, first, Christian heretics in the south of France and, second, the enemies of the pope in Sicily and southern and central Italy weakened the prestige of the popes, and even the actions against Frederick II in 1245 and against his descendants in the following decades elicited criticism from no less imposing a Christian than St. Louis IX of France. Criticism of the pope and the curia, criticism of the Crusade, criticism of the state of Christian society in general all appeared in great volume in the later thirteenth century, and the experience of the papacy between 1260 and 1303 demonstrated the precariousness of papal security and authority in a complex political world in which temporal and spiritual affairs became inextricably confused. The career of Charles of Anjou in Sicily during the late thirteenth century and the conflict between Boniface VIII and Philip IV the Fair of France at the end of the century graphically demonstrate the weakness of the papal position and the growing strength of temporal rulers, even when, as in the case of Charles of Anjou, those rulers were clearly subordinate to the papacy, and even when, as in the case of Philip the Fair, they came from a royal dynasty whose cooperation with the papacy and whose role as Christian kings were outstanding.

The death of Frederick II in 1250 left the kingdom of Sicily in a precarious state. Innocent IV, determined to eradicate the Hohenstaufen family from both empire and kingdom, turned against Frederick's legitimate son and successor, Conrad IV, and against Frederick's illegitimate son, the ablest ruler in the south, Manfred. Conrad IV, however, died in 1254 at the age of twenty-six, leaving only a two-year-old son, Conradin, to succeed to his claims and his illegitimate half-brother, Manfred, to maintain the Hohenstaufen claim to South Italy and Sicily.

As Manfred's power rose in the south, the imperial office itself became the ambition of a number of candidates, including Richard of Cornwall, brother of Henry III of England, Alfonso X of Castile, and others, and while the search for an emperor dragged on, so did the papal search for a king of Sicily. The leading candidate, Edmund of England, the son of Henry III, failed, and other candidates did not meet papal standards. Finally, in 1263 Pope Urban IV came to an agreement with Charles of Anjou, brother of St. Louis IX, over the crown of Sicily.

No prince ever appointed by a pope to temporal rule possessed as satisfactory credentials as Charles of Anjou. Born in 1227, the least regarded of the sons of Louis VIII and Blanche of Castile, Charles had inherited the great princely *appanages* of Anjou and Maine. (In France, the *appanages* were princely states awarded to cadet members of the royal family in the hope that loyalty and family unity would preserve these important commands in the service of the crown.) Charles had acquired the rule of Provence through his wife, and from 1246 on, his life had been one of busy administration, tireless expenditures of intelligence and energy, and, against family and political odds, remarkable success. In 1265, the Languedocian lawyer and servant of Charles, Guy Fulquois, was elected pope as Clement IV (1265–1268), and in 1265–1266 Charles of Anjou's army moved south from France, encountered Manfred's army at Benevento in 1266, and destroyed it. From 1266 on, Charles of Anjou was the effective ruler of Sicily. In 1268, at the battle of Tagliacozzo, Conradin was defeated, and later in the same year Charles of Anjou had him beheaded in Naples. The agent of the papacy had crushed the Hohenstaufen threat.

Yet Charles's victory, pleasing as it was to the pope, generated distrust in the college of cardinals, and after 1268 the power of the papal ruler of Sicily was a matter of considerable suspicion. That suspicion was not misplaced. Charles of Anjou was one of the most meticulous administrators in early Europe. His close supervision of governance, his intelligent appreciation of the minutiae of day-to-day governmental affairs, and his resourceful exploitation of his wealth made him indeed a considerable power to whom the addition of the crown of Sicily only added legitimacy and a new sphere of action.

The papacy, of course, was nominally Charles's master, but the expanding interests of the ruler of Sicily and the popes' dependence on Charles's support led Charles to attempt to influence papal elections in order to guarantee his own autonomy. But Charles's rule was not accepted any more readily in Sicily than in the curia, and in 1282 the population of Palermo rose up and massacred the French garrison. The Sicilian Vespers, as the revolt of 1282 is called, precipitated a general conflict throughout the northern Mediterranean world, and the intervention of the papacy, committed to the cause of Charles of Anjou, further weakened the papacy's prestige throughout Europe, particularly in Aragón, whose expanding Mediterranean interests conflicted with those of the Sicilian Angevins.

The conflict among France, Aragón, Sicily, and South Italy and the papacy further reduced the position of the pope to that of one contender in a complicated game of diplomacy and temporal rivalry. The drawn-out question of Sicily, which finally went to Aragón with Byzantine support, and of South Italy, which remained in the Angevin house, was not resolved until the treaty of Caltabellotta in 1302. During the course of the last quarter of the thirteenth century, however, papal participation in the complex power struggles of the Mediterranean further reduced the universal prestige of the papacy and threatened at times to reduce the papacy itself to the tool of the Capetian house of France. Papal commitment to Louis IX was one thing, to Charles of Anjou, his son Charles II, and to the house of France's involvement in the affairs of Sicily, Aragón, and the rest of the Mediterranean world, quite another. The solution devised by the papacy for the vacant Hohenstaufen throne of Sicily had created a new and ultimately uncontrollable power in the central Mediterranean, the house of Anjou, and had exacerbated the century-old enmity between the crowns of Aragón and France. Not only did the house of Anjou come very close to controlling the papacy, it very nearly succeeded in setting France and Aragón at each other's throats and launching the Angevin rulers of Sicily on a course of expansion whose ultimate goal was the conquest of the Byzantine Empire and the coast of North Africa. The papal triumph over the Hohenstaufen in Sicily must have seemed remote indeed during the reign of Charles II of Sicily in the last quarter of the thirteenth century. The papacy could not even control its loyal son, the king of Sicily and vassal of St. Peter.

Charles of Anjou's grandnephew, Philip IV the Fair, became king of France at the death of his father, Philip III, in 1285. Philip III, the son of Louis IX, had exhausted himself and his resources in the drawn-out conflict with Aragón over the Sicilian question, and he died on a grotesque Crusade into Aragon in 1285. St. Louis had died on an ill-planned Crusade in Tunis in 1270, and his death had struck a further blow to the Crusade idea in the west. The Crusading deaths of three successive kings of France, one of them the most influential king who ever lived, sharpened both the prestige of the Capetian dynasty and the hostility toward the papacy that spread on many levels in France, hitherto the kingdom most supportive of the papacy and most highly regarded by the popes. The sanctity of France and its ruling dynasty had become expensive, however, and the loss of three successive kings, the growing ambition of the Angevin house of Sicily, and the confusion surrounding papal elections in the last decade of the thirteenth century all separated France and the papacy. Never again would they be as close as they were between 1250 and 1280.

Between 1285 and 1295 the cost of the earlier French royal involvement with papal projects became painfully clear. The accession of Philip IV and his attempts to restore French royal control of the kingdom, the two-year scandalous papal interregnum following the death of Pope Nicholas IV in 1292, the election of the holy man, Pietro Morone, to the papacy in 1294 as Celestine V, Celestine's resignation of the papacy six months later, and the election of an old papal lawyer and diplomat,

Benedetto Gaetani, as Boniface VIII in 1294 all set the stage for the consequences of papal and French political, diplomatic, and military activity between 1262 and 1294. The pontificate of Boniface VIII (1294–1303) was not in itself the cause of the conflict between France and the papacy. The events of the preceding half-century had taxed both powers, and the failures, half-victories, differences of policy, and lack of direction of papal affairs after 1262 had all contributed to a kind of mutual exhaustion and distrust. France had, after all, sent its saintly king, his father and son, and innumerable nobles on Crusades throughout the century, and the only profit shown was the acquisition of Occitania and Provence. Aragón, the target of papal opprobrium, Crusades, and charges of heresy, was rapidly expanding its Mediterranean empire, while France was bogged down in conflicts with England, Aragón, and Flanders. Philip IV was acutely aware of the condition of the French monarchy, but he was also acutely aware of its prestige.

Boniface VIII, on the other hand, was not a young and vigorous prince, but an old man, already past eighty, with, as he once acidly remarked to a critic, forty years of service in the law behind him, when he ascended the papal throne. Moreover, he succeeded an extraordinarily complex pope, Celestine V, whose saintly reputation and circumstances of resignation would have colored the pontificate of any but the most utterly self-effacing successor. The major events of the Church in the following century—the weak pontificate of Clement V, the removal of the seat of papal government to Avignon between 1305 and 1375, the catastrophic double election of 1378 and the ensuing Great Schism, ending only with the even more traumatic Council of Constance in 1415—all these have been casually laid at Boniface's doorstep, and his pontificate is conventionally regarded as the beginning of the end of the medieval height of the papacy. Such a view is as unbalanced as that that neglects Boniface's predecessors, from Innocent IV to Celestine V, and their obsession with the problems of Byzantium, Sicily, Aragón, and the Papal States at the expense of Christendom as a whole. Boniface's own generation, after all, was born during the pontificates of Honorius III and Gregory IX, between 1220 and 1240, when the arguments of papal power were produced by one of the most brilliant and able bodies of lawyers and jurists that ever lived. Boniface's own career as a lawyer, diplomat, and teacher connects him with that earlier tradition, and when he confronted Philip IV the Fair in 1296, it was out of his own personal experience that he wrote and acted. But his position had been undercut thirty years before his pontificate had begun by the Sicilian, imperial, and Aragónese involvements, the Crusades against Byzantium and the Cathars and the disruptive nobles of southern and central Italy, and the papal-imperial factions in the northern Italian towns. Boniface was responsible for none of the events and consequences that preceded his pontificate. Neither, of course, was he responsible for the Avignon papacy, the Great Schism, or the ground swell of conciliarism that reached its high point at Constance in 1415. No single pope was capable of wrecking the papacy. But a succession of popes after 1254 had drastically misjudged the proper business of the papacy, and when Boniface found only the law to use as a weapon against Philip the Fair, he witnessed his learned and careful arguments grotesquely distorted in a new political world. The echo of the pope's thundering statements resounded not in a world traditionally obedient to Church law, but in one seeking new security through allegiance to effective powers. And, as Boniface discovered, the greatest power was that of Philip.

The reign of Philip IV the Fair (1285-1314) witnessed great demands made upon the king of France. The vast territories acquired during the thirteenth century—particularly Languedoc, the eastern territories near the Rhine, and the northern principalities—and the oppressive presence of the king of England, Edward I (1272-1307) as duke of Aquitaine called for the expenditure of great royal energy and vast sums of money. The problems of consolidation and diplomacy were considerable, and Philip's wars, his administrative needs, and his conception of the kingship of France made financial affairs the center of his attention. Again and again, his agents scoured the kingdom exploiting every claim the king could possibly make upon the resources of his subjects. Arguments from the old regulations of lordship, from the new vocabulary of public necessity and emergency of state, and from Philip's own conception of the extraordinary prerogatives of the king buttressed these activities, and it is the variety of Philip's claims rather than their exclusively lordly or modern character that is impressive. In addition to his lower-ranking administrative agents, who had to deal with societies as diverse as the rural areas of the south and the highly urbanized and privileged urban areas of the north and of Flanders, Philip attracted a number of accomplished and loyal legal officials who became the king's spokesmen, often to such a degree that some historians have claimed, with considerable exaggeration, that the lawyers, not the king, ruled the kingdom.

The rulers of England and France in the late thirteenth century faced many and varied difficulties. The costs of warfare and administration had risen, although the sources of public finance had not. The perennial quest of Edward I and Philip IV for money led both rulers into areas of experimentation and expediency, in which traditional and exceptional means of eliciting finances were used together. Claiming old rights of lordship and new rights to tax all subjects during an emergency of state, negotiating with large- or small-scale assemblies or subjects, demanding, cajoling, promising, compromising, and, at times, even begging, these rulers were caught in the pressures of rising costs and the absence of a universally accepted legal and ethical framework justifying new taxation. The financial difficulties of thirteenth- and fourteenth-century monarchs were more demanding and uncertain than their constitutional difficulties. Indeed, it was precisely the absence of a right of the monarch to tax his subjects that reminds us of the traditional character of these monarchies. As needs increased, expedients also increased, but these were always temporary, hesitant, and colored both by general social objections to regular taxation and the monarch's own moral uncertainty about the legitimacy of his activities. Such difficulties drove Philip the Fair to be alternately grasping and reluctant, alternately conciliatory and demanding. The administration of the royal government and the advice of Philip's counselors must be regarded in terms of the year-to-year needs of the king and the resistance his demands met.

It was precisely over questions of royal financial needs and practices that the great quarrel between Philip IV and Boniface VIII was launched. Although papal permission had long been required in order for temporal rulers to tax their clergy (and even then only in cases of dire necessity), thirteenth-century rulers had often neglected this rule. In 1296, Philip, facing a war with England and a vexing problem in Flanders, issued new demands for taxes from the clergy, and Boniface VIII responded with a papal letter directing the French bishops not to pay. This letter, *Clericis laicos,* condemned the abuse of temporal authority, and although its legal provisions were on solid ground, its tone was rather more categorical than suited Philip. In the same year, Philip prohibited the export of any money at all, including papal revenues, from France. In 1297, in the letter *Romana mater,* Boniface qualifiedly suspended the provisions of *Clericis laicos* for France, and in a later letter of the same year, *Etsi de statu,* he withdrew slightly from his earlier position. In 1297 Boniface faced difficulties on several fronts. An influential segment of the college of cardinals denounced him as a usurper, and in turn Boniface resorted to the unfortunate device of proclaiming a Crusade against them. Supporters of Celestine V further accused Boniface of canonical irregularity, and in 1298 Boniface published his great lawbook, the *Liber Sextus,* part of which included texts justifying papal resignation and the procedures for providing a successor to a still-living former pope. In 1297 Boniface also proclaimed the canonization of Louis IX of France, and in 1300 the pope announced the Jubilee Year, a year in which the pilgrimage to Rome was surrounded with particular spiritual benefits. By 1301 both parties appeared to have recovered from the earlier encounter, and the success of the Jubilee Year must have been encouraging to Boniface.

In 1301, however, the second conflict broke out. Philip IV arrested the bishop of Pamiers, Bernard Saisset, for treason and heresy, condemned him, and wrote to Boniface requesting papal confirmation of his action. Boniface could, with legitimacy, have modified his position on taxation, but he could not relax the canonical sanctions against any layman who presumed to try and convict a bishop. Boniface refused, and called a council at Rome for 1302, writing to Philip a long letter, *Ausculta fili,* in which he carefully cautioned the king against abusing the age-old liberties of the Church. Philip's agent in turn circulated a forged version of the letter, in which Boniface was made to appear to have claimed complete temporal and spiritual authority. It was one of the first documents in modern propaganda warfare. In addition, Philip called in 1302 a large assembly of nobles, clergy, and people, the first Estates-General in the history of France, to solicit public support in his quarrel with the pope. In 1302 Boniface issued the bull

Unam sanctam, a long, detailed, and wholly traditionalist exposition of papal authority. This bull, one of the most famous documents in the history of the relations between the two powers, elicited no counterarguments from Philip's supporters. Instead, Guillaume de Nogaret, Philip's chief minister, denounced Boniface as a heretic and blasphemer and marched into Italy, where he took the pope captive at Anagni and attempted to force him to repudiate his earlier statements and to renounce the papacy. Although he was released before he was forced to do this, Boniface died a few weeks later, and the questions of the relations between France and the papacy were momentarily suspended.

With the accession of Clement V (1305–1314), the relations between France and the papacy were slowly restored, but at a formidable price. The excommunications against Nogaret and others were lifted, and Philip was formally praised for his devotion in the bull *Rex Gloriae* of 1311. Some of Boniface's arguments in *Clericis laicos, Ausculta fili,* and *Unam sanctam* were formally repudiated by the pope, and Clement had to work very hard to prevent Philip from engineering a church council that would pronounce Boniface VIII an antipope. These concessions terribly weakened the direct authority of the popes after Clement V, and they presaged an even more remarkable incident, the destruction of the Order of the Templars.

In one sense, Boniface's concern over Philip's claims may well have come from his fear that the territorial monarchies in general were acquiring too much direct power over the clergy in their kingdoms. After all, the machinery of governance and communications was more direct and influential within England or France than throughout all of Christendom, and events of the fourteenth and fifteenth centuries proved that such monarchical control over clergy was a real threat to the universal claims of the papacy. No event suggests more clearly the threat constituted by a temporal power than the affair of the Templars. This order, having earned an attractive reputation in the Holy Land, had expanded its role in Europe, particularly in the fields of banking and Crusade financing. The wealth of the Templars and their virtual independence from governmental institutions made them an attractive target for the needy Philip, and their growing concern with financial affairs and their own privileges had doubtless weakened their standing in the eyes of many individual Christians. Between 1307 and 1314 Philip undertook to destroy the order and confiscate its property. In 1307 his campaign began with the arrest of the Templars on charges of heresy and unspecified but enormous and horrible vices. By 1310 a number of Templars were burned at the stake as heretics, and in 1314 the grand master of the order, Jacques de Molai, was executed. The financial resources of the Templars were confiscated by the crown, and papal approval was elicited with difficulty after pressure was exerted upon Clement V in the matter of Boniface VIII and the troubles of the first decade of the fourteenth century. Although not all subjects of Philip IV, clergy and laity, concurred in the destruction of the Templars, the king's success marked, along with his successful conflict with the papacy, one moment in the rise of temporal authority in European history. Despite whatever attractions the power of a universal Church, directing a Christian society whose defense was conducted by such universal orders as the Templars, might still have possessed in the first quarter of the fourteenth century, the powers of the king, enhanced by new administrative agents, financial resources, unquestioned Christian orthodoxy, and the growing cult of the kingdom of France itself, were both more immediately visible and more directly effective.

The relations of the papacy with Charles of Anjou and Philip the Fair, the complex problems of the reigns of Boniface VIII and Clement V, and the destruction of the Templars, one of the last vestiges of a kind of supranational Christian society, by the king of France, an event that heralded the civil theology of territorial monarchy, did not, of course, destroy the traditional separation of powers or unambiguously herald the triumph of the temporal authority of the king. The struggle between the two powers was not that between an archaic church and the "modern" state, but rather between spiritual and temporal authorities in the new circumstances of the late thirteenth and early fourteenth centuries. Both powers were still, in this sense, traditional powers, and the authority of the clergy and the papacy still counted for much throughout the fourteenth century, and continued to do so until the eighteenth century. But temporal authority, with its resources, claims, and spiritual justification, defined the terms of the new relationship. In defining these terms, however, temporal authority still left much room in which spiritual authority could and did function.

23

LATIN CHRISTENDOM AND BEYOND

BYZANTIUM, OUTREMER, AND THE LATIN WEST, 1144–1261

The death of John II Comnenos in 1143, the fall of Edessa in 1144, and the accession to power of Nur-ed-Din in 1146 marked major changes in the worlds of Byzantium, Outremer, and Islam. The accession of Manuel I Comnenos (1143–1180) marked the last serious attempt by a Byzantine emperor to come to terms with the rising world of Latin Christianity until the troubled reign of Michael VIII Palaeologus at the end of the thirteenth century. Between these two reigns, relations between Byzantium and the Latin West deteriorated badly, culminating in the Latin Christian capture of Constantinople in 1204 and the establishment of a brief Latin Empire there between 1204 and 1261. The fall of Edessa called forth the ill-planned and ill-fated Second Crusade of 1148 and signaled the decreasing capacity of the kingdom of Jerusalem to organize its own defense and the growing reluctance of Latin Christians to mount large-scale Crusading invasions. The rise of Nur-ed-Din marked a resurgence of militant Islam, especially on the political front. Under Nur-Ed-Din (1146–1174) and his remarkable successor Saladdin (1174–1193) the combined strength of Syria and Egypt grew greater, culminating in the capture of Jerusalem in 1187 and the reduction of the Crusader kingdom to a few coastal cities. The Third Crusade of 1188 led to little except a temporary truce, and although neither popes nor popular preachers diminished their cries for further Crusades, the history of the Crusades and of Byzantine-Latin relations in the thirteenth century is one of temporary gains and ultimate losses. But the political strength of Nur-ed-Din and Saladdin did not long survive them. In Egypt, Saladdin's successors succumbed to the Turkish Mameluk dynasty in 1250, and the last Abbasid caliph perished in the Mongol siege of Baghdad in 1258. After 1258 the dominant powers in the Near East were the Egyptian Mameluks and the Mongol hordes. After 1261 a dynasty of Byzantine emperors was faced with the daunting prospect of recovering a depopulated and impoverished empire and controlling the growing economic and political power of Venice and Genoa. With the fall of Acre in 1291, the last Christian land in Outremer fell back into Islamic hands. The old structure of powers and relations in the Byzantine, Syrian, and Egyptian worlds gave way before the powers of the Mameluks and Mongols on the one hand, and the vigorous military and entrepreneurial forces of the Latin West on the other.

By the accession of Manuel I Comnenos, his two predecessors, Alexius I and John II, had managed to restore much of the power that the empire had lost during the middle and last years of the eleventh century. Yet pervasive problems still remained. The loss of much of Asia Minor had cut off supplies of men and land from the capital, and the slow process by which rural military aristocratic landlords were driving off the free peasant farmers continued. The army tended to be divided into local commands, which were continually rivaled by the imperial bureaucracy in Constantinople, and the once-great Byzantine navy had to be reconstituted entirely during Manuel's reign, although it declined rapidly after his death. The increased hostility toward Greek Orthodoxy in the West sharpened Latin hostility in the Greek world. Beyond religious scorn, however, lay economic insecurity, for the Byzantines grew more and more to suspect the increasingly prosperous Venetian, Genoese, and Pisan merchants. This mutual dislike flared into open hostility in the anti-Venetian legislation of 1171, the massacre of Venetians in 1182, and Byzantine outrage at the Norman sack of Thessalonica in 1185. Nevertheless, the orderly administration of the empire continued throughout Manuel's reign, taxes were paid in gold, and the aristocracy and the wealthy citizens of Constantinople prospered. Yet the gaps between wealth and poverty were particularly galling to the proud but impoverished lower classes of the capital, and this social discontent also added fuel to their quarrel with the Latins. On the western borders, both Serbia and Bulgaria began to grow more independent at the end of the century, and their power was an important factor in Byzantine diplomacy during the thirteenth and fourteenth centuries.

In spite of Manuel I's pronounced fondness for westerners, his feelings were not echoed by his subjects, and the westerners merely increased their contempt for, and economic superiority over, Byzantium. The blame for the failure of the Second Crusade was laid at Byzantine doors, and the failure of the Third Crusade prolonged this Latin hostility. For, whether the Byzantines recognized it or not, the Latin attitude toward them was pegged to the fortunes of the kingdom of Jerusalem, although the Latins did not, collectively, do much themselves to support "The Kingdom Beyond the Seas." The reigns of Baldwin I and Baldwin II had established a strong monarchy, but problems of succession and the tension between established colonialist nobles and their relatives in Europe weakened the monarchy's resources. The growing power of the military orders created "states" within a state, and in the shaping of individual policy decisions, the voices with a legitimate claim to be heard were too numerous and insufficiently cooperative to form a consistent attitude toward the place of their kingdom in the Near Eastern world. By the reign of Baldwin III (1143–1163), families had begun to establish dynastic claims to their lands, legally guarantee regular succession to titles, and dispose of family properties without having them revert to the king. The king gradually lost his powers as a knightly caste grew up, and during the troubled reign of the leper-king Baldwin IV (1174–1185), the opposing forces in the kingdom increased their hostility. The death of Baldwin in 1185 and of his nephew the infant Baldwin V (1185–1186) a year later led to the succession of Guy of Lusignan (1186–1190), an incompetent noble under whose rule Jerusalem was lost to Saladdin in 1187. Guy was succeeded by Baldwin IV's stepsister Isabelle, who ruled with three of her four husbands in succession until 1205.

The power of such individual lords as Raymond of Tripolis and the power of the orders, particularly the Templars, furthered the turbulent conditions in the kingdom, and only Saladdin's own generosity prevented the utter destruction of the kingdom in the troubled days following the fall of Jerusalem. The power of Nur-ed-Din and Saladdin was primarily political, although both rulers invoked ideas of the *jihad,* or holy war, against their Christian enemies. Yet their power was momentary and exceptional, and the course of political change in Syria and Egypt did not guarantee the establishment of a dynasty. Even though Saladdin's Ayubid descendants ruled Egypt until 1250, the first half of the thirteenth century witnessed new power struggles in Syria, and with the rise of the warlike Mameluks in Egypt after 1250 and the threat of the Mongols after the sack of Baghdad in 1258, the older stability of the caliphate of Baghdad disappeared, and Syria especially was thrown into political upheaval.

The loss of Jerusalem and the diminishing of the Latin kingdom, the success of Nur-ed-Din and Saladin, and Saladin's subsequent reputation in Europe as that of a great and generous opponent fueled the general hostility toward the Crusade movement that had become apparent as early as 1144 and sharpened Latin hostility towards Byzantium. The Crusading ideal of Popes Innocent III and Gregory IX generated new movements, but these had limited success. In the course of the thirteenth century, criticism of the Crusade grew sharply, and criticism of the Byzantines grew sharper still.

In 1198 Pope Innocent III called for the launching of a new Crusade to relieve the Holy Land, and at the same time a number of individual preachers toured Europe, preaching in towns and at tournaments, attempting to ignite some support. By 1200 plans were well under way for a new Crusade, one that would be directed by the pope and would consist of individual lords and their followers. Negotiations were made with Venice to transport the forces, but when the army that turned up in Venice proved to be smaller than the Venetians bargained for, they refused to sail. As negotiations drew on, the Venetians proposed to transport the army if it agreed to aid the Venetians in asserting their rights over the Christian town of Zara on the Adriatic. In spite of papal criticism, the Crusaders helped the Venetians conquer Zara. While they were encamped there, they were approached by Alexius Angelus, the pretender to the throne of Byzantium. In appealing for Crusader aid, Alexius promised Byzantine support of the Crusade in return. Again encountering papal criticism, the Venetians and Crusaders attacked Constantinople, placed the pretender Alexius on the throne, and waited for the aid that had been promised them. Alexius, however, lacking resources, delayed action. In turn, the Crusaders and Venetians concocted between them a plan to capture the city for themselves. In 1204, by siege and indifferent planning, Constantinople was taken by an opposing force for the first time in its nine-hundred-year history. The population, or most of it, fled from the city, and Baldwin of Flanders was elected emperor. The Venetians were allowed to carve out desirable territories from the empire, and the rest was divided among the leaders of the Crusade and their followers.

Innocent III, at first outraged at the attack on fellow Christians, later accepted the conquest and installed a Latin clergy in Constantinople. The Latin Christians who carved out principalities for themselves behaved ruthlessly toward their new subjects, and the city of Constantinople itself was looted of precious materials and relics. The conquest afforded the opportunity to Venetians to enrich themselves and their city beyond their wildest dreams. The accounts that have survived, Geoffrey de Villhardouin's *History of the Conquest of Constantinople* and Robert of Clary's *History*, give remarkably vivid accounts of the events of 1204, and the letters of other prelates recount the looting of relics that so enriched the churches of western Europe.

Yet Byzantine resistance was not dead: in Trebizond on the Black Sea, Byzantine refugees established a kingdom; Cyprus remained independent; another principality was established at Epiros; and in Nicaea in 1205 a new Greek patriarch of Constantinople crowned Theodore Laskaris emperor. The line of Latin emperors of Constantinople had great difficulty in managing their unruly empire. Their own Latin subjects remained largely indifferent, as did the rest of Europe, and Greek resistance increased. Only Henry of Flanders (1205–1216) appears to have been a capable and effective ruler, but after his death a long series of regencies and minorities plagued the house of Flanders. In 1237 Baldwin II of Flanders brought a boatload of relics to the West, seeking to purchase arms and aid, and returned in 1243 on a similar mission. During these years the hatred of Byzantines for Latins grew from scorn and contempt to revulsion, and the prestige of the Laskarid dynasty in Nicaea maintained at least the image of the Orthodox empire in exile.

Theodore Laskaris (1208–1222) was succeeded by his able son-in-law John III Vatatzes (1222–1254), under whose military and diplomatic abilities, with the great weight of Constantinople removed, the kingdom of Nicaea prospered. Asia Minor once again became a focus for Byzantine loyalism and a source of men and money for military campaigns. With the coronation of Michael VIII Palaeologos in 1258, the Laskarid dynasty was displaced, but under Michael the Byzantine reconquest of Constantinople was achieved and the Latin Empire was destroyed in 1261.

The Latin Empire of Constantinople had never attracted the interest in the West that the kingdom of Jerusalem had. The fall of Jerusalem and the diverting of the Fourth Crusade to Constantinople sharpened the hostility to the Crusade idea that had grown up in the twelfth century, and the other uses of the Crusade in the thirteenth century further sharpened and spread this hostility. The Albigensian Crusade of 1209–1229 had once again turned the Crusader's sword against Christians, and the political Crusades launched by the later thirteenth-century papacy against Aragón, the Hohenstaufen, and even opponents within the Papal States themselves further disillusioned men and women about the value of the Crusade. Finally, the traditional forms of Crusade that took place in the thirteenth century also contributed to this disillusionment. In 1217 the Fifth Crusade was launched, with great preparation and careful planning, against Egypt, and in spite of initial success and the capture of Damietta, it dissolved in internal rivalries and dissension. In 1212–1213, a wave of children left their homes in France and Germany claiming that they would march to Jerusalem. Their movement generated great initial piety and great skepticism, and when the Crusade petered out on the coasts of France and Italy, further disillusionment resulted.

The Crusade of Frederick II, successful even though the emperor was under the ban of excommunication, raised further questions about the movement as a whole, and the two great Crusades of Louis IX of France, the most widely venerated Christian of the late thirteenth century, in 1246 and 1270 both ended in failure. If St. Louis failed, men asked, who could succeed? The Holy Land had been won—and lost. Constantinople had been captured—and lost. Excommunicated emperors had succeeded where popular saints had failed. Popes had declared Crusades against Christians and neighbors. The popes were never free from the antipapal satire that devastated the Crusade idea in the thirteenth century.

Byzantium, Outremer, and the Latin West underwent great transformations during the period 1144–1261. The initial confidence and certainty of the first Crusading movements was gone, and in its place there appeared both a dogged desperation to succeed, regardless of the cost, and a bitter hostility to the whole Crusade idea. The occasional breaking down of the relations between Greek and Latin Christians had developed, between 1185 and 1216, into an unremitting hatred, particularly at the lower levels of society and in the Greek and Latin religious orders. The turbulent politics of the Near East had permitted Nur-ed-Din and Saladdin to acquire great power but to found no states. And the history of North Africa and Egypt between 1250 and the fall of the Mameluk dynasty in 1519 is the history of the Mameluks. In Syria and Persia, the growing power of the Mongols and the Byzantine state in Nicaea determined events, and the rise of the Ottoman Turks at the end of the thirteenth century heralded the ultimate successors to Mongol rule in the Near East. The diminished authority and resources of the Byzantine Empire survived, often with grace and vigor, against its eastern and western enemies until 1453. But the world in which Byzantium first faced the Latin Crusaders, in which the Latin kingdom of Jerusalem first took root, in which Moslem particularism might be momentarily welded together by Kurdish adventurers with a genius for politics and warfare—this world passed away in the turbulent events of the period between 1144 and 1261.

KINGDOM AND COMMUNITY IN CENTRAL AND EASTERN EUROPE

The kings of England and France strengthened their authority by exploiting a wealthy and secure royal domain, developing a cadre of loyal and effective royal servants throughout the realm, acquiring the support of the Church and at least part of the support of the nobility, and identifying themselves and their causes with the idea of a common history, language, and culture. In their different ways, such rulers as Richard I, Henry III, Philip II Augustus, and St. Louis IX also conferrred something of their own personal prestige upon their descendants, for descent from a line of well-remembered kings also constituted a support for the monarchy in both kingdoms. In Castile, the circumstances of the *reconquista* gave the king considerable income in tribute and land, but the king in turn distributed much of these to the nobility, offered attractive terms to those who would settle the countryside and the towns, and contributed much to the military orders, in the process developing a kingdom whose finances depended upon continual expansion to the south and whose economic structure did not include essential proportions of agricultural and commercial enterprise. The crown of Castile was well known and widely admired, but its security was uncertain, and its roots went far less deeply into the economic and social life of the kingdom than did those of other monarchies.

In central and eastern Europe, population levels, agricultural and commercial productivity, the power of the nobles, and the resources of the royal houses shaped different kinds of political communities with different systems of rule. Similar in many ways to the kingdoms of England, France, and Castile, the kingdoms of Poland, Bohemia, Hungary, Serbia, Bulgaria, and Kievan Russia also constituted important parts of Christian culture and engaged in different kinds of relations with the powers of the West and the papacy.

By the year 1000 Christian kings had been established in Poland, Bohemia, and Hungary, the conception of the monarchy appears to have been territorial, and in Poland and Hungary the Christian church was generally independent of German ecclesiastical authorities. Hungary's expansion was toward the southwest and south, and it reached the Adriatic Sea and pressed against the Serbs and the Bulgars. Poland, on the other hand, expanded against the pagan Slavic peoples along the Baltic coast, and Bohemia, under the ecclesiastical authority of the bishops of Regensburg and Mainz, the personal protection of King St. Wenceslaus (921–929), and the expansionist aims of Wenceslaus's brother Boleslav I (929–967), faced German and Hungarian frontiers. Under Boleslav II (967–999) in 967, Prague became the ecclesiastical and political center of Bohemia, and long trade routes to the east, to southern Germany in the west, to the north through the Elbe valley, and to the south through Venice crossed in Bohemia and made it a precocious center of trade, particularly the slave trade. The role of Prague as an ecclesiastical center and as the capital of the Premyslids, the rulers of Bohemia, made it the most prosperous town in the dukedom of Bohemia and the center for the transmission of cultural and political influences from the western monarchies and Italy. The Premyslid dukes of Bohemia maintained cautious relations with the powerful empire to the west, and in 1198 Philip of Swabia recognized the duke of Bohemia as a hereditary king, a title confirmed by Frederick II in 1212. Henceforth, the king of Bohemia, throughout the eleventh and twelfth centuries a considerable figure in imperial affairs, became a major prince of the empire, and during the interregnum following the death of Frederick II in 1250, the Bohemian king Premysl Ottakar II (1253–1278) emerged as a strong candidate for the imperial throne itself. The silver strikes in the mountains of Bohemia during the thirteenth century increased

Bohemian prosperity, and the spread and growth of towns, which frequently included many German merchants and colonists, strengthened the power of the king. Throughout the thirteenth and fourteenth centuries Bohemia remained a rich kingdom, one ruled by a powerful king, extraordinarily productive in trade and internal wealth, and closely tied by liturgical language, cultural exchanges, and political alliances to the worlds of Germany, France, and Italy.

Of the three great central European kingdoms whose liturgical language was Latin, Bohemia hewed closely to the political, economic, and cultural world of Germany. Hungary, however, the true frontier between Byzantine and Latin Christianity, was far more socially eclectic. Germans, Italians, Slavs from the southern Slavic world, and Byzantines all contributed to the organization and governance of the kingdom of Hungary. The persistence of Latin as the liturgical and cultural language of Hungary linked that kingdom firmly with the varied influences of both the Latin and Greek worlds. In 1222 the lesser nobility of Hungary, strengthened by several generations of service to the king, made the claims that it had acquired enforceable against the king himself and his greatest lords. It was in the process of guaranteeing some of their rights against the king that the lesser Hungarian nobility appeared to nineteenth-century historians as comparable to the English barons who forced King John to sign the Magna Carta. Both the Magna Carta and the Golden Bull of 1222, however, were far more the attempts on the part of a *nobility* to assure its *own* privileges and rights than an attempt to constitute anything resembling a modern constitutional government, and both documents were severely rejected by the papacy. The agricultural produce of Hungary slowly gave way to horse and cattle breeding and the opening of Hungary's silver and gold mines in the thirteenth century contributed further to enhancing the wealth of the kingdom. With the extinction of the Árpád dynasty in 1301, Hungary proved to be an extremely attractive goal of noble families throughout Europe.

By the end of the tenth century, the economic prosperity of Bohemia and the strength of the German Empire had brought trade and money into Christian Poland. The vigor of the Piast dynasty, from Mieszko I on, placed Poland under the overlordship of St. Peter, where it became, like Hungary, a "vassal" kingdom of the papacy, and the elevation of Gniezno to an archbishopric in 1000 under the patronage of St. Adalbert focused the ecclesiastical and political authority of the Polish king. Protected by their Christianity from the kinds of savage wars waged against heathens, Poland and Bohemia both succeeded in achieving their political independence, while acting against the pagan Slavic peoples on their frontiers. The clashes between Poland and Germany over the lands of the pagan Slavs south of the Baltic Sea came about rather as the result of competing expanding Christian powers than as the result of some imaginary conflict between "Germanic" and "Slavic" spirits.

The activities of Christian Germanic and Slavic kingdoms against pagan Slavs on the southern Baltic coast, the influx of Germans into Bohemia, Hungary, and Poland, and the influence of Latin Germanic ecclesiastical structures on Slavic Christendom have all been regarded by Slavic and German historians as examples of a mythical struggle between "Germanic" and "Slavic" cultures. Such a view is far more the product of the culture of nineteenth- and twentieth-century German and Slavic historians than an accurate picture of the relations between Slavs and Germans in the twelfth and thirteenth centuries. Poland, Bohemia, and Germany were all vigorous, expansive societies during this period, and they all drew not only upon Germanic, but upon Italian, French, and Byzantine influences.

During the twelfth and thirteenth centuries, the rulers of eastern German society led an expansion movement into the territories of the pagan northern Slavic tribes, and this movement, largely successful, produced a particular kind of aristocratic society with strong economic and cultural characteristics. The most striking difference between the expansionist movements on the Baltic and in Spain, at either corner of Europe, was in the conditions of the peoples whose lands were taken over by Christian expansion. Northern Spanish Christians developed a military expansionist society on a far less complex economic and intellectual level than the Moslem and Jewish societies they conquered, and the problem of Christian-Jewish-Moslem relations that colored much of subsequent Spanish history derives from the different cultural levels of the expanding and retreating societies in the Iberian peninsula during the twelfth and thirteenth centuries. In eastern Germany and the lands beyond, however, the differences between Christian Polish and German society, on the one hand, and pagan Slavic tribal society, on the other, were not the same as those between Christians and Moslems in Spain. Polish and Germanic society was far more organized, possessed of a common Christian culture, capable of exploiting new economic and material resources in complex ways, and far more capable of pressing expansion over several generations than the Slavic tribal societies at whose expense their expansion was taking place.

The relations between German powers and Slavic societies must be considered across a long time span and a broad cultural spectrum. The pressures exerted by Germans on the new Slavic kingdoms in the tenth century changed in the eleventh and twelfth centuries as such kingdoms as Poland and Bohemia became Christian and began their own expansion against the Slavic pagans. Not until the twelfth century did continual German expansion to the east begin, and this expansion was against pagan Slavs. The penetration of Germans into Poland, Bohemia, and Hungary was far more peaceful and acceptable to both Germans and non-Germans, and may be considered part of a general series of small-scale migrations that brought economic, cultural, and political influences from many parts of the Latin West into central and eastern Europe in the twelfth and thirteenth centuries. During the late twelfth and thirteenth centuries, for example, such influences as Romanesque architecture, ecclesiastical reform, and canon law came into the Slavic-speaking world from places as diverse as the lower Rhineland, France, and Italy. The western Slavic kingdoms were still Slavic-speaking, but they were also Latin-praying and part of the community of Christian peoples recognized throughout the Latin West. Nor were the Flemish and German immigrants always forceful intruders in Poland, Silesia, and Bohemia after the eleventh century. The foundations of markets, towns, and larger areas of settlement and colonization were usually under the power of Slavic lords, whether dukes or kings, and the structure of markets and towns grew largely out of ducal or royal privileges. Slav princes regulated most market and urban activity, from the flow of money to the sale of wine, the renting of stalls, and the building of larger structures for settled commerce. The immigration of new settlers, traders, merchants, and financiers was regulated by princely authority, and the growth of urbanism in the late twelfth and thirteenth centuries in Slavic lands was generally carried out by foreigners, with princely approval.

The German expansion eastward into pagan Slavic territories had both economic and political dimensions. By the early twelfth century, northern sea trade was flourishing in the North Sea, the Baltic Sea, and the Rhine system. This trade linked England, the Low Countries, Denmark, Sweden, the eastern Baltic, and Novgorod in northern Russia. One of its major crossing points was Cologne. The ecclesiastical sphere witnessed the establishment of independent Scandinavian bishoprics, beginning with the founding of Lund in 1108. Lund, Magdeburg, Bamberg, and Hamburg-Bremen all contributed to the missionary efforts in the lands of the pagan Slavs, and in 1147 St. Bernard obtained papal permission for potential German participants on the Second Crusade to move instead in a northern Crusade against the pagan Wends. This campaign, which was supported by Christian Polish and Danish forces, marked the onset of Crusade, commerce, and politics as the major characteristics of eastward German expansion in the twelfth and thirteenth centuries.

Under the reign of Emperor Lothar III (1125–1137), who had been duke of Saxony and hence strongly concerned with the pagan Slavs on his northern and eastern frontiers, new families became powerful in Holstein, the northern mark, and Saxony—the families of Schauenberg, Brandenburg, and Welf—and their major energies throughout the next century were devoted to the expansion of their power eastward. The expanding population of western Europe and the growing activities of the Cistercian order provided the personnel for this expansion, and the missionary-Crusading character of twelfth-century Christian culture provided a rationale and justification. The economic developments in the North and the Baltic Seas, the growth of towns along the Baltic, and the attractions of the Russian and Polish markets also contributed to the financial stability of the new expansion and colonization. Throughout the period of expansion, the eastward movement was alternately marked by peaceful penetration and bitter hostility: Slavs allied with Germans against other Slavs; Slavs and Danes allied against Germans; towns, bishops, the kings of Germany and Denmark, and the pope allied at various times to push the Christianization of the east.

The founding of Lübeck in 1158–1159, the development of a community of merchants in Gotland during the twelfth century, the efforts of Albert, bishop of Livonia (1199–1229), in founding bishoprics in the newly conquered lands and establishing military orders to support them, and the independent efforts of Henry the Lion, duke of Saxony and Bavaria, and the margraves of Brandenburg extended the conquests still further.

In 1226 the Teutonic Knights, one of the many military orders in the Holy Land, moved to northeastern Germany, where, with the support of Emperor Frederick II and under the leadership of Grand Master Hermann von Salza, they undertook the conquest and occupation of Prussia. In 1236 the Knights incorporated the Livonian orders, and from the mid thirteenth century on, the Knights governed Prussia, pushing frequently into Poland and Russia. From 1309, on, their headquarters and the seat of the grand master was the city of Marienburg. The military aspect of German eastward expansion, however, was not dominant everywhere, nor did military conquest allow the mass immigration of large numbers of German settlers. Migration and settlement were more often peaceful than forceful, and the competition for settlers was brisk among lords of all sorts. By the thirteenth century, a specialized group of men known as *locatores,* who were responsible for the development of the *locatio,* or settlement of colonists, organized movements of settlers in western Europe, and received privileges in the new settlements for themselves. By the end of the thirteenth century, the balance of wealth and political power in Germany had shifted from its Rhineland origins far to the east, a movement signaled by the rise in power of the king of Bohemia, the growth of Prussia, the influence of Cistercian ideas on eastern Germany, and the rapidly growing wealth of the Baltic and Rhenish cities and the city-foundations of Danzig, Riga, and Breslau. The rise of the Bohemian and Polish kingdoms and the eastward expansion of Germans during the twelfth and thirteenth centuries was thus a complex process, one that has far more political and economic characteristics than ethnic or racial ones. Dynastic difficulties and a limited economy, more than German hostility or influence, contributed to the weakening of the Polish monarchy in the thirteenth century and the growing local Bohemian resistance to the Premyslid dynasty in the fourteenth.

To the south and east of Hungary, the principalities of Serbia and Bulgaria both freed themselves from Byzantine control during the twelfth century. The weakness of the last Comneni and the Angelus dynasty, the Christian capture of Constantinople, and the growing economic prosperity of the Balkans contributed to this new independence and to the reassertion of vigorous traditional cultures. During the thirteenth century there arose the Second Bulgarian Empire under the talented Asen dynasty. The rise of the Serbian monarchy under Stephen Nemanja from the mid twelfth century on was characterized by an independent Serbian church that remained closely affiliated with Greek Orthodoxy. The liturgical crowning of the Serbian king was first performed during the reign of Stephen Uros I (1195–1224). The reigns of Stephen IV the Great (1237–1272) and Stephen VI (1275–1321) continued the consolidation of the Serbian kingdom, and under the reign of Stephen Dusan (1336–1356) Serbia emerged as the most powerful Christian state in the east. It had designs upon the imperial throne of Constantinople itself.

The vigorous assertion of strong, independent monarchies in Hungary, Serbia, and Bulgaria during the late twelfth and thirteenth centuries was in part related to the decline of Constantinople and to the growing prosperity of the economic network extending from southern Germany and Venice across the eastern Mediterranean and the Black Seas. Two threats to this independence and prosperity appeared in the thirteenth and fourteenth centuries: the arrival of the Mongols and the growing power of the Turks. Although the Mongol penetration of the Balkans was brief, it upset political development and influenced the eastern end of the economic system. The slow rise to power of the Turks in the fourteenth and fifteenth centuries ultimately removed the independence of Bulgaria, Serbia, and Hungary until the decline of Turkish power in the seventeenth and eighteenth centuries.

During the twelfth and thirteenth centuries, several of the ruling dynasties of European kingdoms survived and strengthened themselves by possessing able ruling successors ready to follow in the footsteps of the ruling king. Some ruling families, however, produced no children, or too many of them, and in an age when the laws of succession were still fluid, the situation in France and Hohenstaufen Germany offered considerable opportunities for the strengthening of the dynastic aspects of monarchy. In the principality of Kiev, however, the proliferation of competitive male children weakened any thought of centralization, and after the death of Iaropolk II in 1139, the fragmenting of the Kievan principality among rival branches of the house of Rurik broke the progress, which had been considerable since the late tenth century, toward the shaping of a central authority in the principality.

The diverse principalities into which the principality of Kiev broke up between 1054 and 1113 permitted no supreme prince to govern Kiev until the successful reign of Vladimir Monomakh (1113–1125). Yet in the generation succeeding Vladimir, that of his sons Msitislav I (1125–1132) and Iaropolk II (1132–1139), princely rivalry and the great diversity of economic and political interests among the princely houses weakened the position of Kiev, and this period witnessed the appearance and increased strength of the principalities of Suzdal and Riazan and the great city of Novgorod, with its economic connections across the Baltic in Scandinavia and northern Germany. Princely rivalries involving Byzantium, the Holy Roman Empire, the Cumans, the Norman rulers of Sicily, and the powers of central Europe, particularly the Teutonic Knights and the kingdom of Poland, weakened the position of Kiev and offered opportunities for economic and political prosperity to eastern as well as southern and northern Russian principalities. The brief reign of Andrei of Suzdal (1169–1174) indicates some of the power inherent in victorious princes whose interests ranged wider than the Kiev-Constantinople trade linkage. The spread of

Venetian commercial power in the world of Kiev and Constantinople, the growing strength of the Cumans in the old Pecheneg lands of South Russia, and the decline of Byzantium created an external instability that increased the anarchy among the princes who contended for authority in Kiev and the south.

The pressures of Slavic and German expansion in northwestern Russia, particularly the pressures of the Teutonic Order in the first quarter of the thirteenth century, challenged Novgorod's crucial place in the economic and political world of the north, and in 1222 the southern Russian armies, allied with the Cumans, encountered the first probing expeditionary forces of the expanding empire of the Mongols. Between 1223 and 1237, the divergent interests of the Russian princes, the growing separation of the worlds of Novgorod, Kiev, and the eastern principalities of Suzdal and Muscovy, and the ominous menace of the Mongols in the east further fragmented the principalities. By the middle of the thirteenth century, Kievan Russia lost its central position, partly because of the growing economic prosperity of the north, particularly Novgorod, and partly because of the divisive character of the principalities of the east and south. As we will see, the advent of the Mongols destroyed forever the predominance of Kiev and resulted in two centuries of Mongol domination of Russia, centuries that saw as well the transformation of Novgorod and the rise of the principality of Muscovy to predominance in fourteenth- and fifteenth-century Russia. The links with Constantinople and Byzantine civilization in the south, and with the trading network of Scandinavian and German cities in the north, slowly weakened with the decline of Constantinople and the growing power of Muscovy. Kievan Russia disappeared in the rise of other principalities among pressures of outside invasion and economic competition that no principality and no single ruling dynasty in the Christian world faced. Russia was far too vast and became far too conscious of competing economic and political tensions for the continued survival of Kievan dominance. In the course of the fourteenth and fifteenth centuries, a new Russia took shape in the north.

THE MONGOL EMPIRE, 1227–1350

The Islamic and eastern Christian worlds encountered in the first quarter of the thirteenth century a new and powerful military force from Asia, the Mongol Empire, first formed by Genghis Khan (1155/62–1227) and later extended by his successors. At the height of its extent and power, around 1300, the Mongol Empire included China and parts of southeast Asia, central Asia, and the Islamic and Christian lands from Persia north and west through South Russia, Poland, and northern Russia. The advent of the Mongol Empire affected the history of China, Persia, and the Christian territories of the east for two centuries. One indirect result of

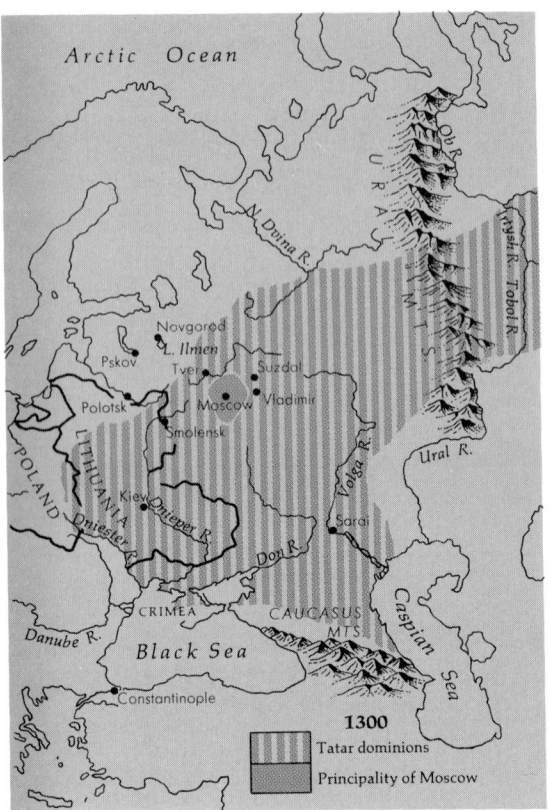

Modern Russia 1190-1505

the Mongol conquests was the access given Europeans to eastern Asia, which in turn led to the growth of trade, a missionary movement to Asia, and the increased knowledge in the west of the geography of eastern Eurasia. Partly as a result of the Mongol conquests, the west discovered the world.

The Mongols were an agglomeration of loosely related Eurasian peoples speaking a common language and living by herding and hunting. From the late tenth century on, the Mongols established short-lived empires in eastern Asia, power among them being held by the leaders of warlike clans. The rise to power of one of these, Temujin, after 1196, first in his own tribe and later among all the tribes of Mongolia, was sudden. By 1206 Temujin, now called Ghengis Khan, had solidified his rule. During the remaining two decades of his life, his military, legal, and fiscal reforms shaped the Mongol Empire into a powerful military unit that occupied northern China in 1215, turned to the west and destroyed the kingdom of Khorezem in 1217, invaded Persia and South Russia by 1223, and, by the time of his death in 1227, had become the greatest power in the world.

Ghengis Khan's sons divided the empire among themselves, electing one among them, Ogodai, to succeed to the title of great khan in 1229. From his capital at Karakorum, Ogodai directed the expansion of the Mongol Empire. In 1236, Mongol armies again moved into eastern Europe, destroying the Volga Bulgars by 1238 and ravaging the Russian principalities on the upper Volga. The Mongols then turned south and besieged and captured Kiev in 1240. From Kiev, the Mongol armies divided, one passing west to sack Cracow, which fell in 1241, Breslau, and Liegnitz. At the same time, the second force passed west through Hungary and destroyed the armies of King Bela IV within several days of the destruction of the forces of Duke Henry II of Silesia far to the north. The Mongols halted this first penetration in order to consolidate their gains, and the death of the Great Kahn Ogodai in 1246 recalled the leaders of the armies to Karakorum, where Guyuk, son of Ogodai, succeeded his father.

Among the observers of the installation of Guyuk Kahn were not only the generals of the Mongol hordes, but a remarkable Dominican diplomat, John del Piano Carpini, whose presence is in itself a tale of heroism. Among the most fanciful anthropology of the early thirteenth-century Christian world was the legend of Prester John, a fabled Christian king ruling somewhere in Asia who would someday join forces with the Christian west to annihilate Islam. The legend of Prester John was probably based upon the real existence of Nestorian Christians in Asia as well as the eschatological dreams of the more imaginative western clergy. At first, the appearance of the Mongols fanned belief in Prester John's arrival—until word came back to the west of the Mongols' activities in Russia, Poland, and Hungary. At the First Council of Lyons in 1245, Pope Innocent IV dispatched a papal agent, John del Piano Carpini, to find out about the Mongols, and John, a middle-aged, overweight lawyer and diplomat who had spent his career in Scandinavia and the Iberian Peninsula, promptly departed on horseback for the east, knowing not a word of the Mongol language, and, as it turned out, bearing a letter to the Great Kahn that could be interpreted as highly insulting. With his companion, a monk named Benedict the Pole, John traveled on relays of horses from Kiev to Karakorum, delivered his message, and returned between 1245 and 1247, a journey whose accomplishment was an astonishing act of bureaucratic heroism. Not only did John rush across Asia, witness the installation of Guyuk, exchange messages and return, but he sat down and wrote a description of his journey that is a stunning piece of travel and diplomatic reporting. Vincent of Beauvais, the court historian of St. Louis IX, incorporated parts of John's account into his world history, and Salimbene, a curious and gossipy Franciscan friar, left a brief account of a conversation he had with John in France in 1247. Louis IX, impressed with the news of the Mongols, sent two missions himself, one by Andrew of Longjumeau in 1248 and another by William of Rubrouck in 1253–1255, from which descriptive accounts have also survived. Although the "mission to Asia" failed to find a Prester John or to convert the Mongol Khans to Christianity, they perhaps helped in securing tolerance for Christians passing into Mongol territory, and their accounts served as the basis for later commercial travelers into the Mongol Empire.

Guyuk Kahn was succeeded by Mongke, who focused his attention on the east—China—and left the expansion of Mongol power in the west to Hulagu, who moved into the Islamic world of Persia, Syria, and Egypt, and to Berke, who succeeded the great general Batu as ruler of the Golden Horde in Russia in 1256. The years 1256–1266 marked permanent changes in the Mongol Empire. The succession to Mongke was finally decided in 1266, when Kubilai Kahn became great Kahn and moved his residence to Peking in China. Hulagu, Kubilai's brother, established the Empire of the Ilkhans in Persia, sacked Baghdad in 1258, but was prevented from moving further west by his defeat at the hands of the Turkish Mameluks of Egypt at Ain Jalut in 1260. From that date the Mameluks of Egypt constituted a powerful state, controlling Palestine and parts of Syria and remaining hostile toward the Buddhist Ilkhans of Persia. The Ilkhans of Persia also encountered the hostility of the Golden Horde after 1258. The Horde, under Berke, adopted Islam around 1260, thus opposing the Buddhist Mongols of Persia, and were inclined to form trading alliances with the Mameluks of Egypt. The Ilkhans of Persia reigned until 1353, when civil wars and the advance of Timur destroyed their khanate. In South Russia the Golden Horde, with its capital at Sarai on the lower Volga, just to the north of the Caspian Sea, dominated the affairs of Russia for two centuries. Although Mongol power was collapsing everywhere around 1360, the strength of the Golden Horde survived in Russia throughout the fourteenth and fifteenth centuries, and not until the end of the fifteenth century was the Horde overthrown by the grand dukes of Muscovy. The Islamic Horde and the Christian Russians shared no cultural sympathies, although the eastern Russian princes ruled in their own domains by Mongol appointment and approval.

By the second half of the fourteenth century, Mongol rule was weakening in much of the old empire. Nomadic empires possessed little staying power, and when the contrast between the conquerors and the conquered was great, the nomads were generally attracted by the culture they found. After 1350 the Ilkhans of Persia collapsed; at the same time the Golden Horde began to weaken, and in 1369 the Ming dynasty's rise to power in China ended the domination of the successors of Kubilai Kahn. Between 1400 and 1500, the Mongol penetration of the worlds of China, Islam, and the Christian west ended. The brief reign of Timur in the late fourteenth and fifteenth centuries had no lasting effects, although the movement into India of Timur's descendant Babur in 1525 led to the formation of the Great Moghul (Mongol) Empire, which lasted until the nineteenth century.

As we will see, the economic consequences of the opening of Asia to Christian travelers were considerable. The growth of Genoese economic activity in the Black Sea and the Crimea through the port of Kaffa, the overland trade routes to China, along which merchants followed missionaries, the increased knowledge of the eastern world that marks the beginning of the western discovery of the world, and the diminishing of the struggle between Christianity and Islam in the face of other peoples and places that seemed far more numerous and more mysterious all grew out of the western European experience of the Mongols. The fall of Kiev and the slow growth of Novgorod and Muscovy, the rigid Russian adherence to a highly formal Christianity in the face of the Moslem beliefs of their Mongol overlords, and the burden of tribute and taxes shaped Russian history for three centuries. The Mongol occupation of Persia and the Mameluk occupation of Egypt contributed to the weakening of Islamic culture, and the slow progress of the Ottoman Turks in the fourteenth and fifteenth centuries weakened Islamic culture still further. China, Russia, and the eastern parts of the Islamic world bore the greatest brunt of the Mongol conquests, and their energies were taken up for centuries in restoring their cultures and power. Egypt and the west had largely been spared.

GEOGRAPHY, TRAVEL, AND COMMERCE: THE OPENING OF CHINA AND THE ATLANTIC

In 1298 Rustichello of Pisa, a writer of knightly romances, shared a Genoese prison cell with a Venetian captive named Marco Polo, who told the writer the story of his eighteen years spent in China in the service of the Great Khan. Rustichello wrote the stories down in a book that came quickly to be called *Il milione,* "The Million," because of its tales of fabulous Asian wealth and possibly also because Marco Polo was alleged to have brought great wealth back with him. Four years earlier, in 1294, two brothers of Genoa, the Vivaldi, had undertaken to outfit several ships and sail west to seek new trade routes. Thirty years earlier, by 1268, regular Genoese and Venetian fleets departed west to sail out of the Mediterranean north into the Atlantic to make commercial connections with the trade networks of northern Europe. The travels to Asia, the establishment of regular maritime contact between the Mediterranean and the Atlantic, and the mystery and interest generated by such adventures as those of the Vivaldi, who disappeared, and Marco Polo, whose story quickly became widely known, suggest a new interest on the part of some Europeans, not only in the wonders of the unknown parts of the world, but also in the more practical aspects of what might be made of them. The time between John del Piano Carpini's journey in 1245–1247 and the embassy of William of Rubrouck in 1253–1255 and the establishment of regular sailing routes to the west was very brief. By the 1270s others had begun to travel to Asia, and by the 1290s the Vivaldi thought it at least possible that a westward voyage might bring them, too, to wealthy lands. The traditional geographical knowledge of Europeans before the thirteenth century was most accurate close to home, fanciful and often wildly imaginative the farther away from Europe it strayed. In the course of the thirteenth century, however, Europeans learned much about the rest of the world, and their geographical ideas, commercial ambitions, systems of communication, and travel reports accumulated more and more knowledge. This knowledge was not, of course, immediately and universally absorbed, but it represented an enormous increment, and it began to chip away, at least, at the received tradition of geographical thought.

The geographical knowledge of eleventh- and twelfth-century Europe was a learned and nonexperimental amalgam of several distinct traditions. The knowledge handed down by Roman literature, from Pliny through Isidore of Seville, constituted one body of tradition. Second, the necessary speculations on such problems as the size and shape of the earth, the habitable and nonhabitable zones, the topography and character of physical features, and climate—problems that had emerged in centuries of commentary on the Hexameral parts of the Book of Genesis—necessarily played a role between science and theology. Third, the efforts of twelfth-century thinkers to describe natural phenomena in terms of Platonic cosmology led to other speculations concerning the nature of the world and its inhabitants. Fourth, there grew up in the twelfth century a large body of literature, ranging from personal travel accounts to stories of the legendary and fabulous journeys of Alexander the Great and others, that made much of these traditions available to a wider circle of readers. The one truly impressive body of geographical knowledge developed between the ninth and the thirteenth centuries, that of the Moslem geographers, was virtually ignored in the west, and the legendary travel stories, including Marco Polo's book itself, tended to be ignored by the learned. The learned, for whom geography was often a branch of theology, tended to regard geographical knowledge as useful insofar as it was consistent with the data from other branches of learning and insofar as it was morally edifying. Jerusalem was at the center of the world, Europe occupied precisely one quarter of the world, and the Mediterranean Sea neatly divided the sections of the world in such a way as to make the physiognomy of the land areas resemble the outline of the letter T within a large circle resembling the letter O. These O–T maps constituted the basis of formal geographical knowledge, and the history of their slow transformation during the fourteenth and fifteenth centuries is one reflection of the new impact of naturalistic geography upon the traditional learning of the twelfth and thirteenth centuries.

The stream of legates, missionaries, adventurers, and merchants who followed John del Piano Carpini into Asia after 1247 swelled quickly. As early as 1260, two Venetian brothers, Maffeo and Nicolo Polo, left the Venetian settlements in the Crimea and traveled with merchandise to the court of Berke at Sarai on the Volga. They then made their way to Bokhara and, in the company of one of Kubilai Khan's envoys, to Shangtu in China. By 1269 they had returned to the west with messages and gifts from Kubilai Khan to the pope. Their son and nephew, Marco (b.ca. 1254), departed with his father and uncle for China, which he reached in 1275, and where, for eighteen years, he served in the administrative section of the Great Khan's court. The Polo brothers had begun as merchants and traders, but the success of their first journey to China, the Khan's welcome, and their return journey with Marco transformed them from traders into gentlemen ambassadors. As a diplomat and administrator, not a trader, Marco Polo served the Great Kahn for eighteen years. The Polos returned to Italy in 1295, a year after the Franciscan John of Monte Corvino arrived in Peking, of which he became the first Christian archbishop, in 1307. Marco Polo settled in Venice as a moderately wealthy nobleman, spent several years in a Genoese jail as a war prisoner, was released in 1299, and died in Venice in 1324. His book, *Il milione*, was widely known, and his mission as papal emissary to the court of the Great Khan was unfulfilled. When Christopher Columbus began to record his plans to reach China two centuries later, he regarded himself as following in Marco's footsteps.

The failure of the Vivaldi expedition was counterbalanced by the success of the Genoese and Venetian sailings into the Atlantic, the linking with the trade routes of the northern seas, and the increased maritime prosperity of European trade. The success of the Polos and the sense of wonder and entertainment in Marco's book was also followed by practical enterprises.

In 1340 Francesco Balduccio Pegolotti wrote a treatise called *On the Divisions of Lands and the Types of Commerce,* a book more commonly called *La Practica della Mercatura,* in which he described very soberly all the things a merchant would need to know in order to do business among the Mongols. The work included a remarkable description of the conditions on the overland route to China (Pegolotti found it much more secure than it has ever been since). As Leonardo Olschki has observed in comparing the two works, "For the Florentine, the whole earth is one vast market. For the Venetian, the world is a spectacle, which he portrays as best he may and recalls in great variety and a multiplicity of manifestations."

PART SIX

THE HUMAN CONDITION

24

THE INDIVIDUAL AND SOCIETY IN THE THIRTEENTH CENTURY

BIRTH AND DEATH, DIET, SICKNESS AND HEALTH

During the twelfth century, the lay condition began to acquire a stature, and the natural order of creation a respectable place, in the minds of thinking people. From the fourth through the twelfth centuries, the literature on the human condition was one that dealt chiefly with its miseries, and the hard spiritual lot of lay society corresponded approximately to an equally hard physical lot. Birth, survival, and death, sickness and health—these stood out, marked by ceremonies and sadness, joy and despair, hysterical elation and sometimes numbed indifference. What was it to be born and to give birth, to eat and starve, and to die seven centuries ago in a distant part of the world?

Childbirth, from the sixth to the twentieth century reflected the vulnerability of the human condition. Children were born at home, often to a woman unattended, and the rate of infant mortality remained high. In a picture in the Moutier-Grandval Bible, produced at Tours around 840, there is depicted a sequence of events from God's creation of Adam to the expulsion of Adam and Eve from Eden. Immediately after their expulsion, Eve and Adam are shown in their new life, which is described in Scripture as hard and laboring. Eve sits with an infant, and Adam strikes at the ground with a mattock. Childbirth and labor are thus graphically portrayed as the two most striking consequences of the expulsion from Eden, and yet, perhaps because of the painter's antique models, Eve looks far from distressed and Adam resembles the hundreds of farmers whose labors were depicted in astrological charts and books of hours. As we have seen, both marriage and family life, on the one hand, and the notion of the dignity of labor, on the other, received particularly strong emphasis during the twelfth century, although the facts of childbirth and labor remained grim.

Infant mortality played a large role in maintaining population levels, and so did childhood mortality. Surviving children were usually given names that were common within a family or a region; sometimes the same forename was repeated several times in a single generation of a single family. The close wrapping of infants in swaddling clothes was followed by the dressing of children like miniature adults, although childhood was certainly recognized as a period in which play and other forms of diversion were particularly needed. Thus, through birth, infancy, and childhood, risk, the attentions of the midwife and wet nurse (when available), and early introduction to an adult world were generally the lot of the child. Learning, and other forms of introduction to the adult world, were taught in hard lessons of apprenticeship and servitude. Peasant children went into the fields early, and noble children learned the domestic and military arts equally early, usually from the tutelage of an adult and through imitation and practice rather than theory. Discipline was often harsh and precipitous, and praise was seldom forthcoming.

Innocent III, in his treatise *On the Contempt of the World,* says little of childhood, except to point out in passing that children are especially helpless, powerless, and subject to grotesque birth defects. The question of children also touches upon the obscure problem of birth control. Families of different social ranks might produce many children and lose many of them in infancy or childhood, for a certain number had to be reared in order for the family to continue. Abstention from sexual intercourse, attempts to abort children through diets, and the later cooperation of midwives in the murder of children by parents, either through studied neglect or willful act, illustrate the variety of means of birth control. One of the chief motifs in later witch trials was the ritual use of children, and midwives were commonly accused of murdering children. Yet, after the twelfth century, pictorial representations of childhood become more naturalistic, reflecting an interest and affection that must be noted. Pictures of the Virgin with the infant Jesus became popular, and the sentimental tales of atrocities committed against children indicate both a consciousness of childhood and an affection for children that we must also consider in discussing the harder aspects of infants' and children's lives in the twelfth and thirteenth centuries.

The thirteenth-century diet usually changed with the rhythms of the agricultural year. Not only the availability of different kinds of food at different times, however, but the grimmer prospect of famine and drought plagued early Europeans. When there was enough food, as there often was not, most people lived largely on grain foods: porridge, ale, and bread. Meat was limited in the peasant household but generally more available in the noble's. But after the early winter slaughtering of animals or between hunts, the meats eaten were usually smoked, salted, and spiced heavily. Vegetable protein appears to have been greater in the diet of the poor, and excessive animal protein may have contributed to the unique diseases that nobles suffered from. Dietary deficiencies often produced a social spectrum of diseases, those at a certain social level suffering from diseases caused in part by dietary deficiencies particular to a class. Food was plentiful at harvest time and through the early fall; bread, cheeses, and meat were generally available for all. As winter wore on, however, the meat for those who could obtain it became more heavily seasoned, the bread became coarser, and the vegetables, where there were any, were boiled. A peasant Christmas feast in thirteenth-century England is described as including bread and broth, two kinds of meat, and "various savoury messes." In the early fifteenth century, after the shortage of labor sent wages soaring, several writers complained of the new demands for food made by the peasants. Peasants in former days, they complained, were satisfied by simple fare such as bread, cheese, and a few boiled vegetables, the bread not made from wheat, but from corn or beans. Now, they complained, peasants demanded meat cut so large that its sides hung over the plate, bread made from finely milled wheat flour, and ale and wine. Food constituted part of the wage for laborers, and the right to attend certain feasts or to dine at the expense of someone else was greatly guarded. From coarse brown bread, cheese, a few vegetables, and an occasional fish or a piece of bacon to season the soup at the lowest level of society, and in a large part of society in hard times, to the elaborate feasts of the nobility, and even of peasant life in times of great prosperity, is a large step. Meat was perhaps the great dividing line; a wide range of fowl and fresh and salt fish appeared in far greater quantities on the tables of the wealthy. What might surprise us particularly is the evidence of highly spiced and seasoned meats, soups, and sauces, and the fondness for certain kinds of fowl, peacocks, for example, that are not now generally considered edible. Many people had dietary problems, and bad teeth were probably extremely common. The diet of early Europeans, when there was enough food to speak of a diet, ranged in kind, variety, and sufficiency across a wider spectrum than do most modern diets.

Just as few women at childbirth had any attendants, save for the occasional midwife or, more commonly, a woman friend or relative, so did few people ever see the doctor when they were ill. Learned medicine was taught in the universities, of which Salerno and Montpellier were well-known centers, but the surgeon's craft was generally handed down, sometimes with its secrets, from father to son or from master to apprentice. Medical practice, outside of surgery, was based on the theory of keeping the humors in balance within the body, and techniques of bloodletting, heating and chilling parts of the body, and using a range of *materia medica* from ointments and salves to various compounded drugs were all designed to maintain the balance of heat and cold, moisture and dryness that was considered ideal health.

The diseases from which people suffered tended to be related to both diet and hygiene. Circulatory and skin diseases, from dietary and vitamin deficiency, traumatic wounds of all sorts in most walks of life, and recurring fevers of various kinds appear to have been most prevalent. In a world with few hospitals and much of what we would call outpatient care, the illnesses of mankind were probably more visible in the streets and fields than they might be now, in the Western world, at least. Beggars, lepers, and the deformed, although restricted, wandered through towns or sat and begged food or alms. And although standards of personal hygiene were high in theory, with bathing, washing, and neatness receiving high praise from all sources, in practice, and among the poor, hygiene was maintained less assiduously. Lack of knowledge of dietary requirements, poor sanitation facilities, and dietary imbalance increased the odds against perfect health even for those lucky enough to avoid disease and wounds.

It was possible, however, to live to an old age, and humans in the eighties and nineties were not uncommon. Actuarily, however, the average life expectancy for a male in thirteenth-century England was around thirty-nine years, for a female somewhat less. Death and its attendant rituals were more evident and visible then than now. Although Innocent III says little in his treatise of childhood and young adulthood, except to catalogue the vices particular to each, he says much about the miseries of the rich and poor, the married and the single, illness, old age, the terrors of dreams, and sudden death. Physical debilitation and emotional disorders constitute the focus of his description of old age. Bodily pain, the clear sight of the dying conscience, self-judgment, and watching the demons ready to carry the soul away torment the dying. The whole of Innocent's third book of *On the Misery of the Human Condition* is devoted to the process of dying and the miseries of eternal punishment. After the thirteenth century, handbooks were prepared dealing with the *ars moriendi,* the proper method of dying. After death, a religious came to prepare the body, and a procession would take the corpse to its burial place, a great tomb in a church in the case of the prominent or wealthy person, a wooden box in a churchyard for most.

There were many claims extended upon the dead, and divine judgment was only one of them. Mortuary dues and items and sums owed to a lord, to a church, or even to those who prepared the body and accompanied it to burial all had to be paid. To visualize the afterlife became easier after the eleventh century, when scenes of the Last Judgment were carved over church doors to remind the penitents of what awaited them. Although artists could occasionally enliven the depiction of life in Heaven, it was the torments of the damned that achieved the greatest attention in sculpture, in manuscript illuminations, and in the enthusiastic rhetoric of preachers, particularly in the fourteenth and fifteenth centuries. The saved ascended to Abraham's bosom, there to await the Last Judgment; the damned descended immediately into Hell. There was, however, another disposition of souls, one with many links to those who still lived. Purgatory purged the spirits of those whose guilt had not been expiated in life. Prayers on earth, intercessions to the saints, masses, and charitable acts could all shorten the time spent in Purgatory; a distinctive link was thereby created between the dead and the living. In Dante's *Purgatorio* many of the dead in Purgatory complain bitterly that their families no longer pray for them and so do nothing to shorten their time of purgation. Many people were entered on the necrologies of monasteries so that prayers for their souls would be continued. Guilds, confraternities, and religious orders, as well as families, sponsored memorial services, and after the thirteenth century many wealthy people built chantries, chapels where memorial masses were continually said. The poor could afford only an occasional mass or offering, but, in one of the rare instances in which ecclesiastical theory might bring genuine consolation, the poor needed such prayers less than the rich. The story of Lazarus and Dives, the pauper and the rich man, was also carved on churches and painted in manuscripts. And even if the intention of this scene was to sober the thoughts of the rich as they passed, it may not be excessive to hope that the scene also consoled the spirits of the poor.

MARRYING AND GIVING IN MARRIAGE, FRIENDSHIP, LOVE, AND HATE

The emotional attitudes that colored personal relationships and social institutions appear to have changed considerably among Europeans between 1050 and 1250. The traditional patristic and scriptural hostility to sexual relationships endured for a long time, and not until 1215 was marriage established as a sacrament. This long history of nonsacramental status made marriage before the thirteenth century a purely lay institution, subject to temporal law only. Thus, marriage might not take place between a man and a woman if the woman wished to retain control of her own property, something she could not do in marriage; from the sixth to the twelfth centuries, in fact, the independence of woman is a striking aspect of European society. Marriage was, it may be suggested, one of those curious interstices in which ecclesiastical attitudes played little part before the late twelfth century; thus the marriage union was left open to change. Married clergy, a considerable problem during the Investiture Contest, disappeared only slowly during the twelfth and thirteenth centuries; before that period, the priest's wife played an important role in local societies. Since the specific process by which the clergy was juridically and socially separated from the laity did not culminate until the twelfth century, the clerical wives and concubines may well have had a quasi-sacral role in the societies in which they lived. Certainly the freedom of aristocratic women to act as regents for absent kings and emperors, to rule monasteries in which both male and female religious lived, to control—in at least one instance in the tenth century— the succession to the papacy itself—all these characteristics suggest that before the late twelfth century, women possessed a status sufficiently undefined to allow them great latitude in the expression of ecclesiastical and temporal power. Before the thirteenth century, women appear to have been fewer in number than men, more intensely sought after, and probably shorter-lived.

Before the thirteenth century, it appears, men brought dowries to the marriage, and after 1200 it seems that women did. This suggests that the ratio of women to men in society had reversed itself and that there were more women than men in the population during and after the thirteenth century. In a passage of the *Divine Comedy,* Dante discusses the Florence "of the good old days"—of the twelfth and early thirteenth centuries—and comments that daughters and sons were equally welcomed at birth into Florentine families; now, however (in the early fourteenth century), people wail and moan whenever a daughter is born, fearing that her dowry will bankrupt them. In the thirteenth and fourteenth centuries one of the most popular forms of charity was the establishment of funds to provide dowries for poor girls; the versatile St. Nicholas became associated with such charity.

One of the most interesting and important topics in the history of European society is that of the shift of sex roles and social status between the eleventh and the fourteenth centuries. Of the position of women, scholars have often pointed enthusiastically to the phenomena of "courtly love," the literary genre of antifeminist satire that sprang up in the twelfth, thirteenth, and fourteenth centuries, and the increasingly realistic and sympathetic depiction of woman in the visual and plastic arts of the twelfth and thirteenth centuries. Yet these avenues of research, which seem to reflect *both* a new sentimental and moral stature for women *and* an increasing savagery against them, certainly do not exhaust the evidence, nor may they always be interpreted unambiguously. The shift in sentiment that allowed poets and other individuals in real life to explore the emotional and psychological relationships between man and woman certainly mark a distinctive stage in the development of European sensibility, but they accompany in time a marked restriction of women's role in society. The statues of graceful Eves, Virgins, and female saints—and even the personifications of female vices—certainly mark a new sensitivity to the human body and a new sense of respect for the dignity of human status. But the rough depictions of woman in the early *chansons de geste* and the fierce representations of women in early sculpture and illumination, though not differentiating sexually between women and men, occurred during a period when women's access to political and ecclesiastical authority was much greater. And against the furious and learned antifeminism of such later tracts as the fifteenth-century *Hammer of Witches* or Johann Nider's *Formicarius*, the conventional patristic antifeminism of the eighth, ninth, and tenth centuries seems mild enough. To be sure, the place of women in society changed drastically in the twelfth and thirteenth centuries in many areas of life. But the gains represented by new emotional and psychological relationships, the sacramental status of marriage, the new perception of physical beauty, and new forms of legal protection must be considered against the indisputable losses: the exclusion from sacerdotal status, the reduction of political and economic power, and the loss of a former freedom as a result of changing sex roles.

To turn from the question of love and women's new status in other areas of activity to a single example of specific change, we may consider the case of Fontevrault. Founded by the popular reforming preacher Robert of Arbrissel around 1100, Fontevrault was part of a wide movement in the late eleventh and early twelfth centuries not only to alleviate the spiritual and material difficulties of women in a changing society, but to permit them to lead a life as a religious in ways uniquely suited to their needs. Of all the orders that developed with these intentions, however—Gilbertines, Premonstratensians, and the later half-affiliated Cistercian nunneries—only Fontevrault survived with its essential institutions intact. Reviving the old institution of the double monastery—one for men and one for women—Fontevrault continued to be ruled by its abbess, who controlled the convent, the monastery of canons attached to it, the leprosarium, and the house of St. Mary Magdalene, for reformed laywomen.

Located in the old diocese of Poitiers—where it was close to Chinon, later made famous by another woman, Joan of Arc, and to the infamous Loudun, which played its own inglorious role in the history of women during the seventeenth century—Fontevrault prospered during the twelfth century and attracted powerful and wealthy women as well as poor ones. The earliest abbesses, Hersende of Champagne and Petronilla, successfully saw to the survival and preservation of the monastery, and the enormous prestige of Robert of Arbrissel supported their work. King John of England spent some time there as a child, and in 1194 Eleanor of Aquitaine assumed the administration of the vast Angevin Empire on behalf of her son Richard I Lionheart from the security of Fontevrault. At Fontevrault she may have died, and at Fontevrault she certainly was buried, next to the tombs of her husband Henry II and her son Richard. The enduring success of Fontevrault helped support other aristocratic convents in France and England, and these institutions, often ignored by historians of religious life, remind us that they constituted an important place of refuge for women who could not or did not wish to participate in society in other ways.

For the question of women's voluntary participation in twelfth- and thirteenth-century society is complex. Convents and monasteries filled a real social need as well as a spiritual one. As women's status was changed, some took to the change less well than others. The social circumstances that produced a Heloise—an ecclesiastical family, ecclesiastical surroundings, a high degree of literacy, individual passion and wit, and an indelible stamp of personal independence—changed in the course of the twelfth century, and a convent emerged as one of the few places in which such women could fulfill their own intellectual and spiritual needs. Heloise died as the abbess of just such a community ruled by women, founded for her by Peter Abelard. Apart from the convent, there were few other roles for dissenting women to play. It is no accident that an extraordinarily high proportion of critics of different social classes were the women of these classes. In the early thirteenth-century epic poem *Parzival,* Parzival's mother, a noblewoman, takes her infant son from the royal court and flees into the forest to live in obscurity, "where he will never hear the name of knight." Of course, Parzival does become a knight, a particularly distinctive sort of knight, but his mother's rejection of her world is pronounced. In the case of heresy too, the heretical sects' willingness to educate girls and women, their lack of differentiation between men and women in the heretical hierarchies of perfection, and their many female patronesses all suggest a lively and troubled position of women in the twelfth and thirteenth centuries, more lively and complex than conventional histories of love and the arts often suggest.

From its early role as a vehicle for the transfer of property and as a strictly lay institution, marriage became the object of much of the devotional and juridical energies of twelfth- and thirteenth-century theologians and canon lawyers. The wide range of personal relationships on the one hand, and of purely family-arranged marriages on the other, gave way before clerical speculation on the nature of marriage, on the human will, on the technicalities of consummation, and on the impossible tangle of annulments, flaws in the relationship between the members of a conjugal union, and the status of marriage as a unique lay *ordo*. Again, in defining marriage the clergy at once *both* reflected aspects of a new sense of human dignity and responsibility *and* redefined the hitherto informal status of women partners in the marriage. Against this growing concern over the character of marriage and the partners' place in it, it is little wonder that many women retired—to convents such as Fontevrault, to heretical sects, to centers of Beguine activity in the Rhineland or southern France or Italy—or remained critics of society while still inside it, thereby feeding not only much antifeminist literature but the handbooks for wives and daughters that fourteenth- and fifteenth-century gentlemen wrote in such great numbers and lugubrious prose.

Sexual relationships, inside or outside of marriage, celibacy, and sex roles in society pose related and difficult questions. Sexual identity and sexual habits are as much a part of historical cultures as economic institutions or political theory, and in spite of much ink spilled over early Europeans' alleged double standards in these matters, it seems clear that celibacy was a viable, attractive, satisfying life for far many more people than it is today. The history of human sexuality has not yet been written, but when it is, those chapters devoted to the world of the Middle Ages will be complex. From the earliest period, the clergy denounced sins of the flesh, and yet sexual practices appear to have varied widely and freely, not only in the demimonde of wanton religious and standard-free laymen, but in the worlds of marriage and friendship as well. Homosexuality and heterosexuality may have seemed less distinct than they have since, and certainly the vocabulary of emotions reflects a sometimes shocking parallelism between devotional and erotic intensity. Certainly, impotence in marriage appears to have exercised the logic of canon lawyers considerably, and both intense revulsion toward and indiscriminate fondness for the flesh characterized the sexual practices of ecclesiastics and laypeople alike.

The range of human relationships is certainly not exhausted by a consideration of sexual and marital relationships and the changing sexual and social roles of women and men. For behind marriage and religious establishments lies the changing pattern of community associations, from the household to the monastery, and behind the heterosexual, homosexual, and asexual characteristics of individuals lies the broader pattern of emotional bonds, ranging from friendship and love to hate. Behind the institutional or personal expression of these relationships lies the question of the human personality itself and the ranges of its motivations and emotional spectrum.

The styles of interpreting Scripture and patristic literature that dominated European thought between the sixth and the thirteenth centuries provided for a limited, although distinctive, concept of human nature and theory of the human personality. Vices and virtues, the nature of sin, and the habit of regarding good and evil people in terms of a rigid set of typologies afforded little room for much expansion of the theory of personality. During the eleventh and twelfth centuries, however, the rise of the study of logic, new devotional movements, the perennial strain of individualism in Christian thought and its Jewish influences, the appearance of an Aristotelian psychology and its influence upon concepts of vices and virtues—all these influenced the general ideas of creation, nature, collective society, and the individual. It is important to remember that both new attitudes toward nature and the other intellectual and emotional changes of the twelfth and the thirteenth centuries shaped not only a new concept of individualism, but new concepts of society as well. The new sense of self and individuation that appeared in the twelfth century had deep and widespread roots in other forms of intellectual and social change, and it is in terms of these that the history of new forms of individualism and new ideas of the self must be considered.

A new idea of the self implies also the concept of other selves, and personal relations are an integral part of any investigation into the history of the individual and society between the twelfth and the nineteenth centuries. The history of friendship begins in the ordered, psychologically precocious society of the monastery, in which the writings of the ancients, the church fathers, and contemporary devotional stylists appealed in different ways to the unique religious communities that possessed different social bonds from those of the countryside or the early towns or courts. In the writings of such twelfth-century figures as Ailred of Riveaulx and St. Bernard, human friendship is explored on levels previously unknown in early European history. Neither the rough comradeship of the battlefield or the rustic court nor the daily personal encounters in villages or towns afforded the kinds of personal associations or the conceptual articulateness that the monasteries did, and monastic friendships offer strong evidence for changing concepts of self and changing forms of human association. Outside the monasteries, the society of court and city after the twelfth century also offered opportunities for new sets of human relationships. The complex life of courtly society, the relationships among students at the new schools and universities, the congregations of patrician elites, religious confraternities, or even heretical sects contained new opportunities for one to discover the self and others. The increasing frequency of personal memorials and family and guild prayers for the dead, and the realism of donor portraits in thirteenth-century church art suggest a change in the most basic forms of human association and in the most basic notions of the human self from the twelfth century on.

CEREMONY AND FESTIVAL: THE HUMAN YEAR

Physical circumstances and personal associations and feelings mark only two of the many aspects that may be said to constitute the human condition in any age. A third is the way societies mark their time, not against an absolute mathematical calendar, but against a functional calendar comprising economic, religious, and social values and expressed in ceremony and festival—in other words, the whole process by which a society perceives the passing of time to be of importance to its normal patterns of life. We have already considered, briefly, one way of perceiving the passage of time—in the work of chroniclers. In the history of organized states, regnal years, succession ceremonies, and other rituals surrounding life in a royal household constitute another form of marking political time. In monasteries, the normal daily round of scheduled prayers imparted an impression of stability and regularity—almost of antitime—at least in those institutions that followed a regular order of prayers. Chronicles, kingdoms, and monasteries, however, offer only a few examples of concepts of time and their importance to people's understanding of their own lives. In this section we will focus upon the human year as it was lived by peasants and townsmen, merchants and clergy, the lower and more numerous orders of society.

Not only were the rhythm and segmentation of the peasant's and townsman's year different, but the marking of the calendar year itself varied throughout early Europe. January 1, the opening of the year according to the Roman calendar, remained widely used in towns, but in other areas the beginning of the year might be March 1 (as it remained in Venice until the end of the eighteenth century), March 25 (as in the Rhineland, Italy, and England from the twelfth to the eighteenth centuries), or, elsewhere in Europe, any of a number of different dates, including Easter (a movable new year), September 1, or December 25. For most people, the 365¼ day solar Julian calendar meant far less than the functional division of the year into seasons and, less important, months. The various institutions that marked social life had calendars of their own: courts often observed a tripartite year; rent payments in rural areas often were made on the basis of a two-season year, winter beginning at Michaelmas (September 29) and summer on Hockday (the second Tuesday after Easter). Many feasts were necessarily movable because they were based on Easter, and so the year could shift perceptibly depending upon the occurrence of the major movable feasts. The months were thought of less as firm parts of a twelve-part year than as phases of the sun's journey through the signs of the zodiac, from Aries through Pisces. On astrological calendars the signs of the zodiac are linked to appropriate labors for each of the months, and illustrations of these labors are among our most important examples of the visual representation of peasant life. At the other end of the social scale, the periodical holding of great formal courts marked out the royal year, and in England the great festivities of Christmas, Whitsuntide, and Pentecost displayed the powerful presence of the king in different parts of his realm.

For the farmer, the great cycle of the year focused upon Michaelmas, September 29, when the harvest had been brought in, accounts had been paid, festivities were held, and the sober thoughts of winter were predominant. From Michaelmas to Martinmas (November 11), winter planting took place. The great twelve-day Christmas feast extended from December 25 to January 6. From January 6 to Easter extended the somber season of Lent, in which Shrove Tuesday, the day before Ash Wednesday, was as important as Ash Wednesday itself, because it represented the last shriving, or confession, before the formal penitential season. Hocktide marked the resumption of work after the Easter festival and opened the most important and busy of the seasons, when plowing, weeding, and the extensive preparations for the harvest were begun. Between St. John's day (July 24) and Lammas (August 1) the farmer's work was most intense, and between Lammas and Michaelmas the reward or poverty of the working year became generally known. Thus, the rural calendar measured a distinctive kind of year from September to Septem-

Plate 19 courtesy Anderson, Art Reference Bureau.

THE ROAD TO THE WORLD. In the fourteenth and fifteenth centuries a number of painters and illuminators succeeded in creating images of the relation between the spiritual and temporal life and the virtues of civil society that still evoke the ideal they sought to serve. The Spanish Chapel in the Church of Santa Maria Novella, painted by Andrea da Firenze around 1366-1368, was not only intended to glorify the Dominican Order but to display the order and hierarchy of the world in which the Order worked (Plate 19). Around 1420, a painter known as The Master of Flémalle produced the Merode altarpiece (Plate 20), whose marvelous depiction of the Annunciation in the setting of fifteenth-century Flanders included the town, the donors, and the irreducible details of concrete daily life in order to heighten the significance of a transcendent spiritual event. For all of the security and stability that these paintings depict, there were other sides as well to fifteenth-century attitudes toward experience, and one of the most popular and compelling figures of late medieval art is the figure of Fortune, who unpredictably disposes earthly affairs, raising and lowering the poor and the mighty at her whim (Plate 21). This depiction of Fortune, from a fifteenth-century manuscript in the British Library, suggests the increasing complexity of fifteenth-century perceptions of life and the leaving room in otherwise tidy systems of causation for the unpredictable and the capricious. In this respect, Medieval and Renaissance writers and painters shared a common attitude.

Plate 20 courtesy the Metropolitan Museum of Art, The Cloisters Collection, purchase.

Plate 21 reproduced by permission of the British Library Board. Royal Ms. 180 II, f.30v.

ber, and was marked by the necessities of the agricultural life rather than by the great ecclesiastical or civil feasts. This was the year familiar to most Europeans before the nineteenth century.

The Church's year did not fit the agricultural year exactly. Its cycle was ritually repetitive of the life of Christ and the Church. From Advent to Christmas, the penitential season of Lent, festive Easter, Pentecost, the great high summer holidays, and back to penitential Advent, which started the next year, the ecclesiastical year altered seasons of penitence with seasons of joy, continually fought against the oversecularization of ecclesiastical feasts, particularly when they coincided with pauses in the work year, and witnessed the subtle blending of ancient and recent festive customs on days that had marked the human year long before the Church redesignated them holy days. All Hallows Eve, Midsummer Day, and Whitsuntide all bore deep marks of pre-Christian festivals, as, of course, did Christmas.

Between the agricultural and the ecclesiastical years there existed other, equally important but less formalized calendars. Feasts at which the normal order of things was turned upside-down, such as the feasts of fools or the plow-days, and the comic dimensions even of formal ecclesiastical or civil holidays are extremely important in understanding the individual's attitude toward himself and society. Many formal feasts had comic dimensions; in particular, the religious plays that were attached to town and rural holidays possessed strongly comic and satiric veins, which were often defended against clerical criticism and upper-class indignation. Medieval festival, comedy, and parody have had few historians, yet in order to understand the immensely important role of the various forms of comic expression in the fifteenth, sixteenth, and seventeenth centuries, some familiarity with the cycle of ceremony and festival, parody and comedy, is essential. As the fine Russian literary historian Mikhail Bakhtin remarked, "To ignore or to underestimate the laughing people of the Middle Ages also distorts the picture of European culture's historic development." Over and against, and yet at the same time a part of, the expansive expressions of penitence in procession, flagellation, and liturgy must be set the laughter, parody, satire, and ritual topsy-turviness that also constituted an important part of life and time.

There were, of course, other calendars as well: winter and summer marked the sailing seasons for mariners and traders; each diocese had its own local calendar of religious feasts; university terms and vacations, the suitable times for pilgrimages, and the great and small feasts of localities and of all Christendom all constituted part of the human year. In 1378, in Beverley in England, this small feast was observed:

> The Guild of St. Helen and St. Mary . . . have yearly on St. Helen's Day [September 3] a procession headed by one old man with a cross and another with a spade and a youth dressed as Queen Helen—all in token of the finding of the cross. The guild brethren and sisters follow to the church where a solemn mass is sung, and each offers one penny.

There were thousands of such small feasts marking out the year throughout Christendom, some accompanied with far more elaborate rituals than the two old men and the youth. On the opposite end of the scale, Pope Boniface VIII instituted the Holy Year in 1300. The original intention to have a Holy Year every hundred years was modified by the disasters of the plague, and the second Holy Year was held in 1350. Subsequent Holy Years were held in 1383, 1400, and 1450, thereby setting the fifty-year cycle of years of special penitential expressions and special indulgences for Christians.

Thus, in the general disorder of precise measurements of space and time, there existed as many ways of marking the passing of time as there existed social ranks, lives, and regions. Yet even beside the great cycles of agricultural and ecclesiastical markings of time, there existed others, some small, some large, and all of them reflect, from various perspectives, the way in which the rhythms of life and work, penitence and joy, birth and death dominated people's perception of time and made the markings of the year indelibly human markings and the year a human year.

25

THE WORLD OF DANTE

ITALY AND THE ITALIAN CITY-REPUBLICS

The wreckage of Hohenstaufen Sicily and South Italy, the troubles of the papacy in central Italy, the rise of Aragón, and the conflicting interests of the great Italian maritime cities of Genoa, Pisa, and Venice during the second half of the thirteenth century framed and influenced the world of the city-republics of northern Italy. From the tenth to the thirteenth centuries the towns of northern Italy had struggled to win the independence of their communal associations from the traditional authority of nobles and bishops. The first communes were composed of urban nobles, and in the course of the late twelfth and thirteenth centuries power within the commune was contested between the earlier town patriciates and the groups of merchant patricians whose economic power backed their bid for political authority. The thirteenth century witnessed the growing economic power of Italian urban banking houses, industrial centers, and merchant oligarchies, as the wool, salt, oil, wine, alum, and moneychanging businesses brought increased wealth into the ruling classes of city after city. The variety of urban response to such economic and political turbulence, however, should be carefully marked. There was no "standard" development of Italian cities. Some, like Florence and Milan, grew great. Others, such as Pisa and, later, Siena, declined. Genoa turned to the western Mediterranean and the Atlantic as Venetian dominance of the eastern Mediterranean trade grew greater. Venice turned itself into a giant communal enterprise whose fortunes were supervised closely by an aristocratic board of directors, the Great Council, membership in which was restricted after 1294 to those who had already had an ancestor on it before that date. The closing of the Great Council of Venice, Genoese entrepreneurial activities in Spain, southern France, and England, Florentine industry, and Sienese finances offer some picture of the economic variety of late thirteenth-century Italy and the world it included, and such narrative histories as Salimbene's *Chronicle* and the later parts of Giovanni Villani's *Chronicle* of Florence reflect much of the life of the northern Italian cities.

Urban statutes, the idea of urban history, local city festivals, pride in city and surrounding countryside, country estates owned and lived in by the urban rich—all these mark the civic consciousness of northern Italian towns in the late thirteenth century. Earlier in the century, the great struggle between popes and emperors had divided the towns and the population within single towns into supporters of the pope (and his Welf protégés; hence the designation of the Guelf party) and of the emperor (the Hohenstaufen castle of Waiblingen had given its name to the Ghibelline party). Some cities became traditionally Guelf, exiling the Ghibelline opponents, and others became Ghibelline. Some cities shifted allegiance many times during the century, as exiles joined enemy cities to oust the incumbents of their own. Both pope and emperors actively supported their own factions in the towns, sometimes with fearsome results. The internal dissension within the cities, however, was not strictly the result of Guelf and Ghibelline rivalry. In fact, the designations Guelf and Ghibelline came to mean less and less as the century wore on, reflecting more and more traditional alignments of local political authority. Not all the nobles were Ghibelline, nor were all the merchants and financiers Guelf.

In regard to economics, the cities also presented a varied picture. Long-distance trade and large-scale finance have long appealed to historians as being characteristic of such cities as Florence and Siena, but local trade and other commercial products besides those of the great wool industry and its affiliated industries also occupied much commercial energy. Grain, salt, oil, and cloth for purely local markets occupied the same families and companies who dealt in long-range commercial and financial exchange, and for every agency such companies managed in

England, France, Germany, or China, they managed many more in the towns of Italy themselves.

The nobles and the great merchants, the *grandi* and the *grassi*, struggled among themselves for power, but more frequently both banded together against the *popolo minuto*, the "little people," those who worked in the lesser crafts or constituted the bulk of the labor force. Political reforms between 1250 and 1350 generally readjusted the ruling component of a given town without offering substantial power to the majority of inhabitants. Family rivalry, neighborhood loyalties, the role of representatives of particular sections of the *contado*—the surrounding countryside—within the central city—all of these elements played crucial roles in day-to-day political affairs. The great oppositions of Guelf-Ghibelline, noble-merchant, and laymen-clergy more often conceal minute political changes than illuminate them. Each city-republic controlled its own affairs and those of a shifting region around it. These small political worlds possessed their own dynamics, far more powerful than those of the great movements that have often been given credit for the political history of the northern Italian cities throughout the thirteenth century.

Civic buildings, walls, bridges, cathedrals, and market places with their appurtenant structures constituted the common enterprises of towns. Taxation, regulation of political participants, recruiting urban militias, and establishing corps of notaries, judges, and teachers defined the individual's place in town society. Many towns with a population of just over 5,000 were overshadowed by a few great towns such as Florence and Milan, each comprising about 100,000 inhabitants in 1300. More towns—for instance, Padua—prospered in the 10,000–40,000 population range. Not only growth, but also wealth on the part of a larger proportion of the citizen body, characterized the towns of northern Italy.

The citizen body, those with political rights, was far smaller than the whole population, and its changing composition constituted the real focus of political rivalry, discontent, and conflict. Not only did those citizens with interests in distant lands have to be able to supervise their interests in their own town, but colonial administrators, men whose business or service in the church took them far away from their own cities, and financiers had both links with distant parts and interests in a single town. The population of the town was frequently replenished from the countryside, not only from the poorer rural classes, the population source most frequently studied, but from the wealthy landholding classes as well. Thus, the identity of an urban population at any given moment might be a mixture of older families, recent arrivals, travelers, merchants, ecclesiastics, and entertainers. The attitudes of the citizens toward such a mixture became important, because they determined the recent arrivals' status. Towns even conferred knightly status when they wished to—or needed to. One of the most frequently used terms in restive communes was that of "new people," *gente nuova*, meaning both newly rich persons scrambling for a share of political power and newly arrived individuals who had difficulty finding unexploited work. Pride of family and pride of city are both reflected in late thirteenth- and early fourteenth-century literature, and family survival as well as family antiquity occupied the concerns of many people on many levels of society. Especially articulate were members of families whose earlier status was higher than at present. These individuals regarded changing populations and changing power structures with acerbic distaste, and some writers, including Dante, attributed the troubles of many cities to the unbridled energies of "new people," who refused to follow the traditionally honorable customs of earlier town cultures. Indeed, the habit of looking back upon "the good old days," in which life appeared to have been simpler and plainer, increased in the late thirteenth and fourteenth centuries—precisely during a period when the wealth and struggles of "new people" were in the process of enriching the towns, patronizing great artists, exercising their own political judgment, and engaging in the old struggle for power between the nobility and the urban mercantile patriciate. Herein lay two of the greatest cultural problems of the northern Italian towns at the turn of the fourteenth century: the adaptation of old wealth and power to the changing population pattern that produced new demands for power, and the failure to conceptualize an explanation for change that did not elevate the past over the present. Dante, for instance, never found a solution, and the constant round of revolution, exile of the defeated, planned reconquest, and shifting loyalties prevented the creation of a tolerated political opposition within the towns. The very concept of a "loyal opposition," a touchstone of modern constitutional theory, was never successfully formulated in the thirteenth century, either in the towns of Italy or in the public assemblies of France and England. Those who opposed the ruling authorities were pejoratively called "parties," "factions," or "traitors." The growth of a concept of party or division within the polity that could remain loyal without compromising its opposition to the ruling party did not emerge in European states until the eighteenth century. "Party" and "faction" remained until then highly pejorative terms. The political universe of the northern Italian towns was unitary.

The forms in which political authority was expressed in many towns varied throughout the north. In some towns, two or more *consuls* ruled, sometimes with the advice of the popular assembly, sometimes with (or under) the direction of a smaller council. The procedure of election to these councils was extremely varied among different towns. Highly complex forms of indirect election, including the drawing of lots, combined with direct balloting, each time with a shifting electorate, reflect the towns' fear of election rigging. A general observation about the political life these institutions and procedures reflect would have to point out that such a fear, although frequently justified, created an unwieldy form of government in many places. The balance of voices reflected in the proliferation of councils is also reflected in the institution of the podestà (derived from the Latin *potestas*, power), a single official, usually appointed for a year and nearly always from another city, who held administrative authority, particularly judicial, within the city. This outsider, who remained subject in policy decisions to the councils, was virtually untouchable: he brought his own staff with him, lived by himself, was prohibited from entertaining or being entertained by citizens during his term of office, and did not receive the last installment of his salary until his records had been carefully checked. More and more of the *podestà,* many of whom made a profession out of such work, became trained lawyers, and their profession, although well paying, was highly dangerous.

Indirect taxes, hearth and property taxes, and, increasingly in the thirteenth and fourteenth centuries, public debts raised the funds necessary to administer the city. Public buildings, walls, fountains, bridges, and some churches all fell within the scope of the commune, as did salaries for officials, military financing, and the salaries for teachers in the city's schools, including, if the city contained a university, the salaries of professors. Citizenship, which was granted with increasing care, was sometimes given to university professors as a mark of respect, and also to hold them in the face of offers from elsewhere. The concept of citizenship, moreover, was one of the most precocious intellectual developments of urban political thought.

At the turn of the fourteenth century, the cities of northern Italy present a variegated picture. They differed widely in size and constitutional structure, in dependence upon other, more powerful towns (some cities were virtually independent), in long-range financial, commercial, and diplomatic affairs, in the degree of city control of social and economic life, in the degree of civic consciousness, in relations with the countryside and neighboring towns, and in levels of education and artistic patronage. They were small societies, but the degree of political energy required to mobilize their resources and conduct policy, their high consciousness of the dangers of the surrounding world, and their control of ecclesiastical authority all reflect their precocious development as political societies. The wealth brought in from trade, industry, and finance, the necessity of having a "foreign" policy and a militia, the needs of public financing, and the concept of what a later lawyer called "the city, a prince unto itself," made many of these cities resemble later larger kingdoms. The political instability and constitutional crises to which the cities were usually prone reflects not so much political immaturity, but political creativity. After the Church, the northern Italian towns may be said to have created the first European states.

CIVIC CULTURE

Population and economic growth, the long struggles for independence, and the very experience of living within the physical city contributed to the development of an urban culture that expressed itself in various ways, from education to history writing, from architecture to public ceremonies. The necessities of town government produced the great town halls that still survive in many of even the smallest towns, as do the carefully planned and maintained public squares. Pride in the physical appearance of the city dates from very early in communal history, and statutes protecting the physical city, from measures concerning hygiene to those concerning aesthetics, appear continually on the statute books of many towns. The towns were responsible too for much church building. Citizen committees managed the work and commissioned the artists who decorated the churches. The contacts many cities had with Byzantium and the east and France and the north and west brought many diverse influences into the towns, and these too contributed to the selection and planning of buildings and the artistic themes that were embodied in them. The cities knew of individual artists by reputation, and many of the greatest works of Duccio di Boninsegna, Arnolfo di Cambio, and Giotto were done on civic commissions. The decoration of churches expressed the spiritual values of the town, and the decoration of public buildings expressed the town's sense of its own history and its own self-image.

There is no more striking example of the liveliness of urban artistic patronage than the series of frescoes produced by Ambrogio Lorenzetti in the Palazzo Publico of Siena in 1338–1340. Lorenzetti's frescoes on the subject of good and bad government offer a vast and extraordinarily detailed exposition of the self-image of the city of Siena. Theological personifications, political abstractions, and gigantic figures are set off against a highly intricate depiction of the life of the city and its inhabitants, from masons and carpenters to farmers, traders, hunters, and governing officials. Although these frescoes present a self-image particularly dear to the rulers of the commune, they focus in a single work the spiritual and secular values that represent the unique urban consciousness of the early fourteenth century.

Fountains, piazzas, public buildings, and bridges were occasions for the city not only to enhance the aesthetic quality of the town plan, but to convey visually that idea of the city held by the dominant classes. Visual propaganda extended also to the "pictures of infamy" that were commissioned by the towns for the purpose of depicting the particular horrors of individual crimes. They consisted of paintings in a public place depicting the criminal in the act for which he was later punished. These pictures seem to have been painted less frequently after 1300. Such pictures also contributed to the images of "bad government" found in public frescoes and sculpture of the period. Evil could be visualized as dramatically as good in the late thirteenth century, and just as the town officials wished to increase the "honor" of the city by beautifying it and portraying its most cherished values in painting, so they wished to remind the citizen body of the unique dangers to which the city was exposed. These "pictures of infamy" may well have influenced some of Dante's descriptions of the *Inferno*.

The culture represented by plastic and visual art, secular and spiritual building, and pride in the city did not cease with the field of literature. The *Biccierna,* the account books of Siena, have as covers lively pictures of city life, and handbooks for the instruction of *podestà* abounded, as did town histories after the late thirteenth century. The most famous of these, Giovanni Villani's *Chronicle* of Florence, reflects pride in both the past and present of the town and joins other literary works "in praise of cities" that survive from Milan, Padua, and elsewhere.

The quality of urban culture, of course, touched private as well as public expression. The schools, intellectuals, clergy, and entertainers of the towns were receptive to outside influences in their verse and thought, and northern Italy experienced two powerful influences in the late thirteenth century. From southern France the diminished Languedocian culture offered verse techniques and cultural values that were adopted by such poets as Sordello da Goito, a northern Italian who lived in Provence and wrote in Occitanian. From the court circle of Frederick II in Sicily and South Italy there emerged, in the poems of Pierre della Vigne and others, the first Italian adaptation of the literary techniques of Occitania. These two influences, both courtly, ornate, and containing ethical as well as lyric and erotic strains, were available to the poets of the northern cities, and in the second half of the thirteenth century several of them took up the themes of their literary predecessors in Occitania and Sicily.

By the late thirteenth century in northern Italy, the literary influence of Occitania and Sicily had shaped what contemporaries called the *dolce stil nuovo*, "the sweet new style," in which amatory, ethical, and philosophical literary themes blended in a kind of lyric poetry that praised love and women while exploiting these experiences as philosophical and spiritual springboards for the male sensibility. Guido Guinizelli (1230–1275) and Guittone d'Arezzo (1225–1293) contributed to the development of these themes in Tuscan verse, and Dante Alighieri (1265–1321) brought them to a high level of achievement. But philosophical lyrics and love songs were not the only literary occupations of learned and talented Florentines at the end of the thirteenth century. In fact, the literary polish of the former has often cast the latter into unjust obscurity. Cecco d'Angiolieri, a correspondent of Dante's, wrote scurrilous lyrics against his family, against the manners of foreigners, against the whole world—bitter, wildly lyrical sonnets that do not easily bear translation and resemble no other literary work as much as that of Dante himself at his most invective and, two centuries later, François Villon. At the opposite end of the lyric spectrum is the brooding lyric genius of the Franciscan poet Jacopone da Todi (1230–1306). Jacopone, who had been a notary before the death of his wife turned him to the spiritual wing of the Franciscans, brought a lyric genius to poems written against worldly vanities, Pope Boniface VIII, and the follies of his own time, but also to lyrics meditating upon the Virgin and the Child Jesus. Jacopone's lyric skills are strangely akin to those of Cecco d'Angiolieri.

The variety of secular and religious culture includes, of course, more than the different ends of the aesthetic and lyric spectrum of verse. St. Francis of Assisi left some meditative lyrics, particularly the *Canticle of the Sun,* which convey vitality and love with a sense of plain-spokenness, and the accomplished Roman lawyer and professor, Cino da Pistoia, also left lyrics of high quality. Lovato dei Lovati, the Paduan judge who was a contemporary of Jacopone's, wrote on both the meters of Seneca's tragedies and the political character of his own age. Albertino Mussato (1261–1329), another contemporary of Dante's, rose from an impoverished childhood to become diplomat, historian, playwright in classical forms, and the first poet to receive the laurel crown since Statius in the fourth century. Thus, in the late thirteenth-century Italian towns, poetry, spiritual expressiveness, invective, wit, and art were common possessions of remarkable people from all walks of life. Not merely the *dolce stil nuovo,* then, but the rich variety of verbal expression, from the *laude* of St. Francis to the scholarly Latin prose of Lovato, created in northern Italy an extraordinarily expressive literary culture, one reflected in prose in the collection of saints' lives by Jacopo da Varazze of Genoa and in the learned encyclopedia of Dante's early friend Brunetto Latini. Two of Dante's contemporaries, aside from those cited above, deserve mention as well.

Dino Compagni and Giovanni Villani were laymen who wrote historical accounts of the Florentine experience at the turn of the fourteenth century. The politically active Compagni (1266–1324) was a friend of Dante's and shared similar literary and intellectual interests with the great poet. Compagni's *Chronicle of Events Occurring in His Own Time* is a vivid account of personalities and political crises in Florence at the end of the thirteenth and beginning of the fourteenth centuries. Villani (1270–1348) spent his life as a merchant and developed great interest in Florence and the world around it. Like many other Florentines, Villani mixed business with political activity, serving in a number of offices in the city until his death from plague. In 1300 Pope Boniface VIII proclaimed a Holy Year, offering particular indulgences to all those making the pilgrimage to Rome. The success of the declaration was spectacular; crowds thronged to the city, and papal prestige was vastly, though briefly, increased. Villani was among those in Rome in 1300, and among his impressions was this:

> Beholding the great and ancient things which are [in the city], reading of the great deeds of the Romans, and considering that our great city of Florence, the daughter and creation of Rome, was ascending to greatness while Rome was declining, [I decided] to bring together in this chronicle all the beginnings of the city of Florence and then to set forth in detail the doings of the Florentines.

Villani's *Chronicle* began with an account of the Tower of Babel in traditional fashion, but the last six books of his work, covering the period from the arrival of Charles of Anjou in 1265 to 1348, offer a detailed and universal portrait of the city of Florence, one that is enriched by Villani's broad interest in such diverse topics as Asia and the complexities of commerce and trade. Villani also depicts well-known figures from Florence, and his portrait of Dante is particularly moving. Like Dante and others, Villani wrote in Tuscan, and the literary flowering of Tuscan that occurred in the late thirteenth and early fourteenth centuries is not the least striking aspect of the urban culture of the northern Italian towns during this period.

The economic, social, and political life of the northern Italian towns afforded much subject matter for these towns' thinkers, as well as preachers, artists, and chroniclers. The portraits in Compagni's and Villani's works are strikingly naturalistic, and in the portraits of donors of churches and of public officials of the same period, we find the same representation of individuality and uniqueness. Dante's *Divine Comedy* owes much to the literary and artistic works of his own lifetime, which reveal that others besides the great poet were vitally concerned with the great and small issues of the day, and that the cultural world of these cities was a lively and exhausting one in which religious and secular values were inextricably intermingled, the one set coloring the other. Eminent and unknown laymen listened to lectures in the Dominican church of Santa Maria Novella, by such distinctive thinkers as Remigio de' Girolami, and in the Franciscan church of Santa Croce. These great churches, as well as the great cathedral of Santa Maria del Fiore and the third circle of city walls, were all built within Dante's lifetime, giving Florence at the turn of the fourteenth century the air not of an ancient city, in spite of Villani, but of a strikingly modern one. Florence literally took shape under the eyes of the writers, artists, and preachers who were among the most eloquent praisers of the city and its life.

Religious fraternities, communal organizations that supervised the construction of urban churches, drinking and gaming clubs, masters' guilds, and literary circles divided and subdivided the social life of the towns. Secular triumphs inspired religious patronage; religious sentiment governed many aspects of secular life. By the fourteenth century, the life of the city, its civic spirit, had come to include religion and secular affairs as well. In the eyes of citizens and strangers alike, the towns of northern Italy possessed a distinctive culture, and such works as Lorenzetti's frescoes on good and bad government and the *Divine Comedy* reflect that culture in all its diversity.

EXUL IMMERITUS

No single figure represents and transcends the cultural world of the northern Italian towns more strikingly than Dante Alighieri, and no single literary or artistic work reflects the intellectual and political movements between 1150 and 1300 in greater detail and artistic force than does Dante's great poem, the *Divine Comedy*.

Dante was born in 1265 to a family that claimed descent from the earlier Florentine nobility but in Dante's youth experienced a brief period of economic prosperity through money lending. Certainly, the family's status remained modest, and Dante's marriage to Gemma di

Manetto, a member of a minor branch of the great Donati family, indicates only a modest social status. Even minor respectability afforded many opportunities to Florentine citizens, however. Dante pursued a course of studies, probably in Florence, and in 1289 he participated in the Florentine defeat of Arezzo at the battle of Campaldino. By that date his earliest literary work, several lyric poems, had attracted the attention of a talented and influential group of Florentine writers, and his friendships with the great lyric poet Guido Cavalcanti, the chronicler Dino Compagni, and the encyclopedist Brunetto Latini date from these years.

Dante was thus exposed both to a wide literary circle, as well as the wider circle of acquaintances that a man of letters encountered in the city, and to the new sensibility expressed in contemporary love lyrics. In his own life, the figure of Bice Portinari, later the wife of Simone dei Bardi, became his ideal woman, and after her death in 1290 Dante wrote a short account of her role in his personal spiritual and intellectual development in verse and prose, *The New Life (La Vita Nuova)*, which he completed in 1292. Not only are the verses in this work the indication of a major poetic talent, but the development of Bice into Beatrice, Dante's own spiritual guide, foreshadows her role in the *Comedy*. Yet Dante's development during this period was not solely that of poet and philosopher. Between 1295 and 1300 he held various political offices, and, as did other men of letters, he enrolled in the guild of apothecaries and physicians. Membership in a guild was essential for holding political office, however, and there is no evidence that Dante ever practiced the craft. The fortunes of Florence were insecure during Dante's terms of public service. Boniface VIII, the Black faction of the Guelf party that dominated Florence, and the royal house of France were involved in complex intrigues, and Dante's term of prior in June and August, 1300, revealed to him the dangers surrounding the city. In 1301, while Dante was serving as ambassador from the city to Rome, the Black Guelfs seized power, attacked their enemies, and banished Dante from the city *in absentia*, citing several charges of political corruption on his part that would have sufficed for his execution had he returned.

From 1302 to 1304, Dante wandered throughout northern Italy, serving as an advisor to the exiled White Guelf faction in its quest to restore itself to power in Florence. Shortly after 1304, however, Dante broke with his fellow exiles, whose shortsightedness, greed, and self-interest he later denounced bitterly in the *Comedy*. Between 1304 and 1310, Dante wandered even wider, moving from court to court, experiencing both the pain of exile and the fitful patronage of local princes. When Emperor Henry VII descended into Italy, Dante joined his cause and became a letter writer on the emperor's behalf. The early years of his exile had produced the unfinished treatise on the Italian vernacular, *De vulgari eloquentia*, and the long, unfinished collection of philosophical poems and commentaries, *The Convivio*. Dante's letters on behalf of Henry VII, however, reflect a more prophetic strain, and his later letters, written when Henry's cause had failed, contain bitter denunciations of those whom Dante held responsible not only for the emperor's failure but for the chaos and disorder of Italian life.

From 1310 to his death in September, 1321, Dante lived at the courts of various patrons, most notably that of Can Grande della Scala at Verona and that of Guido da Polenta at Ravenna, where he died and is buried. During the last decade of his life, and possibly earlier, he worked on his great poem, the *Comedy*, a vast vision of Hell, Purgatory, and Heaven in which he organized and analyzed the events of his life and his time by bringing to bear a vast intelligence and one of the greatest poetic voices the world has ever known. Citizen, scholar, man of letters, philosophical lover, and exile, Dante illuminates, not as a type but as a distinctive, compelling individual, the life of the cities in which he lived and the force of the culture that he shared and helped shape.

Several times he attempted to negotiate with Florence for his return to the city, but the parties never reached terms that Dante could accept. His exile and pilgrimage became for Dante a metaphor of justice; *exul immeritus,* "an undeserving exile," he called himself, condemning in passionate and eloquent language the disorder of justice that, in his vision, prevented mankind from governing itself properly. And from his exile there emerged the great poem that represents the culmination of his visionary genius.

26

MATERIAL CIVILIZATION IN CRISIS:

The Fourteenth Century

FAMINE, PLAGUE, AND WARFARE

The expansion of cultivated land between the tenth and the fourteenth centuries increased Europe's food supply and population, and the increased quantity of food and the variety of cereal and leguminous crops improved the European diet. Population growth and the clearing of wilderness areas, the beginnings of specialized commercial agriculture, and the growth of urban populations established complex patterns of supply and demand, and cities in particular came to depend upon the importation of food from great distances. Neither the population increase nor the growth of agricultural productivity, however, were uniform across Europe, nor were they necessarily uniform even among neighboring regions in the same territory. Prosperous, well-populated villages located on productive, easily cultivated land were rarely far from marginal settlements on land of limited productivity whose populations barely grew at all. The system of food production and supply was extensive, but it was not secure, and it was highly vulnerable. The greatest achievement of the period between the tenth and the fourteenth centuries, the successful cultivation of extensive tracts of forest, swamp, and wasteland, spread human settlements into regions never before cultivated. Even internal colonization, the creation of new communities within settled territories, as we have seen, became a profitable enterprise for lords and peasants alike. But the problem of the overextension of dependence on distant places for food supplies remained considerable, and even small-scale disasters could easily threaten the complex, vigorous, yet demographically and agriculturally fragile world of Europe.

In the Book of Revelations, the figures of the Four Horsemen let loose to afflict the earth had traditionally been associated with death, famine, pestilence, and war. The art of the fourteenth and fifteenth centuries abounds with the depiction of these figures, and in the course of the fourteenth century the effects of famine, pestilence, and war plunged material civilization into a great crisis. Population levels fell, land turned back to waste, and the overextended system of agricultural production virtually collapsed.

The pulsations of climate that had produced a mild period in Europe between 100 B.C and 1200 A.D. began to change in the thirteenth century. The changes that occurred, however, did not instantly create colder temperatures, shorter summers, and more severe winters. The signs of change came, rather, in an increasing unpredictability of weather patterns. Extremely good years were followed by inexplicably bad ones; a series of heavy rains that rotted crops and leached the earth might last for several years, to be followed by improved weather for a decade or more. Europeans began to experience not the sudden reversal of beneficial conditions, then, but the intermittent severe conditions that might freeze or inundate vineyards and grain fields for a season or two.

The effects of such changes were felt most quickly in the former marginal lands that required intensive cultivation and whose margin of productivity was small, even in the best of times. Famine had been a constant danger, even in times of prosperity, and from 1290 on, famine appears to have occurred more regularly. From 1309 to 1314, however, extremely poor crops and a series of long, destructive rains posed a threat of famine on a larger scale than ever before. Not the severity of the famine in a few places, but the general shortage of food everywhere and the immediate crisis on marginal land mark the first of the fourteenth-century crises. The tenuous balance between population and agricultural productivity was particularly threatened. The relatively low seed-to-yield ratio of even the best-tended and most productive fields meant that even a small decline in that ratio had large consequences for the total agricultural output of a region. On lands whose maintenance required intensive labor to prevent erosion or continue drainage, a higher population level was needed than elsewhere, and to sustain that laboring population, agricultural output had to remain high. In addition, other human activities posed threats to agriculture. The extensive deforestation of mountain slopes for shipbuilding in the thirteenth century, the reduction of grazing lands that provided agricultural communities with natural fertilizer, and the overextension of grazing in other areas that made agricultural productivity virtually impossible all contributed to upsetting the balance that climate and crop failure had already attacked.

In the years 1315–1317, the famine reached its greatest extent. Grain prices soared astronomically, regions that depended on distant places for their food witnessed a drastic population loss—as high as 10 percent in some towns—and the seed-to-yield ratio fell, in some cases by half. The 1315–1317 famine was the greatest that Europe experienced, but it was not the only one. The fragile agricultural system, even if it had not reached the limits of its potential output, had nevertheless proved incapable of feeding Europe without profound revision of its practices. Moreover, nearly every succeeding decade of the fourteenth century witnessed either regional or more widespread famine, and hunger became a universal and perennial scourge for the first prolonged period since the end of antiquity.

Hungry people die—or move. In the course of the fourteenth century land that could no longer be worked—because of soil exhaustion, population loss, the ravages of war, or the frequency and extent of pestilential disease—was abandoned. The fourteenth century witnessed an increasing number of deserted farming settlements and towns, in many cases never to be settled again. People moved to other areas where food supplies were likely to be greater—to monasteries, towns, or more productive regions, there to seek food through charity, wage labor, or the assumption of servile status. The physical mobility necessary in the face of famine raised yet other crises. Urban population increased, but urban food supplies were strained, and the new arrivals could contribute little to the quality of town or city life. As we will see later in this section, the extent of the warfare in the fourteenth and fifteenth centuries also disrupted agricultural life, and on the heels of famine and war followed pestilence.

The dangers of reduced harvests, rising grain prices, and widespread famine are many. Death by starvation is not the only consequence of famine, and some of the other consequences have even farther-reaching effects. Medieval people knew little about the different properties of foods, and medieval nutrition was uneven even in the best of times. The wealthy tended, even as late as the seventeenth century, to eat more animal protein and fewer vegetables than they needed, and the poor tended to eat far less animal protein and—because these foods were more readily available—far more vegetables and starchy foods. Animal protein, always expensive, was usually available only periodically—in late fall and early winter, when animals were slaughtered, and as winter progressed, meat was salted more and more heavily and spiced to prevent it from turning rancid. An excessive meat diet, besides producing such diseases as gout, raises the danger of a host of other diseases, as well as the possibility of a severe vitamin deficiency. Wealthy or moderately prosperous Europeans ran these risks until well into modern times. On the other hand, a deficiency of animal protein produces tuberculosis, dysentery, and other diseases, and stunts growth substantially. Vitamin deficiency generally produces enormously painful and prolonged physical conditions—scurvy, rickets, gallstones. Thus the European diet, even in the most prosperous of years, created potential physiological imbalances that afflicted many people, although the particular causes of these were not generally known until the period from the eighteenth century to the present. Starvation and malnutrition raised equally severe problems, and the period between 1300 and 1850 witnessed the greatest effects of malnutrition on the greatest number of people.

Aside from their immediate effects on the individual human, starvation and malnutrition affect the general population. They kill the old and the weak, they maim—as we now know—the entire lives of those who experience them in childhood, and they produce in given regions a drastic change in the demographic composition of society. The number of old and sick people drops, infant mortality increases, and the birth rate decreases. Women die during their most fertile years, and those who survive and leave an area—usually the young and the healthy—take with them another generation, one that will be born elsewhere. Thus, the depopulation of many farms, villages, and towns did not last merely for the duration of a period of famine, but for two or three generations, and sometimes forever.

Those who suffer malnutrition lack resistance to disease. The widespread effects of starvation and malnutrition had already begun to reduce the population of Europe when the next of the Four Horsemen—pestilence—struck with unprecedented fury. And it struck a population already weakened by hunger and lack of resistance, crowded into cities, more physically mobile than in any period of Europe's history since the fifth and sixth centuries, and thus extremely prone to contagion—a principle which it did not understand, carried by a bacillus which was not identified until 1918.

The history of widespread epidemic disease and human society has barely begun to be written. The great plague in Athens during the Peloponnesian War, described by Thucydides, the plague brought back to Italy by Marcus Aurelius's troops in the late second century A.D., and the great plague that struck Constantinople and the West in 542–543, whose description by Procopius consciously echoes that of Thucydides, are the most striking and best-known of the epidemics in early European History. The great epidemics of cholera, smallpox and influenza in nineteenth- and twentieth-century Europe have been better described and their effects more closely analyzed than any earlier epidemic. But the plague of 1348–1350, and its subsequent outbreaks between the mid fourteenth and the late seventeenth centuries, stands as the most memorable and destructive of all. Although its ravages were regional, it reduced the population of Europe by one third, completely depopulated some regions and towns, and further aggravated the earlier effects of agricultural problems, famine, and demographic rearrangement that had begun by the last years of the thirteenth century. It also provoked a prodigious test of the resiliency of European society: the recovery of fifteenth-, sixteenth-, and seventeenth-century Europe, in terms of demography and agricultural output and the amelioration of living conditions offer equally eloquent testimony to the vigor and recuperative powers of European society. The roots of this recovery surely lay in the agricultural, technological, and economic innovations of the tenth through the early fourteenth centuries.

Bubonic plague, carried by the fleas on brown rats, appears to have struck first in China around 1333. By 1340 it had reached Lake Baikal in Siberia, and by 1346 it had crossed the Caucasus and struck the Crimea, the great port center on the Black Sea. Carried by the rats on an Italian fleet from the Black Sea to the Mediterranean, the plague struck first in Europe in Messina and Sardinia in 1347. In 1348 it hit Genoa and Venice, the greatest ports of the West, simultaneously. From the ports, the plague followed the trade routes. In February, 1348, both Lucca and Avignon reported outbreaks, and by April of the same year Siena and Perugia in Italy and Cerdaña and Rousillon in southwestern France were struck. In May, Ancona, Orvieto, and Rimini in Italy, and Barcelona and Catalonia in Spain were afflicted, followed in July by Paris and Antioch and a year later by Germany and Tunisia. By September of 1349 the plague had reached England, by 1350 Prussia, Bremen, and the eastern Netherlands, and by 1351–1352 western Russia. The indescribably swift spread of plague, its erratic destructiveness of human life, and the utter incomprehension of European society not only provoked severe loss of life and economic disruption on a vast scale, but struck the European Christian mind and imagination with a terrible force, and the consequences of the plague were echoed in literature, devotional styles, and the visual arts, as well as in depopulated farms and villages, devastated cities, and disordered economic institutions. Moreover, plague recurred, and survival of the 1348–1351 crisis did not necessarily guarantee immunity to later outbreaks. The years 1362 and 1375 witnessed outbreaks as severe as that of 1348, and plague returned at least once in every decade until 1497. The great plague cycle begun in 1348 did not end until the late seventeenth century, and pestilence followed hunger and malnutrition into the experience of fourteenth- and fifteenth-century men and women.

In addition to the widespread bubonic form of plague, the far more virulent pneumonic and septicemic strains quickly developed; these were vastly more contagious and quicker to kill. The plague, in these three forms, struck a population that had already begun to decline several decades earlier and attacked undernourished populations that were crowded into towns and ecclesiastical centers under the worst possible hygienic conditions, that possessed uncertain food supplies, and that exhibited a demographic imbalance resulting from heavy inroads into the numbers of the very old, the very young, and women in childbearing age. Those who survived one attack of plague were, of course, vulnerable to later epidemics and were vulnerable as well to other infectious diseases, such as tuberculosis.

After great demographic disasters, the birth rate usually increases, as if to offset the population losses. After the mid fourteenth century, however, the frequent recurrence of plague and famine prevented the birth rate from producing a population increase, and, in the aggregate, most of the population increase of European society after 1100 was effectively wiped out. But such population loss did not occur uniformly everywhere. Population densities were redistributed considerably, villages were deserted for centuries, new villages were founded, and the ratio proportion of urban to rural dwellers increased. Cities recovered their populations faster, not through an increased birth rate but by drawing off the rural population increase. The countryside had to populate both itself and the cities.

Famine and plague strike most severely at those least able to provide for themselves. In fourteenth- and fifteenth-century Europe, a society in which material resources had been stretched to their limits, a series of wars broke out between 1337 and the late fifteenth century, and their duration and character were different from those of earlier kinds of warfare. In addition to famine and pestilence, therefore, we must consider the impact of warfare on fourteenth- and fifteenth-century society. Earlier warfare had consisted generally of infrequent pitched battles between small armies that were not assembled for long periods of time. Such wars usually troubled the noncombatant population relatively little, because they did little permanent damage. The wars of England and France, Castile, and northern Italy in the fourteenth and fifteenth centuries, however, had a different character. Recurring campaigns made battlefields out of plowed fields year after year. The constituents of agricultural life that could not be quickly replaced, unlike crops, and that required substantial capital and labor investment—churches, stone barns, mills, manor houses, and ovens—were hurt more deeply. The temporary but often regular destruction of crops and the prolonged effects of the destruction of capital framed the circumstances of warfare. An invading fourteenth-century army, rather like a small expeditionary force, struck into enemy territory on a swift raid, a *chevauchée*, on which it had to support itself from enemy land, capture enemy towns, and destroy opposing forces. The invaded country, its inhabitants temporarily crowded into fortified towns and castles barely large enough to contain them, could only destroy the food in its own fields so that it did not fall into enemy hands and hold out until the invaders, frustrated and hungry, moved on. The open country of northern France was particularly vulnerable to this kind of warfare, and the frequent slowing down of military campaigns by prolonged sieges increased the dangers to the noncombatant population considerably. Enemy armies, particularly when they wished to demoralize a hostile population, could themselves destroy fields and crops, exact large ransoms and bribes, and fail to keep their armies from looting.

Not only did the duration, frequency, and style of warfare prove particularly disastrous to noncombatants, so did the composition of fourteenth-century armies. Soldiers were paid little, and their pay was frequently late or not forthcoming at all. Soldiers were usually recruited from the poorer and least stable elements of society and regarded military activity as a means of self-enrichment. Prisoners were taken for ransom, towns and castles were plundered, and agricultural lands were held for tribute. Financial exigencies usually demanded that armies be disbanded as soon as possible, and large bands of discharged soldiers wandered around the countryside during truces plundering and terrorizing the population. These groups, called *routiers* in the fourteenth century and *écorcheurs* in the fifteenth, posed continual problems, sometimes being reabsorbed into armies when the wars broke out again, as they usually did, and sometimes selling themselves to the highest bidder in local conflicts. France and Italy were plagued the most severely by them, until the end of the fifteenth century.

Closely related to the activities of discharged or deserted soldiers was the increasing prevalence of banditry in the late fourteenth and fifteenth centuries. The companies of mercenaries, *écorcheurs*, took over and controlled territories around the fortified places they had captured on their own, ransomed those they kidnaped, demanded entire harvests, and required "protection" payments from all whose lives they touched. Impoverished and undisciplined lords of castles also found it profitable to raid neighboring areas, particularly after acquiring some military experience—and probably some military personnel—in the numerous wars of the fourteenth century. Finally, although both nobles and displaced peasants sometimes formed their own bands or joined the larger gangs in the French provinces and the north of England, robber bands appear to have formed among the poor themselves, as well as among individuals of yeoman or even noble status. From the fourteenth century to the nineteenth, banditry became a ubiquitous and particularly dangerous aspect of life for those already ravaged by famine, plague, and war.

The disasters of the fourteenth and fifteenth centuries were not new in European history. Famine and pestilence had broken out continually, and warfare, even if conducted on a much smaller scale than in later times, had destroyed people, crops, and mills before the middle of the fourteenth century. The natural isolation of most of Christian European society, however, had served as a kind of control on the spread of the effects of such dangers. Contagion is not epidemic until there are carriers for it; famine may be regional as long as the food chain is not extended beyond local districts; small armies serving for limited periods of time cannot devastate a region irreparably. However, mid fourteenth-century European society was well into the process of overcoming its earlier particularism, in both political and economic terms. Agricultural regions had become more interdependent, and specialized and commercial agriculture had further complicated the problems caused by the expansion of cultivated land and the growth of population. Agricultural and military disorders, trade, travel on official ecclesiastical or commercial business or for the purpose of study at distant schools had all increased the physical mobility of Europeans, and the increasing density of both rural and urban areas had increased the odds for disease to be epidemic. Moreover, the forms of fourteenth- and fifteenth-century plague were the most virulent the world has ever known. Finally, fourteenth- and fifteenth-century armies grew larger and larger, the duration, character, and aims of war changed, and a higher percentage of the increased population was likely to be touched by warfare, either as combatants or noncombatants, contributors to the mobilization of resources for war or its victims.

THE FINANCIAL CRISIS

Between the end of the thirteenth and the end of the fifteenth century the population of Europe declined and redistributed its diminished numbers. Famine, malnutrition, pestilence, war, and the consequences of an overextended economy combined in a massive assault upon the institutions of traditional Europe. Under these pressures, both the economy and the social order underwent extensive transformations. The constant limits of agricultural enterprise, the social structure of the labor force, and the resources of technology did not significantly change, however, and the transformations in the fourteenth- and fifteenth-century economy and social structure remained well within the limits of a primarily agricultural, lightly urbanized preindustrial civilization. The period witnessed a crisis, not a revolution, in the life of traditional Europe.

The changes that occurred in the economic and social life of the fourteenth and fifteenth centuries were, as always, highly localized, having greater effects and distinctive characteristics in some areas and leaving others virtually untouched. As we have seen again and again, general statements concerning demographic and economic history are most helpful when they are set against the relatively sparse data from particular places in particular periods. The considerable increase in the English wool trade, for example, had a considerable impact on several factors of England's economy, but it left many others untouched, and it partially caused a decline in the wool trade of Flanders; thus the European wool market, considered as a whole, was left without a noticeable net gain, although a considerable rearrangement occurred within particular sectors of that market. In northern Italy, the interdependence of the city and the *contado*, its surrounding territory, had deep and enduring roots, the towns immediately surrounded by vineyards, olive groves, and fruit orchards, the grainfields farther away. Townspeople owned extensive rural lands and spent substantial parts of the year in the country. In this area, the demographic and economic crisis struck less severely than it did elsewhere. In the vast agricultural areas of eastern and northern Germany, to consider yet another area, the limited and unstable authority and the irregular finances of rulers allowed the rural nobility, in return for subsidies, considerable authority over the once free peasantry. Armed with virtually limitless powers, the nobility imposed rigorous and effective controls upon its subject population, converted rural farms to large-scale agricultural enterprises, and entered the European food market with cheap grain and other products. England, northern Italy, and eastern Germany are but three large regions, themselves composed of many smaller distinctive areas, and themselves parts of yet larger economic networks. This particularism of the fourteenth- and fifteenth-century European experience must be kept in mind in the following general discussion.

Among the earliest consequences of the changes in material life between 1270 and 1350 in the agricultural sector of the economy were the stabilization and decline of cereal grain prices, a rise in the prices of manufactured or crafted goods, a considerable rise in the prices of commercial agricultural products, and the increasing size of sheep herds at the expense of agricultural land. In the course of the fourteenth century the increasing demand for meat led to the raising of meat prices and to the importation of cattle from northern and eastern Europe. The new mobility of peasant families and the new demands for labor contributed to the changing patterns of inheritance among the peasant population and to the practice of leasing vacant land at a fixed rent for a short period and subcontracting a labor force to work it. Problems in the economic position of the urban craft guilds led entrepreneurs to take different stages of wool production into the countryside, where they found an unregulated labor force in need of income. In much of England, western Germany, the Low Countries, and Savoy the growth of rural craft industry became prominent. The material crises of the fourteenth century opened much land to the profitable raising of sheep, and in Castile the organization of privileged sheepherders, the *Mesta*, grew quickly after 1273. Great herds of fine merino sheep were driven north across the vast Castilian tableland in the spring and south in the fall, thus restricting even further the development of the Castilian agricultural economy.

To the peasants who survived famine, plague, and war the new economic opportunities were in some places considerable. The price of labor in a reduced labor force had gone up, and if old lords were unwilling to renegotiate the price of service and its conditions, other lords or prosperous peasant proprietors would. Statutes against wage increases proved incapable of controlling labor costs, and there appeared thriving peasant agricultural entrepreneurs who themselves became the employers of the available rural wage labor. The old haphazard scatterings of settlements on good land and bad that had spread unchecked between the tenth and the fourteenth centuries began to be tightened into compact new villages, field systems were reorganized, and large farms appeared in peasant possession, worked by a single peasant family with its own employees and servants; these peasants were increasingly resentful of demands made by old lords and royal tax agents, and of the successful enterprise of townspeople and middlemen that seemed to keep grain prices down and allow the towns to grow rich at the expense of rural labor. The new conditions of rural enterprise and the markets of the wider world contributed to the shaping of distinctly particularistic points of view that in turn heightened the tensions of society.

The good fortune of some peasants must not obscure the miserable lot of others. Wage laborers had been forced to trade the security of servile tenure for the instability of a world in which there was opportunity both to earn and to lose money. The increase in the number of wage laborers in the countryside who had no possessions or security of their own led to a widening of the spectrum of the peasant population and to a differentiation of social and economic relationships. For instance, the cereal grain farmer was generally closer to his employees and servants than the commercial farmer or the stock raiser. The new conditions of economic exchange further eroded the old social and economic bonds of dependence and security that had characterized much of rural society before the mid fourteenth century.

The wool and wine trades were perhaps the two most conspicuous instances of the physical transformation of the European countryside in the fourteenth and fifteenth centuries, and the ruralization of some craft industries illustrates in an equally striking manner that the character of labor use changed just as the character of land use changed. What of agriculture proper, the direct cultivation of the land for food and commercial crops? In the thirteenth century, the growing cloth industry had supported the extension of commercial agriculture, and the cultivation of dye-plants, flax, and hemp had begun to spread. The crisis in grain prices and the growth of industry in the late fourteenth and fifteenth centuries increased the spread of commercial agriculture. Barley and hops for the brewing of beer brought better prices then wheat and rye. Flax, hemp, woad, and madder all increased in value as wheat prices remained stable or declined. Yet some of the changes in late medieval agriculture ultimately proved beneficial. The retreat of grain cultivation to good rather than marginal or poor land concentrated the remaining labor force on the most productive lands. The increase of crop rotation and the generally greater proportion of leguminous crops meant that the soil received more nitrogen, animal and human diets improved, and land that now grew grain crops rather than legumes required somewhat less animal manure to fertilize it. Fodder crops, which increased after the fourteenth century, also decreased the frequency of necessary fallow periods; the fallow periods of much land decreased from one year in three sometimes to one year in five or six. These conditions, even if they did not in themselves increase the price of cereal grains, nevertheless made grain cultivation more profitable when the population growth of the late fifteenth and sixteenth centuries increased the demand for grain, and hence its price, during the sixteenth and seventeenth centuries.

Fluctuating crop experimentation, new fertilizing techniques, and soil and technological improvement bettered the quality of late medieval agriculture but did not represent a complete break from earlier experience. In spite of the spread of labor-saving devices (hastened by the shortage of labor) and the improvement of soil productivity, the seed-to-yield ratios remained less than a third of those of modern agriculture, farm and food animals remained small—they were more valuable for wool and leather than for meat—the profit margin of agricultural activity remained small (the general rule appears to have been that one third of the harvest was used for seed, one third for rent, and one third for the farmer's own livelihood), and the inescapable relation between demand and prices and wages persisted in keeping agriculture at a marginal level, even in the best of times and in the most favored areas. The population and the production of the European countryside in the period from the fourteenth to the seventeenth centuries experienced greater and more varied opportunities, more far-raching crises and outright disasters, and a substantial recovery. But European society remained until the eighteenth century tied to a preindustrial, agricultural demographic and economic pattern. The immense growth of the thirteenth century was not to be repeated until the nineteenth century.

The manor, the great farm, and the rural village and market were the modules of agricultural society in preindustrial Europe, and their experience informs us about the experience of the vast majority of the European population. The city was the module of nonagricultural society and economy, and although its population remained small and its political significance often dwindled in the face of the increased power of royal or princely authority, the city remained the hub of the European economy. Between the fourteenth and the seventeenth centuries, the city, not the rural castle, became the seat of royal and princely government. In spite of the catastrophes in the agricultural, industrial, and commercial sectors of the fourteenth- and fifteenth-century economy, the importance of the city persisted and increased. In the concurrent process of the shaping of territorial monarchies, the cities became the critical components of larger states, and the character of the life of the late medieval city influenced in turn the psychology, the politics, and the economy of larger regions. The study of the nonagricultural sectors of the late medieval European economy begins with a consideration of the cities.

The density of population in a medieval city permitted not only the concentration of a productive labor force, but the concentration of economic activities on both a large and a small scale. In Italy, Venice, Genoa, Milan, and Florence became the principal centers of international trade and finance; in England, London and Bristol; in Flanders, Bruges; in the south of France, Marseilles and Avignon; and in the north, the Hanseatic towns of Danzig, Riga, Stralsund, Rostock, Lubeck, Hamburg, and Bremen. These were the international as well as the regional centers of the European economy. These cities also controlled the regional economy in their immediate vicinity: Venice, the Adriatic sea and, increasingly, the towns in the Trevisan March; Genoa, the Ligurian coast and what is now the Riviera with a growing influence in southern Spain; Milan and Florence, the center and north of Italy; London and Bristol, the productive wool trade of southeastern and southwestern England. In international affairs these cities prospered because of their strong coinage, the exclusivity of their control, and the supporting services they offered their merchants and bankers. In regional affairs, their strong political control of the countryside and other cities and the relative prosperity that they provided made them local capitals as well. In such cities as Paris, London, Dijon, Avignon, and Naples, extremely powerful rulers of large territories transformed the city into a political capital, thus enhancing its economic prominence and drawing people to it. Although many medieval cities preserved their older character and their customary political divisions, the economic boom of the twelfth and thirteenth centuries, the growing concentration of political authority, and the stabilizing of local and long-distance trade and finance caused the greatest cities to grow even greater.

Economic prosperity did not, however, guarantee permanent importance. As we will soon see, the predominance of some economic activities, particularly mining, over others, particularly cereal-grain growing, raised some regions to prosperity at the expense of others. Most of the great cities mentioned above remained prominent through the sixteenth century. But already by the fifteenth century others were rising to challenge them. The increased mining activity in central Europe brought the South German cities of Nuremberg, Augsburg, Prague, and Leipzig to degrees of prosperity that foreshadowed their continued growth in the sixteenth century.

In addition to the increased size and prosperity of the greatest European cities and the emergence of lesser cities as prominent political capitals and centers of new industry, the formation of new towns occupied much energy in the late fourteenth and fifteenth centuries. The new wave of colonization that grew in Europe after the fourteenth-century crises was much more markedly urban than the expansion of the tenth, eleventh, and twelfth centuries. Built up now along established trade routes and serving as strategic military and administrative regional centers, the new towns of late medieval Europe lacked the early medieval character given to other cities by the older churches, the ninth- and tenth-century comital castles, and the irregularity of streets and suburbs. Their skylines were more regular, their streets broader and more carefully planned, and their control and rule more assured. The great southern European cities, with their taller buildings, broad plazas, high population density, and active, complex economic and social lives remained in contrast with both the new and older cities of the north.

After the crises of the fourteenth century, most European cities took careful steps to protect themselves against starvation, and the late fourteenth and fifteenth centuries witnessed a new flow of legislation regulating the sale of food both inside the city and in its environs. The provisioning of the early modern European city is still the object of intense and detailed study, and the efforts of medieval towns to regulate the production and consumption of their food supplies was simply one link, although an important one, in the ties that bound cities to the larger regions surrounding them.

The late medieval city had to provision and defend itself, regulate increasingly large bodies of citizens and other inhabitants, and provide a political and juridical climate favorable to both commerce and industry. The late thirteenth and early fourteenth centuries witnessed the first great wave of success in most of these areas, but the demographic, epidemic, and military crises of the late fourteenth century, the changes in the economy that grew more marked in the same period, and the changing political milieu in which the cities found themselves as the fourteenth and fifteenth centuries wore on all altered the character of urban life and the economic role of the city in early modern Europe.

Apart from exploiting, directing, and controlling much of the agricultural sector of the economy, both in provisioning themselves and in selling comestible and commercial agricultural products to others, the late medieval towns contained a large labor force that was both skilled and unskilled, was increasingly regulated during the fourteenth and fifteenth centuries, and, in many towns, was capable of taking and holding political power. In the course of the fourteenth and fifteenth centuries, the members of many craft occupations formed associations of masters and apprentices, of laborers in a particular stage of a long craft process, or of traders—all of which were loosely called guilds. The term *guild,* of course, like the term *university,* did not refer originally to men organized for a particular purpose; it connoted an association in general, and it might refer to religious associations as well as groups of craftsmen and scholars.

Guild regulations appeared in greater numbers—and in greater detail—during this period, and their study reveals the growing tension among different levels of the labor and ownership process, the more stringent controls applied by masters, the attempts of subordinate ranks in the craft process to better their lot, and the relative inability of even the strongest guilds to alter substantially the economic conditions that generated such tensions. Economic pressures also contributed to rendering the guilds less and less able to respond flexibly to new problems. The late medieval guilds aimed at an exclusivity, a highly refined particularism that was designed to regulate all stages of production and reduce the potential of outside competition to zero. The steps taken to achieve this goal, which were under the control of guild masters who also controlled in many places an extraordinary amount of political power, generated further rivalries, sometimes between masters and journeymen, sometimes between cities and their surrounding regions. However, even high prices and wages, urban population densities, increased control over all stages of production, and a large share of political power could not assure social and economic stability in a period when trade routes and industrial techniques were shifting very rapidly, and when increased competition and the decline of the agricultural sector themselves marked substantial social and economic changes. Among the results of the new rationalism and control within guilds were increased social unrest, greater hostility between ranks in the production process, and an intensifying of local control over production. By the fifteenth century, the guilds were compelled to undertake an offensive as well as a defensive role on behalf of their members. That role, however, led to economic and political factionalism and contributed further to the social unrest already evident in late medieval agriculture.

The increasing specialization of production proliferated the number of guild associations, opened avenues to political power to lesser artisans and—briefly—to the lowest ranks of unskilled laborers, and raised new questions concerning monopoly, restraint of trade, and other economic practices. These questions became part of the political life of much of Europe in the fifteenth and sixteenth centuries, and the economic interests of princes, ecclesiastical institutions, guild masters, entrepreneurs, and laborers at all levels of production color the political life of late medieval and early modern Europe profoundly.

Aside from the crises discussed above, European cities and the industrial and commercial economy they controlled were also vulnerable to changes in the world outside Christendom. The mid fourteenth century witnessed the disintegration of the vast Mongol Empire. A new spirit of resistance in China under the leadership of the Ming dynasty, the liberation of Persia, and the breaking up of the Mongol armies under individual leaders, as in Russia and, most spectacularly, under Timur the Lame in the Near East in the early fifteenth century, weakened the economic security of the great trans-Eurasian caravan routes. The rise to power of the Ottoman Turks from the late fourteenth to the early seventeenth century gave Islam a new impetus, one that threatened not only the old eastern trade routes, but the colonial empires of Genoa and Venice in the eastern Mediterranean and the Black Sea and the political security of much of eastern Christendom as well. By the late fourteenth century, the Turks had achieved a foothold in Europe, in 1453 they captured Constantinople, in 1519 they conquered Egypt—a task for which even the greatest of the Mongol armies had been unprepared—and in 1529 they were at the gates of Vienna, having already overrun Hungary, Greece, and the Balkans. The decline of the Mongols, the new resistance of China to any westerners, and the rise of Ottoman Turkish power in the Near East and in eastern Europe defined some of the conditions that had harsh consequences in the economy of Christendom. The closing of the eastern Mediterranean markets left little room for the earlier kind of urban rivalry that had characterized the twelfth and thirteenth centuries. Venice, left virtually alone in the eastern Mediterranean, was drawn into new economic and political relations with the troubled mainland of northeastern Italy and with the rising prosperity of the South German cities. Genoa, militarily humbled in her thirteenth- and fourteenth-century conflicts with Venice, focused her activities on her own smaller colonial empire and among the new activity in central and southern Spain she laid the groundwork for her later role as banker to the kings of Spain. Christopher Columbus was one of the last, not one of the first, Genoese to succeed in the service of the Spanish kings.

The economic rearrangement of Mediterranean powers was only one example of the changes in economic life in the late fourteenth and fifteenth centuries. Throughout much of Europe, cities, princes, and aristocratic dynasties began to construct strong, closely controlled regional areas of provincial prosperity, thereby depressing the independence of towns, seigniories, and other cities, as well as consciously altering their economic profiles.

One of the most striking pieces of evidence of change during this period is the changing character of the economic records that have survived to the present. Two characteristics are immediately evident: first, the increasing presence of political authority in the form of tax registers, verifications of land titles, publication of guild statute-books, the granting of monopolies, and the intervention of political authority in economic and social disputes; second, the extraordinary proliferation of private records, information, suggestions for economic reforms, and complex accounting systems. In short, there is both *more* paperwork and paperwork of a different kind. The records alone tell us that governmental institutions and merchants and financiers themselves established more complex and accurate information systems to record economic activity, and on the basis of their information they determined future courses of action. By the fifteenth century, for example, a true accounting system spread over much of Europe. Not only were monies of account more widely used, but receipts and expenses were more carefully labeled and separately registered and verified. Moreover, accounting systems of considerable complexity began to be used, not only in commerce and finance but in the public treasuries of cities, princes, prelates, and kings. In the fifteenth century the kingdom of France produced the first modern budget constructed according to sound accounting principles. The increased corporate character of economic activity, because of its size and complexity, rendered such economic awareness indispensable. The interests of the great individual merchant or merchant family had set the stage for the affairs of the corporation, the company, and the kingdom. Large-scale public investment in private commercial enterprises, in banks, in funded public debts, and in charitable funds had necessitated one of the most immediately evident transformations of the late medieval economy.

A striking example of the consequences of the spread of complex accounting systems was the transformation of late medieval banking. The word *bank* (like the legal term *bench*) derives from the Latin *bancus,* the bench on which most bankers (and judges) did their work. The simplified banking systems of the twelfth and thirteenth centuries gave way to problems of investment of capital, the need for negotiable paper, and the increasingly complex question of the risk attached to large investments. One of the most perplexing events of the fourteenth century was the increasingly frequent failure of European banks. The increasing amount of capital in the hands of the great Italian and Flemish merchant bankers of the thirteenth century had been let by these banks in the form of large loans, sometimes to individuals or companies, but more often to those who could offer more substantial security—the rulers of the principalities and territorial monarchies. As we will see below, the fiscal and political crises of the early fourteenth century caught European rulers with antiquated fiscal systems in a terrible dilemma: rulers had come to depend on large loans as a regular part of their revenue, and the retarded development of public finance in the late thirteenth and early fourteenth centuries met the new flood of private commercial capital and engorged it indiscriminately. One of the most striking political changes in the late fourteenth and fifteenth centuries was the restructuring of public finances and their influence on political life. The large amounts of capital available to underfinanced rulers in the late thirteenth and early fourteenth centuries led them to borrow on anticipation of revenues, to assign future revenues to their creditors, and to issue monopolies inconsiderately. When even these unwise measures failed to produce enough money to repay their debts and further decreased their operating revenues, the kings of England and France, faced with still more extensive financial needs because of their mobilization for war, refused many of their obligations to the Italian and Flemish bankers who had loaned them money. Thus, in addition to demographic, epidemic, and military crises, Europe witnessed a financial crisis of previously unheard-of dimensions. Banks whose revenues had been committed to government loans quickly failed: the great banking houses of Siena collapsed in 1339, and in 1343 and 1346 the great Florentine banks of the Peruzzi and the Bardi went under. The crisis of the great early banking houses not only seriously incapacitated public finance for most of the century and turned the rulers of Europe to new means of raising money, it also transformed the character of banking itself. Investments in even the most wealthy territorial monarchies had proved to be no more secure than investments in private enterprises. Banks had to take two steps: first, to find a way of minimizing their risks, and, second, to find new investments for their diminished capital.

Until the seventeenth century, the banking houses that survived the crash of the mid fourteenth century operated generally on a smaller scale than their great predecessors. The new banks that rose in the wake of the mid fourteenth-century failures—in Italy, those of the Medici, the Casa di San Giorgio in Genoa, and the Banco di San Ambrogio in Milan—became semipublic, absorbing shares of the increasingly common funded debts of the cities, and acquiring political power that made their investments more secure than they were in the thirteenth century. The surviving banks and the newer institutions were aided by an increasing tendency to make monetary values homogeneous over wider regions. The aligning of currencies throughout larger and larger regions overcame slowly one of the most vexing and time-consuming activities of early medieval moneychangers and bankers. Some areas also insisted on evaluating different currencies according to a stable gold standard determined according to weight. Currency speculation had long provided a profitable area of investment, but currency variation had increased economic risks, and "bad money" persisted in driving out "good money" until well into the early modern period. The great stable coins of the twelfth and thirteenth centuries—the Byzantine solidus, the Venetian ducat, the Florentine florin—all succumbed to currency difficulties in the course of the fourteenth century. By the end of the fourteenth century Italian banks had begun to issue paper currency, but the spread of the new form of money was slow and uneven. Early modern Europe operated on a metallic currency. The scarcity or promiscuity of bullion altered considerably the economic activity of regions, cities, and kingdoms.

The supply of gold and silver bullion in Europe, like that of iron and other metals, was limited to two sources: the importation of gold in bullion, coinage, or metalwork from places outside Europe, and the exploitation of European mines. The fourteenth century witnessed a crisis in both these methods of bullion supply. The decline of Byzantium, the hegemony of Italian towns in the Mediterranean, and the increasing insecurity of the gold route across the western Sahara decreased the amount of bullion arriving in Europe from outside sources, and the balance of trade in Europe itself directed the flow of bullion south to Christian Mediterranean lands—hence, the increasing financial complexity of the Italian city-republics. Second, the mining technology of medieval Europe, though suitable for surface mining, had lost the Roman techniques for deep mining. As the supply of bullion decreased, its value increased, and hoarding always threatened to draw good coinage out of circulation, just as did the increasingly frequent practice of acquiring valuable silver and gold utensils. Thus, both sources of European gold and silver became less productive in the fourteenth century. In those areas in which mining remained a profitable activity—most of which were in central and eastern Europe—the limits of mining technology were rapidly being reached. As mines went deeper, problems of support, drainage, and labor increased exponentially, and the ore became more expensive to get at. The decline in population halted the exploration of new territories, including new mines, and the political conflicts of the fourteenth and fifteenth centuries seriously disturbed both mining production and the population of miners.

Thus, the social and technological difficulties of the fourteenth and fifteenth centuries contributed not only to the crisis in the European economy, but to the crisis in its production and acquisition of precious metals. The influx of precious metals caused by new mining strikes in the tenth and eleventh centuries and the reversal of the balance of trade with Asia during the twelfth and thirteenth centuries had contributed to the economic growth of Christian Europe during the commercial and agricultural revolution of 950–1350. By 1350 the sources of bullion were again on the verge of exhaustion. By the late fourteenth century the surface deposits of gold and silver that had begun to be exploited in the eleventh century had been virtually worked out. The exhaustion of the supply of bullion occurred, of course, at a time when wages rose considerably, and contributes to our understanding of the fearful economic pressures on fourteenth- and fifteenth-century society.

Wool—either in raw form or as finished or semifinished cloth—was the staple trade good of medieval Europe. During the twelfth and thirteenth centuries, those cities that controlled the final stages of the production and distribution of the best cloth—the cities of Flanders and Brabant and the great towns of northern Italy—were the most economically prosperous. Yet they were also the most economically vulnerable. Flanders drew both its food supply and its raw wool supply from far beyond its own regional limits. The interruption of either or both of these could, and did, plunge the Flemish towns into one crisis after another. The Flemish dependence on England for raw wool increased substantially when England curtailed this trade during the early stages of its conflict with France. Moreover, the agricultural problems of the late fourteenth century led to the increased production of raw wool as marginal agricultural land was turned into grazing land. Thus, England might displace Flanders as a prominent wool producer, but the economic crisis, aggravated by an oversupply of wool, did not permit the English economy to flourish as a result of its new enterprise until the late fifteenth and early sixteenth centuries. The enthusiasm of the new English wool entrepreneurs led them to experiment with the parceling out of stages of the production process to rural areas; in the process, they turned away from the rigidified guilds of the great towns. This innovation added freedom of enterprise to the new industry but contributed seriously to the dislocation of older forms of economic regulation, which explains the increasing frequency throughout Europe of regional restrictions on the export and production of woolen cloth. The cities of Italy also felt the new pressures in their greatest industry, and much of the political difficulty of Florence in the fourteenth century may be traced to the collapse of its great banking houses and the reduced fortunes of the woolen industry.

The history of the wool industry in the fourteenth and fifteenth centuries illuminates one aspect of late medieval trade: the shifting areas of production, finishing, and sale and the consequences in terms of economic, social, and political change for those areas that lost and those that gained from such shifts. The rise of the English cloth industry, its relative freedom from restriction, the decline of Flanders, and the weakening of Italian trade all suggest an aspect of late medieval economic life that has long been misunderstood—the problem of economic reorganization within a complex system that many historians have insisted must be labeled uniformly as a "decline." To be sure, there is remarkable evidence of many sorts of decline—from financial to agricultural—during this period. But there are also compelling indications that the rearrangement of the European economy—from finance to agriculture—not only increased prosperity in some places and among some social groups, but ultimately laid the groundwork for the social and economic changes of the seventeenth and eighteenth centuries. The new freedom of different kinds of entrepreneurs, new means of record keeping and accounting, the increasingly prominent role of political authority in economic activity, and the rapidly changing prosperity of many areas offer a confusing picture, but not a picture that can casually be labeled one of uniform decline. Regional variations were still the predominant characteristic of European economic life until well into the eighteenth century, and the decline of one region, town, or family usually meant the rise of another.

Most of the economic changes were misunderstood, and interpreted as acts of God, as signs of the corruption of political or ecclesiastical authority, as the result of greed (the predominant vice in late medieval moral philosophy), or as the consequences of a world turned upside down. Economic complaints were joined indiscriminately to other kinds of complaints and sometimes to the literary or artistic preoccupations of late medieval society, and the resulting picture is often a false one of unrelieved gloom and totally unchecked self-interest. This is a common picture, but certainly not a uniformly accurate one. It does little justice to those who, however novel and incomprehensible their activities, *did* attempt, in bettering their own lot, to be useful to society, to serve their rulers loyally, to be good Christians, and to accommodate as best they could the deepest and most enduring values their society held.

THE PROBLEMS OF THE SOCIAL ORDER

The problems of material life, demographic structure, and the economy that struck Europe between 1270 and 1470 become most clear, as we have seen, when considered in terms of the experience of particular groups of people in particular regions, less clear when attempts are made to generalize about the condition of the European population as a whole over a long period of time. The divinely ordained threefold division of early European society that appeared in writings of the tenth and eleventh centuries distinguished those who fight, those who pray, and those who work. Although such a concept was oversimplified even when it was first enunciated, some of its implications endured for centuries. The rise in the honorific status of the fighting man in the eleventh and twelfth centuries made the status of knight a bond between kings and the high nobility on the one hand, and among individual poor knights on the other. After the Investiture Conflict, clerical status, from pope to clerks in minor orders, was sharply set apart from lay status. And until the fifteenth century, many social thinkers adamantly refused to consider bourgeois, urban patricians, financiers, students, and skilled craftsmen as significantly different from the peasantry—"those who work." Yet within this honorific framework of rudimentary social theory, what is particularly striking is the transformation of different groups of people, variations within a single status, and the complex influences that affected society during the fourteenth and fifteenth centuries.

The aristocracy, already by the thirteenth century showing divisions into families of great magnates, middle ranks of nobles holding power in regions, and lords of single villages or castles, shared the common bonds of knightly rank, oaths of personal loyalty, and economic dependence, but in terms of aristocratic status as a whole it was quite varied. From the twelfth century on, aristocratic status became formalized and surrounded by privilege and ritual, and access to it became strictly regulated. The highest nobility in England and France was close to the rulers, often required some royal counterweight to offset its wealth and power, and was highly selective about its associations. At the other end of the scale, individual knights might be desperately poor, barely living at the subsistence level, and in some areas they might actually drop from knightly rank. In the middle range, the lesser nobility generally improved its position from the thirteenth century on, managed its properties carefully, and derived considerable help from royal or high aristocratic patronage. Many of these nobles entered royal service, and many of them focused their efforts on their rural holdings in the process of turning themselves into country gentry.

Although the numbers of great families often changed, the fortunes of those that survived, in England, for example, appear to have increased. In addition, even the greater nobility was not averse to entering royal service in return for the increase in wealth and power such service entailed. Even the profits of war were sometimes invested successfully in land and other economic enterprises. The greater nobility also displayed a heightened dynastic consciousness in terms of consolidating holdings, arranging marriage alliances, and planning succession. The family and its fortunes, rather than a particular estate, region, or territory, became the focus of aristocratic consciousness from the fourteenth century on. The lesser aristocracy fought tenaciously to survive economically against the falling prices of grain, the high costs of labor, and the shifts in favor that characterized the world of public and private power. Some converted their lands from labor-intensive cereal grain cultivation to stock raising, dairying, and commercial agriculture that produced crops, such as barley for beer, vines, dye-plants, and flax, and some even let their land revert to forest when the market for timber became attractive. By conserving only the best of their land for cereal grains, they slowly increased the yield of grain in proportion to the amount of land sown, and by doing so they conserved the maintenance labor that had been required to make their lesser lands even minimally productive. Although not all lords could create vast estates with a highly controlled peasantry reduced to near-servile status—as could the nobility of northern and eastern Germany and Castile—lords even in England and France could press for statutory control of wages and the mobility of the labor force, as the English did in the Statute of Laborers in 1351. Finally, in their attempts to gain extended control over their labor force, lords could demand meticulous fulfillment of all of the oldest signs of bond service. To a peasantry that had, between the eleventh and the fourteenth centuries, become freer and more mobile than ever before, such demands appeared harsh indeed, and they contributed to the spread of peasant and artisan revolts that mark the end of the fourteenth century throughout Europe. Whether in the greater or lesser aristocracy, vigorous and energetic families and large, extensive estates seem to have held together more efficiently than lax and inept families, no matter how high or powerful, and smaller, weaker estates.

The nobility strove to maintain or expand their power in new arenas. The greatest nobility, and the ambitious lesser nobility, became attached to royal courts and struggled there for favor and fortune in a highly complicated milieu. Other families rooted themselves in their rural holdings, and members of lesser social groups struggled to establish themselves as gentry, whether by accepting distraint of knighthood (the opportunity to purchase knightly status if one's income level was sufficiently high) or by living in "knightly" style without formal status. Several recent historians have argued that the fourteenth and fifteenth centuries were an "age of ambition." In England, for example, "the nobility were criticized and infiltrated by the knightly commons; the gentry were both crystallizing as a class yet being attacked and infiltrated from below; the upper bourgeoisie was assimilating itself to the gentry through intermarriage and the acquisition of possessions. Below this again, the lesser bourgeoisie of shopkeepers and skilled artisans were proliferating and often showing intense hostility to those above them in the social scale."

The shifting character of power and authority, the economic activities of the aristocracy, and the nature of the European economy during the late fourteenth and fifteenth centuries transformed the opportunities and restrictions of other social groups, particularly the urban commercial classes and the rural peasantry. Social experience often outruns social theory. The redistribution of wealth, power, and interests among the higher and lesser nobility, the intrusion of urban entrepreneurs and absentee owners into the countryside, and the changing opportunities open to the peasant classes posed difficulties that traditional social ideas could not easily explain. Tensions between producers and merchants, the slackening of traditional bonds of dependence and mutual obligation, and the turbulent rise and fall of prices and wages weakened the customary composition of the countryside and the towns and substituted uncertainty and insecurity for traditional social relationships. Beside the varying market and the new entrepreneurialism, the devaluation of coinage, exigencies of public finances and taxation, and the new managerial mentality of successful noble or commercial groups, older social views and customs seemed both appealing and remote. Behind many of the social protests of the fourteenth and fifteenth centuries lay the desire to restore a world of limited exchange and dependent social relationships that seemed to be slipping away rapidly.

The ambition of successful people was to fit into the world of their "betters," a world that they often conceived in traditional and archaic ways. Successful merchants left the towns for the countryside, acquired coats of arms and genealogies, and tried to live as they imagined the nobility lived. Sometimes they succeeded. Great financiers funded royalty, rose to the highest social positions, and effectively entered the nobility. Individuals and families also lost wealth, power, and status, however, and those leaving a social rank for a lower one felt bitter toward those rising into it. The vast plurality of interests, techniques, and roads toward success or failure were utilized long before a satisfactory rationale that explained them could be worked out. It is against this background of enterprise, ambition, sudden rises and falls, and new roads to fortune and status that the conflicting views of the individual and society must be considered.

Fourteenth- and fifteenth-century social ideas are found in moral treatises, legal literature, parliamentary records, and imaginative literature, but two of the most revealing sources for changing social thought during this period are the records of sermons and the literature of protest and revolt that appear in great volume throughout the fourteenth and fifteenth centuries. By the late fourteenth century, social movements designed to acquire political power for the newly wealthy had already risen in northern Italy, Flanders, Germany, and France. These early movements, however, were aimed not at overturning society, but in inserting into the ruling ranks new groups whose wealth and enterprise, they claimed, gave them the right to be there. The large capital exchanges, regional power, and individual and family wealth generated by merchants and artisans in the thirteenth century enabled this group to confront, first, the traditional prerogatives of an older social structure. By the late fourteenth century, however, lower economic groups also commenced a series of revolts, not to gain for themselves another rank's ruling prerogatives, but to abolish rank altogether, as some of the rebels claimed, or to turn the world upside down, as some of their critics claimed.

Between 1350 and 1390 a number of revolts led by the rural peasantry and the urban poor broke out in Italy, Castile, France, and England. The rationalization of several of these revolts by their leaders focused upon a dream of evangelical Christian social reform, a restoration of "good old" customs, and sometimes a demand for the abolition of those onerous obstacles to ambition, the gentry and the restricted access to traditional rights. These explanations suggest the increasingly wide division between social thought and social problems. In the new unfettered economic world of the late fourteenth and fifteenth centuries, tradition, expectation, and predictability gave way to novelty, despair, and, so it seemed, the whim of fortune. Indeed, as if as a symbol of the fear and excitement of the fifteenth century, the image of the wheel of fortune abounds in the literature and art of the period. The preachers, whose sermons enunciated again and again the traditional picture of social order, railed against rebellion, disorder, and excessive social movement. But the old rhetorical image of the body politic and social, a stable, unchanging image, contrasted sharply with the image of the wheel of fortune, from whose unsettling revolutions no one, neither king nor peasant, was free. Economic instability, material setbacks, new opportunities and new restrictions—these elements shaped the social views of fifteenth-century people, and they generated deep tensions not only between different social groups but betwen traditional and novel ways of conceiving the order of society and acting within that order.

27

THE ROOTS
OF TRADITIONAL EUROPE

SPIRITUALITY AND SECULARISM

In spite of the many and varied divisions within Christendom between the eleventh and the fourteenth centuries, the concept of a vast territorial community, conceived as spiritual in essence with the pope at its head, continued to flourish throughout the fourteenth and fifteenth centuries and beyond. This common Christian culture of early Europe was the basis of the later secularized European culture that emerged between the fourteenth and the nineteenth centuries. The Investiture Conflict had postulated a new vision of the right order of the world with the Christian community at its center. In 1095 Pope Urban II invoked the same image when he preached the First Crusade, and he went further, by declaring the Peace of God throughout Christendom as a juridical act. Canon law pursued and developed the juridical aspects of the idea of Christendom, and from the writings of St. Bernard to the commentators at the Second Council of Lyons in 1274 the spiritual dimensions of the idea were sustained. Dante had raised the concept, with the figure of the emperor at its head, to the status of a governing motif in the *Divine Comedy,* and throughout the fourteenth and fifteenth centuries proposals for new Crusades, treatises on papal and imperial authority, and other literary works returned again and again to the idea of a universal Christian community. Europeans considered themselves and their culture collectively as a community of Christians long before they conceived of themselves as a community of Europeans.

From the thirteenth century on, however, the concept of Christendom became altered. Questions concerning the legitimacy of non-Christian societies continued to appear in philosophical debates and legal treatises. The loss of Constantinople to the Ottoman Turks in 1453 and the Turkish inroads into Balkan Europe between 1354 and 1689 identified the concept particularly with Latin Europe as a doctrinal and geographical unit. Finally, the struggles over questions of authority, law, and doctrine that troubled the ecclesiastical and spiritual life of fourteenth- and fifteenth-century Europe transformed the concept of Christendom far from its eleventh- and twelfth-century character.

That transformation was neither rapid nor simple. Relations between Latins and Byzantines crumbled, but they crumbled slowly, and the possibility of a reunion between the two parts of the Christian Church remained bright—in the minds of a few, at least—until the fall of Constantinople in 1453. From the eleventh century on, for example, theologians in both churches had agreed that many of the specific points of doctrine at issue between them were based upon misunderstandings, linguistic difficulties, and ambiguities. In the fourteenth century Demetrios Kydones translated St. Thomas Aquinas's *Summa Theologiae* into Greek, inaugurating a new Byzantine appreciation for Latin theology. Byzantine mystical theology of the fourteenth century tended to reduce the central position of Trinitarian differences and opened up ways for the Greeks to accept the *Filioque* clause in the Creed. There were even several occasions, such as the Council of Lyons in 1274 and the Council of Florence/Basel in 1439, when official reunion was indeed proclaimed. Yet formal reconciliation presented problems that extended beyond the efforts of diplomats and theologians. Byzantine popular resentment over the rape of the city of Constantinople between 1204 and 1261 ran deep, as did resentment at the economic power of Genoa and Venice in the Byzantine world. This resentment, which colored the decline of Byzantine political, economic, and military resources, strengthened the Byzantines' loyalty to their one great resource, the image of the empire and its religious orthodoxy, proclaimed in churches from Armenia to the Adriatic, from Muscovy to Nicaea, and revered by Slavs, Greeks, and Armenians in the monasteries, towns, and schools of the greatest and oldest culture of the Western world. Moreover, even diplomacy had its limits.

No formal agreement between powers, not even with the emperor's own participation, could persuade the Byzantines to sacrifice their own orthodoxy in return for western aid, particularly if such an act meant running the great risk of alienating Muscovy, Serbia, and the rest of the Orthodox world, whose aid might, through a sense of duty as well as generosity, ultimately be of more help. Reunion with the Latin church may well have been the Byzantines' only realistic alternative to destruction, but it was not one that they were prepared—or able—to choose.

The failure of reunion between the Greek and Latin churches was one blow to the universal concept of Christendom. Increasing conflicts among temporal powers, particularly England and France, reduced the strength of the notion of a common society. Although the popes discovered new resources in the course of the fourteenth century, particularly in terms of administrative organization, theoretical exposition of papal claims to authority, and finance, a number of crises in the fourteenth and fifteenth centuries seriously impaired the effectiveness of its universal claims. Finally, the Holy Roman Empire, reduced by the conflict between Frederick II and the papacy in the thirteenth century, weakened by the long interregnum between 1250 and 1273 and the succession of weak emperors after the latter date, and constituting after 1300 much more an arena for dynastic expansion and political rivalry, emerged as a much reduced and localized power. Its efforts and presence were most successful in central Europe—Austria, Hungary, and Bohemia—and least successful in the old imperial heartlands of Italy, South Germany, and the Rhine Valley. Thus, no real center that could make unchallenged claims to represent Christendom had survived untouched by the mid fifteenth century. Institutional and spiritual crises, new means of accommodating spiritual and temporal loyalties within the territorial monarchies, and a new separation of the real vitality and creativity of Christian spirituality from large numbers of people through the increasing mediation of ranks of unlearned and incompetent lower ecclesiastical officials all contributed further to the deterioration of the idea of Christendom.

The study of the papacy, the movement known as conciliarism, and the problems of devotional reform reveal some of the most striking examples of the tensions between spirituality and secularism in the fourteenth and fifteenth centuries. Between the death of Boniface VIII in 1303 and that of Pius II in 1464 the increased workload falling upon the office of pope and particular difficulties that succeeded one another with inexorable regularity tended to separate the popes from new devotional movements and to focus their energies upon smaller areas.

Many of the greatest and most controversial popes in history became pope in compromise elections when more formidable candidates failed to obtain a majority of the cardinals' votes. The surprise election of a papal dark-horse candidate has indeed become almost a leitmotif in history writing, journalism, and fiction from the eleventh century to the twentieth. One such momentous election was held in 1304–1305, when divisions within the cardinalate prevented one of the cardinals from being elected pope; the compromise choice of the electors was the archbishop of Bordeaux, Bertrand de Got, who, not being a cardinal, was in France at the time of his election. Taking the title Clement V, the new pope set out for Italy, stopping for his coronation in the city of Lyons. Clement's personal concern for the quarrels between Philip the Fair of France and Edward I of England, the fact that his own native land, Gascony, was at the center of these quarrels, and his own involvement in Philip's charges against the Templars and the memory of Boniface VIII prevented Clement's departure for Italy. The Council of Vienne, called to treat some of these crises, was called for 1311, and Clement remained in the south of France, settling in 1309 in the small city of Avignon near the only extensive papally owned lands north of the Alps; there, Clement was beyond the power of Philip of France. Avignon was a city owned by King Charles of Sicily, who was also count of Provence and a papal vassal for his Italian kingdom. There Clement settled to await the council and to mediate between the rulers of England and France, and there, from such a circumstantial beginning, the popes from 1309 to 1377 took up permanent residence. Clement, kept at Avignon by council business, and then kept out of Italy by the invasion of Emperor Henry VII in 1310, died in 1314. His successor, elected at Lyons, was the former bishop of Avignon, who took the name John XXII and reestablished the papal court in his old episcopal city. The troubled state of Italy and the Romagna prevented a papal return until Italy had been quieted. Pope John's hostility to the new emperor, Louis of Bavaria, and the attractions and efficiency of life in Avignon kept John there through his eighteen-year pontificate. John's successor, Benedict XII, elected in 1334, was a dedicated ecclesiastical reformer, and devoted his intense energies to large-scale correction of ecclesiastical abuses, improvement of the papal administrative system, and the development of Avignon into a permanent seat of papal government. In 1336 he began to build the great palace of the popes there, probably the first government building in Europe specifically designed for the business, as well as the pomp and ceremony of a ruling court. By 1340 the papacy had settled in Avignon for the foreseeable future.

To a great extent, the Avignon residence aided the papacy in its task of directing the spiritual life of Christendom. There is considerable irony in the fact that although the Avignon papacy was probably more disposed, better equipped, and financially stable enough to direct universal Christian society more efficiently than ever before, the Avignon residency was regarded by many as the "Babylonian captivity" of the popes, and the increasing factionalism of national rivalries always tended to place the mediating popes in great disfavor with parties opposed to their activities. Indeed, the Avignon papacy was long widely heralded as the sign of the breakup of medieval Christendom; only recently has scholarship clarified its real accomplishments and begun to estimate some of the fourteenth-century popes as highly as they deserve.

By the end of the fourteenth century the possibility of a move back to Rome became more and more likely, but the enormity of moving the papal bureaucracy postponed such a move until 1377. Then Pope Gregory XI accomplished a task that was a great achievement as much in terms of logistics as in terms of morale: he restored Rome as a papal residence. Gregory's death, however, and a disputed, faction-ridden conclave, resulted in the compromise election of Bartolomeo Prignano, the archbishop of Bari, as Pope Urban VI in 1378. Urban, a vehement opponent of cardinals' privileges, quickly alienated many of the cardinals, particularly the large French faction, who had left Avignon very reluctantly. Part of this faction, claiming that Urban's election had been accomplished by threats from the Roman people, withdrew to Perugia and there elected one of their own number, Robert, bishop of Geneva, as pope, with the title Clement VII. Urban resisted, and beginning in 1378 each man claimed to be the canonically elected pope and each claimed the allegiance of all Christendom.

Papal schism was not, of course, new to the Church. The twelfth century had witnessed over twenty antipopes and several schisms, and the furious attacks upon Boniface VIII that continued long after that pope's death remind us of the frequent instability of the papacy and its vulnerability to certain kinds of forces. The Schism of 1378, however, fell during a time of intense and prolonged division among the powers of Christian Europe. The military conflict between France and England, having burst into war in 1337, divided many of the powers of Europe along lines of sympathy, alliance, or hostility. Much of the energy, skill, and resources of the Avignon papacy had been devoted to restoring the peace between England and France. Moreover, the vastly increased business of the papal administrative bureaucracy had resulted in a structure of papally dispensed privileges, benefices, and rights throughout the kingdoms of Europe. The factional alignments of different forces behind different popes during the schism echoed the wider factionalism among the territorial princes, reduced the papal status as mediator in a series of progressively more devastating wars, and crippled the papal ability to provide for its servants. From 1378 to 1409 the rival popes and their successors had to take sides in other disputes in order to guarantee their own support, they lost their impartial status as peacemakers, and they often duplicated each other's awards of benefices and privileges in an effort to force their opponents to capitulate.

As the schism endured, various steps were taken to put pressure on both sides to reach an understanding. Between 1399 and 1403 the king of France declared a "suspension of obedience" from both sides, and gave the French church an early experience of that independence that later, in the form of special concordats—agreements with the papacy—helped create the highly independent Gallican Church of the sixteenth and seventeenth centuries. In 1409 an abortive council held at Pisa deposed both contenders and elected yet another pope, thereby widening the schism to a field of three. The next six years were spent in dramatic attempts to resolve the claims of three rivals, and only the energy of a number of high prelates, the universities, and Emperor Sigismund determined the direction in which a solution might possibly be found. It was decided that this, the greatest of all the ills of the Church, must be solved—could *only* be solved—by an ecumenical Church council. The council, called to meet at Constance in 1415, was to be the Church's last resort to restore unity in a faction-ridden world and to restore a single pope to the throne of St. Peter.

The dramatic events in the century of papal history between the ascension of Pope Boniface VIII in 1294 to the Council of Constance in 1415 have seemed to many historians sufficient in themselves to account for the decline of the papacy as a spiritually supreme force in the fourteenth and fifteenth centuries. The conflict between Boniface and Philip the Fair, the affair of the Templars, the Avignon residency, the schism, and the beginnings of the conciliar movement—all certainly damaged the papacy as an institution and the popes as individual leaders. Yet their results must not be considered inevitable, nor must their role in papal history be overrated. The memory of Boniface survived the attacks of Philip and others; the Avignon residency witnessed a vigorous, efficient period in papal history; the schism generated the desire to restore once again a single pope to a single body of Christendom; and the Council of Constance was to be concerned as much with the growth of heresy as with the problem of papal unity. The full impact of the events of this century must be considered in terms of other institutions besides the papacy, those that, along with the papacy, constituted the visible expression of Christian unity and were the bonds of a universal concept of Christian society.

Besides papal supremacy in the Christian world, what other institutions reflected that idea of a universal Christian society? The destruction of the Templars by Philip the Fair of France in the first quarter of the fourteenth century signaled the decline of one such institution, the military orders. From the twelfth through the sixteenth centuries, these associations constituted a visible reflection of the new militant Christianity of Crusading Europe. Their resources and their membership were coextensive with Christian civilization. The destruction of the Templars only signaled dramatically a process already well under way by the fourteenth century—the increasing localism that made many of the orders territorial powers rather than symbols of militant universal Christianity. Only the Knights Hospitalers remained in the eastern Mediterranean, where, first from Rhodes, then from Malta, they continued to act against Islamic expansion. Of the other orders, the Teutonic Knights had long since formed an extensive territorial state in the eastern Baltic, the Orders of Santiago and Calatrava were great landholders in Spain, and the universal claims of others were fast becoming shadows. Indeed, the new secular "orders" of knighthood established in the thirteenth- and fourteenth-century royal and princely courts—the Order of the Garter in England and that of the Star in France and the Ship in Naples—reflected, in their new, local, and secularized interests, the fate of the once novel idea of religious associations of fighters, bound together by their common vows and a common dedication to the idea of Christendom.

In other areas as well, deep-rooted change reflected the weakening of universal Christian idealism. Monasticism, long the very fiber of a concept of universal Christian society, had ceased since the thirteenth century to represent significantly any cause but a local one. The increased episcopal and parish enthusiasm of the thirteenth and fourteenth centuries, the popularity of the Orders of Preachers and Friars Minor, the universities' drawing off many men who might once have entered monastic centers all weakened the former exclusivity and prestige of monasticism. Economic changes, changes in the style of living, changing criteria of recruitment, and the increasingly frequent practice of *commendam*—placing an absentee ruler in lieu of an abbot in charge of a monastery for financial reasons—all transformed the demography and the style of monasticism. The last great monastic reforms of the Middle Ages, the series passed by the Cistercian pope Benedict XII in 1335, 1336, and 1339, barely corrected the new developments in monastic life. Limited recruiting, the relaxation of former strenuous dietary regulations, and the increasing popularity and effectiveness of other forms of devotional life weakened the attractions and the effectiveness of monasticism. The decreasing number of monks and nuns during the fourteenth and fifteenth centuries, the transformation of monasteries into houses either of study or of semiworldly retirement, and the increasing variety of new forms of devotional experience heralded the decline of monasticism from its former central role in Christian ecclesiology. In spite of occasional vigorous attempts at local monastic reform and the steady but much smaller stream of monastic theological and mystical writers, the great age of monasticism was over by the beginning of the fifteenth century, a century before many of the physical remains of monasticism were forever destroyed by the Reformation.

The third great symbol of universal Christian society—the orders—also experienced fragmenting change during this period. Furious internal conflicts such as that between the Conventual and Observant wings of the Franciscan Order, between different sides taken by the Dominicans during the papal schism, and increasing popular hostility to the friars weakened the universality of the last recent creations of a vigorous papacy and a responsive Church. In Chaucer's *Canterbury Tales,* a number of fourteenth-century ecclesiastical figures are portrayed, and some are savagely satirized, none more than the Friar, the Monk, and the Pardoner, a hawker of false relics and indulgences of dubious legitimacy. The great age of SS. Francis and Dominic and the second great age of the orders' contribution to learning and theology were both over by the fifteenth century. The forces of economic, ecclesiastical, and devotional change transformed the role of the orders just as they had those of the military orders, monasticism, and the administrative bureaucracy of the Church. The experience of the papacy alone, then, does not adequately convey the depth and extent of change in earlier universal institutions. The chief supports of papal universality all experienced transformation during the fourteenth and fifteenth centuries.

Within this framework of general ecclesiastical history between 1400 and 1471, let us focus upon some of the events of the Council of Constance. The Sixteenth Ecumenical Council of the Church assembled at the imperial city of Constance at the confluence of the Rhine and Lake Constance, and was convoked by Pope John XXIII and Emperor Sigismund on November 5, 1414. Sigismund, emperor since 1410, had been moved to support the idea of a council by the threat of heresy in his Bohemian lands as well as by a general feeling that the schism had to be brought to an end. After suggesting a meeting place in Italy and rejecting French suggestions for a meeting place in France, John XXIII reluctantly agreed to Constance at Sigismund's suggestion. The sheer logistical problems posed to the small city by the prospect of a large assembly were enormous, but for four years little Constance was the capital of Christendom.

Sigismund's local difficulties and John's reluctance were but two of the political problems that remained even after Constance had been decided upon. The wars between France and England, halted during the reigns of Charles VI and Richard II, were about to flare up again under Henry IV and Henry V of England and the fatal quarrel between the regents of France. Cardinals, bishops, and abbots were joined by a large group of laymen, university doctors, representatives of monarchs, conciliar thinkers of all persuasions, and the vast numbers of servants, secretaries, companions, advisors, and men at arms who attended them, and among these there was considerable rivalry. Cardinals feeling opposed by conciliarists, clergy opposed by laymen, popes opposed by popes, burghers attempting to keep good order in the city—all were at least initially, under the nominal control of the emperor in council, which was presided over at first by John XXIII. Everyone knew the great duties of the council—to reestablish unity in the Church and to defend troubled orthodoxy—and the organization of the assembly to accomplish these purposes was the first task at hand.

The council was organized by nations, groups of territories recognized as having a kind of fundamental unity, rather along the lines of the national groupings at some universities. This form of organization, important as it was in recognizing a new basis for ecclesiastical organization, was slow to be perfected and was torn with internal rivalries—rivalries between nations, particularly the English and French, and rivalries between the nations and the College of Cardinals, which thought, perfectly accurately, that its own power was threatened by such novelties. The organization according to nations meant that no matter how numerous or high-ranking a particular delegation might be—Italian clergy, for example, were far more numerous than any other group—or how small or peculiarly constituted others might be—the English nation consisted of twenty persons, and the Portuguese delegation, which alone represented the Spanish nation for a time, consisted solely of laymen—each nation had to achieve internal concord, and each nation's vote counted as much as another's. Such organizational difficulties, especially when they exacerbated existing rivalries, made the council's work slow and weakened conciliar unity, particularly after the removal of the three contending popes. After the election of Martin V in 1417 the pope alone presided over the council, and he concluded its sessions by signing concordats with individual nations, promising reform, making concessions, and perpetuating, in papal diplomacy, the new ecclesiastical organization that had come so close to dissolving the council in political rivalries.

When it became clear to John XXIII that the first issue the council proposed to take up after its organizational sessions was his own removal, he fled from Constance in March, 1415, but he was captured and returned and was deposed by the council on May 29. In the preparation of the articles of deposition, the voices of the great conciliar thinkers, particularly Dietrich of Niem and Jean Gerson, were most effective, and conciliar thought itself was strengthened just over a month later when Gregory XII formally resigned. Not until two years later was Benedict XIII deposed by the council.

The council's early success with two of the three contending popes was matched by its promptness and ferocity in bringing to trial the Bohemian heretic John Hus, thereby establishing its own orthodoxy and expressing its concern over the growth of heresy in general during the late fourteenth and early fifteenth centuries. Hus was born in the small village of Husinec in southern Bohemia. After receiving a local education, he entered the university at Prague around 1390 at the age of eighteen and in extreme poverty. Supporting himself as a singer in churches, he received his Bachelor of Arts degree in 1393, enrolled in the study of theology, and in 1396 began to lecture in the lower faculty of arts. Prague was the first university founded east of the Rhine, and from its foundation in 1348 under Emperor Charles IV, Sigismund's father, to 1400, it served as the principal imperial university. Around 1400, however, new intellectual and social movements, particularly in the field of theology and in the rising national consciousness of the Czech people, gave it a more distinctly Bohemian character. The theological movement owed much to the English theologian and ecclesiastical critic John Wycliffe (1320?-1384), and the upsurge of Czech national feeling centered in late fourteenth-century vernacular preachers, such as Matthew of Janov and John Milic, and in the foundation of the Bethlehem Chapel in Prague in 1391 by Wenceslaus Krix and John of Milheim. In 1402 Hus was named rector and preacher at the Bethlehem Chapel, and when Zbynek Zajic became archbishop of Prague in 1403, he and Hus shared the institution of reform movements in the Czech church. Hus was elected rector of the University of Prague in 1409. The radical wing of the ecclesiastical reformers, led by Jerome of Prague, soon drove a wedge between Hus and Zajic, the archbishop excommunicating Hus in 1411. Hus bitterly denounced John XIII's attempt to call a Crusade in 1411 and again was excommunicated and had to flee Prague in 1412. In spite of Hus's political activities, however, he remained the pastor of the Bethlehem Chapel, delivering careful sermons to his flock and ministering to them in the greatest tradition of Christian pastoralism. Hus not only preached in Czech, but he reformed the orthography of the Czech language.

In 1414 Hus was summoned to Constance to answer for his statements and was granted an imperial safe-conduct by Sigismund. When Hus arrived at Constance, however, the council threw him in prison, denied the validity of his safe-conduct, and after eight months of strict imprisonment brought him to trial for heresy. Not until June 5, 1415, was Hus brought to a hearing before the council. The final trial focused upon Hus's alleged teachings concerning the Church, the ecclesiastical hierarchy, the treatment of heresy, the condition of the clergy, and several other points, all of which Hus protested were misinterpreted from his works. He was condemned as an obstinate heretic on July 6, 1415, degraded from the priesthood, and relaxed to the secular arm, in this case Duke Louis of the Palatinate, who turned Hus over to the executioners. Hus was led outside the city, clothed in the costume of condemned heretics, fastened to the stake, and burned. His ashes were scattered and his clothing was destroyed so that no relics might be returned to Bohemia.

Thus, the rudiments of ecclesiastical unity—the removal of the three popes and the attack upon heresy in the person of John Hus—launched the council upon its path. Yet in spite of these early actions, the council accomplished little in its remaining three years that was entirely satisfactory. Bohemia exploded in a terrible civil war that lasted until 1434. Pope Martin V came to terms with the nations and the cardinals but not with the ardent conciliarists, and his coming to terms with the nations almost unavoidably prevented the possibility of universal reforms. The Council of Constance, in some ways as representative of the new idea of Christendom as the Crusade movement had been of the old idea, found itself unable to perform the very task it had condemned the popes for failing to accomplish. When later councils met at Basel and Florence later in the century, the old ideas were revived, but with even fewer results. Having failed to establish internal unity, the conciliar movement found itself incapable of creating external unity either. The temporal reconciliation with the eastern church of 1439 was repudiated in Constantinople and Russia, and not even the Turkish capture of Constantinople in 1453 could generate a unified response by Christendom. The future of conciliarism lay, like the direction of the Church, with the individual nations, whether as kingdoms or as modern states. The new pope, Martin V, left Constance in 1418 to reestablish some semblance of papal authority in the Papal States.

In spite of the pronounced reform efforts of many churchmen, including popes, during the Avignon period, the divided papacy between 1378 and 1415 and the consequent lack of leadership in the Church could do little to prevent the spread of abuses or eradicate their causes. And it was the Church, as a whole body possessed of a collective well-being, that became the focus of reformers' attentions during the fifteenth century. From the small centers of religious reform in the Netherlands and the lower Rhineland—Deventer and Windesheim—to the great schools of law and theology at Paris, and to the new centers of learning and devotion in central Europe—Vienna, Cracow, Prague— thinkers and writers devoted considerable attention to the dilemmas of both Christian society and the individual Christian. The episcopal order itself, lacking a single head until 1417, veered closer in its loyalty to the secular ruler, although few kings of the late fourteenth and fifteenth centuries were especially able to exploit the resources of this new loyalty. The lower clergy, still generally ignored, often failed to respond to the new devotional movements of the souls in their care.

Yet it is too easy to focus upon ecclesiastical abuses and the exclusively legal and administrative problems of solving them and reestablishing firm and universally recognized ecclesiastical government. If we consider the spiritual history of the period between 1300 and 1525 apart from the difficulties created by the Avignon Papacy and the Great Schism, the number of attempts at real reform and the concern for local clergy are surprisingly extensive. Thirteenth- and fourteenth-century English bishops, for example, did make substantial attempts to administer their dioceses, and with the publication early in the fourteenth century of William of Pagula's *Occulus Pastoralis* and in the fifteenth century of John Mirick's *Instructions for Parish Priests,* we can see the first stages of the slow process by which thirteenth-century theology, moral theology, and canon law began to filter down to a pastoral revolution on the parish level, just as the prestige of the Franciscans and Dominicans was beginning to wane. In the mid fourteenth century Pope Benedict XII made extensive efforts to reform monasticism, the first major attempt to do so since the Cistercian revolution two centuries before. In the course of the fourteenth century a pastoral ideal took shape, one that is perhaps best reflected in the figure of the Parson in Chaucer's *Canterbury Tales* but that was certainly not an invention of Chaucer himself. Indeed, it may be said that a workable interest in pastoral care—aided by ideals of clergy, handbooks of instruction, and helps for sermon writing, and moved by a new and genuine sense of responsibility to the souls of individual Christians on all levels of society—was one of the most important results of the ecclesiastical changes of the thirteenth century. That interest was hard to activate, however, and it is more remarkable in isolated centers than in consistently applied diocesan or metropolitan regulations.

The fourteenth and fifteenth centuries also witnessed a new sophistication and acuteness of conscience on the part of many individuals, women and men, learned and unlearned, in special religious communities and in parishes. The Brethren of the Common Life at Deventer, in particular, stand out as a reflection of a wider and less universally articulate movement in which laypeople from all walks of life expressed the dissonance between their own spiritual anguish and the inability of the Church to assuage it. Some of the remarkable religious figures of the fourteenth and fifteenth centuries—St. Brigit of Sweden, St. Catherine of Siena, San Bernardino of Siena, Thomas à Kempis, John Wycliffe—shared this intense concern for devotional purity and social reform, as well as a new interest in learning and letters, and the consequent mental and spiritual habits they developed had already begun to move out of the towns and into the countryside.

The study of the religious temper of the fifteenth century is often made difficult because we know very well what followed: the Reformation of the sixteenth century and the Church's response at the Council of Trent between 1545 and 1563. Yet it would not be too much to say that the movements that constituted the Reformation would have had no public but for the devotional interests of the fourteenth and fifteenth centuries, would have had no Luther but for the reform movements of the fifteenth century within the Augustinian order and the spread of universities into remote corners of Saxony, would have had no Henry VIII without the clergy's growing loyalty to and respect for the secular power.

For a brief period, many of these concerns became the center of attention at Constance. Besides the aforementioned actions of the council in resolving the papal schism and burning the Bohemian Hus, the council attempted to insure the continuity of conciliar scrutiny of the well-being of the Church by insisting that general councils be called by future popes with meticulous regularity. These solutions, however, proved to be nearly worse than the disease they had set out to cure. Conciliarism, a movement that had made great headway since the thirteenth century, consisted of many different strains of thought, few of which agreed on all issues. After the success of the movement at Constance, the strength of the ideal waned, and part of the result was the long delay in calling what later became the Council of Trent in the sixteenth century. The most outspoken supporters of the superiority of council to pope alienated the papacy throughout the fifteenth century and caused much friction in high ecclesiastical circles. The burning of John Hus touched off the terrible Bohemian wars of the early fifteenth century. The Council's decree *Frequens,* which insisted that regular councils be called in the future, hung around later popes' necks like an albatross, further alienating the popes, from Martin V (1417–1431) to Pius II (1458–1464), from the concept of conciliar usefulness, and leaving their successors, from Paul II (1464–1471) on, to function far more as local Italian princes concerned with consolidating power within the Papal States than as leaders of a universal church. The high-water mark of conciliarism as successful movement was brief, and the price paid by the whole Church for the papal failure to come to terms with it was a Church as localized and headless at the end of the fifteenth century as it had been at the end of the fourteenth. Unlike the conditions of a century earlier, however, the lay rulers of the late fifteenth century were far better able to master "their" churches, and the price of even lip service to Rome was a series of carefully negotiated concordats, signed by the papacy and different rulers in Europe.

Against this series of political and fiscal crises in the government of the Church must be set the new devotional movements of the late fourteenth and fifteenth centuries: new religious communities of clerks and laypeople; an increasing spiritual anguish that was often inextricably mixed with a magical view of the properties of sacred objects and sacred prayers; a new Christian humanism that attempted to plot out an ideal Christian life with the rationality of classical Latin and

Greek writers and the moral force of the early church fathers, a movement that culminated in the career of the great scholar Erasmus (1469–1536); and, finally, a new intensity in the role of the layman in the plan of salvation, an intensity that reached its greatest heights in the brooding, bitter lines of the late fourteenth-century English poem, *Piers Plowman*. The shattered Church organization of the fifteenth century could not deal adequately with these movements, and when Pope Pius II, the great humanist pope, died while setting out on a Crusade against the Ottoman Turks—the first humanist Pope setting out on the last Crusade—it may well seem as if one phase in the history of the idea of Christendom had come to an end.

POWER AND ORDER

The political thought of early Europe was not, as we have seen many times, easily separable from ideas of cosmology, ecclesiology, and general law, on a large scale, nor from minute details of specific legal privilege, private property laws, and custom, on the scale of its day-to-day expression. The idea of a Christian cosmos, whether seen through the eyes of Carolingian and Ottonian emperors or post-Gregorian popes and their supporters, survived the political structures and political thought of early Europeans until the eighteenth and nineteenth centuries. The ecclesiological crises of the twelfth and thirteenth centuries had formally stripped temporal rulers of much of their sacral, liturgical character, but the intricacies of ecclesiastical thought, although perfectly clear to those who formulated them, were not always clearly understood by wider segments of the population. One of the most striking features of the transformation of political thought between the twelfth and the nineteenth centuries is the success with which temporal rulers surrounded themselves and the communities they ruled with a secularized political theology whose elements ranged from nonsacramental coronation ceremonies to the prestige of sainted predecessors. Within the frames of cosmology and the post-twelfth-century secularized legitimation of rulership were fitted, in the twelfth and thirteenth centuries, new ideas of secular public law and, in the thirteenth and fourteenth centuries, the new vocabulary derived from the recovery of Aristotelian political thought. To a great extent, much greater than is generally supposed, these four elements in the order just given constitute the foundations of modern political theory.

In the practical sphere, temporal power too was successful. Royal and nonroyal government became increasingly efficient in many areas, and the spread of royal justice carried the image of the ruler into distant corners of his territory. In theory, kings began to appropriate for themselves qualities formerly attributed only to the Roman emperor—exclusion from a superior authority, the right to make laws, the

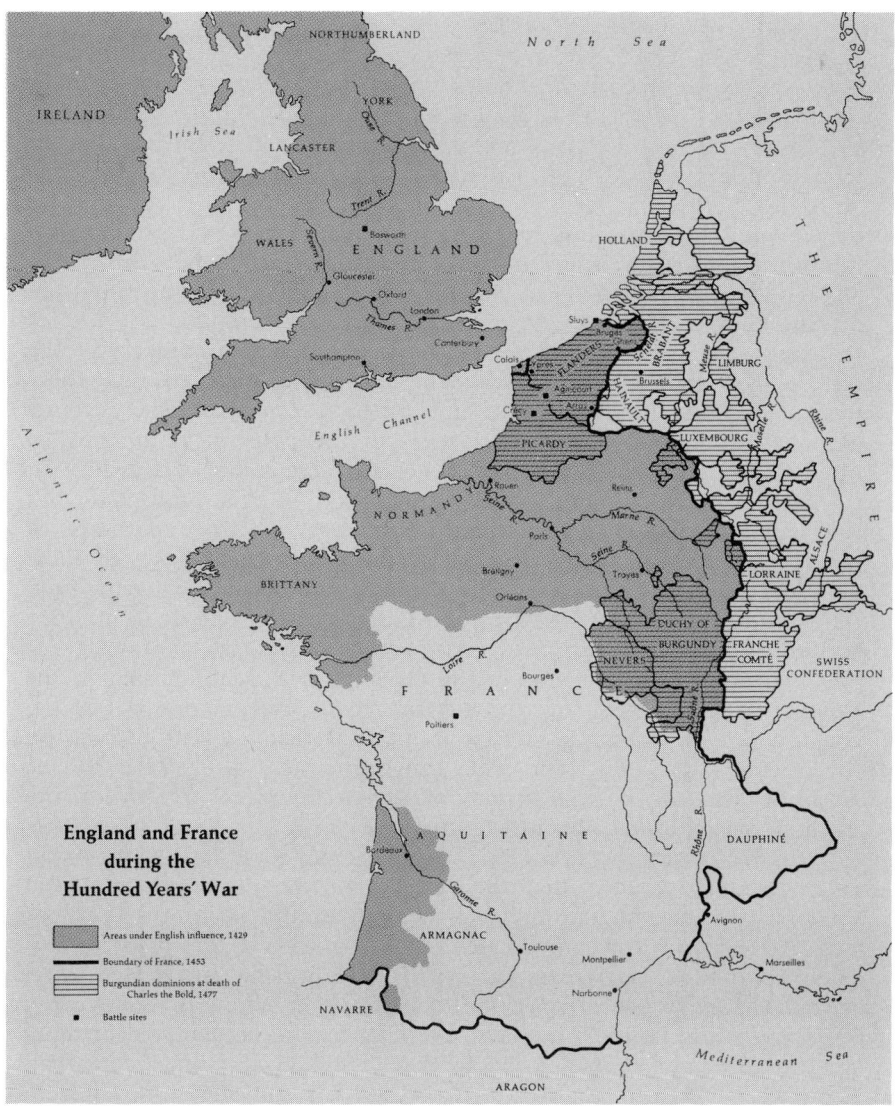

England and France during the Hundred Years' War

- Areas under English influence, 1429
- Boundary of France, 1453
- Burgundian dominions at death of Charles the Bold, 1477
- Battle sites

right to be the object of the public crime of treason. In practice, the worlds of the court and the town hall became more than private households, articulated the public functions of their members, extended patronage and propaganda, and exploited both high theory and the widest possible range of resources, both traditional and novel, to extend and strengthen their power and their legitimacy.

In two treatises on political thought from the early fourteenth century, it is possible to detect the influence of both new theory and new practice. John of Paris's *On Royal and Papal Power* presents a distinctive justification of the royal authority of the kings of France, based upon the experience of the French crown and the papacy in the thirteenth century. Marsiglio of Padua's *Defensor Pacis* (*The Defender of the Peace*) offers a comparative vocabulary of political concepts and terms applicable to all political societies in all periods of history. For Marsiglio, political order has as its end the formation of a new kind of political public, one whose members participate freely and productively in an orderly society. Marsiglio is, of course, not a "liberal" theorist in any modern sense of the term, but his role as a gifted extrapolator from diverse kinds of experience toward a universal comparative view of political society makes him one of the most important thinkers in the history of secularist political thought. To works such as these there were added in the fourteenth and fifteenth centuries new defenses of papal authority, various approaches to the political rationalism of fifteenth-century monarchies, and a general acceptance of the idea of the legitimacy of temporal society and power. In this sense, and with the added attribute of a sharpened awareness of the importance of recent historical changes, the work of thinkers such as John of Paris and Marsiglio of Padua leads to the writings of such fifteenth- and sixteenth-century theorists as Sir John Fortescue, Philippe de Commines, and Machiavelli.

The various movements in the conciliar crisis, culminating in the Council of Constance, contributed further to the exploration of the consequences in temporal society of political theories that had begun in ecclesiastical circles. The wide range and general disorder of the world of ideas may be seen in some of the circumstances of political life in the fourteenth and fifteenth centuries.

In 751, when the Franks rid themselves of their last Merovingian ruler, they said bluntly that they were removing the royal title from their king because he had lost the royal power, and that a title without power was merely an empty name. In 1399, when a group of English nobles and their supporters succeeded in capturing and trying King Richard II, they too attempted to justify their action in removing a legitimate king. In 1399, however, the king had to be deprived of more than a "title" and he had to be accused of losing something more than "power." Richard II was made to declare his subjects absolved from their oaths of fealty, from the bonds of homage, allegiance, regality, and lordship, and he himself renounced not only the title and power of king, but the royal dignity, majesty, crown, lordship, rule, governance, administration, empire, jurisdiction, honor, regality, and highness of king. In the event that they had missed any of the more elusive royal qualities, his prosecutors also declared Richard deprived of any other trace of the royal dignity "as much as any yet remained in him." Now this astonishing proliferation of qualities that had to be renounced by or removed from a king who was abdicating or being deposed did not represent clearly conceptualized characteristics and attributes. Many, if not all, of Richard's opponents would have been hard put to define all or most of them clearly. Yet the sheer increase in the number and variety of essential royal qualities—or at least qualities that royal enemies presumed that kings possessed—does indicate that the institution of kingship had grown vastly more complex. Some of these terms—homage, allegiance, title, lordship—came from an old political vocabulary that reminds us that the king was once considered a type of lord similar to other lords, a "feudal" overlord. Others—dignity, majesty, honor, regality, empire—reflect the increased prestige of the royal figure in the secular and religious thought of the twelfth and thirteenth centuries, deriving from the revived study of Roman law, the activity of rulers and publicists, and the king's secularized liturgical character. Still others—governance, administration, jurisdiction—are yet more interesting, because it is these terms that represent the differentiation of different kinds of royal power as rulers' subjects actually knew it in their daily lives, and it was this access to differentiated and extremely sophisticated kinds of power that men really wanted to take away from King Richard II. To be sure, the other sets of terms—as well as the final catchall designation of other qualities "insofar as any remain in him"—also carried weight, and would continue to do so through the sixteenth century and well into the eighteenth century. But it was this last group that men's attention focused on in 1399. It is important to remember that as late as the eighteenth century, although kings' abstract claims to power grew even more formidable, the personal qualities upon which they based their authority and right had all been developed between the sixth and the thirteenth centuries. The revolutions of the eighteenth and nineteenth centuries against monarchical authority possessed new philosophical justifications and sprang from different political, social, and economic experiences, but they all assumed the existence of an abstract state and certain institutions of governance. What these later revolutionaries attacked was not the state itself, but the role of the king and his government within the state, and that role had been created by the rulers of the thirteenth and fourteenth centuries.

Of what, then, did the king's governance, administration, and jurisdiction consist, and why was it important that the king be separated from them? In the first place, it may be useful to contrast the authority and institutional resources of the Holy Roman Emperor, once the prototype of temporal rule in the west, with those of the territorial monarchs of England, France, Castile, and Naples. The emperor, it will be remembered, had been compelled in the thirteenth century to modify considerably his claims to certain kinds of authority in the face of papal authority and his rights to govern in northern Italy and Germany because of the powers of the city-republics in the one region and that of the German ecclesiastical and secular princes and cities in the other. By 1356, when the Golden Bull was issued, imperial jurisdictional and fiscal resources were virtually reduced to a minimum, the legitimate authority of the great electors was sanctioned by imperial edict, and the emperors, in spite of the ambitious claims still made on their behalf, were forced to develop their own family resources by acquiring other lands and crowns. With no continuing administrative mechanisms and no regular public source of income, the Holy Roman

Emperors were compelled to become dynasts and political adventurers. Other monarchs, faced with far less powerful resistance, grew stronger. The model of monarchical and princely government in the west developed along far different lines. In the twelfth century western monarchs too had faced repositories of legitimate authority and power outside their own hands and, hence, in twelfth-century terms, outside of royal governance. The most successful responses to this problem were those that introduced effective organizational reforms first into the lands that the king held personally and proprietarily, then into other lands in which the kings could claim at least a jurisdictional foothold, and, later, under both the effective power of the kings and the willingness of their subjects to recognize that power, into the kingdom as a whole. The German emperors succeeded fully in the first of these steps, only partially in the second, and never in the third. The success of hereditary monarchy (again, an advantage to which emperors could not lay claim, although they tried to) and the continued influence of the personal, private, king over increasingly public administration maintained the idea of personal monarchical authority and at the same time permitted rulers to develop increasingly complex and effective forms of making that authority abstract and public. The thirteenth century witnessed the increasingly sedentary royal court and the emergence of a capital town in England and France. Alongside traditional public servants, kings continued to exploit the services of those who immediately surrounded them, and specialized departments of governance quickly proliferated, usually to the king's advantage. The power of the prince reached farther and farther into the daily life of his kingdom. By sharpening men's concept of their relation to the prince as that of subjects to a ruler, by extending royal judicial and fiscal agents into local regions, and by publicizing widely the needs of the kingdom and men's responsibility to aid the king in fulfilling those needs, thirteenth- and fourteenth-century rulers furthered the character of the private king whose power was increased by the increasingly regular, stable, and public character of his administration.

The ways in which various kingdoms achieved this kind of governance varied according to the ways in which kings had come to rule in the first place; the experience of royal dynasties, the personal abilities of individual rulers, and the success or failure of governmental experiments were themselves made as often from royal necessity as from royal plan. England had been placed since the Norman Conquest of 1066 into a certain relationship with its king, and the very compactness and lack of serious provincial differences within the kingdom tended to offer to its ruler both a closer association with the great magnates and a more precociously developed sense of acting on behalf of the kingdom as a whole. France, which had added provinces of very differing character to the territories ruled by the king from the twelfth to the fourteenth century, tended to retain this regional sense very late, far later than the fifteenth century. The king of England found it easy (as did his opponents) to call great assemblies in order to inform them of his intentions and needs or in order to exploit their support. In France, regional assemblies long remained localized, and the development of a general assembly took much longer. In England again, these great assemblies became identified with the term *parliament*, which simply meant any assembly gathered for purposes of discussion. As was the case with other collective words—guild and university, for example— the word parliament did not become until much later the exclusive designation of a formally constituted assembly holding clearly specified substantial powers that could challenge or override those of the king and his servants. In France, the term *parlement* moved in another direction. There, general provincial assemblies and the infrequent national assemblies were called Estates-General, referring to the collective assembly of *estates*—that is, ranks—of society. *Parlement* came to mean in France the institutionalized expression of the judicial function of the king's household, a much more specific legal court than the English Parliaments that followed.

In Spain the circumstances of the formation of the kingdoms of Castile and Aragón had resulted in the formation of ambitious claims on behalf of the royal authority, but also in its relative weakness. This weakness was signaled not only by aristocratic and ecclesiastical privilege and the wealth of the military orders, but in the institution of the *Cortes*, the "courts," within each of the kingdoms on the Iberian peninsula. Although each *Cortes* operated individually and was structured individually, they all had in common a clearly defined membership—usually composed of sections including the magnates, the higher clergy, and the representatives of privileged towns. The *Cortes* vigorously preserved the rights of each estate to its traditional privileges and maintained their regular meetings and took steps to assure that their business was continued between meetings, although the strength and continuing of the *Cortes* in each kingdom varied considerably from those of the others.

What is perhaps most noteworthy among all late medieval proto-representative assemblies, however, is their dependence to some extent upon the royal authority, their defense of traditional rights, and their vulnerability to royal evasion of their powers in fiscal and some legislative matters. They were far from constituting, as similar institutions did later, constituent parts of the government of a state working in a system of checks and balances with other parts, of which the royal authority was one. In spite of these novel political institutions, and in spite of frequent royal weakness, the king still stood firmly at the head of early European society, and few political theorists or rebellious subjects, no matter how extreme or how powerful, were able even to conceive of a state in which royal authority did not occupy such a position.

Some of the results of an increasingly sharpened body of political theory and an increasingly widened sphere of political life may be seen in the relationship between power and order in the kingdoms of England and France, in the wide and generally neglected sphere of subnational societies, and in the practice of governance that came, by the fifteenth century, to include international relations, the effective mobilization of state resources, public service, taxation, warfare, and patronage.

The circumstances of public rule in England and France during the fourteenth and fifteenth centuries must be considered not, as those of the empire, in terms of the spread of princely power and the disentanglement with the papacy, but against a growing concept of kingly rule shaped in the process of a series of long, devastating, and expensive wars between 1337 and 1453. In spite of the very different history of each of the two crowns, the reigns of Henry III of England (1216–1270) and St. Louis IX of France (1226–1270) witnessed considerable consolidation of monarchical authority, whereas later reigns, particularly those of Edward I (1270–1307) and Edward II (1307–1327) of England and Philip IV (1285–1314) and Philip VI (1328–1350) of France witnessed the difficulties of monarchical governance both internally and in terms of relations between the two kingdoms. The long reigns and distinctive personalities of Henry III and Louis IX, and their concern for affairs beyond their own kingdoms—St. Louis went on two Crusades and was requested to intervene in the dispute between Henry III and his rebellious barons; Henry III planned to acquire the crown of Sicily for his son and patronized a large number of artists from all over Europe—suggest the older world of wide interests of royal personalities, a world in which the ideas of Christendom and Crusade still constituted the most familiar frames of reference for kings. By the beginning of the fourteenth century, however, both local problems and the growing strains upon relations between the two kingdoms created the backdrop of more than a century of intermittent warfare between the two kingdoms and their allies. The circumstances of those wars sharply influenced internal constitutional changes and paved the way for the revived monarchies of the later fifteenth century.

The articulation of royal government in England had created by the thirteenth century an effective bureaucratic instrument in the king's council, the *curia regis*. The *curia,* Parliament, and the king's legal officers carried royal authority systematically into the countryside in administrative, financial, and legal affairs, and between 1263 and 1485 baronial attempts to check royal power frequently included moments of dominating, or trying to dominate, both individiual rulers and their institutions. Philip IV's fiscal and judicial reforms in France, like those of Edward I in England, created deep-rooted resentments among the great nobles and wealthy taxpayers, and some of the consequences of such resentment became apparent in succeeding reigns, in which France, like England, witnessed the impact of dynastic affairs—minorities, new personal styles of rule, and succession crises—upon the public problems of the kingdom. Edward II of England was deposed in 1327 because he could not control the opposition that his father's policies had engendered. Edward III turned to war in part at least as an attempt to restore the weakened authority of the king. Philip IV died in 1314, leaving three sons, each of whom succeeded to the crown—the two younger ones doing so as an elder brother died without sons—for the first time in the history of the French monarchy since 987. At the death of Charles IV (1322–1328) and the accession of Philip VI (1328–1350), the threat of baronial opposition was great, but the size, diversity, and particularism of the kingdom of France prevented consolidated baronial opposition from gaining the foothold it had in England. But financial difficulties pressed both kingdoms, and disputes concerning royal finances colored both kingdoms for the next century. Moreover, the succession crisis in France in 1328 offered an opportunity for the heightening of tensions between France and England.

The financial and political crises of the late thirteenth and early fourteenth centuries illuminate sharply the growing disparity between new needs and traditional institutions. Few problems illustrate better both the traditional and the novel approaches to political order than those surrounding the outbreak of the Hundred Years War between England and France. The complex dynastic marriage patterns of the late thirteenth century had made Edward II and Edward III legitimate claimants for succession to the crown of France, and the existence of the English claims, which were legally stronger than his own, increased Philip VI's dependence upon those who had supported his bid for the crown. A second "private dimension" to the conflict was Philip VI's status as overlord to Edward III for the English holdings in Gascony and his demand for homage from the English king when he ascended the throne. Yet these "private" affairs existed side by side with very immediate public difficulties, and of these the best example is the problem of Gascony itself.

The English occupation of Gascony had been part of the complex settlement of English royal holdings in France that had been determined in 1258. Technically, the king of England was vassal to the king of France for Gascony, but the roles of lord and vassal became particularly strained when both the lord and the vassal were kings. "The king can be no man's vassal," argued publicists and theorists in both England and France throughout the thirteenth century, and the quarrel over Gascony suggests the practical truth of that maxim. In the course of the thirteenth century the royal governance of England had tended to homogenize the administration of all crown possessions, no matter how they were technically attached to the crown. Gascony was integrated into the system of English governmental administration and, because of the value of its wine harvest, into the English economic world as well. Gascony was part of an increasingly complex English economic sphere that included access to Flemish wool centers, Breton salt processing, and Portuguese trade. The conflict between lord and vassal over the rights of each in Gascony and elsewhere is one way of looking at a set of problems that have equally critical economic and diplomatic dimensions as well. The lord-vassal relationship was not, however, capable of accommodating these with any great success.

French pressure on Gascony and the English claim to succeed to the French throne, coupled with French diplomatic alliances with Scotland, led to a carefully planned and financed French attempt to invade

Scotland and England and to the outbreak of war as a result of the English naval victory at Sluys in 1340. From 1340 to the Treaty of Brétigny in 1360, England launched *chevauchées* into France, winning pitched battles at Crécy and Poitiers in 1346 and 1356 and capturing the Channel Islands in 1345 and the great port of Calais in 1347. The war proved difficult to control, however, and was extraordinarily expensive. Moreover, both kingdoms were struck by the famine and pestilence of the mid fourteenth century. The triumphs of England sustained the power of Edward III, but the French losses, heightened by the capture of King Jean II in 1356, precipitated both intense factionalism among the nobility and in 1356–1358 a social revolution in Paris itself, led by Robert LeCoq, bishop of Laon, and Etienne Marcel, provost of the merchants of Paris.

The reign of Charles V of France (1364–1380) witnessed significant improvements. Between the capture of his father Jean II in 1356 and Jean's death in 1364, Charles was the regent of France. He first subdued the rebels of 1358 and then successfully negotiated his father's release and ransom. By 1369 he was able, through administrative and financial reforms, to resume the war, profiting from the senility of Edward III, the deaths of Edward's son the Black Prince in 1376 and of Edward III himself in 1377, and the minority of Richard II (1377–1381) to lead to another truce. Charles's fiscal and military reforms were only part of his success, however. His artistic and literary patronage virtually inaugurated the role of the French crown as a leader in intellectual and artistic, as well as political life, France itself, however, experienced a minority under Charles's son and successor Charles VI (1380–1422), whose long reign was also troubled after 1392 by the king's periodic fits of insanity. During the reign of Charles VI the great noble families contended for power over the king, thus dividing the realm once again, and after 1415 the English resumption of the war plunged France into far greater misery than it had experienced during the years from 1340 to 1360.

England had made little successful use of its early victories in the war, however, and forces of discontent built through the disabled last years of the reign of Edward III. The loss of the popular Black Prince and the troubled minority of Richard II (1377–1399) permitted great nobles, particularly Edward III's younger brother John of Gaunt, duke of Lancaster, to assume ascendancy over the crown and wage the economic policies that helped precipitate the Peasants' Revolt of 1381. Richard II's peace policy and his intelligent but autocratic attempts to restore royal control over the government and nobles led to his deposition and murder in 1399, the usurpation of the throne by Henry IV (1399–1413), son of John of Gaunt, and the beginnings of the royal house of Lancaster. Henry IV and his son Henry V (1413–1422), facing rebellions in the north and discontent at home, reopened the war with France in 1415; the renewed warfare was signaled by another major English victory at Agincourt.

Between 1415 and 1453, however, the tone of war changed. The length of the conflict, its social and economic consequences, the political instability that ensued, and the character of the fighting made it considerably more savage than earlier wars, and France, the invaded land, bore the brunt of these effects first. The complete and efficient occupation of a conquered nation is difficult in the twentieth century—and it was impossible in the fifteenth. Although England began the fifteenth century by ruling most of northern France, including Paris, it had neither the population nor the ability to "occupy" the kingdom, nor could it support indefinitely an expensive expeditionary force in a distant and economically depleted country. Intimidation of the population had become a matter of English policy, and the economic and social consequences of this intimidation, and the long-range consequences in later wars of the new role of noncombatants generally, had influenced the character of English rule. Thus, as the war aims of the antagonists changed and the costs of war mounted, opportunities for internal dissension increased considerably, whether over traditional problems such as privilege and status or over novelties such as the burden of taxes and the less tangible circumstances of shifting fortunes. France's internal stresses between 1340 and 1430 preceded the internal conflicts of 1380 to 1480 in England. The shifting aims of war, changing political circumstances, and the mutual reluctance of France and England to surrender, respectively, sovereignty and the claim to the French throne, revealed that there was no clear way of ending the conflicts in terms that might satisfy all interested parties.

The opportunities offered to other parties during this prolonged conflict may best be illustrated by the history of the duchy of Burgundy. One technique developed by thirteenth-century French kings was the *appanage*, an extraordinary territorial lordship, sometimes over a newly acquired province, given to younger sons of the royal family, chiefly as a means of ensuring their loyalty to the crown and binding the new territories close to the royal dynasty. After several generations, however, some of these *appanages* took independent courses and emerged virtually as small states in their own right. The duchy of Burgundy was given by King Jean II of France to his son Philip, and when Philip married the heiress of the count of Flanders in 1369, these combined territories made the dukes of Burgundy the strongest princes of France. In the crisis over the insanity of Charles VI, Philip the Bold of Burgundy gradually asserted his ascendancy, and Philip's son and successor John the Fearless (1404–1419) inherited his father's power. Rivalry with another noble faction, the Armagnacs, however, drove Burgundy into the alliance with England that enabled English forces to capture most of northern France after 1415. At the Treaty of Troyes in 1420, Henry V's title to the throne of France was guaranteed. When Charles VI of France died in 1422, he left a shattered kingdom with an English king on its throne, an empty treasury, bitter resentment against the crown and the higher nobility, and a legally disinherited son, the Dauphin Charles, ruling a small part of southern France from an empty, borrowed palace in the old city of Bourges.

In spite of England's initial triumphs, however, the toll of prolonged war and the poverty of English institutional response to its social and economic crises threatened England's hold on France. Not the least important element of French resistance was the disinherited dauphin himself. Charles VII (1422–1461), weakened by the Treaty of Troyes and suffering from the added imputation of illegitimacy, was an unlikely reformer. Sickly, personally unattractive, completely unwarlike, and dominated by ruthless favorites, he at first helplessly witnessed the English armies proceed south from 1422 to 1428, through Maine and Anjou toward Bourges itself. Then, in 1428, French military resistance stiffened. Among the complex causes for the new resistance was the appearance of a young woman from Domrémy, a small town in Champagne, named Joan of Arc, who arrived at Charles's court at Chinon in 1429 claiming that SS. Michael, Catherine, and Margaret "told me of the pitiful state of France and told me that I must go to succor the King of France." In April, Joan and the leaders of the French army relieved the English siege of Orleans, and in July Charles was able to proceed to Reims for his coronation. Not even Joan's capture and burning at the stake for heresy in 1431 reversed the anti-English course of the war. By 1434 Charles VII's legitimacy was pronounced by the Council of Basel and in 1435 he was formally reconciled with Philip the Good, successor to John the Fearless as duke of Burgundy, at the Council of Arras. By 1453 Charles had won back most of northern France, Normandy, and Gascony and had begun to restore many of the reforms instituted by his grandfather, Charles V. In 1456 he initiated the formal process of rehabilitation, the overturning of the verdict of heresy upon Joan of Arc. The last years of Charles's reign were spent restoring royal fiscal and political dominion over a drastically weakened kingdom against the discredited nobility and the rebellious burghers. When he died in 1461 Charles VII had resumed the great reform traditions of his grandfather and laid the foundations for the growth of monarchical power and national order.

France recovered more quickly than England, and in a different way. The overstrained English governmental institutions were not improved by Lancastrian rule, and the collapse of the English occupation of France, coupled with the early death of Henry V in 1423 and the long minority of Henry VI (1423–1461) precipitated political and military struggles that lasted nearly to the end of the fifteenth century. The costs of the wars had been enormous compared to the returns from English victories, and English financial exigencies had led to violent clashes among the high aristocracy. The reign of Henry VI witnessed collapse on both fiscal and political fronts, and the reversals of English fortune in France plunged England into a series of dynastic wars, commonly called the Wars of the Roses, between 1454 and 1485. Overromanticized as these wars have generally been, their economic, military, and social consequences were quite small. Even more important than the change of dynasty that placed Edward IV on the throne in 1461, however, and the subsequent changes that placed the Tudor dynasty on the throne in the person of Henry VII in 1485, was the ability of the English monarchs after 1461 to capitalize upon the ending of foreign, expensive wars and to reorganize both royal finances and aristocratic factionalism in favor of a stable but not particularly strong royal rule.

The reign of Edward IV (1461–1483) witnessed the king's successful attempt to support his rule by enriching loyal nobles and ruthlessly destroying those who would not be loyal and whose private armies made them threats to peace and order. Having witnessed the end of the drain caused by the French wars on English public finance, Edward was intelligent enough not to resume them, and in general he remained independent of the necessity of going to Parliament with requests for more taxes. Hence, Edward drastically reorganized crown finances, partly by tightening traditional royal rights on crown lands, but primarily by forcing economies upon the royal household and exploiting traditional rights such as wardship and marriage. By increasing the king's activity in trade, including the supervision of the customs and actual commercial activity itself, Edward succeeded in maintaining his financial independence from Parliament and greatly expanded the king's independent income. Edward's activities laid the basis for the later financial independence of the English crown through the sixteenth century. Yet Edward's economic and political expedients, both old and new, do not wholly sum up his impact upon England. Personally, the king cultivated an image that was at once appealing and remote, displaying royal largess and splendor, on the one hand, and ruthlessly employing raw force when he could, on the other. The extensive power of the high nobility was not checked by Edward, for he could not, by himself, accomplish such a large task. What he could do, and did, however, was to establish the king's own lordship as the most effective of the many great lordships in England. By the end of the fifteenth century, kings still had to balance the traditional rights and resources of the older "personal" aspect of rulership judiciously against the new "public" attitudes, needs, and dangers of changing kingdoms. The very different developments of the English and French monarchies are thus related, both by their long involvement in wars with each other over a century of social and economic change and by the combination of traditional and novel opportunities that each ruling house had to exploit for its survival and prosperity.

Monarchy in the empire, England, and France may be considered both in terms of individual development and comparatively in terms of general problems and wide-ranging political and economic changes. In detail, in many cases, military and political changes do not explain social and economic movements, and they often had little to do with them. No late fifteenth-century monarchy approached the degree of complex interconnectedness among its social, political, and economic elements that characterizes most modern states.

In maintaining or strengthening their public power, the monarchs of the late fifteenth century explored both traditional and novel means of communicating with each other and with mobilizing their own state resources. Diplomacy, an expanded range of public service, new ideas and institutions of taxation, and the high costs and general social attitudes toward warfare are all important elements in the political order of traditional monarchies, but not until the sixteenth and seventeenth centuries were kings able to systematize both a theory and the practical means to fully exploit these resources. The spread of royal authority throughout the many social levels and institutions of large societies, the efficiency of public power, and the rituals of communication among powerful states took a long time to develop from the straitened monarchies of the late fifteenth century. Long before such large-scale monarchical states dominated the political and diplomatic affairs of Europe, however, other kinds of political orders had begun to successfully exploit these features that much later characterized some aspects of the modern state. Subnational societies—leagues, confederations, individual cities, and principalities—especially when these existed in a particularly crowded region or had a common enterprise, usually economic, had begun to exploit new uses of public power much earlier than the inefficient monarchies of much larger territorial states. It is in the history of some of these smaller but in many respects more thoroughly ruled and more communicative societies that we may see some prototypes of later forms of large-scale public order.

Throughout fourteenth- and fifteenth-century Europe economic and social changes had greatly diversified not only the profound gaps between social ranks and the differences between regions, but the character of similar states of life in different places. Peasant life differed drastically from England to Russia and from Sicily to northern France. The king of Castile, as we have seen, ruled a kingdom that was itself composed of subkingdoms, in each of which his rights, powers, and resources were different. In fourteenth-century Burgundy, as that great duchy was assembled under its Valois dukes after 1363, an enormous variety of customs and practices prevailed, and the individual we designate the duke of Burgundy in fact ruled in different capacities in many different places within the duchy. The practical limitations upon the articulated exercise of great public power over large territorial areas meant that rulers of these areas had to increase their own resources in order to attract servants, without doing so in such a way as to generate excessively widespread resentment. Their first successes were in the fields of practical power and military affairs—in the first case because there were no institutionalized organs of resistance to rulers who increased their power without exceeding traditional limits upon raising money, and in the second case because social and economic circumstances attracted to military service both the aristocracy and the new uprooted military proletariat while offering less resistance to extraordinary demands for increased finances. Even the private expansion of royal resources and the spirit of military cooperation, however, had their limits, but these limits were not reached until monarchical power had increased greatly. Other limits remained in effect longer. The bureaucratization of governmental institutions was still centuries off, and the efficiency of royal servants was often constricted by ideas of office as private property, the resistance to change of those who held office, and the primitive means available to superior powers in actively supervising and correcting the work of their subordinates.

In some smaller public units, however, some of these obstacles were overcome. Small states that, in places such as Italy and the Rhineland, crowded each other's borders and occupied a territory whose supervision was manageable in terms of the communication facilities available to preindustrial Europe, faced early many of the difficulties that larger states faced only later. Control of ecclesiastical and temporal wealth and power, the definition of boundaries that had to be defined exactly by towns or regions that exploited the full territorial extent they occupied, the necessity of formal relations and communication with other political units whose affairs crowded one's own, the careful exploitation of public finance and the judiciary, the finite resources available for public welfare and defense, the tendency for those who held economic power to hold political power, and the high visibility of public dissent and the necessity of the means to suppress it—all these and more faced the town-republics and highly organized principalities of the fourteenth and fifteenth centuries.

A city-principality such as Venice was ruled more thoroughly than any other contemporary European state, and its political form was determined by the necessity of extensive control over state resources in order to exploit its far-flung trading dominions. In a territory such as Switzerland, small regions, physically separated from others, could hardly be governed at all, and regional independence grew after successful combined resistance to the rule of the duke of Austria after 1315. Yet the Swiss confederation was a complicated organism, and the conflicts between local and confederation interests led to general instability. Even the astonishing development of the duchy of Burgundy, which after 1363 was ruled by Valois dukes who attempted to import the governmental techniques of the kingdom of France for use in ruling their wide variety of lands, did not completely overcome the regionalism of its parts; its rich court life, the large number of ducal servants, and the powerful military resources of the dukes were the greatest achievements of its independent existence. During the sixteenth century the duchy was disassembled as if it had never existed. The cities of the Baltic that shared a very loose common association based upon trading interests and control over the trade routes, the Hansa, developed local governmental competence to a high degree. But the diversified interests of individual cities prevented the league from forming a thorough association except in a very few areas of common interest. Finally, the city-republics of Italy, perhaps the most thoroughly and efficiently governed political units before the late seventeenth century, developed financial, diplomatic, and military resources, institutions of public welfare, and governmental administrative and judicial structures that did more to shape a civil society than any other temporal governments.

Smaller political units with highly articulated needs and resources transformed the image and institutions of power and order in a highly rationalistic direction. In larger political units, however, such development was slower and irregular. Not only in kingdoms and empires, but in ecclesiastical units and church councils as well, patronage, dependence, reward, and the blurred distinction between private and public service more readily characterized both ideas of order and the exercise of power.

The great figures who dominated the Council of Constance—the popes, the emperor, Cardinals Gerson, d'Ailly, and Zabarella, and John Hus—afford a useful focus for the analysis of Christian society at its most organized and active. Beneath these figures, however, bustled hundreds of other—and at the time lesser—men whose own careers and circumstances constitute no small part of fifteenth-century history. Secretaries, advisers, courtiers, clergy, and scholars, in greater numbers and prominence than ever before, remind us that the world of the great powers and individuals was increasingly propped up by the patronage it extended to others, and that patronage on a lavish scale in turn created images of court and curial life that were presented to a still wider and interested public. As we have seen, such great gatherings as the Council of Constance—or, earlier, the papal court at Avignon— brought together for varying periods of time many different kinds of individuals, persons who could exchange ideas and insults, acquire books, learn, discuss, dispute, exert mutual influences, and then return to their homes or travel in the service of new masters to Spain or Poland or Prague. Many of the minor functionaries at Constance emerged later as scholars, ecclesiastical leaders, or lay powers in their own right. Poggio Bracciolini, a young secretary, spent his spare time ransacking South German libraries for classical manuscripts and later became one of the most learned humanists of Renaissance Italy. Another, Aeneas Sylvius Piccolomini, became a papal legate and then Pope Pius II. During the fifteenth century, on a scale scarcely ever achieved before, the patronage of educated individuals, artists, and experienced advisers characterized the great and small courts of Christendom. Artists, orators, writers, musicians, heralds, lawyers, and diplomats of all kinds constituted a new and variously talented courtier population whose impact upon the public life of European powers increased into the nineteenth century.

It is this growth in the numbers and functions of people receiving patronage and employment in the service of powerful individuals that casts the fifteenth and sixteenth centuries in such a distinctive light. Donors of churches and church decorations crowd into the scenes painted by the artists who accepted their commissions, kneeling piously outside the house in which the Annunciation is made to the Virgin, or kneeling directly in homage before the Virgin and Infant themselves. The subject of the diplomatic embassy appears in paintings, and court scenes in other paintings reveal the numerous levels of courtiers bustling about the court's business. In 1435, ten years after the Council of Constance, another great assembly was held, this time at Arras, to resolve the diplomatic entanglements of the Hundred Years War. The provost of the Church of St. Vaast in Arras, Antoine de la Taverne, left a long and detailed memoir of the Congress of Arras, which is crowded with depictions of the liveliness of the Congress's external aspects. Indeed, the crowd—of servants, artists, courtiers, and functionaries—characterizes many of the most familiar scenes of the fifteenth century. The crowd was composed of people upon whom the rulers and the powerful men of the period depended more and more for getting work done.

The work that rulers wanted doing varied widely. Any respectable fifteenth-century court required its own image to shine brightly, in details from the costume of its servants to the quality of the Latin written and spoken by its official orator. The history of new and old dynasties had to be rewritten according to the latest requirements of historical fashion; the court itself had to be decorated by artists and architects as well as by elements that would reflect both its wisdom and its power and wealth. Libraries became extremely popular; they ranged from very small ones to quite large ones, such as that assembled by Humphrey, duke of Gloucester, brother of Henry V of England, and that assembled by Platina for the popes. Resident scholar-librarians, orators, musicians, painters, teachers, and chaplains graced and crowded the courts of the mighty, and competition for favor and rewards was intense. By the early sixteenth century, handbooks for courtiers began to be produced, the most famous of which was Baldassare Castiglione's *The Courtier*. As courtiers struggled to achieve something resembling the quality of Castiglione's ideal courtier—an enormously difficult task—artists and poets themselves became the subject matter of a new kind of literature. A lively and costly trade in books and *objets d'art* arose in the fifteenth century, and investment in art—and artists—also characterized the period.

It is in the ubiquitous character of all levels of patronage and the exploitation of most of the varieties of arts and letters that Italian and transalpine courts most strongly resembled each other. The creation of a new level of intellectual, artistic, and service personnel reflected the triumph of two principles whose earlier history we have already seen: the increased status of the lay ruler and the attendant growth and circulation of laypeople's values and interests, on the one hand, and, on the other, the increasing complexity of the world that laypeople ruled. The glittering, often sordid, elaborate courts that directed the fortunes of European society in the fifteenth and sixteenth centuries are thus most striking in their attempts to take control of the affairs of a rapidly changing world. Their remoteness and frequent quaintness should not distract our attention from the substantial work they undertook, the financing and organization they required, and the numerous personnel in their lower reaches, from artists to minor secretaries of diplomatic legations who had undergone long periods of apprenticeship and education in order to compete for a place in the service of their rulers.

THE SHAPE OF EUROPE AND THE NEW WORLD

At the beginning of this book we considered extensively the character of European space and the difficulties many peoples faced in overcoming the limits imposed by the smallness of populations, the speed and nature of communication, and the character of geographical knowledge. After 1150 the "vast, disorganized spaces" of Europe began to close in on one another, and after the Mongol invasions of the early thirteenth century European interests extended far beyond Europe's own borders. In the fifteenth century the internal distances within Europe were shortened, and advances in shipbuilding techniques, the matematics of navigation, and geographical knowledge brought Europeans into distant corners of the world. After the fifteenth century Europe became smaller in several different senses. First, internal communication made more of it regularly accessible to more people, and, second, increasing awareness of just how large the world outside Europe was impressed upon Europeans the relative size of the corner of the globe they inhabited.

From the thirteenth to the seventeenth centuries most of the improvements in land communication and transport consisted of refinements of techniques that had been developed in the twelfth and thirteenth centuries. New techniques in harnessing and shoeing horses, the improvement of wagons' maneuverability and suspension, and the improvements in road and bridge building brought European technology in this field to a state that remained essentially static until the extensive road-building programs and the development of the steam engine in the eighteenth century. Networks of information, in merchants' companies and in kingdoms and other political units, improved the regularity and speed of some communications. By the early fourteenth century cart roads were being built in the Alpine passes, and in 1480 gunpowder was used in the Tyrol to blast rock for the widening of roads. Slowly, the pack animal gave way to the wagon, the track to the road. The increasingly sedentary character of large governments made capital towns and cities centers of new communications networks, from papal Avignon in the fourteenth century to Vienna and Madrid in the sixteenth. Finally, not only did the means of sending information and goods improve during this period, but so did the means of producing information. From the 1440s on, improvements in cheap paper making, the invention and development of movable type, investment in printing, and the growth of a literate public propelled the book trade into a prominent place in fifteenth- and sixteenth-century life. Not only books, of course, but laws and lawbooks, newsletters, and official and unofficial printed matter of all kinds helped increase the speed of dissemination of information. Frequent large-scale public assemblies, from those of regions to the great international congresses and councils, drew many people together and then returned them to their places of origin, their heads full of what they had seen, read, and heard. Diplomatic services, armies, councils, trade, and learning all helped overcome the spatial and temporal limits of preindustrial Europe.

These diverse improvements in communication and transportation touched societies differently, of course. Not all levels of society had access to or were particularly concerned with news from afar. Nevertheless, governments, entrepreneurs, great commercial companies with many branches, individual scholars, and others exploited these old and new resources to accelerate communication and facilitate transportation within the borders of Europe. At the borders, too, a slowly developing awareness of territorial divisions began to influence political, diplomatic, and even cultural attitudes. In the sparsely populated lands of central and eastern Europe political rulers and rivals tested the extent of their territorial influence. The marriage in 1386 of Jadwiga, heiress to the crown of Poland, and Jagiello of Lithuania began the process of the conversion of Lithuania to Christianity, the last major pagan territory to be converted. At the battle of Tannenberg in 1410, Jagiello of Poland and his cousin Witold, grand prince of Lithuania, broke the power of the Teutonic Knights. In 1466 Poland and the Order of the Teutonic Knights signed the Peace of Thorn (Toruń), according to whose terms much of the order's lands went to the Polish crown and the rest was held as a fief of the king of Poland. Although the vigor of Poland and Lithuania in the fifteenth century did not create states that closely resembled those of western Europe, the increasingly successful attempts of their rulers to impose their own authority over large territories in eastern Europe suggest that at the edges of Europe too, the empty lands were slowly being closed in. The brilliance of court life at Prague and Budapest remind us again of the importance of the development of courts as centers of economic and political life and centers of communication as well.

It was a different element that sharply reminded Europeans of the territorial limits of their power, however. In the late fourteenth and fifteenth centuries a new Turkish invasion swept into Asia Minor and the Balkans, and in 1453 Constantinople, the last, shrunken symbol of the idea of a universal Christian empire, fell to the Turkish armies of Sultan Mehmet II. Byzantine resistance to western demands for ecclesiastical reunion and the vastly diminished resources of the restored empire of Michael VIII Palaeologos after 1261 had reduced Byzantine power considerably. A fifteenth-century English chronicler who had observed Emperor Manuel II's visit to the west for aid sadly commented, "How grievous it was that this great Christian prince should be driven by the Saracens from the furthest East to these furthest Western islands to seek aid against them. . . . Oh God, what dost thou now, ancient glory of Rome?" In the fourteenth century the vigorous kings of Serbia, particularly Stephen Dusan (1331–1355), threatened the empire's existence, and the growth of Catalan and Aragonese power in the eastern Mediterranean also reduced Byzantine strength. In the early years of the fourteenth century the Catalan Grand Company brought the first Ottoman Turks to Europe as mercenaries, and in the next several decades the expansion of the emirate in Anatolia and the growing reputation of the Ottoman sultans as supporters of Sunnite orthodoxy increased Ottoman power and prestige in the Islamic world. In 1354 the Turks conquered Adrianople, the site nearly one thousand years before of Emperor Valens's defeat at the hands of the Visigoths. The powerful and well-organized Ottoman armies assaulted Constantinople in 1396 and in 1422. In 1453, when Mehmet II assaulted the city by sea and land with vast armies and massive artillery pieces, the city was defended by only 5,000 native troops and 2,000 foreigners. The assault breached the great Theodosian walls on May 29, 1453, and Constantine XI, the last emperor, died fighting in the streets of the sacred city. The principalities in the Peloponnesus and Trebizond capitulated to the Turks shortly after the fall of Constantinople, and the great city became the capital of a new Turkish Empire. Control of the Black Sea and new influence in South Russia and Poland, as well as in the Balkans and most of Hungary, passed into the hands of the Sultan. On the eastern borders of Europe the frontiers had suddenly become very clear indeed.

In a famous letter, Pope Pius II (1458–1464) complained of Europe's failure to restore Constantinople and blamed the particularism of the Latins for their reluctance to challenge the Turkish lords of southeastern Europe: "Who will understand the different languages? Who will rule the diverse customs? Who will reconcile the English with the French, or join the Genoese to the Aragonese, or conciliate the Germans to the Hungarians and Bohemians?" By the end of the fifteenth century the resources of Christendom as a collective society seemed to have disappeared with Constantinople. Latin Europe indeed fought battles against the Turks, but these were defensive battles. The last emperor was dead and the new patriarch of Constantinople, George Scholarios Gennadios, was an appointee of the sultan.

From the Latin conquest of Constantinople in 1204 to the fall of the city in 1453, the relations between the Byzantine Empire and the peoples of eastern Europe underwent a series of significant changes. We have already seen an example of the ambition of one of Byzantium's culturally dependent peoples, the Serbians, during the early fourteenth-century aggrandizement of the Serbian "Empire" under Stephan Dusan. The early thirteenth century had witnessed an increased Latin attempt to assume the spiritual overlordship of several eastern European peoples, including the Serbians, Bulgars, and Russians. The contest in spiritual diplomacy slowly veered once more in favor of Greek Christianity, as the activity of the patriarchate of Nicaea during the period of the Latin occupation of Constantinople retained the spiritual loyalty of these peoples by effective ecclesiastical concessions. In 1235, for example, Bulgaria received its own patriarch, and after 1250 the metropolitans of Kiev were alternately Greek and native Russians. Indeed, it was during the Latin Empire that the Byzantine church gradually came to assume the diplomatic role that had been once the prerogative of the emperor alone. Thus, in spite of renewed Latin overtures and in spite of the strong trade relations between Serbia and the west, the manifestations of Bulgarian and Serbian strength took the shape and coloring of the Byzantine state. The imperial styles of John Alexander of Bulgaria (1331–1371) and Stephen Dusan of Serbia reflect strongly the influence of Byzantine concepts of court ceremonial and kingship. The duel between east and west was most intense in Serbia and Bulgaria, but the attraction of Byzantium won out. In Russia, however, circumstances were somewhat different. The Mongol occupation of Russia had overrun the ancient city of Kiev in 1240, and during the later thirteenth century Russia was virtually cut off from both Byzantium and the west. In 1300 the metropolitan of Kiev established himself in Vladimir, to the north, and then in 1328 in Moscow. The Russian revival of the fourteenth century that brought it once again into active contact with Byzantium began with Muscovy and signaled a change in the relation between the Russians and Byzantines.

Muscovy's greater distance from Constantinople, its long period under Mongol domination, and its ecclesiastical rivalry with Lithuania all helped weaken the bonds between Byzantium and the most faithful of its cultural dependents. The alternation between Greek and Russian metropolitans of Kiev after 1250, however, helped maintain relations between the two peoples, and the steady stream of Russian pilgrims to Constantinople continued to testify to the great city's religious attraction to the north. In addition to its rivalry with Lithuania over the question of the metropolitan, however, Muscovy also began to criticize Constantinople itself after 1439. The Council of Florence, at which union between the Greek and Latin churches was proclaimed, seemed to the Russians a breach of the faith. The Greek metropolitan of Kiev, Isidore, was arrested upon his return to Muscovy and after his attempts to introduce the Latin rite. In 1448 a synod of Russian bishops took the unprecedented step of electing a metropolitan of Kiev without Byzantine initiation. Although this step must be considered in terms of Russian resistance to Byzantine unionization, it may also be considered as a reflection of the vigor of the Russian state.

The rule of Grand Duke Ivan III (1462–1505) traditionally marks the full coming of independence to Muscovy. Under Ivan's energetic and ambitious rule, the breakup of the Mongol khanate and the western interests of Lithuania were both exploited to Muscovy's advantage. By the mid fifteenth century, the Golden Horde had broken up into three separate khanates, one at Kazan, one in the Crimea, and a third on the lower Volga. Ivan III became the first grand duke of Muscovy to assume his rulership without Mongol permission, and he soon began to exert Muscovite control over other northern Russian principalities. Between 1456 and 1478 the great city of Novgorod, hitherto dependent upon its economy and its Lithuanian neighbors for support, fell to Ivan's armies, and the rise of Muscovy to the domination of all Russia had begun.

The strained ecclesiastical relations between Russia and Byzantium in the fourteenth and fifteenth centuries, the vigor of the principality of Muscovy, and the success of Grand Dukes Vasili (1425–1462) and Ivan III in the face of Lithuanian-Polish, Mongol, and other Russian opposition, developed considerable economic and political power within the Muscovite state, as well as a fierce sense of pride and divine approval. Thus, in 1460 the metropolitan of Moscow could firmly observe that Constantinople had fallen because of God's disapproval of the union of the churches at the Council of Florence. Certainly, the new Muscovite preeminence was a heady experience, and the success of the grand dukes of the fourteenth and fifteenth centuries had acquired for them a preeminence even among the boyars, which hastened political consolidations. Like the earlier rulers of Serbia, Bulgaria, and the Romanian principalities, the grand dukes of Muscovy began to adopt the outward signs of imperial rule. In 1472, partly through the agency of the pope, Ivan III married Zöe Palaeologina, the niece of the Byzantine emperor Constantine XI. Although the pope may have hoped through the marriage to effect the 1439 provisions in Russia, Ivan and the empress, renamed Sophia, adopted an elaborate Byzantine court ceremonial and the imperial device of the double-headed eagle. Under their rule the grand dukes of Muscovy began to evolve into the tsars of Russia (Tsar: Byzantine "Caesar"). Muscovite self-confidence went even further in certain areas. In 1492 Moscow was proclaimed the "New Constantinople," and in 1510 the monk Philotheus of Pskov proclaimed that Moscow was the "Third Rome."

The rise of Muscovy, which, despite its imperial pretensions echoed in the words of Philotheus, recognized its interests as expansionist and its problem as the maintenance of the tsar's authority over the restive boyar class, hints at something of a common experience in the political world of all Christendom by the fifteenth century. The great universalist titles, claims, theories, emblems, and ambitions rang hollow when unsupported by institutional and economic power and carefully managed states. These ideals had always led a precarious existence even during their heyday, and they were perhaps better represented by such institutions as the Crusades and monasticism, the papacy and the Byzantine Empire, than by the Holy Roman Empire. Yet by the fourteenth and fifteenth centuries, all of these institutions had undergone a process of transformation. Sometimes a name survived—a new Crusade, a new movement for monastic reform, the claims for papal authority; sometimes one disappeared—the *Vasileus Rhomaion;* sometimes one survived with its name intact but its power drastically reduced or changed—the Holy Roman Empire. Men were to live with these names for centuries yet, and even after the Reformation and the Wars of Religion, men could invoke an ideal of universal Christian brotherhood in anti-Turkish propaganda or plans for overcoming the effects of the Reformation. But the age of the universals was over. Power—and society—were to be organized in different groups, ones that were characterized by less universal ambitions and much greater efficiency.

New communications systems within western Europe, the fragile but more clearly defined political units of central and eastern Europe, the graphic and sudden establishment of the Ottoman Turkish Empire, and the rise and westward spread of Muscovy indicate some of the most important elements in the relationship between Europe and the world immediately surrounding it and the character of communication within Europe itself. These systems and relationships were established for the most part on the land. It was on the sea, however, that the most striking changes in Europe's address to the world took place. Even the new access to the sea in the fourteenth and fifteenth centuries, however, must be considered in terms of other changes in communication and transport, and their impact must be considered as it appeared to Europeans at the time.

As long as it was forced to remain within the upward limits of animal and human power, land transportation remained generally unchanged between the thirteenth and the nineteenth centuries. On the sea, however, technological and economic influences quickly expanded Europeans' capacities for long-distance travel. Early European ships were of two types, neither very satisfactory. The round-bottomed cog with a square sail was capacious but slow, and the long narrow galley, powered by oars, was fast but had too large a crew for effective cargo transportation. In the fourteenth century in the Baltic, the great hulk was developed; it had a greater carrying capacity but no more speed. At the beginning of the fifteenth century, however, the caravel appeared. The increased proportion of beam to length, the use of two masts, one of which carried a triangular lateen-rigged Mediterranean sail, the construction of the hull by edge-to-edge instead of overlapping planking, the reduced crew, and the enormous cargo volume of around 400 tons produced the most efficient ship the West had ever known. The stern rudder, the increased amount of sail, the reduced crew, the new hull, and the increased carrying capacity made the caravel the most efficient and the most profitable ship afloat. It was also the fastest. The caravel's speed under full sail was only slightly exceeded by the clipper ships of the nineteenth century. By the end of the fifteenth century, not only had sail gone far to replace oar, but the upward limits of sailing speed had very nearly been reached.

Marine technology and practical navigation outreached geography and cartography quickly. The intellectual developments that produced astronomical navigation and the geographical and cartographical knowledge that characterizes more recent marine technology and theory did not come for a century. But practical sailors' use of the compass after the twelfth century, of minutely accurate local charts, the portolans, and of practical trigonometry for course correction—all of which developed by the end of the thirteenth century—gave European mariners impressive tools. The exploitation of the Baltic, North Sea, and Atlantic sailing routes had all been developed by the end of the thirteenth century. In the course of the Spanish *reconquista,* the Atlantic off the western coast of the Iberian peninsula was occupied, and sugar-cane-producing settlements on the Canaries and Madeira developed in imitation of the Venetian and Genoese colonies in the eastern Mediterranean. In spite of these practical achievements, however, knowledge of geography and anthropology was still restricted to the accounts of Marco Polo and the fabulous narratives contained in Sir John Mandeville's *Travels,* a fictionalized account of the author's travels in the Near East between 1332 and 1366. Fourteenth-century learned maps still filled the vast uncharted spaces with semihuman creatures and the catch-all warning, *hic sunt leones*— as the Elizabethans later translated it, "here there bee tygres." Not until the *Dialogue on Geography,* written by the humanist Poggio Bracciolini in 1447–1448 was there an attempt to link formal, learned geography with the actual experience of travelers and sailors. There was no word for "explorer" in any European language.

In the late thirteenth and fourteenth centuries climatic change and economic interests focused Scandinavian maritime activity in the Baltic and the North Seas. In 1291 the brothers Vivaldi from Florence were lost in the first modern attempt to navigate the western coast of Africa, and in 1346 the Catalan Jaume Ferrer probably reached the coast of Senegal before he too disappeared. In 1248 and 1268 Christian forces captured Seville and Cadiz, the greatest ports in southern Spain, and the expansion west and south into the Canaries and Madeira developed Castilian maritime techniques considerably. Those ports and that technical experience took place in a fortunate location—the eastern end of the most climatically favorable route for sailing west, between 35 and 42 degrees north latitude, in which the favorable winds and currents flow west for nine months of the year.

At first, however, the southward thrust of Spanish and Portuguese maritime power turned not to exploration but to recognized trade routes. By 1277 Genoese and Venetian fleets were sailing from the Mediterranean to the Atlantic, and the great northern and southern European maritime trade routes were finally connected at England, Normandy, and Flanders. Along the new Atlantic routes, the discovery and exploitation of the Canaries and Madeira in the first half of the fourteenth century brought Iberian sugar into the European market. By the late fourteenth century, however, the Mediterranean-Atlantic routes had raised Castilian and especially Portuguese interests in yet another area, North Africa.

The Maghreb, the western coast of North Africa, was since the tenth century the northern terminus of the route of gold caravans that originated in Ghana and crossed the western edge of the Sahara to Ceuta, Oran, Algiers, and Tunis. Copper and salt also came up this route, and these products, along with North African wheat, enriched the North African cities and made them attractive—either for trade or for conquest, or both—to other Mediterranean powers, from Norman Sicily in the twelfth century, to the Italian maritime cities in the thirteenth and fourteenth, to the Crusading army of St. Louis of France in 1270, and, finally, to the Castilian and Portuguese rulers in the fourteenth and fifteenth centuries. In the fourteenth century the gold of the Sudan became a particularly important prize among Christian and North African Moslem powers, and Christians began to obtain clearer information concerning its sources. In 1339 a Majorcan *portolan* map noted, "Below the Sahara, on the banks of a river that is the Niger, there is a king whose riches are counted in gold; it is the king of Mali." One chronicler's account of Jaume Ferrer's voyage to West Africa in 1346 stated that his purpose was "to go to the river of gold." By the mid fourteenth century, Europeans knew that the source of the gold traded in the cities of the Maghreb was the West African Sudan and that it was extracted from rivers by black men, about whom a number of legends had circulated among Moslem traders. Europeans also knew that there were powerful, advanced black kingdoms in West Africa whose power rested upon their rulers' role in controlling the gold trade. The great kings of Ghana and Mali controlled access to the gold-mining natives and only permitted their own subjects to trade salt for gold, which they then carried north and traded to the North African caravan merchants. The greatest of all black Moslem rulers of this period was, as the Majorcan map of 1339 had observed, the king of Mali. By 1375, when Abraham Cresques drew his great Catalan atlas, the brief reference of 1339 had been expanded to a large picture of the black king seated on a throne, holding (somewhat improbably) the royal scepter of France with a fleur-de-lis at its end and a globe, the new legend reading:

> This black lord is called Musa Melly, lord of the blacks of Guinea. This king is the richest and most noble lord by reason of the abundance of gold that is found in his country.

The black king of the 1339 and 1375 Catalan maps was Mansa Musa, who had made a pilgrimage in 1321 to Mecca, where his display of wealth and piety astonished his Moslem coreligionists.

The crisis of the late fourteenth century had drastically increased Europeans' need for gold, and the new knowledge of the sources of West African gold raised the possibility of circumventing the Saharan-Maghreb trade routes by sailing directly to the source of the gold. The new maritime importance of Castile and Portugal on the Mediterranean-Atlantic trade routes, the new security of Christian Iberia, and the experience of sugar-cane production in the eastern Atlantic islands had greatly increased Iberian maritime skill and experience and had brought the enterprising genius and technological skills of the Italian city-republics to bear on the peninsula as well. Finally, in Portugal first and later Castile, the gap between practical maritime experience and scholarly knowledge appears to have been less than elsewhere.

The central, but still obscure, figure in the first Portuguese voyages to the west coast of Africa was Prince Henry the Navigator (1394–1460), the son of King John I of Portugal. Henry, little different in world view or character from other fifteenth-century princely knights, appears to have been particularly interested in the legends of mysterious lands in Africa, especially the reports that Prester John, the legendary Christian king, was to be found in Africa, perhaps in Ethiopia. Interested in measuring the extent of Moslem power and imbued with the Crusade mentality that had driven the earliest stages of the *reconquista,* Henry was also seriously concerned with the possibility that his own dynasty and kingdom might be the first to tap African gold at its source. With this mixture of motives—none of which, it may be added, was particularly "scientific" or, worse, "modern"—Henry spent vast sums of his own wealth in assembling at Sagres a group of cartographers, scholars, and sailors of all faiths and many languages. Henry was driven by an important youthful experience. When he was nineteen, a military expedition under his father had captured Ceuta on the North African coast, the first Christian landfall in Moslem Africa. From the capture of Ceuta in 1415 until his death in 1460, Henry conceived that event as the beginning of Portuguese expansion, as much for the injury of Islam as for any particular increases in scientific knowledge that it might make. By 1431 Portuguese had discovered and settled in the Azores, and Henry, armed with royal and papal privileges to carry on the *reconquista* in Africa, began his annual dispatches of fleets to the west coast of Africa. Shortly after the middle of the fifteenth century, Portuguese sailors had landed in Guinea and begun to exploit the gold reserves and the large numbers of black slaves that had once been the exclusive right of the Sahara caravans. By the death of Henry the Navigator in 1460, many of the Prince's ambitions had been fulfilled. Gold had begun to flow into Portugal, and just before Henry's death Portugal had issued its first gold coin, appropriately called the *crusado*.

The beginnings of Portuguese exploitation of the Gold Coast of Africa produced two remarkable developments: the direct acquisition by the Portuguese of large amounts of gold, and the beginnings of the trade in black slaves that was to remain a source of income first in Mediterranean and transalpine Europe, and later, and to a much greater degree, in the agricultural and mining settlements in the Spanish New World.

THE FRAMES OF TIME:
VISIONS OF A NEW PAST AND PRESENT

The various frames, or divisions, of time within which historians try to make human experience in the past intelligible and coherent provide us with different kinds of information, depending upon the length of time periods and the subject matter they include. Sometimes they tell us more about the minds of those who design them than they do about the past they contain. Since the particular purpose of this book has been to explain as many of the circumstances surrounding the settlement and culture of early Europe as possible, that particular part of the story called the Middle Ages as it is conventionally conceived does not fit tightly at all points within the largest frames with which we have been concerned. The chief cause of this imprecise fit lies in the way in which the idea of the Middle Ages was invented and discovered between the fifteenth and the twentieth centuries, a partial account of which was given in the Introduction and another part of which is considered just below. Other causes have other explanations. The longest and largest frames we have considered, those dealing with geological and climatic change, and the next longest, those dealing with long periods in the history of the cultures and civilizations in the Mediterranean and Eurasian worlds, can only contain early European history as part of a much larger time span and can only cast light upon certain aspects of the human condition. The longest and largest frames are very difficult to use in explaining individuals and particular events, although they tell us much about the circumstances within which individuals and events may be partially understood. The opposite problem, that particular individuals and events and very short time frames do not explain or connect very well to larger sets of circumstances, is also apparent in the preceding pages. Finding no point in trying to look exclusively from one point or another, I have tried in the preceding chapters to shift back and forth between them, considering other-sized frames as well along the way. This technique has obliged me to leave out much that I would have liked to include and to spend more time on particular points of detail than anyone will be entirely satisfied with. Nor will be selection of details satisfy everyone, nor will the omissions. This introduction to the history of early Europe is extensive, but it is far from exhaustive, and I envy the interested reader who goes on to discover that "hole worlde of things very memorable" that I have managed to neglect totally or only to brush by in passing. When faced with hard choices, which is nearly all the time, I have chosen to look at as long a time period and as wide a space and as many different societies as possible, and when I have had to narrow the focus of the narrative, particularly in dealing with great issues in the traditional sense, I have tried always to suggest some of the underpinning and sometimes mundane structural supports and individual men and women behind political, ecclesiastical, and economic movements and events. It always seemed helpful, for example, to consider the actual resources of political powers before discussing the flights of theory, to explain something of literacy and book production before considering the intellectual glories of the twelfth and thirteenth centuries, and to say something of liturgy, clerical life, and pastoralism in preparation for the wider issues of ecclesiastical life. Being unable to talk about the life of a single individual from the largest population group—the workers and peasants—I tried to speak generally about birth and death, love and hate, and the measuring of time. Finally, in an ideal book of this kind the proper time frame would be one that extended from the settlement of transalpine Europe to the Industrial Revolution, a frame that is acquiring among economic and demographic historians and others the designation of Traditional Europe. It is in that frame that most of early and much "modern" European history seems to me most intelligible.

Why, then, the "Middle Ages" and not "Traditional Europe"? The answer to this question leads us back to the frames of time and to the interests and abilities of those who first designed them.

Among the most influential fashions in literary scholarship during the late thirteenth and early fourteenth centuries was the one that generated a new understanding of and admiration for the antique past of Greece and Rome. The search for classical antiquity took place on many levels, and in many places. Scholars hunted down ancient manuscripts in cathedral and monastic libraries, storage rooms, and royal treasuries. Ancient monuments and buildings were regarded with a new kind of vision. Students of Roman law began to complain that the commentators of the twelfth and thirteenth centuries did not understand the institutions and relationships described in the *Corpus* of Justinian. They even suspected that an older and more interesting Roman law lay behind Justinian's collection. Late in the thirteenth century, a grave was opened in Padua that was thought to be that of Antenor, the legendary antique founder of the city; at around the same time, the city of Mantua struck a medallion with the portrait of the Roman poet Vergil on its face; in Padua, Florence, and other northern Italian cities, interested laymen gathered in informal groups to study and discuss the Roman past. The disciplines of philology were sharpened to the point at which they could easily distinguish among the various stages of linguistic history, particularly the history of the Latin language. Philology helped people to read and understand Roman history, philosophy, and literature in a way that was much more distinctive and precise than ever before. As the image of the Roman past emerged sharply, people began to perceive for the first time some of the enormous changes that had taken place in the Roman world in the period between the late second and the fifth centuries, and as the Roman world looked brighter and nobler and marvelously articulate, the world that had succeeded it in Europe appeared drabber, more confused, and infinitely less articulate. The golden age of Vergil, Cicero, and Horace appeared to offer not only superior art, language, and literature, but superior moral values as well, values that an increasingly laicized European world perceived more clearly and valued more highly as the fourteenth and fifteenth centuries wore on.

The Latin that people had learned in school seemed clumsy and imprecise next to the spare, economical Latin of the prose writers of the first century B.C., and where philologists and literary figures led, representatives from other disciplines soon followed. Writers on painting and, later, on sculpture and architecture soon spoke of recapturing the classical Roman and Greek past after the distortions of what they sometimes contemptuously called "modern" art. Between 1350 and 1550, an arsenal of criticism of the arts and letters of the period 400–1350 evolved and lay at the disposal of those who wished to strengthen the tie between their own time and the artistic and literary modes of expression of classical Rome. They even developed a terminology for the past that they wished to imitate and recapture: *antiquitas*, antiquity, soon became a commonplace designation for the culture of classical Rome and Greece, and after some indecision, *modernus*, modern, a late antique construction, became applied to their own time, generally the period after 1350–1450. Between antiquity and modernity, which marked out for the history of arts and letters the twin poles of admired technique and experience, there remained an ungainly period that was conceived and defined less and less in terms of its own character than in terms of its remoteness from the glories of the Greco-Roman past and the accomplished classicism and naturalism of the "modern" present. For this period, a name was long in becoming generally accepted, probably because the period itself was not the center of many people's interests, as were antiquity and modernity. *Media aetas, media tempestas,* "a middle age," "a middle time" were the most commonly and casually used labels for the long period between the age of Constantine the Great and the flowering of Patrarca, Boccacio, and Giotto. Not until the seventeenth century did the expression "Middle Ages" acquire common currency, and by that time the new model of human cultural history had been firmly established: from the literary humanists came the decline of good Latin letters around the fourth century and their revival in the fourteenth and fifteenth; from the art historians came the decline of classical principles in the representational arts and architecture, the loss of naturalism at around the same time, and the rediscovery of these principles and the emergence of the new naturalism during the fourteenth and fifteenth centuries. For fifteenth- and sixteenth-century ecclesiastical critics, the evangelical Christianity of the first three centuries A.D. gave way to the monstrous church of the age of Constantine and beyond, which itself survived with undisputed authority until the days of the critics of the fifteenth century and the reformers of the sixteenth. Thus, the discovery of *antiquitas,* originally the historical view of a small circle of philologists and literary historians, came to accumulate new weight and to exercise its fascination in many other areas of thought and life.

Writers of history also picked up the distinction. For Petrarca in the mid fourteenth century, history was divided into "ancient" and "modern," the dividing line lying across the Christianization of the Roman Empire in the fourth century. Writers wrote a new history of Rome, deriving much help from philologists and antiquarians, and even "modern" historians took to recasting the writing of the history of Europe after 400 A.D. in classical form. Petrarca's highly charged vocabulary, however, did more than suggest a new division of historical periods. Borrowing terms with particularly strong spiritual associations, such as "rebirth," and applying the metaphors of darkness and light, blindness and sight, to the history of culture, Patrarca brought to that history some of the veneration and spiritual associations attending this terminology. Thus, the discovery of *antiquitas* and *modernitas* carried with it from the first a sort of spiritual intensity that heightened the paradox between the increasing Christianization of the Roman world and its cultural degeneration. This was a paradox that did not sit easily in fifteenth- and sixteenth-century minds, but it could be explained by the religious reformers who claimed that the church of the age of Constantine perverted, rather than spread, the teachings of Christ.

From a small circle of literary men, philologists, and antiquarians, there evolved a new way of looking at the western past, and that new way, marked by the discovery of antiquity, both the word and the thing meant, influenced their views of the early European past for centuries to come. Antiquity and modernity, indissolubly linked, left little room for any middle ground except for *the* "middle period," the Middle Ages, the middle between the two admirable periods of human originality and rediscovery. "Middle" also in its apparent distance from the values reflected in Roman and fifteenth-century Italian and later European culture, "middle" in what men considered its drabness and barbarity, "middle" in its artistic incompetence and lack of naturalistic representation, the "Middle Ages" acquired both its name and its first and in many ways most lasting characterization from thinkers whose vision was focused upon the distant past and the challenging present. Between these two, the early history of Europe, as if by default, acquired its first name and shape.

BIBLIOGRAPHY

The bibliography is divided into two parts. Part I is a general survey of selected topics. Part II is a selective bibliography arranged to correspond to the six parts of this book. For medieval studies generally, see J. M. Powell, *An Introduction to Medieval Studies* (Syracuse: Syracuse University Press, 1976).

I. GENERAL BIBLIOGRAPHIES

A. General Histories

The most complete history of the Middle Ages is *The Cambridge Medieval History,* ed. J. B. Bury et al., 8 vols. (Cambridge: Cambridge

University Press, 1911–1936); Volume IV of this history, *The Byzantine Empire,* ed. J. M. Hussey, appeared in a new edition in 1966. Among a number of modern series, one of the best and most thorough is the *General History of Europe Series,* ed. Denys Hay (New York: Longmans), which includes works by A. H. M. Jones, Donald Bullough, Christopher Brooke, John Mundy, and Denys Hay dealing with the period 300–1500. Two superbly illustrated collaborative works are David Talbot Rice, ed., *The Dark Ages* (London: Thames and Hudson, 1965), and Joan Evans, ed., *The Flowering of the Middle Ages* (London: Thames and Hudson, 1966).

B. Individual Histories

The first individual history of medieval Europe—and in the opinion of many, still the greatest—is Edward Gibbon, *The Decline and Fall of the Roman Empire,* the most complete edition of which is that by J. B. Bury (London: Methuen, 1909–1914); there are also many abridgements of Gibbon's work.

Among recent surveys, distinctive and particularly good ones are Robert S. Lopez, *The Birth of Europe* (New York: Evans, World, 1967); Jacques Le Goff, *La Civilisation de l'Occident Médiéval* (Paris: Arthaud, 1964); R. H. C. Davis, *A History of Medieval Europe* (London: Longmans, 1957), and Lynn White, ed., *The Transformation of the Roman World* (Berkeley and Los Angeles: University of California Press, 1966).

C. Sources of Medieval History in Translation

C. P. Farrar and Austin P. Evans, *Bibliography of English Translations from Medieval Sources* (New York: Columbia University Press, 1946), is an authoritative guide to translations before its date of publication. M. A. Ferguson, *Bibliography of English Translations from Medieval Sources, 1944–1968* (New York: Columbia University Press, 1973), brings Farrar-Evans up to date. Brian Pullan, *Sources for the History of Medieval Europe* (New York: Barnes & Noble, 1966), is the best single collection of annotated documents in translation.

D. Encyclopedias

Although most popular encyclopedias now rely upon modern scholarly writers, the most useful encyclopedias are particularly specialized compendia. The *Dictionnaire d'archéologie chrétienne et de liturgie,* 15 vols. (Paris: Letouzey et Ané, 1907–1953), the *Dictionnaire du droit canonique,* 7 vols. (Paris: Letouzey et Ané, 1935–1965), and the *Dictionnaire de théologie catholique,* 15 vols. (Paris: Letouzey et Ané, 1903–1950) are excellent examples of specialized but highly professional and useful reference works. *The New Catholic Encyclopedia* (New York: McGraw-Hill, 1967–1974), the *Encyclopedia of Islam* (Leiden: Brill, 1960–1961), *The Jewish Encyclopedia* (New York: Funk & Wagnalls, 1901–1906), and the *Encyclopedia Judaica* (New York: Macmillan, 1971–1972) are also excellent reference works, and they contain frequent helpful suggestions for further reading. For biographical materials, the British *Dictionary of National Biography* (London: Oxford University Press, 1921–1922), is excellent; on a lower level, the *McGraw-Hill Encyclopedia of World Biography* (New York: McGraw-Hill, 1974) contains brief biographical articles with up-to-date suggestions for further reading. John Fines, *Who's Who in the Middle Ages* (New York: Stein, 1971), offers one hundred short lives of random saints, popes, and political rulers.

E. Atlases

The most readily available atlases for the student of early European history are those of Colin McEvedy, *The Penguin Atlas of Medieval History* (Baltimore: Penguin, 1961), H. E. Stier et al., *Westermanns grosser Atlas zur Weltgeschichte* (Braunschweig: Westermann, 1969); J. Engel, ed., *Grosser historischer Weltatlas,* Vol. II, *Mittelalter* (Munich: Bayerischer Schulbuch-Verlag, 1970).

Besides these works, however, there are a number of specialized, well-illustrated, and documented atlases that, although sometimes not translated into English, are easy and helpful to use. Among the best of these are S. de Vries et al., *An Atlas of World History* (London: Nelson, 1965); Frederic Van Der Meer, *Atlas of Western Civilization*, trans. T. A. Birrell, 2nd ed. (Princeton: Van Nostrand, 1960); F. Vercauteren, *Atlas historique et culturel de l'Europe* (Paris: Elsevier, 1962); Frederic Van Der Meer and Christine Mohrmann, *Atlas of the Early Christian World* (London: Nelson, 1958); Jacques Boussard, *Atlas historique et culturel de la France* (Paris: Elsevier, 1957); Pierre Kovalevsky, *Atlas historique et culturel de la Russie et du monde Slave* (Paris: Elsevier, 1961); A. F. Chew, *An Atlas of Russian History* (New Haven: Yale University Press, 1970).

One of the best of all specialized atlases is the monumental *Atlas zur Kirchengeschichte,* eds. Hubert Jedin, K. S. Latourette, and J. Martin (Freiburg: Herder and Herder, 1970). A superb example of extremely detailed historical geography and cartography is the French *Atlas Historique Belfram,* a publication in progress under the direction of F. Michel, B. A. Angliviel, A. Rigade, and R. H. Bautier. The first volume to have appeared is the *Atlas historique: Provence,* eds. E. Baratier, Georges Duby, and E. Hildesheimer (Paris: Belfram, 1969).

For the world of Islam, see R. Roolvink, et al., *Historical Atlas of the Muslim Peoples* (Cambridge, Mass.: Harvard University Press, 1957).

F. Chronology

A good extensive chronology is that of R. L. L. Storey, *Chronology of the Medieval World, 400–1491* (New York: D. McKay, 1973). For England there are fine guides by F. M. Powicke and E. B. Fryde, *Handbook of British Chronology* (London: Royal Historical Society, 1961), and C. R. Cheney, *Handbook of Dates for Students of English History* (London: Royal Historical Society, 1945). A general reference is W. L. Langer, *An Encyclopedia of World History* (Boston: Houghton Mifflin, 1948).

G. Bibliographies and Guides to Medieval Studies

When it is completed, the most thorough guide to medieval bibliography will be A. Potthast, *Repertorium fontium historiae medii aevi*, 3 vols. to date (Rome: Instituto storico per il medioevo, 1962–), an international bibliography and a complete revision of Potthast's *Bibliotheca historica medii aevi*, 2nd ed. (Berlin, 1896). L. J. Paetow, *A Guide to the Study of Medieval History*, rev. ed. (Cambridge, Mass.: Medieval Academy of America, 1959), is an old but useful aid, now being brought up to date by Gray C. Boyce. E. B. Graves, *Bibliography of English History to 1485* (Oxford: Oxford University Press, 1974), is a modern revision of the classic work by C. Gross. *Bibliographical Handbooks*, sponsored by the Conference on British Studies, is a series of up-to-date bibliographies of British history, a good example of which is Michael Altschul, *Anglo-Norman England, 1066–1154* (Cambridge: Cambridge University Press, 1969). There are several useful essays in Elizabeth Chapin Furber, ed., *Changing Views on British History* (Cambridge, Mass.: Harvard University Press, 1963).

Beyond such detailed bibliographical surveys as exist for medieval England, the beginning student is confined to brief bibliographical surveys, such as R. H. C. Davis, *Medieval European History: A Select Bibliography* (London: The Historical Association, 1963), and Bryce Lyon, *The Middle Ages in Recent Historical Thought: Selected Topics* (Washington, D.C.: The American Historical Association, 1959). For France, the standard work is A. Molinier, *Les sources de l'histoire de la France des origines aux guerres d'Italie* (Paris: Picard et fils, 1902); for Germany, B. Gebhardt, *Handbuch der deutschen Geschichte*, 8th ed. rev. H. Grundmann (Stuttgart: Union Verlag, 1954). Many scholarly journals offer annual bibliographical surveys of their particular fields. In the United States, the *American Historical Review* offers such a survey annually.

A recent survey of the whole field is Donald Finlay, "Current Trends in Medieval Bibliography: A Progress Report," *Medieval Studies*, 30 (1968). The *International Medieval Bibliography* (Minneapolis, 1967–), published by the University of Minnesota, and R. Rouse, *Annotated Guide to Serial Bibliography* (Berkeley and Los Angeles: University of California Press, 1969–), are fine current reference works.

H. Journals

There are a number of traditional scholarly journals that publish exclusively in the area of medieval studies, and each discipline has its own further specialized journals. Medievalists also publish in general journals, particularly newer interdisciplinary ones. Among the best-known of the traditional journals are *Speculum* (Cambridge, Mass., 1926–), *Traditio* (Washington, D.C., 1942–), *Cahiers de Civilisation médievale* (Poitiers, 1958–), *Annales: économies, sociétés, civilisations* (Paris, 1946–), *Deutsches Archiv für Erforschung des Mittelalters* (Frankfurt, 1820–), *Le Moyen Age* (Brussels, 1888–), *Studi Medievali* (Spoleto, 1928–), and *Medieval Studies* (Toronto). General scholarly journals, such as the *American Historical Review* and the *English Historical Review*, usually publish articles of interest to medievalists.

Such modern journals as *Past and Present*, *The Journal of Interdisciplinary History*, *Comparative Studies in Society and History*, and *History and Theory* sometimes include studies by medievalists.

Two very new journals, *Viator* (Berkeley and Los Angeles, 1970–) and *The Journal of Medieval History* (London, 1975–), are also useful. Longer articles and short monographs are printed in *Medieval and Renaissance Studies* (Lincoln, Nebr.).

I. Economic and Social History

The best general survey is the *Cambridge Economic History of Europe*, J. Clapham et al., eds., Vols. I–III (Cambridge: Cambridge University Press, 1941–1961). Among recent shorter works, there is the profusely illustrated volume of Robert-Henri Bautier, *The Economic Development of Medieval Europe* (New York: Harcourt, Brace, Jovanovich, 1971), and Guy Fourquin, *Histoire Économique de l'occident médiéval* (Paris: A. Colin, 1969).

For the early period, see Robert Latouche, *The Birth of the Western Economy* (New York: Harper & Row, 1966), and A. F. Havighurst, *The Pirenne Thesis* (Lexington, Mass.: D. C. Heath, 1975).

For the period after 900, see Robert S. Lopez, *The Commercial Revolution of the Middle Ages, 950–1350* (Englewood Cliffs, N.J.: Prentice-Hall, 1971); R. S. Lopez and Irving Raymond, *Medieval Trade in the Mediterranean World* (New York: Columbia University Press, 1955); Carlo M. Cipolla, ed., *The Fontana Economic History of Europe: The Middle Ages* (London: Fontana, 1972); Harry A. Miskimin, *The Economy of Early Renaissance Europe* (Englewood Cliffs, N.J.: Prentice-Hall, 1969). Most of these works offer extensive bibliographies. See also Carlo M. Cipolla, *Before the Industrial Revolution* (New York: W. W. Norton, 1976).

The literature of economic history is particularly large, but the following specialized works offer lively approaches to circumscribed topics: Benjamin Nelson, *The Idea of Usury*, 2nd ed. (Chicago: University of Chicago Press, 1969); John W. Baldwin, *The Medieval Theories of the Just Price* (Philadelphia: American Philosophical Society, 1956); Carlo M. Cipolla, *Money, Prices, and Civilization in the Mediterranean World* (Princeton, N.J.: Princeton University Press, 1956); George Duby, *Rural Economy and Country Life in the Medieval West* (Columbia, S.C.: University of South Carolina Press, 1968); E. W. Bovill, *The Golden Trade of the Moors* (rpt., New York: Oxford University Press, 1970); Bryce Lyon and A. E. Verhulst, *Medieval Finance* (Providence, R.I.: Brown University Press, 1967); Georges Duby, *The Early Growth of the European Economy* (Ithaca: Cornell University Press, 1975).

The best recent comprehensive social history of medieval Europe is Robert Fossier, *Histoire Sociale de l'occident médiéval* (Paris: A. Colin, 1970). On the individual, see Colin Morris, *The Discovery of the Individual, 1050–1200* (New York: Harper & Row, 1973), and Walter Ullmann, *The Individual and Society in the Middle Ages* (Baltimore: Johns Hopkins University Press, 1966). A good anthology of documents is Jeremy duQuesnay Adams, *Patterns of Medieval Society* (Englewood Cliffs, N.J.: Prentice-Hall, 1969). Marc Bloch, *Feudal Society* (Chicago: University of Chicago Press, 1961), and Eileen Power, *Medieval People* (New York: University Books, 1966), are classic works. An excellent example of modern social history is A. H. de Oliveira Marques, *Daily Life in Portugal in the Late Middle Ages* (Madison, Wis.: University of Wisconsin Press, 1971).

J. Political and Regional History

More distortion than illumination has been produced by the nineteenth-century habit of forcing "national" histories upon the materials of early European history. In considering some general works dealing with the history of regions, kingdoms, and other territories between the tenth and the fifteenth centuries, the following remarks should be read in a greater spirit of casualness than the general labels might seem to indicate. For many "modern" nations did not exist during the Middle Ages, and those that still exist do so in a very different form from their medieval predecessors, and some medieval regions do not now exist as nations. The following works indicate both historical reliability and, unfortunately, the convenience of using some recent labels to describe entities that existed in a different form ten centuries or so ago. See H. Mitteis, *The State in The Middle Ages* (New York: North-Holland Publishing Company, 1975).

England. Standard and exhaustive, although now somewhat out of date, is the *Oxford History of England:* Vol. I, R. G. Collingwood and J. N. L. Myres, *Roman Britain and the English Settlements*, 2nd ed. (1937); Vol. II, Frank Stenton, *Anglo-Saxon England*, 2nd ed. (1947); Vol. III, A. L. Poole, *From Domesday Book to Magna Carta*, 2nd ed. (1955); Vol. IV, F. M. Powicke, *The Thirteenth Century*, 2nd ed. (1962); Vol. V, May

McKisack, *The Fourteenth Century* (1959); Vol. VI, E. F. Jacob, *The Fifteenth Century* (Oxford: Oxford University Press, 1961). The series *English Historical Documents*, ed. David C. Douglas (New York: Eyre & Spottiswoode, 1955–), complements the general Oxford series with extensively annotated historical sources in translation. There is an enormous and constantly increasing bibliography on medieval English history.

France. The best comprehensive histories of medieval France remain in French. E. Lavisse, ed., *Histoire de France,* 9 vols. (Paris: Hachette, 1900–1911), and G. Glotz, *Histoire Générale* (Paris: Presses universitaires de France, 1937–1941), are still the standard histories. In English, Robert Fawtier, *The Capetian Kings of France* (New York: Barnes & Noble, 1962), is a good survey, and may be complemented by John B. Henneman, *The Medieval French Monarchy* (Hinsdale, Ill.: Dryden Press, 1973). A. Luchaire, *Social France at the Time of Philip Augustus* (New York: Harper & Row, 1967), is old but still valuable, and may be complemented by Joan Evans, *Life In Medieval France* (New York: Phaidon, 1969). P. S. Lewis, *Later Medieval France: The Polity* (New York: St. Martin's Press, 1968), is a good guide to the political problems of later medieval France. Marc Bloch, *French Rural History* (Berkeley and Los Angeles: University of California Press, 1970), is a fine introduction to one aspect of medieval France. J. F. Lemarignier, *La France médiévale: Institutions et société* (Paris: A. Colin, 1970), is an important recent survey.

Germany. The best general introduction to medieval Germany is Geoffrey Barraclough, *The Origins of Modern Germany* (rpt., New York: Oxford University Press, 1963). *Medieval Germany,* 2 vols. (Oxford: Basil Blackwell, 1948), by the same author, is also helpful. Franz H. Bäuml, *Medieval Civilization in Germany, 800–1273* (New York: Praeger, 1969), is a helpful cultural introduction. Karl Hampe, *The German Empire under the Salian and Hohenstaufen Emperors,* trans. R. F. Bennett (Oxford: Oxford University Press, 1973), is a classic history now available in English. Boyd Hill, *Medieval Monarchy in Action* (New York: Barnes & Noble, 1972), deals with the tenth and eleventh centuries.

Hungary. A good introduction is C. A. Macartney, *Hungary: A Short History* (Oxford: Oxford University Press, 1962).

Ireland. A good short introduction is A. J. Otway-Ruthven, *A History of Medieval Ireland* (New York: Barnes & Noble, 1968). Kathleen Hughes, *The Church in Early Irish Society* (Ithaca, N.Y.: Cornell University Press, 1968), is a fine introduction to a particularly important period. J. F. Lydon, *The Lordship of Ireland in the Middle Ages* (Dublin: University Presses of Ireland, 1972), considers political history after the eleventh century.

Italy. The most recent thorough treatment is J. K. Hyde, *Society and*

Politics in Medieval Italy, 1000–1300 (New York: St. Martin's Press, 1969), a useful guide among the tangled regional histories that constitute Italian history for this period. T. Hodgkin, *Italy and Her Invaders*, 8 vols. (Oxford: Oxford University Press, 1880–1899), is still the most thorough survey of post-Roman Italy. Gino Luzzato, *An Economic History of Italy* (New York: Barnes and Noble, 1961), and Leonardo Olschki, *The Genius of Italy* (Ithaca, N.Y.: Cornell University Press, 1954), are two good studies of particular problems.

Central and Eastern Europe. A useful short introduction to Polish history may be found in V. L. Benes and N. J. G. Pounds, *Poland* (New York: Praeger, 1970), which is part of the series, *Nations of the Modern World*. The older work by O. Halecki, *A History of Poland* (rpt., New York: Roy, 1956), is also useful. The best recent long survey is A. Gieysztor et al., *History of Poland* (Warsaw: Polish Scientific Publishers, 1968). Reference should be made to the important collection of essays in G. Barraclough, ed., *Eastern and Western Europe in the Middle Ages* (New York: Harcourt, Brace, Jovanovich, 1970), which contains a helpful bibliography. A good recent specialized work is Paul W. Knoll, *The Rise of the Polish Monarchy* (Chicago: University of Chicago Press, 1972).

Frederick G. Heymann, *Poland & Czechoslovakia* (Englewood Cliffs, N.J.: Prentice-Hall, 1966), deals partly with the general question of the western Slavs in the Middle Ages, as do Francis Dvorník, *The Slavs in European History and Civilization* (New Brunswick, N.J.: Rutgers University Press, 1962); and the uneven collected work represented by *The Cambridge History of Poland*, Vol. I (Cambridge: Cambridge University Press, 1950).

The best study of the emergence of the Slavic peoples is A. P. Vlasto, *The Entry of the Slavs into Christendom* (Cambridge: Cambridge University Press, 1970). O. Halecki, *Borderlands of Western Civilization* (New York: Ronald Press, 1952), and T. Stoianovich, *A Study in Balkan Civilization* (New York: Knopf, 1967), are also important. There remain wide gaps in the literature in English on Slavic Europe, but these works constitute a good introduction.

Scandinavia. D. M. Wilson and P. G. Foote, *The Viking Achievement* (New York: Praeger, 1970), is a thorough recent study. P. H. Sawyer, *The Age of the Vikings* (London: A. E. Arnold, 1962), and Gwyn Jones, *A History of the Vikings* (New York: Oxford University Press, 1968), are good shorter treatments, as is the well-illustrated volume by D. M. Wilson, *The Vikings and their Origins* (New York: Praeger, 1970). Lucien Musset, *Les invasions: Le second assaut contre l'Europe chrètienne (VIIe–XIe siècles)* (Paris: Presses universitaires de France, 1965), sets the Viking attacks in their contemporary context, and Musset's *Les peuples scandinaves au Moyen Age* (Paris: Presses universitaires de France, 1951), is the best general history of medieval Scandinavia. Individual studies include Palle Lauring, *A History of the Kingdom of Denmark* (Copenhagen:

Høst, 1973); Karen Larsen, *A History of Norway* (Princeton, N.J.: Princeton University Press, 1948).

Sicily. Good popular introductions may be found in John J. Norwich, *The Normans in the South* and *The Kingdom in the Sun* (London: Longmans, 1968, 1970), both of which contain good bibliographies. Steven Runciman, *The Sicilian Vespers* (Cambridge: Cambridge University Press, 1958), covers much of the thirteenth-century Mediterranean world. For the reign of Frederick II, see the provocative and controversial biography by E. Kantorowicz, *Frederick II* (New York: Frederick Ungar, 1957), or the more up-to-date but less intriguing work of Thomas C. Van Cleve, *The Emperor Frederick II of Hohenstaufen* (Oxford: Oxford University Press, 1973).

Spain. Several short works offer sensible approaches to the general region of Spain, and all have good bibliographies. Gabriel Jackson, *The Making of Medieval Spain* (New York: Harcourt, Brace, Jovanovich, 1972); J. Vicens Vives, *Approaches to the History of Spain* (Berkeley and Los Angeles: University of California Press, 1970), all are suggestive and informative. The long, brilliant, and perplexing study of Américo Castro, *The Spaniards* (Berkeley and Los Angeles: University of California Press, 1970), incorporates much of the author's earlier *The Structure of Spanish History* (Princeton, N.J.: Princeton University Press, 1954), and offers the most engaging introduction to Spanish culture available in English. An important longer study is that of J. F. O'Callaghan, *A History of Medieval Spain* (Ithaca: Cornell University Press, 1975).

Switzerland. See E. Bonjour, H. S. Offler, and G. R. Potter, *A Short History of Switzerland* (Oxford: Oxford University Press, 1952).

K. The Church

The history of the Church touches so many aspects of early European life and thought that its study is indispensable for those who wish to understand something of the history of Europe. There are many histories of the Church available, but those that take the broadest approach and invite the most serious thought are considerably fewer. Probably the greatest history is the multivolume work edited by A. Fliche and V. Martin, *Histoire de l'Église* (Paris: Bloud & Gay, 1935-), now in the slow process of completion and translation. Equally substantial is the monumental *Handbuch der Kirchengeschichte,* ed. Hubert Jedin. Of this work, not yet completed, Volume III, *The Church in the Age of Feudalism,* ed. by F. Kempf, H.-G. Beck, E. Ewig, and J. A. Jungmann, trans. Anselm Biggs (New York: Herder and Herder, 1969), is certainly the best single study of the period, 700–1123. A comparable work, less consistent and better in its original French sections than in English translation, is *The*

Christian Centuries, ed. Louis Rogier et al., Vol. I, *The First Six Hundred Years,* by Jean Danielou and Henri Marrou (New York: McGraw-Hill, 1964), and Vol. II, *The Middle Ages,* by David Knowles and Dimitri Obolensky (New York: McGraw-Hill, 1969). All of the works cited above contain extensive bibliographies.

Among shorter studies, Henry Chadwick, *The Early Church* (Baltimore: Penguin, 1967), and R. W. Southern, *Western Society and the Church in the Middle Ages* (Baltimore: Penguin, 1970), constitute the first two volumes in the fine series, *The Pelican History of the Church.* Both are superbly readable and reliable, although selective in their approach. A handy reference work is F. L. Cross, ed., *The Oxford Dictionary of the Christian Church* (rpt., London: Oxford University Press, 1966). A comprehensive recent bibliography, in addition to those in the works cited above, is H. Chadwick, *The History of the Church: A Select Bibliography,* 2nd ed. (London: The Historical Association, 1966). The best atlases are F. Van Der Meer and Christine Mohrmann, *An Atlas of the Early Christian World* (London: Nelson, 1958), and the *Atlas zur Kirchengeschichte,* eds. H. Jedin, K. S. Latourette, and J. Marten (Freiburg: Herder and Herder, 1970).

L. Islamic History

A good brief introduction to Mohammed and the rise of Islam is the work of Francesco Gabrieli, *Muhammad and the Conquests of Islam* (New York: McGraw-Hill, 1968). The best biography of the Prophet is Tor Andrae, *Mohammed, The Man and His Faith* (rpt., New York: Harper and Row, 1960). Other excellent short introductions include Bernard Lewis, *The Arabs in History* (rpt., New York: Harper and Row, 1960); G. E. von Grunebaum, *Medieval Islam* (rpt., Chicago: University of Chicago Press, 1961).

For the Qur'an, see R. Bell, *Introduction to the Qur'an* (Edinburgh: Edinburgh University Press, 1970). For general information on Islam, see *Encyclopedia of Islam,* new ed. (Leiden: Brill, 1960–).

Two distinctive and very different approaches to various aspects of Islamic thought are F. I. J. Rosenthal, *Political Thought in Medieval Islam* (Cambridge: Cambridge University Press, 1962), and E. W. Lane, *Arabian Society in the Middle Ages* (rpt., New York: Barnes & Noble, 1971). *The Islamic City,* eds. A. H. Hourani and S. M. Stern (Oxford and Philadelphia: Oxford University Press and University of Pennsylvania Press, 1970), collects much important recent scholarship, as does D. S. Richards, ed., *Islam and the Trade of Asia* (London: Oxford University Press and University of Pennsylvania Press, 1971).

A good recent study of Islamic culture is D. M. Dunlop, *Arab Civilization to 1500* (London: Longmans, 1971), and there is much related material in several essays included in K. M. Setton, gen. ed., *A History of the Crusades,* Vols. I and II, 2nd ed. (Madison, Wis.: University of Wisconsin Press, 1969). Norman Daniel, *The Arabs and Medieval Europe*

(London: Longmans, 1974), is a good introduction to Islamic-Christian relations. D. Sourdel and J. Sourdel-Thomine, *La civilisation de l'Islam classique* (Paris: Arthaud, 1968), is, however, the best book on the subject. For Moslem Spain, see A. Chejne, *Muslim Spain* (Minneapolis: University of Minnesota Press, 1974).

A classic work, now available in English, is Maurice Lombard, *The Golden Age of Islam* (New York: North-Holland Publishing Co., 1975).

M. The Jews in Medieval Europe

A good short introduction to the history of the Jews in the world of late antiquity is Michael Grant, *The Jews in the Roman World* (New York: Scribner, 1973). Volumes III–VIII of Salo W. Baron's *A Social and Religious History of the Jews*, 2nd ed. (New York: Columbia University Press, 1957), deal with most of the Middle Ages and represent the work of one of the greatest modern historians. The range of Baron's concerns is also reflected in his collected essays, *Ancient and Medieval Jewish History* (New Brunswick, N.J.: Rutgers University Press, 1972).

The period between the fifth and the twelfth centuries is brilliantly explored in Bernard Blumenkranz, *Juifs et Chrétiens dans le monde occidental, 430–1096* (Paris: Mouton, 1960), and the Christian literature on the Jews is described by the same author in his *Les auteurs Chrétiens latins du moyen âge sur les juifs et le judaïsme* (Paris: Mouton, 1963). The most exhaustive recent work on the early period is Cecil Roth and I. H. Levine, eds., *The Dark Age: Jews in Christian Europe 711–1096*, Vol. II of *The World History of the Jewish People*, gen. ed. Cecil Roth; Second Series: The Medieval Period (New Brunswick, N.J.: Rutgers University Press, 1966). Among particularly useful detailed studies is Joshua Starr, *The Jews in the Byzantine Empire, 641–1204* (rpt., New York: Burt Franklin, 1970).

A good collection of documentary evidence is assembled and expertly commented upon in Jacob Marcus, *The Jew in the Medieval World* (rpt., New York. Harper and Row, 1965). A useful depiction of community existence is found in Israel Abrahams, *Jewish Life in the Middle Ages* (New York: Atheneum, 1969).

Among studies of Jewish history in regions of Europe, a classic work is Guido Kisch, *The Jews in Medieval Germany* (Chicago: University of Chicago Press, 1949). Good studies of aspects of Jewish-Arab relations are S. D. Goitein, *Jews and Arabs* (rpt., New York: Schocken, 1964), and James Kritzeck, *Sons of Abraham* (Baltimore: Helicon Press, 1965). A fine study of the roots of anti-Semitism is Joshua Trachtenberg, *The Devil and the Jews: The Medieval Conception of the Jew and its Relation to Modern Antisemitism* (New Haven: Yale University Press, 1943).

An immensely important review of the question of the Jews in medieval Europe and the methodology of research into medieval Jewish history is the study of Gavin Langmuir, "The Jews and the Archives of Angevin England: Reflections on Medieval Anti-Semitism," *Traditio*, 19

(1963), 183–244. Most of the works cited above, and particularly that of Langmuir, contain useful bibliographies.

The most thorough study of a single Jewish community in the Middle Ages is S. D. Goitein, *A Mediterranean Society: The Jewish Communities of the World as Portrayed in the Documents of the Cairo Geniza*, Vol. I, *Economic Foundations;* Vol. II, *The Community* (Berkeley and Los Angeles: University of California Press, 1968, 1971). Equally important in studying the impact of Judaism on a very different kind of society is D. M. Dunlop, *History of the Jewish Khazars* (Princeton, N.J.: Princeton University Press, 1954).

N. Byzantine History

The standard reference work is now *The Cambridge Medieval History*, Vol. IV, *The Byzantine Empire*, ed. Joan M. Hussey (Cambridge: Cambridge University Press, 1966). The best single shorter history is that of George Ostrogorsky, *A History of the Byzantine State*, 2nd ed. (New Brunswick, N.J.: Rutgers University Press, 1968). Norman Baynes and H. St. L. B. Moss, *Byzantium: An Introduction to East Roman Civilization* (rpt., Oxford: Oxford University Press, 1961), consists of essays by a series of experts on various aspects of Byzantine civilization. An excellent recent survey of Byzantine civilization is H. W. Haussig, *A History of Byzantine Civilization* (New York: Praeger, 1971). J. M. Hussey, *The Byzantine World* (New York: Harper and Row, 1961), is a fine brief introduction.

On Constantinople, see David Talbot Rice, *Constantinople: From Byzantium to Istanbul* (New York: Stein and Day, 1965); Philip Sherrard, *Constantinople: Iconography of a Sacred City* (London: Oxford University Press, 1965); Dean A. Miller, *Imperial Constantinople* (New York: John Wiley, 1969). On Byzantine art, see David Talbot Rice, *Byzantine Art* (Harmondsworth: Penguin, 1968). On religion, see the chapters by Hans-Georg Beck in *The Church in the Age of Feudalism*, eds. Friedrich Kempf et al. (New York: Herder and Herder, 1969), and George Every, *The Byzantine Patriarchate, 451–1204* (London: Society for the Promotion of Christian Knowledge, 1947).

Byzantium's impact upon neighboring societies is outlined in the important study by Dimitri Obolensky, *The Byzantine Commonwealth* (New York: Weidenfeld and Nicholson, 1971).

O. The History of Ideas

A good general introduction is M. L. W. Laistner, *Thought and Letters in Western Europe*, A.D. *500–900*, 2nd ed. (Ithaca, N.Y.: Cornell University Press, 1957). Laistner may well be followed by the fine general study of Philippe Wolff, *The Awakening of Europe*, Vol. I in *The Pelican History of European Thought* (Baltimore: Penguin, 1968). David Knowles, *The Evolution of Medieval Thought* (New York: Vintage, 1962), and Gordon Leff, *Medieval Thought: St. Augustine to Ockham* (Baltimore: Penguin, 1962), are somewhat conventional intellectual histories. Friedrich Heer, *The Intellectual History of Europe*, Vol. I, *From the Beginnings of Western Thought to Luther* (Garden City, N.Y.: Anchor, Doubleday, 1968), is wildly idiosyncratic but occasionally exciting and provocative.

Particular aspects are treated by R. R. Bolgar, *The Classical Heritage and Its Beneficiaries* (New York: Cambridge University Press, 1964); Charles Homer Haskins, *The Renaissance of the Twelfth Century* (rpt., Cleveland, Meridian, 1961); Christopher Brooke, *The Twelfth Century Renaissance* (New York: Harcourt, Brace, Jovanovich, 1969); John W. Baldwin, *The Scholastic Culture of the Middle Ages, 1000–1300* (Lexington: D. S. Heath, 1971).

In their various ways, the following books offer diverse and often exciting introductions to various aspects of medieval thought. C. S. Lewis, *The Discarded Image* (Cambridge: Cambridge University Press, 1964), considers medieval cosmology and literature with an ease and magisterial skill few historians can muster. Beryl Smalley, *The Becket Conflict and the Schools: A Study of Intellectuals in Politics in the Twelfth Century* (Oxford: Basil Blackwell, 1973), is an engaging examination of one case of the involvement of intellectuals with wider forces. R. W. Southern, *Medieval Humanism and Other Studies* (New York: Harper and Row, 1971), considers a number of aspects of medieval thought in an original, perceptive, and often provocative manner. M. D. Chenu's *Toward Understanding St. Thomas* (Chicago: University of Chicago Press, 1964), trans. A. M. Landry, O.P. and D. Hughes, O.P., and *Nature, Man, and Society in the Twelfth Century*, trans. Jerome Taylor and Lester K. Little (Chicago: University of Chicago Press, 1968) are two classic works by one of the great masters.

P. Transportation and Technology

A. P. Newton, *Travel and Travellers of the Middle Ages* (New York: K. Paul, Trench, Trubner & Co., 1930), is a good general introduction. More recent works are G. Hindley, *A History of Roads* (Secaucus, N.J.: P. Davies, 1972), and Albert C. Leighton, *Transport and Communication in Early Medieval Europe, A.D. 500–1100* (Newton Abbot: David and Charles, 1972).

There are a number of good general histories of technology, a subject long neglected and extremely important in early European history. Two particularly lively studies are Lynn White, *Medieval Technology and Social Change* (Oxford: Oxford University Press, 1962), and idem, *Machina ex Deo* (Cambridge, Mass.: M.I.T. University Press, 1969).

Q. Mathematics, Science, and Medicine

Loren C. MacKinney, *Early Medieval Medicine with Special Reference to France and Chartres* (Baltimore: Johns Hopkins University Press, 1937), and idem, *Medical Illustrations in Medieval Manuscripts* (Berkeley and Los Angeles: University of California Press, 1965) constitute a good introduction to the history of medieval medicine; each includes bibliographical guides. B. Lawn, *The Salernitan Questions* (Oxford: Oxford University Press, 1963), is a good introduction to the conceptualization of medical and scientific problems in the Middle Ages. C. H. Talbot, *Medicine in Medieval England* (London: Oldbourne, 1967), is extremely wide-ranging and informative. A more extensive bibliography may be found in Edward Grant, *A Sourcebook in Medieval Science* (Cambridge, Mass.: Harvard University Press, 1974). A particularly good popular account of a single problem that was in large part medical is Philip Ziegler, *The Black Death* (New York: Harper and Row, 1969). Another particular account, a classic in the history of medicine, is Hans Zinsser, *Rats, Lice, and History* (rpt., New York: Bantam, 1957).

Standard histories of medieval science are A. C. Crombie, *Medieval and Early Modern Science*, rev. ed., 2 vols. (New York: Doubleday, 1959), and George Sarton, *Introduction to the History of Science*, 3 vols. (Baltimore: Johns Hopkins University Press, 1947–1958). Edward Grant, *Physical Science in the Middle Ages* (New York: John Wiley, 1971), contains an excellent bibliography. Richard Dales, *The Scientific Achievement of the Middle Ages* (Philadelphia: University of Pennsylvania Press, 1973), offers a fine selection of documents in translation and includes an introduction and bibliography.

No general history of mathematics deals at all adequately with the Middle Ages. A short popular introduction is provided to some extent in Joseph Gies and Frances Gies, *Leonardo of Pisa and the New Mathematics of the Middle Ages* (New York: Crowell, 1969).

R. Archaeology and Anthropology

A good introduction to the nature of the discipline and its methodology is Rainer Berger, ed., *Scientific Methods in Medieval Archaeology* (Berkeley and Los Angeles: University of California Press, 1970). The journal *Medieval Archaeology* is the best ongoing survey of archaeological research. A sample of some of the contributions of anthropologists and archaeologists to historical problems is Brian Spooner, ed., *Population Growth: Anthropological Implications* (Cambridge, Mass.: M.I.T. University Press, 1972), especially the essay by Bernard Wailes.

Among the increasing number of studies by anthropologists that touch upon medieval Europe or that medievalists have found useful are the following: Max Gluckman, *Politics, Law and Ritual in Tribal Society* (New York: New American Library, 1968); Laura Nader, ed., *Law in Culture and Society* (Chicago: University of Chicago Press, 1969); Mary

Douglas, ed., *Witchcraft Confessions and Accusations* (London: Tavistock, 1971). An interesting but far from satisfactory approach to medieval European history from an anthropologist's point of view is Robert T. Anderson, *Traditional Europe: A Study in Anthropology and History* (Belmont, Calif.: Wadsworth, 1971). A fascinating study that touches considerably upon early European views of the European past, as well as non-European societies, is Margaret T. Hodgen, *Early Anthropology in the Sixteenth and Seventeenth Centuries* (rpt., Philadelphia: University of Pennsylvania, 1971).

Desmond Collins, *The Origins of Europe* (London: Allen & Unwin, 1974), includes several important archaeological contributions to the history of early medieval Europe.

II. SELECTIVE BIBLIOGRAPHY
PART I

The best extensive studies of European historical geography are C. T. Smith, *An Historical Geography of Western Europe before 1800* (London: Longmans, 1967), and Norman J. G. Pounds, *An Historical Geography of Europe, 450* B.C.–A.D. *1330* (Cambridge: Cambridge University Press, 1973). For English-speaking readers, a good detailed study of a single area is H. C. Darby et al., *Historical Geography of England before 1800* (Cambridge: Cambridge University Press, 1951).

The easiest introduction to recent work on the history of climate is the wise and witty book by Robert Claiborne, *Climate, Man, and History* (New York: W. W. Norton, 1970), but the reader should then consult the superb survey of Emmanuel Le Roy Ladurie, *Times of Feast, Times of Famine: A History of Climate Since the Year 1000*, trans. Barbara Bray (New York: Doubleday, 1971). A good example of a more technical study is H. H. Lamb, *The Changing Climate* (London: Methuen, 1966).

Two excellent introductions to human geography are Emrys Jones, *Human Geography: An Introduction to Man and His World*, (rev. ed. New York: Praeger, 1965), and Derwent Whittlesey, *Environmental Foundations of European History* (New York: Appleton-Century-Crofts, 1949). A brilliant example of working such data into the fiber of a great historical study is Fernand Braudel, *The Mediterranean and the Mediterranean World in the Age of Phillip II*, trans. Siân Reynolds, 2 vols. (New York: Harper & Row, 1972). See also W. Gordon East, *The Geography Behind History* (London: W. W. Norton, 1965).

On Celtic society, see Nora Chadwick, *The Celts* (Baltimore: Penguin, 1970), a good short introduction. At greater length, there is Nora Chadwick and Myles Dillon, *The Celtic Realms* (New York: Weidenfeld & Nicholson, 1967). For Celtic art and culture, see J. Hatt, *Celts and Gallo-Romans* (New York: Hippocrene, 1970). See also J. Filip, *Celtic*

Civilization and Its Heritage (Prague: Publishing House of the Czechoslovak Academy of Sciences and Artia, 1962).
For the earliest period that can be spoken of as European, see V. Gordon Childe, *The Prehistory of European Society* (Baltimore: Penguin, 1958), and, more recently, Stuart Piggott, *Ancient Europe* (Chicago: University of Chicago Press, 1965), Glyn Daniel; *The Idea of Prehistory* (Baltimore: Penguin, 1965).
E. A. Thompson, *The Early Germans* (Oxford: Oxford University Press, 1965) is a good introductory essay.
There are numerous studies of Roman European provincial history. A recent survey is Fergus Millar, *The Roman Empire and Its Neighbors* (London: Weidenfeld & Nicholson, 1967). See also R. E. M. Wheeler, *Rome Beyond the Imperial Frontiers* (rpt., Westport, Conn.: The Greenwood Press, 1972).
For the whole period, see A. H. M. Jones, *The Late Roman Empire, 284–602*, 4 vols. (Oxford: Oxford University Press, 1964), and Jones's shorter work, *The Decline of the Ancient World* (New York: Holt, Rinehart & Winston, 1966). A good brief political survey is F. E. Adcock, *Roman Political Ideals and Practice* (Ann Arbor, Mich.: University of Michigan Press, 1959). Peter Brown, *The World of Late Antiquity* (New York: Harcourt, Brace, Jovanovich, 1970), is a brilliant and stimulating essay.
A good survey of various aspects of the third- and fourth-century Roman world is A. Momigliano, ed., *Paganism and Christianity in the Fourth Century* (Oxford: Oxford University Press, 1963). See Ramsay MacMullen, *Constantine* (New York: Harper & Row, 1971), and Anthony Birley, *Marcus Aurelius* (London: Eyre & Spottiswoode, 1966), for studies of two important emperors. Ramsay MacMullen, *Enemies of the Roman Order: Treason, Unrest, and Alienation in the Empire* (Cambridge, Mass.: Harvard University Press, 1966), and idem, *Soldier and Civilian in the Later Roman Empire* (Cambridge, Mass.: Harvard University Press, 1963) offer important social and cultural insights into later imperial culture. A. Alföldi, *A Conflict of Ideas in the Late Roman Empire* (Oxford: Oxford University Press, 1952), examines the critical period between Constantine and Theodosius. F. W. Walbank, *The Awful Revolution* (Toronto: University of Toronto Press, 1969), is a short treatment of the general problem.
A brilliant study of the emergence of Christian thought is Charles N. Cochrane, *Christianity and Classical Culture* (Oxford: Oxford University Press, 1957). For the early Church, see especially Karl Baus, *From the Apostolic Community to Constantine* (London: Burns & Oates, 1965). For St. Augustine, see Peter Brown, *Augustine of Hippo: A Biography* (Berkeley and Los Angeles: University of California Press, 1969), and idem, *Religion and Society in the Age of Saint Augustine* (New York: Barnes & Noble, 1972). Michael Gough, *The Early Christians* (London: Thames & Hudson, 1961), has much to say about Christian art and society, as does R. A. Markus, *Christianity in the Roman World* (London: Thames & Hudson, 1974).

M. Rostovtzeff, *Iranians and Greeks in South Russia* (rpt., New York: Russell & Russell, 1969), and T. Sulimirski, *The Sarmatians* (London: Thames & Hudson, 1970), offer insights into the northeastern corner of the Mediterranean and Black Sea worlds. Cyril Toumanoff, *Studies in Christian Caucasian History* (Washington, D.C.: Georgetown University Press, 1963) is an interesting description of a neglected part of the ancient and medieval world.

In addition to sources already cited, see John E. N. Hearsey, *The City of Constantine, 324–1453* (London: J. Murray, 1963); A. Momigliano, ed., *The Conflict Between Paganism and Christianity in the Fourth Century* (Oxford: Oxford University Press, 1963); Walter Kaegi, *Byzantium and the Decline of Rome* (Princeton, N.J.: Princeton University Press, 1968).

PART II

For the late Roman world see particularly H. St. L. B. Moss, *The Birth of the Middle Ages, 395–814* (New York: Oxford University Press, 1964). F. Lot, *The End of the Ancient World and the Beginnings of the Middle Ages* (rpt., New York: Harper & Row, 1961); W. C. Bark, *Origins of the Medieval World* (Stanford, Calif.: Stanford University Press, 1958), and Joseph Vogt, *The Decline of Rome* (London: Weidenfeld & Nicholson, 1968), all offer distinctive, stimulating views.

The best introduction in English to the history of the migrations is Lucien Musset, *The Germanic Invasions* (State College, Pennsylvania: The Pennsylvania State University Press, 1975). Particular studies of early invaders are Bernard S. Bacharach, *A History of the Alans in the West* (Minneapolis: University of Minnesota Press, 1973); J. Otto Maenchen-Helfen, *The World of the Huns* (Berkeley and Los Angeles: University of California Press, 1973); E. A. Thompson, *The Visigoths in the Time of Ulfila* (Oxford: Oxford University Press, 1966). A fine short survey is J. M. Wallace-Hadrill, *The Barbarian West* (New York: Harper & Row, 1962).

For Galla Placidia, see Steward I. Oost, *Galla Placidia Augusta* (Chicago: University of Chicago Press, 1968). An extremely important collection of source materials and commentary is J. N. Hillgarth, *The Conversion of Western Europe, 350–750* (Englewood Cliffs, N.J.: Prentice-Hall, 1969). See also Noel Q. King, *The Emperor Theodosius and the Establishing of Christianity* (New York: Westminster Press, 1962).

For the periods covered by Parts II, III, IV, see Romilly Jenkins, *Byzantium: The Imperial Centuries, 610–1071* (New York: Vintage, 1969). The most extensive study of Theodoric is T. Hodgkin, *Theodoric the Great* (London: G. P. Putnam's Sons, 1891). J. B. Bury, *The Invasion of Europe by the Barbarians* (rpt., New York: Russell and Russell, 1963) is old but comprehensive.

On the Franks, see J. M. Wallace-Hadrill, *The Long-Haired Kings* (New York: Barnes & Noble, 1962). On Britain, see Peter Hunter-Blair, *Anglo-Saxon England* (Cambridge: Cambridge University Press, 1960). Peter Lasko, *The Kingdom of the Franks* (New York: McGraw-Hill, 1971), is particularly strong on art and archaeology. For Visigothic Spain, see E. A. Thompson, *The Goths in Spain* (Oxford: Oxford University Press, 1969).

On early monasticism, see the short general work of David Knowles, *Christian Monasticism* (New York: McGraw-Hill, 1969) with bibliography.

There are many biographies of Justinian, but the best short introduction is John W. Barker, *Justinian and the Later Roman Empire* (Madison, Wis.: University of Wisconsin Press, 1966), which contains a good bibliography. For the city of Constantinople, see the General Bibliographies.

On the Slavs, see A. P. Vlasto, *The Entry of the Slavs into Christendom* (Cambridge: Cambridge University Press, 1970). Steven Runciman, *The First Bulgarian Empire* (London: G. Bell & Sons, 1930), and Sirarpie Der Nersessian, *Armenia and the Byzantine Empire* (Cambridge: Cambridge University Press, 1953), are good introductions. R. N. Frye, *The Heritage of Persia* (New York: New American Library, 1966), offers a general introduction.

Peter Llewellyn, *Rome in the Dark Ages* (New York: Praeger, 1970), offers considerable material on Lombard, Italy. Katherine Fischer Drew, ed. and trans., *The Lombard Laws* (Philadelphia: University of Pennsylvania Press, 1973) has a good introductory section, as does William Dudley Foulke's translation of Paul the Deacon, *History of the Lombards* (rpt. Philadelphia: University of Pennsylvania Press, 1974).

On Gregory the Great, see F. H. Dudden, *Gregory the Great: His Place in History and Thought* (rpt., New York: Russell & Russell, 1967), and Llewellyn, *Rome in the Dark Ages*.

On England and Ireland, see Charles Thomas, *Britain and Ireland in Early Christian Times* (New York: McGraw-Hill, 1971), and H. R. Loyn, *Anglo-Saxon England and the Norman Conquest* (New York: Harper & Row, 1962).

On Spain, in addition to E. A. Thompson, *The Goths in Spain* (Oxford, 1969), see P. D. King, *Law and Society in the Visigothic Kingdom* (Cambridge: Cambridge University Press, 1972).

PART III

Aside from the *Cambridge Medieval History,* there is no single work in English dealing exclusively with this period. When it appears, Donald Bullough's volume in the series, *A General History of Europe,* ed. Denys Hay, should be the standard work in English.

For early England, see Peter Hunter Blair, *The World of Bede*

(London: Secker and Warburg, 1970), for a general introduction. W. Levison, *England and the Continent in the Eighth Century* (Oxford: Oxford University Press, 1946), is a classic, as is S. J. Crawford, *Anglo-Saxon Influence on Western Christendom, 600–800* (Cambridge: Cambridge University Press, rpt., 1966).

For the Continent, see J. M. Wallace-Hadrill, *The Long-Haired Kings* (New York: Barnes & Noble, 1962), F. Kempf, et al, eds., *The Church in the Age of Feudalism* (New York: Herder and Herder, 1969), H. Fichtenau, *The Carolingian Empire*, trans. P. Munz (New York: Harper & Row, 1964), and F. L. Ganshof, *Frankish Institutions with Charlemagne* (New York: W. W. Norton, 1972), offer different approaches. Donald Bullough, *The Age of Charlemagne* (New York: Putnam, 1966) offers a fine text and further references. B. Scholz, *Two Carolingian Chronicles* (Ann Arbor, Mich.: University of Michigan Press, 1971), and Einhard, *The Life of Charlemagne* (Ann Arbor, Mich.: University of Michigan Press, 1960) are useful translated source materials. Jacques Boussard, *The Civilization of Charlemagne* (New York: McGraw-Hill, 1971), is the most recent general survey.

See R. Latouche, *The Birth of the Western Economy*, 2nd ed, trans. E. M. Wilkinson (New York: Harper & Row, 1967), and A. C. Leighton, *Transport and Communications in Early Medieval Europe, 500–1100* (Newton Abbot: David and Charles, 1974).

See Dimitri Obolensky, *The Byzantine Commonwealth* (London: Weidenfeld & Nicholson, 1973), and A. P. Vlasto, *The Entry of the Slavs into Christendom* (Cambridge: Cambridge University Press, 1972), as well as works cited in the general bibliographies. On Byzantium, see the general bibliographies. For the western invasion, see Lucien Musset, *Les invasions: le second assaut contre l'Europe* (Paris: Presses universitaires de France: Nouvelle Clio, 1951), and E. S. Duckett, *Death and Life in the Tenth Century* (Ann Arbor, Mich.: University of Michigan Press, 1971).

PART IV

Robert S. Lopez, *The Commercial Revolution of the Middle Ages, 950–1350* (Englewood Cliffs, N.J.: Prentice-Hall, 1971) is a good short introduction to the revolution in material culture during the period, as are the relevant sections of *The Fontana Economic History of Europe: The Middle Ages*, ed. Carlo M. Cipolla (London: Fontana, 1972), and Robert-Henri Bautier, *The Economic Development of Medieval Europe* (New York: Harcourt, Brace, Jovanovich, 1971). See also Georges Duby, *Rural Economy and Country Life in the Medieval West* (Columbia, S.C.: University of South Carolina Press, 1968).

The best general history of the period 950–1150 is Christopher Brooke, *Europe in the Central Middle Ages, 962–1154* (New York: Holt,

Rinehart & Winston, 1968). The works by R. W. Southern and Marc Bloch are classics, each emphasizing different but complementary elements of the period. There are a number of important studies in Fredric L. Cheyette, ed., *Lordship and Community in Medieval Europe* (New York: Holt, Rinehart, & Winston, 1968). On the German monarchy, see Boyd Hill, *Medieval Monarchy in Action* (New York: Barnes & Noble, 1972), and Karl Hampe, *Germany under the Salian and Hohenstaufen Emperors,* trans. R. F. Bennett (Totowa, N.J.: Rowman & Littlefield, 1973). On northern and eastern Europe, see the works on Scandinavia and central and eastern Europe cited in the general bibliographies. The classic work on kingship remains Fritz Kern, *Kingship and Law in the Middle Ages* (rpt., New York: Harper & Row, 1956).

The literature on the Gregorian reform is vast. A good introduction is K. F. Morrison, *Tradition and Authority in the Early Church, 300–1140* (Princeton, N.J.: Princeton University Press, 1969), and a classic is Gerd Tellenbach, *Church, State, and Christian Society at the Time of the Investiture Contest* (Oxford: Harper & Row, 1948). On pilgrimage, see Vera Hell and Helmut Hell, *The Great Pilgrimage of the Middle Ages* (New York: C. N. Potter, 1967). On monasticism in general, see Joan Evans, *Monastic Life at Cluny, 910–1157* (Oxford: H. Milford, 1931), and J. Leclerq, *The Love of Learning and the Desire for God* (New York: New American Library, 1961). The world of the Crusades may now be followed in *A History of the Crusades,* gen. ed. Kenneth M. Setton, Vols. I and II (rpt. ed., Madison, Wis.: University of Wisconsin Press, 1969), and in Hans Eberhard Mayer, *The Crusades* (New York: Oxford University Press, 1972). On the problem of the legitimacy of war, see Frederick H. Russell, *The Just War in The Middle Ages* (Cambridge: Cambridge University Press, 1975) and James T. Johnson, *Ideology, Reason, and the Limitation of War* (Princeton, N.J.: Princeton University Press, 1975).

PART V

The best general views are those of Christopher Brooke, *Europe in the Central Middle Ages, 962–1154* (New York: Holt, Rinehart, 1968), and J. H. Mundy, *Europe in the High Middle Ages, 1150–1309* (New York: Basic Books, 1973).

The best brief account of the importance of logic in the twelfth-century curriculum and the early transformation of the schools is R. W. Southern, *The Making of the Middle Ages* (New Haven: Yale University Press, 1953). The best short account of the relationship among educational curricula, ideas of cosmology, and philosophy is C. S. Lewis, *The Discarded Image* (Cambridge: Cambridge University Press, 1964). A general introduction to the history of literacy is Carlo Cipolla, *Literacy and Development in the West* (Baltimore: Penguin, 1969). There is a large literature on the manufacture of books, and one of the most convenient starting points is David Diringer, *The Illuminated Book: Its History and Production* (New York, Washington, D.C.: Praeger, rpt. 1967). On medieval libraries, the standard work is J. W. Thompson, *The Medieval Library* (New York: Hafner, rpt. 1967). The history of medieval handwriting is a discipline in itself, paleography, and has a large literature. An excellent introduction is E. A. Lowe, *Handwriting* (Rome: Edizioni di storia e letteratura, 1969), which includes many clear plates and transcriptions of the hands by J. Braxton Ross.

The best introduction to medieval Latin is Karl Strecker, *Introduction to Medieval Latin,* trans. and rev. Robert B. Palmer, 2nd ed. (Berlin: Weidmannische Verlags Buchhandlungen, 1963). Helen Waddell, *The Wandering Scholars* (New York: Doubleday, rpt. 1968), is a stimulating account of Latin's place in medieval culture. More formidable and scholarly, with an immensely wide imaginative range, is E. R. Curtius's classic *European Literature and the Latin Middle Ages* (New York: Harper & Row, 1953). See also R. R. Bolgar, *The Classical Heritage* (New York: Cambridge University Press, rpt., 1964).

On the origins and development of western languages in general, see Philippe Wolff, *Western Languages,* A.D. *100–1500* (New York: McGraw-Hill, 1971), a superb guide for the beginner. More specialized studies include Erich Auerbach, *Introduction to Romance Languages and Literature* (New York: Capricorn, 1961), and Otto Jespersen, *The Growth and Structure of the English Language* (New York: Doubleday, rpt., 1955). For translations, see Charles Homer Haskins, *Studies in the History of Medieval Science* (Cambridge, Mass.: Harvard University Press, 1924); R. Walzer, *Greek into Arabic* (Oxford: Oxford University Press, 1962); F. E. Peters, *Aristotle and the Arabs* (New York: New York University Press, 1968); James Kritzeck, *Peter the Venerable and Islam* (Princeton: Princeton University Press, 1964).

There exist a number of concise histories of medieval thought. A particularly good introduction is David Knowles, *The Evolution of Medieval Thought* (New York: Vintage, 1963). For philosophy proper, see E. Gilson, *A History of Christian Philosophy in the Middle Ages* (London: Random House, 1955). The best introduction to Anselm is R. W. Southern, *St. Anselm and His Biographer* (Cambridge: Cambridge University Press, 1963), and Eadmer, *The Life of St. Anselm, Archbishop of Canterbury,* ed. and trans. R. W. Southern (London: Nelson, 1962). A convenient guide to translations and studies is Jasper Hopkins, *A Companion to the Study of St. Anselm* (Minneapolis: University of Minnesota Press, 1972). The literature on Abelard is immense. The standard introduction is J. G. Sikes, *Peter Abailard* (Cambridge: Cambridge University Press, 1932). A very good shorter work is Leif Grane, *Peter Abelard* (New York: Harcourt Brace Jovanovich, 1970). An interesting reconstruction of the sentimental lives of Heloise and Abelard is Regine Pernoud, *Heloise and Abelard* (New York: Stein and Day, 1973); however, the authenticity of their correspondence has been challenged by Professor John Benton. There is an excellent essay defending the authenticity of the correspondence in the fine collection by R. W. Southern, *Medieval Humanism and Other Essays* (New York: Harper and Row, 1971). Abelard's influence is described by D. Luscombe, *The School of Peter Abelard* (Cambridge: Cambridge University Press, 1969).

The best short introduction to the twelfth-century transformation of theology is M. D. Chenu, *Nature, Man, and Society in the Twelfth Century*, trans. Jerome Taylor and Lester K. Little (Chicago: University of Chicago Press, 1968). On Bernard Sylvester, see Brian Stock, *Myth and Science in the Twelfth Century* (Princeton: Princeton University Press, 1972).

For the importance of Gratian and ecclesiastical law in general, see Stephan Kuttner, *Harmony from Dissonance* (Latrobe, Pa.: St. Vincent's Abbey, 1960). A more specialized study is C. Duggan, *Twelfth-Century Decretal Collections and Their Importance in English History* (London: Athlone, 1963). An excellent example of modern scholarship on a particular topic is R. L. Benson, *The Bishop-Elect* (Princeton, N.J.: Princeton University Press, 1968). For Roman Law, see Paul Vinogradoff, *Roman Law in Medieval Europe*, 3rd ed (Oxford: Oxford University Press, 1961). For Glanvil, see G. Hall, *Glanvil's Treatise on the Laws and Customs of England* (London: Nelson, 1966). For Sicilian law, see James M. Powell, *The Liber Augustalis* (Syracuse: Syracuse University Press, 1971).

The standard history of universities is Hastings Rashdall, *The Universities of Europe in the Middle Ages*, ed. F. Powicke and A. B. Emden, 3 vols. (Oxford: Oxford University Press, 1936). Good short works are Helène Wieruszowski, *The Medieval University* (New York: Van Nostrand, 1966); L. J. Daly, S.J., *The Medieval University, 1200–1400* (New York: Sheed & Ward, 1961); Gordon Leff, *Paris and Oxford Universities in the Thirteenth and Fourteenth Centuries* (New York: John Wiley, 1968). An excellent collection of source materials is Lynn Thorndike, *University Records and Life in the Middle Ages*, rpt. (New York: W. W. Norton, 1975).

Of the many general works on twelfth-century learning in its full range, Charles Homer Haskins, *The Renaissance of the Twelfth Century* (New York: Meridian, rpt., 1961), Christopher Brooke, *The Twelfth-Century Renaissance* (New York: Harcourt, Brace, Jovanovich, 1969), and R. R. Bolgar, *The Classical Heritage* (New York: Cambridge University Press, 1964), should be particularly noted. The introduction to biblical studies in the Middle Ages is Beryl Smalley, *The Study of the Bible in the Middle Ages* (Notre Dame, Ind.: Notre Dame University Press, 1964). On the culture of monasticism, see the brilliant study of Jean Leclerq, *The Love of Learning and the Desire for God* (New York: New American Library, 1962).

On the question of "renaissances" in general, see E. Panofsky, *Renaissance and Renascences in Western Art* (New York: Harper & Row, rpt. 1972). Georges Duby, *The Europe of the Cathedrals, 1140–1280* (Cleveland: World, 1964), is a fine blending of visual and verbal analysis.

The best general introduction to the complex development of early

European society is the great work of Marc Bloch, *Feudal Society* (Chicago: University of Chicago Press, 1961); many of Bloch's views have been modified by later scholarship. The most recent comprehensive sketch is Robert Fossier, *Histoire sociale de l'occident médiéval* (Paris: A. Colin, 1970). A fine particular study is John W. Baldwin, *Masters, Merchants and Princes: The Social Views of Peter the Chanter and His Circle*, 2 vols. (Princeton, N.J.: Princeton University Press, 1970).

There is a good introduction to the setting of much Latin and vernacular literature and a good bibliography in Christopher Brooke, *The Twelfth-Century Renaissance* (New York: Harcourt, Brace, Jovanovich, 1969). See W. T. H. Jackson, *The Literature of the Middle Ages* (New York: Columbia University Press, 1960).

There has recently been a renewed interest in medieval historiography. There is a pertinent and interesting chapter in Brooke, *The Twelfth-Century Renaissance*. See also William Brandt, *The Shape of Medieval History* (New Haven: Yale University Press, 1966). Most of the works cited in the text exist in English translations.

On the complex question of the place of nature, see first M. D. Chenu, *Nature, Man, and Society in the Twelfth Century*, trans. Jerome Taylor and Lester K. Little (Chicago: University of Chicago Press, 1968). On Aquinas, see M. D. Chenu, *Toward Understanding St. Thomas*, trans. A. M. Landry, O.P. and D. Hughes, O.P. (Chicago: University of Chicago Press, 1964), which contains a complete bibliography. The work of Theophilus has been translated by C. R. Dodwell, *De diversis artibus* (London: Nelson, 1961). See also E. Panofsky, *Gothic Architecture and Scholasticism* (rep. New York: Doubleday, 1960), and O. von Simson, *The Gothic Cathedral* (rpt. New York: Harper & Row, 1964). Henry Kraus, *The Living Theater of Medieval Art* (rpt. Philadelphia: University of Pennsylvania Press, 1972) is a lively and discursive introduction to several social and cultural themes and their relation to the visual arts. On scholastic culture in general, see John W. Baldwin, *The Scholastic Culture of the Middle Ages, 1000–1300* (Lexington, Mass.: D. C. Heath, 1971), which includes an extensive bibliography.

There is a large literature on theories of economic and social relationships between the tenth and the fourteenth centuries. See Gabriel LeBras's long essay in the third volume of the *Cambridge Economic History of Europe*, J. Clapham et al., eds. (Cambridge: Cambridge University Press, 1941–1961). John W. Baldwin, *Medieval Theories of the Just Price* (Philadelphia: American Philosophical Society, 1959), and Benjamin N. Nelson, *The Idea of Usury* (rpt. Chicago: University of Chicago Press, 1959), deal with two important aspects of economic history. For a fine introduction to the relationships among economic experience and moral thought, see Lester K. Little, "Pride Goes Before Avarice: Social Change and the Vices in Latin Christendom," *American Historical Review*, 76 (1971), 16–49.

The formation of the political public of the thirteenth and fourteenth centuries has not yet found its historian. A good introduction to the early development of representative assemblies is Antonio Marongiu,

Medieval Parliaments: A Comparative Study, trans. and adapted by S. J. Woolf (London: Eyre & Spottiswoode, 1968). On Magna Carta, see J. C. Holt, *Magna Carta* (Cambridge: Cambridge University Press, rpt., 1969). An excellent introduction to some of the complex legal problems involving representation and many other topics is Gaines Post, *Studies in Medieval Legal Thought* (Princeton, N.J.: Princeton University Press, 1964).

There is as yet little in English on the relations between the physical city and the culture of the people who live in it. See David Herlihy, *Pisa in the Early Renaissance* (New Haven: Yale University Press, 1958), and *Medieval and Renaissance Pistoia* (New Haven: Yale University Press, 1967). On technology, see, besides the works cited earlier, Lynn White, Jr., *Machina ex Deo* (Cambridge, Mass.: M.I.T. University Press, 1970).

The best short introduction to the changes in monasticism and their consequences is David Knowles, *Christian Monasticism* (New York: McGraw-Hill, 1969). The letters of St. Bernard have been translated by B. S. James (Chicago: H. Regnery, 1963). On the development of canon law, see Stephan Kuttner, *Harmony from Dissonance* (Latrobe, Pa., 1960). On the military orders, see the popular work by Desmond Seward, *The Monks of War* (Hamden, Conn.: Archon Books, 1972), which includes a bibliography. Among the many studies of the origins of heresy, one of the most original is J. B. Russell, *Dissent and Reform in the Early Middle Ages* (Berkeley and Los Angeles: University of California Press, 1965). Most of the major scholarship on twelfth-century heresy is in French and German. The standard works are Herbert Grundmann, *Religiöse Bewegungen im Mittelalter* (rev. ed. Hildesheim: Georg Olms Verlagsbuchhandlungen, 1961), and Henri Maisonneuve, *Études sur les origines de l'Inquisition* (rev. ed. Paris: J. Vrin, 1960). The most extensive work in English is Henry C. Lea, *A History of the Inquisition of the Middle Ages,* 3 vols. (New York: Harper & Row, 1887). For Catharism and the Albigensian Crusade, see W. L. Wakefield, *Heresy, Crusade and Inquisition in Southern France, 1100–1250* (Berkeley and Los Angeles: University of California Press, 1974), an excellent introduction. On the history of heresy, a superb collection of documents in translation is W. L. Wakefield and A. P. Evans, *Heresies of the High Middle Ages* (New York: Columbia University Press, 1969).

For Franciscan history, see John Moorman, *A History of the Franciscan Order* (Oxford: Oxford University Press, 1968), and Rosalind B. Brooke, *Early Franciscan Government* (Cambridge: Cambridge University Press, 1959). For the Dominicans, see M. H. Vicaire, *St. Dominic and His Times* (London: Oxford University Press, 1964), and R. F. Bennett, *The Early Dominicans* (Cambridge: Cambridge University Press, 1937).

The problem of papal authority and the struggle between papacy and empire has an immense literature. A good bibliography is appended to Geoffrey Barraclough, *The Medieval Papacy* (New York: Harcourt, Brace, Jovanovich, 1968). On Frederick Barbarossa, see Peter Munz, *Frederick Barbarossa* (Ithaca, N.Y.: Cornell University Press, 1969). For Frederick II, see Ernst Kantorowicz, *Frederick II* (rpt. New York: Frederick Ungar, 1957), and Thomas C. Van Cleve, *Frederick II of Hohen-*

staufen (Oxford: Oxford University Press, 1973). Frederick's study of falconry is available in English: Casey A. Wood and F. Marjorie Fyfe, eds. and trans., *The Art of Falconry* (rpt. Stanford: Stanford University Press, 1975).

Besides the works listed in the general bibliography, the following studies offer important views. Charles M. Brand, *Byzantium Confronts the West, 1180–1204* (Cambridge, Mass., 1968), treats Byzantine-Latin relations on the eve of the Fourth Crusade. Donald Queller, *The Latin Conquest of Constantinople* (New York: John Wiley, 1971), provides a good sampling of the scholarly problems concerning the Fourth Crusade and a fine short bibliography. Robert Lee Wolff and Harry Hazard, eds., *The Later Crusades, 1189–1311,* Volume II of *A History of the Crusades,* ed. K. M. Setton, 2nd ed. (Madison, Wis.: University of Wisconsin Press, 1969), is now the standard authority on many aspects of eastern Mediterranean history for this period. For the later Byzantine Empire, see Donald M. Nicol, *The Last Centuries of Byzantium: 1261–1453* (London: Hart Davis, 1972). Two particularly good recent studies are Deno J. Genakoplos, *The Emperor Michael Palaeologos and the West, 1258–1282* (Cambridge, Mass.: Harvard University Press, 1959), and Angeliki E. Laiou, *Constantinople and the Latins: The Foreign Policy of Andronicus II, 1282–1328* (Cambridge, Mass.: Harvard University Press, 1972).

On the Mongols, see J. J. Saunders, *The Story of the Mongol Conquest* (London: Routledge & Kegan Paul, 1971), and B. Spuler, *The Mongols in History* (London: Pall Mall, 1971); both contain bibliographies. Many sources are available in translation. Christopher Dawson, ed. *Mission to Asia* (New York: Harper & Row, 1966), and B. Spuler, *History of the Mongols Based on Eastern and Western Accounts of the Thirteenth and Fourteenth Centuries,* trans. Helga Drummond (Berkeley and Los Angeles: University of California Press, 1972), offer many selections. For Russia, see George Vernadsky, *The Mongols and Russia* (New Haven: Yale University Press, 1953).

For the expansion to Asia, see Leonardo Olschki, *Marco Polo's Asia,* trans. John A. Scott (Berkeley and Los Angeles: University of California Press, 1960), and Olschki, *Guillaume Boucher: A French Artist at the Court of the Khans* (Baltimore: Johns Hopkins University Press, 1946). For expansion on the Atlantic, see Robert S. Lopez, *The Commercial Revolution of the Middle Ages* (Englewood Cliffs, N.J.: Prentice-Hall, 1971).

PART VI

A good recent introduction to the fourteenth and fifteenth centuries is Denys Hay, *Europe in the Fourteenth and Fifteenth Centuries* (New York: Holt, Rinehart & Winston, 1966). Daniel Waley, *Later Medieval Europe* (London: Longmans, 1964), is shorter and more selective. Jacques

Heers, *L'Occident aux XIVe et XVe siècles: Aspects économiques et sociaux* (Paris: Presses Universitaires de France: Nouvelle Clio, 1970), is a brilliant survey of social and economic history. Georges Duby, *Foundations of a New Humanism, 1280–1440* (Cleveland: World, 1966), is a fine introduction to cultural history, as is the classic by Johann Huizinga, *The Waning of the Middle Ages* (New York: Doubleday, 1953). Margaret Aston, *The Fifteenth Century: The Prospect of Europe* (New York: Harcourt, Brace, Jovanovich, 1968), is a good introduction to a difficult period. *Europe in the Late Middle Ages*, ed. John Hale, J. R. L. Highfield, and Beryl Smalley (Evanston, Ill.: Northwestern University Press, 1965), combines the recent research of many scholars on selected important topics. Among many surveys focusing on the later aspects of this period, Wallace K. Ferguson, *Europe in Transition, 1300–1520* (Boston: Houghton Mifflin, 1962), is comprehensive. The series *History of Mankind* has published Volume IV, Parts I and II, *The Foundations of the Modern World, 1300–1775,* eds. Louis Gottschalk, L. C. McKinney, and E. H. Pritchard (London: Harper & Row, 1969), a large work well worth consulting. Particularly important, although not without its shortcomings, is Fernand Braudel, *Capitalism and Material Life, 1400–1800* (New York: Harper & Row, 1973). Theodore K. Rabb, *The Struggle for Stability in Early Modern Europe* (New York: Oxford University Press, 1975) considers the general problem of political organization and culture.

There exist many studies of various aspects of medieval life, but there are few specific studies on women, childhood, and family life. T. S. R. Boase, *Death in the Middle Ages* (London: McGraw-Hill, 1972), is an interesting and well-illustrated introduction to a complex topic, as is P. Ariès, *Western Attitudes Towards Death* (Baltimore: Johns Hopkins University Press, 1975). The treatise of Pope Innocent III may be found in a translation by Donald Howard (New York: Bobbs–Merrill, 1969). An introduction to several topics concerning social structure may be found in Jeremy DuQuesnay Adams, *Patterns of Medieval Society* (Englewood Cliffs, N.J.: Prentice-Hall, 1969), and Marjorie Rowling, *Life in Medieval Times* (New York: Capricorn, 1973).

Two excellent studies of rural life are H. S. Bennett, *Life on the English Manor* (Cambridge: Cambridge University Press, 1937), and George C. Homans, *English Villagers of the Thirteenth Century* (rpt., New York: W. W. Norton, 1970). Homans's study in particular is highly suggestive of further investigation of rural life. R. T. Morewedge, ed., *The Role of Woman in the Middle Ages* (Albany: State University of New York Press, 1975) and Susan M. Stuard, ed., *Women in Medieval Society* (Philadelphia: University of Pennsylvania Press, 1976) are good collections of recent studies on the history of women.

Derek Pearsall and Elizabeth Salter, eds., *Landscapes and Seasons of the Medieval World* (Toronto: University of Toronto Press, 1974) is a good introduction to the medieval perception of time. Although it deals with a later period, Natalie Z. Davis, *Society and Culture in Early Modern France* (Stanford: Stanford University Press, 1975) is a model for future research in cultural history.

A good although idiosyncratic introduction to the Mediterranean world in the late thirteenth century is Steven Runciman, *The Sicilian Vespers* (Cambridge: Cambridge University Press, 1958). The best recent short histories of the Italian towns are Daniel Waley, *The Italian City-Republics* (New York: McGraw-Hill, 1969), and J. K. Hyde, *Medieval Italy, 1000–1350* (New York: St. Martin's, 1974). The economic life of Italy is reflected in Robert S. Lopez and Irving Raymond, *Medieval Trade in the Mediterranean World* (rpt., New York: W. W. Norton, 1967). A recent survey of Italian culture is Helène Nolthenius, *Duecento: The Late Middle Ages in Italy* (New York: McGraw-Hill, 1968); however, John Larner, *Culture and Society in Italy, 1290–1420* (New York: Scribner's 1971), is more reliable for the social history of culture during this period. Translations from primary sources dealing directly with the place and period are rare, but a lively group of materials is gathered together in G. G. Coulton, *From St. Francis to Dante: Translations from the Chronicle of the Franciscan Salimbene (1221–1288)* (rpt., with new introduction and bibliography, Philadelphia: University of Pennsylvania Press, 1972). The interested reader should also consult the fine collected papers of Helène Wieruszowski, *Politics and Culture in Medieval Spain and Italy* (Rome: Edizioni di storia e letteratura, 1971).

On Florence, see the short work of Paul C. Ruggiers, *Florence in the Age of Dante* (Norman, Okla.: University of Oklahoma Press, 1964), and the older but detailed history of Ferdinand Schevill, *Medieval and Renaissance Florence*, Vol. I (rpt. New York: Harper & Row, 1963). More recent and more controversial is the work of Marvin Becker, *Florence in Transition*, 2 vols. (Baltimore: Johns Hopkins University Press, 1967, 1968). The history of other towns is noted by Waley. Mention should also be made of J. K. Hyde, *Padua in the Age of Dante* (Manchester: Manchester University Press, 1966).

The bibliography of Dante scholarship is immense and seems to be growing unceasingly larger. A good introduction to Dante's life is Michele Barbi, *Life of Dante*, trans. P. C. Ruggiers (Berkeley and Los Angeles: University of California Press, 1954), and to his works, Umberto Cosmo, *A Handbook to Dante Studies* (Oxford: Basil Blackwell, 1950). Of the many studies on specialized topics, Erich Auerbach, *Dante: Poet of the Secular World* (Chicago: University of Chicago, 1961), and Charles T. Davis, *Dante and the Idea of Rome* (Oxford: Oxford University Press, 1957), offer fine introductions to complex aspects of the poet's mind and work. A good general introduction to the works is Thomas G. Bergin, *Dante* (Boston: Houghton Mifflin, 1965).

The question of translations is complex, because Dante's works have attracted many translators of varying abilities and interests. A good prose translation of the *Comedy*, with facing Italian text and modest notes, is John D. Sinclair, *The Divine Comedy of Dante Alighieri*, 3 vols. (rpt. New York: Oxford University Press, 1968). A contemporary poetic translation is that of John Ciardi, in three volumes (New York: New American Library, 1954, 1961, 1970). Most of the works listed offer further bibliographical suggestions.

On the economic problems in general of this period, see Harry A. Miskimin, *The Economy of Early Renaissance Europe, 1300–1460* (Englewood Cliffs, N.J.: Prentice-Hall, 1969). For war, see Kenneth Fowler, ed., *The Hundred Years War* (New York: St. Martin's, 1971), and E. Perroy, *The Hundred Years War* (New York: Oxford University Press, 1951). A number of social crises are considered in F. R. H. Du Boulay, *An Age of Ambition* (New York: Viking, 1970); Sylvia Thrupp, *The Merchant Class of Medieval London* (rpt. Ann Arbor, Mich.: University of Michigan Press, 1962); Michael Mollat and Philippe Wolff, *The Popular Revolutions of the Late Middle Ages* (London: Allen & Unwin, 1972).

Good introductions to the impact of increasing European knowledge of the world may be seen in J. K. Wright, *The Geographical Lore of the Time of the Crusades* (rpt., New York: Dover, 1965); Pierre Chaunu, *L'Expansion européenne du XIIIe au XVe siècle* (Paris: Presses Universitaires de France: Nouvelle Clio, 1969); J. H. Parry, *The Age of Reconnaissance* (rpt., New York: New American Library, 1964); see also the extensive collection of essays in F. M. Chiapelli, R. L. Benson, and M. J. B. Allen, eds., *First Images of America*, 2 vols. (Berkeley and Los Angeles: The University of California Press, 1975).

There is much stimulating material in Margaret Aston, *The Fifteenth Century: The Prospect of Europe* (New York: Harcourt, Brace, Jovanovich, 1968), Jacques Heers, *L'Occident aux XIVe et XVe siècles. Aspects économiques et sociaux* (Paris: Presses Universitaires de France: Nouvelle Clio, 1970), and Bernard Guenée, *L'Occident aux XIVe et XVe siècles. Les États* (Paris: Nouvelle Clio, 1973).

On the early stages of the restored Byzantine Empire and its relations with the west, see Deno J. Geanakoplos, *Emperor Michael Palaeologus and the West: A Study in Byzantine-Latin Relations* (Cambridge, Mass.: Harvard University Press, 1959), and *The Cambridge Medieval History*, Vol. IV: *The Byzantine Empire*, Part 1: *Byzantium and Its Neighbors;* Part 2: *Government, Church, and Civilization*, ed. J. M. Hussey (Cambridge: Cambridge University Press, 1967). On the Latins in the east, see W. Miller, *The Latins in the Levant: A History of Frankish Greece, 1204–1566* (London: Murray, 1908). The best recent study of the Byzantine influence outside Byzantium is Dimitri Obolensky, *The Byzantine Commonwealth: Eastern Europe, 500–1453* (London: Weidenfeld & Nicholson, 1971). The best short history of later Byzantium is Donald M. Nicol, *The Last Centuries of Byzantium, 1261–1453* (London: Hart-Davis, 1972). A good account of the fall of the city is Stephen Runciman, *The Fall of Constantinople, 1453* (Cambridge: Cambridge University Press, 1965).

The best survey of Ottoman history in this period is now Halil Inalcik, *The Ottoman Empire: The Classical Age, 1300–1600* (New York: Weidenfeld & Nicholson, 1973).

Besides the works in Church history cited in the general bibliographies, see G. Mollat, *The Popes at Avignon, 1305–1378,* trans. Janet Love (New York: Harper & Row, 1965), and Yves Renouard, *The*

Avignon Papacy, 1305–1403, trans. D. Bethell (London: Faber & Faber, 1970). Walter Ullmann, *The Origins of the Great Schism* (rpt. Hamden, Conn.: Archon Books, 1973), is a particularly important study, as are several of the essays collected in Beryl Smalley, John Hale, and J. R. L. Highfield, eds., *Europe in the Late Middle Ages* (Evanston, Ill.: Northwestern University Press, 1965). W. A. Pantin, *The English Church in the Fourteenth Century* (Cambridge: Cambridge University Press, 1955), is a study of a single kingdom. On the empire, see Geoffrey Barraclough, *The Origins of Modern Germany* (rpt., New York: Oxford University Press, 1963).

A brilliant introduction to conciliar thought is Brian Tierney, *Foundations of the Conciliar Theory* (Cambridge: Cambridge University Press, 1955). Aspects of the general period are illuminated by the works of E. F. Jacob, particularly *Essays in the Conciliar Epoch*, 2nd ed. (Manchester: Manchester University Press, 1953), and *Essays in Later Medieval History* (New York: Manchester University Press, 1968). For the Council of Constance, the best introduction in English is John H Mundy and K. M. Woody, eds., Louise Ropes Loomis, *The Council of Constance* (New York: Columbia University Press, 1961). For John Hus, see Matthew Spinka, *John Hus: A Biography* (Princeton, N.J.: Princeton University Press, 1968), which contains a good bibliography, and idem, *The Letters of John Hus* (Manchester: Manchester University Press, 1972).

The life of court functionaries in the fifteenth century has yet to find its historian. Otto Cartellieri, *The Court of Burgundy* (New York: Knopf, 1929), offers a brilliant picture of one great court. Johann Huizinga, *The Waning of the Middle Ages* (rpt., New York: Doubleday, 1956), offers a panoramic and highly suggestive view of the culture of the fifteenth century. See also F. du Boulay, *An Age of Ambition* (New York: Viking, 1970).

The best introduction to the question of the Renaissance is Erwin Panofsky, *Renaissance and Renascences in Western Art* (rpt., New York: Harper & Row, 1972), a book that examines far more than its title suggests.

Among several good recent studies of the late fifteenth and early sixteenth centuries, the work of J. R. Hale, *Renaissance Europe: The Individual and Society, 1480–1520* (New York: Harper & Row, 1971), offers a particularly original approach to the continuity of some of the problems described at the end of this book.

Two recent reevaluations of thought and learning are C. Trinkaus and H. Oberman, eds., *The Pursuit of Holiness in Late Medieval and Renaissance Religion* (Leiden: Brill, 1974), and Paul O. Kristeller, *Medieval Aspects of Renaissance Learning* (Durham, N.C.: Duke University Press, 1974). Steven E. Ozment, ed., *The Reformation in Medieval Perspective* (Chicago: University of Chicago Press, 1971), offers a highly suggestive collection of essays by a number of authorities on the relation between medieval and Reformation religion. Keith Thomas, *Religion and the Decline of Magic* (New York: Scribner's, 1971), offers an extensive review of popular religious culture that is highly suggestive.

INDEX

Aachen, 208, 216, 222, *Plate 7*
Abbasid caliphate, 165-67, 347, 476
Abelard, Peter, 370-72, 374-83, 388, 397, 406, 409, 410, 426, 504
Abu Bakr, 163
Acta Sanctorum, 5
Adelard of Bath, 367-68
Adelbert of Bremen, 316
Adhémar of Le Puy, 341-42
Adso, 309
Agriculture:
  early, 19-20
  medieval, 41, 226-30, 257-68, 506-12, 528-30

Albertus Magnus, 440-41
Alcuin, 207-19
Alexander II, Pope, 321, 322, 324
Alexander III, Pope, 386, 402, 421-24, 427, 428, 458
Alexius I, Emperor, 335, 337, 344-45, 476
Alfonso VI, of Castile, 332, 334, 340
Alfred the Great, 101, 246, 270, 283, 287, 297, 310, 339, 366
Almohades, 462
Almoravides, 462
Ambrose, St., 68-72, 83-85, 113, 142, 324
Anselm, St., 327, 356, 369, 374-81

Anthony, St., 72-73, 143
Arius, 65
Arnold of Brescia, 426, 467
Arthur, King, 107, 433, 436-37
Athaulf, 87-88
Augustine, St., 51, 54, 72, 84-85, 87, 91-92, 113, 143, 339, 375, 411
Avars, 130-36, 198-99, 236

Basil, St., 73, 84, 111, 335, 337
Basil II, Emperor, 293, 335, 337
Becket, Thomas, 372, 430, 457
Bede, St. 146, 171-76, 178, 205, 339
Benedict, St., 113-14, 143-44, 312, 394, 407
Benedict of Aniane, 312, 393
Beowulf, 434
Bernard, St. 379, 394-95, 396-411, 444, 484, 506, 547 ,,
Bernard Silvester, 379, 439
Bishop, 64, 112, 221-22, 225-26, 269-70, 288-89
Boethius, 99-100, 140, 355
Boniface, St., 175, 176-79
Boniface VIII, Pope, 403, 447, 466, 470-74, 510, 518-19, 521, 548, 550, 551
Bulgars, 124, 129, 217, 237-40, 247-49, 293, 476

Caesar, Julius, 25, 30, 32, 37
Calixtus II, Pope, 328, 402, 416
Cassiodorus, 99-102, 113-14, 139-40, 186
Chalcedon, Council of, 118-19
Charlemagne, 182-86, 188-222, 272, 283, 288, 307, 308-10, 312, 332, 339, 353-55, 366, 393, 422, 434, 435
Charles the Bald, Emperor, 176, 221-26, 283, 285, 301, 366
Charles of Anjou, 467-69, 474, 519
Charles Martel, 156, 165, 176, 179, 283
Chaucer, Geoffrey, 277, 435, 438, 552, 556
Chrétien de Troyes, 436-37
Cicero, 48, 142
Cistercian Order, 394-96, 397-406, 411
Clovis, 103-6, 109, 143, 151-52, 283
Cluny, 313-15, 317, 322, 324, 326, 329, 331, 341, 371, 393, 407, 409
Columba, St., 116, 147, 172
Columbanus, St. 172, 176, 319
Concordat of Worms, 380, 410
Conrad I, Emperor, 286, 288-89, 302
Conrad II, Emperor, 291, 316, 328

Conrad III, Emperor, 397, 420-21
Constantine, Emperor, 56-65, 67, 74-76, 106, 112, 125, 585

Damasus, Pope, 83, 85
Damian, St. Peter, 323-24
Dante Alighieri, 101, 501-2, 512-22, 547
Dictatus Papae, 323
Diocletian, Emperor, 57-59, 61, 75
Dominic, St., 404, 411-14
Donation of Constantine, 225, 424
Donatism, 64-66

Einhard, 208-10
Eugenius III, Pope, 380, 395, 404, 426-27, 428

Flanders, 285-86
Francis of Assisi, St., 404, 412-14, 437
Franks, 102-6, 109, 151-57
Frederick I Barbarossa, Emperor, 418-22, 424, 427, 458
Frederick II, Emperor, 418, 422, 467, 479-80, 481, 485, 518, 548

Gaiseric, 89-91, 108
Galla Placidia, 86-91
Gerbert of Aurillac, 291, 318-19, 356, 369
Gratian, 382, 385, 386, 402-3
Gregory I, Pope, 85, 139-45, 147, 178, 330
Gregory VII, Pope, 304, 322-29, 338, 340, 380, 393, 402, 404, 418
Gregory IX, Pope, 389, 402-4, 412, 414, 427-29, 478
Gregory of Tours, 104, 154, 178, 205, 265, 339
Guiscard, Robert, 304, 322, 326

Hadrian IV, Pope, 372, 381, 402
Haghia Sophia, 121-22, 338
Henry I, Emperor, 289
Henry II, Emperor, 291, 325
Henry III, Emperor, 291-92, 306, 308, 316, 319-21, 325, 333
Henry IV, Emperor, 299, 303, 316, 321, 323, 325-28, 342, 425, 459
Henry VII, Emperor, 521, 549
Henry I, of England, 299-301, 370, 383, 451
Henry II, of England, 300-302, 327, 387, 451-58, 503

Henry III, of England, 457, 468, 480, 564
Henry the Lion, 421-22, 485
Heraclius, Emperor, 132-34, 159, 200
Heresy, 118-19, 129-30, 159, 201, 211, 316-18, 405-15, 443, 467
Huns, 45, 75, 89-91
Hus, John, 554-55, 572

Iconoclasm, 201-3
Innocent II, Pope, 402
Innocent III, Pope, 402-3, 410, 412, 413, 428, 456, 467, 478, 498-500
Innocent IV, Pope, 402-3, 414, 429, 489
Irene, Empress, 211, 216-17, 238, 239
Isidore of Seville, 151, 180, 355, 492

Jadwiga of Poland, 575
Jagiello of Poland, 575
Jerome, St., 63, 72, 85-86, 100, 113, 174, 363
Joan of Arc, 503, 568
John VIII, Pope, 252
John, of England, 454-59, 482, 503
John of Salisbury, 372, 381
Judaism, 48-51, 149-50, 311-12, 334, 343, 368, 390, 397, 415-17 461
Julian, Emperor, 67-68, 102
Justinian, Emperor, 98, 102, 108, 117-29, 135-36, 139, 148, 158, 384, 584

Kerularios, Michael, Patriarch, 338
Khazars, 200, 237, 293-95, 311
Kiev, 294-97, 486, 489, 576-77

Latifundia, 41, 57
Law:
  Canon, 206, 317, 318, 320, 323-24, 381, 383-91, 402, 423-27
  Carolingian, 191-92
  Islamic, 162
  Lombard, 148-49
  of the manor, 265
  Roman, 97, 122, 384-85, 413
  study of 383-88
  Visigothic, 109, 149
Leo I, Pope, 83, 91, 119, 141
Leo III, Pope, 211-19, 251, 308
Leo IX, Pope, 304, 319-21, 322, 326, 338, 340, 380
Leo I, Emperor, 93
Leo III, Emperor, 210-13, 216, 240
Lombards, 132, 135-41

Lothar I, 221-22
Lothar III, 418-19, 424, 484
Louis the Pious, Emperor, 184, 194-96, 204, 220-23, 283, 301, 306, 312, 393, 434
Louis VI, of France, 303, 328, 457, 460
Louis VII, of France, 303, 458, 460
Louis VIII, of France, 459, 468
Louis IX, St., of France, 387, 433, 460, 467, 469, 480, 489, 564
Louis the German, 221-24, 366

Magyars, 241-43
Manuel I Comnenus, Emperor, 475-76, 575
Marcomanni, 42-43
Marco Polo, 491-93, 580
Marcus Aurelius, Emperor, 43, 256
Marsiglio of Padua, 560
Methodios, St., 225
Michael VIII Palaeologos, Emperor, 475, 575
Mieszko, 482
Missi dominici, 192-93
Mohammed, 161-63
Monasticism:
  development of, 110-16
  origins of, 71-73
Mongols, 476, 478, 480, 486-90, 536, 574, 577
Moravia, 236-38, 241
Muscovy, 576-78

Nicholas II, Pope, 321
Nika Riot, 120

Odovacar, 93-94, 97
Ostrogoths, 94-102, 123-24, 150
Otto I, Emperor, 289-90, 318
Otto II, Emperor, 291-92, 308
Otto III, Emperor, 291-308, 313, 319
Otto IV, Emperor, 425
Ottoman Turks, *See* Turks

Pachomius, St., 73
Paschal II, Pope, 327-28, 402
Patrick, St., 115-16
Paul, St., 50, 71
Peace of God, 333, 339
Pepin II, 156, 195
Pepin III, 157, 176, 179-80, 182-83, 196, 203-4

Persia, 46-47, 93-94, 123, 129, 130-34, 163, 164, 167, 293
Philip I, of France, 301-2, 328, 341-42, 480
Philip II Augustus, of France, 301, 389, 451, 455, 458-59
Philip III, of France, 469
Philip IV the Fair, of France, 447, 466, 469-74, 549, 564
Philip VI, of France, 564-66
Philo Judaeus, 49-50
Photios, Patriarch, 239-41, 252
Piers Plowman, 435, 558
Pseudo-Isidore, 225

Raymond of Peñafort, 403
Raymond of Toulouse, 341-42
Richard I, of England, 451-58, 480, 503
Richard II, of England, 560-61, 566
Robert, of Arbrissel, 394
Roger, the Great Count, 304
Roger II, of Sicily, 368, 383, 422-23
Roscellinus, 357, 370

Slavs, 130-31, 236-39
Song of Roland, 332, 404, 435
Sorbonne, 390
Stephen Dusan, of Serbia, 486, 576-77
Stephen Harding, 394
Stilicho, 87-88, 89
Symmachus, 68-69

Tacitus, 51, 69
Templars, 405, 549, 551
Theoderic, 94, 96-102, 105, 110, 117, 123, 139, 148, 439
Theodora, 119-20, 124

Theodosius I, Emperor, 70, 75, 76, 79, 83, 86
Theodosius II, Emperor, 90, 97, 125
Thomas Aquinas, 100, 377, 440-42, 547
Truce of God, 333, 339
Turks:
  Ottoman, 490, 576-78
  Seljuk, 335-37, 347, 348-49

Urban II, Pope, 327-29, 338, 339-44, 380, 402, 546

Valentinian I, Emperor, 67-68
Valentinian II, Emperor, 75
Valentinian III, Emperor, 90, 108
Vandals, 85-91, 94, 95, 106, 107, 108, 110, 123, 158-59
Vatican, 251
Venice, 272-73, 274, 292, 346-47, 422, 476, 478, 486-87, 513, 533-34, 571
Vergil, 47-48, 101, 584
Visigoths, 44, 75, 86-89, 96, 105, 106, 108, 109-10, 148-51
Vladimir I, of Kiev, 121, 296-97, 307-8, 310

Wilfrid of Ripon, 171-72, 179
William, of England, 5, 259, 285, 287, 298-301, 340, 451

York, 36

Zacharias, Pope, 179-80
Zangi, 348
Zeno, Emperor, 93-94, 117